Public choice II

Public choice II

A revised edition of *Public Choice*

DENNIS C. MUELLER
University of Maryland

PUBLISHED BY THE PRESS SYNDICATE OF THE UNIVERSITY OF CAMBRIDGE
The Pitt Building, Trumpington Street, Cambridge CB2 1RP, United Kingdom

CAMBRIDGE UNIVERSITY PRESS
The Edinburgh Building, Cambridge CB2 2RU, United Kingdom
40 West 20th Street, New York, NY 10011-4211, USA
10 Stamford Road, Oakleigh, Melbourne 3166, Australia

First published 1989
Reprinted 1990, 1991, 1993 (twice), 1995, 1996, 1997

Printed in the United States of America

Typeset in Times

A catalogue record for this book is available from the British Library

Library of Congress Cataloguing-in-Publication Data is available

ISBN 0-521-37083-3 hardback
ISBN 0-521-37952-0 paperback

Public choice II

A revised edition of *Public Choice*

DENNIS C. MUELLER
University of Maryland

CAMBRIDGE
UNIVERSITY PRESS

PUBLISHED BY THE PRESS SYNDICATE OF THE UNIVERSITY OF CAMBRIDGE
The Pitt Building, Trumpington Street, Cambridge CB2 1RP, United Kingdom

CAMBRIDGE UNIVERSITY PRESS
The Edinburgh Building, Cambridge CB2 2RU, United Kingdom
40 West 20th Street, New York, NY 10011-4211, USA
10 Stamford Road, Oakleigh, Melbourne 3166, Australia

First published 1989
Reprinted 1990, 1991, 1993 (twice), 1995, 1996, 1997

Printed in the United States of America

Typeset in Times

A catalogue record for this book is available from the British Library

Library of Congress Cataloguing-in-Publication Data is available

ISBN 0-521-37083-3 hardback
ISBN 0-521-37952-0 paperback

To the memory of my parents,
Catherine and Anthony

Contents

Contents   ix

Part III Public choice in a representative democracy

Contents

Preface

By the time this book is in print some 15 years will have elapsed since I first began the survey of public choice for the *Journal of Economic Literature*, from which this volume evolved. A certain resemblance to that original piece remains, as a grandson resembles the grandfather, but much of the present volume will be unfamiliar to the reader of that article. Less than half of *Public Choice II* is taken from *Public Choice,* and even the material that overlaps the first edition has been changed in most instances.

As with its predecessors, *Public Choice II* is thought of more as a survey of the literature than as a textbook. But the frequent use of its predecessors in the classroom has led me to try to write *Public Choice II* in such a way that it would be more "student friendly." The exposition of some topics has been expanded, more proofs of important propositions have been included, sections denoted by an asterisk cover more difficult topics. These asterisk-denoted sections can be omitted without any loss of continuity.

Several institutions and individuals have helped in the production of *Public Choice II*. Vito Tanzi's invitation to visit the International Monetary Fund during the Winter of 1986 gave me time to write Chapter 17 and I thank him and the IMF for their support, as well as for permission to republish this chapter, which originally appeared in the *IMF Staff Papers,* March 1987.

Chapter 18 was originally written for a conference sponsored by the Liberty Fund and published in *Democracy and Public Choice* (Charles K. Rowley, ed., Basil Blackwell, 1987). My thanks to the Liberty Fund for its support and Basil Blackwell for permission to republish.

Writing of much of the book has been facilitated by a grant from the Thyssen Foundation of Cologne, West Germany. Some parts of the book were written during the second half of 1986 when I visited the Centre for Policy Studies and the Economics Department at Monash University (Victoria, Australia), and during the first half of 1987 when I was a Fulbright Professor at Marmara University, Istanbul, Turkey. My thanks go to these institutions and my accommodating bosses, Michael Porter, Richard Snape, and Ahmet Serpil.

Several people were kind enough to read and comment upon all or parts of earlier drafts. Special thanks for their help go to Peter Coughlin, Bruno Frey, Brendan Kennelly, Peter Murrell, Yew-Kwang Ng, Wallace Oates, Joe Oppenheimer, Todd Sandler, Murat Sertel, Vito Tanzi, Robert Tollison, and Gordon Tullock. I thank Elizabeth Reardon for cross-checking all of the references.

The size of the manuscript, number of references, and the fact that it was written over two years on three different continents led to more than the usual number of problems in producing a final, typed manuscript. I have been extremely fortunate during this period to have had the help of Rebecca Flick in this task. To her I owe a major note of thanks.

College Park

CHAPTER 1

Introduction

Man is by nature a political animal.

Aristotle

This division of labour . . . is the necessary, though very slow and gradual, consequence of a certain propensity in human nature which has in view no such extensive utility; the propensity to truck, barter, and exchange one thing for another.

Whether this propensity be one of those original principles in human nature . . . or whether, as seems more probable, it be the necessary consequence of the faculties of reason and speech, it belongs not to our present subject to enquire. It is common to all men and to be found in no other race of animals, which seem to know neither this nor any other species of contracts.

Adam Smith

Aristotle, observing the Greeks in the fourth century B.C., thought that man's natural proclivities were toward discourse and political activity. Adam Smith, observing the Scots in the eighteenth century A.D., saw instead a propensity to engage in economic exchange. From the observations of these two intellectual giants, two separate fields in the social sciences have developed: the science of politics and the science of economics.

Traditionally, these two fields have been separated by the types of questions they ask, the assumptions they make about individual motivation, and the methodologies they employ. Political science has studied man's behavior in the public arena, economics has studied man in the marketplace. Political science has often assumed that political man pursues the public interest. Economics has assumed that all men pursue their private interests, and has modeled this behavior with a logic unique among the social sciences.

But is this dichotomy valid? Could both Aristotle and Smith have been right? Could political man and economic man be one and the same? In the field of public choice, it is assumed that they are.

Public choice can be defined as the economic study of nonmarket decision making, or simply the application of economics to political science. The subject matter of public choice is the same as that of political science: the theory of the state, voting rules, voter behavior, party politics, the bureaucracy, and so on. The methodology of public choice is that of economics, however. The basic behavioral postulate of public choice, as for economics, is that man is an egoistic, rational, utility maximizer.[1] This places public choice within the stream of political philosophy extending at least from Thomas Hobbes and Benedict Spinoza, and within political science from James Madison and Alexis de Tocqueville. Although there is much that is useful and important in these earlier contributions, and much that anticipates later developments, no effort is made here to relate these earlier works to the modern public choice literature, for they are separated from the modern literature by a second salient characteristic. The modern public choice literature employs the analytic tools of economics. To try to review the older literature using the analytic tools of its descendants would take us too far afield.[2]

Public choice has developed as a separate field largely since 1948. During the thirties, disenchantment with market processes was widespread, and models of "market socialism" depicting how governments could supplant the price system and allocate goods as efficiently as markets do, if not more so, came into vogue. Abram Bergson's (1938) seminal analysis of social welfare functions appeared to indicate how the economist's individualistic, utilitarian ethics could be incorporated into the government planner's objective function and help him to achieve a social welfare maximum as he managed the state.

Kenneth Arrow's 1951 book was a direct follow-up to both Bergson's article and Paul Samuelson's parallel discussion of social welfare functions in Chapter 8 of *Foundations* (1947). Arrow's concern was to characterize the process, whether market or political, through which the social welfare function Bergson and Samuelson had described was achieved (rev. ed. 1963, pp.

1. For a detailed justification of this postulate in the study of voting, see Downs (1957, pp. 3–20); Buchanan and Tullock (1962, pp. 17–39); Riker and Ordeshook (1973, pp. 8–37). J. A. Schumpeter's (1950) early use of the postulate also should be mentioned. One of the curiosities of the public choice literature is the slight *direct* influence that Schumpeter's work appears to have had. Downs claims that "Schumpeter's profound analysis of democracy forms the inspiration and foundation for our whole thesis" (1957, p. 27, n. 11), but cites only one page of the book (twice), and this in support of the "economic man" assumption. Most other work in the field makes no reference to Schumpeter at all.

Gordon Tullock has made, in correspondence, the following observation on Schumpeter's influence on his work: "In my case, he undeniably had immense impact on me, although it was rather delayed. Further, although I read the book originally in 1942, I didn't reexamine it when I wrote *The Politics of Bureaucracy* (1965). In a sense, it gave me a general idea of the type of thing that we could expect in government, but there weren't any detailed things that could be specifically cited." I suspect that Schumpeter's work has had a similar impact on others working in the public choice field.

For an interesting discussion of the public choice content of Schumpeter's work, see Mitchell (1984a,b).

2. See, however, Black (1958, pp. 156–213); Buchanan and Tullock (1962, pp. 307–22); Haefele (1971); Ostrom (1971).

1–6). Since Arrow's book, a large literature has grown up exploring the properties of social welfare or social choice functions.[3] It focuses on the problems of aggregating individual preferences to *maximize* a social welfare function, or to satisfy some set of normative criteria, that is, on the problem of which social state *ought* to be chosen, given the preferences of the individual voters. This research on optimal methods of aggregation has naturally spurred interest in the properties of *actual* procedures for aggregating preferences via voting rules, that is, on the question of which outcome will be chosen for a given set of preferences under different voting rules. The problem of finding a social choice function that satisfies certain normative criteria turns out to be quite analogous to establishing an equilibrium under different voting rules. Thus, both K. J. Arrow's study (1963) of social welfare functions and D. Black's (1948a,b) seminal work on committee voting procedures build on the works of J. C. de Borda (1781), M. de Condorcet (1785), and C. L. Dodgson (Lewis Carroll) (1876). We discuss the most directly relevant parts of the social welfare function literature as part of normative public choice in Part V.

The models of market socialism developed in the thirties and forties envisioned the state as largely an allocator of private goods. State intervention was needed to avoid the inefficient shortfalls in private investment, which Keynesian economics claimed were the cause of unemployment, and to avoid the distributional inequities created by the market. The immediate prosperity of the post–World War II years reduced the concern about unemployment and distributional issues. But concern about the efficiency of the market remained high among academic economists. The seminal works of the forties and fifties gave rise to a large literature on the conditions for efficient allocation in the presence of public goods, externalities, and economies of scale. When these conditions were unmet, the market failed to achieve a Pareto-optimal allocation of goods and resources. The existence of these forms of market failures provides a natural explanation for why government exists, and thus for a theory of the origins of the state. It forms the starting point of our analysis and is reviewed in Part I.

If the state exists as a sort of analogue to the market to provide public goods and eliminate externalities, then it must accomplish the same preference revelation task for these public goods as the market achieves for private goods. The public choice approach to nonmarket decision making has been (1) to make the same behavioral assumptions as general economics (rational, utilitarian individuals), (2) often to depict the preference revelation process as analogous to the market (voters engage in exchange, individuals reveal their demand schedules via voting, citizens exit and enter clubs), and (3) to ask the

3. For surveys, see Sen (1970a, 1977a,b); Fishburn (1973); Plott (1976); Kelly (1978); Riker (1982b).

same questions as traditional price theory (Do equilibria exist? Are they stable? Pareto efficient? How are they obtained?).

One part of the public choice literature studies nonmarket decision making, voting, as if it took place in a direct democracy. The government is treated as a black box or voting rule into which individual preferences (votes) are placed and out of which outcomes emerge. This segment of the literature is reviewed in Part II. Chapter 4 examines criteria for choosing a voting rule when the collective choice is restricted to a potential improvement in allocative efficiency. Chapters 5 and 6 explore the properties of the most popular voting rule, the simple majority rule. Chapters 7 and 8 present a variety of alternatives to the majority voting rule, some equally simple, others more complex. Part II closes with a discussion of how individuals can reveal their preferences for public goods not through the voice mechanism of voting, but by choosing to join different polities or public good clubs (Chapter 9).

Just as Arrow's book was stimulated in part by Bergson's essay, Downs's 1957 classic was obviously stimulated by the works of both Bergson and Arrow (pp. 17–19). To some extent, Downs sought to fill the void Arrow's impossibility theorem had left by demonstrating that competition among parties to win votes could have the same desirable effects on the outcomes of the political process as competition among firms for customers has on the outcomes of the market process. Of all the works in public choice, Downs's book has had perhaps the greatest influence on political scientists.

In the Downsian model, the government appears not merely as a voting rule or black box into which information on voter preferences is fed, but as an institution made up of real people – representatives, bureaucrats, as well as voters – each with their own set of objectives and constraints. The Downsian perspective on government underlies Parts III and IV of this book. Chapters 10 and 11 examine the properties of two-party representative democracies, while Chapter 12 discusses the reasons for multiparty systems and their properties. The redistributive potential of representative government is the subject of Chapter 13. Part III closes with a review of several theories of the state in which the state itself – in the form of the bureaucracy, the legislature, or an autocratic leadership – increasingly dictates outcomes with the citizenry relegated to playing a more passive role.

In arguing that government intervention is needed to correct the failures of the market when public goods, externalities, and other sorts of impure private goods are present, the economics literature has often made the implicit assumption that these failures could be corrected at zero cost. The government is seen as an omniscient and benevolent institution dictating taxes, subsidies, and quantities so as to achieve a Pareto-optimal allocation of resources. In the sixties, a large segment of the public choice literature began to challenge this "Nirvana model" of government. This literature examines not how governments may or ought to behave, but how they do behave. It reveals that governments too can fail. This literature on how governments do perform is reviewed in Chapters 13–17.

One of the major justifications for an increasing role for government in the economy has been the Keynesian prescription that government policies are required to stabilize the macroeconomic performance of a country. The evidence that governments' macroeconomic policies are affected by their efforts to win votes is examined in Chapter 15 along with the impact of electoral politics on macroeconomic performance.

In Chapter 16 the emphasis shifts from the competition between political parties to the competition among interest groups. The hypothesis of interest here is that the rent-seeking and wealth-transferring efforts of interest groups retard the economic growth of a nation and cause stagflation.

One of the most debated topics of the past 15 years has been the growth in the size of governments. Is this growth a response to the demands of citizens for greater government services because of rising incomes, changes in the relative price of government services, or a change in "tastes"? Does it reflect the successful efforts of some groups to redistribute wealth from others by means of the government? Or is it an unwanted burden placed on the backs of citizens by a powerful government bureaucracy? These and other explanations for the growth of government are presented in Chapter 17.

In Chapter 18 we descend from the heights of macroeconomic performance and the growing government pyramid to examine the calculus of the individual voter as she decides whether or not to go to the polls. This turns out to be a far more complex issue than the more grandiose ones taken up earlier.

The Bergson–Samuelson social welfare function, which helped spark interest in preference aggregation procedures, is discussed in Chapter 19. The Arrowian social welfare function literature is reviewed in Chapter 20. Although both of these approaches build their aggregate welfare indexes on individual preferences, both tend to shift attention from the preferences of the individual to the aggregate. Moreover, in both cases, the aggregate (society) is expected to behave like a rational individual, in the one case by maximizing an objective function, in the other by ordering social outcomes as a rational individual would do. Therefore, the social welfare function literature bears more than a passing resemblance to organic views of the state in which the state has a persona of its own.

James Buchanan's first article (1949) appearing before Arrow's essay was an attack upon this organic view of the state; Buchanan (1954a) renewed this attack following the publication of Arrow's book. In place of the analogy between the state and a person, Buchanan offered the analogy between the state and a market. He suggested that one think of the state as an institution through which individuals interact for their mutual benefit, that one think of government, as Knut Wicksell (1896) did, as a quid pro quo process of exchange among citizens (Buchanan, 1986, pp. 19–27). The view of government as an institution for reaching agreements that benefit all citizens leads naturally to the perspective that the agreements are contracts binding all individuals. The contractarian approach to public choice is developed in Buchanan and Gordon Tullock's *Calculus of Consent* (1962) and Buchanan's *The Limits of Liberty* (1975a). It is reviewed in Chapter 22, following a discussion of John Rawls's influential contribution to contractarian theory (Chapter 21).

One of Knut Wicksell's important insights concerning collective action was that a fundamental distinction exists between allocative efficiency and redistribution and that these two issues must be treated separately, with separate voting rules.[4] This insight reappears in Buchanan's work in which the constitutional and legislative or parliamentary stages of government are separated, and in Richard A. Musgrave's *Theory of Public Finance* in which the work of government is divided into allocative and redistributive branches. The distinction is also featured in this book and constitutes the theme of Chapter 24, which follows a review of the public choice literature on redistribution (Chapter 23).

The important differences that arise when alternative voting rules and democratic procedures are used illustrate the single, most important lesson public choice teaches – institutions do matter. The outcomes of a democratic process vary with the types of issues decided, the methods of representation, and the voting rules employed. The interrelationships among these various elements are sometimes subtle and intricate. Public choice seeks to explicate these intricacies. Let us see how it does so.

---

4. Wicksell's 1896 essay is part of the contribution of the "continental" writers on public economics. Besides Wicksell's work, the most important papers in this group are those of Eric Lindahl. Of the two, Lindahl has had greater influence on public goods theory, Wicksell on public choice and public finance. Their works, along with the other major contributions of the continental writers, are in Musgrave and Peacock (1967).

PART I

Origins of the state

CHAPTER 2

The reason for collective choice – allocative efficiency

> Had every man sufficient *sagacity* to perceive at all times, the strong interest which binds him to the observance of justice and equity, and *strength of mind* sufficient to persevere in a steady adherence to a general and a distant interest, in opposition to the allurements of present pleasure and advantage, there had never, in that case, been any such thing as government or political society; but each man, following his natural liberty, had lived in entire peace and harmony with all others. (Italics in original)
>
> David Hume

> Government is a contrivance of human wisdom to provide for human *wants*. Men have a right that these rights should be provided for by this wisdom. (Italics in original)
>
> Edmund Burke

A. Public goods and prisoners' dilemmas

Probably the most important accomplishment of economics is the demonstration that individuals with purely selfish motives can mutually benefit from exchange. If *A* raises cattle and *B* corn, both may improve their welfare by exchanging cattle for corn. With the help of the price system, the process can be extended to accommodate a wide variety of goods and services.

Although often depicted as the perfect example of the beneficial outcome of purely private, individualistic activity in the absence of government, the invisible hand theorem presumes a system of collective choice comparable in sophistication and complexity to the market system it governs. For the choices facing *A* and *B* are not merely to trade or not, as implicitly suggested. *A* can choose to steal *B*'s corn, rather than give up his cattle for it; *B* may do likewise. Unlike trading, which is a positive-sum game benefiting both participants in an exchange, stealing is at best a zero-sum game. What *A* gains, *B* loses. If stealing, and guarding against it, detract from *A* and *B*'s ability to produce corn and cattle, it becomes a negative-sum game. Although with trading each seeks to improve his position and both end up better off, with stealing the selfish pursuits of each leave them both worse off.

The example can be illustrated with strategy Matrix 2.1. To simplify the discussion, let us ignore the trading option and assume that each individual

9

Matrix 2.1. *Stealing as prisoners' dilemma*

B A	Does not steal	Steals

Does not
steal
	1
	    (10, 9)
		4
		    (7, 11)

Steals	2
	    (12, 6)
		3
		    (8, 8)

grows only corn. Square 1 gives the allocation when *A* and *B* both refrain from stealing (*A*'s allocation precedes *B*'s in each box). Both are better off when they both refrain from stealing, but each is still better off if he alone steals (cells 2 and 4). In Matrix 2.1, stealing is a dominant strategy for both players, so defined because it dominates all other strategy options by promising a higher payoff for the chooser than any other strategy, given any choice of strategy by the other player. In an anarchic environment, the independent choices of both individuals can be expected to lead both to adopt the dominant stealing strategy with the outcome cell 3. The distribution of corn in cell 3 represents a "natural distribution" of goods (so named by Winston Bush, 1972), namely, the distribution that would emerge in an Hobbesian state of nature.

From this "natural" state, both individuals become better off by tacitly or formally agreeing not to steal, provided that the enforcement of such an agreement costs less than they jointly gain from it. The movement from cell 3 to cell 1 is a Pareto move that lifts the individuals out of a Hobbesian state of nature (Bush, 1972; Bush and Mayer, 1974; Buchanan, 1975a; Schotter, 1981). An agreement to make such a move is a form of "constitutional contract" establishing the property rights and behavioral constraints of each individual. The existence of these rights is undoubtedly a necessary precondition for the creation of the "postconstitutional contracts," which make up a system of voluntary exchange (Buchanan, 1975a). Problems of collective choice arise with the departure from Hobbesian anarchy, and are coterminous with the existence of recognizable groups and communities.

A system of property rights and the procedures to enforce them are a Samuelsonian public good in "that each individual's consumption leads to no subtraction from any other individual's consumption of that good."[1] Alter-

---

1. Samuelson (1954, p. 386). The extent to which individuals can be excluded from the benefits of a public good varies. One man's house cannot be defended from foreign invasion without defending another, but a house may be allowed to burn down without endangering another. Gordon Tullock (1971c) has suggested that voluntary payment schemes for excludable public goods could introduce cases resembling the latter.

natively, a pure public good can be defined as one that *must* be provided in equal quantities to all members of the community. Familiar examples of pure public goods are national defense and police and fire protection. National defense is the collective provision against external threats; laws and their enforcement safeguard against internal threats; fire departments against fires. Nearly all public goods whose provision requires an expenditure of resources, time, or moral restraint can be depicted with a strategy box analogous to Matrix 2.1. Replace stealing with paying for an army, or a police force, or a fire department, and the same strategy choices emerge. Each individual is better off if all contribute to the provision of the public good than if all do not, and each is still better off if only he does not pay for the good.

A pure public good has two salient characteristics: jointness of supply, and the impossibility or inefficiency of excluding others from its consumption, once it has been supplied to some members of the community (Musgrave, 1959, pp. 9–12, 86; Head, 1962). Jointness of supply is a property of the production or cost function of the public good. The extreme case of jointness of supply is a good whose production costs are all fixed, and thus whose marginal production costs are zero (e.g., a public monument). For such a good, the addition of more consumers (viewers) does not detract from the benefits enjoyed by others. Even a good with falling average costs, although positive marginal costs, has elements of jointness that raise collective provision issues.

The joint supply characteristic creates the potential gain from a cooperative move from cell 3 to 1. Given jointness of supply, a cooperative consumption decision is necessary to provide the good efficiently. If it took twice as many resources to protect *A* and *B* from one another as it does to protect only one of them, collective action would be unnecessary in the absence of nonexclusion. Each could choose independently whether or not to provide his own protection.

People can be excluded from the benefits from viewing a statue placed within a private gallery if they do not pay to see it. But people cannot be prevented from viewing a statue or monument placed in the central city square. For many public goods, the exclusion of some members of the community from their consumption is impossible or impractical. Failure of the exclusion principle to apply provides an incentive for noncooperative, individualistic behavior, a gain from moving from cell 1 to either cell 2 or cell 4. The impossibility of exclusion raises the likelihood that purely voluntary schemes for providing a public good will break down. Thus, together, the properties of public goods provide the raison d'être for collective choice. Jointness of supply is the carrot, making cooperative-collective decisions beneficial to all, absence of the exclusion principle the apple tempting individuals into independent noncooperative behavior.

Although the purest of pure public goods is characterized by both jointness of supply and the impossibility of exclusion, preference revelation problems arise even if only the first of these two properties is present. That is, an alternative definition of a public good is that it *may* be provided in equal quantities to all members of the community at zero marginal cost. The substitution of "may" for "must" in the definition implies that exclusion may be possible. A classic example of a public good fitting this second definition is a bridge. In the absence of crowding, once built, the services of the bridge can be supplied to all members of the community, but they need not be. Exclusion is possible. As long as the marginal cost of someone's crossing the bridge remains zero, however, excluding anyone who would experience a marginal benefit from crossing violates the Pareto principle. Jointness of supply alone can create the need for collective action to achieve Pareto optimality.

Matrix 2.1 depicts the familiar and extensively analyzed prisoners' dilemma. The salient feature of this game is that the row player ranks the four possible outcomes $2 > 1 > 3 > 4$, while the column player has the ranking $4 > 1 > 3 > 2$. The noncooperative strategy is dominant for both players. It is the best strategy for each player in a single play of the game regardless of the other player's strategy choice. The outcome, square 3, is a Cournot–Nash equilibrium. It has the unfortunate property of being the only outcome of the prisoners' dilemma game that is not Pareto optimal. From each of the other three squares a move must make at least one player worse off, but from 3 a move to 1 makes both better off.

Despite the obvious superiority of the cooperative nonstealing outcome to the joint stealing outcome, the dominance of the stealing strategies ensures that the nonstealing strategies do not constitute an equilibrium pair, at least for a single play of the game. The cooperative solution may emerge, however, as the outcome of a "supergame" of prisoners' dilemma games repeated over and over by the same players. The cooperative solution can arise, even in the absence of direct communication between the players, if each player chooses a supergame strategy that effectively links his choice of the cooperative strategy in a single game to the other player's choice of this strategy. One such supergame strategy is for a player to play the same strategy in the present game as the other player(s) played in the previous game. If both (all) players adopt this strategy, *and* all begin by playing the cooperative strategy, the cooperative outcome will emerge in every play of the game. This "tit-for-tat" strategy beats all others proposed by a panel of game theory experts in a computer tournament conducted by Robert Axelrod (1984).

An alternative strategy, which achieves the same outcome, is for each player to play the cooperative strategy as long as the other player(s) does, and then to *punish* the other player(s) for defecting by playing the noncooperative strategy for a series of plays following any defection before returning to the cooperative strategy. Again, if all players begin by playing cooperatively, this outcome continues throughout the game (Taylor, 1976, pp. 28–68). In both of these cooperative strategies, equilibrium solutions to the prisoners' dilemma supergame, the equilibrium comes about through the *punishment* (or threat thereof) of the noncooperative behavior of any player, in this case by noncooperation of the other player(s). This idea that noncooperative (antisocial, immoral) behavior must be punished to bring about conformity with group mores is to be found in most, if not all, moral philosophies, and forms a direct linkage between this large literature and the modern theory.[2]

In experimental studies the appearance of cooperative solutions in prisoner's dilemma games has been found to depend on the number of players, number of plays of the game, and size of gain from adopting the cooperative strategy relative to both the loss from the noncooperative outcome and the gain from successful playing of the noncooperative strategy. The latter two need no elaboration. The first two factors combine to determine the predictability of the response of the other player(s). When the number of other players is small, it is obviously easier to learn their behavior and predict whether they will respond to cooperative strategy choices in a like manner. It is also easier to detect noncooperative behavior and, if this is possible, single it out for punishment, thereby further encouraging the cooperative strategies. When numbers are large, it is easy for one or a few players to adopt the noncooperative strategy and either not be detected, since the impact on the rest is small, or not be punished, since they cannot be discovered or it is too costly to the cooperating players to punish them. Thus, voluntary compliance with behavioral sanctions or provision of public goods is more likely in small communities than in large (Coase, 1960; Buchanan, 1965b). Reliance on voluntary compliance in large communities or groups leads to free riding and the under- or nonprovision of the public good (Olson, 1965).

In game experiments, cooperative solutions are reached only after a series of plays of the game. In the absence of direct communication and agreement, time is needed to learn the behavior of the other player(s). Generalizing from these findings, one can expect the voluntary provision of public goods and cooperative behavioral constraints to be greater in small, stable communities of homogeneous behavior patterns.

In the large, mobile, heterogeneous community, a formal statement of what behavior is mutually beneficial (e.g., how much each must contribute for a public good) may be needed even for individuals to know what behavior is consistent with the public interest. Given the incentives to free ride, compliance may require the implementation of individualized rewards or sanctions. Mancur Olson (1965, pp. 50–1, 132–67) found that individual par-

2. For classical discussions of moral behavior and punishment, which are most modern and in line with the prisoners' dilemma discussion, see Thomas Hobbes, *Leviathan* (1651, chs. 14, 15, 17, 18); David Hume (1751, pp. 120–7).

ticipation in large, voluntary organizations like labor unions, professional lobbies, and other special interest groups was dependent not on the collective benefits these organizations provided for all of their members, but on the individualized incentives they provided in the form of selective benefits for participation and attendance, or penalties in the form of dues, fines, and other individualized sanctions.

Thus, democracy, with its formal voting procedures for making and enforcing collective choices, is an institution that is needed by communities of only a certain size and impersonality. The family makes an array of collective decisions without ever voting; a tribe votes only occasionally. A metropolis or nation state may have to make a great number of decisions by collective choice processes, although many of them may not correspond to what we have here defined as a democratic process.[3] Similarly, small, stable communities may be able to elicit voluntary compliance with group mores and contributions for the provision of local public goods by the use of informal communication channels and peer group pressure. Larger, more impersonal communities must typically establish formal penalties against asocial behavior (like stealing), levy taxes to provide for public goods, and employ a police force to ensure compliance.

The size of the community, its reliance on formal sanctions and police enforcement, and the breakdown of the prisoner's dilemma may all be dynamically related. Detection of violators of the prisoners' dilemma takes time. An increase in the number of violations can be expected to lead to a further increase in violations but only with a time lag. If, because of an increase in community size, or for some other reason, the frequency of violations were to increase, the frequency of violations in latter periods could be expected to increase even further, and with these the need for and reliance on police enforcement of the laws. James Buchanan (1975a, pp. 123–9) has described such a process as the erosion of a community's legal (i.e., rule-abiding) capital.[4] Michael Taylor (1976, pp. 132–40) has presented a similar scenario. Taylor relates the breakdown of the cooperative solution to the prisoners' dilemma not to the size of the community, however, but to the level of government intervention itself.[5] Intervention of the state in the provision of a community want or in the enforcement of social mores, psychologically

3. It must also be kept in mind that democracy is but one, *potential* means for providing public goods. Autocracies and oligarchies also provide public goods to "their" communities. This survey has little to say about them, except to the extent that oligarchs resolve their differences by voting. Autocracies are briefly discussed in Chapter 14.

4. See also Buchanan (1965b).

5. Indeed, at several points he seems on the verge of arguing that the likelihood of a cooperative outcome to the game is not dependent on the size of the community (1976, pp. 23–5, 27 n. 16, 61, 92). But eventually he does concede its dependence on size (p. 92), and his discussion of anarchy is clearly couched in terms of the small, stable community (ch. 7).

"frees" an individual from responsibility for providing for community wants and preserving its mores. State intervention leads to increased asocial behavior requiring more state intervention, and so on. The theories of Buchanan and Taylor might constitute one explanation for the rising government expenditures that have occurred in this century. Their theories would link these expenditures directly to the increasing mobility and urbanization that has occurred during the century, and the consequent increases in government intervention this has caused.

The scenarios by Buchanan and Taylor of the unraveling of the social fabric mirror to a remarkable degree the description by John Rawls (1971, pp. 496–504) of the evolution of a just society, in which the moral (just, cooperative) behavior of one individual leads to increasingly moral behavior by others, reinforcing the cooperative behavior of the first and encouraging still more. The dynamic process in these scenarios is the same, only the direction of change is reversed.

B.   Public goods and chickens

The prisoners' dilemma is the most frequently used characterization of the situations to which public goods give rise. But the technology of public goods provision can be such as to generate other kinds of strategic interactions. Consider the following example.

The properties of two individuals share a common boundary. G owns a goat that occasionally wanders into D's garden and eats the vegetables and flowers. D has a dog that sometimes crosses into G's property, chasing and frightening the goat so that it does not give milk. A fence separating the two properties could stop both from happening.

Matrix 2.2 depicts the situation. With no fence, both D and G experience utility levels of one. The fence costs $1,000 and each would be willing to pay the full cost if necessary to get the benefits of the fence. The utility levels of each (2) are higher with the fence than without it, even when they must pay the full cost alone. This assumption ensures that the utility levels of both individuals are still higher if each must pay only half the cost of the fence (square 1). Last of all, each is, of course, best off if the fence is built and he pays nothing (payoffs of 3.5 to G and D, respectively, in squares 2 and 4).

Matrix 2.2 depicts the game of "chicken." It differs from the prisoners' dilemma in that the outcome in which no one contributes (cell 3), which is Pareto inferior to the outcome that both contribute (cell 1), is not an equilibrium. Since each individual is better off even if he must pay for the fence alone, each would be willing to move to square 2 or 4, as the case may be, rather than see the outcome remain at cell 3. Cells 2 and 4 are both equilibria in this game, and they are the only two. The ordering of payoffs in a game of

Matrix 2.2. *Fence building as a game of chicken*

	D Contributes to building fence	Does not contribute
Contributes to building fence	1 (3, 3)	4 (2, 3.5)
Does not contribute	2 (3.5, 2)	3 (1, 1)

chicken for the row player is cell $2 > 1 > 4 > 3$, whereas in a prisoners' dilemma it is $2 > 1 > 3 > 4$. The interchange of the last two cells for both players causes the shift in the equilibrium.

In cells 4, 1, and 2, the fence is built. These cells differ only in who pays for the fence and the resulting utility payoffs. In cell 4, G pays the full \$1,000 cost of the fence and experiences a utility level of 2. In cell 1, G pays \$500 and receives a utility level of 3, while in cell 2 G pays nothing for a utility level of 3.5. The lower increment in utility in going from a \$500 fall in income to no change in income, compared with going from a \$1,000 fall in income to a \$500 fall, reflects an assumption of the declining marginal utility of income. If both G and D have declining marginal utilities of income, as assumed in the figures in Matrix 2.2, then the solution that they share the cost of the fence is welfare maximizing as well as equitable. Under alternative assumptions, a stronger, higher fence may be built when the cost is shared, and the result may be an efficiency gain from the cost-sharing solution in cell 1. But the outcome in cell 1 is not an equilibrium. Both D and G will be better off if they can convince the other to pay the full cost of the fence. One way to do this is to precommit oneself not to build the fence, or at least to convince one's neighbor that one has made such a commitment so that the neighbor, say D, believes that her choice is between cells 2 and 3, and thus naturally chooses cell 2.

The chicken game is often used to depict the interactions of nations (Schelling, 1966, ch. 2). Let D be a superpower, which favors having other countries install democratic institutions, C a country favoring communist institutions. A civil war rages in small country S between one group seeking to install a communist regime and another group wishing to install a democratic constitution. The situation could easily take on the characteristics of a game of chicken. Each superpower wants to support the group favoring its ideology in S, and wants the other superpower to back down. But if the other superpower, say C, is supporting its group in S, then D is better off backing off than supporting its group in S and thereby being led into a direct confrontation with the other superpower. Both powers are clearly better off if they both back off than if the confrontation occurs.

Given this game of chicken configuration of payoffs, each superpower may try to get the other to back off by precommiting itself to defending democracy (communism) wherever it is threatened around the world. Such a precommitment combined with a reputation for "toughness" could force the other superpower to back down each time a clash between communist and noncommunist forces occurs in a small country.

The danger in a chicken situation, however, is that both superpowers may become so committed to their strategy of supporting groups of their ideology, and so committed to preserving their reputations for toughness, that neither side will back down. The confrontation of the superpowers is precipitated by the civil war in S. The fence does not get built.

As in prisoners' dilemma situations, the joint cooperation solution to the chicken game can emerge from a chicken supergame, if each player recognizes the long-run advantages to cooperation and adopts the tit-for-tat supergame strategy or an analogous one (Taylor and Ward, 1982; Ward, 1987). Alternatively, the two superpowers (neighbors) may recognize the dangers inherent in the noncooperative, precommitment strategy and thus may directly approach one another and agree to follow the cooperative strategy. Thus, although the structure of the chicken game differs from that of the prisoners' dilemma, the optimal solutions of the game are similar, requiring some sort of formal or tacit agreement to cooperate. As the number of players increases, the likelihood that a formal agreement is required increases (Taylor and Ward, 1982; Ward, 1987). Thus, for the chicken game, as for the prisoners' dilemma game, the necessity of having democratic institutions to achieve the efficient, cooperative solution to the game increases in likelihood as the number of players of the game rises.

C.* Voluntary provision of public goods with constant returns to scale

In this section we explore more formally the problems that arise in the voluntary provision of a public good. Consider as the pure public good a levy or dike built of bags of sand. Each member of the community voluntarily supplies as many bags of sand as she chooses. The total number of bags supplied is the summation of the individual contributions of each member. The more bags supplied, the higher and stronger the dike, and the better off are all members of the community.

Letting G_i be the contribution to the public good of individual i, then the total quantity of public good supplied is

$$G = G_1 + G_2 + G_3 + \cdots G_n. \tag{2.1}$$

Let each individual's utility function be given as $U_i(X_i, G)$, where X_i is the quantity of private good i consumes.

Now consider the decision of i as to how much of the public good to supply, that is, the optimal G_i, given her budget constraint $Y_i = P_x X_i + P_g G_i$, where Y_i is her income and P_x and P_g are the prices of the private and public goods, respectively. In the absence of an institution for coordinating the quantities of public good supplied, each individual must decide independently of the other individuals how much of the public good to supply. In making this decision, it is reasonable to assume that the individual takes the supply of the public good by the rest of the communities as fixed, and chooses the level of G_i that maximizes U_i, given the values of G_j chosen by all other individuals j, in the community. Her objective function is thus

$$O_i = U_i(X_i, G) + \lambda_i(Y_i - P_x X_i - P_g G_i). \tag{2.2}$$

Maximizing (2.2) with respect to G_i and X_i yields

$$\frac{\partial U_i}{\partial G} - \lambda_i P_g = 0 \tag{2.3}$$

$$\frac{\partial U_i}{\partial X_i} - \lambda_i P_x = 0, \tag{2.4}$$

from which we obtain

$$\frac{\partial U_i / \partial G}{\partial U_i / \partial X_i} = \frac{P_g}{P_x} \tag{2.5}$$

as the condition for utility maximization. Each individual purchases the public good as if it were a private good, taking the purchases of the other members of the community as given. This equilibrium is often referred to as a Cournot or Nash equilibrium, as it resembles the behavioral assumption Cournot made concerning the supply of a homogeneous private good in an oligopolistic market.

Now let us contrast (2.5) with the conditions for Pareto optimality. To obtain these, we maximize the following welfare function:

$$W = \gamma_1 U_1 + \gamma_2 U_2 + \cdots + \gamma_n U_n, \tag{2.6}$$

where all $\gamma_i > 0$. Given the positive weights on all individual utilities, any allocation that was not Pareto optimal – that is, from which one person's utility could be increased without lowering anyone else's – could not be at a maximum for W. Thus, choosing X_i and G_i to maximize W gives us a Pareto-optimal allocation.

Maximizing (2.6) subject to the aggregate budget constraint

$$\sum_{i=1}^{n} Y_i = P_x \sum_{i=1}^{n} X_i + P_g G, \tag{2.7}$$

we obtain the first-order conditions

$$\sum_{i=1}^{n} \gamma_i \frac{\partial U_i}{\partial G} - \lambda P_g = 0 \tag{2.8}$$

and

$$\gamma_i \frac{\partial U_i}{\partial X_i} - \lambda P_x = 0, \quad i = 1, n, \tag{2.9}$$

where λ is the Lagrangian multiplier on the budget constraint. Using the n equations in (2.9) to eliminate the γ_i in (2.8), we obtain

$$\sum_i \frac{\lambda P_x}{\partial U_i / \partial X_i} \cdot \partial U_i / \partial G = \lambda P_g, \tag{2.10}$$

from which we obtain

$$\sum_i \frac{\partial U_i / \partial G}{\partial U_i / \partial X_i} = \frac{P_g}{P_x}. \tag{2.11}$$

Equation (2.11) is the familiar Samuelsonian (1954) condition for Pareto optimality in the presence of public goods. Although independent utility maximization decisions lead each individual to equate her marginal rate of substitution of public for private good to their price ratios, as if the public good were in fact private (2.5), Pareto optimality requires that the summation of the marginal rates of substitution over all members of the community be equated to this price ratio (2.11).

That the quantity of public good provided under the Cournot–Nash equilibrium (2.5) is likely to be less than the Pareto-optimal quantity can be seen by rewriting (2.11) as

$$\frac{\partial U_i / \partial G}{\partial U_i / \partial X_i} = \frac{P_g}{P_x} - \sum_{j \neq i} \frac{\partial U_j / \partial G}{\partial U_j / \partial X_j}. \tag{2.12}$$

If G and X are normal goods in each individual's utility function, then

$$\sum_{j \neq i} \frac{\partial U_j / \partial G}{\partial U_j / \partial X_j} > 0,$$

and the marginal rate of substitution of public for private good for individual i defined by (2.12) will be less than that defined by (2.5), which implies that a greater quantity of G and a smaller quantity of X_i are being consumed when (2.12) is satisfied than when (2.5) is.

To gain a feeling for the quantitative significance of the differences, consider the special case where U_i is a Cobb–Douglas utility function, that is, $U_i = X_i^\alpha G^\beta$, $0 < \alpha < 1$, and $0 < \beta < 1$. Under this assumption (2.5) becomes

$$\frac{\beta X_i^\alpha G^{\beta-1}}{\alpha X_i^{\alpha-1} G^\beta} = \frac{P_g}{P_x},$$

(2.13)

from which it follows that

$$G = \frac{P_x}{P_g} \frac{\beta}{\alpha} X_i.$$

(2.14)

Substituting from (2.1) and the budget constraint yields

$$\sum_i G_i = \frac{P_x}{P_g} \frac{\beta}{\alpha} \left(\frac{Y_i}{P_x} - \frac{P_g}{P_x} G_i \right),$$

(2.15)

from which we obtain

$$\left(1 + \frac{\beta}{\alpha} \right) G_i = - \sum_{j \neq i} G_j + \frac{\beta}{\alpha} \frac{Y_i}{P_g}$$

(2.16)

or

$$G_i = - \frac{\alpha}{\alpha + \beta} \sum_{j \neq i} G_j + \frac{\beta}{\alpha + \beta} \frac{Y_i}{P_g}.$$

(2.17)

Equation (2.17) implies that individual i voluntarily chooses to supply a smaller amount of the public good, the larger she believes the amount of public good provided by the other citizens to be. With only two individuals in the community, (2.17) defines the familiar reaction curve from duopoly theory. In this situation, it is a negativity-sloped straight line.

If all members of the community have identical incomes, Y, then all will choose the same levels of G_i, and (2.17) can be used to find the contribution in equilibrium of a single individual:

$$G_i = - \frac{\alpha}{\alpha + \beta} (n - 1)G_i + \frac{\beta}{\alpha + \beta} \frac{Y}{P_g},$$

(2.18)

from which we obtain

$$G_i = \frac{\beta}{\alpha n + \beta} \frac{Y}{P_g}.$$

(2.19)

The amount of the public good provided by the community through independent contributions then becomes

$$G = nG_i = \frac{n\beta}{\alpha n + \beta} \frac{Y}{P_g}.$$

(2.20)

These quantities can be compared to the Pareto-optimal quantities. With all individual incomes equal, all individuals contribute the same G_i and have the same X_i left over, so that (2.11) becomes

$$n \frac{\beta X_i^\alpha G^{\beta-1}}{\alpha X_i^{\alpha-1} G^\beta} = \frac{P_g}{P_x} \, . \tag{2.21}$$

Using the budget constraint to eliminate the X_i and rearranging yields for the Pareto-optimal contribution of a single individual

$$G_i = \frac{\beta}{\alpha + \beta} \frac{Y}{P_g} \tag{2.22}$$

and

$$G = nG_i = \frac{n\beta}{\alpha + \beta} \frac{Y}{P_g} \, . \tag{2.23}$$

Let us call the Pareto-optimal quantity of public good defined by (2.23), G_{PO}, and the quantity under the Cournot–Nash equilibrium (2.20), G_{CN}. Their ratio is then

$$\frac{G_{CN}}{G_{PO}} = \frac{\dfrac{n\beta}{\alpha n + \beta} \dfrac{Y}{P_g}}{\dfrac{n\beta}{\alpha + \beta} \dfrac{Y}{P_g}} = \frac{\alpha + \beta}{\alpha n + \beta} \, . \tag{2.24}$$

This ratio is less than one, if $n > 1$, and tends toward zero as n becomes increasingly large. Thus, for all communities greater than a solitary individual, voluntary, independent supply of the public good leads to less than the Pareto-optimal quantity being supplied, and the relative gap between the two quantities grows as community size increases.

The extent of underprovision of the public good at a Cournot–Nash equilibrium depends on the nature of the individual utility functions (Cornes and Sandler, 1986, ch. 5). For the Cobb–Douglas utility function, the extent of underprovision is *smaller,* the greater is the ratio of β to α. With $\alpha = 0$ – that is, when the marginal utility of the private good is zero – $G_{CN} = G_{PO}$. This equality also holds with right-angled indifference curves, where again the marginal utility of the private good, holding the quantity of the public good fixed, is zero (Cornes and Sandler, 1986, p. 81). But with the familiar, smooth, convex-to-the-origin indifference curves, one can expect an underprovision of a voluntarily provided public good, and an underprovision whose relative size grows with the size of the community. To achieve the Pareto-optimal allocation, some institution for coordinating the contributions of each individual is needed.

D.* Voluntary provision of public goods with varying supply technologies

Many public goods might be depicted using the summation technology of the previous section. Public goods of a prisoners' dilemma type – for example, community order, environmental quality – are provided by each individual contributing to the "production" of the public good by not stealing or not polluting. For the typical public good of this kind, the quantity supplied is to some degree additive with respect to each individual's contribution. The more people there are who refrain from stealing, the more secure is the community, and the greater the benefits consumed by all members.

There are other public goods, however, for which the participation of all members is necessary to secure *any* benefits. The crew of a small sailboat, two-man rowboats, and bobsleds are examples. For the rowboat to go in a straight line each rower must pull the oar with equal force. Under- or over-contributions are penalized by the boat's moving in a circle. Only the equal contribution of both rowers is rewarded by the boat's moving forward. With such goods, cells 2, 4, and 3 collapse into one and cooperative behavior is voluntarily forthcoming.

Goods such as these are produced by what Jack Hirshleifer (1983, 1984) has named the "weakest-link" technology. The amount of public good provided is equal to the smallest quantity provided by any member of the community. At the other pole from weakest-link technology one can conceive of a best-shot technology for which the amount of public good provided is equal to the largest quantity provided by any one member of the community. As an example of the best-shot technology, one can think of a community first having each member design a boat (bridge) for crossing a given body of water, and then the best design being selected and constructed.

The weakest-link technology is like a fixed coefficients production function for public goods. Individual i's marginal contribution to public good supply, $\partial G / \partial G_i$, is zero, if his contribution exceeds that of any other member of the community ($G_i > G_j$ for some j). But $\partial G / \partial G_i$ equals the community supply function when $G_i < G_j$ for all j. The summation technology assumes an additive and separable production function, whereas the best-shot technology assumes a sort of discontinuously increasing returns. The latter seems the least plausible of the three, so we consider only the cases falling in the range between the weakest-link and summation production technologies.

Consider a community of two Australian farmers whose fields are adjacent to one another and border on a segment of the bush. Each night the kangaroos come out of the bush and destroy the farmers' crops. The farmers can protect their crops, however, by erecting fences along the border between their property and the bush. Each farmer is responsible for buying fence for his own segment of the border. The following technologies can be envisaged.

> *Weakest link:* Kangaroos adapt quickly to changes in their environ-
> ment, and discover the lowest point in the fence. The number
> of kangaroos entering both farmers' fields is determined by the
> height of the fence at its lowest point.

Unweighted summation: Kangaroos are very dumb and probe the fence at random. The number of kangaroos entering the two fields varies inversely with the average height of the two fences.

Diminishing returns: If one farmer's fence is lower than the other's, some kangaroos learn to probe only the lower fence, but not all learn, and the higher fence stops some kangaroos from going over.

Now consider the following general formulation of public good supply: Let G be the number of units of public good provided, defined in this case as the number of kangaroos prevented from entering the fields. Let the units of fence purchased at price P_f be defined so that

$$G = F_1 + wF_2, \quad 0 \leq F_1 \leq F_2, \, 0 \leq w \leq 1, \tag{2.25}$$

where F_i is farmer i's purchase of fence. If $w = 0$, we have the weakest link case, and $G = F_1$, the smaller of the two contributions. The larger w is, the more 2's contribution beyond 1's contributes to the supply of G, until with $w = 1$, we reach the unweighted summation supply function examined above.

To simplify the problem, assume that both farmers have identical utility functions and both G and the private good X are noninferior. Then the farmer with the lower income will always choose to purchase the smaller quantity of fence, so that farmer 1 is the farmer with the smaller income of the two. He maximizes his utility $U_1(X,G)$ by choosing a level of private good consumption X_1 and contribution to the public good F_1 satisfying his budget constraint, $Y_1 = P_x X_1 + P_f F_1$. The solution is again equation (2.5), with the price of the public good now P_f.

The solution to the utility maximization problem for farmer 2 is, however,

$$\frac{\partial U_2 / \partial G}{\partial U_2 / \partial X} = \frac{P_f}{wP_x} \tag{2.26}$$

as long as $F_2 > F_1$. In effect, farmer 2 faces a higher relative price for the public good F, since his contributions do not contribute as much on the margin as 1's, owing to the technology defined by (2.25). The smaller w is, the less fence 2 buys (the smaller his optimal contribution to the public good). With small enough w, the solution to (2.26) would require $F_2 < F_1$. But then 2 would be the smaller contributor and his optimal contribution would be defined by (2.5). Since 2 favors a greater contribution than 1, he simply matches 1's contribution if satisfying (2.26) violates $F_2 > F_1$.

To determine the condition for the Pareto-optimal level of G, we choose levels of X_1, X_2, and G to maximize 1's utility, holding 2's utility constant, and satisfying (2.25) and the individual budget constraints; that is, we maximize

$$L = U_1(X_1,G) + \gamma[\bar{U}_2 - U_2(X_2,G)] + \lambda[G - F_1 - wF_2], \tag{2.27}$$

from which it follows that

$$\frac{\partial U_1/\partial G}{\partial U_1/\partial X} + w\,\frac{\partial U_2/\partial G}{\partial U_2/\partial X} = \frac{P_f}{P_x}. \tag{2.28}$$

Only in the extreme weakest-link case, where $w = 0$, is the condition for Pareto optimality for the community (2.28) satisfied by the two individuals acting independently, for then (2.28) collapses to (2.5), and both farmers purchase the amounts of fence satisfying (2.5).[6] With $w = 1$, on the other hand, we have the unweighted summation supply of public good, and (2.28) becomes (2.11), the Samuelsonian (1954) condition for Pareto optimality, and too little public good is being supplied.

Moreover, the difference between the quantity of public good supplied voluntarily when each farmer acts independently and the Pareto-optimal quantity increases with w. To illustrate this, again let both individuals have identical incomes Y, and identical utility functions $U = X^\alpha G^\beta$. Both then purchase the same quantity of fence F and private good X. From (2.5) and (2.25) we obtain the Cournot–Nash equilibrium quantity of public good supplied through the independent utility-maximizing decisions of the two farmers:

$$G_{CN} = \frac{\beta Y(1 + w)}{P_f[\alpha(1 + w) + \beta]}. \tag{2.29}$$

In the same way, (2.28) can be used to obtain Pareto-optimal G:

$$G_{PO} = \frac{\beta}{\alpha + \beta}\,\frac{Y}{P_f}\,(1 + w). \tag{2.30}$$

Dividing (2.29) by (2.30) we obtain the ratio of independently supplied to Pareto-optimal quantities of public good;

$$\frac{G_{CN}}{G_{PO}} = \frac{\alpha + \beta}{\alpha(1 + w) + \beta}. \tag{2.31}$$

With $w = 0$, the ratio is one, but it falls as w increases.

With n individuals, (2.28) generalizes to

$$\frac{\partial U_1/\partial G}{\partial U_1/\partial X} + w_2\,\frac{\partial U_2/\partial G}{\partial U_2/\partial X} + w_3\,\frac{\partial U_3/\partial G}{\partial U_3/\partial X} + \cdots + w_n\,\frac{\partial U_n/\partial G}{\partial U_n/\partial X} = \frac{P_f}{P_x} \tag{2.32}$$

---

6. This conclusion is contingent on the initial incomes of the two farmers and the implicit constraint that farmer 2 cannot transfer money to 1 or purchase fence for him. With w low enough or Y_2/Y_1 high enough, unconstrained Pareto optimality may require that 2 subsidize 1's purchase of fence. See Hirshleifer (1984).

and (2.31) generalizes to

$$\frac{G_{CN}}{G_{PO}} = \frac{\alpha + \beta}{\alpha(1 + w_2 + w_3 + \cdots + w_n) + \beta} . \tag{2.33}$$

The gap between the independently provided and Pareto-optimal quantities of public good increases as the number of members of the community increases, and the weights on the additional contributions increase.

Experiments by Harrison and Hirshleifer (1986) with two players indicate that individuals will voluntarily provide nearly the Pareto-optimal quantity of public good in weakest-link ($w = 0$) situations, but underprovide in summation and best-shot situations. Experimental results by van de Kragt, Orbell, and Dawes (1983) with small groups also indicate that efficient public good provision is forthcoming in situations resembling the weakest-link technology. Thus, voluntary provision of public goods without coordination or coercion at Pareto-optimal levels is possible when the technology of public good provision conforms to the weakest-link condition. Unfortunately, with large communities it is difficult to think of many public goods for which voluntary provision is feasible, and all w_i for contributions greater than the minimum are zero or close to it. In large communities, therefore, some institutional mechanism for coordinating and coercing individual contributions to the supply of public goods seems likely to be needed.

E.   Externalities

Public goods are a classic example of the kinds of market failures economists cite as justification for government intervention. Externalities are the second primary category of market failure. An externality occurs when the consumption or production activity of one individual or firm has an *unintended* impact on the utility or production function of another individual or firm. Individual A plants a tree to provide herself shade, but inadvertently blocks her neighbor's view of the valley. The pulp mill discharges waste into the river and inadvertently raises the costs of production for the brewery downstream. These activities may be contrasted with normal market transactions in which A's action, say, buying the tree, has an impact on B, the seller of the tree, but the impact is fully accounted for through the operation of the price system. There is no market for the view of the valley, or the quality of water in the river, and thus no price mechanism for coordinating individual actions. Given the existence of externalities, a non-Pareto-optimal allocation of resources often results.

To see the problem more clearly, let us consider a situation in which two individuals each consume private good X, and A consumes externality creating good E. Individual A then purchases X and E so as to maximize her utility subject to the budget constraint, $Y_A = X_A P_x + E_A P_e$; that is, A maximizes

$$L = U_A(X_A, E_A) + \lambda(Y_A - X_A P_x - E_A P_e). \tag{2.34}$$

Maximization of (2.34) with respect to X and E yields the familiar first-order condition for individual utility maximization when there are two private goods:

$$\frac{\partial U_A/\partial E}{\partial U_A/\partial X} = \frac{P_e}{P_x}. \tag{2.35}$$

But E is an activity that produces an externality and thus enters B's utility function also, even though B does not buy or sell E. We can solve for the Pareto-optimal allocation of X and E by maximizing one individual's utility, subject to the constraints that the other individual's utility is held constant, and the combined budget of the two individuals is not exceeded.

$$L_{PO} = U_A(X_A, E_A) + \lambda(\bar{U}_B - U_B(X_B, E_A)) + \gamma(Y_A + Y_B - P_x X_A - P_x X_B - P_e E_A). \tag{2.36}$$

The presence of A's consumption of E, E_A, in B's utility function represents the externality nature of the E activity. Maximizing (2.36) with respect to X_A, X_B, and E_A yields

$$\frac{\partial L_{PO}}{\partial X_A} = \frac{\partial U_A}{\partial X} - \gamma P_x = 0 \tag{2.37}$$

$$\frac{\partial L_{PO}}{\partial X_B} = \lambda \left(-\frac{\partial U_B}{\partial X} \right) - \gamma P_x = 0 \tag{2.38}$$

$$\frac{\partial L_{PO}}{\partial E_A} = \frac{\partial U_A}{\partial E} - \lambda \frac{\partial U_B}{\partial E} - \gamma P_e = 0. \tag{2.39}$$

Eliminating λ and γ from (2.37), (2.38), and (2.39), we obtain as the condition for Pareto optimality

$$\frac{\partial U_A/\partial E}{\partial U_A/\partial X} + \frac{\partial U_B/\partial E}{\partial U_B/\partial X} = \frac{P_e}{P_x} \tag{2.40}$$

or

$$\frac{\partial U_A/\partial E}{\partial U_A/\partial X} = \frac{P_e}{P_x} - \frac{\partial U_B/\partial E}{\partial U_B/\partial X}. \tag{2.41}$$

Equation (2.41) gives the condition for Pareto optimality; equation (2.35), the condition for individual A's optimal allocation of her budget. Equation (2.35) governs the determination of the level of E, since only A decides how much E is purchased. If activity E creates a positive externality,

$$\frac{\partial U_B/\partial E}{\partial U_B/\partial X} > 0$$

then

$$\frac{\partial U_A/\partial E}{\partial U_A/\partial X}$$

is larger than is required for Pareto optimality. A purchases too little E (and too much X) when E produces a positive external economy. Conversely, when E generates a negative externality,

$$\frac{\partial U_B/\partial E}{\partial U_B/\partial X} < 0$$

and A buys too much of E.

Although seemingly a separate category of market failure, the Pareto-optimality condition for an externality is identical to that for a pure public good, as a comparison of (2.40) and (2.11) reveals (Buchanan and Stubblebine, 1962). The difference between a pure public good and an externality is that in the case of a public good all members of the community consume the same good, whereas for an externality the good (bad) consumed by the second parties may differ from that consumed by the direct purchaser. When A contributes to the purchase of flowers for the town square, she helps finance a public good. When A plants flowers in her backyard, she creates a positive externality for those neighbors who can see and enjoy them. If some of A's neighbors are allergic to pollen from the flowers, A's plantings create a negative externality. What is crucial to the issue of Pareto optimality is not that A and B consume precisely the same good, but that A's consumption alters B's utility in a manner not accounted for through the price system. B is not excluded from the side effects of A's consumption, and it is this nonexcludability condition that joins public goods and externalities by one and the same Pareto-optimality condition. It is this nonexcludability condition that necessitates some coordination of A and B's activities to achieve Pareto optimality.

One way to adjust A's consumption of E to bring about Pareto optimality is for the government to levy a tax or offer a subsidy to the E activity. If, for example, E generates a negative externality, a tax on E equal to

$$-\frac{\partial U_B/\partial E}{\partial U_B/\partial X}$$

will raise the price of E relative to X by precisely the amount necessary to achieve Pareto optimality. Alternatively, a subsidy to A for each unit of E she consumes less than the amount implied by (2.35) achieves the same effect. The existence of a government to correct for externalities by levying taxes and offering subsidies is a traditional explanation for government intervention most frequently associated with the name of Arthur Pigou (1920).

In most discussions of Pigouvian taxes, the government is assumed to "know" the marginal rate of substitution schedules of the different parties generating and affected by the externalities. Often the government is referred to as an individual, the policy maker, who possesses all of the information relevant to determine the Pareto-optimal allocation of resources and who then announces the optimal taxes and subsidies. But where does the policy maker obtain this information? In some situations – for example, when one factory's activities affect the costs of another – one might think of the government policy maker as gathering engineering data and using these to make a decision. But when individual utilities are affected, the engineer's information-gathering problem is greatly complicated. Much of this book is concerned with describing how democratic institutions reveal information concerning individual preferences on externality-type decisions. The next section discusses a more direct approach to the question.

F.   The Coase theorem

Ronald Coase in a classic article published in 1960 challenged the conventional wisdom in economics regarding externalities, taxes, and subsidies. Coase argued that the existence of an external effect associated with a given activity did not inevitably require government intervention in the form of taxes and subsidies. Pareto-optimal resolution to externality situations could have been and were often worked out between the affected parties with the help of the government. Moreover, the nature of the outcome was independent of the assignment of property rights, that is, in the case of a negative externality associated with E whether the law granted the purchaser of E the right to purchase E in unlimited quantities, or the law granted B the right to be protected from any adverse effects from A's consumption of E.

Although Coase develops his argument by example, and neither states nor proves any theorems, the main results of the paper are commonly referred to as the Coase theorem. The theorem can be expressed as follows:

The Coase theorem: *In the absence of transactions and bargaining costs, affected parties to an externality will agree on an allocation of resources that is both Pareto optimal and independent of any prior assignment of property rights.*

Pigou was wrong; government intervention is not needed to resolve externality issues.

Consider first a discrete case of the theorem. Let A be a factory producing widgets with a by-product of smoke. Let C be a laundry whose costs are raised by A's emissions of smoke. Given that A is in business, C's profits are $24,000, but if A were to cease production altogether, C's profits would rise to $31,000. A's profits are $3,000. Assuming A's factors can be costlessly redeployed, society is better off if A ceases production. C then earns a net surplus over costs of $31,000, while the combined surplus when A and C both operate is only $27,000.

But suppose that there are no laws prohibiting smoke emissions. A is then free to produce, and the socially inferior outcome would appear to ensue. It would, however, pay C to bribe the owners of A to cease production by promising to pay them $3,000 per annum. Alternatively, C could acquire A and close it down. If i is the cost of capital, and the market expects A to earn $3,000 profits per year in perpetuity, then the market value of A is $3,000/i$. The present discounted value to C of shutting A down is $7,000/i$, however. The owners of C will realize an increase in wealth of $4,000/i$ by acquiring and closing A.

To see that the socially efficient outcome arises regardless of the assignment of property rights, assume that A's annual profit is $10,000 and the figures for C are as before. Now the efficient solution requires that A continue to operate. Suppose, however, that the property rights lie with C. Strict air pollution laws exist and C can file a complaint against A and force it to cease production. The profits of A are now such, however, that it can offer C a bribe of $7,000 + \alpha$, $0 \leq \alpha \leq $3,000, not to file a complaint. The owners of both firms are as well or better off under this alternative than they are if A closes, and the socially efficient outcome can again be expected to occur.

Note that under the conditions of the first example, where A's profits were only $3,000, it would not pay A to bribe C to allow it to continue to produce, and the socially efficient outcome would again occur.

When the externality-producing activity has a variable effect on the second party as the level of the activity changes, the Coase theorem still holds. If A's marginal rate of substitution of E for X (MRS_{EX}^A) falls as E increases, then $MRS_{EX}^A - P_e/P_x$ is negative sloped, as in Figure 2.1. The point where $MRS_{EX}^A - P_e/P_x$ crosses the horizontal axis, E_I, is the level of E that A chooses when she acts independently of B. It is the level of E satisfying equation (2.35).

If E creates a negative externality on B, then $-MRS_{EX}^B$ is positive. In Figure 2.1, $-MRS_{EX}^B$ is drawn under the reasonable assumption that B is willing to give up an increasing amount of X to prevent A from consuming another unit of E, the higher E is. E_{PO} is the Pareto-optimal level of E, the level satisfying equation (2.41).

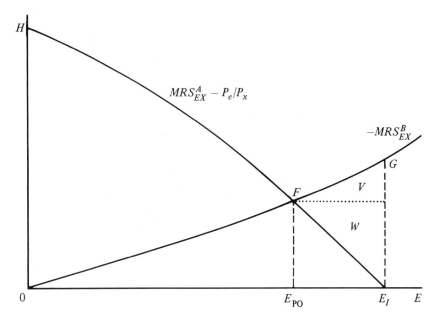

Figure 2.1. Pareto-optimal quantity of a good with external effects.

The area $E_{PO}FGE_I$ measures the utility loss to B from A's consumption of E_I instead of E_{PO}. $E_{PO}FE_I$ measures A's utility gain from these extra units of E. Both B and A will be made better off if A accepts a bribe of Z from B to consume E_{PO} rather than E_I, where $E_{PO}FE_I < Z < E_{PO}FGE_I$. In particular, if B were to offer A a bribe of $E_{PO}F$ for each unit of E she refrained from consuming, A would choose to consume exactly E_{PO} units of E, and A would be better off by the area W, and B by the area V as against the independent action outcome at E_I.

With the property rights reversed, B could forbid A from consuming E and force the outcome at 0. But then A would be forgoing $OHFE_{PO}$ benefits, while B gains only OFE_{PO}, as opposed to the Pareto-optimal allocation E_{PO}. Self-interest would lead A to propose and B to accept a bribe Z', to allow A to consume E_{PO}, where $OFE_{PO} < Z' < OHFE_{PO}$.[7]

Coase (1960) demonstrated his theorem with four examples drawn from actual cases. Several recent experiments have been run with student subjects

---

7. For the quantity of E bought to be the same, whether A receives or pays the bribe, no income effects must be present. When they exist, precise solutions require the use of compensated demand functions (Buchanan and Stubblebine, 1962).

   I also abstract from the large numbers problems and the difficulty of people moving close to a negative externality to receive a bribe, as discussed by Baumol (1972).

in which the students are given payoff tables that resemble those one would observe in an externality situation. Pareto-optimal outcomes are observed in well over 90 percent of the experiments.[8] The Coase theorem offers a logical and empirically relevant alternative to government action in externality situations. But does it hold up as the number of parties involved in the externality increases? We now turn to this question.

G.* Coase and the core

The examples presented by Coase and those discussed above involve but two parties. Does the theorem hold when more than two parties are involved? Hoffman and Spitzer (1986) present experimental results in which Pareto-optimal allocations are achieved in Coasian bargains among as many as 38 parties. But Aivazian and Callen (1981) present an example in which the theorem breaks down with only 3 parties. Let us consider their example.

They deal with a factory, A, producing smoke and a laundry, C, as in our example above. Representing company profits using the characteristic function notation of game theory, we can restate the above example as having the following attributes: $V(A) = \$3,000$, $V(C) = \$24,000$ and $V(A,C) = \$31,000$, where $V(A,C)$ is a coalition between A and C, that is, a merger of A and C that results in A's ceasing production.

Now assume the existence of a second factory, B, producing smoke. Let the characteristic functions for this problem be defined as follows:

$$
\begin{array}{lll}
V(A) = \$3,000 & V(B) = \$8,000 & V(C) = \$24,000 \\
V(A,B) = \$15,000 & V(A,C) = \$31,000 & V(B,C) = \$36,000 \\
& V(A,B,C) = \$40,000. &
\end{array}
$$

The Pareto-optimal outcome is that the grand coalition $V(A,B,C)$ forms; that is, A and B cease production. If the property right lies with C, the Pareto outcome occurs, C forbids A and B to produce, and neither a coalition between A and B ($V[A,B] = \$15,000$) nor the two firms independently ($\$3,000 + \$8,000$) can offer C a large enough bribe to offset its $\$16,000$ gain from going from $V(C)$ to $V(A,B,C)$.

Suppose, however, that A and B have the right to emit smoke. C offers A and B $\$3,000$ and $\$8,000$, respectively, to cease production. Such a proposal can be blocked by A offering to form a coalition with B and share $V(A,B) = \$15,000$ with allocations, say, of $X_A = \$6,500$, $X_B = \$8,500$. But C in turn can block a coalition between A and B by proposing a coalition between itself and B, with, say, $X_B = \$9,000$ and $X_C = \$27,000$. But this allocation can also be blocked.

8. See Hoffman and Spitzer (1982, 1986), Harrison and McKee (1985), and Coursey, Hoffman, and Spitzer (1987).

To prove generally that the grand coalition is unstable, we show that it is not within the *core*. Basically, a grand coalition is within the core if no subset of the coalition can form, including an individual acting independently, and provide its members higher payoffs than they can obtain in the grand coalition. If (X_A, X_B, X_C) is an allocation in the core, then it must satisfy conditions (2.42), (2.43), and (2.44):

$$X_A + X_B + X_C = V(A,B,C) \tag{2.42}$$

$$X_A \geq V(A), X_B \geq V(B), X_C \geq V(C) \tag{2.43}$$

$$X_A + X_B \geq V(A,B), X_A + X_C \geq V(A,C), X_B + X_C \geq V(B,C). \tag{2.44}$$

Condition (2.44) implies that

$$X_A + X_B + X_C \geq \tfrac{1}{2}[V(A,B) + V(A,C) + V(B,C)], \tag{2.45}$$

which from (2.42) implies that

$$V(A,B,C) \geq \tfrac{1}{2}[V(A,B) + V(A,C) + V(B,C)]. \tag{2.46}$$

But the numbers of the example contradict (2.46):

$$\$40,000 < \tfrac{1}{2}(\$15,000 + \$31,000 + \$36,000) = \$41,000.$$

The grand coalition is not in the core.

The primary issue in the present example is the externality of smoke caused by factories A and B imposed upon the laundry C. That there are gains from internalizing this externality is represented by the assumptions that

$$V(A,C) > V(A) + V(C) \tag{2.47}$$

$$V(B,C) > V(B) + V(C) \tag{2.48}$$

$$V(A,B,C) > V(A) + V(B,C) \tag{2.49}$$

$$V(A,B,C) > V(B) + V(A,C). \tag{2.50}$$

In their example, Aivazian and Callen also make the assumption that an externality exists between the two smoking factories; that is, there are gains to their forming a coalition independent of the laundry C:

$$V(A,B) > V(A) + V(B). \tag{2.51}$$

Now this is clearly a separate externality from that involving C and either or both of the two factories. Aivazian and Callen (p. 177) assume the existence of an economy of scale between A and B. But the existence of this second externality is crucial to the proof that no core exists. Combining (2.49) and (2.50) we obtain

$$V(A,B,C) > \tfrac{1}{2}[V(A) + V(B) + V(B,C) + V(A,C)]. \tag{2.52}$$

If now $V(A,B) \leq V(A) + V(B)$ – that is, there are no economies to forming the A,B coalition – then

$$V(A,B,C) > \frac{1}{2}[V(A,B) + V(B,C) + V(A,C)] \qquad (2.53)$$

and condition (2.46) is satisfied. The grand coalition is now in the core. Aivazian and Callen's demonstration that no core exists when property rights are assigned to the factories comes about not simply because a third player has been added to the game, but because a second externality has also been added, namely the gain from combining A and B. Moreover, the absence of the core hinges on the requirement that both externalities be eliminated simultaneously with the help of but one liability rule.

To what extent does this example weaken Coase's theorem? As long as we are concerned with eliminating the inefficiency caused by a single externality, I do not think that the example has much relevance. Suppose, for example, that the property rights are with A and B, but that the law allows C to close them if it pays just compensation. C offers the owners of A and B \$3,000 and \$8,000 per annum in perpetuity if they cease to operate. They refuse, demanding \$15,000. If the matter went to court, should the court consider an argument for awarding \$15,000 on the grounds that A and B could earn that much if they continued to operate *and if they decided to merge?* I doubt that any court would entertain such an argument. Nevertheless, by including the value of the coalition between A and B in the examination of the existence of the core, we have given legitimacy to a threat by A and B to merge and eliminate one externality as a hindrance to the formation of a coalition among C, A, and B to eliminate another. Conceptually, it seems preferable to assume that either A and B definitely will merge, absent agreement with C, or they will not. If they will, negotiation is between C and the coalition A,B, and the Coase theorem holds since $V(A,B,C) > V(C) + V(A,B)$. If A and B will not merge, (2.52) is the relevant condition for determining the existence of the core, and the theorem again holds.[9]

A generalization of the Coase theorem must exist for m externalities and n individuals that states that the allocative effects of the elimination of each externality is independent of the assignment of property rights, as long as there is a separate liability rule for each externality, bargaining on one externality is independent of bargaining on all others, and the zero transactions costs assumption holds.[10] When each externality is resolved individually,

9. The combined market values of A and B must lie between \$11,000/i, the value the market places on the firms if it assigns a zero probability to their merging (\$3,000/i + \$8,000/i), and \$15,000/i, the value of a merged firm. Thus, the option of C buying A and B and forming the grand coalition through merger must exist if ownership claims to A and B are for sale.

10. The actual allocations obtained would not be independent of the order in which the externalities issues were resolved. Moreover, the allocation resulting from the sequential elimina-

natural coalitions exist among the perpetrators of the externality and their victims (beneficiaries). The zero transactions costs assumption ensures that these coalitions form. Each externality situation becomes bilateral. The core with respect to any given externality is never empty. An empty core can arise only if one attempts to resolve multiple externality situations with but a single agreement.

The natural appeal of individuals unable to strike a Pareto-optimal bargain is to the courts, and the courts are inherently restricted to resolving bilateral disputes. The logical way to expand the number of individuals involved is to increase either the number of perpetrators or number of victims of an externality, or both. Such a generalization does not change the problem fundamentally, and does not overturn the theorem. Only the plausibility of the zero transactions costs assumption becomes strained as the number of individuals on each side of the externality expands.

H.   Externalities with large numbers of individuals

Suppose that California had no laws regarding emissions from autos or the kinds of fuel one is allowed to burn in cars. One fine smoggy day in Los Angeles, D arises, takes a deep breath of morning air and with tears in her eyes and a burning in her throat decides that something must be done about the level of air pollution. D realizes that she alone cannot afford to bribe all automobile drivers to install antipollution devices on their cars, use unleaded gas, and drive fuel-efficient cars. But D suspects correctly that there are many others like her who would be willing to offer motorists a bribe to improve the quality of air. To make the example simple, assume that the population is divided roughly equally into two groups: (1) motorists who drive about wearing gas masks and (2) joggers, bicyclists, and others who desire cleaner air. We have a typical bilateral externality situation and the Coase theorem applies. Absent transactions costs, the nonmotorists can bribe the motorists to adopt measures to improve the quality of air.

But consider the task confronting D. She must first approach all of those who, like herself, desire cleaner air. Perhaps they form a club – the Right to Breathe Club. Then they must contact all motorists and get them to agree to undertake the measures necessary to improve air quality in exchange for the bribes. The zero transactions costs assumption is clearly untenable. The transactions costs of organizing these two groups of individuals are mind-boggling.

Desolate D contemplates returning to bed. But then she remembers that she

tion of m externalities might be Pareto inferior to a possible allocation that might be proposed for simultaneously eliminating all. Thus, the absence of a core remains a potential problem lurking in the background, as the next section makes evident.

is already a member of several clubs that include the relevant parties. They are called the city of Los Angeles, state of California, and the United States. Although formed to provide the public goods of police protection, national defense, and the like, they could be used to work out the necessary bribes to motorists to achieve Pareto optimality in this situation, and at a considerable savings in the costs of bringing the different groups together. Thus, given that governments exist to resolve one set of market failures, they may economize on transactions costs when used to resolve others.[11]

Note that this conclusion holds if the presumption on property rights is reversed. The costs of potential motorists forming a club and offering a bribe to clean-airers to be allowed to drive with antipollution devices installed would be equally great.

The parallel between public goods and externalities, noted with respect to the Pareto-optimality condition, is again apparent. Suppose that every motorist is also a jogger and everyone has the same tastes for driving and jogging. Each individual would then realize that she would be better off installing the antipollution devices and taking the other necessary steps to improve air quality, *assuming everyone else did.* We have again a prisoners' dilemma situation, and the likelihood exists that many would free ride by not incurring the extra expense of installing the antipollution equipment. Even the costs of reaching an agreement on the measures to be taken, setting aside the free-rider problem, would be large.

Thus, our examination of both public goods and externalities has brought us to the same conclusion as to the reason why governments exist. The government, as an institution for achieving a Pareto-optimal allocation of resources, exists to economize on the transactions and bargaining costs of obtaining information on individual preferences regarding public goods and externalities when the number of individuals is large.[12]

11. When one uses the government to correct for more than one externality and to determine public goods levels *simultaneously,* one confronts head on the problem raised by Aivazian and Callen (1981), and discussed in Section G. One might then anticipate that the absence of a core – i.e., the absence of an equilibrium – will be a problem with respect to government decisions on public goods and externalities. This anticipation is correct.

12. Hoffman and Spitzer (1986) do not find a deterioration in the extent to which Pareto-optimal results are obtained in Coasian experiments as the number of participants rises as high as 38. But the main transactions costs of a large-number Coasian bargain have already been incurred in their experiments, i.e., the costs of bringing the relevant parties together. Their experiments suggest that bargaining strategies do not stand in the way of achieving Pareto improvements, once the parties are brought together.

A more pessimistic appraisal of the potential for governmental resolution of public goods–externalities issues emerges from Libecap and Wiggins's (1985) study of oil field unitization. They found that asymmetries in information stood in the way of Coasian agreements to share the gains from the unitized development of oil fields. But these same asymmetries also blocked achieving regulatory solutions to the problem through government action.

Bibliographical notes

The best, short introduction to the prisoners' dilemma game is probably R. Duncan Luce and Howard Raiffa (1957, pp. 94–113). Anatol Rapoport and Albert Chammah (1965) have a book on the subject. Michael Taylor (1976, pp. 28–97) presents in a collective choice context an exhaustive discussion of the possibilities of the cooperative solution emerging as an equilibrium in a prisoners' dilemma supergame. Russell Hardin (1982) also discusses the prisoners' dilemma in a public choice context. Robert Axelrod (1984) explores in depth the tit-for-tat solution to the prisoners' dilemma supergame and its relevance to the achievement of cooperative outcomes in real-world situations.

Other works that link the prisoners' dilemma to public goods include Runciman and Sen (1965); Hardin (1971, 1982); Riker and Ordeshook (1973, pp. 296–300); Taylor (1976, pp. 14–27). Robert Inman (1987, pp. 649–72) discusses several additional explanations of a prisoners' dilemma kind for why government intervention may improve allocative efficiency in his excellent survey of the public choice field.

Alan Hamlin (1986) reviews the normative issues surrounding a rational choice theory of the state placing heavy emphasis on prisoners' dilemma-type rationales for collective action.

Some interesting examples of real-world situations that take on the characteristics of the chicken game, as well as an analysis of solutions to the game, are given by Taylor and Ward (1982).

Classic discussions of externalities include the essays by James Meade (1952) and Tiber Scitovsky (1954) as well as Buchanan and Stubblebine's (1962) paper, and William Baumol's book (1967b). Mishan (1971) surveys the literature and Ng (1980, ch. 7) has a nice discussion of both externalities and the Coase theorem. Cornes and Sandler (1986) provide an integrated analysis of externalities and both pure and quasi-public goods.

The core is discussed and defined in Luce and Raiffa (1957, pp. 192–6).

Carl Dahlman (1979) links transactions costs and government intervention to the Coase theorem. Frohlich and Oppenheimer (1970) show that more than individual rationality and self-interest (e.g., transactions costs) are needed to conclude that the extent of free-riding increases with group size.

CHAPTER 3

Allocative efficiency or redistribution

Political organization is to be understood as that part of social organization which constantly carries on directive restraining functions for public ends. . . .

That the cooperation into which men have gradually risen secures to them benefits which could not be secured while, in their primitive state, they acted singly, and that, as an indispensable means to this cooperation political organization has been, and is, advantageous, we shall see on contrasting the states of men who are not politically organized with the states of men who are politically organized in less or greater degrees.

Herbert Spencer

As the state arose from the need to keep class antagonisms in check, but also arose in the thick of the fight between the classes, it is normally the state of the most powerful, economically dominant, class which by its means becomes also the politically dominant class and so acquires new means of holding down and exploiting the oppressed class. The ancient state was, above all, the state of the slave owners for holding down the slaves.

Friedrich Engels

It is easy to envisage government arising out of pristine anarchy to fulfill a collective need of the community (say, protection from a predator) or to coordinate hunting or other food-gathering activity. But it is just as easy to envisage a distributional motivation behind the origin of the state. The best hunter or warrior becomes the chief of the tribe and eventually acquires sufficient authority to extract tribute from his fellow tribesmen. War and police activity begin as the primary activities of "government" but gains from these activities are claimed by the authoritarian leader(s) of the tribe.

Thus, the state can be envisaged as coming into existence either to satisfy the collective needs of *all* members of the community, or to help gratify the wants of only a part of it. The first explanation corresponds to the achievement of allocative efficiency; the second to redistribution.[1]

The distinction between allocative efficiency and redistribution is fundamental in economics and public choice. In the allocation of private goods,

---

1. It is interesting to note that political anthropologists have engaged in the same debate regarding the origins of the state as modern public choice scholars have regarding its current activities. For an excellent review of the debate in political anthropology, see Haas (1982).

market exchange can guide society "as if by an invisible hand" from points inside of the Pareto-possibility frontier to a point upon it. However, this point is chosen blindly. How the gains from trade are distributed is determined arbitrarily, but since this distributional issue is resolved as a by-product of a process benefiting all parties, it need not become a bone of contention.

To obtain Pareto efficiency in the allocation of public goods, a collective choice process that is less anarchic than the market is required. A conscious choice of the quantities of each public good to be produced must be made and along with it the choice of means for paying for them. The issue of the distribution of the gains from collective action is more clearly visible in the allocation of public goods by a political process than it is in the allocation of private goods by a market exchange process. And the possibility arises that this and *other* distributional issues become dominant in the political process.

Although allocative efficiency and distributional issues are inevitably intertwined, it is useful analytically to keep them separate, and we shall endeavor to do so wherever possible throughout the book. Within public choice, one can also point to theories of the role of government that focus almost exclusively on either the allocative efficiency–public good activities of government, or its redistributional activities. Knut Wicksell's (1896) essay on taxation is a prime example of the former. Wicksell assumes that government activity is justified only if it is to the benefit of all citizens and thus advocates the use of the unanimity rule. Wicksell assumes the existence of a just distribution of income upon which the gains from collective action will be built. The redistributional role of government (via majority rule) is relegated to a footnote.

In contrast, Aranson and Ordeshook (1981) regard all of government activity as redistributionally motivated. A bridge does not only benefit those who seek to cross a river. Its construction provides income for the contractors, architects, engineers, and workers who build the bridge; profits for the steel, concrete, and other manufacturers who supply materials for its construction. The incomes of those who own restaurants and other shops at both entrances to the bridge rise, as do property values. According to Aranson and Ordeshook, it is these transfers of income and wealth that explain government activity with the provision of public goods a mere by-product to the primary government activity of redistributing income and wealth. Meltzer and Richard (1978, 1981, 1983) and Peltzman (1980) have also modeled government activity as if it was all directed at redistributing income.

The hypothesis that individuals will use and even create the institution of the state to transfer wealth from their neighbors to themselves achieves verification almost tautologically from the assumption that individuals are driven by self-interest. No elaborate modeling is required to show that selfish individuals take as much as the institutional environment allows them to take.

Therefore we shall not pause to develop this hypothesis here. Rather, we shall keep it in mind as we discuss the properties of democratic institutions throughout the book.

It is tempting to regard Wicksell's essay as a contribution to normative public choice – a theory of what the role of government *ought* to be, and the works of Aranson and Ordeshook, Meltzer and Richard, and Peltzman as contributions to positive public choice – descriptions of government as it is. For the latter do emphasize the purely positive character of their analysis, and Wicksell's essay has a normative ring to it. But such a classification provides too easy an answer to a difficult question, namely the question of the nature of government activity. There is enough similarity among the types of activities that the government does engage in across countries (defense, police, postal and telephone service) and does not (the production and distribution of clothing, furniture, and other household items), and a close enough resemblance between the characteristics of these activities and the definitions of public and private goods to suggest that there is some element of truth to the public good–allocative efficiency explanation for government activity. The question is, how important is this element?

This question is addressed at various points in the book, most notably in Chapters 17, 23, and 24.

PART II

Public choice in a direct democracy

CHAPTER 4

The choice of voting rule

Decision by majorities is as much an expedient as lighting by gas.
William Gladstone

There are two general rules. First, the more grave and important the questions discussed, the nearer should the opinion that is to prevail approach to unanimity. Second, the more the matter in hand calls for speed, the smaller the prescribed difference in the number of votes may be allowed to become: when an immediate decision has to be reached, a majority of one should suffice.

Jean-Jacques Rousseau

This and the next four chapters explore the properties of various voting rules. These rules can be thought of as governing the polity itself, as when decisions are made in a town meeting or by referendum, or an assembly, or a committee of representatives of the citizenry. Following Duncan Black (1958), we shall often refer to "committee decisions" as being the outcomes of the voting process. It should be kept in mind, however, that the word "committee" is employed in this wider sense, and can imply a committee of the entire polity voting, as in a referendum. When a committee of representatives is implied, the results can be strictly related only to the preferences of the representatives themselves. The relationship between citizen and representative preferences is taken up later.

A.   The unanimity rule

Since all can benefit from the provision of a public good, the obvious voting rule for providing it would seem to be unanimous consent. Knut Wicksell (1896) was the first to link the potential for all to benefit from collective action to the unanimity rule. The unanimity rule coupled with the proposal that each public good be financed by a separate tax constituted Wicksell's "new principle" of taxation. To see how the procedure might work, consider a world with two persons and one public good. Each person has a given initial income, Y_A and Y_B, and a utility function defined over the public and private goods, $U_A(X_A,G)$ and $U_B(X_B,G)$, where X is the private good, and G the public good. The public good is to be financed by a tax of t on individual A, and $(1 - t)$ on individual B. Figure 4.1 depicts individual A's indifference

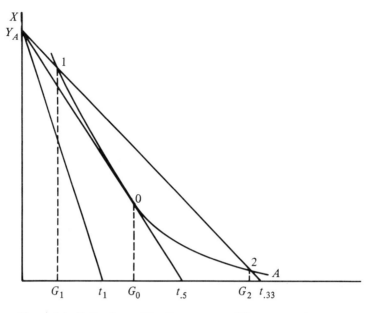

Figure 4.1. Optimal quantities for a voter at different tax prices.

curves between the private and public good. Let the prices of the private and public good be such that if A had to pay for all of the public good ($t = 1$), A's budget constraint line would be $Y_A t_1$. If A must pay only half of the cost of the public good, his budget constraint line would be $Y_A t_{.5}$, and so on. With a tax share of 0.5 A's optimal choice for a quantity of public good would be G_0. Note, however, that the tax–public good combinations $(t_{.33}, G_1)$ and $(t_{.33}, G_2)$ are on the same indifference curve as $(t_{.5}, G_0)$, and that one could calculate an infinite number of tax–public good quantity combinations from Figure 4.1 that lie upon indifference curve A. It is thus possible to map indifference curve A into a public good–tax space (Johansen, 1963).

Figure 4.2 depicts such a mapping. Points 0, 1, and 2 in Figure 4.2 correspond to points 0, 1, and 2 in Figure 4.1. Indifference curve A in Figure 4.2 is a mapping from the corresponding curve of Figure 4.1.

To map all points from Figure 4.1 into public good–tax space, we redefine each individual's utility function in terms of G and t alone. From the budget constraint, we obtain

$$\begin{aligned} X_A &= Y_A - tG \\ X_B &= Y_B - (1 - t)G. \end{aligned} \tag{4.1}$$

Substituting from (4.1) into each individual's utility function, we obtain the desired utility functions for A and B defined over G and t:

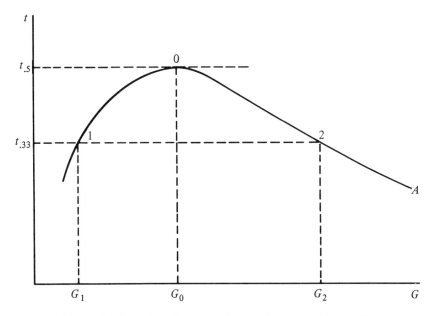

Figure 4.2. Mapping of voter preferences into tax–public good space.

$$U_A = U_A(Y_A - tG, G)$$
$$U_B = U_B(Y_B - (1 - t)G, G). \qquad (4.2)$$

Figure 4.3 depicts a mapping of selected indifference curves for A and B from public good–private good space into public good–tax space. A's share of the cost of the public good runs from 0, at the bottom of the vertical scale, to 1.0 at the top. B's tax share runs in the opposite direction. Thus, each point in Figure 4.3 represents a set of tax shares sufficient to cover the full cost of the quantity of public good at that point. Each point is on an indifference curve for A, and one for B. Embedded in each point is a quantity of private goods that each individual consumes as implied by his budget constraint (4.1), the quantity of the public good, and his tax share. A_1 and B_1 are the levels of utility, respectively, if each individual acted alone in purchasing the public good, and thus bore 100 percent of its cost.[1] Lower curves for A (higher for B) represent higher utilities. The set of tangency points between A and B's indifference curves, CC', represents a contract curve mapping the Pareto-possibility frontier into the public good–tax share space.

1. To simplify the discussion, we ignore spillovers from one individual's unilateral provision of the public good on the other's utility. One might think of the public good as a bridge across a stream. A_1 and B_1 represent the utilities that each individual can obtain if each builds his own bridge. Within A_1 and B_1 are points of higher utility for both that can be obtained by cooperating and building but one bridge.

Percentage Percentage
of tax of tax
paid by paid by
B *A*

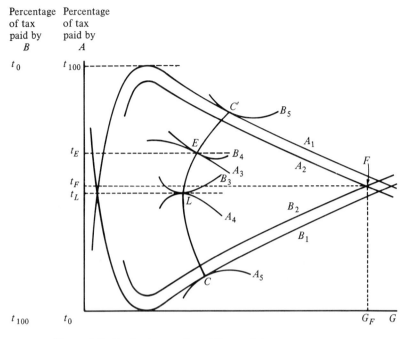

Figure 4.3. Contract curve in public good–tax space.

To see that each point on CC' is a Pareto-efficient allocation, take the total differentials of each individual's utility function with respect to t and G, holding the initial incomes (Y_A, Y_B) constant:

$$\Delta U_A = \frac{\partial U_A}{\partial X}(-t)\mathrm{d}G + \frac{\partial U_A}{\partial G}\mathrm{d}G + \frac{\partial U_A}{\partial X}(-G)\mathrm{d}t$$

$$\Delta U_B = \frac{\partial U_B}{\partial X}(-1+t)\mathrm{d}G + \frac{\partial U_B}{\partial G}\mathrm{d}G + \frac{\partial U_B}{\partial X}(G)\mathrm{d}t. \tag{4.3}$$

Setting the total change in utility for each individual equal to zero, we can solve for the slope of each individual's indifference curve:

$$\left(\frac{\mathrm{d}t}{\mathrm{d}G}\right)^A = \frac{\partial U_A/\partial G - t\partial U_A/\partial X}{G(\partial U_A/\partial X)}$$

$$\left(\frac{\mathrm{d}t}{\mathrm{d}G}\right)^B = -\frac{\partial U_B/\partial G - (1-t)(\partial U_B/\partial X)}{G(\partial U_B/\partial X)}. \tag{4.4}$$

Equating the slopes of the two indifference curves, we obtain the Samuelsonian condition for Pareto efficiency (1954):

$$\frac{\partial U_A/\partial G}{\partial U_A/\partial X} + \frac{\partial U_B/\partial G}{\partial U_B/\partial X} = 1. \tag{4.5}$$

Now consider the following public choice process. An impartial observer proposes both a pair of tax shares, t_F and $(1 - t_F)$, and a quantity of the public good, G_F. If the combination falls within the eye formed by A_1 and B_1, both individuals prefer this proposal to share the cost of the public good to having to provide all of the public good themselves. Both will vote for it, if they vote sincerely. F now becomes the status quo decision and new tax share–quantity pairs are proposed.[2] When a combination falling within the eye formed by A_2 and B_2 is hit upon, it is unanimously preferred to F. It now becomes the status quo and the process is continued until a point on CC', like E, is obtained. Once this occurs, no new proposal will be unanimously preferred, that is, can make both individuals better off, and the social choice has been, unanimously, made.

Note that for the tax shares inherent in the allocation E, each individual's optimal quantity of public good differs from the quantity of the public good selected. A prefers less of the public good, B prefers more. Given the tax shares t_E and $(1 - t_E)$, therefore, each is being "coerced" into consuming a quantity of the public good that differs from his most preferred quantity (Breton, 1974, pp. 56–66). This form of coercion can be avoided under a slightly different variant of the voting procedure (Escarraz, 1967; Slutsky, 1979). Suppose, for an initially chosen set of tax shares t and $(1 - t)$, that voters must compare all pairs of public good quantities, and a given quantity is chosen only if it is unanimously preferred to all others. This will occur only if the two individuals' indifference curves are tangent to the tax line from t at the same point. If no such quantity of public good is found for this initially chosen t, a new t is chosen, and the process repeated. This continues until a t is found at which all individuals vote for the same quantity of public good against all others. In Figure 4.3, this occurs at L for tax shares t_L and $(1 - t_L)$. L is the Lindahl equilibrium.

The outcomes of the two voting procedures just described (E and L) differ in several respects.[3] At L, the marginal rate of substitution of public for private goods for each individual is equal to his tax price:

$$\frac{\partial U_A/\partial G}{\partial U_A/\partial X} = t \qquad \frac{\partial U_B/\partial G}{\partial U_B/\partial X} = (1 - t). \tag{4.6}$$

2. Of course, the rule for selecting a new tax share or a new public good–tax share combination in the procedure described above must be carefully specified to ensure convergence to the Pareto frontier. For specifics on the characteristics of these rules, the reader is referred to the literature on Walrasian-type processes for revealing preferences on public goods as reviewed by Tulkens (1978).

3. For a detailed discussion of these differences, see Slutsky (1979).

L is an equilibrium then, in that *all* individuals prefer this quantity of public good to any other, *given each individual's assigned tax price*. *E* (or any other point reached via the first procedure) is an equilibrium in that at least one individual, and perhaps only one, is worse off by a movement in any direction from this point. Thus, *L* is preserved as the collective decision through the unanimous *agreement* of all committee members on the quantity of public good to be consumed, *at the given tax prices; E* is preserved via the *veto* power of each individual under the unanimity rule. How compelling these differences are depends upon the merits of constraining one's search for the optimum public good quantity to a given set of tax shares (search along a given horizontal line in Figure 4.3). The distribution of utilities at *L* arrived at under the second process depends only on the initial endowments and individual preferences, and has the (possible) advantage of being independent of the sequence of tax shares proposed, assuming *L* is unique. The outcome under the first procedure is dependent on the initial endowments, individual utility functions, *and* the specific set and sequence of proposed tax–public good combinations. Although this "path dependence" of the first procedure might be thought undesirable, it has the (possible) advantage of leaving the entire contract curve *CC'* open to selection. As demonstrated above, all points along *CC'* are Pareto efficient, and thus cannot be compared without additional criteria. It should be noted in this regard that if a point on *CC'*, say *E*, could be selected as most preferred under some set of normative criteria, it could always be reached via the second voting procedure by first redistributing the initial endowments in such a way that *L* was obtained at the utility levels implied by *E* (McGuire and Aaron, 1969). However, the informational requirements for such a task are obviously considerable.

We have sketched here only two possible *voting* procedures for reaching the Pareto frontier. Several papers have described Walrasian/tâtonnement procedures for reaching the Pareto frontier when public goods are present. These procedures all have in common the existence of a "central planner" or "auctioneer" who gathers information of a certain type from the citizen-voter, processes the information by a given rule, and then passes a message back to the voters to begin a new round of voting. These procedures can be broadly grouped into those in which the planner calls out tax prices (the *ts* in the above example), and the citizens respond with quantity information, the process originally described by Erik Lindahl (1919) (see also Malinvaud, 1970–1, sec. 5); and those in which the planner-auctioneer calls out quantities of public goods and the citizens respond with price (marginal rate of substitution) information, as in Malinvaud (1970–1, secs. 3 and 4), and Drèze and de la Vallée Poussin (1971). A crucial part of all of these procedures is the computational rule used to aggregate the messages provided by voters and generate a new set of signals from the planner-auctioneer. It is this rule that determines if, and when, and where on the Pareto frontier the process leads. Although there are obviously distributional implications to these rules, they are in general not designed to achieve any specific normative goal. The central planner-auctioneer's single end is to achieve a Pareto-efficient allocation of resources. These procedures are all subject to the same important distinction as to whether they allow the entire Pareto frontier to be reached or always lead to an outcome with a given set of conditions, like the Lindahl equilibrium. As such, they also share the other general properties of the unanimity rule. One particularly attractive variant on these procedures is discussed in the next section.

B.*   Vernon Smith's auction mechanism

Whereas most of the tâtonnement-type procedures ask voters to state *either* a willingness-to-pay tax price or a desired quantity, Smith's (1977, 1979a,b, 1980) mechanism requires the voter to announce *both*. Each individual i announces both a bid, b_i, which is the share of the public good's cost that i is willing to cover and a proposed quantity of the public good, G_i. The tax price actually charged i is the difference between the public good's costs, c, and the aggregate bids of the other $n - 1$ voters, B_i, that is,

$$t_i G = (c - B_i)G, \tag{4.7}$$

where $B_i = \Sigma_{j \neq i} b_j$, and $G = \Sigma_{k=1}^n G_k/n$. The procedure selects a quantity of public good only when each voter's bid matches his tax price and each voter's proposed public good quantity equals the mean:

$$b_i = t_i \text{ and } G_i = G, \text{ for all } i. \tag{4.8}$$

After each iteration of the procedure, voters are told what their tax prices and the public good quantity would have been had (4.8) been achieved at that iteration. If a voter's bid fell short of his tax price he can adjust either his bid or proposed public good quantity to try to bring about an equilibrium. Only when all unanimously agree to both their tax prices and the public good quantity does the procedure stop.

At an equilibrium (4.8) is satisfied, and i's utility can be written as

$$V_i = U_i(G) - t_i G, \tag{4.9}$$

where the utility from consuming G is expressed in money units. Maximizing (4.9) with respect to G_i we obtain the condition for i's optimal proposed quantity for the public good

$$dV_i/dG_i = U_i'/n - t_i/n = 0$$
$$U_i' = t_i. \tag{4.10}$$

Each voter equates his marginal utility from the public good to his tax price. Summing (4.10) over all voters, we obtain

$$\sum_{i=1}^{n} U_i' = \sum_{i=1}^{n} t_i = \sum_{i=1}^{n} (c - B_i) = c.$$

(4.11)

Equations (4.10) and (4.11) define the conditions for the Lindahl equilibrium.

The auction mechanism induces individuals to reveal their preferences for the public good by charging each voter a tax based not on his stated preference for the public good, but on the aggregate of all other stated preferences (bids). In this respect, it resembles the demand-revealing procedures discussed in Chapter 8. Each voter must be willing to make up the difference between the public good's costs at the aggregate bids of the other voters for the good to be provided. The ultimate incentive to state one's preferences honestly is provided by the knowledge that the good will not be provided unless all unanimously agree to a single quantity and set of tax prices.

C.   Criticisms of the unanimity rule

The unanimity rule is the *only* voting rule certain to lead to Pareto-preferred public good quantities and tax shares, a feature that led Wicksell (1896) and later Buchanan and Tullock (1962) to endorse it. Two main criticisms have been made against it. First, a groping search for a point on the contract curve might take considerable time, particularly in a large community of heterogeneous tastes (Black, 1958, pp. 146–7; Buchanan and Tullock, 1962, ch. 6). The loss in time by members of the community in discovering a set of Pareto-optimal tax shares might outweigh the gains to those who are saved from paying a tax share exceeding their benefits from the public good. An individual who was uncertain over whether he would be so "exploited" under a less than unanimity rule might easily prefer such a rule rather than spend the time required to attain full unanimity. The second objection against a unanimity rule is that it encourages strategic behavior.[4] If A knows the maximum share of taxes, B will assume rather than go without the public good, A can force B to point C on the contract curve, by voting against all tax shares greater than t_C. All gains from providing the public good then accrue to A. If B behaves the same, the final outcome is dependent on the bargaining strengths of the two individuals. The same is true of the other equilibria along the contract curve (Musgrave, 1959, pp. 78–80). Bargaining can further delay the attainment of the agreement as each player has to "test" the other's willingness to make concessions.

4. See Black (1958, p. 147); Buchanan and Tullock (1962, ch. 8); Barry (1965, pp. 242–50); Samuelson (1969).

The "bargaining problem" under the unanimity rule is the mirror image of the "incentive problem" in the voluntary provision of a public good. The latter is a direct consequence of the joint supply-nonexclusion properties of a public good. Given these properties, each individual has an incentive to understate his preferences and free-ride, since the quantity of public good provided is largely independent of his single message. The literature on voluntary preference revelation procedures has by and large sidestepped this problem by assuming honest preference revelation in spite of the incentives to be dishonest. The strongest analytic result to justify this assumption has been that sincere message transmittal is a minimax strategy; that is, sincere revelation of preferences maximizes the minimum payoff that an individual can obtain (Drèze and de la Vallée Poussin, 1971). But a higher payoff might be obtained through a misrepresentation of preferences, and some individuals can be expected to pursue this more daring option. If to remove this incentive one compels all citizens to vote in favor of a public good quantity–tax share proposal before it is provided, the free-rider problem does disappear. Each individual's vote is now essential to the public good's provision. This reversal in the individual's position in the collective decision alters his strategic options. Where an individual might, under a voluntary revelation scheme, gamble on the rest of the group providing an acceptable quantity of the public good without his contributing, under the unanimity rule he might gamble on the group's reducing the size of his contribution rather than risk his continual blocking of the collective outcome. Although the strategy options differ, both solutions to the public good problem are potentially vulnerable to strategic behavior.

Recent experimental results of Hoffman and Spitzer (1986) and Smith (1977, 1979a,b, 1980) indicate that strategic bargaining on the part of individuals in unanimity rule situations may not be much of a problem. The Hoffman-Spitzer experiments were designed to see whether the ability of individuals to achieve Pareto-optimal allocations in Coase-type externality situations deteriorates as the number of affected parties increases. Since all affected parties had to agree to a bargain before it could be implemented, the experiments essentially tested whether strategic bargaining by individuals would overturn Pareto-optimal allocation proposals under the unanimity rule. Hoffman and Spitzer (1986, p. 151) found that "if anything, efficiency improved with larger groups" (with groups as large as 20 on a side).

Unanimous agreement is required on the final iteration under Smith's auction mechanism, as already noted. Experiments with small numbers of voters were characterized by fairly rapid convergence on the Lindahl equilibrium, with bids also falling near the Lindahl tax prices. Strategic misrepresentation of preferences was not observed.

Even if strategic behavior does not thwart or indefinitely delay the achievement of a unanimous collective decision, one might object to the unanimity rule on the grounds that the outcome obtained depends on the bargaining abilities and risk preferences of the individuals (Barry, 1965, p. 249; Samuelson, 1969). Such a criticism implicitly contains the *normative* judgment that the proper distribution of the gains from cooperation *should not* be distributed according to the willingness to bear risks. One can easily counter that they *should*. An individual who votes *against* a given tax share to secure a lower one risks, under a unanimity rule, not having the good provided at all, or if so in a less than optimum quantity. Voting in this manner expresses a low preference for the public good, in much the same way as voting against the tax share does, because it is "truly" greater than the expected benefits. Someone not willing to vote strategically might be said to value the public good higher, and therefore perhaps ought to be charged a higher price for it.

We are clearly in the realm of normative economics here, as we were in comparing points E and L above, and need criteria as to how the gains from cooperation *ought* to be shared.[5] Indeed, in a full evaluation of the unanimity rule its normative properties must be considered. Wicksell's advocacy of the unanimity rule was based on its normative properties. The unanimity rule would protect individuals from being coerced by other members of the community, he argued. Wicksell used "coerced" not in the sense employed by Breton, who took it to mean having a different evaluation of the public good *at the margin* from one's tax price, but in the sense of being coerced through a collective decision to pay more for a public good than its benefits are in toto. This argument for the unanimity rule stems directly from Wicksell's view of the collective choice process as one of mutually beneficial voluntary exchange among individuals, as is Buchanan and Tullock's (1962) (see also Buchanan, 1975b). This emphasis on the "voluntary exchange" nature of collective choice underlies the classic essays by both Wicksell and Lindahl and forms an intellectual bond between them, leading in Wicksell's case to the unanimity principle, in Lindahl's to a set of tax prices equal to each individual's marginal evaluation of the public good. It also explains the reference to "just" taxation in the titles of each of their essays. We shall return to these issues in Chapter 6.

D.   The optimal majority

When a less than unanimous majority is sufficient to pass an issue, the possibility exists that some individuals will be made worse off via the committee's decision; Wicksell's coercion of the minority can take place. If the

---

5. At least two normative proposals for sharing these gains are dependent on the bargaining or risk preferences of the individuals (Nash, 1950; Braithwaite, 1955).

issue is of the public good–prisoners' dilemma variety, and there exist reformulations of the issue that could secure unanimous approval, the use of a less than unanimity rule can be said to impose a cost on those made worse off by the issue's passage, a cost that could be avoided through the expenditure of the additional time and effort required to redefine the issue so that its passage benefits all. This cost is the difference in utility levels actually secured, and those that would have been secured under a full unanimity rule. Buchanan and Tullock were the first to discuss these costs and refer to them as the "external costs" of the decision rule (1962, pp. 63–91; see also Breton, 1974, pp. 145–8).

Were there no costs associated with the unanimity rule itself, it would obviously be the optimal rule, since it minimizes these external decision costs. But, the time required to define an issue in such a way as to benefit all may be considerable. In addition to attempting to find a formulation of the proposal benefiting all, time may be required to explain the nature of the benefits of the proposal to some citizens unfamiliar with its merits. On top of these costs must be added the time lost through the strategic maneuvering that might take place as individuals jockey for more favorable positions along the contract curve, as described earlier.

Most observers, including those most favorably disposed toward the unanimity rule like Wicksell and Buchanan and Tullock, have considered these latter costs sufficiently large to warrant abandoning this rule. If all need not agree to a committee decision, what percentage should agree? The above considerations suggest a trade-off between the external costs of having an issue pass against which the individual is opposed, and the costs of time lost through decision making. At the one pole stands unanimity, under which any individual can block any agreement until he has one with which he is satisfied, or which he feels is the best he can obtain. The external decision costs under this rule are zero, but the decision time costs may be infinite. At the other extreme, each individual decides the issue alone. No delays may occur, as with a pure private good decision, but the external costs of allowing each individual to decide unilaterally for the community are again potentially infinitely large.

These various possibilities are depicted in Figure 4.4, which is taken from Buchanan and Tullock (1962, pp. 63–91). The costs of a particular collective decision are presented along the vertical axis; the number of people 0 up to N, the committee size, required to pass the issue are presented along the horizontal axis. Curve C is the external cost function representing the expected loss of utility from the victory of a decision to which an individual is opposed under the committee decision rule. Curve D depicts the decision-time costs of achieving the required majority to pass the issue as a function of the size of the required majority. The optimal majority is the percentage of the committee at

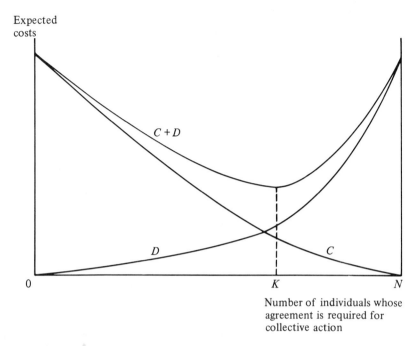

Figure 4.4. Choosing the optimal majority.

which these two sets of costs are together minimized. This occurs at K, where the vertical addition of the two curves reaches a minimum. The optimal majority to pass the issue, given these cost curves, is K/N. At this percentage, the expected gain in utility from redefining a bill to gain one more supporter just equals the expected loss in time from doing so.

Since these costs are likely to differ from issue to issue, one does not expect one voting rule to be optimal for all issues. The external costs will vary depending upon both the nature of the issues to be decided and the characteristics of the community deciding them. Ceteris paribus, when opinions differ widely, or information is scarce, large amounts of time may be required to reach a consensus, and if the likely costs to opposing citizens are not too high, relatively small percentages of the community might be required to make a decision. Again, the extreme example here is the pure private good. In contrast, issues for which large losses can occur are likely to require higher majorities (e.g., issues pertaining to the Bill of Rights). The larger the community, the greater the number of individuals with similar tastes, and thus, the easier it is likely to be to achieve a consensus among a given *absolute* number of individuals. Thus, an increase in N should shift the curve D rightward and downward. But, the fall in costs of achieving a consensus among a given number is unlikely to be fully proportional to the rise in community size. Thus, for issues of a similar type, the optimal *percentage* of the community required to pass an issue K/N is likely to decrease as the community increases in size (Buchanan and Tullock, 1962, pp. 111–16).

Individuals whose tastes differ widely from most others in the community can be expected to favor more inclusive majority rules. Individuals with high opportunity costs of time should favor less inclusive majority rules. Buchanan and Tullock assume that the choice of the optimal majority for each category of issues is made in a constitutional setting in which each individual is uncertain over his future position, tastes, and so on. Therefore, each views the problem in the same way, and a unanimous agreement is achieved as to which less than unanimity rule to use for which set of issues. When such a consensus does not exist, the knotty question that must be faced is what majority should be required to decide what majorities are required on all other issues? Having now faced this question, we shall move on.

E.   A simple majority as the optimal majority

The method of majority rule requires that at least the first whole integer above $N/2$ support an issue before it becomes the committee decision. Nothing we have said so far can indicate why $K/N = N/2$ should be the optimal majority for the bulk of a committee's decisions; and yet it is. As Buchanan and Tullock (1962, p. 81) note, for any one rule, such as the majority rule, to be the optimal majority for a wide class of decisions, there must exist some sort of a kink in one of the cost functions at the point $N/2$, causing the sum of two curves to obtain a minimum in a substantial proportion of the cases at this point.

A possible explanation for a kink in the decision-making cost curve, D, at $N/2$ can be obtained by considering further the internal dynamics of the committee decision process. When less than half of a committee's membership is sufficient to pass an issue, the possibility exists for both the issue A and the issue's converse ($\sim A$) to pass. Thus, a proposal to increase school expenditures by 10 percent might first achieve a winning majority (of, say, 40 percent) and a counterproposal to cut expenditures by 5 percent may also receive a winning majority. The committee could, when less than half of the voters suffice to carry an issue, become deadlocked in an endless series of offsetting proposals absorbing the time and patience of its members. The method of simple majority rule has the smallest possible required majority to pass an issue, which avoids the possibility of self-contradictory issues simultaneously passing (Reimer, 1951).

In Figure 4.5, decision costs and external costs curves have been drawn

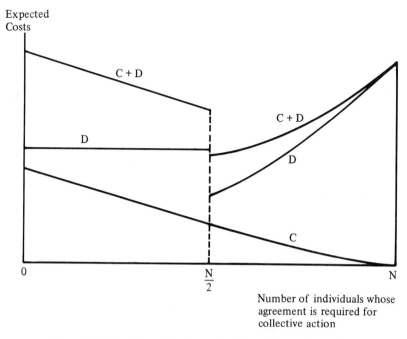

Figure 4.5. Conditions favoring a simple majority as the optimal majority.

such that their minimum would lie to the left of $N/2$ were D to continue to decline as it moves leftward from $N/2$. But the D curve is higher to the left of $N/2$ owing to the extra decision costs of having conflicting issues pass. This portion of the D curve has been drawn as a straight line, but it could conceivably be U- or inverted U-shaped to the left of $N/2$. The discontinuity at $N/2$ makes this majority the optimal majority for this committee.

Absent a discontinuity, a minimum for $C + D$ occurs to the left of $N/2$ only when the D curve rises more rapidly as it moves to the right than C does moving to the left; that is, decision costs vary much more over the range of committee sizes than do the external costs of collective decision making. $N/2$ is the optimal majority for the committee because of the discontinuity in the D curve. Thus, the choice of $N/2$ as the optimal majority is driven by the shape of the D curve. The method of simple majority rule will be selected as *the* committee decision rule by a committee whose members place a relatively high value on the opportunity costs of time. Were it not for the loss of time involved in having conflicting proposals like A and $\sim A$ pass, the minimal cost majority for the committee would be less than 0.50. The simple majority is optimal because it is the smallest majority one can select and still avoid having conflicting proposals both obtain winning majorities.

Speed is not the majority rule's only property, however. So important is the simple majority rule as a voting procedure that we shall devote most of the next two chapters to discussing its other properties.

Bibliographical notes

Henry Tulkens (1978) presents an excellent review of the literature on tâtonnement procedures for revealing preferences on public goods. Milleron (1972) reviews the literature on public goods more generally.

The seminal discussions of the "voluntary exchange" approaches of Lindahl and Wicksell are by Richard Musgrave (1939) and James Buchanan (1949). See also Head (1964).

The relationship between Wicksell's voting theory and the Lindahl equilibrium is taken up by Donald Escarraz (1967), who first described a way in which the Lindahl equilibrium could be reached under a unanimity voting rule. Escarraz argues that the unanimity rule was a necessary assumption underlying Lindahl's belief that the equilibrium would be reached and might have been implied in Lindahl's concept of an "even distribution of political power." Under this interpretation, Lindahl's even distribution of political power, Wicksell's freedom from coercion, the unanimity rule, and a set of tax prices equal to the marginal rates of utility for the public good all become nicely integrated.

Figure 4.3 corrects the analogous figure in the first edition of this book reflecting the note of Geoffrey Philpotts (1980). Figure 4.4 removes an ambiguity in the version of this figure appearing in the first edition.

CHAPTER 5

Majority rule – positive properties

But as unanimity is impossible, and common consent means the vote of the majority, it is self-evident that the few are at the mercy of the many.

John Adams

A.   Majority rule and redistribution

As Chapter 4 indicated, a committee concerned only with providing public goods and correcting for externalities might nevertheless choose as its voting rule the simple majority rule, if it placed enough weight on saving time. But speed is not the only property that majority rule possesses. Indeed, once issues can pass with less than unanimous agreement, the distinction between allocative efficiency and redistribution becomes blurred. Some individuals are inevitably worse off under the chosen outcome than they would be were some other outcome selected, and there is in effect a redistribution from those who are worse off because the issue has passed to those who are better off.

To see this point more clearly, consider Figure 5.1. The ordinal utilities of two groups of voters, the rich and the poor, are depicted on the vertical and horizontal axes. All of the members of both groups are assumed to have identical preference functions. In the absence of the provision of any public good, representative individuals from each group experience utility levels represented by S and T. The point of initial endowment on the Pareto-possibility frontier with only private good production is E. The provision of the public good can by assumption improve the utilities of both individuals. Its provision thus expands the Pareto-possibility frontier out to the curve $XYZW$. The segment YZ corresponds to the contract curve in Figure 4.3, CC'. Under the unanimity rule, both groups of individuals must be better off under the provision of the public good for them to vote for it. So the outcome under the unanimity rule must be a quantity of public good and tax share combination leaving both groups somewhere in the YZ segment along the Pareto-possibility frontier.

But there is no reason to expect the outcome to fall in this range under majority rule. A coalition of the committee's members can benefit by redefining the issue to increase their benefits at the expense of the noncoalition

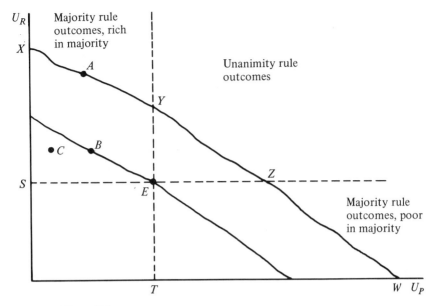

Figure 5.1.

members, say, by shifting the tax shares to favor the coalition members. If the rich were in the majority, they could be expected to couple the public good proposal with a sufficiently regressive tax package so that the outcome wound up in the *XY* segment. If the poor were in the majority, the taxes would be sufficiently progressive to produce an outcome in *ZW*. Given the opportunity to redefine the issue proposed through the alteration of either the quantity of the public good provided, the tax shares, or both, one can expect with certainty that the outcome of the collective choice process *will* fall outside of the Pareto-preferred segment *YZ* (Davis, 1970). As long as the issue could be continually redefined in such a way that a majority still benefited, it would pass, and a stable majority coalition could, in principle, push a minority back as far along the Pareto-possibility frontier as their consciences or the constitution allowed.

The process of transforming a proposal unanimously supported into one supported by only a simple majority resembles that described by William Riker (1962) in which "grand" coalitions are transformed into minimum winning coalitions. In developing his theory of coalitions, Riker makes two key assumptions: that decisions are made by majority rule, and that politics is a zero-sum game. He assumes that the allocational efficiency decisions (quantities of public goods) are all optimally resolved as a matter of course, and that the political process is left with the distributional issue of choosing from among the Pareto-efficient set (pp. 58–61). Thus, Riker (pp. 29–31) takes the extreme position that politics involves *only* redistribution questions, and is a pure zero-sum game. Given that the game is to take from the losers, the winners can obviously be better off by increasing the size of the losing side, as long as it remains the losing side. Under majority rule, this implies that the losing coalition will be increased until it is almost as large as the winning coalition, until the proposal passes by a "bare" majority. In Riker's description, the committee is made up of several factions or parties of different sizes, rather than two "natural" coalitions, as depicted earlier, and the process of forming a minimum winning coalition consists of adding and deleting parties or factions until two "grand" coalitions of almost equal size are formed. In regular committee voting, the process would consist of adding and deleting riders to each proposal, increasing the number of losers, and increasing the benefits to the remaining winners.

Several writers have described ways in which majority rule can lead to redistribution other than via the obvious route of direct cash transfers. The pioneering effort in this area was by Gordon Tullock (1959). Tullock described a community of 100 farmers in which access to the main highway is via small trunk roads, each of which serves only 4 or 5 farmers. The issue comes up as to whether the entire community of 100 should finance the repair of all of the trunk roads out of a tax on the entire community. Obviously one can envisage a level of repairs and set of taxes on the individual farmers under which such a proposal would be unanimously adopted. But, under majority rule it is to the greater advantage of some to propose that only one-half of the roads are repaired out of a tax falling on the entire population. Thus, one can envisage a coalition of 51 of the farmers forming and proposing that only the roads serving them are repaired out of the community's general tax revenue (Tullock discusses other possible outcomes, which we take up shortly). Such a proposal would pass under majority rule, and obviously involves a redistribution from the 49 farmers who pay taxes and receive no road repairs to the 51 farmers whose taxes cover only slightly more than one-half of the cost of the road repairs.

In the Tullock example, redistribution to the 51 farmers in the majority coalition takes place through the inclusion in the entire community's budget of a good that is of benefit to only a subset of the community. Each access road benefits only 4 or 5 farmers and is a public good with respect to only these farmers. The optimal size of jurisdiction for deciding each of these "local" public goods would seem to be the 4 or 5 farmers on each access road. The inclusion of private goods in the public budget as a means of bringing about redistribution was first discussed by James Buchanan (1970) and has been analyzed by several other writers. Building on Buchanan's paper, Robert Spann has demonstrated that the collective provision of a private good fi-

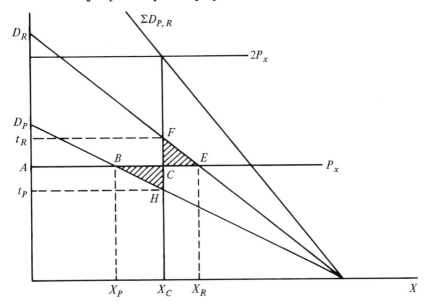

Figure 5.2. Redistribution with the public provision of a private good.

nanced via a set of Lindahl tax prices leads to a redistribution from the rich to the poor (Spann, 1974). To see this, consider Figure 5.2. Let D_P be the demand schedule for the poor, D_R for the rich. Let X be a pure private good with price = marginal social cost = P_X. If the good is supplied to the market privately, the poor purchase X_P at price P_X, the rich purchase X_R. Assume next that the good is collectively purchased and supplied to the community in equal quantities per person, as if it were a public good. The optimal quantity of X is then given by the intersection of the community demand schedule, obtained by vertically summing the individual demand schedules. (We ignore here income effect considerations. The argument is not substantively affected by this omission.)

The supply schedule under collective provision is obtained by multiplying the market price of the good by the number of members of the community. If we assume for simplicity an equal number of rich and poor, the community will purchase X_C units of the good for each individual. At this quantity, a poor individual places a marginal evaluation on the good of $X_C H$, and his Lindahl tax is t_p. A member of the rich group pays t_R. In effect, the poor receive a subsidy of $ACHt_P$, the difference between the price they pay for the good and its social cost multiplied by the quantity they consume. But their consumer surplus gain from the collective provision of the private good is only $ABHt_P$. Thus, there is a deadweight loss of BCH through the collective provision of X.

In addition to the direct transfer of income from R to P ($t_P HCA$) via the subsidization of P's purchase of X, R is worse off by being forced to consume a less than optimal amount of X. R loses the consumer surplus triangle FCE (Buchanan, 1970, 1971; Spann, 1974).

This loss in efficiency comes about through the constraint placed on each individual's behavior, when all are forced to consume the same quantity of the private good. Given the costs of producing the private good, all could be made better off by being allowed to maximize their individual utilities at the set of market prices for this and the other goods. The additional constraint that all consume the same quantity lowers the set of utilities possibly attainable. But, the poor are better off receiving the redistribution in this form than not at all, and if it is not feasible for them to obtain direct cash subsidies via lump-sum transfers, and it is possible to obtain them through the collectivization of private good supply, then the latter is worth pursuing.

The above illustration does not imply that redistribution will inevitably be from the rich to the poor,[1] or that it will take place at a set of Lindahl prices. It does help to emphasize, however, that the Pareto-efficiency properties of the Lindahl prices are contingent on the constraint that all consume an equal quantity of the good being a natural (physical) constraint, and not one artificially imposed, as in the collective provision of an essentially private good (see Buchanan, 1970, 1971; Spann 1974).

Barzel (1973) and Barzel and Deacon (1975) have taken up the specific case of education as a private good purchased and supplied as a public good and have illustrated both the allocational inefficiencies and redistributive properties of this activity. Education is an example of a good that can involve redistribution from the bottom to the top (or middle) of the distribution. And redistribution may occur on the basis of criteria other than income (e.g., occupation, sex, race, geographic location, recreational preferences, political affiliation). What is required for redistribution to take place under majority rule is that the members of the winning coalition be clearly identifiable, so that the winning proposal can discriminate in their favor, either on the basis of the distribution of the benefits it provides (e.g., Tullock's unequal distribution of roads at equal taxes) or the taxes it charges (e.g., Buchanan and Spann's equal quantities of private good X at unequal taxes).

Regardless of what form it takes, and regardless of whether political choice under majority rule is a pure zero-sum game, as Riker assumes, or involves allocational efficiency changes *plus* redistribution, the fact remains that the redistributional characteristics of any proposal will figure in its passage, and that majority rule creates the incentive to form coalitions and redefine issues

---

1. Davis (1970) and Meltzer and Richard (1978, 1981, 1983) argue that redistribution is generally toward the poor. We take up alternative arguments in Chapter 23.

to achieve these redistributional gains. Indeed, from the mere knowledge that an issue passed with some individuals in favor and others opposed, one cannot discern whether it really was a public good shifting the Pareto-possibility frontier out to *XYZW* in Figure 5.1 coupled to a tax unfavorable to the poor, say, resulting in an outcome at *A;* a pure redistribution along the private-good Pareto-efficiency frontier resulting in *B;* or an inefficient redistribution from the poor to the rich via the collective provision of a private good resulting in, say, *C.* All one can say with much confidence is that the rich appear to believe that they will be better off, and the poor that they will be worse off from passage of the proposal; that is, the move is into the region *SEYX*.

Let us now consider again the issue of the origins of the state, which we took up in Chapter 3. Even if the emergence of states is best explained as cooperative efforts undertaken to benefit all members of the community, it is now clear that the use of the majority rule to make collective decisions must transform the state at least in part into a redistributive state. Since all modern democracies use the majority rule to a considerable degree to make collective decisions – indeed the use of the majority rule is often regarded as the mark of a democratic form of government – all modern democratic states must be redistributive states in part if not in toto.

B.   Cycling

Given that majority rule must induce some element of redistribution into the collective decision process, we take up next an attribute of majority rule when a pure redistribution decision is to be made. Consider a three-man committee that must decide how to divide a gift of $100 among them using majority rule. This is a pure distributional issue, a simple zero-sum game. Suppose that V_2 and V_3 first vote to divide the $100 between themselves, 60/40. V_1 now has much to gain from forming a winning coalition. He might propose to V_3 that they split the $100, 50/50. This is more attractive to V_3, and we can expect this coalition to form. But now V_2 has much to gain from trying to form a winning coalition. He might now offer V_1 a 55/45 split forming a new coalition, and so on. When the issues proposed involve redistribution of income and wealth, members of a losing coalition always have a large incentive to attempt to become members of the winning coalition, even at the cost of a less than equal share.

The outcome of a 50/50 split of $100 among a pair of voters is a von Neumann–Morgenstern solution to this particular game (Luce and Raiffa, 1957, pp. 199–209). This game has three such solutions, however, and there is no way to predict which of these three, if any, would occur. Thus, the potential for cycles, when issues involve redistribution, seems quite large. It is always possible to redefine an issue so as to benefit one or more members

Table 5.1.

Voters	Issues			
	X	Y	Z	X
1		>	>	<
2		>	<	>
3		<	>	>
Community		>	>	>

and harm some others. New winning coalitions containing some members of the previously losing coalition and excluding members of the previously winning coalition are always feasible. But, as we have seen from the discussion of majority rule, when issues can be amended in the committee, any pure allocative efficiency decision can be converted into a combination of a redistribution and an allocative efficiency change via amendment. Thus it would seem that when committees are free to amend the issues proposed, cycles must be an ever-present danger.

The possibility that majority rule can lead to cycles across issues was recognized over two hundred years ago by the Marquis de Condorcet (1785). C. L. Dodgson (1876) analyzed the problem anew one hundred years later, and it has been a major concern of the modern public choice literature beginning with Duncan Black (1948b) and Kenneth Arrow (1951, rev. ed. 1963).[2] Consider the following three voters with preferences over three issues, as in Table 5.1 (> implies preferred). X can defeat Y, Y can defeat Z, and Z can defeat X. Pairwise voting can lead to an endless cycle. The majority rule can select no winner nonarbitrarily.[3]

If we define Z as a payoff to voters V_2 and V_3 of 60/40, Y as the payoff (50, 0, 50), and X as (55, 45, 0), the ordinal rankings of issues in Figure 5.3 corresponds to the above zero-sum pure distribution game. But it is also possible to get orderings as in Table 5.1 and Figure 5.3 for issues involving allocational efficiency. If X, Y, and Z are sequentially higher expenditures on a public good, then the preferences of Voters 1 and 3 can be said to be single-peaked in the public good–utility space (see Figure 5.3). Voter 2's preferences are double-peaked, however, and herein is a cause of the cycle. Change 2's preferences so that they are single-peaked, and the cycle disappears.

One of the early important theorems in public choice was D. Black's (1948a) proof that majority rule produces an equilibrium outcome when voter preferences are single-peaked. If voters' preferences can be depicted along a

---

2. For a discussion of these and other early contributions, see Black (1958) and William Riker (1961).
3. See A. K. Sen's discussion (1970a, pp. 68–77).

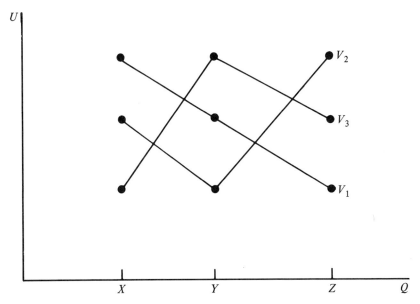

Figure 5.3. Voter preferences that induce a cycle.

single dimension, as with an expenditure issue, this equilibrium lies at the peak-preference for the median voter. Figure 5.4 depicts the single-peaked preferences for five voters. Voters 3, 4, and 5 favor *m* over any proposal to supply less. Voters 3, 2, and 1 favor it over proposals to supply more. The preference of the median voter decides.

C.* The median voter theorem – one-dimensional issues

The proof follows Enelow and Hinich (1984, ch. 2). The two key assumptions for the median voter theorem are (1) that issues are defined along a single dimensional vector *x* and (2) that each voter's preferences are single-peaked in that one dimension. Let voter *i*'s preferences be represented by a utility function $U_i(\ )$ defined over x, $U_i(x)$. Let x_i^* be voter *i*'s most preferred point along the *x* vector. Call x_i^* *i*'s ideal point.

Definition: x_i^* *is i's ideal point if and only if (iff)* $U_i(x_i^*) > U_i(x)$ *for all* $x \neq x_i^*$.

Definition: *Let* y *and* z *be two points along the* x *dimension, such that either* $y,z \geq x_i^*$ *or* $y,z \leq x_i^*$. *Then voter* i'*s preferences are single-peaked iff* $[U_i(y) > U_i(z)] \leftrightarrow [|y - x_i^*| < |z - x_i^*|]$.

Utility

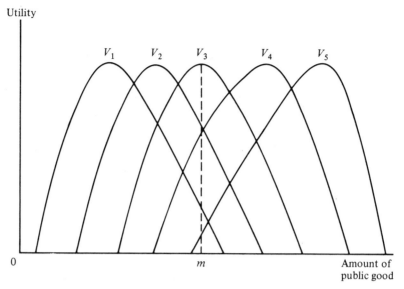

Figure 5.4. The median voter decides.

In other words, the definition of single-peaked preferences says that if y and z are two points on the same side of x_i^* then i prefers y to z if and only if y is closer to x_i^* than z. If all preferences are single-peaked, then preferences like those of Voter 2, in Figure 5.3, cannot occur (note z is 2's ideal point in this figure.

Definition: *Let* $\{x_1^*, x_2^*, \cdots, x_n^*\}$ *be the* n *ideal points for a committee of* n *individuals. Let* N_R *be the number of* $x_i^* \geq x_m$, *and* N_L *be the number of* $x_i^* \leq x_m$. *Then* x_m *is a median position iff* $N_R \geq n/2$, *and* $N_L \geq n/2$.

Theorem: *If* x *is a single-dimensional issue, and all voters have single-peaked preferences defined over* x, *then* x_m, *the median position, cannot lose under majority rule.*

PROOF: Consider any $z \neq x_m$, say $z < x_m$. Let R_m be the number of ideal points to the right of x_m. By definition of single-peaked preferences, all R_m voters with ideal points to the right of x_m prefer x_m to z. By definition of median position, $R_m \geq n/2$. Thus, the number of voters preferring x_m to z is at least $R_m \geq n/2$. x_m cannot lose to z under majority rule. Similarly, one can show that x_m cannot lose to any $z > x_m$. □

D.   Majority rule and multidimensional issues

Single-peakedness is a form of homogeneity property of a preference ordering (Riker, 1961, p. 908). People who have single-peaked preferences on an issue *agree* that the issue is one for which there is an optimum amount of the public good, and that the further one is away from the optimum, the worse off one is. If quantities of defense expenditures were measured along the horizontal axis, then a preference ordering like the ordering in Figure 5.4 would obviously imply that Voter 1 is somewhat of a dove and Voter 5 a hawk, but a consensus of values would still exist with respect to the way in which the quantities of defense expenditures were ordered. The median voter theorem states that a consensus of this type (on a single-dimensional issue) is sufficient to ensure the existence of a majority rule equilibrium. During the Vietnam War, it was often said that some people favored *either* an immediate pullout or a massive expansion of effort to achieve total victory. Preferences of this type resemble Voter 2's preferences in Figure 5.3. Preference orderings such as these can lead to cycles. Note that the problem here may not be a lack of consensus on the way of viewing a single dimension of an issue, but on the dimensionality of the issue itself. The Vietnam War, for example, raised issues regarding both the U.S. military posture abroad and humanitarian concern for the death and destruction it wrought. One might have favored high expenditures to achieve the first, and a complete pullout to stop the second. These considerations raise, in turn, the question of the extent to which any issue can be viewed in a single dimension.

If all issues were unidimensional, multipeaked preferences of the type depicted in Figure 5.3 might be sufficiently unlikely so that cycling would not be much of a problem. In a multidimensional world, however, preferences of the type depicted in Table 5.1 seem quite plausible. Issues X, Y, and Z might, for example, be votes on whether to use a piece of land for a swimming pool, tennis courts, or a baseball diamond. Each voter could have single-peaked preferences on the amount to be spent on each activity, and a cycle would still appear over the issue of how the land should be used. The introduction of distributional considerations into a set of issues can, as already illustrated, also produce cycles.

A great deal of effort has been devoted to defining conditions under which majority rule does yield an equilibrium. Returning to Figure 5.4 we can see, somewhat trivially, that m emerges as an equilibrium because the other four voters are evenly "paired off" against one another regarding any move from m. This condition has been generalized by C. R. Plott (1967), who proved that a majority rule equilibrium exists, if it is a maximum for one (and only one) individual, and the remaining even number of individuals can be divided into pairs whose interests are diametrically opposed; that is, whenever a

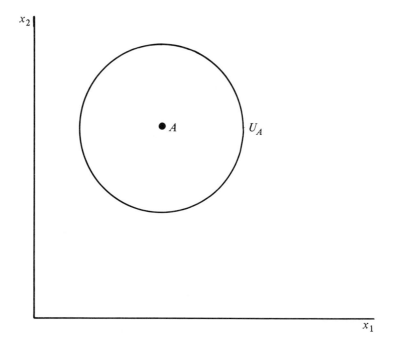

Figure 5.5.

proposal is altered so as to benefit a given individual A, a given individual B must be made worse off.

To see the intuition behind Plott's important result, consider first Figure 5.5. Let x_1 and x_2 be two issues, or two dimensions of a single issue. Let individual preferences be defined over x_1 and x_2, with point A the ideal point, the most preferred point in the x_1x_2 quadrant for individual A. If one envisages a third dimension, perpendicular to the x_1x_2 plane, with utility measured in this third dimension, then point A is a projection of the peak of individual A's utility "mountain" onto the x_1x_2 plane. Pass a second plane through the mountain between its peak and floor and it will intersect the mountain in curves representing equal levels of utility. One such curve, drawn as a circle, is presented in Figure 5.5.

If we thought of individual A as a committee of one making choices using majority rule, then rather obviously and trivially she would choose point A. For her it is the dominant point in the x_1x_2 quadrant; that is, *it is a point that cannot lose to any other point*. What we seek to determine are the conditions for the existence of a dominant point under majority rule for committees larger than one.

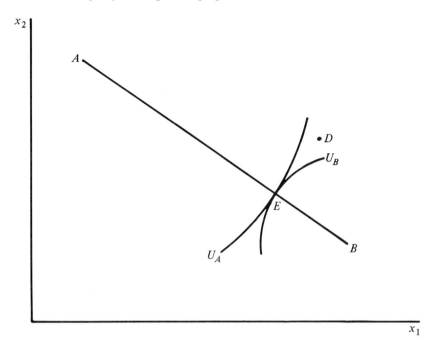

Figure 5.6.

Let B join A to form a committee of two. Under majority rule, any point that is off the contract curve, like D in Figure 5.6, can be defeated by a point on the contract curve, like E, using majority rule. Thus, no point off the contract curve can be a dominant point. At the same time, points like E on the contract curve cannot lose to other points on the contract curve like A and B. In a choice between A and E, voter A chooses A, B chooses E, and the result is a draw under majority rule. For a committee of two, the set of dominant points under majority rule is the contract curve. With circular indifference curves, the contract curve is the straight line segment joining A and B.

It should be clear from this example that dominance and Pareto optimality are closely related. Indeed, for E to be a dominant point, it must be in the Pareto set of every majority coalition one can construct for were it not, there would exist some other point Z in the Pareto set for a majority coalition, which is Pareto preferred to E. This coalition will form and vote for Z over E.

Now consider a committee of three. Let C's ideal point be at C in Figure 5.7. The Pareto sets for each majority coalition are again the straight line segments joining each pair of ideal points, AC, BC, and AB. There is no point common to all three line segments, and thus no point is contained in all three

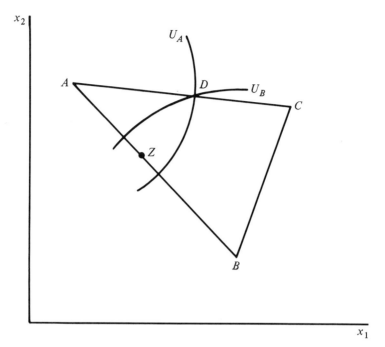

Figure 5.7.

Pareto sets. By the logic of the previous paragraph, there is no dominant point under majority rule. A point like D in A-C's Pareto set lies outside of A-B's Pareto set. There thus exist points on AB, like Z, that can defeat D.

The triangle ABC inclusive of its borders constitutes the Pareto set for the committee of three. Were the unanimity rule employed, the committee would be led to some point within ABC or on its boundary. Once there, the committee would be stuck, unable to move unanimously to another point. All points in and on ABC are potential equilibria. Under the majority rule, however, only the Pareto sets for the majority coalitions are relevant. There are three of them, but with no common point among them, no equilibrium exists.

The situation would be different if the third committee member's ideal point fell on the segment AB or its extension, say at E (Figure 5.8). The three majority coalition Pareto sets are again the segments joining the three ideal points, AB, AE, and EB. However, now they have a point in common, E, and it is the dominant point under majority rule.

When the third committee member's ideal point falls on the ray connecting the other two members' ideal points, what was a multidimensional choice problem collapses into a single-dimensional choice problem. The committee

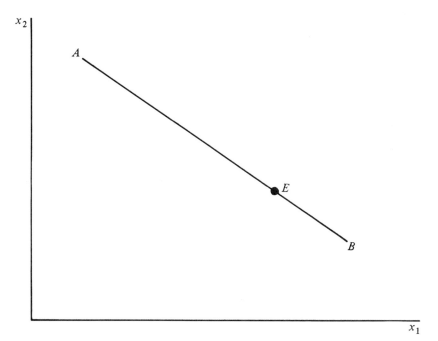

Figure 5.8.

must select a combination of x_1 and x_2 from along the ray through A and B. The conditions for the median voter theorem are applicable, and the committee choice is at the ideal point for the median voter, point E. Note also that the interests of the remaining committee members, A and B, are both diametrically opposed and "balanced" against one another as Plott's theorem asserts.

Now consider adding two more members to the committee. Obviously, if their ideal points were to fall along the ray through AB, an equilibrium would still exist. If one point were above and to the left of E and the other below and to the right, then E would remain the single dominant point under majority rule. But if both points fell outside of AB but were still on its extension, say, above and to the left of A, an equilibrium would still exist. In this case, it would be at A.

But the ideal points of the new members do not have to fall along AB extended for a dominant point to continue to exist. Suppose the two new committee members had ideal points falling on a line segment passing through E, but not coinciding with AB, say, like F and G in Figure 5.9. With a committee of five, three are needed to form a majority coalition. The Pareto

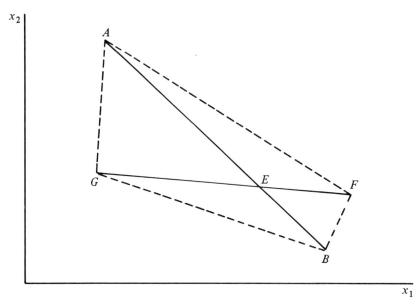

Figure 5.9.

sets for the majority coalitions are the triangles formed by three ideal points and the straight line segments formed by three ideal points, that is, *AEF*, *AEG*, *GEB*, *BEF*, and the line segments *AEB* and *GEF* (see Figure 5.9). These six Pareto sets have but one point in common, *E*, and it is the dominant point under majority rule. *E* remains the equilibrium because the two new members' interests are symmetrically positioned on opposite sides of *E*, and are thus balanced one against the other. As long as new committee members would continue to be added in pairs with ideal points on line segments passing through *E*, and on opposite sides of it, this balance would not be upset and *E* would remain the committee's equilibrium choice under majority rule.

The dominance of *E* in Figure 5.9 does not follow as it did in Figure 5.8 from a direct application of the median voter theorem. The issue space cannot be collapsed to a single-dimensional representation in Figure 5.9. But *E* is a median point in a more general sense. Pass any line through *E*, like *WW* in Figure 5.10, and there are three points on or to the left of (above) this line, as well as three points on or to the right of (below) it. A movement from *E* to the left will be opposed by a majority of the committee (*EBF*) as will a movement to the right (*EAG*). Since this is true for all possible lines that one can draw through *E*, all possible moves from *E* are blocked – hence its equilibrium nature. *E* satisfies the definition of a median point presented in Section C*, with respect to directions along the perpendicular to *WW* through *E*, the

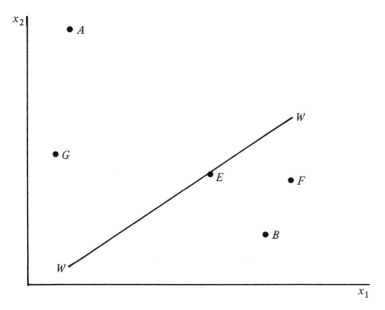

Figure 5.10.

number of ideal points at or to the left of E is greater than $n/2$, as is the number at or to the right, where n, the committee size, in this case is 5. Since this property holds for every WW one can draw through E, E is a median point *in all directions*. The theorem – that the necessary and sufficient conditions for E to be a dominant point under majority rule is that it be a median in all directions – is proved in the next section.

E.*   Proof of the median voter theorem – multidimensional case

This theorem was first proved by Davis, DeGroot, and Hinich (1972); we again follow Enelow and Hinich (1984), ch. 3.

We begin by generalizing the definitions of N_R and N_L. N_R is the number of ideal points to the right of (below) any line passing through E, N_L is the number of ideal points to the left of (above) this line. Continue to assume circular indifference curves.

Theorem: E *is a dominant point under majority rule iff* $N_R \geq n/2$ *and* $N_L \geq n/2$ *for all possible lines passing through* E.

SUFFICIENCY: Pick any point $Z \neq E$ (see Figure 5.11). Draw ZE. Draw WW perpendicular to ZE. Given that all indifference curves are circles, E

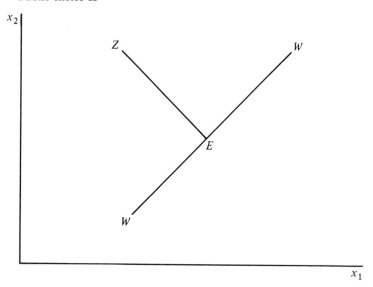

Figure 5.11.

is closer to any ideal point to the right of (below) WW than Z. N_R voters prefer E to Z. By assumption, $N_R \geq n/2$. E cannot lose to Z.

□

NECESSITY: We must show that if Z is a point not satisfying the $N_R \geq n/2$ and $N_L \geq n/2$ condition for some WW line drawn through it, then it cannot be a dominant point. Let Z and WW in Figure 5.12 be such that $N_R < n/2$. Then $N_L > n/2$. Now move WW parallel to its original position until it reaches some point Z' on the perpendicular to WW such that N'_L just satisfies the condition $N'_L \leq n/2$ for the line $W'W'$ through Z'. Clearly, some point Z' satisfying this condition must eventually be reached. Now choose Z'' between Z and Z' on the line segment ZZ'. N''_L defined with respect to the line through Z'' parallel to WW must satisfy $N''_L > n/2$. But the N''_L voters with ideal points to the left of $W''W''$ must all prefer Z'' to Z. Thus, Z cannot be a dominant point.

□

F.   Majority rule equilibria when preferences are not defined in spatial terms

So far, the results of this chapter regarding an equilibrium under majority rule have been derived in the context of a spatial model of choice. This is perhaps a natural way to approach choice questions for economists since they often analyze individual choices assuming utility functions defined over continuous

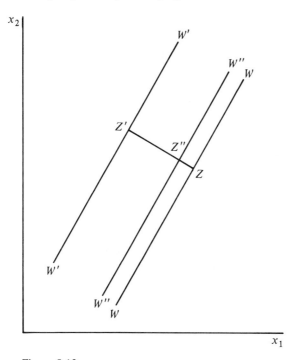

Figure 5.12.

variables and illustrate their results using geometry. But, whether one views the results so far in a positive light (an equilibrium does exist under majority rule) or in a negative one (but only under very stringent assumptions), one might wonder how sensitive the results are to the formulation of the questions in spatial terms? Might better or worse results ensue if one abandoned the spatial context for examining majority rule? After all, voters do not typically think in spatial terms. These questions echo an attack on the public choice approach to politics levied by Donald Stokes (1963), when public choice spatial models first began to intrude into the political science literature.

All of the major results concerning consumer behavior can be derived without the help of geometry or calculus, if one assumes that individual preferences satisfy certain basic rationality axioms (Newman, 1965). Since the theorems regarding consumer behavior derived from these axioms closely resemble those derived from using calculus, one might suspect that the same will be true regarding collective decision functions like majority rule. And this suspicion is borne out.

The concept of an ideal point for an individual carries over directly into the axiomatic approach if we assume that individual preferences satisfy the three axioms of reflexivity, completeness, and transitivity. Using R to denote the relationship "at least as good as," that is, either strict preference P, or indifference, I, then the axioms are

> *Reflexivity:* For every element x in the set S, xRx.
> *Completeness:* For every pair of elements x and y in the set S, $x \neq y$, either xRy, or yRx, or both.
> *Transitivity:* For every triple x, y, and z in S, $(xRy$ and $yRz) \rightarrow (xRz)$.

If individual preferences satisfy these three axioms, then they define an ordering over the set of alternatives, S. The individual is assumed to be capable of ranking all of the alternatives in S, and the ideal point is then the alternative ranked highest, that is, the alternative preferred to all others.

Given that individual preferences are assumed to define an ordering, a natural way to approach the issue of whether an equilibrium exists under majority rule is to ask whether majority rule defines an ordering, in particular, to ask whether majority rule satisfies transitivity. If it does, then an alternative that beats (or at least ties) all others must exist in any set, and this is our dominant (equilibrium) outcome.

Majority rule does define an ordering over the set of alternatives S if individual preferences, in addition to satisfying the three axioms that define an ordering, also satisfy the extremal restriction axiom.[4]

> *Extremal restriction:* If for any ordered triple (x,y,z) there exists an individual i with preference ordering xP_iy and yP_iz, then every individual j who prefers z to x (zP_jx) must have preferences zP_jy and yP_jx.

There are several things to observe about this axiom. First, although it does not require a spatial positioning of alternatives, it does require that individuals view alternatives in a particular way. Individuals must order issues x,y,z or z,y,x; they cannot order them y,x,z, for example.

Second, the condition does not require that all individuals have either the xP_iyP_iz ordering or the zP_jyP_jx ordering. The second part of the condition is only triggered if some individual prefers z to x. But no one may prefer z to x. All may either prefer x to z or be indifferent between them. If they are, then the theorem states that no cycle can occur.

Third, if one wants to think of the issues as ordered in a left-to-right way (x,y,z), then the condition resembles single-peakedness but is not equivalent to it. In particular, the condition allows for the preferences xI_jzP_jy when the preferences xP_iyP_iz are present. If y is the middle issue, then the preference ordering xI_jzP_jy implies twin peaks at x and z. The condition does mandate, however, that the two peaks at x and z must be of equal altitude.

---

4. Sen and Pattanaik (1969). Other variants on this axiom (all equally restrictive) and on the basic theorem are discussed by Sen (1966, 1970a, chs. 10, 10*).

Although the extremal restriction avoids defining the issues in spatial terms, it is in other respects a severe constraint on the types of preference orderings people can have if majority rule is to satisfy transitivity. If a committee must decide whether a vacant lot is to be used to build a football field (x), tennis courts (y), or a swimming pool (z), then some individuals may reasonably prefer football to tennis to swimming. But equally reasonably, others may prefer tennis to swimming to football. If both types of individuals are on the committee, however, the extremal restriction is violated and a voting cycle under majority rule may ensue. This theorem is proved in the next section.

G.* Proof of extremal restriction – majority rule theorem

Theorem: *Majority rule defines an ordering over any triple (x,y,z) iff all possible sets of individual preferences satisfy extremal restriction.*

The proof follows Sen (1970a, pp. 179–81).

Sufficiency: The most interesting cases involve those in which at least one voter has preferences

1. $xP_iyP_iz.$

With at least one voter of type 1, all other voters must have either the same ordering over the triple or one of the following four sets of preference orderings if extremal restriction is to be satisfied:

2. zP_jyP_jx
3. yP_jzI_jx
4. zI_jxP_jy
5. $zI_jxI_jy.$

Voters of type 5 can be assumed to abstain, so we are left with four possible sets of preference orderings if extremal restriction is to be satisfied, when one voter's preferences are of type 1. Assume that the theorem does not hold; that is, assume the existence of a forward cycle

$xRy, \ yRz, \ \text{and} \ zRx,$

where the unsubscripted R implies the social ordering under majority rule. Call $N(zP_ix)$ the number of individuals who prefer z to x:

$$(zRx) \rightarrow [N(zP_ix) \geq N(xP_iz)]. \tag{5.1}$$

By assumption, at least one individual has the ordering xP_iyP_iz. Thus,

$$N(xP_iz) \geq 1 \tag{5.2}$$

and from (5.1)

$$N(zP_ix) \geq 1. \tag{5.3}$$

Call N_1 the number of individuals with preferences as given in (1), N_2 as in (2), and so on.

$$(xRy) \rightarrow (N_1 + N_4 \geq N_2 + N_3) \rightarrow [N_4 \geq (N_2 - N_1) + N_3] \tag{5.4}$$

$$(yRz) \rightarrow (N_1 + N_3 \geq N_2 + N_4) \rightarrow [N_3 \geq (N_2 - N_1) + N_4] \tag{5.5}$$

$$(zRx) \rightarrow (N_2 \geq N_1). \tag{5.6}$$

For both (5.4) and (5.5) to hold,

$$N_2 = N_1 \tag{5.7}$$

and thus

$$N_3 = N_4. \tag{5.8}$$

But then

$$(N_2 + N_3 \geq N_1 + N_4) \rightarrow (yRx) \tag{5.9}$$

$$(N_2 + N_4 \geq N_1 + N_3) \rightarrow (zRy) \tag{5.10}$$

$$(N_1 \geq N_2) \rightarrow (xRz). \tag{5.11}$$

But (5.9)–(5.11) imply a backward cycle. Thus, if extremal restriction is satisfied, a forward cycle can exist only in the special case when a backward cycle does. A cycle ensues because society is indifferent among all three issues. The number of voters preferring x to y equals the number preferring y to x, the number preferring y to z equals the number preferring z to y, and the number preferring x to z equals the number preferring z to x.

If one assumes the theorem is violated by a backward cycle, an analogous argument demonstrates that extremal restriction also implies a forward cycle.

Necessity: We must show that violation of the extremal restriction axiom can lead to intransitive social preferences under the majority rule.

Assume one i with

$$xP_iyP_iz. \tag{5.12}$$

Extremal restriction is violated if one j has the ordering

$$zP_jx \text{ and } zP_jy \text{ and } xR_jy \tag{5.13}$$

or the ordering

$$zP_jx \text{ and } yP_jx \text{ and } yR_jz. \tag{5.14}$$

Assume (5.12) and (5.13) hold. Then under majority rule

$xPylzIx,$

which violates transitivity.

Next assume (5.12) and (5.14) hold. Then under majority rule

$xlyPzIx,$

which is again in violation of the transitivity axiom. When the extremal condition is not satisfied, majority rule may be incapable of producing a complete ordering over all alternatives.

H.   Preference homogeneity and majority rule equilibrium

For the reader who is unfamiliar with the public choice literature, the results on majority rule equilibrium must seem both surprising and disconcerting. Can the most frequently employed voting rule really produce the kind of inconsistency implied by its violation of the transitivity property? Are the types of preferences needed to bring about an equilibrium under majority rule really as unlikely to arise naturally as the above theorems suggest?

Unfortunately, the answers to these questions appear to be yes. That this is so is nicely illustrated in Gerald Kramer's (1973) generalization of the single-peakedness condition to more than one dimension. Kramer's theorem is particularly revealing to economists because he explores voter choices in the familiar environment of budget constraint lines and convex indifference curves.

In Figure 5.13, let x_1 and x_2 represent the quantities of two public goods, or two attributes of a single public good. BB is the budget constraint line for the committee. All points on or within BB are feasible alternatives. Let U_1^A and U_2^A be two indifference curves for individual A. A's preferences over the triple (x,y,z) are $xP_A yP_A z$. Let C have the dotted indifference curve U^C. C's preferences over (x,y,z) are $yP_C zP_C x$. The extremal restriction defined in Section F is violated. With individuals like A and C on the committee, majority rule may produce a cycle over triples like (x,y,z) selected from the feasible set. But there is nothing unusual about A and C's indifference curves other than that they intersect. When can we be certain that we avoid all preference orderings that violate extremal restriction over the feasible set? Only when all individuals have identical indifference maps, or as Kramer (1973, p. 295) puts it, when there is "complete unanimity of individual preference orderings."[5]

---

5. Were we to allow pairwise comparisons among all points along BB and exclude all points within BB from consideration, then convex utility functions would imply single-peaked preferences along the one dimension BB defines, and the median voter theorem would apply. Allow points interior to BB to be chosen under majority rule, or add a third dimension to the issue set and this escape hatch is closed, however.

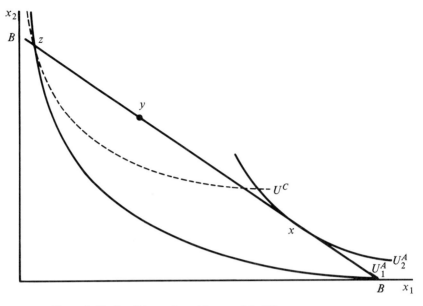

Figure 5.13. Possible cycles with normal indifference curves.

And so we return to a unanimity condition. If what we seek is a voting rule to reveal individual preferences on public goods, the options would appear to be as follows. A unanimity rule might be selected that possibly requires an infinite number of redefinitions of the issue until one that benefited all citizens was reached. Although each redefinition might, in turn, be defeated until a point on the Pareto-possibility frontier had been reached, once attained, no other proposal could command a unanimous vote against it, and the process would come to a halt. The number of times an issue must be redefined before a passing majority is reached can be reduced by reducing the size of the majority required to pass an issue. Although this "speeds up" the process of obtaining the *first* passing majority, it slows down, perhaps indefinitely, the process of reaching the *last* passing majority, that is, the one that beats all others. For under a less than unanimity rule, some voters are made worse off. This is equivalent to a redistribution from the opponents of a measure to its proponents. As with any redistribution measure, it is generally possible to redefine an issue transferring the benefits among a few individuals and obtain a new winning coalition. The Plott "perfect balance" condition ensures an equilibrium under majority rule by imposing a form of severe symmetry assumption on the distribution of preferences that ensures that any redefinition of an issue always involves symmetric and offsetting redistributions of the benefits. The same counterbalancing of interests is contained in the median-in-all-directions condition, while extremal restriction also tends to limit the contest to those with strictly opposing interests (e.g., xP_iyP_iz types against zP_jyP_jx types). The Kramer "identical utility functions" condition removes all conflict, and thereby eliminates all questions of redistribution.

The redistributive characteristics of less than unanimity rules explain the similarities between the proofs and conditions for a majority rule equilibrium, and those establishing a social welfare function (or the impossibilities thereof). Both flounder on their inability to choose among Pareto-preferred points, that is, to handle the question of redistribution (see A. K. Sen, 1970a, chs. 5, 5*).

These theorems all establish the *possibility* of a cycle when their restrictive conditions are not met. They do not establish the inevitability of a cycle. As Kramer (1973) notes, the existence of a majority with identical preferences is sufficient to ensure a majority rule equilibrium regardless of what the preferences of all other voters are (see also Buchanan, 1954a). More generally, we might wish to inquire as to how often in practice a set of preferences arises that leads to a cycle. A large number of studies have explored this question using simulation techniques. When no special restrictions are placed on the types of preference orderings individuals may have, the probability of a cycle is high, and approaches one as the number of alternatives increases.[6] We have noted that a cycle cannot occur if a majority of voters have identical preferences. Thus, we might expect that as various homogeneity assumptions are made about voter preferences, the probability of a cycle occurring decreases. And this is so. Niemi (1969) and Tullock and Campbell (1970) have found the probability of a cycle declines as the number of single-peaked preferences increases. Williamson and Sargent (1967), and Gehrlein and Fishburn (1976a) have found the probability of cycles declines with the proportion of the population having the same preferences,[7] and similarly Kuga and Nagatani (1974) have discovered that it increases with the number of pairs of voters whose interests are in conflict. Although these results are comforting, it is not clear how comforting they are.[8] To the extent that the collective choice process involves only movements from off the contract curve to points on it – that is, the kinds of decisions the unanimity rule might be able to handle – voter interests tend to coincide, and the probability of a cycle under majority rule will be low. But to the extent that the issues to be decided involve

6. Garman and Kamien (1968); Niemi and Weisberg (1968); DeMeyer and Plott (1970); Gehrlein and Fishburn (1976b). This literature is reviewed in Niemi (1969); Riker and Ordeshook (1973, pp. 94–7); Plott (1976).
7. See also Abrams (1976) and Fishburn and Gehrlein (1980).
8. Under rather stringent conditions, median voter outcomes will satisfy the Pareto-optimality requirement, however. See Bowen (1943) and Bergstrom (1979).

redistribution, interests will not coincide, indexes of "voter antagonism" will be high, and so too will the probability of cycles.

I.   Logrolling

When faced with a simple binary choice between X and $\sim X$ under majority rule, an individual's obvious best (dominant) strategy is to state honestly his preference for X or $\sim X$. Majority rule records only these ordinal preferences for each individual on the issue pair. The condition for the Pareto optimality of the supply of public goods requires information on the relative intensity of individual preferences; however, the marginal rates of substitution of public for private goods must sum to the ratio of their prices. Since this information is not directly gathered under majority rule, it is not particularly surprising that the outcomes under majority rule may not satisfy the Pareto-optimality condition.

The Pareto-optimal allocation of private goods also requires information on individual preference intensities, but this information is elicited by the "voting" process for private goods as individuals selfishly engage in the exchange of goods and services to maximize their own utilities. But with voting on public issues, each individual is constrained to cast but one vote for or against a given issue, unless, of course, one allows individuals to exchange votes.

The buying and selling of votes by individual citizens is outlawed in all democratic countries. That such laws exist, and are occasionally violated, suggests that individual intensities of preference regarding the value of a vote do differ. Although buying and selling votes is also prohibited in parliamentary bodies, the more informal process "you vote for my pet issue and I'll vote for yours" is difficult to police. Exchanges of this sort have occurred in the U.S. Congress for as long as it has been in existence. That they do exist, in spite of a certain moral stigma to their use, has two implications. Intensities of preference on issues must differ across congressmen. The assumption that congressmen's actions can be explained as the pursuit of self-interest is buttressed. The natural inclination to engage in trade, "to truck and barter," as Adam Smith called it, seems to carry over to the parliamentary behavior of elected representatives.

To understand the process, consider Table 5.2. Each column gives the utility changes to three voters from an issue's passage; defeat produces no change. If each is decided separately by majority rule, both fail. Voters B and C have much to gain from X and Y's passage, however, and can achieve this if B votes for Y in exchange for C's vote for X. Both issues now pass to B and C's mutual benefit.

The existence of beneficial trades requires a nonuniform distribution of intensities. Change the two 5s to 2s and B and C gain nothing by trading. This

Table 5.2.

| | Issues | |
	X	Y
A	−2	−2
B	5	−2
C	−2	5

equal intensity condition is often invoked in arguments in favor of simple (without trading) majority rule, and are taken up in Chapter 6 when we consider the normative case for majority rule.

The trade between B and C can be said to have improved the welfare of the community of three voters, if the numbers in Table 5.2 are treated as cardinal, interpersonally comparable utilities. Without trading, the majority tyrannizes over the relatively more intense minority on each issue. Through vote trading, these minorities express the intensity of their preferences, just as trading in private goods does, and improve the total welfare change of the community. With trading there is a net gain of 2 for the community.

An obvious condition for an improvement in community welfare through the changes in outcomes that vote trading brings about is that the cumulative potential utility changes for the (losing) minority members exceed the cumulative potential utility changes for the winning majority members on the issues involved. Change the 5s to 3s or the −2s of A to −4s, and the same trades emerge as before, since the pattern of trades depends only on the *relative* intensities of preferences of the voters. The sum of utilities for the community with trading is then negative, however. An exchange of votes increases the likelihood of the participants winning on their relatively more important issues. It *tends,* therefore, to increase their realized gains. These increases *can* increase the utility gain for the entire community. However, trading also imposes externalities (utility losses) on the nontraders who would have been better off in the absence of trading,[9] and, if these are negative and large, they can outweigh the gains to the traders, lowering the community's net welfare. Critics of logrolling have typically envisaged situations such as these. They assume that the cumulative potential gains of the majority exceed those of the minority. Vote trading that reverses some of the outcomes of simple majority rule lowers collective welfare when this is true.

Gordon Tullock's (1959) argument that majority rule *with trading* can lead

---

9. See Taylor (1971, p. 344), and Riker and Brams (1973).

to too much government spending is of this type. Let *A, B,* and *C* be three farmers, and *X* be a road of use to only farmer *B, Y* a road of use to only *C.* If the gross gains to a farmer from the access road are 7 and the cost is 6, which is shared equally, we have the figures of Table 5.3. With these costs and benefits, total welfare is improved by logrolling. But a bill promising a gross gain of 5 at a cost of 6, equally shared, also passes. Such a bill lowers community welfare by excessively constructing new roads, roads whose total benefits are less than their total costs. Again, the problem arises because majority rule can involve allocation and redistribution at the same time. The two bills involve both the construction of roads with gross benefits of 5 and costs of 6, and the redistribution of wealth from *A* to *B* and *C,* and the latter can be sufficient to pass the bills.

An important difference separating logrolling's critics and proponents is their views as to whether voting is a positive- or negative- (at best zero-) sum game. If the latter, the game is obviously bad to begin with, and anything that improves its efficiency can only worsen the final outcome. The numerical examples that Riker and Brams (1973) present in their attack on logrolling are all examples of this type, and the examples they cite of tariff bills, tax loopholes, and pork barrel public works are all illustrations of bills for which a minority benefits, largely from the redistributive aspects of the bill, and the accumulative losses of the majority can be expected to be large.[10] The worst examples of logrolling cited in the literature are always issues of this type in which private or local public goods are added to the agenda for redistribution purposes to be financed out of public budgets at a higher level of aggregation than is appropriate (Schwartz, 1975). The best the community can hope for is the defeat of all of these issues. Riker and Brams (1973) logically recommend reforms to eliminate logrolling opportunities.

A private good or a very local public good will of course be of great interest to a few and little interest to the majority. The conditions necessary for logrolling are likely to be satisfied, therefore, through the incorporation of these goods into the community's agenda. But, preference intensities can also vary considerably across individuals on what are truly pure public goods, for example, defense, education, and the environment. On issues such as these, vote trading can be a superior way for revealing individual preference intensities over the public goods.

One of the most positive and influential discussions of vote trading's potential has been presented by James Coleman (1966b). He depicts the members of the committee or legislature as entering into logrolling agreements on all public good issues. Each voter forms agreements to swap votes with other voters of the type described above. Each voter increases his ability to *control*

10. See also Schattschneider (1935); McConnell (1966); Lowi (1969).

Table 5.3.

			Utilities		
Winning pair	Losing pair	Trading voters	A	B	C
X,Y	$\sim X,\sim Y$	B and C	-4	3	3
$X,\sim Y$	X,Y	A and B	-2	5	-2
$\sim X,\sim Y$	$X,\sim Y$	A and C	0	0	0

those *events* (issues) about which he feels most intense in exchange for a loss of control over those events about which he cares little. A form of ex ante Pareto optimum is reached in which no voter feels he can increase his expected utility by agreeing to exchange another vote. This equilibrium is the optimum of Coleman's social welfare function.

Unfortunately, whatever potential a vote trading process has for revealing relative intensities of preference, and thereby improving the allocation of public goods, may go unrealized, because the trading process may not produce stable coalitions, nor be free from strategic misrepresentation of preferences. When vote trades are parts of only informal agreements and take place in sequence, voters are motivated both to misstate their preferences at the time an agreement is formed and to violate the agreement after it is made. A voter who would benefit from X might pretend to oppose it and secure support for some other issues he favors in "exchange" for his positive vote for X. If successful, he wins on both X and the other issue. But the other "trader" might be bluffing too, and the end results of trading become indeterminate (Mueller, 1967).

Even when bluffing is not a problem, cheating may be. When issues are taken up seriatim, there is an obvious and strong incentive for the second trader to renege on his part of the bargain. This incentive must be present, since the same preference orderings that produce a logrolling situation imply a potential voting cycle. Consider again the example in Table 5.3. In addition to X and Y with payoffs as in Table 5.3, we have the issues $\sim X$ and $\sim Y$, which "win" if X and Y fail. Both have payoffs for the three voters (O, O, O). Thus, four combinations of issues might result from the voting process, (X,Y), $(\sim X,Y)$, $(X,\sim Y)$, and $(\sim X,\sim Y)$. The committee must choose one of these four combinations. If we envisage voting as taking place on the issue pairs, then a cycle exists over the three pairs $(\sim X,\sim Y)$, (X,Y), $(X,\sim Y)$. In terms of the vote-trading process, the existence of this cycle implies that no stable trading agreements may be possible. We have seen that a trade between B and C to produce (X,Y) would make them both better off than the no trade outcome $(\sim X,\sim Y)$ (see Table 5.3). But A can improve her position by offering to vote for X if B refrains from voting for Y. Thus, (X,Y) can be beaten (blocked) by $(X,\sim Y)$. But C can then offer A the option of no loss of utility if they both agree to vote sincerely and reestablish the victory of $(\sim X,\sim Y)$. From here the trading cycle can begin again. Moreover, the only condition under which a potential logrolling situation is certain not to create the potential for a cycle is when a unanimity rule is imposed (Bernholz, 1973). Allowing for individual intensity differences as in a logrolling process does not allow us to escape the cycling problem. On the contrary, the existence of the one implies the presence of the other, as we shall now demonstrate.

J.*   Logrolling and cycling

We illustrate the theorem following Bernholz (1973) with the simple example of the previous section. The key assumptions are that voters have well-defined preference orderings, which satisfy the following independence condition for voter i over the relevant issues:

Independent issues: If $XP_i\sim X$, then $(XY)P_i(\sim XY)$.
All voters vote sincerely at each juncture.

Definition: *A logrolling situation exists if*

$$\sim XRX \tag{5.15}$$

$$\sim YRY \tag{5.16}$$

$$XYP\sim X\sim Y, \tag{5.17}$$

> *where* R *and* P *are the social preference orderings defined by whatever voting rule is being used. In a pairwise vote,* $\sim$X *defeats* X *and* $\sim$Y *defeats* Y. *But the pair* XY *can defeat* $\sim$X$\sim$Y.

Theorem: *The existence of a logrolling situation implies intransitive social preferences. The existence of a transitive social preference ordering implies the absence of a logrolling situation.*

PROOF OF FIRST PROPOSITION: Assume a logrolling situation exists [i.e., (5.15), (5.16), and (5.17) hold]. Then winning coalitions h must exist (i.e., majority coalitions under majority rule) for which

$$\sim XR_hX \tag{5.18}$$

$$\sim YR_hY \tag{5.19}$$

$$XYP_h\sim X\sim Y. \tag{5.20}$$

From (5.18) and (5.19) and the independent issues assumption,

$$\sim X\sim YR_hX\sim Y \tag{5.21}$$

$X \sim YR_h XY.$ \hfill (5.22)

Since each respective h is a winning coalition,

$\sim X \sim YRX \sim Y$ \hfill (5.23)

$X \sim YRXY.$ \hfill (5.24)

Combining (5.17), (5.23), and (5.24), we have

$\sim X \sim Y \; R \; X \sim Y \; R \; XY \; P \; \sim X \sim Y.$ \hfill (5.25)

The existence of a logrolling situation implies intransitive social preferences. □

PROOF OF SECOND PROPOSITION: We assume the first part of a logrolling situation exists and demonstrate that transitive social preferences imply the absence of the second part (5.17); that is, assume

$\sim XRX$ \hfill (5.15)

$\sim YRY.$ \hfill (5.16)

This implies

$\sim XR_h X$ \hfill (5.26)

$\sim YR_h Y.$ \hfill (5.27)

By independent issue assumption,

$\sim XYR_h XY$ \hfill (5.28)

$\sim X \sim YR_h \sim XY.$ \hfill (5.29)

Since each h is a winning coalition,

$\sim XYRXY$ \hfill (5.30)

$\sim X \sim YR \sim XY.$ \hfill (5.31)

But then

$\sim X \sim Y \; R \; \sim XY \; R \; XY.$ \hfill (5.32)

The last part of a logrolling situation is not satisfied. The existence of a transitive social preference ordering implies the absence of a logrolling situation. □

K.   Agenda manipulation

Surely by now the patient reader has grown weary of cycling theorems. Yet we have but scratched the surface of a vast literature establishing cycling and

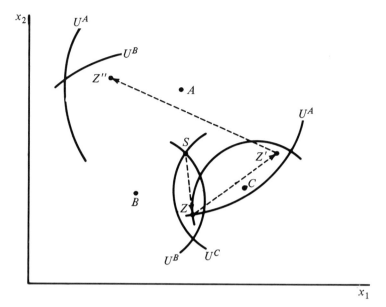

Figure 5.14. Agenda manipulation possibilities.

instability results of one form or another. That majority rule leads to cycles is a (some would say *the*) major theme of the public choice literature. Yet is the problem that serious? Do committees really spin their wheels endlessly as the cycling results seem to suggest? Probably not, and we shall consider several reasons why committees avoid endless cycles in the next section. But before we do, let us examine a result that illustrates the potential significance of the cycling phenomenon.

In an important paper, Richard McKelvey (1976) first established that, when individual preferences are such as to produce the potential for a cycle with sincere voting under majority rule, then an individual who can control the agenda of pairwise votes can lead the committee to any outcome in the issue space he chooses. The theorem is developed in two parts. First, it is established that with a voting cycle it is possible to move the committee from any starting point S an arbitrarily large distance d from S. In Figure 5.14, let A, B, and C be the ideal points for three voters and S the starting point. If each individual votes sincerely on each issue pair, the committee can be led from S to Z to Z' to Z'' in just three steps. The further one moves away from S, the larger the voter indifference circles and the larger the steps will become. The process can continue until one is any d one chooses from S.

Now let r be the radius of a circle around S such that (1) the target point of the agenda setter is within the circle (say, ideal point A) and (2) at least $n/2$

ideal points for the committee (in this case two) are within the circle of radius r. Now choose d such that $d > 3r$ and one is certain that a majority of the committee favors A over the last Z^n obtained in the cycle, the Z^n d distance from S. The last pairwise choice offered the committee is then Z^n versus A, and A wins. The agenda setter then either calls a halt to the voting or picks new proposals that will lose to A. Thus, a member of a committee with the power to set the agenda can bring about the victory of his most preferred outcome.

McKelvey's theorem has two important implications. First, and most obviously, the power of the agenda setter may be substantial. If this power is vested in a given individual or subcommittee, then one must take precautions lest those with agenda-setting power secure a disproportionate share of the gains from collective action. Second, the existence of a voting cycle introduces a degree of unpredictability to the voting outcomes that may provide an incentive for some to manipulate the process to their advantage. The fact that a committee has reached a decision may in itself not have much normative significance until one learns by what route it got there.

L.   Why so much stability?

If cycling problems are as pervasive as the public choice literature implies, then why do committee outcomes in Congress and in state legislatures seem to be so stable, both in the sense that the committees do reach decisions and that these outcomes do not gyrate from one meeting of the committee to the next, and from one session of the legislature to the next? This challenging question was put forward by Gordon Tullock (1981) and we shall take it up on more than one occasion in this book.

We have in the previous section already encountered one answer to this question, and not a comforting one. An agenda setter may lead the committee to an outcome particularly pleasing to the agenda setter, and keep it there. This solution to the cycling problem is one of several possible answers to Tullock's question, which rely on a particular institution like the agenda setter to structure the voting sequence so as to avoid cycles. Roberts' Rules of Order are probably the most familiar example of an institutional constraint on a committee, which by restricting the possibility of defeated proposals reappearing on the agenda tends to limit the scope for cycles. We discuss two additional examples of structure-induced equilibria in this section.

1.   Voting one dimension at a time

Black's median voter theorem is the first and still the most compelling demonstration of the existence of a majority rule equilibrium. Given that we have a single-dimensional issue, single-peakedness does not seem to be that strong

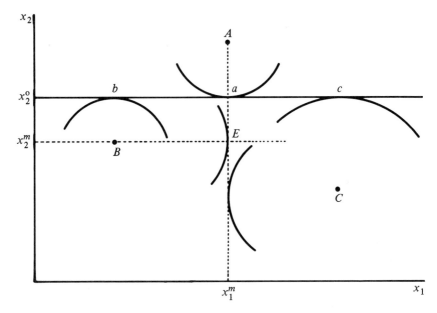

Figure 5.15. Equilibrium outcomes with sequential votes.

an assumption. What is implausible is the assumption that the issue space is one dimensional.

Suppose, however, that in a two-dimensional issue space we limit voting to but one dimension at a time. Consider Figure 5.15, where x_1 and x_2 are two public goods vectors. Tax rates to finance the public goods are assumed given, so that A, B, and C are again the ideal points of our three voters. With each voter free to propose any point in the positive orthant, a cycle can ensue. But let the committee rule be that voting must take place one dimension at a time. Take x_2^o as initially given and have the committee vote on the level of x_1, given x_2^o. With circular (or ellipsoid) indifference contours, each voter has single-peaked preferences along the horizontal line x_2^o. B favors point b, A favors a, and C favors c. A is the median voter in the x_1 dimension and x_1^m is the quantity of x_1 chosen under majority rule. Now fix x_1 at x_1^m and allow the committee to decide the quantity of x_2. B is now the median voter and x_2^m is the quantity of x_2 chosen. Point E is an equilibrium under majority rule given the constraints that x_1 and x_2 must be voted upon one dimension at a time.[11]

With tax shares fixed, the Pareto set is the triangle with apexes at A, B, and

---

11. E is a median in two directions. To be an unconstrained equilibrium, it must be a median in all directions, which it is not. Allow the committee to vote on combinations of x_1 and x_2 along a ray through E running in a northeast direction, and E will not be the chosen point.

C. *E* falls inside this triangle and is Pareto optimal under the constraint that tax shares are fixed. But taxes are one of the important variables a committee must decide. If the choice of tax rate can be formulated as a one-dimensional issue – say, the degree of progressivity of an income tax – then tax progressivity can be voted upon as a separate issue, holding x_1 and x_2 constant, and an equilibrium outcome chosen in these three dimensions. But this equilibrium outcome need not be Pareto optimal (Slutsky, 1977b). To find the Pareto-optimal quantities of x_1 and x_2, one chooses x_1, x_2 and the individual tax shares so as to maximize the sum of the utilities of the committee. The resulting solution must satisfy the Samuelsonian condition for the Pareto-optimal allocation of a public good. Choosing quantities of each public good and tax rates one dimension at a time in effect adds further constraints to the maximization problem. There is no reason to suspect that this constrained committee choice will coincide with what the unconstrained solution would be, and in general it will not. The price of an equilibrium under majority rule can be high.

2.   *Logrolling equilibria*

The theorems, that logrolling situations imply voting cycles and that agenda setters can achieve their ideal points in cyclic situations, assume that every voter at each step of a voting sequence votes sincerely. Voters, like the children of Hamlin, follow the agenda setter blindly wherever he goes. These theorems assume a seemingly unrealistic degree of myopia on the part of voters.

Consider again the trading cycle illustrated with the help of Tables 5.2 and 5.3. *B* first agrees to trade votes with *C*, then deserts her for *A*, who in turn jilts *B* for *C*. For a true cycle to enfold, *B* and *C*, not having learned their lessons, must again agree to swap votes and we repeat the cycle. But surely rational individuals should not allow themselves to be dragged through too many revolutions of this cycle before they begin to foresee the short-run nature of each trade. Once each trader realizes that an apparently advantageous trade is likely to be overturned, he might try to stick to a *relatively* advantageous pair of trades once made, or never allow himself to be talked into a trade to begin with. Note, in this regard, the inherent instability of the outcome pairs $(X, \sim Y)$ and $(\sim X, Y)$. Under each of these two outcomes one individual (*B* or *C*) gets her maximum potential gain. Thus, were the coalition *A–B* to form the produce $(X, \sim Y)$ as an outcome pair, *A* can threaten to leave *B*, since both *A* and *C* are better off when they form a coalition than when *A* stays with *B*. But *B*'s only alternative to *A* is a coalition with *C*, which makes *B* worse off. Thus, *B* prefers preserving the *A–B* coalition, but if *A* is rational, *B* will be incapable of doing so. Now consider the *B–C* coalition to produce

(X,Y). Either B or C could become better off by joining A to produce $(X,\sim Y)$ or $(\sim X,Y)$, respectively. Both have the identical threats to make against the B–C coalition. Thus, if one individual begins to waver in her support for the B–C coalition, the other can issue the counter threat to bolt and join with A. Since both are confronted by the same threats and counterthreats, each may decide that it is better to remain in the B–C coalition.

Considerations such as these lead one to predict a coalition between B and C with outcomes (X,Y), even though no core exists. This outcome is contained in the main solution concepts, which have been proposed to solve simple bargaining games (e.g., the von Neumann–Morgenstern solution, the bargaining set, the kernel, and the competitive solution). If vote trading in parliamentary committees resembles the kinds of bargaining deliberations that underlie these different solution concepts, then stable, predictable outcomes from a logrolling process can be expected even though no core exists and myopic trading would produce a cycle. Joe Oppenheimer (1979) has argued in favor of the bargaining set as predictor of outcomes from logrolling, whereas McKelvey and Ordeshook (1980) have found that outcomes from vote-trading experiments conform to the competitive solution.

In the game depicted in Tables 5.2 and 5.3, either voter B or C could ensure the outcome $(\sim X,\sim Y)$ that arises when each voter sincerely states her true preferences by voting against both issues. If B, say, votes against X and Y, A can achieve her most preferred outcome $(\sim X,\sim Y)$ by voting sincerely. C can make her no better proposal and $(\sim X,\sim Y)$ will be the committee choice. Thus, if B or C were fearful that trading would produce an outcome that left them worse off than the sincere voting outcome $(\sim X,\sim Y)$, they could make sure that this outcome comes about by following the *sophisticated* strategy of voting against both issues.[12] Enelow and Koehler (1979) show that the majority, which produces the sincere voting outcome, always can preserve this outcome by the appropriate sophisticated voting strategy, even when logrolling with sincere voting would overturn it.

Thus, there is reason to suspect that either (X,Y) or $(\sim X,\sim Y)$ would emerge as the committee outcome in the example from Tables 5.2 and 5.3. Although either B or C can preserve $(\sim X,\sim Y)$ by sophisticated voting, the temptation to join with one another to produce (X,Y) must be strong. What might prevent them from ever doing so is the fear that once the B–C coalition has formed, the other trading partner will fail to deliver on her part of the trade (or join with A). This danger is particularly likely when issues X and Y are decided sequentially. We have here another example of a prisoners' dilemma (Bernholz, 1977). Matrix 5.1 depicts the strategic options for voters B and C

---

12. The distinction between sincere and sophisticated voting was introduced by Farquharson (1969).

Matrix 5.1.

| | | Voter C | |
		Vote for X and Y	Vote for Y and against X
Voter B	Vote for X and Y	1 $(+3, +3)$	2 $(-2, +5)$
	Vote for X, and against Y	3 $(+5, -2)$	4 $(0, 0)$

when issues X and Y must be decided as before. Both voters are better off with the trade (square 1) than without it (square 4), but the incentive to cheat is present. If issue X is decided before issue Y and voter C lives up to her part of the bargain by voting for X, the outcomes in column 2 become infeasible. Voter B must choose between squares 1 and 3 and her choice is obvious, if there is no possibility for voter C to retaliate.

As we have seen in Chapter 2, the cooperative solution to the prisoners' dilemma emerges only if the player thinks that her choice of the cooperative strategy is likely to induce the corresponding strategy choice of the other player. If the strategy options are played in sequence and the game is played but once, the first player has no means by which to influence the second player's decision at the time the latter is made. Thus, one would not expect vote trading to take place over issues decided sequentially among coalitions that form but a single time. A stable, cooperative vote-trading game can be expected only when the issues on which votes are traded are all decided simultaneously, say, as part of an omnibus highway bill; or when the same constellations of issues come up time and time again, and a prisoners' dilemma supergame emerges. Peter Bernholz (1978) has discussed the latter possibility. Under the assumption that the same types of issues do arise again and again, he shows that the likelihood of a stable prisoners' dilemma supergame emerging is positively related to both the net potential gains from cooperation and the probability that the same players reappear in each successive game. As Bernholz notes, the depiction of logrolling situations as single plays of a prisoners' dilemma supergame is plausible for a legislative assembly, whose members continually represent the same interests and have reasonably long tenure.

Arranging vote trades and ensuring that bargains are kept is the job of party leaders and their whips. These "agenda setters" are elected to their posts by their fellow party members presumably in part on the basis of how capable they are at avoiding cycles and satisfying the goals of all party members, not just the leaders. Both Haefele (1971) and Koford (1982) see party leadership as effectively guiding the legislature to outcomes that maximize the welfare of the party membership. Their rather optimistic description of how the legislative process functions stands in sharp contrast to most of the logrolling–majority rule–cycling literature.

So, too, do the experimental results of Fiorina and Plott (1978). They find that when committee preferences are such that a majority rule equilibrium exists, that is, an outcome is in the core, a committee does indeed select it. Moreover, even when no core outcome exists, committees using majority rule do not flounder "all over the map" in choosing outcomes, but rather cluster their choices relatively closely together.

Although McKelvey and Ordeshook's (1980) experimental results are less encouraging with respect to the magnetism of the core, they are reassuring in other respects. The most dire prediction regarding logrolling, that it can lead to Pareto-inferior outcomes, is not borne out. Even when no core exists, the outcomes from vote-trading experiments tend to conform to those one would expect from the kinds of game-theoretic arguments presented in this chapter. For better or worse, the outcomes from committees that use majority rule tend in practice to be more stable than the theoretical literature on majority rule leads one to expect.

Bibliographical notes

A rigorous proof of the median voter theorem is presented by G. H. Kramer (1972). Kramer and A. K. Klevorick (1974) established a similar result for local optima, and A. Kats and S. Nitzan (1976) have shown that a local equilibrium is likely to be a global equilibrium under fairly mild conditions.

Following Plott (1967), the major papers on stability conditions in multidimensional models have been Kadane (1972), Sloss (1973), Slutsky (1977a), Schofield (1978), and Cohen (1979).

Hoyer and Mayer (1974) prove the median-in-all-directions theorem using elliptical indifference curves.

The literature on axiomatic restrictions on preference orderings to produce majority rule equilibria is reviewed in Inada (1969); Sen (1970a); Plott (1971); and Taylor (1971).

The seminal discussions of logrolling in public choice are by Downs (1957), Tullock (1959), and most extensively by Buchanan and Tullock (1962). In political science, the classic reference is Bentley (1907).

Arguments that logrolling can, in the proper structural setting, improve on the outcomes from simple, sincere majority voting have been presented by Coleman (1966a,b, 1970); Mueller (1967, 1971, 1973); Wilson (1969, 1971a,b); Mueller, Philpotts, and Vanek (1972); and Koford (1982).

The negative side of logrolling has figured more prominently in the political science literature (Schattschneider, 1935; McConnell, 1966; Lowi, 1969; Riker and Brams, 1973; Schwartz, 1975).

The theorem relating logrolling to cycling appears in various forms in Park (1967); Kadane (1972); Oppenheimer (1972, 1975); Bernholz (1973, 1974a, 1975); Riker and Brams (1973); Koehler (1975); and Schwartz (1981). A very useful review of this literature with additional proofs is given by Nicholas Miller (1977).

Shepsle and Weingast (1981) discuss several possible institutions to bring about "structure-induced" equilibria. Niemi (1983) emphasizes the potential importance of limiting the issue set to a few choices and presents a weakened version of the single-peakedness condition.

Bernholz (1974b) was the first to propose limiting consideration to a single dimension at a time to induce equilibria. Both Slutsky (1977b) and Shepsle (1979) offer proofs of the result.

Coleman (1983) emphasizes the importance of the long-run context in which logrolling takes place in bringing about stability, as Bernholz proves (1977, 1978).

CHAPTER 6

Majority rule – normative properties

Unanimity is impossible; the rule of a minority, as a permanent arrangement, is wholly inadmissible; so that, rejecting the majority principle, anarchy or despotism in some form is all that is left.

Abraham Lincoln

. . . unless the king has been elected by unanimous vote, what, failing a prior agreement, is the source of the minority's obligation to submit to the choice of the majority? Whence the right of the hundred who do wish a master to speak for the ten who do not? The majority principle is itself a product of agreement, and presupposes unanimity on at least one occasion.

Jean-Jacques Rousseau

In Chapter 4 we argued that the ubiquitous popularity of majority rule might be attributable to the speed with which committees can make decisions using it. This quickness defense was undermined considerably in Chapter 5 by the results on cycling. A committee caught in a voting cycle may not be able to reach a decision quickly, and the outcome at which it eventually does arrive may be arbitrarily determined by institutional details, or nonarbitrarily determined by a cunning agenda setter. Is this all one can say in majority rule's behalf? Does the case for the majority rule rest on the promise that quasi-omniscient party leaders can arrange stable trades to maximize the aggregate welfare of the legislature as just discussed?

When asked to explain majority rule's popularity, students unfamiliar with the vast public choice literature on the topic usually mention justness, fairness, and egalitarian and similar normative attributes that they feel characterize majority rule. Thus, to understand why majority rule is so often *the* committee rule, one must examine its normative as well as its positive properties. In doing so, we shall contrast the majority and the unanimity rules.

A.   May's theorem on majority rule

A most important theorem concerning majority rule was proved some 35 years ago by Kenneth O. May (1952). May begins by defining a *group decision* function:

$$D = f(D_1, D_2, \cdots, D_n),$$

where n is the number of individuals in the community. Each D_i takes on the value 1, 0, −1 as voter i's preferences for a pair of issues are xP_iy, xI_iy, yP_ix, where P represents the strict preference relationship and I indifference. Thus, the D_i serve as ballots, and $f(\ )$ is an aggregation rule for determining the winning issue. Depending on the nature of the voting rule, f( ) takes on different functional forms. Under the simple majority rule, f( ) sums the D_i and assigns D a value according to the following rule:

$$\left(\sum_{i=1}^{n} D_i > 0 \right) \rightarrow D = 1$$

$$\left(\sum_{i=1}^{n} D_i = 0 \right) \rightarrow D = 0$$

$$\left(\sum_{i=1}^{n} D_i < 0 \right) \rightarrow D = -1.$$

May defines the following four conditions.[1]

> *Decisiveness:* The group decision function is defined and single valued for any given set of preference orderings.
> *Anonymity:* D is determined only by the values of D_i, and is independent of how they are assigned. Any permutation of these ballots leaves D unchanged.
> *Neutrality:* If x defeats (ties) y for one set of individual preferences, and all individuals have the same *ordinal* rankings for z and w as for x and y (i.e., $xR_iy \rightarrow zR_iw$, etc.), then z defeats (ties) w.
> *Positive responsiveness:* If D equals 0 or 1, and one individual changes his vote from −1 to 0 or 1, or from 0 to 1, and all other votes remain unchanged, then $D = 1$.

The theorem states that a group decision function is the simple majority rule *if and only if* it satisfies these four conditions. It is a most remarkable result. If we start from the set of all possible voting rules one can conceive of, and then begin imposing conditions we wish our voting rule to satisfy, we shall obviously reduce the number of viable candidates for our chosen voting rule as we add more and more conditions. May's theorem tells us that once we add these four conditions, we have reduced the possible set of voting rules to but one, the simple majority rule. All other voting rules violate one or more of these four axioms.

1. The names and definitions have been changed somewhat to reflect subsequent developments in the literature and to simplify the discussion. In particular, the definition of neutrality follows Sen (1970a, p. 72).

This result is both surprising and ominous. It forebodes that if we were to demand more of a voting rule than that it satisfy only these four axioms, that is, were we to demand a fifth axiom, then even majority rule would not qualify and we would have no voting rule satisfying the proposed conditions. Chapter 5 also gives us a strong hint as to what that fifth condition might be – transitivity. But for the moment we are concerned with the choice between just two issues, and we need not concern ourselves with transitivity. The foreboding can be suppressed until Chapter 20.

The equivalence between majority rule and these four conditions means that all of the normative properties majority rule possesses, whatever justness or egalitarian attributes it has, are somewhere captured in these four axioms, as are its negative attributes. We must examine these conditions more closely.

Decisiveness seems uncontroversial. If we have a *decision* function, we want it to be able to decide at least when confronted with only two issues. But this axiom does eliminate all probabilistic procedures in which the probability of an issue's winning depends on voter preferences. Positive responsiveness is also a reasonable property. If the decision process is to reflect each voter's preference, then a switch by one voter from opposition to support ought to break a tie.

The other two axioms are less innocent than they look or their names connote. The neutrality axiom introduces an issue independence property.[2] In deciding a pair of issues, only the ordinal preferences of each voter over this issue pair are considered. Information concerning voter preferences on other issue pairs is ruled out, and thereby one means for weighing intensities is eliminated. The neutrality axiom eliminates voting rules like the Borda count and point voting described in the next two chapters. It requires that the voting rule treat each issue pair alike regardless of the nature of the issues involved. Thus, the issue of whether the lights on this year's community Christmas tree are red or blue is decided by the same kind of weighing of individual preference orderings as the issue of whether John Doe's property should be confiscated and redistributed among the rest of the community.

Although the neutrality axiom guarantees that the voting procedure treats each *issue* alike, anonymity assures that each *voter* is treated alike. On many issues this is probably a desirable property. On the issue of the color of the Christmas lights, a change of one voter's preferences from red to blue and another from blue to red probably should not affect the outcome. Implicit here is a judgment that the color of the tree's lights is about as important to one voter as to the next. This equal intensity assumption is introduced into the voting procedure by recording each voter's expression of preference, no matter how strong, as a plus or minus one.

2. Sen (1970a, p. 72); Guha (1972).

But consider now the issue of whether John Doe's property should be confiscated and distributed to the rest of the community. Suppose John is a generous fellow and votes for the issue and the issue in fact passes. Suppose now that John changes his vote to negative, and that his worst enemy, who always votes the opposite of John, switches to a positive vote. By the anonymity condition, the issue still should pass. A voting procedure satisfying this procedure is blind as to whether it is John Doe or his worst enemy who is voting for the confiscation of John Doe's property. In some situations this may obviously be an undesirable property.

B.*   Proof of May's theorem on majority rule

Theorem: *A group decision function is the simple majority rule iff it satisfies the 4 conditions on page 97.*

That majority rule implies the four conditions is rather obvious.

1. It always adds to an integer, which by the decision function is transformed into -1 or 0 or $+1$, and thus is decisive.
2. Change any $+1$ to -1, and any -1 to $+1$, and the sum is left unchanged.
3. If the rankings are the same on any two pairs of issues, then so too will be the vote summations.
4. If $\Sigma D_i = 0$, increasing any D_i will make $\Sigma D_i > 0$, and decide the contest in favor of x. If $\Sigma D_i > 0$, increasing any D_i will leave $\Sigma D_i > 0$, and will not change the outcome.

Now we must show that the four conditions imply the majority rule. We first show that the first three conditions imply

$$[N(-1) = N(1)] \rightarrow D = \Sigma D_i = 0, \qquad (6.1)$$

where $N(-1)$ is the number of votes for y and $N(1)$ is the number for x.

Assume that (6.1) does not hold, for example, that

$$[N(-1) = N(1)] \rightarrow D = 1. \qquad (6.2)$$

When the number of votes for y equals the number of votes for x, the outcome is x.

Now relabel y to z and x to w, where a vote for z is now recorded as a -1 and a vote for w as a $+1$. Reverse all $+1$s to -1s, and -1s to $+1$s. By anonymity, this latter change should not affect the group decision. All individuals who originally regarded x at least as good as y (xR_iy) will now regard z as at least as good as w. By the neutrality axiom, the collective outcome must be z if it was originally x. But z is equivalent to y not x. The decisiveness axiom is violated.

Thus, (6.2) is inconsistent with the first three axioms. By an analogous argument one can show that (6.3) is inconsistent with the first three axioms:

$$[N(-1) = N(1)] \rightarrow D = -1. \tag{6.3}$$

Thus, (6.1) must be valid.

From (6.1) and positive responsiveness, we have

$$[N(1) = N(-1) + 1] \rightarrow D = +1. \tag{6.4}$$

When the number of votes for x is one greater than the number for y, then x must win. Now assume that when the number of votes for x is $m-1$ greater than the number for y, x wins. A change in preferences of one voter so that the number preferring x to y is now m greater than the number preferring y to x cannot reverse the outcome by positive responsiveness. By finite induction, the four conditions imply the method of simple majority rule.

C.   The Rae–Taylor theorem on majority rule

Although on the surface they seem quite different, May's theorem on majority rule is quite similar in its underlying assumptions to a theorem presented by Douglas Rae (1969) and Michael Taylor (1969).

Rae (1969, pp. 43–4) sets up the problem as one of the choice of an optimal voting rule by an individual who is uncertain over his future position under the voting rule. Thus, the discussion is set in the context of constitutional choice of a voting rule as introduced by Buchanan and Tullock (1962, pp. 3–15).[3] Politics, as Rae and Taylor depict it, is a game of conflict. Some individuals gain from an issue's passage, some inevitably lose. The representative individual in the constitutional stage seeks to avoid having issues he opposes imposed upon him, and to impose issues he favors on others. He presumes that the gains he will experience from a favorable issue's passage will equal the loss from an unfavorable issue's passage, that is, that all voters experience equal intensities on each issue.[4] Issues are impartially proposed so that each voter has the same probability of favoring or opposing any issue proposed. Under these assumptions, it is reasonable to assume that the representative voter selects a rule that minimizes the probability of his supporting an issue that is defeated, or opposing an issue that wins. Rae (1969) illustrates and

3. See, also, Buchanan (1966).
4. Rae (1969, p. 41, n. 6). The importance of this equal intensity assumption has been recognized by several writers. Additional references for each assumption are presented in the notes to Table 6.1, where the assumptions are summarized.

Taylor (1969) proves that majority rule is the only rule that satisfies this criterion.[5]

The full flavor of the theorem can best be obtained by considering an example of Brian Barry (1965, p. 312). Five people occupy a railroad car that contains no sign either prohibiting or permitting smoking. A decision must be made as to whether those occupants of the car who wish to smoke are to be allowed to do so. If an individual placed himself in the position of one who was uncertain as to whether he would be a smoker or nonsmoker, the natural assumption is that nonsmokers suffer as much from the smoking of others as smokers suffer from being stopped from smoking. The equal intensity assumption seems defensible in this case. With this assumption, and uncertainty over whether one is a smoker or nonsmoker, majority rule is the best decision rule. It maximizes the expected utility of a constitutional decision maker.

This example illustrates both the explicit and implicit assumptions underlying the Rae–Taylor theorem on majority rule. First, the situation is obviously one of conflict. The smoker's gain comes at the nonsmoker's expense, or vice versa. Second, the conflictual situation cannot be avoided. The solution to the problem provided by the exit of one category of passenger from the wagon is implicitly denied.[6] Nor does a possibility exist to redefine the issue to remove the conflict and obtain a consensus. Each issue is unidimensional and must be voted up or down as is. Fourth, the issue has been randomly or impartially selected. In this particular example, randomness is effectively introduced through the chance assemblage of individuals in the car. No apparent bias in favor of one outcome has been introduced via the random gathering of individuals in the car. The last assumption contained in the example is the equal intensity assumption.

The importance of each of these assumptions to the argument for majority rule can perhaps best be seen by contrasting them with the assumptions that have typically been made in support of its antithesis, the unanimity rule.

D.   Assumptions underlying the unanimity rule

As depicted by Wicksell (1896) and Buchanan and Tullock (1962), politics is a cooperative, positive-sum game. The committee's business is the collective satisfaction of needs common to all members. The committee (or community) is a voluntary association of individuals brought together for the purpose of

---

5. The "only" must be qualified when the committee size, n, is even. With n even, majority rule and the rule $n/2$ share this property. See Taylor (1969).
6. Rae (1975) stresses this assumption in the implicit defense of majority rule contained in his critique of unanimity.

satisfying these common needs.[7] Since the association is voluntary, each member is guaranteed the right to preserve his own interests against those of the other members. This right is preserved by the power contained in the unanimity rule to veto any proposal that runs counter to an individual's interest, or through the option to exit from the community, or both.

Given that the purpose of the committee is the satisfaction of the wants of the committee members, the natural way for issues to come before the committee is from the individuals themselves. Each individual has the right to bring before the committee issues that will benefit him and that he thinks might benefit all. Should an initial proposal fail to command a unanimous majority, it is redefined until it does, or until it is removed from the agenda. Thus, the political *process* implicit in the unanimity rule argument is one of discussion, compromise, and amendment, continuing until a formulation of the issue is reached benefiting all. The key assumptions underlying this view of politics are both that the game is cooperative and positive sum, that is, that a formulation of the issue benefiting all exists, *and* that the process can be completed in a reasonable amount of time, so that the transaction costs of decision making are not prohibitive.[8]

Let us also illustrate the type of voting process that the proponents of unanimity envisage through the example of fire protection in a small community. A citizen at a town meeting proposes that a truck be purchased and a station built to provide fire protection and couples his proposal, in Wicksellian fashion, with a tax proposal to finance it. Suppose that this initial tax proposal calls upon each property owner to pay the same fraction of the costs. The citizens with the lowest-valued property complain. The expected value of the fire protection (the value of the property times the reduction in the risk of fire) to some property owners is less than their share of the costs under the lump-sum tax formula. Enactment of the proposal would make the poor subsidize the protection of the property of the rich. As an alternative proposal, a proportional tax on property values is offered. The expected benefits to all citizens now exceed their share of its cost. The proposal passes unanimously.

---

7. See also Buchanan (1949).
8. Both Wicksell (1896) and Buchanan and Tullock (1962) recognize that decision time costs may be sufficiently high to require abandonment of a full unanimity rule in favor of a near unanimity rule (Wicksell) or some even lower fractional rule. Indeed, much of Buchanan and Tullock's book is devoted to the choice of the optimal "nonunanimity" rule, as discussed here in Chapter 4. Thus, one might question whether they can legitimately be characterized as champions of unanimity. I have chosen them as such because I think their arguments can be fairly characterized as stating that *were it not for these transaction costs,* unanimity would be the best rule, and, therefore, that some rule approaching unanimity, or at least greater than a simple majority is likely to be the best in many situations. In contrast, Rae (1975) and Barry (1965) both argue that their critique of unanimity is not based solely on the decision cost criterion.

E.   Assumptions underlying the two rules contrasted

Fire protection, the elimination of smoke from factories, and similar examples used to describe the mutual benefits from collective action all pertain to public goods and externalities – activities in which the market fails to provide a solution beneficial to all. The provision of these public goods is an improvement in allocative efficiency, a movement from a position off the Pareto frontier to a point on it. Proponents of unanimity have assumed that collective action involves collective decisions of this type.

In contrast, the advocates of majority rule envisage conflictual choices in which no mutually beneficial opportunities are available, as occurs when a community is forced to choose from among a set of Pareto-efficient opportunities. In the fire protection example, there might be a large number of tax share proposals that would cover the cost of fire protection and leave all better off. All might receive unanimous approval when placed against the alternative of no fire protection. Once one of these proposals has achieved a unanimous majority no other proposal from the Pareto-efficient set can achieve unanimity when placed against it. Any other proposal must make one voter worse off (by raising his tax share), causing him to vote against it.

Criticisms of unanimity and defenses of majority rule often involve distributional or property rights issues of this type. In Barry's example, the train car's occupants are in conflict over the right to clean air and the right to smoke; Rae (1975, pp. 1287–97) uses the similar example of the smoking factory and the rights of the nearby citizens to clean air in criticizing the unanimity rule. In both cases, a property rights decision must be made with distributional consequences. If the smokers are given the right to smoke, the seekers of clean air are made worse off. Even in situations in which the latter can be made better off by bribing the smokers to reduce the level of smoke, the nonsmokers are worse off by having to pay the bribe than they would be if the property right had been reversed and the smokers had to offer the bribe (Rae, 1975). Buchanan and Tullock (1962, p. 91) discuss this same example, but they assume that the initial property rights issue has already been fairly resolved at the constitutional stage. This illustrates another difference between the proponents of unanimity and majority rule. The former typically assume decision making takes place *within* a set of predefined property rights; the latter, like Barry and Rae, assume that it is the property rights decision itself that must be made. In Barry's example it is the *only* decision to be made. Rae's argument is more complicated. He argues that the constitution cannot resolve all property rights issues for all time, so that technological and economic changes cause some property rights issues to *drift* into the resolution of public goods and externalities. In either case, however, unanimous agreement on the property rights issue of who has the initial claim on the air is obviously unlikely under the egoistic man assumptions that all writers have made in this discussion. A less than unanimity rule *seems* necessary for resolving these initial property rights–distributional issues.

The last statement is qualified because it requires the other assumptions introduced in the discussion of majority rule: exit is impossible (or expensive); the issue cannot be redefined to make all better off. The need for the first assumption is obvious. If the occupants of the railroad car can move to another car in which smoking is explicitly allowed or prohibited, the conflict disappears, as it does if either the factory or the nearby residents can move costlessly. The importance of the second assumption requires a little elaboration.

Consider again the example of smoking in the railway car. Suppose the train is not allowed to proceed unless the occupants of this car can decide whether smoking is to be allowed or not. If the unanimity rule were employed, the potential would exist for the type of situation critics of unanimity seem to fear the most – a costly impasse. Out of this impasse, the minority might even be able to force the majority to capitulate, if the benefits to the majority from the train's continuation were high enough. Under these assumptions, majority rule is an attractive alternative to unanimity.

Now change the situation slightly. Suppose that *all passengers of the entire train* must decide the rules regarding smoking before the train may proceed. Since there is undoubtedly some advantage in having the entire train from which to choose a seat rather than only part of it, a rational egoist can be expected to prefer that the entire train be declared an area that accords with his preferences regarding smoking. If majority rule were used to decide the issue, then smoking would be either allowed or prohibited throughout the train. But, if a unanimity rule were employed, the train's occupants would be forced to explore other alternatives to having the entire train governed by the same rule. The proposal of allowing smoking in some sections and prohibiting it in others might easily emerge as a "compromise" and win unanimous approval over having the train remain halted. Members of the majority would be somewhat worse off under this compromise than they would have been had the entire train been designated according to their preferences, but members of the minority would be much better off. An impartial observer might easily prefer the compromise forced on the group by the unanimity rule to the outcome forthcoming under majority rule.

The arguments in favor of majority rule implicitly assume that such compromise proposals are not possible. The committee is faced with mutually exclusive alternatives.[9] Mutually beneficial alternatives are assumed to be

---

9. Buchanan and Tullock (1962, p. 253); Rae (1969, pp. 52–3).

Table 6.1. *Assumptions favoring the majority and unanimity rules*

Assumption	Majority rule	Unanimity rule
1. Nature of the game[a]	Conflict, zero sum	Cooperative, positive sum
2. Nature of issues	Redistributions, property rights (some benefit, some lose)	Allocative efficiency improvements (public goods, externality elimination)
	Mutually exclusive issues of a single dimension[b]	Issues with potentially several dimensions and from which all can benefit[c]
3. Intensity	Equal on all issues[d]	No assumption made
4. Method of forming committee	Involuntary; members are exogenously or randomly brought together[e]	Voluntary; individuals of common interests and like preferences join[f]
5. Conditions of exit	Blocked, expensive[g]	Free
6. Choice of issues	Exogenously or impartially proposed[h]	Proposed by committee members[i]
7. Amendment of issues	Excluded, or constrained to avoid cycles[j]	Endogenous to committee process[i]

[a]Buchanan and Tullock (1962, p. 253); Buchanan (1966, pp. 32–3).
[b]Barry (1965, pp. 312–14); Rae (1975, pp. 1286–91).
[c]Buchanan and Tullock (1962, p. 80); Wicksell (1896, pp. 87–96).
[d]Rae (1969, p. 41, n. 6); Kendall (1941, p. 117); Buchanan and Tullock (1962, pp. 128–30).
[e]Rae (1975, pp. 1277–8).
[f]Wicksell (1896, pp. 87–96); Buchanan (1949). This assumption is common to all contractarian theories of the state, of course.
[g]Rae (1975, p. 1293).
[h]This assumption is implicit in the impartiality assumed by Rae (1969) and Taylor (1969) in their proofs, and in Barry's example (1965, in particular on p. 313).
[i]Wicksell (1896); Kendall (1941, p. 109).
[j]Implicit.

technologically infeasible or the voting process is somehow constrained so that these issues cannot come before the committee.

Table 6.1 summarizes the assumptions that have been made in support of the majority and unanimity decision rules. They are not intended to be necessary and sufficient conditions, but are more in the nature of the most favorable conditions under which each decision rule is expected to operate. It is immediately apparent from Table 6.1 that the assumptions supporting each decision rule are totally opposed to the assumptions made in support of the alternative rule. The importance of these assumptions in determining the normative properties of each rule can be easily seen by considering the consequences of applying each rule to the "wrong" type of issue.

F.   The consequences of applying the rules to the "wrong" issues

1.   Deciding improvements in allocative efficiency via majority rule

On an issue that all favor, nearly one-half of the votes are "wasted" under majority rule. A coalition of the committee's members could benefit from this by redefining the issues to increase their benefits at the expense of noncoalition members. In the town meeting example, one could easily envisage a reverse scenario. An initial proposal to finance fire protection via a proportional property tax is made. All favor the proposal and it would pass under the unanimity rule. But, the town meeting now makes decisions under majority rule. The town's wealthiest citizens caucus and propose a lump-sum tax on all property owners. This proposal is opposed as being regressive by the less well-to-do members of the community, but it manages to secure a majority in its favor when placed against the proportional tax proposal. A majority coalition of the rich has succeeded in combining the provision of fire protection with a regressive tax on the poor. Wicksell's (1896, p. 95) belief that the unanimity rule would favor the poor was probably based on similar considerations.

But there are other ways in which de facto redistribution can take place under majority rule. A coalition of the residents of the north side of the town might form and propose that the provision of fire protection for the entire town be combined with the construction of a park on the north side, both to be financed out of a proportional tax on the entire community.[10] On the assumption that the south siders do not benefit from the park, this proposal would redistribute income from the south siders to the north siders just as clearly as a proposal to lower the taxes of the north siders and raise the taxes of the south siders would.

Thus, under majority rule, a process of issue proposal and amendment internal to the committee can be expected to convert purely positive-sum games of achieving allocational efficiency into games that are a combination of an allocational change and a redistribution. As Buchanan and Tullock (1962, pp. 190–2) have shown, when logrolling games allow side payments of money, the redistribution of wealth for and against any proposal will balance out. In logrolling games where direct side payments are not allowed, the exact values of the net income transfers are more difficult to measure. Nevertheless, when stable coalitions cannot be formed, the dynamic process of issue redefinition under majority rule to produce winning and losing coalitions of nearly equal size and differing composition can be expected to result

10. This example resembles Gordon Tullock's (1959) example in his demonstration that majority rule can lead to *over*expenditure in government, as discussed earlier.

in essentially zero *net* redistribution in the long run. Riker's assumption that all politics is a zero-sum game of pure redistribution might characterize *the long-run redistributive aspects of the outcomes* of the political process under majority rule.

This potential of majority rule must be stressed. The redistributive properties of majority rule can have a dynamic such that the winning majority only barely defeats the losing majority, thus justifying Rae's assumption that the probability that one favors the winning issue equals the probability that one favors the losing issue. Add to that the equal intensity assumption that Rae makes, and May's axioms build in, and we have the expected utility gains for the winners on any issue equaling the expected utility losses of the loser. Thus, the assumptions underlying the normative properties of majority rule imply that there are no expected utility gains from the passage of any issue. The game is zero sum in expected utilities as well as dollar payoffs. But then why play the game? The normative assumptions building a case for majority rule when applied to any issue pair undermine its use in the long run. This feature of majority rule may help explain why some observers like Samuel Brittan (1975) are frustrated with the long-run benefits to society from majority rule democracy.

We have seen that the redistributive characteristics of majority rule can make stable winning coalitions difficult to maintain and can lead to cycles. If a stable, winning coalition can form, however, the transaction costs of cycling and of forming and destroying coalitions can be greatly reduced or eliminated. If committee members are free to propose and amend issues, a stable majority coalition can engage in continual redistribution from the losing committee members. This "tyranny of the majority" outcome may be even more undesirable than a futile, but more or less impartial, redistribution emerging under a perpetual cycle (Buchanan, 1954a).

Thus, implicit in the arguments supporting majority rule we see the assumption that no stable majority coalition forms to tyrannize over the minority, and a zero transaction costs assumption, analogous to the zero decision time assumption supporting a unanimity rule. The issue proposal process is to be established so that cycles either cannot form or, if they do, they add a purely redistributive component to a set of allocational efficiency decisions that are predetermined or somehow unaffected by the cycling-redistribution process. Whether this issue of redefinition-coalition-formation-cycling process results in any net welfare gains remains an open question.

2. *Deciding redistribution by unanimity*

Any issue over which there is unavoidable conflict is defeated under a unanimity rule. Redistribution of income and wealth, redefinitions of property rights, are all blocked by this rule.

Critics of unanimity have found two consequences of this outcome particularly disturbing. First is the possibility that all progress may halt.[11] The train cannot proceed until the five occupants of the car have reached a consensus on the smoking issue. Most technological progress leaves some people worse off. Indeed, almost any change in the economic or physical environment may make someone worse off.[12] Although in principle each proposed change, down to the choice of color of my tie, could be collectively decided with appropriate compensation paid to those injured, the decision costs of deciding these changes under a unanimity rule are obviously prohibitive. The decision costs objection to the unanimity rule reappears. In addition, as an implicit defense of majority rule, this criticism seems to involve the assumption that technological change, or those changes involving de facto redistributions of income and property rights, are impartial. The utility gain to any individual favoring a change equals the utility loss to an opponent. And, over time, these gains and losses are impartially distributed among the population. Behind this assumption is another, that the process by which issues come before the committee is such that it is impossible to amend them so they will benefit one group systematically at the expense of the others. Time and the environment cast up issues involving changing property rights and redistribution impartially, and the committee votes these issues up or down as they appear, using majority rule. All benefit in the long run from the efficiency gains inherent in allowing technological progress to continue unencumbered by deadlocks in the collective decision process.

The second concern about using the unanimity rule to decide redistribution and property rights is that the veto power this rule gives a minority benefits one particular minority, violating a generally held ethical norm. The abolition of slavery is blocked by the slave owners, the redistribution of income by the rich. If one group achieves a larger than average share of the community's income or wealth via luck, skill, or cunning, the unanimity rule ensures that this distribution cannot be upset by collective action of the community. Under the unanimity rule, those who gain from the maintenance of the status quo always succeed in preserving it.[13]

G.   Conclusions

A follower of the debate over majority and unanimity rule could easily be forgiven for concluding that there is but one type of issue to be decided

---

11. See Reimer (1951); Barry (1965, p. 315); Rae (1975, pp. 1274, 1282, 1286, 1292–3).
12. This would appear to be the point behind Rae's arguments with respect to property rights drift in the smoking chimney example (1975, pp. 1287–93). As Gordon Tullock (1975) points out, however, these criticisms do not suffice as a justification for majority rule to decide this issue. The other assumptions we have discussed are needed.
13. Barry (1965, pp. 243–9); Rae (1975, pp. 1273–6, 1286).

collectively, and one best rule for making collective decisions. Thus, Wicksell (1896, p. 89) argues:

> If any public expenditure is to be approved . . . it must generally be assumed that this expenditure . . . is intended for an activity useful to the whole of society and so recognized by all classes without exception. If this were not so . . . I, for one, fail to see how the latter can be considered as satisfying a collective need in the proper sense of the word.

A similar position is inherent in all contractarian positions, as in John Locke (1939, p. 455, § 131):

> Men . . . enter into society . . . only with an intention in everyone the better to preserve himself, his liberty and property (for no rational creature can be supposed to change his condition with an intention to be worse), the power of the society, or legislative constituted by them, can never be supposed to extend farther than the common good, but is obliged to secure everyone's property.[14]

On the other extreme, we have Brian Barry (1965, p. 313):

> But a *political* situation is precisely one that arises when the parties are arguing not about mutually useful trades but about the legitimacy of one another's initial position. (Italics in original)

And in a similar vein William Riker (1962, p. 174):

> Most economic activity is viewed as a non-zero-sum game while the most important political activity is often viewed as zero-sum.

But, it should now be clear that the collective choice process is confronted with two fundamentally different types of collective decisions to resolve, corresponding to the distinction between allocation and redistribution decisions (Mueller, 1977). Some important political decisions involve potentially positive-sum game decisions to provide defense, police and fire protection, education, environmental protection, and so on. These decisions are made neither automatically nor easily. It is similarly obvious that part of political decision making must and should concern itself with the basic questions of distribution and property. The inherent differences between the underlying characteristics of these two types of decisions suggests both that they should be treated separately conceptually and, as a practical matter, that they should be resolved by separate and different collective decision processes.

In some ways, it is an injustice to Wicksell to have quoted him in the

---

14. Wilmore Kendall (1941) depicted Locke as a strong defender of majority rule. The only explicit reason Locke (p. 422, § 98) gives for using the majority rule in place of unanimity is a sort of transaction cost problem of assembling everyone, analogous to the Wicksell–Buchanan–Tullock decisions cost rule for choosing some less than unanimity rule. In this sense, Locke is a consistent unanimitarian.

present context, for it was one of Wicksell's important insights, and the most influential contribution to the subsequent development of the literature, to have recognized the distinction between allocation and redistribution decisions, and the need to treat these decisions with separate collective decision processes. Indeed, in some ways he was ahead of his modern critics, for he recognized not only that the distribution and allocation issues would have to be decided separately, but also that unanimity would have to give way to majority rule to resolve the distribution issues (1896, p. 109, note *m*). But, Wicksell did not elaborate on how the majority rule would be used to settle distribution issues, and the entire normative argument for the use of the unanimity rule to decide allocation decisions is left to rest on the *assumption* that a just distribution has been determined prior to the start of collective decision making on allocation issues.

Unfortunately, none of the proponents of majority rule has elaborated on how the conditions required to achieve its desirable properties are established. Somewhat ironically, perhaps, the normative case for using majority rule to settle property rights and distributional issues rests as much on decisions taken *prior to* its application, as the normative case for using the unanimity rule for allocation decisions rests on an already determined just income distribution. The Rae–Taylor theorem presupposes a process that is impartial, in that each voter has an equal chance of winning on any issue and an equal expected gain (or loss) from a decision's outcome. Similar assumptions are needed to make a compelling normative case for May's neutrality and anonymity conditions. But what guarantees that these conditions will be met? Certainly they are not met in the parliaments of today, where issue proposals and amendments are offered by the parliamentary members, and the outcomes are some blend of cycles, manipulated agendas, and tyrannous majorities. To realize majority rule's potential for resolving property rights and redistribution issues, some new form of parliamentary committee is needed that satisfies the conditions that majority rule's proponents have assumed in its defense. A constitutional decision is required.

But what rule is used to establish this new committee? If unanimity is used, those favored by the status quo can potentially block the formation of this new committee, whose outcomes, although fair, would run counter to the status quo's interest. But if the majority rule is employed, a minority may dispute both the outcomes of the distribution process and the procedure by which it was established. What argument does one use to defend the justness of a redistribution decision emerging from a parliamentary committee to a minority that feels the procedure by which the committee was established was unfair and voted against it at that time? This question seems as legitimate when raised against a majority rule decision, whose justification rests on the fairness of the issue proposal process, as it does when raised against a unanimity rule that rests its justification on some distant, unanimous agreement on property rights. At some point, the issue of how fairness is introduced into the decision process, and how it is agreed upon, must be faced.

We have run up against the infinite regress problem. The only satisfactory way out of this maze is to assume that at some point unanimous agreement on a set of rules and procedures was attained.[15] If this agreement established a parliamentary committee to function under the majority rule, then the outcomes from this committee could be defended on the grounds that all at one time must have agreed that this would be a fair way of resolving those types of issues that are allowed to come before the committee. This interpretation places the majority rule in a secondary position to the unanimity rule at this stage of the analysis and reopens the question of how unanimous agreement, now limited perhaps to establishing the parliamentary procedures to decide both distributional and allocation efficiency issues, is reached. We take up this question in Part V.

Bibliographical notes

Sen (1970a, pp. 71–3) offers another proof of May's (1952) theorem, and Campbell (1982) presents a related result.

15. See Buchanan and Tullock (1962, pp. 6–8).

CHAPTER 7

Simple alternatives to majority rule

My scheme is intended only for honest men.

Jean-Charles de Borda

Several alternatives to the majority rule have been proposed down through the years. Three of the newest and most complicated of these are taken up in Chapter 8. Here we discuss some of the simpler proposals.

These voting procedures are usually not considered a means of revealing preferences on a public good issue, but a means of choosing a candidate for a given office. All issues cannot be chosen simultaneously. Only one of them can be. Although such choices are perhaps most easily envisaged in terms of a list of candidates for a vacant public office, the procedures might be thought of as being applied to a choice from among any set of mutually exclusive alternatives – such as points along the Pareto-possibility frontier.

A.   The alternative voting procedures defined

Majority rule: Choose the candidate who is ranked first by more than half of the voters.

Majority rule, runoff election: If one of the m candidates receives a majority of first-place votes, this candidate is the winner. If not, a second election is held between the two candidates receiving the most first-place votes on the first ballot. The candidate receiving the most votes on the second ballot is the winner.

Plurality rule: Choose the candidate who is ranked first by the largest number of voters.

Condorcet criterion: Choose the candidate who defeats all others in pairwise elections using majority rule.

The Hare system: Each voter indicates the candidate he ranks *highest* of the m candidates. Remove from the list of candidates the one ranked highest by the fewest voters. Repeat the procedure for the remaining m-1 candidates. Continue until only one candidate remains. Declare this candidate the winner.

The Coombs system: Each voter indicates the candidate he ranks *lowest* of the *m* candidates. Remove from the list of candidates the one ranked lowest by the most voters. Repeat the procedure for the remaining *m*-1 candidates. Continue until only one candidate remains. Declare this candidate the winner.

Approval voting: Each voter votes for the *k* candidates ($1 \leq k \leq m$) he ranks highest of the *m* candidates, where *k* can vary from voter to voter. The candidate with the most votes is the winner.

The Borda count: Give each of the *m* candidates a score of 1 to *m* based on the candidate's ranking in a voter's preference ordering; that is, the candidate ranked first receives *m* points, the second one *m*-1, . . . , the lowest-ranked candidate one point. The candidate with the highest number of points is declared the winner.

B.   The procedures compared – Condorcet efficiency

This array of procedures is already lengthy and we could easily add to the list, although these cover the most frequently discussed procedures. Each has a certain intuitive appeal. How can one decide which is best?

There are several criteria for defining "best." First, we might define the axiomatic equivalents to each procedure, as we did with majority rule in Chapter 6, and compare the procedures on the basis of their axiomatic properties. These axioms are often rather abstract, however, and thus it may be somewhat difficult to declare procedure *A* superior to *B* just by looking at its axiomatic properties. We might declare one property most important, and compare the procedures on the basis of their ability to realize this property. The literature has proceeded in both ways, and we shall discuss the procedures in both ways.

The first of the axioms May (1952) requires of a voting procedure is that it is *decisive;* that is, it must pick a winner. Majority rule satisfies this criterion when there are but two candidates, a restriction May imposed on the problem. Choosing from a pair of alternatives is, however, the simplest *choice* one can conceptualize, and all of the above procedures select the same winner when *m* = 2. Interesting cases involve $m \geq 3$. With $m > 2$ no candidate may receive a majority of first-place votes, and no candidate may defeat all others in pairwise contests. Thus, when $m > 2$, both majority rule and the Condorcet criterion may declare no candidate a winner. Each of the other procedures will pick a winner.[1] Thus, for those who, on the basis of the arguments of Chapter 6, feel the majority rule ought to be the community's decision rule, interest in the other procedures arises only when $m > 2$.

1. We ignore ties. With large numbers of voters, ties are unlikely. The Borda count can easily be changed to accommodate ties in rankings (Black, 1958, pp. 61–4).

Table 7.1.

V_1	V_2	V_3	V_4	V_5
X	X	Y	Z	W
Y	Y	Z	Y	Y
Z	Z	W	W	Z
W	W	X	X	X

Table 7.2.

V_1	V_2	V_3	V_4	V_5
X	X	X	Y	Y
Y	Y	Y	Z	Z
Z	Z	Z	X	X

Although the other procedures always pick a winner, even when a Condorcet winner does not exist, they do not always choose the Condorcet winner when one does exist. Table 7.1 presents a set of preference orderings for five voters in which X is the winner under the plurality rule, although Y is a Condorcet winner. Since a single vote for one's most preferred candidate is a possible strategy choice for voters under approval voting, X might also win under this procedure with the preference orderings of Table 7.1.

In Table 7.2, X is the Condorcet winner, while Y would be the winner by the Borda count. In Table 7.3, X is again the Condorcet winner, while issue W wins under the Hare system. Under each of the procedures other than majority rule, a winner may be chosen who is not the Condorcet winner even when the latter exists.

If one finds the properties of majority rule most attractive, then failure to select the Condorcet winner when one exists may be regarded as a serious deficiency of a procedure. One way to evaluate the different procedures is to compute the percentages of the time that a Condorcet winner exists and is selected by a given procedure. Merrill (1984, 1985) has made these percentage calculations and named them Condorcet efficiencies, that is, the efficiency of a procedure in actually selecting the Condorcet winner when one exists. Table 7.4 reports the results from simulations of an electorate of 25 voters with randomly allocated utility functions and various numbers of candidates.[2]

---

2. Merrill (1984, p. 28, n. 4) reports that Condorcet efficiency is not very sensitive to the number of voters.

Table 7.3.

V_1	V_2	V_3	V_4	V_5
Y	W	X	Y	W
X	Z	Z	Z	X
Z	X	W	X	Z
W	Y	Y	W	Y

Table 7.4. *Condorcet efficiency for a random society (25 voters)*

	Number of candidates				
Voting system	3	4	5	7	10
Runoff	96.2	90.1	83.6	73.5	61.3
Plurality	79.1	69.4	62.1	52.0	42.6
Hare	96.2	92.7	89.1	84.8	77.9
Coombs	96.3	93.4	90.2	86.1	81.1
Approval	76.0	69.8	67.1	63.7	61.3
Borda	90.8	87.3	86.2	85.3	84.3
Social utility maximizer	84.4	80.2	77.9	77.2	77.8

Source: Merrill (1984, p. 28).

The first six rows report the Condorcet efficiencies for six of the procedures defined in Section A. Voters are assumed to maximize expected utility under approval voting by voting for all candidates whose utilities exceed the mean of the candidates for that voter (Merrill, 1981). With 2 candidates, all procedures choose the Condorcet winner with efficiency of 100. The efficiency of all procedures is under 100 percent with 3 candidates. The biggest declines in efficiency in going from 2 to 3 candidates are for the plurality and approval voting procedures. When the number of candidates is as large as 10, the six procedures divide into three groups based on their Condorcet efficiency indexes: the Hare, Coombs, and Borda procedures all achieve about 80 percent efficiency; majority rule with one runoff and approval voting achieve about 60 percent efficiency; and the plurality rule selects the Condorcet winner only 42.6 percent of the time.

It is implausible to assume that an electorate would go to the polls nine separate times, as would be required under either the Hare or Coombs systems with 10 candidates. Therefore, if either of these procedures were actually used, as a practical matter one would undoubtedly simply ask voters to write down their complete rankings of the candidates, and use a computer to determine a winner following the prescribed rule. Thus, the informational requirements of the Hare, Coombs, and Borda procedures are identical; they differ only in how they process this information. Given that they rely on the same information sets, it is perhaps not surprising that they perform about the same.

Of the six procedures listed in Table 7.4, the runoff and plurality procedures are the only ones in common use today. Thus, another way to look at the results of Table 7.4 is to calculate the gains in Condorcet efficiency in abandoning the plurality or runoff rule in favor of one of the other four procedures. The biggest gains obviously come in going to the Hare, Coombs, or Borda procedures, particularly if the number of candidates exceeds five. But much more information is demanded of the voter at the election. Approval voting might then be compared with the runoff and plurality systems as a relatively simple procedure with Condorcet efficiency properties that exceed those of the plurality rule and approach those of the runoff system as the number of candidates expands. An important advantage of approval voting over the majority rule–runoff procedure is that approval voting requires that voters go to the polls only once (Fishburn and Brams, 1981a,b).

C.   The procedures compared – utilitarian efficiency

Although the relative achievement of Condorcet efficiency may be an important property for those who favor majority rule as the voting procedure, for others it may not be the decisive factor in choosing a rule. Consider again Table 7.2. Issue X is the Condorcet winner, and indeed wins a majority against all three candidates. But this voting situation is clearly one that has some characteristics of a "tyranny of the majority." Under majority rule, the first three voters are able to impose their candidate on the other two, who rank him last. Y, on the other hand, is more of a "compromise" candidate, who ranks *relatively* high on all preference scales, and for this reason Y might be the "best" choice from among the three candidates. Y would be chosen under the Borda procedure, and under approval voting if any two of the voters (V_1, V_2, V_3) thought highly enough of Y to vote for both X and Y under approval voting, and not just for X. The closer Y stands to X, and the further it stands from Z, the more likely it is that one of these voters will vote (X,Y) under approval voting and not just X.

An alternative normative criterion to that of Condorcet efficiency for a voting procedure is that it should maximize a utilitarian welfare function of, say, the form

$$W = \sum_i U_i, \tag{7.1}$$

Table 7.5. *Utilitarian efficiency for a random society (25 voters)*

Voting system	Number of candidates				
	3	4	5	7	10
Runoff	89.5	83.8	80.5	75.6	67.6
Plurality	83.0	75.0	69.2	62.8	53.3
Hare	89.5	84.7	82.4	80.5	74.9
Coombs	89.7	86.7	85.1	83.1	82.4
Approval	95.4	91.1	89.1	87.8	87.0
Borda	94.8	94.1	94.4	95.4	95.9
Condorcet	93.1	91.9	92.0	93.1	94.3

Source: Merrill (1984, p. 39).

where the U_i are cardinal interpersonally comparable utility indexes for each voter i defined over the issue set. The bottom row of Table 7.4 reveals that the candidate whose choice would maximize (7.1) is the Condorcet winner only about 80 percent of the time. How then do the six procedures measure up against this utilitarian yardstick?

Table 7.5 presents further simulation results for a 25-person electorate. Note first that the Condorcet winner measures up rather well against the utilitarian maximum W criterion. But so, too, does the Borda count. It achieves a higher aggregate utility level for any number of candidates greater than two than the Condorcet winner would, if the Condorcet winner could always be found, or greater than any of the other five procedures would. Bordley (1983) presents analogous results. Although not providing full cardinal utility information, as is needed to achieve 100 percent efficiency in maximizing W, the Borda count, by providing a much richer informational base, is able to come fairly close to this objective.

Of additional interest in Table 7.5 is the performance of approval voting relative to the informationally more demanding Coombs and Hare systems. Given its performance by this utilitarian yardstick and its greater simplicity, we confine further attention to the Borda and approval voting procedures.

D.   The Borda count

Judged by the simulation results of Section C, the Borda count would appear to be a potentially attractive voting procedure. What are its other normative properties?

Suppose we were to proceed as May (1952) did and seek an axiomatic representation of the Borda count. The first axiom May imposed was decisiveness – the procedure must be able to pick a winner from a binary pair. Some property like decisiveness is obviously attractive for any voting procedure. We can do this more formally by saying that we want the voting procedure to define a set of best elements, which we shall define as a choice set (Sen, 1970a, p. 10).

Definition of choice set: *An element* x *in S is a best element of S with respect to the binary relation R if and only if for every y in S, xRy. The set of best elements in S is called its choice set* C(S,R).

Thus, we wish to have a voting rule that defines a choice set. H. Peyton Young (1974) proved that the Borda count was the only voting rule that defines a choice set and satisfies the four properties of neutrality, cancellation, faithfulness, and consistency.

As in May's theorem, the neutrality property is a form of impartiality with respect to issues or candidates. The names of the candidates or the nature of the issues do not matter.

The cancellation property, like anonymity in May's theorem, is a form of impartiality toward voters. Any voter i's statement "x is preferred to y" is balanced or canceled by any other voter j's statement "y is preferred to x" (Young, 1974, p. 45). What determines the social ordering of x and y is the number of voters who prefer x to y versus the number preferring y to x. The identities of the voters do not matter.

The faithfulness property is the totally innocuous condition that the voting procedure, when applied to a society consisting of only one individual, chooses as a best element that voter's most preferred element, that is, is faithful to that voter's preferences.

The above properties seem inherently reasonable. Indeed, they are all satisfied by majority rule. The more novel property is consistency.

> *Consistency:* Let N_1 and N_2 be two groups of voters who are to select an alternative from the set S. Let C_1 and C_2 be the respective sets of alternatives that the two groups select using voting procedure B. Then if C_1 and C_2 have any elements in common (i.e., $C_1 \cap C_2$ is not empty), then the winning issue under procedure B when these two subgroups are brought together ($N_T = N_1 \cup N_2$) is contained in this common set of elements ($C_T = C_1 \cap C_2$).

This consistency property has obvious intuitive appeal. If two groups of voters agree on an alternative when choosing separately from a set of alternatives, they should agree on the same alternative when they are combined.

Now majority rule also satisfies the consistency condition when the issue space and voter preferences are such as to ensure that a Condorcet winner

Table 7.6.

	N_1			N_2		
V_1	V_2	V_3	V_4	V_5	V_6	V_7
z	x	y	z	z	x	x
x	y	z	x	x	y	z
y	z	x	y	y	z	y

always exists (Young, 1974, p. 44). Suppose, for example, that all issues were single dimensional and all voter preferences single peaked. Let m_1 be the median voter outcome for a committee of size N_1, where N_1 is odd. Let the interval $m_2 - m_2'$ be the choice set under majority rule for another committee of size N_2, where N_2 is even. If m_1 falls in the interval $m_2 - m_2'$, then m_1 will be the majority rule winner if the two committees combine, since one voter from N_1 has m_1 as a most preferred point, and $[(N_1 - 1)/2 + N_2/2]$ voters have preference peaks to the left of m_1 and the same number have peaks to the right of m_1. In this situation, majority rule satisfies the consistency property.

But we cannot always be assured that the conditions guaranteeing a Condorcet winner are satisfied for every subset of voters. When they are not, then a cycle can arise of the form $xRyRzRx$. If in such situations we define the choice set as (x, y, z), the majority rule violates the consistency property, as the following example from Plott (1976, pp. 562–3) illustrates.

Let N_1 and N_2 be groups of voters with preference orderings as in Table 7.6. For N_1, a cycle over x, y, and z exists and we define the choice set as (x, y, z). For N_2, x and z tie and both beat y so its choice set is (x, z). The intersection of these two choice sets is (x, z) and the consistency criterion requires that x and z tie under majority rule when N_1 and N_2 are combined. But they will not tie. The committee $N_1 + N_2$ selects z as the unique winner using majority rule thus violating the consistency condition.

An alternative way to look at the problem is to note that those versions of majority rule that do satisfy the consistency criterion, like the Condorcet principle, do not always define a nonempty choice set. Thus, if in going from two to three or more elements in our issue set, we wish the voting rule to continue to be capable of picking a winner, and we wish to have the properties of neutrality, cancellation, faithfulness, and consistency, more information is required than is provided under simple majority rule. Young's theorem demonstrates that the information needed is the complete preference ordering of every voter over the full issue set.

Although the Borda count has axiomatic properties, which seem at least the equal of majority rule, and it performs well when measured by the yardstick of the utilitarian welfare function, its Achilles' heel is commonly felt to be its vulnerability to strategic behavior (Pattanaik, 1974; Sen, 1984). Consider again Table 7.2. Issue Y wins using the Borda count when all voters vote sincerely. If the first three voters were to state their rankings of the issues as XP_iZP_iY, however, the Borda count would select X as the winning issue. Thus, an incentive exists for voters 1–3 to misstate their preferences, *if they know the preferences of other voters, and expect the other voters to vote sincerely.*

If the electorate is large, it is unlikely that a voter knows the preferences of many other voters. Moreover, if one group of voters can behave strategically, so can another. If voters 4 and 5 in Table 7.2 suspect that the other voters are trying to manipulate X's victory, they can try to avoid having their worst alternative, X, win, by misstating their preferences as $ZPYPX$. With both groups of voters now misstating their preferences, Z wins under the Borda rule.

Thus, voters 1–3 take a chance when they raise Z above Y in their stated preference orderings of bringing about not X's victory, but Z's. The Borda count satisfies a nonnegativity or monotonicity condition (Smith, 1973). Lifting Y above Z in a voter's stated preference ordering either raises or leaves unchanged Y's position in the social ordering, while having the reverse effect on Z. A risk-averse voter, uncertain of the relative chances of X, Y, and Z winning, either due to ignorance of other voter preferences, or uncertainty about their possible strategic behavior, maximizes her expected utility under the Borda procedure by honestly stating her true ranking of the three issues.

E.   Approval voting

In addition to its possible vulnerability to strategic behavior, the most serious disadvantage of the Borda procedure is its complexity. The voter must list her complete ranking of the set of alternatives. When this set is fairly large (say, 10), this requirement could discourage individuals from voting.

In contrast, approval voting asks voters only to draw a line through their preference ordering so as to separate the candidates into those they approve of and those they do not. If the candidates are relatively evenly spaced from one another in terms of expected utility payoffs, then this line will divide the set of candidates roughly into two equal-sized groups (Merrill, 1981). Voters need not concern themselves with how the two sets of candidates stack up against one another within the approval and disapproval subsets.

When the number of candidates is few, or voters are indifferent between various pairs of candidates, approval voting also has some advantages over other procedures in discouraging strategic behavior. Brams and Fishburn (1978) have proven that when voter preferences are dichotomous in the sense that it is possible for every voter i to divide the set of all candidates S into two subsets S_{i1} and S_{i2} such that i is indifferent among all candidates in S_{i1} and among all in S_{i2}, then under approval voting there is a single undominated strategy – vote for all candidates in the subset S_{ij} who are ranked higher than those in the other subset. Approval voting is the only voting procedure to have a unique, undominated strategy for all possible dichotomous preference relationships.

When voter preferences are trichotomous – that is, candidates are divided into three indifference groups, S_{i1}, S_{i2}, S_{i3} – then the only undominated strategies under approval voting are to vote sincerely for either (1) all candidates in the most preferred group, or (2) all candidates in the two most preferred groups. Approval voting is the only voting system that is sincere in this sense for every possible trichotomous preference relationship.

When voter preferences are multichotomous – that is, four or more indifference groups are required – no voting procedure is sincere or strategy-proof for all possible multichotomous preference relationships.

Since all procedures discussed in this chapter are identical to majority rule when there are only two candidates, the importance of the results for dichotomous candidates rests on the plausibility of assuming voter indifference between various pairs of candidates in a multicandidate race. On this issue opinions will differ (Niemi, 1984). Beyond whatever advantages it possesses in discouraging strategic behavior, however, approval voting deserves serious attention as a possible substitute for the plurality and majority rule–runoff rules, because of its superior performance, as judged by the Condorcet or utilitarian efficiency criteria, and greater simplicity than the Hare, Coombs, Borda, and to some extent majority rule–runoff procedures.

F. Implications for electoral reform

State presidential nominating elections and elections of representatives to the House and Senate in the United States are based on a first-past-the-post criterion, that is, the plurality rule. Yet the plurality rule scores worst of all by the Condorcet and utilitarian efficiency criteria. This observation has led to recommendations that an alternative rule be introduced, particularly in presidential primaries where the number of candidates may be large (Kellett and Mott, 1977).

The possible significance of such a reform is revealed in Richard Joslyn's (1976) study of the 1972 Democratic presidential primaries. Joslyn argued that the plurality rule favored extremist candidate George McGovern, who was the first choice of a plurality of voters in many states but was ranked relatively low by many other voters, over "middle-of-the-road" Edmund Muskie, who was ranked relatively high by a large number of voters. Joslyn's

Table 7.7. *Delegate totals under various decision rules*

Candidate	Plurality rule	Double election	Condorcet choice	Borda count	Adjusted[a] Borda count
McGovern	1,307	766	766	766	584
Muskie	271	788	869	869	869

[a]Adjusted Borda count is modified to allow for ties. See Black (1958, pp. 61–4).
Source: Joslyn (1976, Table 5, p. 12).

most striking result is his recalculation of final delegate counts under the various voting rules presented in Table 7.7 (double election is a two-step runoff procedure). The interesting feature of this table is the dramatic increase in Muskie's delegate strength under any of the voting procedures other than the plurality rule.[3]

One might *argue* that Muskie *should* have been the Democratic Party's nominee in 1972, and that, therefore, one of the other voting procedures is preferable to the plurality rule. Muskie would have had a better chance to defeat Nixon than McGovern, and McGovern's supporters would probably have preferred a Muskie victory to a McGovern defeat in the final runoff against Nixon. And, with the infinite wisdom of hindsight, one can argue that "the country" would have been better off with a Muskie victory over Nixon.

The rules of the game do matter.

Bibliographical notes

The seminal discussion of the various voting rules is by Duncan Black (1958, pp. 55–75). Duncan Black also presents biographical discussions of the work of the Marquis de Condorcet (pp. 159–80) and Jean-Charles de Borda (pp. 156–9, 178–90).

The Borda count is also discussed by Plott (1976, pp. 560–3), Sen (1982, pp. 187–7, 239–40, 376–7), and Schwartz (1986, pp. 179–81).

The properties of approval voting were first discussed by Steven Brams (1975, ch. 3) with important extensions presented by Brams and Fishburn (1978), and Fishburn and Brams (1981a,b). The major results on approval voting are pulled together in their book (Brams and Fishburn, 1983).

3. Muskie would undoubtedly also have faired much better against McGovern had approval voting been used. See Kellett and Mott (1977) and Brams and Fishburn (1978, pp. 840–2).

CHAPTER 8

Complicated alternatives to majority rule

In this Method [the Method of Marks], a certain number of marks is fixed, which each elector shall have at his disposal; he may assign them all to one candidate, or divide them among several candidates, in proportion to their eligibility; and the candidate who gets the greatest total of marks is the winner.

This method would, I think, be absolutely perfect, if only each elector wished to do all in his power to secure the election of *that candidate who should be the most generally acceptable,* even if that candidate should *not* be the one of his own choice: in this case he would be careful to make the marks exactly represent his estimate of the relative eligibility of *all* the candidates, even of those he *least* desired to see elected; and the desired result would be secured.

But we are not sufficiently unselfish and public-spirited to give any hope of this result being attained. Each elector would feel that it was *possible* for each other elector to assign the entire number of marks to his favorite candidate, giving to all the other candidates zero: and he would conclude that, in order to give his *own* favorite candidate any chance of success, he must do the same for him.

Charles Dodgson (Lewis Carroll)

In 1954 in what has become the classic paper on public goods, Paul Samuelson both defined the necessary conditions for Pareto optimality in the presence of public goods and cast a pall over the field of public economics by asserting that no procedure could be constructed to reveal the information on preferences required to determine the quantities of public goods that would satisfy the Pareto optimality condition. In a section entitled "Impossibility of Decentralized Spontaneous Solution," Samuelson (1954, p. 182) stated that "*no decentralized pricing system can serve to determine optimally these levels of collective consumption*" (italics in original).

So influential was this article, that for a generation economists merely repeated Samuelson's words and lamented the absence of a satisfactory procedure for revealing individual preferences. And with good reason. Traditional voting schemes seemed vulnerable to the transaction costs and strategic incentives inherent in the unanimity rule, or the paucity of information and onus of compulsion characterizing less than unanimity rules, most notably the majority rule.

But then in the seventies, a revolution suddenly erupted. New procedures began to appear one after the other, which claimed to have solved the preference revelation problem. As so often happens in the mechanical arts, once one scientist demonstrated that the impossible might be possible, others were moved to follow, and a wave of developments ensued. In this chapter we review this literature, focusing upon three rather different types of procedures. We begin with the procedure that has attracted the greatest attention.

A.   The demand-revealing process

This procedure was first described by William Vickrey in 1961, although he attributed the idea to "an interesting suggestion" Abba Lerner threw out in *Economics of Control* (1944). Consequently, the procedure might be said to antedate Samuelson's paper by 10 years. But neither Lerner nor Vickrey applied the procedure to the problem of revealing preferences for public goods, and the potential importance of the procedure was not recognized until the appearance of papers by Edward Clarke (1971, 1972) and Theodore Groves (1973).

To understand how the procedure works, consider the collective choice between the two issues P and S. Assume a committee of three with preferences as given in Table 8.1. Voter A expects to be the equivalent of $30 better off from the victory of P, voter C $20, and voter B prefers S by the equivalent of $40. The procedure for selecting a winner is to first ask all three voters to state in dollars the amount of benefits they expect from the victory of their preferred issue, and then add these figures, declaring the issue with the most expected benefits the winner. In the present example this is P, since it promises gains of 50 to voters A and C, whereas S benefits B by only 40.

The voters are induced to declare their true preferences for the issues by announcing that they will be charged a certain tax, depending on the responses they make and their impact on the final outcome. This tax is calculated in the following way. The dollar votes of all other voters are added up and the outcome determined. The voter-in-question's dollar votes are now added in to see if the outcome is changed. If it is not, he pays no tax. If it is, he pays a tax equal to the *net* gains expected from the victory of the other issue in the absence of his vote. Thus, a voter pays a tax only when his vote is decisive in changing the outcome, and then pays not the amount he has declared, but the amount needed to balance the declared benefits of the other voters on the two issues. The last column of Table 8.1 presents the taxes on the three voters. Without A, there are 40 dollar votes for S and 20 for P. A's vote is decisive in determining the outcome, and imposes a net cost of 20 on the other two voters, and that is A's tax. B's vote does not affect the outcome, and he pays no tax. Without C's vote, S would again win, so C pays a tax

Table 8.1.

		Issue	
Voter	P	S	Tax
A	30		20
B		40	0
C	20		10
Total	50	40	30

equal to the net benefits the other voters would have received had he not voted $(40 - 30 = 10)$.

Under the tax each voter has an incentive to reveal his true preferences for the two issues. Any amount of benefits from P that voter A declared equal to or greater than 21 would leave the collective decision, *and his tax,* unchanged. If he declared net benefits of less than 20, S would win, and A's tax would fall from 20 to 0, but his benefits of 30 would also disappear. A voter pays a tax only if his vote is decisive, and the tax he pays is always equal to or less than the benefits he receives. Thus, there is no incentive to understate one's gains, for then one risks forgoing a chance to cast the deciding vote at a cost less than the benefits. And, there is no incentive to overstate one's preferences, since this incurs the risk of casting the decisive vote and receiving a tax above one's actual benefits, albeit less than one's declared benefits. The optimal strategy is honest revelation of preferences.

To maintain this desirable incentive property, the tax revenue raised to induce honest revelation of preferences cannot be returned to the voters in such a way as to affect their voting decision. The safest thing to do with the money to avoid distorting incentives is to waste it. But this implies that the outcome from the procedure will not be Pareto optimal (Groves and Ledyard, 1977a,b; Loeb, 1977). The amount by which the procedure falls short of Pareto optimality can be stated explicitly: It is the amount of revenue raised by the incentive tax. In the example above, this amount is substantial, equaling three times the net gains from collective action.

Fortunately, the amount of taxes raised under the demand-revealing procedure should decline as the number of voters increases (Tideman and Tullock, 1976, 1977). To see why this is so, consider Table 8.2, in which the preferences of three other voters, A', B', and C', identical to those of A, B, and C have been included. The issue P still wins, of course, now by a surplus of 20. Voter C's tax has fallen from 10 to 0, however, and A's from 20 to 10. Without voter C, the net benefits on the two issues over the other voters are 0 (80 for P and 80 for S). Although his vote tips the outcome in favor of P, his

Table 8.2.

Voter	Issue		
	P	*S*	Tax
A	30		10
B		40	0
C	20		0
A'	30		10
B'		40	0
C'	20		0
Total	100	80	20

gain of 20 does not come at the *net* expense of the other voters. So *C* pays no tax. *A* still pays a positive tax, but the amount has been reduced, since the net cost of his vote on all other voters has fallen. With the addition of three more voters (*A''*, *B''*, *C''*) with preferences identical to *A*, *B*, and *C*, the outcome would again not change, and the taxes on all voters would now be zero. Thus, the collective decision of this committee of nine would be Pareto optimal. Although the procedure does allow for a weighing of intensities in determining the outcome, the effect of any one voter's preferences on the final outcome will dwindle, as with other voting procedures, as the number of voters increases. Since a voter's tax equals his impact on the other voters, it, too, dwindles as the size of the group increases.

Groves and Ledyard (1977c, p. 140) claim to be able to construct counterexamples in which the incentive tax surplus is arbitrarily large, and Kormendi (1979, 1980) has pressed the same point. But such examples rely on expanding the committee by adding equal numbers of voters who favor *P* and *S*. If the committee were equally divided between voters favoring *P* and voters favoring *S*, every vote might be decisive and the amount of tax revenue raised would be large, whereas the *net* social benefit would be very small. However, we would then have essentially a distributional issue, the *P*'s versus the *S*'s. For a pure public good that all favor, the incentive-tax revenue should vanish as *n* increases. For a rigorous demonstration, see Rob (1982).

The procedure can reveal individual demand schedules for a public good, from whence its name arises. We follow here the exposition of Tideman and Tullock (1976). Each individual is asked to report his complete demand schedule for the public good. These schedules are then vertically added to obtain the aggregate demand for the public good. The intersection of this schedule and the supply schedule for the good determines the quantity provided. If each individual has honestly reported his demand schedule, the procedure determines the Pareto-optimal quantity of public good, as defined by Samuelson (1954) and Bowen (1943).

Individuals are again induced to reveal their true preferences via a special tax imposed upon them. In fact, there are two taxes imposed upon the individual, one designed to cover the full costs of producing the public good, the other to ensure honest revelation of preferences. In our first example, the first of these two taxes was implicitly assumed to be part of the proposals P and S. Let us assume that the public good can be supplied at constant unit costs C, and that each voter is assigned a share of these costs, T_j, such that $\sum_{j=1}^{n} T_j = C$. These T_j's are the first components of each individual's tax. The other component is computed in a way analogous to that used to assign each individual a tax in the preceding example. Namely, one first determines the quantity of public good that would be demanded in the absence of individual i's demand schedule and contribution to the public good's total costs. The quantity with his demand schedule and contribution is next determined. The difference represents the impact of this individual's preferences on the collective outcome. The cost to the other voters of the shift in quantity that recording his preferences brings about is the absolute value of the difference between the costs of producing these extra units and the sum of the individual demand schedules over these units. Thus, if i forces the community to consume more than it would have without this demand-schedule vote, the costs of the extra output will exceed their willingness to pay for it, and i is charged the difference. Conversely, if voter i causes the community to consume less than they would have, their aggregate demand for the extra units of public good will exceed the good's costs, and the difference, the loss in consumer surplus to the other voters, is charged to the ith voter.

The latter possibility is illustrated with the help of Figure 8.1. Omitting i's demand schedule, aggregate demand for the public good is $D - D_i$. Subtracting his preassigned tax share, the cost of the public good is $C - T_i$. With i's preferences removed, the community would purchase A. With i's preferences included, the community purchases Q, the quantity at which aggregate demand and supply are equal. The cost imposed on the other voters of this shift in outcomes is the difference between the amount that the other voters would be willing to pay for the extra units $(A - Q)$, and the taxes they would have to pay $(C - T_i)(A - Q)$ for these units, which is the cross-hatched triangle above the line $C - T_i$. This triangle represents the additional tax, apart from T_iQ, that the ith voter must pay.

That the ith voter's optimal strategy is to reveal his true demand schedule in the presence of this incentive tax becomes clear when we construct an effective supply schedule of the public good, S_i, to the ith voter, by subtracting the $D - D_i$ schedule from C. The intersection of the individual voter's demand for the public good, D_i, and this S_i schedule is for him the optimal quantity of

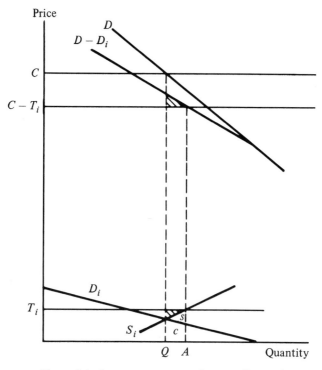

Figure 8.1. Some new processes for revealing preferences.

public good, which, of course, is Q. By stating his demand schedule as D_i, voter i forces the community to consume Q instead of A, and thereby saves himself the rectangle $T_i(QA)$ in taxes. He must pay the incentive tax represented by the cross-hatched triangle below T_i, which equals the cross-hatched triangle above $C - T_i$, and loses the consumer surplus represented by the quadrilateral, c. His net gain from forcing the community to Q rather than leaving it at A is thus the triangle s. That there is nothing to be gained by stating a demand schedule below D_i can be seen by observing that the triangle s vanishes at Q. To the left of Q, i's incentive tax plus consumer surplus loss would exceed his tax saving T_i. If he states any demand schedule above D_i, T_i exceeds his consumer surplus gain and incentive tax saving. The honest revelation of his true demand schedule D_i is i's optimal strategy.

   To see how the procedure works algebraically, write $U_i(G)$ as voter i's utility from consuming G. Let t_i be i's incentive tax. We ignore income effects, so we can assume that the marginal utility of money is constant and measure $U_i(G)$ in dollar units. Voter i's objective is thus to maximize utility,

U_i, net of i's share of the cost of the public good, T_iG, and incentive tax, t_i; that is,

$$O_i = U_i(G) - T_iG - t_i. \tag{8.1}$$

The incentive tax that i must pay is the cost that i's vote imposes on all other voters by bringing about G; it is the difference between the other voters' utilities at G and their cost shares:

$$t_i = \sum_{j \neq i} (T_jG - U_j(G)). \tag{8.2}$$

Substituting (8.2) into (8.1) and maximizing with respect to G, one obtains

$$dO_i/dG = U_i'(G) - T_i - \sum_{j \neq i} (T_j - U_j'(G)). \tag{8.3}$$

Setting (8.3) equal to zero, we can solve for the optimal G for i to state, given i's tax share T_i and the incentive tax t_i. Rearranging this first order condition, we obtain the Samuelsonian condition for the Pareto-optimal provision of G:

$$\sum_i U_i'(G) = \sum_i T_i = C. \tag{8.4}$$

Note that although the quantity of the public good selected is Pareto optimal, it is also generally true that $U_i'(G) \neq T_i$, $i=1,n$, as can also be seen in Figure 8.1. An important element of the procedure is that an individual's share of the cost of a public good is independent of his stated demand schedule. This independence is necessary to ensure the honest revelation of preferences. Only the (probably rather small) incentive tax, represented by the cross-hatched triangle in Figure 8.1 is directly related to the individual's reported demand schedule, and the funds raised here are to be wasted, or at least not returned in any systematic way to the payer.

The idea of a two-part tariff to ensure an efficient allocation of resources in industries characterized by economies of scale, or large fixed costs, has been around for some time. The most obvious examples are probably the electric and gas industries (see, e.g., Kahn, 1970, pp. 95–100). The principles underlying these pricing schemes are analogous to those of the demand-revealing process. A proportional charge is made to each customer for his use of the service, and an extra charge is made for the costs on other buyers that a customer's demand imposes at the peak (margin) of the system's capacity. Public goods are also characterized by high fixed costs, the joint supply property; and the demand-revealing process is thus a perhaps not too surprising, if somewhat long-awaited, extension of the idea of the two-part tariff into the public good area.

Green and Laffont (1977a) have demonstrated that the class of demand-revealing processes first developed by Groves (1973) in effect defines the full set of procedures of this type, of which the above examples are but one variant, for which honest revelation of preferences is the dominant strategy. That is, regardless of what message the other voters supply to the message-gathering agent, it is always an individual's optimal strategy to reveal his true preferences. This property of the procedure is dependent upon an absence of interaction between an individual's fixed tax share, revealed demand schedule, and the revealed demand schedules of the other individuals. There is no way, direct or indirect, by which individuals can influence the taxes that they pay other than through the immediate effect of their revealed demand schedules. Thus, the procedure is a purely partial equilibrium approach that abstracts from any interactions among voters via income effects or other means.

Although honest preference revelations and the Samuelson efficiency conditions are ensured under the partial equilibrium variants of the demand-revealing process, budget balance is not, and so Pareto efficiency cannot be presumed. As already noted, the size of the total tax intake from the incentive tax is a matter of some controversy, and so, too, therefore the significance of the Pareto-inefficiency property. Groves and Ledyard (1977a) have developed a general equilibrium version of the demand-revealing process in which budget balance is achieved. Each individual reports a quadratic approximation to his true demand function of the following form,

$$m_i = \beta_{iy} - \frac{\gamma}{2n} y^2,$$

where γ is a constant across all individuals, y is the quantity of public goods, and n is the number of consumers. The individual's tax is given as

$$T_i = a_i y^*(m) + \frac{\gamma}{2} \left[\left(\frac{n-1}{n} \right) \left(m_i - \mu_i \right)^2 - \sigma_i^2 \right],$$

where a_i is a preassigned tax share, $y^*(m)$ is the quantity of public good chosen as a result of the aggregation of all individual messages, μ_i is the mean of all of the *other* voters' messages, and σ_i is the standard error of all of the other voters' messages. Each individual pays a fixed tax share, a_i, and a variable tax that increases with the size of the difference between his proposed quantity and the proposed quantity of all other voters, and decreases in proportion to the amount of dispersion among the other proposals. Thus a voter is again penalized to the extent that his proposed public good quantity differs from that of all other voters, but his penalty is smaller, the more disagreement there is among the other voters over the desired quantity of public good. To supply his optimal message, a voter must know his preassigned tax share, the fixed constant, and the mean and standard error of all other voters' messages. Thus, a sequential adjustment procedure is required in which each voter is supplied with the computed mean and standard error of the other voters' messages on the preceding round of calculations to make a calculation on the present one. The present messages then become the data for making new mean and standard error statistics for each voter. The process continues until equilibrium is obtained.[1]

Under the Groves–Ledyard procedure, the tax on each individual can be designed to ensure budget balance, and if each voter treats the messages of the others as given, each has the incentive to reveal his own preferences honestly, and a Pareto-optimal equilibrium can be established (1977a, pp. 794–806). But, it may not be in each voter's best interests to treat the messages of all other voters as given. The achievement of budget balance and individual equilibrium via a multistep adjustment process makes each individual's message at one step of the process dependent on the other individuals' messages at the preceding stage. A voter who could deduce the effect of his message on the messages of other voters in subsequent rounds of voting might have an incentive to manipulate their messages in later rounds via dishonest indication of his own demand schedule in earlier rounds. The proofs of Pareto optimality that Groves and Ledyard offer assume essentially Cournot-type behavior: Each voter treats the messages of the other voters as fixed at each stage of the adjustment process. Once voters begin to take the reactions of other voters into account, Stackleberg-type behavior may be individually optimal, and both the honest-revelation and Pareto efficiency properties of the mechanism may be lost (Groves and Ledyard, 1977b, pp. 118–20; Groves, 1979; Margolis, 1983).

Although honest revelation of individual preferences is not the dominant strategy under the Groves–Ledyard balanced budget variant of the demand-revealing procedure, it is a Nash equilibrium. That is, given that all other individuals honestly reveal their preferences at each step in the process, it is in each voter's best interest to do so. The significance of this property of the procedure rests heavily on whether it is reasonable to expect voters to adopt a Cournot-type frame of mind when sending messages, at least when the number of voters is fairly large. This issue cannot be settled on the basis of *a priori argument*.[2] Experimental work conducted by Vernon Smith (1977, 1979a,b, 1980) using a variant of the Groves–Ledyard process, albeit one without the budget balance constraint, indicated a fairly fast convergence of the process on the Lindahl equilibrium. Smith also obtained encouraging results using an "auction process" with properties analogous to the demand-revealing process

---

1. Groves and Loeb (1975) first discussed the possibility of achieving budget balance when the consumer's, in this case a firm's, demand schedule is a quadratic function of the form given above.
2. The basic result is established by Groves and Ledyard (1977a). For a discussion of its significance, see Greenberg, Mackay, and Tideman (1977); Groves and Ledyard (1977c).

(see Chapter 4, Section B*). Harstad and Marrese (1982) reported convergence to efficient outcomes in nine experiments with the Groves–Ledyard procedure. Thus, the vulnerability to individual strategizing of processes requiring sequential adjustment mechanisms may not be serious. The Public Broadcasting System successfully employs another form of preference revelation procedure to allocate program space (Ferejohn, Forsythe, and Noll, 1979), and Tideman (1983) obtained some success with fraternity students using the demand-revealing process. These real-world experiments with demand-revealing procedures further buttress our confidence that its theoretical liabilities can be overcome in practice.

Of the many criticisms and caveats that have been raised about the demand-revealing process, the most serious would appear to be the failure of the various partial equilibrium variants to allow for income effects; that is, the amount of money being collected from an individual is assumed to be too small to affect his stated demand schedule. This is obviously an extreme assumption and one not typically found in other economic models. Once income effects are allowed, however, we move into the general equilibrium framework first explored by Groves and Ledyard (1977a). To handle income effects adequately, one needs even stronger assumptions and a more complicated voting procedure than Groves–Ledyard (Conn, 1983),[3] and the dominance property of preference revelation vanishes.[4]

The remaining difficulties of the process are shared by most if not all other voting processes:

Information incentives: To the extent that the size of the incentive tax levied on any individual falls as the number of voters increases, the incentive to provide information conscientiously dwindles.[5] Thus, the demand-revealing process is caught in a form of numerical dilemma. If the numbers involved are small, the incentive taxes may be large, but so too, then, is the potential Pareto inefficiency arising out of the existence of this unutilized tax revenue. If the numbers are large, the Pareto inefficiency may be relatively small, but so too is the incentive to supply the needed information. Much of the information coming from the process could be inaccurate, although not systematically dishonest. Clarke (1977), Green and Laffont (1977b), Tullock (1977a), and Brubaker (1986) have discussed ways to circumvent this problem by relying on representative systems or sampling techniques.

3. For further discussion of the problems raised by income effects or nonseparable utility functions, see Groves and Ledyard (1977b); Green and Laffont (1977a, 1979); and Laffont and Maskin (1980). For a defense of the assumption, see Tideman and Tullock (1977).
4. For the most general discussion of this problem, see Hurwicz (1979).
5. See Clarke (1971, 1977); Tideman and Tullock (1976); Tullock (1977a, 1982); Margolis (1982a); Brubaker (1983).

Coalitions: A coalition of voters who felt they would be 100 better off from the victory of *P* could increase the chances of *P*'s winning significantly by all agreeing to claim that they were 200 better off under *P*'s victory. As long as *P* won by more than 200, they would be better off under the coalition than acting independently. If *P* won by less than 100 or lost, they are no worse off. Only if *P* won by between 100 and 200, an unlikely event if the coalition is very large, would a voter be worse off under the outcome with the coalition than without it. Thus, incentives to form coalitions to manipulate outcomes exist under the demand-revealing process (Bennett and Conn, 1977; Riker, 1979).

Gordon Tullock (1977c) is undoubtedly correct in arguing that the problem of coalition formation is unlikely to be serious if the number of voters is large and voting is by secret ballot (1977c). For then the same incentives to free-ride will exist within the coalition as now exist and will thwart the functioning of a pure voluntary-exchange voting mechanism. A single voter's optimal strategy is to urge the formation of a 200-vote coalition and then vote 100, himself. If all voters follow this strategy, we are left with honest preference revelation.[6]

But with small numbers of voters and publicly recorded votes, as in a representative body, the conditions for coalition formation are more favorable. This is particularly true because we usually elect representatives as members of parties, which are natural coalition partners. Again we find ourselves confronted by a numerical dilemma: In a direct democracy with a large number of voters, no one has an incentive to gather information *or* join a coalition; in small committees of representatives, incentives exist to gather information about not only one's own preferences, but also those of others who may be potential coalition members.

Bankruptcy: Under the demand-revealing process it is possible for an outcome to emerge in which the entire private wealth of an individual is confiscated (Groves and Ledyard, 1977b, pp. 116–18). This is true of almost any voting procedure other than the unanimity rule, however, and is probably not a serious, practical problem. It does point up the need to view the process as taking place within some sort of system of constitutional guarantees and constraints upon the types of issues that come before the committee.[7]

Thus, the demand-revealing process is very much in the spirit of the Wicksellian approach to collective choice. Collective decision making is *within* a system of prescribed property rights, and *upon* a just distribution of income.

6. For further discussion, see Tideman and Tullock (1981).
7. For further discussion of the bankruptcy issue, see Tullock (1977a); Tideman and Tullock (1977); Groves and Ledyard (1977b,c).

The goal of collective action is to improve allocative efficiency, not to achieve distributive justice. Such redistribution as will take place is of the Pareto-optimal variety and is more appropriately viewed as part of the "allocation branch" of the public weal than of the "distribution branch."[8]

We discuss some of these points further in Section E, but first we review another procedure that shares many of the Wicksellian attributes of the demand-revealing process.

B.   Point voting

We seek from a voting process two pieces of information, the quantity of the public good that satisfies the Pareto-optimality condition, and the set of tax shares that finances the purchase of this quantity. The demand-revealing process sidesteps the second question by starting with a preassigned set of tax shares that suffice to cover the cost of supplying the public good. It induces honest preference revelation to determine the Pareto-optimal quantity of public good by means of the special incentive tax.

The need to charge a tax to induce honest preference revelation creates the problem of disposing of the revenue raised by the incentive tax and makes the normative properties of the process dependent on the normative properties of the initial income distribution. These disadvantages could be avoided by giving each voter a stock of vote money that would be used to reveal preferences for public goods and would have no other monetary value. No problem of disposing of the money collected would exist, and the initial distribution of vote money could be made to satisfy any normative criterion one wished. Aanund Hylland and Richard Zeckhauser (1979) have proposed such a procedure.

The idea of giving each citizen a stock of vote points and of allowing the citizen to allocate these points across the public goods issue set in accordance with the citizen's preference intensities is not a new one.[9] The difficulty with point voting has always been that it does not provide the proper incentives for honest preference revelation, as Dodgson was well aware in the passage quoted at the beginning of this chapter. Individuals can better their realized outcomes by overstating their preferences on their most intense issues (Phil-

8. Tullock (1977d) has explored the redistributive potential of the process and claims somewhat more for it. On the distinction between Pareto-optimal redistribution and other kinds, see Hochman and Rodgers (1969, 1970).
9. Dodgson's comment at the beginning of this chapter suggests that he did not invent the procedure, so it is probably over 100 years old. See more recent discussions by Musgrave (1959, pp. 130–1); Coleman (1970); Mueller (1971, 1973); Intriligator (1973); and Nitzan (1975).

potts, 1972; Nitzan, Paroush, and Lampert, 1980; Nitzan, 1985). The important innovation of Hylland and Zeckhauser is their vote-point aggregation rule that provides voters with the proper incentive for honest preference revelation. They are able to show that with the appropriate determination of the vote points assigned to each citizen, voters will reveal their true preferences for public goods when the government aggregates the *square roots* of the vote points of each voter. The main steps in this demonstration are outlined in the next section.

C.*   An explication of the Hylland–Zeckhauser point-voting procedure

We again assume the existence of preassigned tax shares for each citizen for each public good. Each citizen can calculate her total tax bill for each quantity of public good provided, and thus can determine the optimal quantities of each public good given her tax shares and money income. This point-voting procedure, like the demand-revealing process, does not address the question of what the tax shares for each citizen should be. Its objective is to reveal preference intensities to determine the Pareto-optimal quantities of the set of public goods.

There are K public goods whose quantities must be determined. Each voter i is given a stock of vote points, A_i, to be allocated across the K public goods issues according to the voter's preference intensities. If voters wish to increase the quantity of the public good, they allocate a positive number of vote points to the issue; if they wish to decrease the quantity, they allocate a negative number of vote points. If $|a_{ik}|$ is the absolute number of vote points that voter i allocates to issue k, then the a_{ik}s must satisfy

$$\sum_{k=1}^{K} |a_{ik}| \leq A_i. \tag{8.5}$$

The government converts an individual's vote points into increments or decrements in the proposed quantity of public good using the rule

$$b_{ik} = f(a_{ik}), \tag{8.6}$$

where b_{ik} takes on the sign of a_{ik} and $(b_{ik} = 0) \leftrightarrow (a_{ik} = 0)$. The most straightforward rule is, of course, $b_{ik} = a_{ik}$, but, as we shall see, this rule does not provide the proper incentive for honest preference revelations. The quantities of public goods are determined through an iterative procedure. The government-auctioneer announces an initial proposal of public good quantities, perhaps the levels provided last year.

$$G_1^0$$
$$G_2^0$$

.
.
.

$$G_K^0.$$

Each voter responds by stating an allocation of vote points across the K issues, which satisfies (8.5). If a voter wants a larger quantity of G_k than G_K^0, she allocates positive vote points to issue k, that is, $a_{ik} > 0$, and vice versa. The government determines a new vector of proposed public good quantities using (8.6); that is,

$$G_1^1 = G_1^0 + \sum_{i=1}^{n} b_{i1}$$

$$G_2^1 = G_2^0 + \sum_{i=1}^{n} b_{i2}$$

.
.
.

$$G_K^1 = G_K^0 + \sum_{i=1}^{n} b_{iK}$$

The process is repeated until a vector of public good quantities is obtained such that the aggregated votes for changing each public good quantity all sum to zero; that is,

$$\sum_{i=1}^{n} b_{ik} = 0, \qquad k = 1, K. \tag{8.7}$$

There are three questions of interest concerning the procedure.

1. Does it converge?
2. What are the normative properties of the bundle of public goods quantities it selects?
3. What form does f( ) take?

Demonstrating that an iterative procedure converges is never an easy task. Hylland and Zeckhauser (1979) make a reasonable case for the convergence of this procedure, and we leave this issue aside.

The normative property we seek is Pareto optimality. This property is assured if we can choose a vector of public good quantities $G = (G_1, G_2, \cdots, G_K)$, which maximizes

$$W(G) = \sum_{i=1}^{n} \lambda_i U_i(G), \tag{8.8}$$

where $U_i(G)$ is voter i's utility defined over the public good quantity vector G (see Section 2.C*). For $W(G)$ to be at its maximum, the following first-order condition must be satisfied for each of the K public goods:

$$\sum_{i=1}^{n} \lambda_i \frac{\partial U_i}{\partial G_k} = 0, \qquad k = 1, K. \tag{8.9}$$

The appropriately weighted marginal utilities must just balance, so that any change in G_k results in offsetting changes in weighted $\partial U_i / \partial G_k s$. We now have two conditions that our equilibrium vector of public goods must satisfy, (8.9) and (8.7). Clearly we could ensure the Pareto optimality of any equilibrium vector to which the procedure converged, if

$$b_{ik} = \lambda_i \frac{\partial U_i}{\partial G_k}. \tag{8.10}$$

Then whenever convergence was achieved, that is,

$$\sum_{i=1}^{n} b_{ik} = 0, \qquad k = 1, K,$$

(8.9) would also be satisfied, and Pareto optimality would be ensured. We now have a clue as to the form f( ) should take. It must be chosen to satisfy (8.10).

Now consider i's decision for allocating her stock of vote points, A_i, at any step in the iterative procedure. She wishes to maximize her utility defined over the vector of public goods, given her vote-point budget constraint as given by (8.5); that is, she must at the $t + 1$th iteration maximize

$$O_i = U_i \left(G_1^t + \sum_{j \neq i} b_{j1} + b_{i1}, \cdots, G_k^t + \sum_{j \neq i} b_{jk} + b_{ik} \cdots \right.$$

$$\left. G_K^t + \sum_{j \neq i} b_{jK} + b_{iK} \right) + \mu_i \left(A_i - \sum_{k=1}^{K} |a_{ik}| \right). \tag{8.11}$$

Now the G_k^t are the announced quantities of public goods from the previous iteration and are fixed. The $\sum_{j \neq i} b_{jk}$ are the aggregated vote points of the other voters on this iteration, and are not subject to i's control. Thus, i can change only the b_{ik}. Equation (8.11) obtains a maximum when the following K equations are satisfied:

$$\frac{\partial U_i}{\partial G_k} f'(a_{ik}) = \mu_i, \ k = 1,K \tag{8.12a}$$

when $a_{ik} > 0$, or

$$\frac{\partial U_i}{\partial G_k} f'(a_{ik}) = -\mu_i, \ k = 1,K \tag{8.12b}$$

when $a_{ik} < 0$. Substituting for $\partial U_i/\partial G_k$ in (8.10), we obtain

$$b_{ik} = f(a_{ik}) = \frac{\lambda_i \mu_i}{f'(a_ik)} \tag{8.13}$$

when $a_{ik} > 0$. Now λ_i is the weight i gets in W, and μ_i is the Lagrangian multiplier from (8.11). Thus, $\lambda_i \mu_i = C$, a constant. The function f( ) must be such that

$$f(a_{ik})f'(a_{ik}) = C. \tag{8.14}$$

From the observation that

$$\frac{df(a_{ik})^2}{da_{ik}} = 2f(a_{ik})f'(a_{ik}) \tag{8.15}$$

we obtain

$$\frac{df(a_{ik})^2}{da_{ik}} = 2C. \tag{8.16}$$

If we integrate (8.16), we obtain

$$f(a_{ik})^2 = 2Ca_{ik} + H, \tag{8.17}$$

where H is an arbitrary constant of integration. Setting $H = 0$, we obtain

$$f(a_{ik}) = \sqrt{2Ca_{ik}} = \sqrt{2\lambda_i\mu_i a_{ik}}. \tag{8.18}$$

Since μ_i represents the marginal utility of a vote point to i, μ_i can be changed by changing i's stock of vote points, A_i. In particular, if A_i is chosen such that

$$\mu_i = 1/(2\lambda_i), \tag{8.19}$$

then $f(a_{ik})$ takes on the simple form

$$f(a_{ik}) = \sqrt{a_{ik}}. \tag{8.20}$$

The utility-maximizing vote-point allocations of each voter will be such as to maximize the weighted welfare function W, (8.8), for appropriately chosen

A_i's, if the government-auctioneer determines the quantities of public goods by aggregating the square roots of each voter's vote-point allocations. Taking the square root of a voter's vote-point allocation provides a sufficient penalty to overallocating vote points to more intense issues to offset the tendency to misrepresent preferences under naive point voting [$f(a_{ik}) = a_{ik}$] mentioned earlier.

Note that an egalitarian assignment of vote points, $A_i = A$ for all i, is consistent with giving each individual equal weight in the social welfare function, W, if and only if the marginal utility of a vote point is the same for all voters. This condition can, in turn, be interpreted as being equivalent to assuming that all voters have an equal stake, that is, an equal expected utility gain from collective action (Mueller, 1971, 1973; Mueller, Tollison, and Willett, 1975). Alternatively, an egalitarian assignment of vote points can be interpreted as an implicit decision to give lower weights (λ_i's) in the social welfare function to those with more intense preferences (higher μ_i's).

The equilibrium obtained in the Hylland–Zeckhauser point-voting scheme is a Nash equilibrium, and strategizing on intermediary steps or coalitions could overturn the results. On the other hand, strategies for "beating the system" are not readily apparent.

D.   Voting by veto

The demand-revealing and point-voting procedures call to mind analogies with market mechanisms in that real money or vote money is used to express preferences, and equilibrium is achieved through a tâtonnement process. The welfare properties of the procedures depend in part on the implicit interpersonal, cardinal utility comparisons that arise from the aggregating of dollar or point votes. In contrast, voting by veto (hereafter VV) utilizes only ordinal utility information.[10] Pareto optimality is achieved, as with the unanimity rule, through the rejection of Pareto-inferior outcomes. The procedure also resembles majority rule in important respects.

VV differs from the two procedures discussed earlier in this chapter in that it allows one to determine both the quantities of public goods and the tax shares to finance it. It differs from all voting procedures as typically analyzed in formally including the issue proposal process in the procedure, rather than assuming that voting takes place on a predetermined issue set.

The procedure has two steps. In the first, each member of the committee makes a proposal for the outcome of the committee process. These proposals could be the quantity of a single public good and the tax formula to finance it,

10. This procedure was first discussed by Mueller (1978), with further development by Moulin (1979, 1981a,b, 1982) and Mueller (1984).

or a whole vector of quantities of public goods with accompanying tax for-mulas. At the end of step 1, an $n + 1$ proposal set exists consisting of the proposals of the n committee members and a status quo issue s (what was done last year, zero levels of all public goods, . . .). A random process is then used to determine an order of veto voting. The order of veto voting is announced to all members of the committee. The individual placed first in the veto sequence by the random process begins by eliminating (vetoing) one proposal from the $n + 1$ element proposal set. The second veto-voter elimi-nates one proposal from the remaining n proposals. Veto voting continues until all n members of the committee have vetoed one proposal. The one unvetoed proposal remaining in the issue set is declared the winner.

To see the properties of VV consider the following example for a commit-tee of three. The voters, A, B, and C, propose issues a, b, and c, which together with s form the issue set. Let the individual preference orderings be as in Table 8.3, ignoring the two entries in parentheses.

Assume that each individual knows the other voters' preference orderings. Suppose that the randomly determined order of veto voting is A then B then C. A can make his proposal a winner by vetoing b. If B then vetoes either a or s, C will veto the other issue in this pair (s or a), and c wins. Since B prefers a to c, B's best strategy is to veto c, leaving C to veto s, making a the winner.

Now suppose that the randomly determined voting order is ACB. A no longer can get his proposal to win. If A vetoes c, C vetoes a or s, and b wins. If A vetoes b, C vetoes a, and c wins. Since A prefers c to b, he will veto b, leaving c to become the winner. The winners for the six possible permutations of voting sequences are as follows:

$$ABC \rightarrow a \qquad\qquad BCA \rightarrow b$$
$$ACB \rightarrow c \qquad\qquad CAB \rightarrow c$$
$$BAC \rightarrow a \qquad\qquad CBA \rightarrow b.$$

Each issue proposed by a committee member has a one-in-three chance of winning.

The preferences in Table 8.3 produce a cycle over a, b, and c in pairwise voting under majority rule. Thus, in this opening example, the parallel be-tween majority rule and VV seems close. Where the former produces a cycle over three issues, VV selects a winner at random with equal probability.

Now replace the two entries for C in Table 8.3 by those in parentheses; that is, assume that C now prefers a to b, all other rankings remaining the same. With this one change, the probability of a's winning jumps to 5/6. The only order of veto voting that selects a different issue than a is CAB, which leads to c's victory.

Table 8.3. *Rankings of issues in voting by veto example*

| | Voters | | |
Issues	A	B	C
a	1	2	3(2)
b	3	1	2(3)
c	2	3	1
s	4	4	4

This example illustrates an important incentive property of VV. *A* increases the probability of his proposal winning by advancing it in the preference ordering of another voter. Thus, the procedure establishes incentives to make proposals that, although perhaps favoring oneself, stand relatively high in the other voters' preferences. Of course, the same incentive exists for all voters, and a competition ensues to make the proposal standing relatively highest in all voters' preferences.

The procedure can be shown to select a unique winning proposal out of any $n + 1$ element proposal set, given the randomly determined veto-voting sequence (Mueller, 1978, 1984). Moreover, the chances that an issue will win vary directly with its position in each voter's ranking of the $n + 1$ proposals. The lower a proposal is ranked by any voter, the lower are its chances of winning.

To see the latter point and further illustrate the properties of the procedure, consider the following example. A committee of n is offered a gift of G dollars if they can agree on a distribution of the gift. If they cannot agree, they retain the status quo distribution of nothing. Although the issue here is basically how to distribute G, the example resembles a public good decision under the unanimity rule in that all are better off only if they can all agree on a single proposal. The issue is one for which majority rule would produce a cycle. Let us examine the outcome under VV.

The initial, selfish instinct of a voter might be to propose that all of G go to himself and nothing to the other $n - 1$ committee members. But this would make his proposal no better than the status quo and almost ensure his defeat. He must offer some of G to the other voters.

What defeats a proposal is a low rank in another voter's preference ordering. Thus, whatever amount of G a voter sets aside for the other committee members will be divided equally, since to discriminate against any one voter greatly increases the probability that that voter will veto the proposal. Assum-

Table 8.4. *The elimination of proposals and voting by veto: example 2*

Voter	Rejects, r_i	Sets of possible winning proposals
V_1	p_3 or p_2 or p_1	$\{p_1\}$ or $\{p_2\}$
V_2	p_4 or p_3 or p_2	$\{p_1, p_2\}$ or $\{p_1, p_3\}$
.		
.		
.		
V_{n-3}	p_{n-1} or p_{n-2} or p_{n-3}	$\{p_1, \cdots p_{n-4}, p_{n-3}\}$ or $\{p_1, \cdots, p_{n-4}, p_{n-2}\}$
V_{n-2}	p_n or p_{n-1} or p_{n-2}	$\{p_1, \cdots p_{n-3}, p_{n-2}\}$ or $\{p_1, \cdots, p_{n-3}, p_{n-1}\}$
V_{n-1}	p_n or p_{n-1}	$\{p_1, \cdots p_{n-2}, p_{n-1}\}$ or $\{p_1, \cdots, p_{n-2}, p_n\}$
V_n	s	$\{p_1, p_2, \cdots, p_n\}$

ing that i selfishly desires a bit more of G for himself than he sets aside for others, i's proposal will look like the following:

$$\left(\frac{G}{n} - \frac{e_i}{n-1}, \frac{G}{n} - \frac{e_i}{n-1}, \cdots, \frac{G}{n} + e_i, , \cdots, \frac{G}{n} - \frac{e_i}{n-1} \right). \quad (8.21)$$

Voter i proposes an egalitarian distribution of G with something extra for himself, $G/n + e_i$, and divides the remainder equally among the other $n - 1$ voters, giving each $G/n - e_i/(n - 1)$. Assume that all proposals other than s take this form. We can now designate the proposals according to their degree of egalitarianism. Call p_1 the proposal with the smallest e_i (i.e., the most egalitarian), p_2 the proposal with the second smallest e_i, and so forth. Assume no two proposals have the same e_i.

Now let the order of veto voting be determined as in Table 8.4. V_1 is the first to vote, V_2 the second, and so on. Once the veto-voting sequence is determined, it is announced to all voters. Given the nature of the proposals, any voter can easily determine the complete rankings of the $n + 1$ proposals for all other voters. All voters rank the status quo proposal s last. All know that the last to go in the veto-voting sequence, V_n, ranks s last. Given a choice between s and any other proposal, V_n rejects s. Thus, none of the voters will waste their veto on s, and s is left for V_n to veto. We can designate s with V_n as the proposal he definitely rejects. Considering V_n we can determine the set of possible winning issues as $\{p_1, p_2 \ldots p_n\}$. Voter V_{n-1} receives three proposals, one of which is s, and rejects the lower ranked of the two other proposals. Of the possible winning proposals, $\{p_1, p_2, \ldots p_n\}$, V_{n-1} would veto the proposal ranked lowest by him in this set against any other proposal. Call this proposal r_{n-1}. If any voter who precedes V_{n-1} were to reject r_{n-1}, he would waste his veto. All will leave r_{n-1} for V_{n-1} to reject. Given the nature of the proposals, we can narrow the list of possible candidates for r_{n-1}. V_{n-1} ranks the least egalitarian of the proposals, p_n, lowest since it promises him the lowest payoff, unless p_n is his proposal. If V_{n-1} proposed p_n, he did not propose p_{n-1}, and ranks it lowest. Thus, V_{n-1} must reject either p_n or p_{n-1}.

Proceeding thus we can work our way up the list of voters, associating with each an issue to be rejected. If V_{n-1} proposed p_n, then V_{n-2} did not, and V_{n-2} rejects p_n. Considering both V_{n-1} and V_{n-2}, one or both did not propose p_n, and p_n is definitely rejected by one of the last three voters. Considering the last three voters, s and p_n are definitely eliminated as possible winning issues. As we work our way up the veto-voting sequence, we discover that all proposals are eliminated as possible winners except p_1 and p_2, the two most egalitarian proposals!

The most egalitarian proposal, p_1, wins most of the time because all voters other than its proposer rank it second to their own proposal. If the proposer of p_2 happens to come first in the voting sequence (is V_1), he can make his proposal the most egalitarian of the proposals by rejecting p_1; p_2 can win only if its proposer is V_1.[11] Since the probability that a given individual will come first in the voting sequence approaches zero as n increases, the probability that any proposal other than the most egalitarian proposal will win approaches zero as the committee grows.

More generally, VV selects proposals ranked relatively high on all preference orderings. When the issue space is single dimensional, and voter preferences single peaked, VV assigns nonzero probabilities of winning to only the middle $\frac{1}{3}$ proposals, with the highest probability going to the median proposal. This tendency to pick proposals "in the middle" is reinforced by the incentives facing voters at the proposal stage.

Let x and y be quantities of two public goods, or quality dimensions of a single public good to be decided by the committee. Let $U_i(x,y)$ be i's utility function reaching a maximum at some point I in the positive orthant. Assume circular indifference curves around I. Proposals take the form of combinations of x and y, $p_i(x_i, y_i)$. The probability that any other voter j will reject p_i is higher the further p_i is from j's utility maximum, J; call this probability $\pi^i_j(x_i, y_i)$. The probability that any of the other $n-1$ voters will reject p_i is

$$\pi^i = \sum_{j \neq i} \pi^i_j. \tag{8.22}$$

Although π^i is not continuous, it is reasonable to assume that it approaches a continuous function with a minimum at C, the center of the distribution of peak utilities of the other $n-1$ voters, as n grows large. Let $\bar{U}_i$ be i's

11. Note that p_2 does not always win when its proposer votes first. When he is followed by the proposer of p_3, p_2's proposer will not veto p_1, because then p_3's proposer would veto p_2.

expected utility if his proposal does not win. His task is to propose a pair of characteristics (x_i, y_i) to maximize his expected utility, $E(U_i)$.

$$E(U_i) = (1 - \pi^i)U_i(x_i, y_i) + \pi^i \bar{U}_i. \tag{8.23}$$

Maximizing (8.23) with respect to x_i and y_i and setting each equation equal to zero, we derive

$$\frac{\partial U_i}{\partial x_i}(1 - \pi^i) - U_i \frac{\partial \pi^i}{\partial x_i} + \frac{\partial \pi^i}{\partial x_i} \bar{U}_i = 0$$

$$\frac{\partial U_i}{\partial y_i}(1 - \pi^i) - U_i \frac{\partial \pi^i}{\partial y_i} + \frac{\partial \pi^i}{\partial y_i} \bar{U}_i = 0 \tag{8.24}$$

$$\frac{\partial U_i / \partial x_i}{\partial U_i / \partial y_i} = \frac{\partial \pi^i / \partial x_i}{\partial \pi^i / \partial y_j}.$$

Equation (8.24) defines a point of tangency between an indifference curve of i, and an isoprobability of rejection locus around C (see Figure 8.2), a point on a pseudocontract curve running from i's optimum point, I, to the center of the density function defined over the other voters' optima. In making a proposal, i is pulled along this contract curve in the direction of C by the knowledge that the probability of his proposal's rejection is higher, the further it lies from C. Application of VV will lop off the proposals lying furthest from the center of the density function defined over all optima, leaving as possible winners only a subset of proposals clustered around the center.

VV suffers from some of the same shortcomings as other procedures. As the number of participants grows, the incentive to participate declines. The process is also vulnerable to coalitions. If two of the three committee members in the above example could agree to discriminate against the third, they could combine redistributive elements into their proposals, making themselves better off, and the third person even worse off than under the status quo. The excluded member could veto but one of the proposals, and the other would win. As with other voting rules, however, the coalition problem will be less important the larger the number of voters.

E.   A comparison of the procedures

When Paul Samuelson (1954, p. 182) proclaimed the task of revealing individual preferences for public goods impossible, he was assuming that a form of benefit tax would be used to finance the purchase of the public good. An individual's share of the costs of the public good would be tied to his stated preference for it. The demand-revealing process and point voting solve the preference revelation problem by severing the link between stated preference

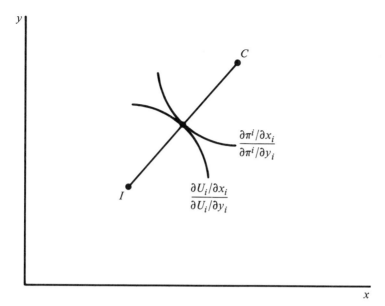

Figure 8.2. Determination of voter i's proposal.

and share of cost, as do other related processes like Vernon Smith's (1977) auction process.

Although these processes do not make a voter's share of the costs of a public good directly related to his stated preferences for it, they do impose a cost upon the voter for moving the committee outcome in a given direction. As Theodore Groves (1979, p. 227) has observed, "The idea of a 'quid pro quo' is fundamental to an economic theory of exchange." With the exception of the logrolling models, the idea of a quid pro quo has not been part of either theoretical or real-world democratic processes; perhaps this explains their limited success at achieving Wicksell's goal of a *voluntary* exchange process of government. In most democratic procedures, votes are distributed as essentially free goods, with the only real constraint on their use being the ticking of the clock.

The procedures discussed in this chapter all break with this tradition in a fundamental way. The demand-revealing and point-voting schemes require that the voter be prepared to spend real money or fungible vote money to change the committee outcome. Under VV, vetoes are no longer free goods. Each individual has but one proposal to make, and one veto to cast.

Each of the procedures is also in the Wicksellian tradition in that the key equity issues are assumed to have been resolved prior to the application of the procedures.[12] For both the demand-revealing and point-voting procedures, the individual shares of the costs of the public good are predetermined. With demand revelation, the outcomes are further dependent on the initial distribution of income; with point voting, on the distribution of vote points. Voting by veto leaves aside the issue of initial income distribution.

Given a just starting point, the goal of collective action is to increase the welfare of all, and the task of the collective decision process is to indicate those situations where that is possible. The proposals differ, however, in the way that the gains from collective action are distributed. The demand-revealing process moves individuals out along their demand or offer curves to maximize the sum of consumer surpluses across individuals. The gains from collective action are distributed to those with the lowest shares of the public good costs and the highest initial incomes.[13] With point voting, the gains go to those with the lowest initial tax shares and highest initial stocks of vote points. With voting by veto, the analogy is the cake-cutting exercise, as brought about by the random determination of an order of veto voting. The gains from collective action will tend to be equal across individuals, and the normative characteristic of the process is set by this egalitarian property.

The Wicksellian voluntary exchange approach is ineluctably tied to philosophical individualism (Buchanan, 1949). Each individual enters the collective choice process to improve his own welfare, and the process is established so that all may benefit. Implicit here are a set of constitutional guarantees or constraints upon the collective decision process, and, I believe, an assumption that coalitions of one group *against* another do not form. Each man strives *for* himself, but, as in the market, does not strive, collectively at least, against any other. The three proposals here all assume some form of constitutional constraints on the issues coming before the committee, and explicitly rule out coalitions. Under the demand-revealing process, the tax charged an individual is exactly equal to the cost that his participation in the process imposes on all others. Under voting by veto, an individual can protect himself against a discriminatory threat to his well-being by any other voter's proposal through the veto he possesses.

In addition to the inherently individualistic orientation of these three proposals, they also resemble one another in the demands they place upon the individual who participates in the process. A simple yes or no will not do. The individual must evaluate in dollars his benefits under various possible alternatives, and, in the case of voting by veto, also the benefits for other voters.

---

12. For a discussion of this in the context of the demand-revealing process, see Tideman (1977).
13. Gordon Tullock (1977b) has elaborated on the normative properties of the demand-revealing process.

This task is made easier by another Wicksellian characteristic of the procedures; each assumes that an expenditure issue and the tax to finance it are tied together. Although this latter feature might actually make the voter's decision task easier, the kind of information required of him under the three procedures is far more sophisticated than obtained under present voting systems. It is also more sophisticated than one might expect "the average voter" to be capable of supplying, at least if one accepts the image of him gleaned from the typical survey data regarding his knowledge of candidates and issues. To many, the information required of voters will constitute a significant shortcoming of these processes. In my own mind it does not. If we have learned one thing from the sea of work that has emerged following the classic contributions on public goods and democratic choice by Samuelson and Arrow, it is that the task of preference revelation in collective decisions is not an easy one. If we must further assume that the individuals whose preferences we seek to reveal are only capable of yes or no responses, the task is hopeless from the start.

Much of the discussion of these procedures, pro and con, has been in the context of their use by the citizens themselves, as in a direct democracy. A more plausible application of them would appear to be by a committee of representatives, as in a parliament. Here the charge that the procedures are "too complicated" for the voters would carry less weight. Viewed as parliamentary procedures, both point voting and voting by veto would appear to have an advantage over demand revelation, since they do not depend on the use of real money incentives. (Who pays the incentive tax, the citizens or the representatives?) The allocation of a representative's vote points or the characteristics of his proposals under VV would also be useful information for voters when evaluating their representatives. Only the assumption that there are no coalitions would appear to constitute a major problem, requiring the elimination of political parties (each representative would be an independent), or limiting applications of the procedures to committees without party affiliations (e.g., many city councils and school boards).

Although each has its weak points, the three procedures reviewed in this chapter suggest that the knotty problem of preference revelation in collective choice can be resolved as both a theoretical and practical matter. Whether the optimal solution will be a variant on one of these processes, or on a process yet to be discovered, cannot at this point be ascertained. But the basic similarities running across these three processes are so strong, despite the inherently different procedural mechanics by which they operate, that one is led to suspect that these same characteristics will be a part of any "ultimate" solution to the preference revelation problem. And, if this is true, it further highlights Knut Wicksell's fundamental insight into the collective choice process.

Bibliographical notes

In addition to the procedures discussed in this chapter, mention should be made of those proposed by Thompson (1966), Drèze and de la Vallée Poussin (1971), and Bohm (1972).

CHAPTER 9

Exit, voice, and disloyalty

Among the laws that rule human societies there is one which seems to be
more precise and clear than all others. If men are to remain civilized or to
become so, the art of associating together must grow and improve in the
same ratio in which the equality of conditions is increased.

Alexis de Tocqueville

In his book *Exit, Voice, and Loyalty* (1970), Albert Hirschman developed the
useful distinction between processes in which individuals express their preferences via entry or exit decisions, and those in which some form of written,
verbal, or voice communication is employed. An example of the first would
be a market for a private good in which buyers indicate their attitudes toward
the price-quality characteristics of the good by increasing or decreasing (entry
or exit) their purchases. An example of the exercise of voice to influence a
price-cost nexus would be a complaint or commendation of the product deliv-
ered to the manufacturer. A necessary condition for the effective use of exit is
obviously that the potential users of this option be mobile: and full mobility of
both buyers and sellers (free entry and exit) is an assumption underlying all
demonstrations of market efficiency. In contrast, the literature focusing on
voting processes, public choice, and political science has almost exclusively
assumed (most often implicitly) that exit is not an option. The boundaries of
the polity are predefined and inclusive, the citizenry is fixed. A citizen is at
most allowed to abstain from participating in the political process, but he
cannot leave the polity to avoid the consequences of its decisions.

Given the assumption of fixed boundaries and citizenry, the characteristics
of a pure public good, nonexcludability, and jointness of supply require that a
collective *voice* or nonmarket decision process be used to reveal individual
preferences and achieve Pareto efficiency, as Samuelson (1954) emphasized.
But many goods are "pure" public goods in a limited sense only. For these
goods, the nonexclusion principle and/or the jointness of supply property may
not be applicable over the full range of possible distribution and production
alternatives. For these quasi- or local public goods, the possibility may exist
for employing *exit* as an alternative or complement to the *voice* process. These
possibilities are reviewed in the present chapter.

149

A.   The theory of clubs

Consider the effect of retaining only the joint supply property of public goods. That is, assume that exclusion is possible, but addition of a new member lowers the average cost of the good to all other members; that is, there are economies of scale. If average costs fall indefinitely, the optimal size of the consumption group is the entire population, and the traditional public good problem exists. If they eventually stop falling or rise, either because scale economies are exhausted or because of the additional costs of crowding, the optimal size of the consumption group may be smaller than the population. When those who do not contribute to the costs of providing the public good can be excluded from its consumption, the potential exists for a group of individuals to agree voluntarily to provide the public good only to themselves. We shall define such a voluntary association established to provide excludable public goods as a *club*. Although we shall generally assume that the provision of the public good to club members involves at least some fixed costs, and perhaps some falling variable costs, it should be noted that the public good provided by some *social* clubs consists entirely of the presence of the other members of the club. A bridge club is an example. Here there may be no costs, other than time, to providing the public good, and no benefits other than those arising from the association with the other bridge-playing members. But exclusion is possible, and the analysis of these clubs parallels that of the more general case of interest here. Voluntary associations to provide (or to influence the provision of) nonexcludable public goods do not meet the definition of a club employed here, although these associations sometimes call themselves clubs (e.g., the Sierra Club). These associations typically attempt to influence the provision of the public good by some other body, such as a state or national legislature, and are treated here as interest groups rather than clubs. They are discussed in Chapters 13, 16, and 17.

James M. Buchanan (1965a) was the first to explore the efficiency properties of voluntary clubs using a model in which individuals have identical tastes for both public and private goods. To see what is involved, consider the example Buchanan first employed, the formation of a swimming club. Assume first that the size of the pool, and thus its total cost (F), is fixed and the only issue to be decided is the size of the club. Figure 9.1 depicts the marginal benefits and marginal costs from an additional member as seen by any other member. Given identical tastes and incomes, it is reasonable to assume equal sharing of the costs. The marginal benefit to the first member from adding the second member to the club is the saving of one-half the cost of the pool, that is, $MB = F/2$. The marginal benefit of a third member to the first two is the additional saving of $\frac{1}{3}$ of the cost of the pool $(F/3)$. The additional benefits from adding new members, the savings to the other members from further

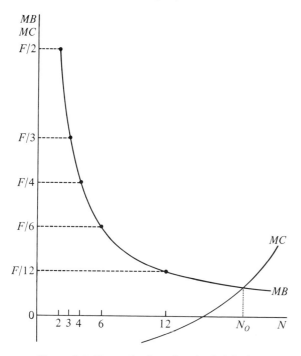

Figure 9.1. Determination of optimal club size.

spreading the fixed costs, continue to fall as the club size (N) increases, as depicted by MB in Figure 9.1. The marginal costs of a new member are given by MC. These are psychic costs. If individuals prefer to swim alone, these will be positive over the entire range. If individuals enjoy the company of others in small enough numbers, the marginal costs of additional members will be negative over an initial range of club sizes. Eventually, the positive costs of crowding will dominate, however, and the optimal club size, N_O, is determined where the marginal cost of an additional member from enhanced crowding just equals the reduction in the other members' dues from spreading the fixed costs over one more club member.[1]

Figure 9.1 can also be used to depict the polar cases of pure private and pure public goods. For a pure public good, the addition of one more member to the club never detracts from the enjoyment of the benefits of club membership to the other members. The marginal cost schedule is zero everywhere and coincides with the horizontal axis. The optimal club size is infinity. For a pure private good, say, an apple, crowding begins to take place on the first unit. If

1. See McGuire (1972, pp. 94–7); Fisch (1975).

a consumer experiences any consumer surplus from the apple, the foregone utility from giving up half of his apple exceeds the gains from sharing its costs and optimal club size is one. Even with such seemingly private goods as apples, however, cooperative consumption may be optimal. If, for example, the unit price of apples is lower when sold by the bushel, the distribution of apples exhibits joint supply characteristics, and might dictate optimal-sized buying clubs of more than one.

The theory of clubs can be extended to take into account the choice of quantity and other characteristics of the collective consumption good. This extension is, perhaps, most easily undertaken algebraically. Let a representative individual's utility be defined over private good X, public good G, and club size N, $U = U(X,G,N)$. Let the cost of providing the public good to the club include a fixed cost, F, and a unit cost (price) of P_g. Assume that each individual has not only the same utility function U, but the same income Y, and that each pays the same fee, t, for membership in the club. In deciding what level of public good to provide and what size of club to establish, we assume that the utility of a representative club member is maximized. This objective might arise as the conscious choice of the founding club members, or be imposed by a competitive market for club memberships. When competition for membership exists, any club that did not provide maximum utility to its members, given the technology of providing the excludable public good, would not survive. Taking into account the budget constraint of a representative member, we obtain the following Lagrangian function to be maximized:

$$L = U(X,G,N) + \lambda(Y - P_x X - t). \tag{9.1}$$

If the club must operate under a balanced budget constraint, then t must satisfy $tN = F + P_g G$. Using this equation to replace t in (9.1), we obtain

$$L = U(X,G,N) + \lambda(Y - P_x X - F/N - P_g G/N). \tag{9.2}$$

Maximizing (9.2) with respect to X, G, and N yields first-order conditions

$$\frac{\partial L}{\partial X} = \frac{\partial U}{\partial X} - \lambda P_x = 0 \tag{9.3}$$

$$\frac{\partial L}{\partial G} = \frac{\partial U}{\partial G} - \lambda P_g/N = 0 \tag{9.4}$$

$$\frac{\partial L}{\partial N} = \frac{\partial U}{\partial N} + \frac{\lambda(F + P_g G)}{N^2} = 0. \tag{9.5}$$

From (9.3) and (9.4) we obtain

$$N \frac{\partial U/\partial G}{\partial U/\partial X} = \frac{P_g}{P_x}. \tag{9.6}$$

The quantity of public good provided to club members must be chosen so that the Samuelsonian condition for Pareto-optimal provision is satisfied; that is, the summation of the marginal rates of substitution of public for private goods over all club members must equal the ratio of their prices.

From (9.4) and (9.5) we obtain

$$N = -\frac{\partial U/\partial G}{\partial U/\partial N} \cdot \frac{F + P_g G}{P_g} . \tag{9.7}$$

If an expansion of club size induces unwanted crowding, $\partial U/\partial N < 0$, and (9.7) implies an $N > 0$. The larger the disutility from crowding relative to the marginal utility of the public good, the smaller the optimal club size. The greater the fixed costs of providing the public good to club members, the larger the optimal size of the club, owing to the advantages of spreading these fixed costs over a larger club membership.

The assumption that individuals have identical tastes and incomes is more than just an analytic convenience. It is often inefficient to have individuals of different tastes in the same club, if this can be avoided. If all individuals are identical, except that some prefer rectangular pools and others oval ones, then the optimal constellation of clubs sorts individuals into oval and rectangular pool clubs.[2] Some differences in tastes for the public good can be accommodated efficiently in a single club, however. For example, if some individuals wish to swim every day and others only once a week, this heterogeneity of preferences can be efficiently handled by charging the different members different fees for the club service. If the costs of providing the public good are positively related to use, then differences in preferences for the intensity of consumption of the public good require user fees to obtain an optimal allocation of costs and use (Sandler and Tschirhart, 1984; Cornes and Sandler, 1986, pp. 179–84).

If the constellation of preferences and technologies for providing excludable public goods is such that the number of optimally constituted clubs, which can be formed in a society of a given size, is large, then an efficient allocation of these excludable public goods through the voluntary association of individuals into clubs can be envisaged. Pauly (1967, p. 317) compares the rules or charter of the club to a social contract unanimously accepted by all members, and the theory of clubs, under these assumptions, is obviously much in the spirit of the contractarian and voluntary exchange approaches to public choice and public finance. With large numbers of alternative clubs available, each individual can guarantee himself the equal benefits for an equal share of the costs assumed above, since any effort to discriminate against him will induce his exit into a competing club, or the initiation of a

2. Buchanan (1965a), and McGuire (1974).

new one. If optimal club sizes are large relative to the population, however, discrimination is possible and stable equilibria may not exist. With an optimal club size of two-thirds of the population, for example, only one such club can exist. If it forms, those not in it are motivated to lure members away by offering disproportionate shares of the benefits gained from expanding the smaller club. But the remaining members of the larger club are motivated to maintain club size, and can attract new members by offering the full benefits of membership in the big club. And so on. No stable distribution of club sizes and benefits need exist (Pauly, 1967, 1970). Analytically, the problem is identical to the emptiness of the core in the presence of externalities discussed in Chapter 2, or more generally the cycling problem (see Section D*).

Even when a stable constellation of clubs exists, when optimal club sizes are large relative to the population's size, not all individuals may be part of an optimally constituted club. Although the voluntary association of individuals to form clubs increases their utilities, it may not maximize the aggregate utility of the entire population, defined to include those not a part of optimally sized clubs (Ng, 1974; Cornes and Sandler, 1986, pp. 179–84). We illustrate this point in Section C with a slightly different form of club.

B.   Voting-with-the-feet

In the theory of clubs, exclusion from the consumption of the public good is assumed to be possible through some institutional device. A fence is built around the swimming pool and only club members are allowed inside the fence. Even when there is no fence around the swimming pool, however, those individuals who live a great distance from the pool are effectively excluded from its use by the costs of getting to it. When the consumption of a public good requires that one be at a certain location, distance can serve as an exclusionary device. If different bundles of public goods of this type are offered at different locations, a spatial division of the population into "clubs" of homogeneous tastes would arise from individuals choosing to reside in that local polity, which offered them their ideal constellation of public goods. No ballots would have to be cast. All preferences would be revealed through the silent voting-with-the-feet of individuals exiting and entering communities, a possibility first noted by Charles Tiebout (1956).

In contrast to the disappointing promise of majority rule, the utopian quality of the unanimity rule, and the imposing complexity of the newer, more sophisticated procedures, Buchanan's clubs and Tiebout's voting-with-the-feet seem to accomplish the task of revealing individual preferences by the surprisingly simple device of allowing people to sort themselves out into groups of like tastes. The efficiency and mutual gain Wicksell sought from the unanimity rule in his voluntary exchange approach to collective action arise through the voluntary association of individuals in clubs or local polities.

Buchanan described the properties of a single club, and the optimality conditions (9.6 and 9.7) for membership in a single, isolated club. Tiebout described the process of voting-with-the-feet as one that could achieve Pareto optimality with respect to the entire population. But a local polity is a form of club, and clubs are a type of polity. Thus, conditions 9.6 and 9.7 must also hold for a single local polity, and a world of clubs must in principle offer the same potential as the Tiebout model does for achieving Pareto efficiency defined over the entire population. Moreover, any problems of stability or Pareto inefficiency that one can show exist with respect to one model, probably hold for the other.

The following conditions to ensure the global optimality of excludable public goods provision thus apply to both the clubs and voting-with-the-feet models.[3]

1. Full mobility of all citizens.
2. Full knowledge of the characteristics of all communities (clubs).
3. Availability of a range of community (club) options spanning the full range of public good possibilities desired by citizens.
4. Absence of scale economies in producing the public good and/or smallness of the optimum scale of production relative to the population size.
5. Absence of spillovers across communities (clubs).
6. Absence of geographical constraints on individuals with respect to their earnings.

Assumptions 1 and 6 are peculiar to the voting-with-the-feet model, but some sort of freedom-of-association assumption is certainly implicit in the clubs model as a model of global optimality. Some special difficulties with respect to assumption 6 are discussed below. Assumptions 1 and 5 tend to work at cross-purposes. The larger the community, the more costly it is to leave it, and the lower mobility is. Thus, exit is a more reasonable alternative from small than from large communities. On the other hand, the smaller the community, the more likely it is that the benefits from the provision of any specific public good will spill over onto other communities and cause externalities across communities and non-Pareto allocations.

Assumptions 2 and 3 raise complementary issues. The basic argument assumes a full range of possible baskets of public goods available at the start. But how is this spectrum of opportunities established? Two possibilities come to mind: Some central authority or auctioneer could set up different local communities and clubs with different baskets of public goods and inform all potential citizens of the characteristics of each community club. There are two obvious difficulties to this resolution of the problem, however. First, assum-

---

3. See Tiebout (1956); Buchanan and Wagner (1970); Buchanan and Goetz (1972); McGuire (1972); Oates (1972); Pestieau (1977).

ing a central authority knows what baskets of public goods must be supplied disposes of a large portion of the preference revelation problem, which the model is supposed to solve. If the central authority knew which people had which preferences, it could simply assign individuals to the appropriate club or local polity. Second, even if it is to some extent feasible, this solution to the preference revelation problem violates the decentralized spirit of the Buchanan and Tiebout models.[4]

More appropriate is the assumption that entrepreneurs exist who create clubs and polities, where needed, for a share of the "profits" generated from providing a desired quantity or package of public goods. These clubs and polities could be set up on a not-for-profit basis, in which case the rewards to the entrepreneurial founders would, presumably, come in a nonpecuniary form, for example, the power and prestige associated with founding an organization. Tiebout uses the term "city managers" rather than mayors for the local polities' leadership, presumably in recognition of their entrepreneurial role.

It must also be stressed, however, that many goods with significant joint supply characteristics, but for which exclusion is practicable, are provided by profit-seeking entrepreneurs. Television program production and broadcasting is a good example of an activity with significant joint supply properties, but for which exclusion is possible with the help of scrambling devices and coaxial cables. Thus, one finds private firms offering packages of television programs for fees alongside publicly provided program packages. The former are basically consumption clubs formed to consume a particular bundle of television programs, while the publicly broadcast programs are available to citizens only near the points of transmission. Land developers receive an entrepreneurial return for the particular constellation of public and private good characteristics that they combine in the communities they create.

As always with a market-provided good or service, full Pareto optimality cannot be assumed unless the good is provided competitively. Moreover, the provision of excludable public goods by a monopoly raises efficiency issues that go beyond those that exist for the private good monopoly (Brennan and Walsh, 1981; Burns and Walsh, 1981). Nevertheless, the presence of many profit-making firms in competition with nonprofit clubs and local polities in providing excludable public goods (television, recreation and sports, education, travel, health care) attests to the importance of the entrepreneurial function in providing excludable public goods.

Although clubs can be single (swimming) or multiple (tennis, golf, and swimming), local polities inevitably supply a number of goods and services with the potential for supplying many more. As the number of public good dimensions increases, the plausibility of assumption 3 declines. With one

4. See Pauly (1970) and McGuire (1972).

public good issue to decide, such as the proportion of tulips in the public square, 101 communities suffice to allow each individual to consume his optimal fraction of tulips to the nearest percentile. With two issues, the proportions of oaks and tulips, the number of communities needed to ensure Pareto optimality leaps to 101 squared. Each additional public good raises the number of polities required to a higher exponent. If the number of public goods is very large, one reaches a solution in which the number of communities equals the size of the population. Each community individual becomes a polity with a basket of public-private goods (garden, woods) tailored to his own tastes, a possible consequence of the model that Tiebout himself recognized.[5]

C.   Global optimality via voting-with-the-feet

Pareto optimality in a global sense requires that the incremental change in net benefits to the community that an individual joins equal the incremental loss to the community he leaves:

$$\sum_{i=1}^{n} \Delta U_A^i = -\sum_{i=1}^{m} \Delta U_B^i. \tag{9.8}$$

The change in utility of the nth individual to join community A is his total utility from being in $A(U_A^n)$, just as his loss from leaving B is his total utility in B, U_B^m. Equation (9.8) can thus be rewritten as

$$U_A^n + \sum_{i=1}^{n-1} \Delta U_A^i = U_B^m + -\sum_{i=1}^{m-1} \Delta U_B^i. \tag{9.9}$$

In a world of pure competition, each factor owner's marginal product is the same in all industries and areas. If externalities and other market failures are not present, the welfare of others is unaffected by one's location. All ΔU^i are zero except for the moving individual, and he naturally locates in his most favored community. With public goods present, the ΔU^i for individuals in a community are positive for an additional entrant, as the total costs of the public good become spread over a larger number of individuals. A new entrant thus confers positive externalities for a community producing a locally pure public good. Alternatively, a new entrant can produce "congestion" costs, negative externalities, to a community that has grown beyond the optimal size for its locally provided public goods. In either case, since the moving individual compares only his utility levels in the two communities and

---

5. See also Pestieau (1977).

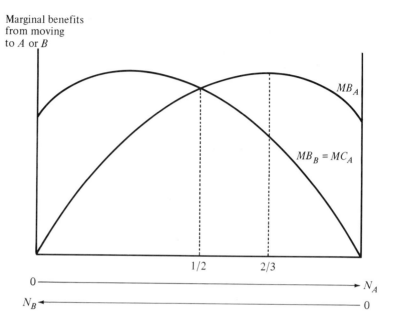

Figure 9.2. Marginal benefit from migration curves.

ignores the marginal effects of his move on the others (the ΔU^i's in A and B), voting-with-the-feet in general will not produce Pareto optimality in the presence of public goods and externalities.[6]

To see how a non–Pareto-efficient equilibrium can emerge, assume that there exist only two communities in which an individual can live, A and B. Each community is identical as are all of the residents. Each community provides a public good, which is optimally provided when $\frac{2}{3}$ of the potential residents of the two communities consume it. Thus, there are enough individuals for only one, optimally sized community. The situation is depicted in Figure 9.2. Curve MB_A represents the *average* benefits to a member of community A from membership in the community as a function of community size. These first rise as a result of the economies of scale property of the public good, and then begin to fall as crowding costs begin to outweigh the benefits from cost sharing. The curve MB_A also represents the *marginal* benefits to a member of community B, from migrating to A. MB_B is the mirror image of MB_A defined with respect to the population of B.

6. See Buchanan and Wagner (1970); Buchanan and Goetz (1972); Flatters, Henderson, and Mieszkowski (1974); Pestieau (1977).

The population of B is read from right to left along the horizontal axis. MB_B is also the marginal cost (MC_A) to a citizen of B from migrating to A. As usual, individual equilibrium occurs where marginal cost intersects marginal benefits *from below*. No such intersection exists in the figure. The intersection at an equal division of population is a local minimum. At any distribution in which one community has a higher population than the other, benefits are higher from membership in the larger community. Migration is from the smaller to the larger community, and this continues until all of the population enters into one of the communities. If congestion costs rise significantly, MB_A might decline fast enough following its peak to intersect MC_A. This would yield an equilibrium for the larger of the two cities at a size above its optimum, but below that of the entire population. In either case, however, the equilibrium city sizes achieved via voluntary migration are not those that maximize the average utility level of all individuals in the two communities. The latter would occur in this example when the population is equally divided between the two communities. This distribution of population maximizes the *average* benefits from *being* in either community. But, once this point is left, the *marginal* benefits from switching to the larger community exceed those of staying, and population redistributes itself until the stable but inefficient equilibrium is obtained (Buchanan and Wagner, 1970).

Although the assumption that the optimal-sized community is more than half the total population may seem unrealistic when one thinks of an area and population as large as the United States, often the potential migrant may not be considering such a wide spectrum of options. The relevant choice may be staying in small town B or moving to nearby large city A. Within this circumscribed range of choice, the optimal-sized community may be more than half the combined populations of the two communities, and the tendency for overpopulating the central city may become evident.

If the optimal-sized polity is less than half the population, the marginal benefits and cost schedules intersect and yield a stable equilibrium with the population evenly divided between the two communities. This equilibrium does result in a maximization of the potential benefits to each citizen, given the constraint that there should be but two communities. When additional communities can be created, and the optimal-sized community is small relative to the total population, we return to a Tieboutian world in which free migration and the creation of new fiscal clubs can be envisaged as resulting in a set of communities, each of optimal size.

Additional complications are introduced into the Tieboutian world, however, if individuals earn part of their incomes outside the community. Assume again two communities with identical production possibilities, and individuals of identical tastes. Within any community, each individual receives the same wage, w, from supplying his services to the local production process, and a differential income, $r_i \geq 0$, that is tied to him and not to his location. This income can be thought of as coming from dividends, as in Tiebout's example, or as rents on assets peculiar to the individual, such as the income of a recording star. We shall refer to this income as simply rental income, covering all nonlocation-specific sources. Now consider two communities with equal numbers of workers, identical production possibility frontiers, and identical tax structures. In equilibrium the total private and public good production in community A must equal the sum of its rental and wage income:

$$\sum_{}^{N_A} Y_i + X = N_A w_A + \sum_{}^{N_A} r_i. \tag{9.10}$$

The utility of a resident of A is given by

$$U_i(Y_i, X, N_A), \tag{9.11}$$

as before. Substituting for X from (9.10) into (9.11), we have

$$U_i(Y_i, N_A w_A + \Sigma r_i - \Sigma Y_i, N_A). \tag{9.12}$$

The assumption of identical tax structures implies that the individual can purchase the same bundles of private goods, Y_i, in both communities. With equal populations and production possibilities, N_A and w_A equal N_B and w_B, respectively. Assuming the public good is not an inferior good, some of any additional rental income in A will go to increased public good production. Thus, $\Sigma r_i - \Sigma Y_i$ is larger in A than in B if Σr_i is larger in A than in B. Since public goods enter an individual's utility function with a positive sign, an individual is better off joining the community with the higher rents, assuming all other community characteristics are the same.

If the communities have different rental incomes, the same set of tax structures may not be optimal in both communities. Nevertheless, if tastes are the same, an individual always receives a more attractive tax–public good package from the community with higher rental income.

Higher rental incomes thus play the same role in attracting individuals from the other community as does a larger population in the presence of joint supply characteristics. Indeed, from (9.12) it can be seen that rental income, the wage rate, and the population size all enter the utility function in the same way through the public good term. Thus, any increase in population, the wage rate, or rental income, ceteris paribus, increases an individual's utility by increasing the quantity of public goods available. An increase in population also enters the utility function negatively, however, through the congestion effect represented by the third argument in the utility function. Increasing population can also be expected to drive the wage rate down, reducing an individual's command over private goods, and thereby his welfare. In contrast, higher rental income has an unambiguous positive impact.

Just as an individual's welfare is higher if he enters the community with the higher rental income, the community's welfare is higher, the higher the rental income of any new entrant. The depressing effect on wages and costs in terms of increased congestion from a new member are identical, but the benefits in terms of increased tax revenue to finance public good provision are obviously greater, the greater the newcomer's rental income.[7] If the community has expanded to the point where the marginal gain from spreading the public good's costs over another taxpayer just equals the marginal cost in terms of reduced wages and congestion, adding another individual who is just a wage earner makes the community worse off. But, if he has a high enough rental income, the additional gains from financing an expansion of public good supply out of this rental income outweigh these costs. Regardless of what the community's size is, an additional member can always increase the welfare of all existing members, if he brings with him a high enough rental income.

In the same way that full mobility between communities may not bring about a Pareto-optimal distribution of the population, where economies of scale in public good production are large, full mobility is unlikely to bring about a Pareto-optimal distribution of the population in the presence of rents. In the example above, the socially optimal distribution of the population is that which equates the marginal product of a worker in each community. This occurs at equal community sizes. But if the distribution of rents differs between the two communities, migration toward the community with the higher rents will occur. This migration will continue until the fall in marginal product and rise in congestion costs is large enough to offset the advantage that this community has from higher rents, and average utility levels in the two communities are equal.

To achieve the socially optimal distribution of population, taxes and subsidies must be levied on either residence in or movement in and out of a given community. One possibility is to grant a central authority the right to make transfers across communities. Such an authority would then determine what the socially optimum distribution of population was, and levy taxes and subsidies to achieve this optimum distribution. In the general case, the central authority would attempt to achieve the equilibrium condition given in equation (9.9). This requires a tax equal to $\Sigma_{i=1}^{n} \Delta U_A^i$ on community A, if A is the community that is, or would become, too large, and a subsidy equal to $\Sigma_{i=1}^{m} \Delta U_B^i$ to community B if it would lose population. If the only difference between the two communities were the level of rental income, the policy would be simple to implement. The central authority would levy a tax on

7. This effect is particularly apparent in the Flatters et al. (1974, pp. 101–2) model in which a golden rule is obtained in which all rents go to public good production and all wages to private good production. This model is based on different assumptions from those of the discussion here, however.

rental income in the community with higher initial rental income and offer a subsidy to the community with lower rental income to bring about equal rental incomes and populations in both communities.[8]

Alternatively, Pareto optimality can be achieved in a decentralized way, by granting each community the right to tax immigration and emigration. If the externalities for community A from immigration were positive, it could offer a subsidy to newcomers equal to $\Sigma \, \Delta U^i_A$ and levy an identical tax on emigration. If B did the same, all individuals would be forced to internalize the external costs their moving entailed, and Pareto efficiency would be obtained.[9]

Although these alternatives have identical efficiency outcomes, they differ both in spirit and in their equity properties. The latter weds Tiebout's decentralized voting-with-the-feet with the theory of exclusive clubs to produce a decentralized solution to the population allocation problem. The enactment of such a system of taxes and subsidies by local communities immediately provides communities favored by natural characteristics, population size, income, and so on with a valuable property right, which they exercise by taxing members outside their community (i.e., those who would have entered in the absence of the tax-subsidy scheme). The centralized solution vests the entire population with a property right in both communities and achieves allocational efficiency by taxing *all* members of the favored community to subsidize the disfavored community.

The difference in policies can be most easily seen by considering again our rent example but assuming that individual rents are not tied to given individuals but are locational rents accruing to all residents of a given community. Granting the right to tax migration into the community with higher rents to its residents would allow them to achieve permanently higher utility levels than would be achieved in the less-favored community. Those who were lucky enough or quick enough to be born or move into a geographically more desirable area would forever be better off than those left in the less desirable areas. In contrast, the centralized solution would equate utility levels across communities by taxing the higher rent areas and subsidizing the low-rent ones.

Even when rental incomes are tied to individuals rather than locations, Tieboutian revelation of preferences coupled with local taxes and subsidies can raise equity issues. As noted earlier, a community can always be made better off by admitting someone whose rental income is high enough. Once a community has reached its optimal size for sharing the costs of public goods, it might adopt a policy of, say, admitting only new members who bring with them a rental income above the average. This can be accomplished by estab-

8. Flatters et al. (1974), McMillan (1975).
9. Buchanan (1971); Buchanan and Goetz (1972).

lishing zoning requirements on lot sizes and apartment dwellings that effectively screen out those with incomes below a given level. The mobile individual, on the other hand, is better off joining a community with greater rental income than he receives. The intersection of these two strategies could be a sorting out of individuals into communities of equal rental incomes. The identical incomes and preferences assumption that Buchanan assumed for convenience in initiating the study of clubs is a plausible outcome to a Tieboutian search for optimum communities (Buchanan and Goetz, 1972).

D.*   Clubs and the core

The above discussion raises three issues with regard to the global properties of a world of clubs and voting-with-the-feet preference revelation: (1) whether an equilibrium distribution of the population among the clubs (communities) exists, (2) whether any equilibrium that occurs is Pareto efficient, and (3) what the redistributive-equity properties of the outcomes are. To further illustrate these issues we consider a simple example first presented by Brian Ellickson (1973).

Assume that each individual i has the hyperbolic utility function $u_i = x_i g$ defined over private good x and public good g. Each individual in a club consumes the same quantity of g. Since $\partial u_i / \partial x_i = g$, the marginal utility of the private good is the same for all individuals within a club. We are working with transferable utility in x.

The unit costs of providing the good g to clubs of size 1, 2, and 3 are respectively a, b, and c. If $a = b = c$, we have a pure public good. If $a = \frac{1}{2}b = \frac{1}{3}c$ we have a pure private good. If the good is a pure public good, the optimal club size is the population. If it is a pure private good, optimal club size is one. We assume a public good with congestion costs so that

$$a < b < 2a$$

$$b < c < (3/2)b.$$

Consider first the quantity of g chosen and utility level obtained when an individual acts alone. Let w_i be i's wealth. We maximize u_i subject to the budget constraint $w_i = x_i + ag$; that is,

$$L_i = x_i g + \lambda(w_i - x_i - ag). \tag{9.13}$$

Maximizing with respect to g and x_i,

$$\partial L_i / \partial g = x_i - \lambda a = 0 \tag{9.14}$$

$$\partial L_i / \partial x_i = g - \lambda = 0. \tag{9.15}$$

Solving for x_i,

$$x_i = ag. \tag{9.16}$$

From the budget constraint and (9.16)

$$w_i = x_i + ag = 2ag, \tag{9.17}$$

from which

$$ag = \frac{w_i}{2} \tag{9.18}$$

and

$$u_i = x_i g = ag^2 = \frac{w_i^2}{4a} . \tag{9.19}$$

Equation (9.19) gives the security level of utility for any individual i, the level of utility i can achieve acting alone. No individual joins a club or community unless she can secure a utility of at least $w_i^2/4a$.

Let us now derive the conditions under which a club of two forms. The Samuelsonian condition for Pareto optimality requires that the sum of the marginal rates of substitution (MRS) for the two club members equals the marginal cost of the public good; that is,

$$MRS_i + MRS_j = b. \tag{9.20}$$

Now

$$MRS_i = \frac{\partial u_i/\partial g}{\partial u_i/\partial x} = \frac{x_i}{g} , \tag{9.21}$$

so that

$$\frac{x_i}{g} + \frac{x_j}{g} = b \tag{9.22}$$

or

$$x_i + x_j = bg. \tag{9.23}$$

The combined budget constraint for the club is

$$w_i + w_j = x_i + x_j + bg. \tag{9.24}$$

From (9.23) and (9.24) we obtain the Pareto-optimal quantity of the public good for a club of two.

$$g = \frac{w_i + w_j}{2b} . \tag{9.25}$$

To be induced to join a club of two, each individual must achieve a utility level of at least what she can achieve acting alone. From (9.24) we can write i's utility as

$$u_i = x_i g = (w_i + w_j - x_j - bg)g = (w_i + w_j)g - bg^2 - x_j g. \tag{9.26}$$

Now $x_j g$ is j's utility. If we set that at $w_j^2/4a$, the minimum level j is willing to accept and be in the club, then whether a club of two forms can be determined by seeing whether i's utility in the club exceeds her security level, that is, whether

$$u_i = (w_i + w_j)g - bg^2 - \frac{w_j^2}{4a} \geq \frac{w_i^2}{4a} . \tag{9.27}$$

Using (9.25) to replace g and some algebra yields

$$\frac{(w_i + w_j)^2}{b} \geq \frac{w_i^2 + w_j^2}{a} \tag{9.28}$$

as the necessary condition for a club of two to form. Whether a club forms depends on the respective wealth of i and j and the relative costs of supplying g in the two contexts. To see what is involved, assume that $w_j = \alpha w_i$, where $0 \leq \alpha \leq 1$. Then for (9.28) to hold the following condition must be satisfied

$$\frac{1 + 2\alpha + \alpha^2}{1 + \alpha^2} \geq \frac{b}{a} . \tag{9.29}$$

Now both sides of (9.29) lie in the range between 1 and 2, but the lower α is the lower the left-hand side of (9.29) is. For a club of two to form, j's income must be sufficiently high relative to i's to allow her share of the costs of g to be large enough to compensate i for the crowding effect j's joining the club has (i.e., b's being greater than a).

The condition for the Pareto-optimal provision of the public good to a club of three requires that

$$g = \frac{w_i + w_j + w_k}{2c} . \tag{9.30}$$

In a manner analogous to the above demonstrations, one can show that the value of a coalition of three, $V(ijk)$, is $(w_i + w_j + w_k)^2/4c$. For the grand coalition to form, (9.31) and (9.32) must be satisfied:

$$V(ijk) \geq V(i) + V(j) + V(k) \tag{9.31}$$

$$V(ijk) \geq V(ij) + V(k)$$

$$V(ijk) \geq V(jk) + V(i)$$
$$V(ijk) \geq V(ik) + V(j),$$

(9.32)

where $V(i) = w_i^2/4a$, and $V(ij) = (w_i + w_j)^2/4b$. Suppose now that i and j have the same incomes, and k's income is α fraction of i's; that is,

$$w_i = w_j = w$$

$$w_k = \alpha w.$$

Consider just the implications of (9.32). Note first that an outcome in which i and j form a club dominates an outcome in which either i or j play alone and the other forms a club with k:

$$V(ij) + V(k) > V(jk) + V(i) = V(ik) + V(j)$$

(9.33)

since

$$\frac{(2w)^2}{4b} + \frac{\alpha^2 w^2}{4a} > \frac{(1 + \alpha)^2 w^2}{4b} + \frac{w^2}{4a}$$

if $b/a < 2$ and $\alpha < 1$. Thus, if only a club of two forms, it will be the wealthier two individuals that form the club. For the poorer k to be admitted, (9.34) must hold:

$$\frac{(2 + \alpha)^2 w^2}{4c} > \frac{4w^2}{4b} + \frac{\alpha^2 w^2}{4a}.$$

(9.34)

The smaller c is relative to b and a, and the larger α is, the more likely (9.34) is to be satisfied. The poorer k will be invited to join the club by i and j, if her income is high enough.

Now assume that $\alpha = \frac{1}{3}$, $a = 1$, $b = \frac{3}{2}$, and $c = 2$. Given these parameter values, (9.34) does not hold and a club of three does not form. A club of the two wealthier individuals will form, however, since $4w^2/4b > 2w^2/4a$ with $b = \frac{3}{2}$ and $a = 1$. If the two wealthier individuals can both form a club and keep k out, they will. If, however, it is not possible to prevent individuals from moving into the community, k may choose to do so. Whether she chooses to join the community will depend on her assigned tax share once there. If, for example, the community were required to finance g by charging all members the Lindahl tax price for g, k would be better off in the community than if she remained outside and provided g for herself. Her Lindahl tax price is her *MRS*, which is x_k/g. Thus, from the budget constraint,

$$w_k = x_k + \frac{x_k}{g} \cdot g$$

(9.35)

or

$$x_k = w_k/2. \tag{9.36}$$

Half of k's income goes to pay for g, and half is left for private good consumption. Given her Lindahl tax share, her utility in the community of three is

$$u_k = x_k g = \frac{\alpha w}{2} \frac{(2 + \alpha)w}{2c} = \frac{7}{72} w^2, \tag{9.37}$$

while playing the game alone she has only

$$u_k = \frac{\alpha^2 w^2}{4a} = \frac{w^2}{36}. \tag{9.38}$$

Thus, k will choose to join the community if she can, even though the aggregate utility of the community is lower with her in it than it is when she is outside it. It should also be obvious that k could choose to move to the richer community even if she left behind other k's who were made worse off by her departure from their community.

Even though the club of three provides lower aggregate utility than the club of two plus k playing the game alone, the effective redistribution from the richer two members to the poorer one when g is provided to all three members and financed at Lindahl tax prices makes her entry into the community to her advantage. We witness here exactly the same kind of Pareto-inefficient redistribution that we observed in Chapter 4 when a pure private good was provided to a community at equal quantities *as if* it were a public good and financed at Lindahl tax prices.

The Pareto inferiority of the club-of-three solution in this example implies that i and j would be better off bribing k to stay out of the community, if her entry requires that she be charged only the Lindahl tax price for g. They would be still better off, of course, if they could prevent her from entering by forcing her to pay more than her Lindahl price, by charging her an entrance fee, or by some other institutional device (e.g., a zoning requirement).

Finally, we show that when the grand coalition is not in the core, no core may exist, even though a coalition of two can provide its members with higher utilities than when they play alone. Assume $w_i = w_j = w_k = w$. Let a, b, and c be such that

$$V(ijk) = \frac{(3w)^2}{4c} < \frac{4w^2}{4b} + \frac{w^2}{4a} = V(ij) + V(k) > \frac{3w^2}{4a}$$

$$\frac{3w^2}{4a} = V(i) + V(j) + V(k). \tag{9.39}$$

At least one member of the $i - j$ coalition must pay at most her Lindahl tax price so that this individual's utility is at least

$$u_i = \frac{w}{2} \cdot \frac{2w}{2b} = \frac{2w^2}{4b} \ . \tag{9.40}$$

But (9.39) implies that

$$\frac{4w^2}{4b} > \frac{2w^2}{4a} = 2V(k). \tag{9.41}$$

Thus, a member of the i-j coalition who pays at most her Lindahl tax price must have higher utility than the individual left outside of the coalition. The outside individual k must be able to offer the member of i-j paying at least the Lindahl tax price a more attractive proposal to form a two-person coalition and i-j cannot be sustained. We have here precisely the same kind of instability we confronted in Chapter 2 in the presence of multiple externalities (Aivazian and Callen, 1981).

E.   Voting-with-the-feet: empirical evidence

Two implications of the Tiebout model are readily testable: (1) whether or not individuals do move in response to local government expenditure-tax offerings, and (2) whether the effect of this migration process is to sort people out into groups of homogeneous tastes consuming the bundles of public goods of their choice.[10] Both of these implications have received strong empirical support.

An examination of responses to survey questions in the Columbus, Ohio, area in 1966 indicated a significant correlation between individual perceptions that there were problems facing the neighborhood and intentions to move (Orbell and Uno, 1972). Moreover, there was a greater tendency in urban areas to resort to exit instead of voice than there was in the suburbs. Individuals appeared to feel that voice is a more effective option in suburbs than it is in the city.

Some evidence exists linking migration patterns to the levels of local public services. People move toward communities supplying greater levels of non-welfare public services, and less consistently away from communities with high tax rates.[11]

As in so many areas, California has led the world in the increasing trend toward greater mobility, with Los Angeles being the archetypical late-twentieth century city. If the Tiebout process succeeds at sorting people into

10. A third possible implication, that housing values are bid up in high expenditure/tax communities (Oates, 1969) is more problematic and is not reviewed here. See, however, Edel and Sclar (1974), Hamilton (1976), and Epple, Zelenitz, and Visscher (1978).
11. For a review of the literature up to 1979, see Cebula (1979). For an update, see Cebula and Kafoglis (1986).

Table 9.1. *Frequency distribution of income homogeneity indexes, Los Angeles County municipalities, 1950, 1970*

	0.333–0.339	0.340–0.349	0.350–0.369	0.370–0.379	0.400+	Total
1950	25	5	5	3	4	42
	(0.60)	(0.12)	(0.12)	(0.07)	(0.10)	(100)
1970	9	13	11	4	5	42
(old cities)	(0.21)	(0.31)	(0.26)	(0.10)	(0.12)	(100)
1970	1	9	12	1	7	30
(new cities)	(0.03)	(0.30)	(0.40)	(0.03)	(0.23)	(100)
1970	12	22	23	5	13	75
(all cities includ-	(0.16)	(0.29)	(0.31)	(0.07)	(0.17)	(100)
ing 3 old 1950						
cities for which						
1950 data were						
missing)						

Note: Percentages in parentheses.
Source: Miller, *Cities by Contract*, Cambridge, MA: MIT Press, 1981, p. 134.

more homogeneous local communities, then the effects of the process should be apparent in Los Angeles. They are.

Gary Miller (1981, chs. 6, 7) computed Herfindahl-like indices of income inequality (the sum of the squares of the percentages of the population in different income strata) for municipalities in Los Angeles County in 1950 and 1970. Since he used only three income strata, complete income heterogeneity would imply an index of 0.333, while complete homogeneity (all residents in the same income strata) would imply an index of 1.0. In 1950, 60 percent of the 42 cities for which data were available were virtually indistinguishable from the maximum degree of heterogeneity, and from Los Angeles County as a whole (index = 0.335) (see Table 9.1). Only 10 percent of 1950 municipalities fell into the most homogeneous category (0.400+).

The distribution of indices in 1970 is shifted distinctly toward greater homogeneity, with only 16 percent of the municipalities in the most heterogeneous category and 17 percent in the most homogeneous category, even though Los Angeles County as a whole remained heterogeneous in income in 1970 (index = 0.334), as it was in 1950. Perhaps the strongest evidence that the Tiebout process does result in increased income homogeneity comes from the 30 newly created municipalities. To the extent that new municipalities come into existence to satisfy demands unmet by existing communities, their composition should accord most closely, in an age of high mobility, with the Tiebout hypothesis. Only 1 of the 30 newly created municipalities had income heterogeneity comparable to that of the entire county; almost one-fourth of the new municipalities fell into the most homogeneous category. In Miller's study, it appears to be largely a common preference for lower taxes and the avoidance of the redistributive outlays of the larger, older cities that drives the formation of new, suburban communities. Miller also presents evidence of increasing racial homogeneity within, and increasing heterogeneity across Los Angeles municipalities between 1950 and 1970.

Hamilton, Mills, and Puryear (1975) find less inequality of income within SMSAs, the greater the number of school districts from which citizens can choose, and in general a better fit to Tiebout-model variables for suburban than for central city observations. Similar results have been reported by Eberts and Gronberg (1981). The Tiebout process is again found to work as predicted, and in so doing to produce less dispersion of incomes within the local polity.

Further, corroborative evidence is presented by Munley (1982) and Gramlich and Rubinfeld (1982a). Tiebout sorting should be more complete the greater the number of different political jurisdictions in which a mobile citizen can choose to live. Consistent with this prediction is Munley's finding that the dispersion of voter demands for education in Long Island, New York, decreased as the number of school jurisdictions in a geographic area increased. Similarly, Gramlich and Rubinfeld find a smaller residual variance in expenditure demands in the Detroit metropolitan area than in other parts of Michigan where a smaller number of local communities are available to the citizen.

Implicit in the Tiebout process is the assumption that when homogeneous demand citizens form a community, the community supplies the level of expenditures that the community demands. This part of the Tiebout model is supported by Gramlich and Rubinfeld's (1982a, p. 556) finding that two-thirds of Detroit metropolitan area voters surveyed wished to see no change in government expenditures, and the average desired change was only -1 percent. Although the percentage of voters desiring no change in expenditures (60) was high throughout the rest of Michigan, that this percentage is lower than for Detroit suggests that the greater number of communities in which Detroit metropolitan area residents can choose to reside allows them to locate in communities that better provide them with the level of expenditures they demand.

Jan Brueckner (1982) found that property values in 54 Massachusetts communities suggested neither an over- nor an underprovision of local public goods, as the Tiebout hypothesis predicts.

F.   Voluntary association, allocational efficiency, and distributional equity

Wicksell's voluntary exchange approach achieves allocational efficiency by imposing a unanimity rule on the polity so that each collective decision must benefit all before it can pass. The approach assumes from the beginning that a predefined polity and citizenry exist.

The theory of clubs and voting-with-the-feet seek to determine a Pareto-optimal distribution of public goods through the voluntary association of individuals of like tastes. Here the dimensions of the polity and citizenship are outcomes of the "voting" process. These processes generally achieve Pareto optimality by grouping individuals into clubs and polities of homogeneous tastes. In the extreme, they satisfy Kramer's (1973) severe condition for consistent majority rule decisions, that all individuals have identical indifference maps, through the imposition of a silent unanimity rule.[12] These processes can realistically be assumed to come close to satisfying this goal, when, relative to the size of the population, (1) the number of public goods is small, and/or (2) the number of distinct preferences for combinations of public goods is small. Since *the* task of public choice is the revelation of (differing) individual preferences for public goods, club formation and voting-with-the-feet, in part, solve the public choice problem by limiting its scope.

Despite these qualifications, the ability to exclude some individuals from the benefits of a public good remains a potentially powerful mechanism for revealing individual preferences. If A seeks the construction of tennis courts and B a golf course, then in a community in which all must consume the same bundle of public goods and preferences are revealed by voting, regardless of what the eventual outcome is, it is likely to involve nonoptimal quantities of at least one good for one of the voters. This voter, say, A, is then worse off than she would have been had B also preferred tennis to golf and was willing to bear a larger share of this sport's costs. If A were incumbent to the community and B outside, A would clearly prefer that others with preferences closer to hers join the community, and, if it were in her power might discriminate in their favor over B.

None of this is very troubling if the public goods are tennis and golf, and the polities private clubs. No one objects too strenuously to a tennis club's restricting membership to those who want to play tennis. But the implications are less comforting for more general definitions of public goods. As we have seen, when individuals have positive income elasticities of demand for public goods, they can benefit from being in a community with incomes higher on average than their own from the additional units of the public good it provides. Even when each individual is taxed her marginal evaluation of the public good—that is, the Lindahl price—an effective redistribution from rich to poor occurs through the egalitarian distribution of the public good that of necessity occurs when rich and poor consume it together. But, one's income

---

12. See, also, McGuire (1974), and on the relationship between voting-with-the-feet and the unanimity rule, see Pauly (1967, p. 317).

elasticity of demand can be regarded as a sort of "taste" for a public good. If the incumbent membership of a local polity is free to exclude new members, then one can expect a sorting out of individuals into local polities of identical tastes *and* incomes, thus thwarting the possibility for this type of redistribution.

Wicksell assumed that voting on allocational issues took place following the determination of a just distribution of income. The same assumption could be made to support a voluntary association solution to the public good problem. But, here it must be recognized that the voluntary association approach is likely to affect the distribution of income, while revealing preferences for public goods. A given distribution of private incomes might be considered just when individuals reside in communities of heterogeneous income strata, so that the relatively poor benefit from the higher demands for public goods by the relatively well-to-do. The same distribution of income might be considered unjust if individuals were distributed into communities of similar income and the relatively poor could consume only those quantities of public goods which they themselves could afford to provide.

The latter is the logical outcome of the voting-with-the-feet process, and one that is coming to pass. If the resulting distribution from this process were thought to be unjust, one could correct it by making transfers across communities, but here one runs directly into the issue of the proper bounds of the polity and the rights of citizenship.

In a federalist system there are two possible ways to view citizenship. Primary citizenship can reside with the local polity, and the central polity can be thought of as a mere union or confederation of the local polities with certain powers delegated to it. Conversely, primary citizenship can reside with the central state, with the local polities being merely administrative branches of the central government and having powers delegated from above. Under the first view of the polity, it would seem that the rights of the local polity to define its own citizenship and to pick and choose entrants would dominate the right of citizens in the larger confederation to migrate, free of hindrances, to any local polity. Here we see a direct clash between two of the conditions for achieving a decentralized, efficient allocation of public goods: the full mobility assumption, and the right of the local polity to tax and subsidize migration. If primary citizenship lies with the central state, then presumably individuals would be free to enter and exit local communities without incurring locally imposed penalties. Equity issues would be viewed from the perspective of the central polity, and it would be free to engage in intergovernmental transfers.

The same distinction exists with respect to clubs. The freedom to form voluntary associations can be regarded as one of the basic rights of the individual. To exercise this right in an optimal way, club members must be free to determine the quality and quantity characteristics of the excludable public good supplied to themselves *and* the size of the club's membership. When the supply functions for excludable public goods and the size of the population allow for the formation of many, individually optimally sized clubs, voluntary club formation can achieve a Pareto-optimal allocation of resources across the whole community. The outcome is entirely analogous to the Pareto-optimal allocation of resources that voluntary actions in the market achieve when large numbers of buyers and sellers exist. Indeed, firms are merely clubs of factor owners formed to achieve the economies of joint supply in production, where the clubs discussed in this chapter arise to achieve the economies from joint supply in consumption. Once again as in the market, however, when technology and population size combine to yield but a small number of optimally sized clubs, the independent utility-maximizing decisions of individuals may not achieve an outcome that is optimal from the perspective of the entire community.

In Chapter 2 we argued that the state emerges as a low transactions costs institution for achieving the cooperative agreements necessary for Pareto optimality in the presence of public goods and externalities. By extension, clubs, local polities, and the whole federalist institutional structure of the state might be formed to minimize the transactions costs of making collective decisions (Tullock, 1969; Breton and Scott, 1978).[13] But the discussion of this chapter reveals that the creation of new political jurisdictions within the state, the assignment of functions and revenue sources to different units, and the definition of citizen rights within a federated state raise issues that go beyond transaction costs savings and allocative efficiency. They go to the heart of the normative characteristics of the polity.

G.   The theory of revolution

When neither the ballot nor the feet constitute adequate modes of expression, there is still Chairman Mao's barrel of the gun. One might expect to find more said about revolutions than has been the case, given their role in real-world politics. For the public choice analyst, the puzzle of revolutions is why individuals participate in them, and thus why they ever occur.

Consider the decision of individual i as to whether to participate in a revolution in her country, and if so how much time to contribute. She is unhappy with the present regime and anticipates benefits of β_i should the revolution succeed and a new order be imposed. The probability of this occurring is a function of the time i contributes to the revolution, t_{ir}, and the

---

13. By further analogy, clubs of factor owners, firms, arise to minimize transaction costs in production (Coase, 1937).

time all other citizens contribute, $O_{ir} = \Sigma_{j\neq i}t_{jr}$. Call this probability $\pi(t_{ir}, O_{ir})$. In addition to the gains, should the revolution succeed, i may receive personal pleasure from participating in the revolutionary movement, whether it succeeds or not, $P_i(t_{ir}, O_{ir})$.

Against these benefits must be weighed the costs of participation. Should i be caught and punished, she faces a fine or imprisonment promising a utility loss F_i. The probability that she will be caught, C_i, is a function of the time she devotes to the revolution, t_{ir}, the time others devote, O_i, and the resources expended by the regime to crush the revolution, R, that is, $C_i(t_{ir}, O_i, R)$ with expected partial derivatives

$$\frac{\partial C_i}{\partial t_{ir}} > 0, \ \frac{\partial C_i}{\partial O_i} < 0, \ \frac{\partial C_i}{\partial R} > 0.$$

In addition, by devoting time to the revolution, i forgoes income. If w is the market wage, then this opportunity cost is wt_{ir}.

The expected benefits from participating in the revolution are then

$$E_i = \beta_i\pi_i(t_{ir}, O_{ir}) + P_i(t_{ir}, O_{ir}) - F_iC_i(t_{ir}, O_i, R) - wt_{ir}. \quad (9.42)$$

Maximizing (9.42) with respect to t_{ir}, we obtain

$$\beta_i\frac{\partial \pi_i}{\partial t_{ir}} + \frac{\partial P_i}{\partial t_{ir}} = F_i\frac{\partial C_i}{\partial t_{ir}} + w \quad\quad (9.43)$$

as the condition i must satisfy when determining her optimal level of revolutionary activity. The marginal expected gain in public good benefits (β_i) from an extra hour of participation plus the marginal personal enjoyment must equal the added risk of being caught when spending another hour in the revolution plus the forgone wage from not having worked that hour.

With O_i large, the change in both π_i and C_i from an additional hour of participation for the average person will be negligible. Whether someone participates or not, and if so to what degree, thus depends almost solely on the purely personal satisfaction from participation in the revolutionary movement weighed against the forgone income from taking time away from market activity (Tullock, 1971a, 1974), a result resembling that in the voting literature.

For the average citizen, the benefits from the revolution's success are the pure public good benefits from living under one regime rather than under another. But for a few, β_i represents the benefits from a position in the new government formed after the revolution. For these leaders, both β_i and $\partial\pi/\partial t_{ir}$ may be much larger than for the average individual. Thus, it is easier to explain the participation of the leaders of a revolutionary movement using a rational choice model than the participation of the rank and file (Silver, 1974; Tullock, 1974). Note, however, that for the leaders, F_i and $\partial C_i / \partial t_{ir}$ may also be higher. Under a rational choice theory, leaders of a revolution are like entrepreneurs in the theory of the firm, risk takers with extreme optimism regarding their ability to beat the odds.

The marginal effect of an average individual's contribution to the revolution's success should fall with the aggregate contributions of others, O_i. This free-rider effect will lower t_{ir} (Olson, 1965; Austen-Smith, 1981a). But there is also safety in numbers. The marginal risk of being caught, $\partial C_i / \partial t_{ir}$, may also shift downward with an increase in the revolutionary activity of others, thereby encouraging more revolutionary participation (Gunning, 1972; De-Nardo, 1985). The personal rewards from participating in the revolution may also be characterized by the bandwagon effect and rise as others join the movement. Thus, participation levels could be characterized by increasing or diminishing returns to scale.

An increase in the resources devoted to crushing the revolution should lead to an increase in the marginal probability of getting caught, and thus discourage participation. Participation should be lower the higher the pecuniary costs, w.

Although the rational behavior approach to revolutionary activity gives some insights into why revolutions occur, it does not generate a rich harvest of testable implications. It does appear that a revolution's success is greatly affected by the resources that the regime devotes to stopping it and thereby to curbing participation (Silver, 1974; DeNardo, 1985).

Perhaps the most distinctive implication of the theory is the prediction that participation declines with the wage rate. David Austen-Smith (1981a) has also shown that it declines with a reduction in uncertainty about the wage if participants are risk-averse. Preliminary testing of these implications by Louis D. Finney (1987) indicates that the number of deaths from political violence in a country is negatively related to both the level and growth in national income, and is positively related to the standard deviation of the growth rate (a measure of uncertainty).

Although results such as Finney's are encouraging, it is yet to be seen how far a rational behavior model can go in explaining such extreme behavior as occurs in revolutions. Nevertheless, these models fill an analytical gap in the public choice literature. In a closed polity, an individual is always in danger of being "exploited" or "tyrannized" by a majority or minority of her fellow citizens. Her choices in such situations are to continue to rely on voice in the hope that the outcomes will change; to seek a new polity by migration; or to create a new one by revolution. The goal of public choice theory must be to explain all three choices.

Bibliographical notes

The discussion of efficiency and equity in a federalist system predates the public choice–Tiebout literature. See, e.g., Buchanan (1950, 1952); Scott (1950, 1952a, b); and Musgrave (1961).

Ng (1985b) shows that one cannot have efficiency with clubs formation without violating *either* equity as argued above or freedom (voluntary association).

The clubs–Tiebout literatures have been surveyed by Henderson (1979), and Sandler and Tschirhart (1980).

The properties of markets in price-excludable public goods are analyzed in Oakland (1974); Burns and Walsh (1981); Brennan and Walsh (1981); and Walsh (1986).

PART III

Public choice in a representative democracy

CHAPTER 10

Two-party competition – deterministic voting

Politicians neither love nor hate. Interest, not sentiment, governs them.

Earl of Chesterfield

. . . a candidate for the Presidency, nominated for election by the whole people, will, as a rule, be a man selected because he is not open to obvious criticism, and will therefore in all probability be a mediocrity.

Sir Henry Sumner Maine

With large numbers of voters and issues, direct democracy is impossible. Even in polities sufficiently small so that all individuals can actually come together to debate and decide issues – say, a polity of 500 – it is impossible for all individuals to present their own views, even rather briefly, on every issue. Thus the "chairman's problem" is to select individuals to represent the various positions most members of the polity are likely to hold (de Jouvenal, 1961). When the polity is too large to assemble together, representatives must be selected by some means.

The public choice literature has focused on three aspects of representative democracy: the behavior of representatives both during the campaign to be elected and while in office; the behavior of voters in choosing representatives; and the characteristics of the outcomes under representative democracy. The public choice approach assumes that representatives, like voters, are rational, economic men bent on maximizing their utilities. Although it is natural to assume that voters' utilities are functions of the baskets of public goods and services they consume, the "natural assumption" concerning what maximizes a representative's utility is not as easily made. The fundamental hypothesis of Anthony Downs's (1957, p. 28) model is that "parties formulate policies in order to win elections, rather than win elections in order to formulate policies." His study was the first to explore systematically the implications of this assumption, and the literature has developed around the framework he laid. Only recently has this assumption been seriously challenged (Wittmann, 1973, 1977), but the Downsian model remains the most frequently employed formulation of the problem.[1]

Much of the literature on public choice and political science has centered on

1. For a well-documented defense of the vote-maximizing assumption, see Mayhew (1974).

representative democracy because it is the dominant mode of political expression. Although many of the issues discussed in this literature have been described here in the context of a model of direct democracy or committees, the committees in mind are often assemblies of representatives and the coalitions are parties. Many of the problems and results already discussed carry over almost directly into the area of representative democracy. Thus, the reader will perhaps not be surprised to find the median outcome, cycling, and logrolling all reappearing.

A.   Outcomes under two-party democracy

Harold Hotelling first presented the median voter theorem as an outcome of two-party representative democracy in 1929, and this paper is a clear intellectual antecedent to both Downs's and, more directly, Black's work. Indeed, it could be regarded as *the* pioneering paper in public choice, for it was the first direct attempt to use economics to analyze a political process.

In the Hotelling–Downs model, political opinion is depicted as lying along a single liberal-conservative (left-right) dimension. Each voter is assumed to have a most preferred position along the spectrum for his candidate or party[2] to take. The further the candidate is from this position, the less desirable his election is to the voter; thus the Hotelling–Downs model assumes single-peaked preferences. Figure 10.1a depicts a frequency distribution of most preferred candidate positions. We assume, first, that this frequency distribution is unimodal and symmetric. If every voter votes, and votes for the candidate closest to the voter's most preferred position, L receives all the votes of individuals lying to the left of X, the midpoint of the segment LR. R receives all votes to the right of X. If L and R are the positions that the two candidates take, R wins. L can increase his vote total by moving toward R, shifting X to the right, as can R. Both candidates are thus driven toward the position favored by the median voter. The logic of the argument is the same as that demonstrating the victory of the *issue* favored by the median voter, for in the Hotelling–Downs model there is only one issue to be decided: how far to the left or right the winning candidate will be.

The assumptions underlying this initial result are so unrealistic (one-issue dimension; a unimodal, symmetric preference distribution; all individuals vote; two candidates) that many researchers were naturally led to examine the consequences of relaxing them. As long as all voters vote, the median outcome holds regardless of the distribution of preferences. As long as all voters vote, the voters lying between a candidate's position and the furthest extreme

---

2. The words "candidate" or "party" can be used interchangeably here, for the implicit assumption when discussing parties is that they take a single position in the voter's eyes.

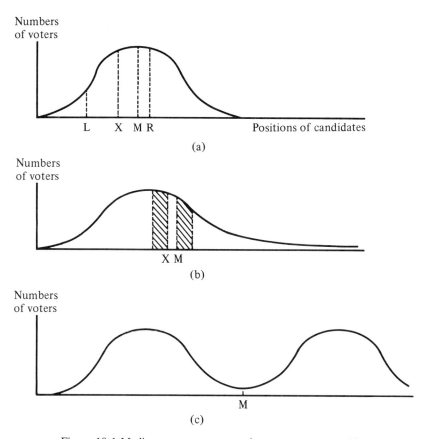

Figure 10.1 Median voter outcomes under two-party competition.

on his side of the other candidate are "trapped" into voting for him. Thus, a candidate can "go after" the votes of the other candidate by "invading his territory" and both continue to move toward the median.

Arthur Smithies (1941) pointed out in an early extension of Hotelling's model, however, that voters might leave a candidate as he moved away from them to support another (third) candidate or simply not vote at all. Two reasonable assumptions about abstentions are that (1) candidate positions can be too close together to make voting worthwhile (indifference), and (2) the nearest candidate may still be too far away to make voting attractive (alienation). If the probability that a voter does not vote is an increasing function of the closeness of two candidates' positions, a movement toward the center of a symmetric distribution of preferences has a symmetric effect on the two candidates' vote totals. The pull of the median remains, and the equilibrium is again at the median. Indifference does not affect this result. If the probability that a voter will abstain is an increasing function of a candidate's distance from him, the candidate is pulled toward the mode of the distribution. If the distribution is symmetric and unimodal, the median and mode coincide, however, and again the median voter result is not upset. Thus, neither indifference nor alienation, nor the two combined will affect the tendency of two candidates to converge on the position most favored by the median voter when the frequency distribution of voter preferences is symmetric and unimodal (Davis, Hinich, and Ordeshook, 1970).

The median voter result can be upset, however, if the distribution of voter preferences is either asymmetric or multimodal. If the distribution is asymmetric, but unimodal, the optimal position for each candidate is pulled toward the mode if voters become alienated as candidates move away from them (Comanor, 1976). This can be seen by considering Figure 10.1b. Suppose that both candidates are at *M,* the median of the distribution. A move of one to *X* decreases the probability that the voters in the cross-hatched region to the right of *M* will vote for him. The move also increases the probability by the same amount that the voters in the cross-hatched region to the left of *X* will vote for him (the two cross-hatched areas having equal bases). Since there are more voters in the region to the left of *X* than in the region to the right of *M,* the net effect of a move toward the mode taking into account only the effect of alienation must be to increase a candidate's expected vote. But, since *M* is the median, the same number of voters must lie to the left and right of this point, and the effect of alienation on the candidate's vote must dominate for small moves from *M.* As Comanor (1976) has shown, however, the distance between the median and mode is not likely to be great enough to cause a significant shift in candidate positions owing to alienation away from those predicted under the median voter hypothesis.

Figure 10.1c depicts a bimodal symmetric distribution. As one might expect, the presence of alienation *can,* via the logic just discussed, lead the candidates away from the median toward the two modes (Downs, 1957, pp. 118–22). But it need not. If weak, alienation can leave the median outcome unchanged or produce no stable set of strategies at all; such is the strength of the pull toward the middle in a two-party, winner-take-all system (Davis et al., 1970).

A spreading out of candidates may occur if elections consist of two steps: competition for nomination within parties, competition among parties. To win the party's nomination, the candidate is pulled toward the *party* median; the need to win the election pulls him back toward the *population* median. If he treats the other candidate's position as fixed, a Cournot strategy game results, with equilibria generally falling between the party and population medians (Coleman, 1971, 1972; Aranson and Ordeshook, 1972).

Table 10.1.

	Voter		
Issue	*A*	*B*	*C*
I	4	−2	−1
II	−2	−1	4
III	−1	4	−2

In Chapter 5 we noted that single-peakedness ensures a majority rule equilibrium in general only when issues are defined over a single dimension. When this occurs, single-peakedness ensures that Plott's perfect balance criterion is met for an outcome at the peak preference of the median voter. But, the single-peakedness condition does not ensure the existence of an equilibrium when we move to more than one dimension. The reader will not be surprised to learn, therefore, that the results concerning the instability of majority rule equilibria in a multidimensional world carry over directly for the literature on representative democracy.[3] The problem a candidate faces in choosing a multidimensional platform that defeats all other platforms is, under majority rule, the same as finding an issue in multidimensional space that defeats all other issues.

One can combine the assumptions of multimodal distributions and alienation and envisage a candidate presenting a platform of extreme positions on several issues and winning the support of a sufficient number of minorities to defeat another candidate taking median positions on all. When this happens, a minority, which supports a candidate for the position he takes on a couple of key issues, regardless of his position on others, is essentially trading away its votes on the other issues to those minorities feeling strongly about these other issues.[4]

Unfortunately, the possibility of logrolling to produce cycles persists. Consider the voter preferences in Table 10.1. Suppose that two candidates vie for election on three issues. If the first takes a position in favor of all three, the outcome that maximizes the net utility gains for all voters, he can be defeated by a candidate favoring any two issues and opposing the third (say, PPF), since two of the three voters always benefit from the defeat of an issue. PPF

---

3. For surveys of this literature, see Taylor (1971); Riker and Ordeshook (1973, ch. 12); Enelow and Hinich (1984).
4. Downs (1957, pp. 132–7); Tullock (1967, pp. 57–61); Breton (1974, pp. 153–5). Note that this form of logrolling is even easier to envisage when issues are arrayed in more than one dimension. When this occurs, one need not assume alienation to get a dominant logrolling strategy.

can be defeated by PFF, however, and PFF by FFF. But all three voters favor PPP over FFF, and the cycle is complete. Every platform can be defeated.

In a single election, candidates cannot rotate through several platforms, and cycling is not likely to be evidenced. Over time it can be. To the extent that incumbents' actions in office commit them to the initial platform choice, challengers have the advantage of choosing the second, winning platform. Cycling in a two-party system should appear as the continual defeat of incumbents (Downs, 1957, pp. 54–62).[5]

Thus we confront again the political instability issue, appearing now as the danger of revolving-door political representation. Yet how well supported is this prediction? Although it is difficult to discern a cycle from a committee's actions, the predication that incumbent candidates are regularly defeated is rather easily tested. In Table 10.2 data are presented on the frequency with which the incumbent *party's* candidate is defeated in a gubernatorial election. To the extent that candidates of the party holding the governor's chair must run on the record of the previous governor, whether that is the same person now running for office or a new one, the cycling theorem predicts the defeat of the candidate whose party currently is represented in the governor's chair.

In addition to the cycling theorem's prediction that the probability of a change in control of the governorship is one, two other "naive" hypotheses can be put forward.

1. *A random hypothesis:* The elections are random events, perhaps because voters do not take the trouble to gather information about the candidates, because the incentive to do so is low. This hypothesis leads to the prediction that the probability of a change in the party of the governor is 0.5 in the U.S. two-party system.[6]
2. *A conspiracy hypothesis:* The incumbents can manipulate the system or voter preferences so that they are never defeated. The probability of their defeat is zero.

Since the birth of the Republic, the party of the incumbent governor has failed to regain the governorship only one-fourth of the time. Gubernatorial elections produce turnover in the governor's chair falling halfway between the elections being rigged for the incumbent party and a coin toss. The revolving-door hypothesis of the cycling theory is resoundingly rejected.[7] As with the

---

5. Of course, one of the advantages of being an incumbent is that one can rewrite the election laws to favor the incumbents.
6. Some states have at times had more than two parties with candidates for the governorship, but the appropriate probability figure is only slightly less than 0.5.
7. Of course, in many states only one party has put forward a gubernatorial candidate. But this fact still seems more in keeping with the conspiratorial hypothesis than with the cycling hypothesis. Given the inherent vulnerability of the incumbent predicted by cycling theory, why is it that the Democrats in Vermont and Republicans in Alabama have been so ineffective in coming up with platforms and candidates to challenge the incumbents?

Table 10.2. *Election outcomes and growth rates, 1775–1984*

Time period (1)	Number of elections (2)	Fraction of changes in party[a] (3)	Winning party's vote fraction (4)	Difference between 1st and 2nd parties (5)	Minority party totals (6)
1775–93	41	.273	.708[b]	.489[b]	.073[b]
1794–1807	85	.133[b]	.700[b]	.426[b]	.026
1808–19	95	.211	.637[b,c]	.297[c]	.022[b]
1820–34	163	.190[b]	.675[b]	.406[b,c]	.055[b]
1835–49	201	.292[c]	.551[b,c]	.142[b,c]	.039
1850–9	156	.296	.541[b]	.137[b]	.056[b]
1860–9	176	.260	.627[b,c]	.271[c]	.017[b,c]
1870–9	167	.259	.571[b,c]	.177[b,c]	.035
1880–9	160	.244	.580	.196	.036
1990–9	178	.299	.551[b,c]	.172[b]	.070[b,c]
1900–9	184	.143[b,c]	.588[c]	.218[c]	.043[c]
1910–19	185	.315[c]	.565[b]	.215	.085[b,c]
1920–9	187	.211[c]	.619[c]	.269[b]	.031[c]
1930–9	180	.320[c]	.608	.248	.032
1940–9	178	.243	.633[b]	.272	.010[b]
1950–9	173	.236	.612	.232	.009[c]
1960–9	156	.372[b,c]	.568[b,c]	.146[b,c]	.010[b]
1970–9	151	.391[b]	.596	.160[b]	.024[b]
1980–4	66	.364	.572	.162	.018
1775–1984	2,882	.268	.598	.229	.037

[a]Adjusted by removing first election in each state, since no party change is possible in this election.
[b]Significantly different (5 percent two-tail) from mean of remainder of sample.
[c]Significantly different (5 percent two-tail) from mean of preceding subsample.
Sources: Glashan (1979), Mueller (1982), Election Research Center (1985).

outcomes from committee voting, Tullock's question, "Why so much stability?" is appropriate.

B.   Two-party competition in a constrained policy space

One explanation for the apparent stability of electoral politics, at least as judged by the policy outcomes of the process, may be that candidates do not choose platforms from the entire feasible policy space, but restrict their choices to a particular subset of the policy space.

Consider Figure 10.2, where the ideal points of three voters are again depicted assuming a two-dimensional issue space. If voter indifference curves are concentric circles centered at the ideal points, then the lines $\overline{AB}$, $\overline{BC}$, and

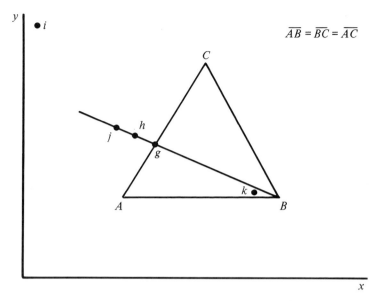

Figure 10.2 Three-voter electorate with equilateral triangle as Pareto set.

$\overline{AC}$ are contract curves for each respective pair of voters, and form the sides of the Pareto set.

As indicated in Chapter 5, no point in the x-y orthant can defeat all other points under majority rule, and the cycling property of majority rule could lead to a sequence of pairwise votes that leads anywhere in the feasible policy space, for example, to point i. Moreover, some points like j lying outside of the Pareto set can defeat points like k inside it in a direct majority rule vote. But do we really expect candidates in a two-party election to pick platforms like i or even j? Will the inherent attractiveness of platforms near the voter ideal points not manifest itself somehow?

Gordon Tullock (1967a,b) was one of the first to argue that cycling would be restricted to a fairly circumscribed space near the point where the voters' median lines intersect.[8] Theoretical justification for this prediction has been provided by Nicholas Miller's work on the uncovered set.[9]

8. A median line divides the issue space so that no more than half of the voter ideal points are on either side of it (see Chapter 5, Sections D and E).
9. The initial exposition is in Miller (1980), with a correction in Miller (1983). Further explication is given by Ordeshook (1986, pp. 184–7), and Feld, et al. (1987).
   Other papers that argue that observed outcomes under majority rule will fall in a circumscribed area within the policy space include McKelvey and Ordeshook (1976), Kramer (1977), and McKelvey, Ordeshook, and Winer (1978).

Definition: *The uncovered set is the set of all points* y *within the set of feasible alternatives* S, *such that for any other alternative* z *in* S, *either* yPz *or there exists some* x *in* S *such that* yPxPz, *where* aPb *means* a *beats* b *under majority rule.*

Absent a Condorcet winner, no platform is unbeatable. But if a candidate chooses a platform from the uncovered set, she knows she is at most "once removed" from defeating any platform her opponent chooses. At worst, her platform will be involved in a cycle of length three with any platform that defeats it. Conversely, if she chooses a platform that is covered, not only can this platform be defeated, but the platforms that defeat it include some that her platform cannot defeat. Thus, her platform can be contained in a transitive triple in which it is the least preferred of the three platforms.

To see this point more clearly, assume that there are but four distinct choices, x, y, z, and w, from which two candidates must choose one as a platform. Majority rule establishes the following binary relationships:

$$xPy \qquad yPz \qquad zPx$$

$$xPw \qquad yPw \qquad wPz.$$

Outcomes x, y, and z are all uncovered. For example, although z beats x, z is in turn beaten by y, which x can beat. Similarly, neither x nor z covers $w - z$ because it loses to w, x because it is defeated by z. However, y does cover w, since it both beats w and is defeated by x, which w cannot beat; y defeats both z and w, w defeats only z. The outcomes that w defeats are a subset of the outcomes that y defeats. Thus, y dominates w as a strategy choice; y defeats every outcome w can defeat, and y defeats w also. The uncovered set, in this case (x,y,z), consists of the undominated set of platforms.[10]

Returning to Figure 10.2, we can easily see that j is covered by h, since h beats j and is in turn defeated by g, but j cannot defeat g. Every point that j defeats is also defeated by h, so that no candidate should choose j over h.

When there are three voters and the Pareto set is an equilateral triangle, as in Figure 10.2, the uncovered set is the Pareto set (Feld, et al., 1987). But the uncovered set can be much smaller than the Pareto set. McKelvey (1986) has proved that the uncovered set is always contained within a circle of radius $4r$, where r is the radius of the circle of minimum radius that intersects all median lines.[11] This latter circle has been defined as the yolk. With an equilateral triangle, the yolk is tangent to each side at its midpoint. But consider now the three voter ideal points, which form an isosceles triangle with a height $2\frac{1}{2}$

---

10. This property holds in general; see Ordeshook (1986, pp. 184–6).

11. Feld, et al. (1987) prove that the uncovered set is always within $3.7r$ of the center of the yolk, and conjecture that for three voters it is within $2.83r$ of the center.

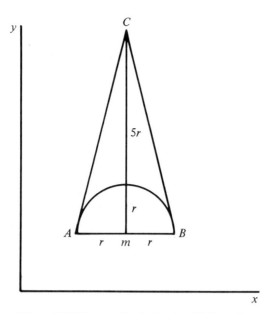

Figure 10.3 Three-voter electorate with isosceles triangle as Pareto set.

times its base (Figure 10.3). McKelvey's theorem implies that ideal point *C*, although still within the Pareto set, is now outside the uncovered set and thus is dominated by points near and along $\overline{AB}$.

In Figure 10.4, two more voters have been added with ideal points to either side of *m*, the median of the segment $\overline{AB}$. The radius of the yolk shrinks, and so, too, the dimensions of the uncovered set. As more and more voters are added to either side of *m* along $\overline{AB}$, the uncovered set converges on *m*. The outcome under two-candidate competition, when candidates restrict their choices to the uncovered set, approaches in this case what one would expect from the median voter theorem, if voter *C* were not present, even though *C*'s presence suffices to destroy Plott's (1967) perfect balance condition and the guarantee of an equilibrium it provides.

As a final example, consider Figure 10.5. Voter ideal points are all arrayed on the circumference of the circle with radius *c* centered at *o*. Plott's (1967) condition ensures an equilibrium at *o* only when voter ideal points occur in pairs at the opposite ends of lines of length 2*c*, which pass through *o*, as for example *A* and *B*, *and* one voter's ideal point is at *o*. Even with no voter's ideal point at *o*, however, the uncovered set shrinks in toward *o* as more voter ideal points are added at random to the perimeter of this circle, yielding *o* or

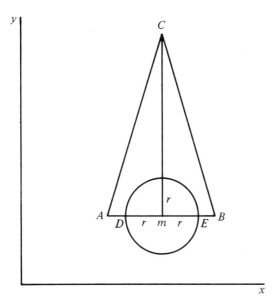

Figure 10.4 Five-voter electorate with isosceles triangle as Pareto set.

points very near it as the predicted outcomes under two-party competition when candidates choose their platforms from the uncovered set.

With voter ideal points as in Figures 10.4 and 10.5, one's intuition suggests that candidates will choose platforms at or near points m and o. But both m and o can be defeated under majority rule, as can every other point in the x-y space. Most of the literature in public choice has been content to leave the discussion at that, the implication being that any and all outcomes in x-y space are (equally) likely. The dominance property of the uncovered set seems a compelling reason to choose points within it, however, and this in turn draws our attention back to points near m and o. In Chapter 11 we discuss yet another reason to expect candidates to focus upon a single point or a constrained set of points. But first we describe still another approach.

C.   Testing the median voter hypothesis

A second explanation for not observing a wide scatter of chosen platforms under two-candidate competition may be that the multidimensional assumption upon which the result depends is inappropriate. All political issues can be arrayed along a single left-right, liberal-conservative dimension as the

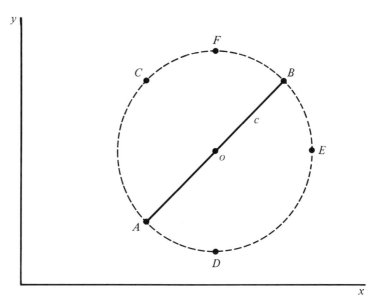

Figure 10.5 Six-voter electorate with circular Pareto set.

Downs–Hotelling model assumes.[12] Numerous studies have attempted to penetrate the "veil of representative democracy" by modeling government expenditure decisions as if they were the private choices of the median voter.[13]

A typical variant on the median voter model assumes that voters maximize utility subject to a budget constraint that includes their tax price for the public good, and derive the following demand equation for the median voter:

$$\ln G = a + \alpha \ln t_m + \beta \ln Y_m + \gamma \ln Z + \mu, \qquad (10.1)$$

where G is government expenditures, t_m and Y_m are the tax price and income of the median voter, respectively, and Z is a vector of taste parameters (number of children, Catholic or non-Catholic, etc.). Equation (10.1) is then tested using cross-sectional data on local expenditures of some kind.

12. Poole and Romer (1985) employ a least-squares multidimensional unfolding technique to map the ratings of members of the House of Representatives by 36 interest groups into a multidimensional policy space. They find that three dimensions suffice to obtain all of the predictive power inherent in the ratings, with a single liberal conservative dimension providing 94 percent of the explanatory power. Thus, it may be possible to represent candidate positions adequately using a single policy dimension if one uses a sufficiently accurate procedure for determining positions.
13. For surveys of this literature, see Deacon (1977a,b) and Inman (1979).

A large number of studies have tested some variant on the median voter hypothesis as given by (10.1). The overwhelming majority claim support for the median voter hypothesis on the basis of statistically significant coefficients on both Y_m and t_m of the correct sign. Denzau and Grier (1984) provide further evidence in support of the hypothesis by demonstrating that these coefficients vary over a narrow range when 12 "conditioning" (Z-) variables gleaned from the literature are included in equations incorporating data on New York school districts.

The merits of the public choice approach can perhaps be best assessed by comparing its findings with those of the "traditional approach," which related government expenditures to urbanization, population size and density, mean community income, and perhaps several other socioeconomic variables, depending on the good in question.[14] Most of these variables might be included in the Z vector of taste or shift variables, and many have reappeared in public choice studies. The key innovations of the public choice approach have been to replace mean income with median income and to add the median voter's tax price. The inclusion of the tax price variable is a clear improvement over previous studies that did not include tax shares in the demand equation, because it indicates that the purchase of public goods is the outcome of some form of collective choice process in which the *cost* of the public good to the voter, as well as its value to him as reflected by socioeconomic characteristics, is important.

The good performance of median income in explaining local public expenditures cannot be interpreted as readily as lending support to the public choice approach. As already noted, most existing studies have assumed that local public good demand is related to *mean* incomes, and it would take a rather peculiar model of local public finance to obtain a prediction that these variables were unrelated. Therefore, the contribution of the public choice approach must be to argue that it is *median* voter income that determines public good demand, not *mean* voter income. Most studies have not tested this hypothesis. Indeed, it is very difficult to test, given the other assumptions needed to test a median voter demand equation using cross-sectional data. As Bergstrom and Goodman (1973, pp. 286–7) point out, to estimate this equation on cross-sectional data one must assume a certain *proportionality* between the distributions of voters across local communities to ensure that the quantity demanded by the voter with the median income always equals the median quantity of public goods demanded in each community. But, if this proportionality holds, the means of the distributions will also be proportional, the correlation between mean and median income across communities will be perfect, and there will be no way to discriminate between the public-choice-

14. For a survey of this literature, see Edward Gramlich (1970).

approach demand equation and its rivals on the basis of this variable. The only way for the public choice approach to yield different predictions from other models is if the ratio of median to mean incomes differs across communities; that is, if there are different degrees of skewness across communities, and these differences in skewness are important in determining the demand for public goods.

Pommerehne and Frey (1976) have tested this latter hypothesis. They found that the median income variable did work somewhat better at explaining local public expenditures than mean income did, although the superiority of median income as an explanatory variable was not particularly dramatic. More convincing support for the superiority of median income over mean income was obtained in a follow-up study by Pommerehne (1978), who used data on 111 Swiss municipalities to test the hypothesis. These data have the important and singular advantage of allowing one to ascertain the effect of having representative democracy, since the sample contains municipalities that make decisions via direct, town-meeting procedures and those that rely on representative assemblies. Pommerehne found that median income performed significantly better than mean income at explaining public expenditures in cities employing direct democracy. In the cities employing representative democratic procedures, median income led "to somewhat superior results," but its "explanatory power is not significantly better in any expenditure category."

Thus, the introduction of representatives into the democratic decision process does seem to introduce a sufficient amount of "white noise" to disguise or almost disguise the relationship between median voter preferences and final outcomes. This throws a cloud of doubt over the U.S.-based estimates, which rely entirely on representative election outcomes. Interestingly enough, Pommerehne found that even the existence of an optional or obligatory referendum on expenditure bills in cities governed by representative assemblies added enough of a constraint on the representatives' behavior to make the median voter model perform perceptibly better than for those cities in which representative democracy was able to function unchecked.

A further cloud on the predictive power of the median voter model is provided by the *range* of estimates of the key parameters that have been reported. The income elasticities in the Bergstrom and Goodman (1973) study ranged from 0.16 to 1.73, while the tax price elasticities ranged from −0.01 to −0.50 (Romer and Rosenthal, 1978, p. 159), and these are for a single model applied to comparable bodies of data.

Gramlich and Rubinfeld (1982a) have also presented evidence suggesting that the performance of median voter income in most studies may be an artifact of aggregation in the cross-sectional data used to test the hypothesis. Using survey data for Michigan, they found that "higher-income individuals within a community . . . do not appear to have any greater taste for public spending" than lower-income individuals. The income elasticity of demand for expenditures "is very close to zero" when measured within communities (1982a, p. 544). The positive elasticities estimated in cross sections are due entirely to a positive association between community income and expenditures, precisely the relationship that the "traditional approach" estimated and the public choice approach sought to improve upon.

All of this underlines the point that caution must be exhibited when interpreting the empirical results from public choice models. As in all areas of economics, the sophistication and elegance of the theoretical models of public choice far exceed the limits placed by the data on the empirical models that can be estimated. In going from the theoretical models to the empirical "verifications," additional assumptions and compromises must often be made that further hamper a clear interpretation of the results as constituting direct support for a hypothesis. What one is willing to conclude boldly on the basis of results analytically derived from *assumed* behavioral relationships, one must conclude circumspectly on the basis of estimated behavioral equations.

This same caution must be exercised in drawing the broader conclusion that a given set of results from a model based on public choice supports the public choice approach. It is common practice in economics to "test" a hypothesis by checking whether the results are "consistent" with it without exploring whether they are also consistent with other, conflicting hypotheses. Although it is perhaps unfair to hold public choice to higher standards than the other branches of economics, I do not think that this methodology suffices here. To demonstrate that public choice has something useful to contribute to the existing empirical literature on public finance and public policy, its models must be tested against the existing models, which ignore public choice considerations. Unless public choice–derived models can outperform the "traditional, ad hoc" models against which they compete, the practical relevance of public choice theories must remain somewhat in doubt. To date, few studies have attempted such comparisons. Two of those reviewed in this section that do make such comparisons (Pommerehne and Frey, 1976; and Pommerehne, 1978) present evidence that is hardly encouraging as to the potential for predicting the outcomes of *representative government* with a model that treats the median voter as if he were dictator.

D. Are local public expenditures public or private goods?

In addition to estimating median income and tax price elasticities, several papers in the literature on median voters estimate a "degree-of-publicness" parameter based on the coefficients of the tax price and population variables.

This parameter is defined in such a way that "if [it] were nearly zero, there would be substantial economies to large city size since in larger cities, more consumers could share in the costs of municipal commodities with only minor crowding effects. Where [it] is about one, the gains from sharing the cost of public commodities among persons are approximately balanced by the disutility of sharing the facility among more persons" (Bergstrom and Goodman, 1973, p. 282). All of the studies discussed here find that this parameter is typically close to one. Borcherding and Deacon (1972, p. 900) urge that "great care should be exercised in interpreting" this coefficient, and in particular note that "normative conclusions drawn from the finding that the goods appear better classified as private or quasi-private rather than public are highly conjectural." Nevertheless, the temptation to make these normative conjectures is obviously appealing to many, and more than one writer has succumbed to it.[15] Such conclusions are not warranted, however. The coefficients upon which this degree-of-publicness parameter is estimated are obtained from cross-sectional equations based on observations from communities of differing sizes, each of which supplies these services (assumed homogeneous across communities) collectively to all members. A parameter estimate of one for police protection implies that a citizen living in a city of two million is no better off after weighing the reduced costs of spreading additional police protection across more taxpayers against the additional costs (crime?) resulting from crowding than a citizen living in a city of one million. It does *not imply* that individuals in the larger city can contract for "private" police protection as efficiently as municipal police departments can supply it. Since no private-contract police service systems are included in the studies, nothing can be said about their costs relative to public police protection. Nor can one even say that citizens in a part of the city of two million can efficiently form a club and provide their own police protection. If there are heavy spillovers from one part of a city to another, there may be no efficient way to supply police protection to a city of two million other than to supply it to all collectively, even though the net benefits from police protection to a citizen in a city of two million may be no greater than those to a citizen of a city half as large. The conclusion that the results of these studies imply that police protection is a private good comes from a confusion of the joint supply and nonexclusion characteristics of public goods. The studies cited above show that the net joint supply benefits of public good provision have generally been exhausted for the range of community sizes considered. Whether subsets of these communities can efficiently be excluded from the benefits of providing these services to other subsets, so that they can be provided via private or local clubs, is another, as yet untested, hypothesis.

15. See, e.g., Niskanen (1975, pp. 632–3); Borcherding, Bush, and Spann (1977).

Bibliographical notes

Recent textbook treatments of political competition models are by Borooah and van der Ploeg (1983), Enelow and Hinich (1984), Calvert (1986), and Ordeshook (1986, ch. 4). An early critic of spatial models was Donald Stokes (1963).

Barr and Davis (1966) and Davis and Haines, Jr. (1966), made the pioneering efforts to apply the median voter model, and their work has been followed up by more sophisticated attempts by Borcherding and Deacon (1972), Bergstrom and Goodman (1973), Peterson (1973, 1975), Clotfelter (1976), Pommerehne and Frey (1976), Deacon (1978), Inman (1978), Pommerehne (1978), and Holcombe (1980).

The critical remarks in Sections C and D parellel in many respects the review by Romer and Rosenthal (1979a).

For further discussion and critiques of the degree-of-publicness parameter, see Inman (1979, p. 296) and Oates (1988a).

CHAPTER 11

Two-party competition – probabilistic voting

It suffices for us, if the moral and physical condition of our own citizens qualifies them to select the able and good for the direction of their government, with a recurrence of elections at such short periods as will enable them to displace an unfaithful servant, before the mischief he mediates may be irremediable.

Thomas Jefferson

The social meaning or function of parliamentary activity is no doubt to turn out legislation and, in part, administrative measures. But in order to understand how democratic politics serve this social end, we must start from the competitive struggle for power and office and realize that the social function is fulfilled, as it were, incidentally – in the same sense as production is incidental to the making of profits.

Joseph Schumpeter

The cycling problem has haunted the public choice literature since its inception. Cycling introduces a degree of indeterminacy and inconsistency into the political process that hampers the observer's ability to predict outcomes, and clouds the normative properties of the outcomes achieved. The median voter theorem offers a way out of this morass of indeterminateness, a way out that numerous empirically minded researchers have seized. But the median voter equilibrium remains an "artifact" of the implausible assumption that issue spaces have a single dimension (Hinich, 1977). If candidates can compete along two or more dimensions, the equilibrium disappears and with it the predictive power of the econometric models that rely on this equilibrium concept.

Not surprisingly, numerous efforts to avoid these dire implications of assuming multidimensional issue spaces have been made. We do not review all of them here, but rather focus upon one set of models that makes a plausible modification to the standard two-party spatial competition model and produces equilibrium outcomes.[1] But first we discuss why the standard model fails to achieve an equilibrium.

1. In addition to the models reviewed here, see in particular the sequential election models of Aranson and Ordeshook (1972) and Kramer (1977).

196

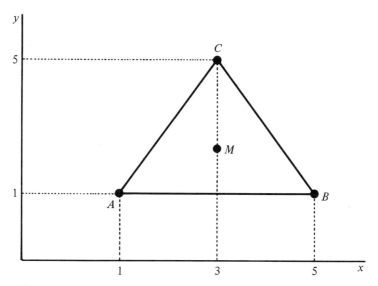

Figure 11.1. Ideal points of three voters.

A. Instability with deterministic voting

Consider again a situation in which there are three voters with ideal points at *A, B,* and *C* in the two-dimensional issue space, *x-y* (Figure 11.1). With separable utility functions, voter indifference contours are concentric circles and the Pareto set is the triangle with apexes at *A, B,* and *C.* The two candidates compete by choosing points in the *x-y* positive orthant.

Our intuition suggests that the candidates choose points inside *ABC.* Could a point outside the triangle win more votes than a point inside the triangle, given that the former must always provide lower utility to *all three* voters than some points inside the triangle? Intuition further suggests that competition between the candidates for the three votes will drive the two candidates toward the middle of the triangle, to some point like *M.*

But we have seen in Chapter 5 that point *M* cannot be an equilibrium if candidates seek to maximize their votes and voters vote for the candidate who takes the closest position to a voter's ideal point. If candidate 1 is at *M,* then 2 can defeat 1 by taking any position within the three lenses formed by U_A and U_B, U_A and U_C, and U_B and U_C (see Figure 11.2). Note that these lenses include points like *N* outside the Pareto set. But any point that 2 chooses can be defeated by a countermove by 1, and so on, ad infinitum.

Let us consider again the assumption that each voter votes with certainty for the candidate whose platform is closest to the voter's ideal point. Candidate 1

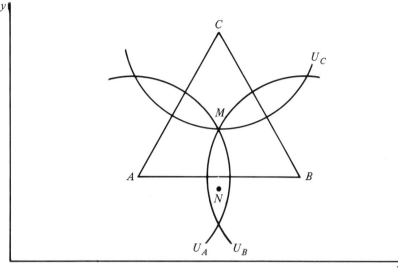

Figure 11.2. Cycling possibilities.

has taken a position at P_1 in Figure 11.3, and candidate 2 is considering taking positions along the ray AZ. In deciding what point along AZ to choose, 2 contemplates the effect of this choice on the probability of winning A's vote. Under the deterministic voting assumption that voter A votes for the candidate closest to point A, this probability remains zero as long as 2 remains outside U_A, and then jumps to one as 2 crosses the U_A contour. The probability of A's voting for 2 is a discontinuous step function equaling zero for all points outside U_A and one for all points inside.

That a candidate expects voters to respond to changes in her platform in such a jerky manner seems implausible for a variety of reasons. First of all, A is unlikely to be perfectly informed about the two candidates' positions, and thus A may not realize that 2 has moved closer to his ideal point. Second, other random events may impinge upon A's decision, which either change his preferences or change his vote in an unpredictable way. Third, 2 may not know with certainty where A's ideal point lies. Thus, a more realistic assumption about 2's expectation of the probability of winning A's vote is that it is a continuous function of the distance 2's position lies from A, increasing as 2 moves closer to A.[2]

With this plausible alternative to the deterministic voting assumption, two-party competition for votes can produce equilibrium outcomes.

2. For further justification of the probabilistic voting assumption, see Hinich (1977) and Coughlin, Mueller, and Murrell (1988).

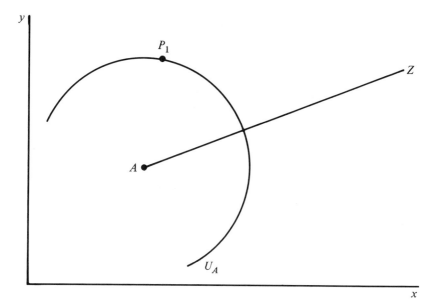

Figure 11.3. Voter A's response to candidate 2's moves.

B.   Equilibria under probabilistic voting

Deterministic voting models assume that voter choices gyrate schizophrenic-
ally as candidates move about competing for votes. A slight movement to the
left loses A's vote, but wins B's and C's. Candidates seek to maximize their
expected number of votes, and these in turn are simply the sum of the probabilities that each voter will vote for the candidate. Define π_{1i} as the probability that voter i will vote for candidate 1, and EV_1 1's expected vote. Then
candidate 1 seeks to maximize

$$EV_1 = \sum_{i=1}^{n} \pi_{1i}. \tag{11.1}$$

Under deterministic voting, π_{1i} and π_{2i} take the following step-function form.

$$(\pi_{1i} = 1) \leftrightarrow U_{1i} > U_{2i}$$

$$(\pi_{1i} = 0) \leftrightarrow U_{1i} \leq U_{2i} \tag{11.2}$$

$$(\pi_{2i} = 1) \leftrightarrow U_{1i} < U_{2i},$$

where U_{1i} and U_{2i} are i's expected utilities under the platforms of 1 and 2,
respectively.

Probabilistic voting models replace (11.2) with the assumption that the probability functions are continuous in U_{1i} and U_{2i}; that is,

$$\pi_{1i} = f_i(U_{1i}, U_{2i}), \; \frac{\partial f_i}{\partial U_{1i}} > 0, \; \frac{\partial f_i}{\partial U_{2i}} < 0. \tag{11.3}$$

The task of finding a maximum for equation (11.1) will be much easier if the π_{1i} are smooth, continuous concave functions, rather than discontinuous functions. The probabilistic voting assumption makes this substitution, and it lies at the heart of the difference between the characteristics of the two models.

The utility functions of each voter can be thought of as mountains with peaks at each voter's ideal point. The probabilistic voting assumption transforms these utility mountains into probability mountains, with the probability of any voter voting for a given candidate reaching a peak when the candidate takes a position at the voter's ideal point.

Equation (11.1) aggregates these individual probability mountains into a single aggregate probability mountain. The competition for votes between candidates drives them to the peak of this mountain.

That the positioning of the candidates at the peak of this mountain is an equilibrium can be established in a variety of ways. For example, the zero-sum nature of competition for votes, combined with the continuity assumptions on the π_{1i} and π_{2i} (implying the continuity of EV_1 and EV_2) can be relied upon to establish a Nash equilibrium (Coughlin and Nitzan, 1981a). If the probability functions are strictly concave, the equilibrium is unique, with both candidates offering the same platforms.

C.   Normative characteristics of the equilibria

Let us examine the properties of the equilibria further by making some specific assumptions about the probability functions. First of all, we assume that all voters vote so that the probability that i votes for candidate 2 is one minus the probability that i votes for 1; that is,

$$\pi_{2i} = 1 - \pi_{1i}. \tag{11.4}$$

In addition to satisfying (11.3), the probability functions must be chosen so that

$$0 \le f(\;) \le 1 \tag{11.5}$$

for all feasible arguments. As a first illustration, let us assume that $f_i(\;)$ is a continuous and concave function of the differences in utilities promised by the two candidates' platforms:

$$\pi_{1i} = f_i(U_{1i} - U_{2i}) \, , \; \pi_{2i} = 1 - \pi_{1i}. \tag{11.6}$$

Consider now a competition for votes between the two candidates defined over a policy space that consists simply of the distribution of Y dollars among the n voters.[3] Each voter's utility is a function of his income, $U_i = U_i(y_i)$, $U_i' > 0$, $U_i'' < 0$. Candidate 1 chooses a vector of incomes $(y_{11}, y_{12}, y_{1i}, \text{etc.})$ to maximize her expected vote, EV_1, subject to the total income constraint; that is, she maximizes

$$EV_1 = \sum_i \pi_{1i} = \sum_i f(U_i(y_{1i}) - U_i(y_{2i})) + \lambda \left(Y - \sum_i y_{1i} \right). \qquad (11.7)$$

Candidate 2 chooses a vector of incomes that maximizes $1 - EV_1$, which is to say a vector that minimizes EV_1. If the $f(\ )$ and $U(\ )$ functions are continuous and strictly concave, both candidates will choose the same platforms. These platforms will in turn satisfy the following first-order conditions:

$$f_i' U_i' = \lambda = f_j' U_j', \quad i,j = 1,n. \qquad (11.8)$$

Each candidate equates the weighted marginal utilities of the voters, with the weights (f_i') depending on the sensitivity of a voter's voting for a candidate to differences in the utilities promised by the candidates. The greater the change in the probability of voter i's voting for 1 in response to an increase in $U_{1i} - U_{2i}$, the higher the income promised to i by both candidates.

If the probabilistic response of all voters to differences in promised utilities were the same – that is, $f_i'(\ ) = f_j'(\ )$ for all i,j, – then (11.8) simplifies to

$$U_i' = U_j' \text{ for all } i,j = 1,n. \qquad (11.9)$$

This condition is the same one that must be satisfied to maximize the Benthamite welfare function

$$W = U_1 + U_2 + \cdots + U_i + \cdots + U_n. \qquad (11.10)$$

Thus, when the probabilistic response of all voters to differences in the expected utilities of candidate platforms is the same, the competition for votes between the candidates leads them to choose platforms that maximize the Benthamite welfare function.[4] When the probabilistic responses of voters differ, candidate competition results in the maximization of a weighted Benthamite welfare function.

A reasonable alternative to the assumption that voter decisions depend on the *differences* in expected utilities from the candidates' platforms is that they depend upon the *ratios* of utilities, that is, that π_{1i} is of the form

$$\pi_{1i} = f_i(U_{1i}/U_{2i}). \qquad (11.11)$$

Substituting (11.11) into (11.7), and recalling that $U_{1i} = U_{2i}$ at the equilibrium, we obtain

3. Peter Coughlin (1984, 1986) has analyzed this problem.
4. Ledyard (1984) obtains the Benthamite SWF using an assumption analogous to (11.6).

$$f'_i \frac{U'_i}{U_i} = \lambda = f'_j \frac{U'_j}{U_j} \qquad i,j = 1,n \tag{11.12}$$

as the first-order conditions for expected vote maximization for each of the candidates. When the marginal probabilistic responses are identical across all voters, this simplifies to

$$\frac{U'_i}{U_i} = \frac{U'_j}{U_j}, \qquad i,j = 1,n, \tag{11.13}$$

which is the first-order condition obtained by maximizing the Nash social welfare function

$$W = U_1 \cdot U_2 \cdot U_3 \cdots U_n. \tag{11.14}$$

Once again, candidate competition is seen to result in the implicit maximization of a familiar social welfare function.[5]

As a final example, consider again the spatial competition example with the three voters depicted in Figure 11.1. Let us assume that the probabilities of i supporting candidates 1 and 2 are defined by (11.6). Since we know this problem is equivalent to the maximization of (11.10), we can find the equilibrium platform that maximizes (11.10). We write the three voters' utility functions as $U_a = Z_a - (1 - x)^2 - (1 - y)^2$, $U_b = Z_b - (5 - x)^2 - (1 - y)^2$, $U_c = Z_c - (3 - x)^2 - (5 - y)^2$, where the Z_i's represent the utility levels achieved at each voter's respective ideal point. The two first-order conditions are

$$2(1 - x) + 2(5 - x) + 2(3 - x) = 0 \tag{11.15}$$
$$2(1 - y) + 2(1 - y) + 2(5 - y) = 0,$$

from which we obtain the expected vote-maximizing platform for both candidates $(3,7/3)$, the point M in Figure 11.1. Competition for votes does drive the two candidates into the Pareto set to a point in the middle of the triangle.

When one assumes that the probabilities of voter support depend on differences in expected utility, competition drives candidates toward the (weighted) arithmetic mean of the voters' utilities. When the probabilities depend on ratios of utilities, the equilibrium is driven toward the geometric mean. Still other assumptions about the relationship between the probability of a voter's support and his expected utility under the competing platforms would produce equilibria at still other points. But as long as the probability of winning an individual's vote responds positively to increases in the voter's utility from a candidate's platform, then equilibria can be expected to be found within the

---

5. Coughlin and Nitzan (1981a) obtain the Nash SWF from an assumption about the $\pi_i s$ analogous to (11.11).

Pareto set, and thus have desirable normative properties of some sort (Coughlin, 1982).

D.   Equilibria with interest groups

The previous section describes a set of results under the probabilistic voting assumption that are indeed salutary. Political competition can produce equilibrium outcomes, and these outcomes can have potentially attractive normative properties. In this section we discuss an extension to the probabilistic voting model that sheds additional light on the nature of the outcomes obtained. The following section raises issues casting a shadow over the results.

Coughlin, Mueller, and Murrell (1988) have extended the probabilistic voting model to allow for the impact of interest groups on political competition. Interest groups are defined as groups of individuals with identical tastes and incomes. If U_{ij} is the utility function of voter j who is a member of interest group i, then $U_{ij} = U_i$, for all $j = 1, n_i$, where n_i is the size of the ith interest group. Each individual is a member of one interest group.

The deterministic voting assumption (11.2) is replaced with the following assumption

$$(\pi_{1ij} = 1) \leftrightarrow (U_{1i} > U_{2i} - b_{ij})$$
$$(\pi_{1ij} = 0) \leftrightarrow (U_{1i} \leq U_{2i} - b_{ij}) \qquad (11.16)$$
$$(\pi_{2ij} = 1) \leftrightarrow (U_{1i} < U_{2i} - b_{ij}).$$

The b_{ij} are "bias" terms. A $b_{ij} > 0$ implies a positive bias in favor of candidate 1 on the part of the jth voter in the ith interest group. The utility this voter expects from candidate 2's platform must exceed that expected from 1's platform by *more* than b_{ij}, before 1 loses this individual's vote to 2.

A probabilistic element is introduced into the model by assuming that the bias terms are random variables drawn from a probability distribution with parameters known to both candidates. Figure 11.4 depicts a uniform probability distribution for an individual in a given interest group. This group can be said to be biased in favor of candidate 1, since the bulk of the distribution lies to the right of the zero bias line. Nevertheless, some members of this group will be associated with negative bias terms. If candidate 1 matches 2's platform, she wins most but not all of the votes of interest group i.

The assumption that interest groups are biased toward or away from certain candidates or parties accords with observed voting patterns. Whites in the South and blacks everywhere in the United States tend to vote Democratic. Yankee farmers tend to vote Republican. On the other hand, not every Yankee farmer votes Republican.

The assumption that candidates know the distributions of bias terms, but

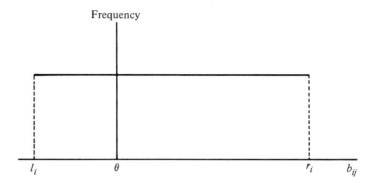

Figure 11.4. A uniform distribution of biases.

not the individual bias terms, implies that neither candidate can say with certainty how a given member of a particular interest group will vote. What they can predict is that they will pick up a greater fraction of an interest group's vote, the greater the difference in the utility their platform promises the representative interest group member over that of their opponent.

Assumption (11.16) makes the probability of i's supporting candidate 1 dependent on the difference between the utilities promised by the platforms of the two candidates. The first-order condition for expected vote maximization is thus of the form in (11.8). When the biases are drawn from the uniform distribution, however, f_i', the change in probability of winning the vote of a member of interest group i, is just the height of the uniform distribution, h_i, from which the b_{ij} are drawn, since the area of the uniform distribution equals one, $h_i = 1/(r_i - l_i)$. Thus, under the assumption that the bias terms are uniformly distributed, two-candidate competition for votes leads each candidate to offer platforms that maximize the following welfare function.

$$W = \alpha_1 n_1 U_1 + \alpha_2 n_2 U_2 + \cdots + \alpha_m n_m U_m, \qquad (11.17)$$

where the $\alpha_i = f_i' = 1/(r_i - l_i)$. The greater the difference between r_i and l_i, the boundaries on the uniform distribution for interest group i, the greater the range over which the b_{ij} are distributed. The greater this range, the more important the b_{ij} become in determining how an interest group's membership votes, and the less important the promised utilities are. Given the latter, both candidates give less weight to this group's interests in choosing platforms.

The results from this probabilistic voting model with interest groups resemble those of the earlier models in that equilibria exist and are Pareto optimal. In fact, an additive welfare function is maximized, albeit one that assigns different weights to the different interest groups.

This latter property raises important normative issues about the equilibria obtained in the competitive struggle for votes. Although candidates are uncertain about how the members of different interest groups will vote, they are uncertain in different degrees about different groups. One way in which interest groups attempt to influence public policy is to make candidates aware of the potential votes to be won from their interest group by taking certain positions in their platforms. Interest groups try to increase the welfare of their membership by reducing candidate uncertainty over how their membership votes.

But this in turn implies that different interest groups receive different weights in the candidates' objective functions and thus receive different weights in the social welfare function, which is implicitly maximized through candidate competition. When candidates are unsure of the votes of different groups, and these groups have different capabilities in approaching candidates, then one's benefits from political competition depend in part upon the interest group to which one belongs. The egalitarianism inherent in the slogan "one man, one vote" is distorted when interest groups act as intermediaries between candidates and citizens.

E.   The quality of a vote

The probabilistic voting models promise that democratic institutions can achieve normatively defensible outcomes. Indeed, they imply that the cumbersome institutional baggage of electing representatives to Congress or Parliament, parliamentary voting, and the like could be abolished. All that one requires is two vote-maximizing candidates for the office of chief executive, with an institutional apparatus that enables the winning candidate to implement her platform upon taking office.

But the probabilistic voting assumption that makes all of this possible is a two-edged sword. Although it cuts cleanly through the forest of cycling results, it simultaneously undercuts the normative authority of the preferences aggregated – for it presumes uncertainty on the part of candidates about voter preferences, or on the part of voters of candidate positions, or both. Indirectly, it raises the question of the quantity and quality of information available to candidates and voters.

One of Anthony Downs's most influential contributions to the science of politics was the concept of "rational ignorance."[6] When two candidates compete for the votes of a large electorate, each individual's vote has a negligible

---

6. Although Downs deserves the credit for making "rational ignorance" part of the parlance of the science of politics, the idea is clearly present in Schumpeter's (1950, pp. 256–64) classic discussion of democracy. It is presumably one of the ideas of Schumpeter from which Downs gained "inspiration" (Downs, 1957, p. 27, n. 1). For an excellent analysis of Schumpeter's writings on democracy, see Mitchell (1984a).

probability of affecting the outcome. Realizing this, rational voters do not expend time and money gathering information about candidates. They remain "rationally ignorant" of both the issues in the election and the opposing candidates' positions on these issues.

If this description of voter knowledge is accurate, as considerable survey evidence suggests it is,[7] then the dimensions of the policy space over which candidates compete are not clear. What exactly are the x's and y's that candidates promise to supply, and how faithful to these promises must they be, given the rational ignorance of a large fraction of the electorate?

Brennan and Buchanan (1984) have recently raised a related issue.[8] They liken individual voter participation in the electoral process to a fan's "participation" in a sporting match. By attending the match and cheering for one of the competing teams, the fan expresses a preference for that team. But the fan is not deluded into thinking that his support *contributes* to the team's chances of success. Even if the volume of cheering by all fans at the game is positively related to a team's performance, the single fan's cheers cannot be heard.

Brennan and Buchanan (1984) argue that voting, like cheering at a sporting game, is an expressive act, not an instrumental one. When an individual decides to cast his dollar votes for a Ford rather than a Toyota, this decision is instrumental in bringing about the final outcome. He drives a Ford. But a vote for candidate Ford over candidate Carter has no consequence upon the outcome of the election. The inconsequential nature of a single vote frees the individual to allow other considerations to intrude upon his choice of candidates. Peer pressure, the lingering memory of a campaign slogan, the picture on a poster seen when approaching a polling booth – all can be allowed to have decisive influence on the individual's vote, with the comforting knowledge that the vote will not have any subsequent impact on the voter's welfare. Brennan and Buchanan argue that the likelihood that random and extraneous factors will determine an individual's vote weakens the public choice scholar's ability to develop predictive models of the political process and undermines the normative conclusions one can draw from them. Even if political competition achieves a welfare maximum based upon the expressed preferences of voters, the question remains as to what these votes express.

F.   Empirical models of candidate competition

The probabilistic voting models introduce uncertainty into political competition and raise issues concerning candidate and voter information. If voters

7. Mayhew (1974, p. 49) claims that "only about half the electorate, if asked, can supply their House members' names."
8. The following argument in different forms has appeared in several of Buchanan's writings as far back as 1954b.

have no incentive to gather information, candidates have an incentive to supply it. The situation is analogous to that for many consumer goods where the cost of providing information is borne by the sellers. In consumer goods markets, we refer to seller provision of information as advertising, and the models of campaign expenditures bear a close resemblance to advertising models.[9]

1.   A model

Assuming that candidates seek to maximize votes, a candidate's objective function can be written as

$$V_c = f(P_c, P_o, C_c, \cdots), \tag{11.18}$$

where V_c are the votes *expected* for candidate c, P_c is the position (platform) of c on the issues, P_o is the platform of the opposition candidate, and C_c are c's campaign expenditures.[10] The dots following C_c indicate that other variables may be relevant. One of these is obviously the campaign expenditures of the opponent, since vote getting is to a considerable degree a zero-sum game. Thus, we rewrite (11.18) as

$$V_c = f(P_c, P_o, C_c, C_o, \cdots), \tag{11.18'}$$

where $\partial V_c / \partial C_c > 0$, and $\partial V_c / \partial C_o < 0$. Although much of the formal theory assumes that V_c and V_o are functions only of P_c and P_o, the empirical literature has focused on the relationship between the Vs and the Cs.

Although some campaign expenditures may come out of a candidate's own wealth, most tend to be covered by contributions from individuals or organizations. An individual can have basically two motives for contributing to a candidate, and they correspond to the distinction between allocative efficiency and redistribution. When tastes for a public good differ intensely, individuals or groups may be willing to contribute funds to help those candidates win who take positions on the quantity or quality of public goods matching those of the contributor. Peace groups contribute to dovish candidates, hawks to hawks. We can define this as the ideological motive for making a campaign contribution.

Alternatively, a contributor may be seeking legislation or government expenditures that directly enhance the contributor's income or wealth. The contributions of the Political Action Committee (PAC) of a defense contractor may be intended to influence both the level of defense expenditures and the direction of their flow. If we think of a contributor's objective function as

---

9. It is not surprising, therefore, to find one of the pioneers in modeling consumer good advertising, Kristian Palda, also making leading contributions to this field.

10. This model resembles that presented by Kau, Keenan, and Rubin (1982). See also Ben-Zion and Eytan (1974), Bental and Ben-Zion (1975), and Kau and Rubin (1982).

being either expected profits or expected utility measured in dollar units, then we can write interest group or individual i's objective function as

$$O_i = \pi_c(V_c - V_o)g(P_c) + (1 - \pi_c(V_c - V_o))g(P_o) - C_{ic} - C_{io},$$
(11.19)

where $\pi_c(V_c - V_o)$ is the probability that candidate c will win, a function of the difference in the expected votes for c and o, and $g(P_c)$ and $g(P_o)$ are the expected profits or utility from the platforms of c and o, respectively. If we assume that the candidates' platforms are fixed, then only π_c will change as i contributes to c or o, in accordance with the impact of contributions on V_c and V_o, as given by (11.18').

$$\frac{\partial O_i}{\partial C_{ic}} = \pi_c' \left(\frac{\partial V_c}{\partial C_{ic}} - \frac{\partial V_o}{\partial C_{ic}} \right) g(P_c) - \pi_c' \left(\frac{\partial V_c}{\partial C_{ic}} - \frac{\partial V_o}{\partial C_{ic}} \right) g(P_o) - 1 = 0,$$
(11.20a)

from which

$$\pi_c' \left(\frac{\partial V_c}{\partial C_{ic}} - \frac{\partial V_o}{\partial C_{ic}} \right) = \frac{1}{g(P_c) - g(P_o)},$$
(11.20b)

with an analogous condition following from $\partial O_i / \partial C_{io}$. If only the expected votes of the two candidates are affected by contributions, at most one C_i will be greater than zero. Contributions will go to increase the expected vote of that candidate, whose platform promises i the highest benefits.

It is also possible, however, that the platforms of the candidates themselves depend on the levels of contributions. Acceptance of a large contribution may obligate a candidate to promote legislation favored by the contributor, which the candidate might not otherwise follow. To see the implications of this assumption, assume that the expected votes for the candidates are not affected by contributions, but the platforms are; that is, π_c is a constant, $g' > 0$ and

$$P_c = h(C_{ic}) , P_o = m(C_{io}).$$
(11.21)

Under these assumptions, i's optimal strategy can be to contribute to *both* candidates.

$$\frac{\partial O_i}{\partial C_{ic}} = \pi_c g'h' - 1 = 0$$

$$\frac{\partial O_i}{\partial C_{io}} = (1 - \pi_c)g'm' - 1 = 0.$$
(11.22)

The higher a candidate's probability of winning, and the more sensitive his platform position is to the level of contributions, the greater will be the contributions from contributor i.

Equations (11.18) to (11.22) describe an interactive model of candidate and contributor behavior. The only major actor left out is the individual voter, whose expected utility depends on the candidates' positions and the levels of campaign expenditures:

$$U_{vc} = \mu(P_c, C_c, C_o) \ , \ U_{vo} = \mu(P_o, C_c, C_o). \tag{11.23}$$

The behavior of voters can be subsumed in the functional form chosen to represent the expected votes of the two candidates. Typically, this has been done by having $\mu(\ )$ include various characteristics of voters, which are assumed to measure their "tastes" for government programs: union membership, educational levels, geographic characteristics, and so on.

This simple model leads to several empirically testable predictions. From (11.18') it follows that the votes for a candidate are a function of his campaign expenditures and those of his opponent

$$\frac{\partial V_c}{\partial C_c} > 0, \ \frac{\partial V_c}{\partial C_o} < 0 \tag{11.24}$$

as well as his platform position, that of his opponent, and the characteristics of voters in his electoral district. From (11.19) and (11.20) it follows that the contributions from a given individual or group are a function of the positions of the candidates and the closeness of the expected vote. Empirical testing of these predictions must examine contributions from particular groups to particular candidates. The contributions of conservative groups will be greater, the more conservative the candidate's position and the closer the expected vote.

Finally, the model predicts that the platforms themselves are endogenous variables. If we treat an incumbent's voting record as his platform in a given election, then this voting record should depend upon the characteristics of those supporting the candidate by both their votes and their contributions to his campaign.

2. *Votes for a candidate as a function of expenditures*

The hypothesis that money can buy votes (i.e., that the number of votes a candidate receives is a function of his level of campaign expenditures) is a simple, direct consequence of the assumption that politicians are rational individuals seeking to maximize their vote totals or margins. If money did *not* buy votes, why would anyone spend it? Of the three relationships outlined in the previous section, this one is perhaps the most extensively researched.[11]

---

11. See Palda (1973, 1975), Welch (1974, 1976, 1981), Glantz et al. (1976), Jacobson (1978, 1985), Johnston (1978), Kau and Rubin (1982), Kau, Keenan, and Rubin (1982), Chapman and Palda (1984), and Palda and Palda (1985).

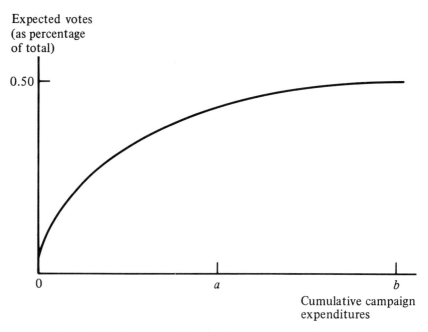

Figure 11.5. Assumed relationship between votes and expenditures across all candidates.

The empirical results generally confirm the hypothesis that money does buy votes, at least for the challenger in an election. Although Palda and Palda (1985) have estimated significant but smaller positive coefficients for incumbent candidates in federal elections in Ontario, other studies have failed to observe significant positive effects of incumbent expenditures (e.g., Glantz, Abramowitz, and Burkart, 1976; Jacobson, 1978, 1985; Welch, 1981; Kau, Keenan, and Rubin, 1982). There are at least two explanations for this apparent asymmetry.

Campaign expenditures, like product advertising, familiarize citizens with the characteristics of the product. They build up a stock of goodwill, which can be written as a function of cumulated past campaign expenditures. Challengers have typically spent less in the past than incumbents, and thus have smaller stocks of goodwill. If the votes a candidate receives increase with the level of the stock of his cumulated campaign expenditures, but are subject to diminishing returns, we obtain the relationship depicted in Figure 11.5. Welch (1976) and Jacobson (1985) have both reported results suggesting diminishing returns to campaign expenditures, which are consistent with the relationship in Figure 11.5. For some of Jacobson's estimates the curve even

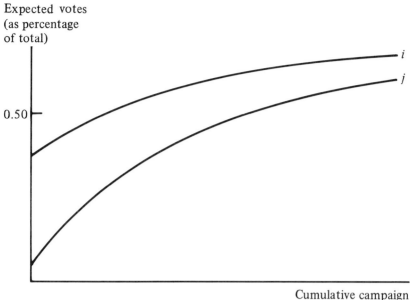

Figure 11.6. Vote–expenditure relationships for different candidates.

turns down. Given that challengers have smaller cumulative stocks of good-will, most observations for them will be to the left of those for their incumbent opponents. If the bulk of observations for challengers fall in the interval between the origin and point *a,* while observations for incumbents are drawn from the interval *a–b,* then the observed statistical results would be consistent with there being a single relationship between campaign expenditures and votes, as in Figure 11.5, and as assumed when estimating the relationship across representative election campaigns.

The same functional relationship may not hold for all candidates, however. Let *i* be an ex–basketball player or movie star who begins his political career with considerable "brand recognition" and goodwill, while *j* is a college professor with noble ideas and no prior exposure (see Figure 11.6). To win, *j* must spend a bundle, while *i* may need to spend very little at all. If *i* and *j*'s expenditures and votes are included in the same cross-sectional regression, it will appear that votes are unrelated to expenditures, even though they are related in both cases, albeit to differing degrees.

This problem is magnified by bringing in the simultaneous relationship between expenditures and votes. Most incumbents win. For example, in the Glantz et al. (1976) study of contests for seats in the California legislature, only 16 of 511 incumbents lost. Many are almost certain winners regardless of what they spend, and thus will receive and spend little. Those who face stiff challenges may receive more funds to help fight off the challenge. The relationship between expenditures and votes for the former candidates will resemble i, for the latter j. At low levels of expenditures, the marginal impact of expenditures for incumbents facing stiff challenges will be higher than for shoo-in candidates, and they will spend more. A cross-sectional regression that includes the two types of candidates will suggest no relationship, however.[12]

The model sketched in subsection 1 implies both a positive coefficient on own expenditures and a negative coefficient on one's opponent's expenditures. Evidence supporting the latter hypothesis exists, although the two expenditures tend to be highly correlated, so that the two effects are difficult to disentangle (Jacobson, 1978, 1985).

3.   Determinants of campaign contributions

Two variables should be important in explaining the direction and levels of campaign contributions: the expected benefits from the candidate's victory as measured by the positions one expects the candidate to take on issues, and the expected impact of the contributions on the outcome of the election as measured by the closeness of the vote. Both predictions have been tested and consistently supported in a burgeoning literature.[13]

In a study that is noteworthy both for the sophistication of its methodology and the size of its sample, Poole and Romer (1985) found a strong relationship between the ideological positions of contributors and the ideological positions of the candidates to whom they offer contributions. Corporate and trade association PACs give to conservative candidates and labor unions to liberal candidates. Moreover, within these broad interest group categories campaign contributions break down even further into consistent ideologic patterns; some corporate PACs give exclusively to the most conservative candidates, others to moderate conservatives and liberals.

As such, these results can be interpreted as supporting either a tastes-for-public-goods view of contributor motivation or a redistributive-favors view.

12. Johnston (1978) emphasizes the difficulty of estimating the expenditure–vote relationship with cross-sectional data, and Welch (1981) and Jacobson (1985) review the simultaneity issue.
13. Ben-Zion and Eytan (1974), Bental and Ben-Zion (1975), Crain and Tollison (1976), Jacobson (1978, 1985), Welch (1980, 1981), Kau and Rubin (1982), Kau et al. (1982), Palda and Palda (1985), and Poole and Romer (1985).
    Also relevant are the studies that find that the total contributions of a firm or industry are positively related to their potential gains from public policies (Pittman, 1976, 1977; Mann and McCormick, 1980; Zardkoohi, 1985).

Welch (1980) claims empirical support exclusively for the redistributive-favors hypothesis on the basis of evidence that interest groups like corporate PACs and unions heavily favor likely winners in their giving. Although Poole and Romer (1985) also find that corporate PACs and unions favor likely winners (i.e., incumbents), they also find that the size of contributions to incumbents is significantly higher in races likely to be close. They go on to state that "this result, together with a parallel one on challenger contributions, appears to be the most robust finding in the empirical literature on campaign contributions" (p. 101), citing Jacobson (1985) and Kau and Rubin (1982) in support of their statement. I tend to agree. Although interest group giving clearly favors likely winners, both incumbents and challengers receive more contributions, ceteris paribus, when they are involved in close contests.

The importance of ideological tastes is apparent in yet another finding of Poole and Romer. If contributors were devoid of ideology and so too were candidates, the former would give to those promising the biggest favors, while candidates would sell favors to anyone who was willing to pay for them. In this ideology-free world, contributors would find it optimal to give to both candidates in some close races, as equation (11.20b) implies. But Poole and Romer (1985) report that few PACs give to both candidates in the same race. That some do certainly supports the pure redistributive-favors hypothesis, but that most do not suggest that we should regard both ideological tastes and redistributive favors as motivations behind individual and interest group giving.

4.   *Determinants of representative voting behavior*

If campaign contributions are rational allocations of contributor income, then there should be payoffs in terms of the votes that winning candidates cast on issues of importance to the contributor. The cleanest test of this prediction comes on those issues that have a simple and obvious economic payoff to certain contributors, such as legislation on the minimum wage or cargo preference. A small, although rapidly increasing, number of studies find empirical support for this prediction.[14]

14. See Silberman and Durden (1976), Chappell (1981), Kau et al. (1982), Kau and Rubin (1982), and Peltzman (1984).

   This fact may seem to contradict the conclusion reached at the end of the previous subsection. Evidence also exists that a representative's ideological position has an independent effect on his voting (Kau and Rubin, 1979; Kau et al., 1982; Kalt and Zupan, 1984). Chappell (1982) finds that the effect of campaign contributions on the voting behavior of congressmen nearly disappears when estimated in a two-equation simultaneous system.

   Even if Peltzman (1984) were to be proven correct and existing ideology indexes merely proxy constituent interests, his results do not demonstrate that only the economic, as opposed to ideological, interests of constituents are represented.

5.   Evaluation

All three legs of the political competition model have gained some empirical support. As is almost always the case with empirical work, however, anomolies abound in the studies cited. The relationships are inherently simultaneous and cry out for simultaneous estimation procedures. But when applied, simultaneous estimation techniques often yield results that (1) differ trivially from the ordinary least squares (OLS) estimates (Jacobson, 1985, p. 33), (2) fail to pass statistical tests that would imply joint endogeneity (Palda and Palda, 1985), or (3) yield differences with respect to the OLS estimates that run *counter* to the predicted simultaneity bias (Jacobson, 1985, p. 33). Multicollinearity is often present. But all of this is par for the empirical course. The results to date are strong enough to sustain the plausibility of the hypotheses that (a) candidates spend money to win votes, and (b) contributors give money to obtain more preferred political outcomes.

G.   Commentary

When Anthony Downs put forward his economic theory of democracy, he seemed to suggest that the outcomes from a political system in which candidates competed for the votes of the electorate would somehow avoid the nihilistic implications of the cycling literature, and more generally Arrow's impossibility theorem (see, e.g., Downs, 1957, pp. 17–19). Downs did not succeed in demonstrating any normative results concerning the outcomes from political competition, however, and the subsequent literature on spatial voting models proved in one paper after another that cycling is potentially just as big a problem when candidates compete for votes as it is for committee voting.

The literature on probabilistic voting drives a giant wedge between the public choice literature on committee voting and that on electoral competition. Committee voting is inherently deterministic, and cycling problems will continue to confound the outcomes from committee voting under rules like the simple majority rule. But if voters reward a candidate who promises them a higher utility, by increasing the likelihood of voting for the candidate, then competition for votes between candidates leads them "as if by an invisible hand" to platforms that maximize social welfare. The analogy between market competition and political competition does exist. Both result in Pareto-optimal allocations of resources. Downs's faith in the efficacy of political competition has at long last been vindicated.

But the probabilistic voting models raise additional normative issues of a less salutary nature. The probabilistic voting model with interest groups implies that different groups receive different weights in the welfare function, which candidate competition implicitly maximizes. The empirical literature underscores the importance of this issue by providing ample evidence of a two-way exchange relationship between candidates and interest groups. At the same time, this literature demonstrates that the vote-maximizing and profit-utility–maximizing assumptions lead to models with predictive content.

Downs's *Economic Theory of Democracy* raised the promise that political competition might achieve attractive outcomes and at the same time undermined that promise by persuasively arguing that rational voters would remain ignorant of the issues. If the probabilistic voting models succeed in laying to rest the issue of the inherent "rationality" of the *process* of aggregating individual preferences, they also underline the question posed by Brennan and Buchanan (1984) as to whether the outcomes of the political process do not remain inherently "irrational" owing to the nature of the inputs.[15]

Bibliographical notes

The first articles to establish the existence of equilibria under probabilistic voting assumptions were by Davis et al. (1970) and Hinich, Ledyard, and Ordeshook (1972, 1973). Although the equilibrium result was clearly there, the significance of the result was not appreciated by this observer, because the probabilistic element in the models was assumed to be due to abstentions when candidates were too far from a voter's ideal point. Thus, equilibria appeared to emerge as a sort of accidental consequence of some voters refusing to vote. This seemed a shaky foundation upon which to build a strong normative case for the outcomes from electoral competition. As the literature has evolved, however, the emphasis has shifted from abstentions to uncertainty on the part of candidates and/or voters. Relevant papers in this evolution include Comanor (1976), Denzau and Kats (1977), Hinich (1977), Coughlin and Nitzan (1981a,b), Coughlin (1982, 1984, 1986), and Ledyard (1984). Enelow and Hinich (1984, ch. 5) and Ordeshook (1986, pp. 177–80) provide overviews of this literature.

The normative significance of the results is brought out most clearly in the articles by Coughlin and Nitzan (1981a), Coughlin (1982, 1984), and Ledyard (1984).

Wittman (1984) extends the equilibrium results to competition among three or more candidates, Austen-Smith (1981b) to multiconstituency party competition.

Samuelson (1984) assumes that candidates begin at different starting points and are constrained in how far from these starting points they can move in any election.

15. Donald Wittman (1986) argues that the issue of voter ignorance, like that of stockholder ignorance in the separation of ownership and control literature, has received too much emphasis. He argues that just as takeover raiders can capitalize on managerial failures and win stockholder support, political entrepreneurs can call failures of incumbent politicians to the attention of voters and win their support.

The analogy is overdrawn. The takeover raider provides stockholders with a single piece of information that is fairly easy to evaluate – a bid for the stockholder's shares at substantially more than their pre-bid market value. In contrast, the voter cannot simply sell her vote. She must evaluate the challenger's promises of a better program against the performance of the incumbent. This task is difficult if the voter remains rationally ignorant.

Equilibria occur with the candidates adopting different platforms and having different expected vote totals. Hansson and Stuart (1984) obtain similar results by assuming that candidates have utility functions defined over the strategy choices.

David Austen-Smith (1987) includes interest groups and campaign expenditures in a probabilistic voting model.

Frans van Winden (1983, ch. 7) also employs a model of political competition in which interest groups are assumed to receive different weights from the political process.

Donald Wittman (1986) presses the analogy between political competition and market competition and argues forcefully that the two processes are equally (in)efficient.

Finally, mention must be made of an important related work of Gary Becker (1983). Becker does not model the process of political competition, but assumes that government is a form of market for equilibrating interest group demands for favors. At the assumed equilibrium, Pareto optimality holds as in the equilibria of the probabilistic voting models.

CHAPTER 12

Multiparty systems

There is a radical distinction between controlling the business of government and actually doing it.

John Stuart Mill

A.   Two views of representation

Views are divided on the role and function of elections in the democratic process and, therefore, on one of the basic constitutive elements of democratic theory. In one view, elections serve primarily to choose a government – a cabinet, administration, or executive – and only secondarily, if at all, to reflect the preferences or opinions of citizens. In that view, a cabinet governs as long as it retains the confidence (reflects the preferences or opinions) of the elected parliament. . . . There is a tendency for those who opt for that view – which we should note provides the foundation for the theory of *responsible* government – to focus on questions and issues that pertain to cabinets more than on those related to parliament and to citizens.

According to a second view, elections are primarily instruments in the hands of the public to signal particular preferences or opinions to competing representatives and only secondarily to fulfill the function of choosing a government. The basis of that view, which provides the foundation for the theory of *representative* government, is the assumption that governments seek to meet the preferences of citizens for public policies which would otherwise be unavailable in sub-optimal quantities. (Breton and Galeotti, 1985, pp. 1–2)

The two-party or two-candidate competition model of Chapters 10 and 11 provides a theoretical foundation for the first view of government. As long as the two parties or candidates must from time to time compete for the votes of the citizens, they will remain responsive to citizens' preferences. Each citizen's preference receives a positive weight in the competing candidates' objective functions. But with a large electorate, that weight will be small, and the equilibrium at which the candidates arrive may be a great distance from the citizen's most preferred platform. Moreover, since the government governs for several years, the "issues" over which the candidates compete are not specific proposals for expenditures and programs, but more general policy positions. Thus, in voting for a particular candidate the citizen does not vote for someone who will closely and directly represent the citizen's preferences. The citizen votes for the candidate or party to whom he wishes to entrust the power to govern for the upcoming electoral period. This view of the process of government resembles somewhat Hobbes's selection of a sovereign, with the amendment that the sovereign must periodically stand for reelection.

The "ideal type" for the second view of government is Athenian democracy. Government outcomes should reflect the preferences of the people as in a direct democracy. One needs representative democracy only if the polity is too large for all citizens to assemble and decide issues directly. In choosing representatives, one seeks to select those whose voting duplicates that which would occur were all of the citizens to assemble and vote directly on the issues.

As the founding fathers of the United States appreciated, an ideal system of representative government must accomplish both functions. Those chosen to govern must be empowered with sufficient discretion and authority to implement their policies. Those chosen as representatives should advocate policies that correspond to some degree to the policies favored by the citizens they represent. Most countries, including the United States, have adopted institutional structures that are best suited to accomplishing but one task. Thus, observed outcomes fall short of the theoretical ideals in at least one dimension.

A model of the first view of democracy was presented in Chapters 10 and 11. We sketch a model of the second kind in the next section.

B.   Selecting a representative body of representatives

We seek an assembly in which each citizen is represented by someone whose preferences are identical to those of the citizen.[1] Such a representative assembly cannot be formed, however, unless some citizens have preferences identical to others. Otherwise the only truly representative assembly would have to include all of the citizens. Assume, therefore, that the citizenry can be divided into s groups with all members of each group having perfectly homogeneous preferences on public issues. Let the number of citizens with preferences of the ith type by n_i. Then a fully representative body can be formed by selecting s individuals, one from each group, giving each representative votes in the assembly proportional to the number of individuals represented, for example, the representative of the ith group has n_i votes. Such an assembly would have each citizen represented by someone whose preferences were identical to

---

1. The model in this section resembles that discussed by Tullock (1967a, ch. 10); and Mueller, Tollison, and Willett (1972, 1975).

those of the citizen, and all citizens' preferences represented in proportion to their frequency in the polity.

The simplest way to form such an assembly would be to make the rewards for serving sufficiently attractive so that members of each group were induced to run for office. Assuming citizens vote for representatives with preferences identical to their own, a fully representative assembly would be formed.

If s were so large as to make the assembly itself unwieldy, then its size could be limited by (a) fixing the number of seats at some figure m and allowing only the m candidates with the highest vote totals to take seats, or (b) setting a minimum on the number or percentage of votes a candidate must receive to be allowed to take a seat in the assembly. The first proposal guarantees that at most m seats are filled in the assembly. The second allows a variable number of seats to be filled, but a number less than s can be guaranteed by setting the number of votes required to be elected high enough.

The second two proposals would both result in some citizens having voted for candidates who did not win seats in the assembly. This feature could be avoided by having a second, runoff election among the winners on the first round to determine the number of votes each could cast in the assembly. Each citizen could then vote for the representative elected in the first round whose preferences came closest to those of the citizen.[2] Although representation would then not be perfect, it would come much closer to the ideal than the outcome from a two-candidate winner-take-all contest.

Finally, if the feasible size of an assembly m were large relative to s, one could simply choose m citizens at random from the population and rely on the law of large numbers to ensure that the assembly formed consists of members whose preferences are in the same proportions as those of the polity at large (Mueller, Tollison, and Willett, 1972).

C.   Proportional representation

PR – Proportional Representation Systems

Although none of the ideal representational systems described above exists in the real world, the proportional representation (PR) systems in use in most countries approximate the ideal systems to varying degrees. The key feature of these systems is that the individual parties receive votes in the national assembly in rough proportion to the percentage of the votes they receive in the national election. Moreover, the members of each party tend to vote en bloc on issues, at least in contrast to the way congressmen vote in the United States. Thus, if we think of the individual parties as representing the policy

---

2. The stability of a given set of strategies cannot be demonstrated (Hinich and Ordeshook, 1970, pp. 785–8; Lindeen, 1970; Selten, 1971). However, if alienation leads voters to abstain when no candidates come close to their ideal points, a spreading out of candidates can be expected.

positions of a group of voters with homogeneous preferences, then PR sys-tems approximate the ideal system with each party acting as a representative. The most important difference with the ideal systems, other than the random selection assembly, is that the ideal systems would have one representative for each group and would give representatives votes in the assembly in proportion to the number of votes they received in the election.[3] Real-world PR systems give each representative one vote in the parliament and assign seats to parties in proportion to the number of votes each party receives in the election.

Under the ideal representational system, the number of seats in the assem-bly required to represent all individuals would depend on the number of different sets of preferences. This number could be large or small, and would presumably differ across countries and perhaps within countries over time. But there is no obvious optimal number that would hold for all countries. In particular, there is no compelling reason to expect two candidates or parties to be adequate to represent the major clusters of individual preferences. Almost all PR systems do have more than two parties represented in the national assembly.[4] The reason they do is directly related to an important difference between their election laws and those of the two-party systems, like those of Canada, the United Kingdom, and the United States.

D.   Electoral rules and the number of parties

PR systems allocate seats in the assembly in approximate proportion to the votes cast for each party.[5] In Canada, the United Kingdom, and the United States, representatives to the national assembly are elected from local districts using the plurality rule. The candidate receiving the most votes in a district is its representative in the assembly.[6] These two methods of electing representa-

3. In addition to representing citizens' preferences in the legislation, U.S. congressmen act as ombudsmen for their constituents and represent their interests before the various government bureaucracies (Ferejohn, 1974; Fiorina, 1977b). Such activity might be inadequately per-formed if representatives had differing numbers of constituents, although representative staff sizes could also vary with the number of their supporters. An "ideal system" might then require that each representative represent roughly the same number of voters. Note that this system would be "ideal" only because one requires that representatives perform two functions, repre-sentation of preferences in the assembly and ombudsmen. The "ideal" in the text could be retained if a separate ombudsman institution were adopted.
4. Austria has a PR parliamentary system that has nevertheless produced two viable parties since World War II. One infers from this that the diversity of opinion on major public issues in Austria is adequately captured by two different party positions.
5. The specifics of the various allocation rules vary considerably. For a formal analysis of their properties, see Balinski and Young (1978, 1982).
6. A variant on this rule sometimes used (e.g., in the election of French presidents) is to have a second, runoff election between the top two vote-getters, when the top vote-getter does not receive an absolute majority of the votes.

Table 12.1. *Percentage of national vote received by five parties*

Party	Vote
A	30
B	25
C	20
D	15
E	10

tives differ dramatically in their effects on the party composition of the assembly. Although PR systems allocate seats more or less in proportion to the votes cast for the parties, a wide range of possibilities exists under the plurality rule. Suppose, for example, there were five parties in a country with percentages of the vote as given in Table 12.1. Under PR, these figures would also be the percentages of seats that each party held in the assembly. If, however, the distribution of votes within each district also corresponds to the figures in Table 12.1, party A would win *all* of the seats in the assembly under the plurality rule. More generally, when voters from each party are randomly distributed across electoral districts, even small percentage advantages in popular support for a given party can translate into large percentage advantages in seats held under the plurality rule (Segal and Spivak, 1986). But, it can also have the opposite effect. In Table 12.2 the distribution of voters by party in each of 10 districts is depicted for a polity of 100 million. Each district has 10 million voters. Under the plurality rule, the two largest parties nationally, *A* and *B,* would win no seats. Party *C* would win half of the seats, $2\frac{1}{2}$ times its share of the national vote, and parties *D* and *E* would each win a fraction of seats that doubled their shares of the national vote.

Under PR, each citizen votes for a party that wins seats in the assembly. Thus every citizen is represented by a party for which he voted.[7] Under the plurality rule, when there are three or more parties, more than half of the citizens are represented by someone they did not vote for (Buchanan and Tullock, 1962, p. 242). This characteristic of the plurality rule can lead to alienation and abstention from the political process. It can also induce voters to switch to one of the larger parties, which has a greater chance of winning.

Under the plurality rule, minority parties whose support is evenly distributed across the country do not win seats. Over time, the continual lack of success of these parties can be expected to dry up their financial support and

7. Parties must obtain constitutionally set minimum fractions of the vote to obtain their first seat. Thus, citizens who vote for parties with very little support go unrepresented.

Table 12.2. *Distribution of votes across 10 electoral districts (numbers of votes in millions)*

Party	District									
	1	2	3	4	5	6	7	8	9	10
A	3	3	3	3	3	3	3	3	3	3
B	3	3	2	2	3	0	3	3	3	3
C	0	0	0	0	0	4	4	4	4	4
D	0	0	4	4	4	3	0	0	0	0
E	4	4	1	1	0	0	0	0	0	0
Total	10	10	10	10	10	10	10	10	10	10

discourage both their members and leaders. Thus, under the plurality rule one expects minority parties to disappear, unless their supporters are concentrated in particular geographic areas. One expects the plurality rule to produce two-party systems.

In 1951 Maurice Duverger claimed that this tendency under the plurality rule in fact "approaches most nearly perhaps to a true sociological law."[8] And so it does. Where exceptions exist, as in Canada, they generally are for parties with heavy concentrations of support in certain geographic areas, as noted above (Rae, 1971, pp. 92–6). The reverse hypothesis, that PR leads to multi-party systems also receives considerable empirical support, although there are again exceptions, like Austria, as already noted (Rae, 1971, pp. 96–100).

Thus, the two views on representation lead logically to two alternative electoral rules for choosing representatives. If the purpose of the election is to select a government, a chief executive, a single party to rule the country, then the plurality rule for electing representatives, or for electing the chief executive, should be employed. This rule will tend to produce two parties or candidates, who compete for votes as in the models of Chapters 10 and 11. If the purpose of the election is to select a body of representatives that mirrors as closely as possible the preferences of the citizenry, then PR is the appropriate electoral rule.

E.   Coalition formation in multiparty systems

When more than two parties hold seats in the assembly, it frequently happens that no single party holds a majority of the seats. Since "the government" in

---

8. As quoted by William Riker (1982a, p. 754). Riker reviews both the intellectual history of the "law" and the evidence gathered on its behalf.

parliamentary systems – that is, the cabinet, which will control the executive functions of the state – must be formed by a party or coalition of parties in the parliament, the question then arises as to which set of parties will succeed in forming a coalition and creating a government.

William Riker (1962) predicted that all single and multiparty systems converge to two parties, or two coalitions of parties, of almost equal size. The hypothesis rests on modeling politics as a zero-sum game. The plausibility of this assumption is best appreciated by thinking of all political issues as involving zero-sum redistributions of wealth. In such a game, the optimal strategy is to allow the opposing coalition to be as large as possible, while remaining a losing-paying coalition. With respect to the formation of parliamentary majorities, one can think of the prize to be divided as the fixed number of positions in the cabinet. Each party wants to have as many cabinet posts as it can, and thus wants to let as small a number of additional parties into the government as it can and still secure a majority.[9]

Riker (1962) presents convincing support for his theory from the rapid break-up of "grand coalitions" into minimum winning coalitions in U.S. political history. If the only goal of a party were winning the election, there would be no reason for a grand coalition to disintegrate. There is always some risk of losing a vote, and the bigger the coalition the safer its position. But, if the gains from winning must be taken out of the pockets of the losers, the rationale for forcing some members of the grand coalition over to the losing side is established.

Considerable evidence in support of the minimum winning coalition hypothesis has been garnered from the records of government formation in European parliamentary systems. Riker's hypothesis, or Robert Axelrod's (1970) extension of it to predict that only minimum-connected-winning coalitions form, explains the bulk of the coalitions that have formed when no single party obtained a majority of the seats. The difference between the two predictions is illustrated in Table 12.3 with data on the allocation of seats to the four Belgian parties following the February 1946 election. The parties are listed from top to bottom according to their position on a left-right ideological scale. The minimum-connected-winning coalition hypothesis predicts that only adjacent groups of parties will combine in numbers just large enough to secure a majority of the seats in the parliament, for example, the Liberals and the Christian Social Party. The minimum-winning coalition hypothesis allows "disconnected" coalitions like the Communists, Socialists, and Liberals to form a government. The latter coalition did in fact form and lasted for 13 months, when it was replaced by the minimum-connected-winning coalition

9. Minority governments sometimes form, but they tend to be short-lived and often serve simply as caretakers of the government until an election can be held and new alignments can be found. See Taylor and Herman (1971), Warwick (1979), and Schofield (1987).

Table 12.3. *Distribution of seats
in Belgian Parliament, February 1946*

Party	Percentage of seats
Communists	11
Socialists	34
Christian Social Party	45
Liberals	8

Source: Schofield (1987, Table 5).

(also minimum winning) of the Socialists and the Christian Social Party. The latter coalition lasted 27 months to the election in June 1949 (Schofield, 1987).

Determining when a minimum-winning or minimum-connected-winning coalition has formed is not always an easy task. Party positions do not always fall neatly along a single ideological dimension, and some minority coalitions govern with the support of parties that might be regarded as tacit members of the winning coalition, although they hold no cabinet positions. Thus, observers differ as to how well the two theories predict the coalitions observed. Taylor and Laver (1973), De Swaan (1975), and De Swaan and Mokken (1980) all claim that the minimum-connected-winning hypothesis provides the best explanation for the observed data. But Warwick (1979) finds that the hypothesis adds no explanatory power to the predictions given by the minimum-winning coalition hypothesis, and Schofield also favors the simpler minimum-winning coalition hypothesis on the basis of Occam's razor.[10]

F.   Political performance and the number of parties

In a parliamentary system, the government survives only as long as it can preserve its support from a majority of the members of the parliament. When there are but two parties this task is relatively easy, as the majority party's leadership must only maintain the support of the members of its own party. But when a coalition of parties forms the government, the task becomes more difficult. The different parties have different views as to what the government's program should be, and perhaps different views as to the costs, or benefits, from having a government fall and either a new coalition of parties take over or a new election called. Thus, one expects multiparty systems to have more difficulty forming stable governments.

10. In addition to presenting detailed results of his own, Schofield (1981, 1987) surveys the work of others on this topic.

The criticism of PR, that it leads to unstable government, is the most frequently and forcefully leveled criticism of this system (e.g., Schumpeter, 1950, pp. 272–3; Black, 1958, pp. 81–2). It is a well-founded criticism. Using data for 196 governments from the post–World War II period, Taylor and Herman (1971) found that government stability, measured as the duration of the government in days, was negatively correlated with both the number of parties in the parliament ($r = -0.39$) and the number in the coalition forming a government ($r = -0.307$). A Herfindahl-type index of party fractionalization ($F = 1 - \Sigma p_i^2$, p_i = proportion of the seats held by the ith party) was negatively correlated with government stability when measured for the full parliament ($r = -0.448$), or for the government ($r = -0.302$). One-party governments lasted on average 1107.9 days, almost twice as long as coalition governments (624.5 days).

Warwick (1979) focused upon the durability of *coalition* governments, and found that majority coalitions lasted longer than minority coalitions, and that minimum-winning coalitions lasted much longer than other types. Government durability was inversely related to the number of parties in the government. These findings were reconfirmed by Schofield (1987). Powell (1981) found that the durability of the chief executive (president, prime minister) was significantly and negatively correlated with political fractionalization ($r = -0.41$). Given the linkage between PR and the number of parties in the parliament (Rae, 1971), the proposition that PR systems have less stable (shorter-lived) governments seems well established.[11]

But stability is not the only indicator of a political system's performance. As noted above, alienation can be expected to be higher in a two-party system, as some voters perceive the party positions to be too distant from their own. If alienation leads voters to abstain, then it will evidence itself in the form of lower voter turnouts at the polls. Powell (1981) did report significantly lower turnouts in the aggregative (two-party) democracies like Canada and the United States than in representative (PR) systems like West Germany and the Netherlands.

Alienation can also lead citizens to seek other, more violent modes of political expression. Powell (1981) also reported significantly higher numbers of riots and deaths due to political violence in the aggregative systems than occurred in the representational ones.

Thus, it would appear that there exists a stability trade-off across the different types of political systems. The plurality rule favors two-party sys-

---

11. For additional references to the literature, see Warwick (1979) and Schofield (1987).

   Midlarsky (1984) presents additional evidence in support of the stability of minimum-winning coalitions by demonstrating a tendency for both presidential and House votes by party to cycle around 50 percent. His model predicts that minimum-winning coalitions in multiparty systems, where one party has at least 44–5 percent of the vote, approach two-party systems in their stability properties.

tems and provides disproportional power to the largest party. These systems are more stable when one defines stability in terms of the life expectancy of the government. But they induce greater alienation in the citizens and higher levels of politically motivated violence. Representational systems like PR allow minorities a greater opportunity to voice dissent regarding political outcomes, and thus channel this dissent out of the streets and into the national assembly.

G.   Commentary

We began this chapter with a quotation from Albert Breton and Gianluigi Galeotti (1985) regarding two views of representation. It should be clear from this chapter and the two preceding ones that both two-party, winner-take-all systems and PR systems are representative in the sense that each citizen's preferences receive weight in the final outcomes of the political process. In the two-party competition systems, the individual citizen's preferences influence the platforms upon which the candidates run and the outcomes to the extent that the necessity to stand for reelection forces the winners to implement the platforms upon which they run. In the PR systems, each citizen is represented by a party for which he has voted, and which, to a greater extent than in the two-party systems, represents his preferences. His preferences thus pass through the votes of his party and are reflected in the outcomes of parliamentary votes.

It can be argued that both systems will produce about the same set of final outcomes from the political process. Although extremists on the far left and right are represented in the assemblies of PR systems, their votes do not carry the day. Outcomes on single-dimensional issues are presumably near the median representative's preferences. But competition between candidates in the two-party systems also results in outcomes at the median in one-dimensional contests, and at the mean in multidimensional issue spaces. If majority rule is the ultimate decider of issues, fringe minorities always lose.

Although the final outcomes from the two systems might plausibly be the same, their underlying rationales and logic are quite different. The two-party system is essentially a device for choosing a chief executive, or the executive branch's cabinet. The two candidates or parties compete on the basis of promises of what they will do if entrusted with executive branch power. Upon election, the winners must be free to carry out the platforms that brought about their victories if the system is to achieve its potential.

PR is a system for choosing *representatives,* not for picking between final packages of outcomes. When the citizen votes for a given party or representative, he votes for someone who he thinks will vote in the assembly in the same way that the citizen himself would vote were he there. He cannot know when he votes for a representative what the final outcomes from the assembly votes will be, and considerations about these outcomes can influence the citizen's vote only in the most indirect way.

Which of the arguments underlying the two systems one finds most compelling is a matter of considered judgment and political taste. But whichever one is preferred, obviously its rationale is quite different from that of the other system and requires a quite different set of institutions if it is to achieve its potential. One cannot combine both modes of representation into one system, and yet most countries do.

Presidential elections in the United States resemble the competitions described in Chapters 10 and 11. If one feels that the system these models describe is the preferred one, then the U.S. system would be optimal *if* the president had the power to implement the policies promised in the election campaign. But he does not. He must get Congress to agree to his program, which it does only in part.

Congress would constitute a reasonable approximation to a parliament elected under PR, if voter preferences were perfectly homogeneous within congressional districts and states but differed across these jurisdictions. On *national* issues, this condition is clearly violated. The only issues upon which all of a congressman's constituents have reasonably similar preferences are redistributional issues favoring their district. Not surprisingly, a good deal of a congressman's efforts goes toward securing the victory of these issues, as well as ombudsman work for individual constituents.[12]

The use of the plurality rule to elect members of Congress leads to inadequate representation of minority views in the legislature. But Congress is also too large and unwieldy to effectuate the executive function. The president is elected in such a way that would legitimate his sole undertaking of this function, but he is frustrated in this endeavor by the Congress.

The Canadian and British parliamentary systems correspond to the two-party competition model to the extent that they are two-party states, which is true only in part, and party discipline forces party members to support their party leaders on all parliamentary votes. The real contests for office are then between the prime ministerial candidates and their prospective cabinets. The main function of the other party members is to supply information to the party leadership concerning voter preferences and to train for the party leadership.

The PR systems would fit the pure representation model if the only function of their assemblies was to vote upon legislation. If a separate, administrative branch existed for implementing the actions of the assembly, the assembly could serve as the kind of representational town meeting; the logic underlying

---

12. See Ferejohn (1974), Mayhew (1974), Fiorina (1977b), Fenno (1978), and Weingast, Shepsle, and Johnsen (1981).

the system dictates it should be. But most PR systems require that the assembly not only vote upon legislation, but also form the executive branch. This requirement blurs the purely representational role of the parties, as voters must also now consider the executive potential of the leaders of the major parties, and leads to the instability problems that have been PR's Achilles' heel since its invention. Thus, in varying degrees, most political systems actually combine elements of both views of representation, and thereby are incapable of achieving the full benefits of either.

Bibliographical notes

The standard format for articles on PR or multiparty systems is to begin with one or more lengthy quotations from classic works. I know of no other area in public choice in which the average age of a source quoted is so great. Whether this tendency reflects the brilliance of the first writers on the topic or the paucity of talent devoted to the topic since, I am not sure. Perhaps it merely reflects the lack of interest in the topic by Anglo-Saxon scholars. I defer in part to this tradition with my opening quotation from the recent article by Breton and Galeotti (1985).

Among the classics, John Stuart Mill's *Considerations on Representative Government*, first published in 1861, is worth reading for its discussion of both PR and political theory more generally. Other early writings on PR are discussed in Pitkin (1967), Riker (1982a), Chamberlin and Courant (1983), and Sugden (1984).

institutions induce
friction, induce
stability

CHAPTER 13

Rent seeking

The *positive* evils and dangers of the representative, as of every other form of government, may be reduced to two heads: first, general ignorance and incapacity, or, to speak more moderately, insufficient mental qualifications, in the controlling body; secondly, the danger of its being under the influence of interests not identical with the general welfare of the community. (Italics in original)

John Stuart Mill

In Chapter 11 we discussed a model of political competition in which politicians provide policies or legislation to win votes, and voters and interest groups provide campaign funding as well as votes. From the discussion up to this point, it seems reasonable to think that the legislation consists of either public goods with characteristics that appeal to given groups of voters or income transfers from one sector of the population to another. The latter might be a tax loophole benefiting a particular group coupled with a rise in the average tax rate to make up for the revenue lost through the loophole. Income can be transferred from one group to another by other, more subtle means, however.

The government can, for example, help create, increase, or protect a group's monopoly position. In so doing, the government increases the monopoly rents of the favored groups, at the expense of the buyers of the group's products or services. The monopoly rents that the government can help provide are a prize worth pursuing, and the pursuit of these rents has been given the name of rent seeking.

A.   The theory of rent seeking

Rent seeking was first discussed systematically by Gordon Tullock (1967c). The term "rent seeking" was first used to describe the activity in question by Anne Krueger (1974). Figure 13.1 depicts the demand schedule for a monopolized product. If the monopoly charges the monopoly price P_m instead of the competitive price P_c, the rectangle R of monopoly rents is created, as is the welfare triangle L of lost consumers' surplus on the output of the monopolized product, which would have been produced under perfect competition, but is not provided by the monopolist.

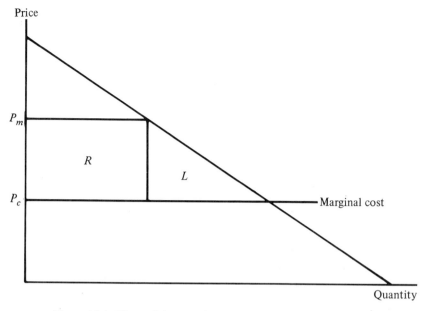

Figure 13.1. The social costs of monopoly with rent seeking.

In the traditional discussion of monopoly, it has been customary to treat L as a measure of the efficiency loss due to monopoly, and R as a pure redistribution of income from the consumers of the monopolized product or service to its producers. Suppose, however, that the monopoly has been created and is protected by an action of the government. For example, an airline might have been granted a monopoly over the routes between two or more cities. If there is more than one airline in the country that could service the routes, then R, or the present discounted value of R, is a prize to be awarded to the airline that succeeds in inducing the government to grant it the monopoly over the routes. If the airlines can invest resources and increase the probability of obtaining the monopoly, it will pay them to do so. Tullock's (1967c) initial insight revealed that these invested resources may constitute a social cost of monopoly in addition to the welfare triangle L.

James Buchanan (1980a, pp. 12–14) has identified three types of rent-seeking expenditures that may be socially wasteful: (1) the efforts and expenditures of the potential recipients of the monopoly, (2) the efforts of the government officials to obtain or to react to the expenditures of the potential recipients, and (3) third-party distortions induced by the monopoly itself or the government as a consequence of the rent-seeking activity. As examples of each of these, assume that the airlines employ lobbyists to bribe the government official who awards the routes. It becomes known that the income of this government official is supplemented by bribes, and thus lower-level government officials invest time studying the airlines industry to improve their chances of obtaining this position. Finally, assume that the government's additional tax revenue from creating the monopoly leads to a competition among other interest groups for subsidies or tax breaks. The lobbying effort of the airlines industry is an example of the first type of social waste. The extra efforts of the bureaucrats to be promoted is an example of the second category (assuming that they do not improve the route allocation process, which is a reasonable assumption if the awards are determined by the bribes). The expenditures induced by the other interest groups to capture the extra tax revenue generated is an example of the third category of social waste.

Note that the bribe itself is not regarded as a social waste. If an airline could win a monopoly position simply by offering a bribe, and this bribe could be costlessly transmitted to the government official awarding the routes, and this was all that the bribe brought about, then no social waste would be created by the bribe. It would simply be a further redistributional transfer from the passengers of the airline, through the airline to the government official. The social waste in passing the bribe comes in the transaction costs of making the bribe, the fee of the lobbyist, and the wasted time and money of the bureaucrats competing for the promotion that places them in the position to receive the bribes.[1]

Considerable attention has been devoted in the literature to the issue of whether the rents of monopoly are totally dissipated by socially wasteful expenditures to capture them.[2] That they might be can easily be illustrated for the case when all rent seekers are risk-neutral. Let us measure utility in monetary units, so that an individual's initial utility equals her income, $U = Y$. Let the amount invested be I, and the potential rent be R. If all rent seekers have the same initial incomes, each will choose to invest the same amount I, and each will have an equal probability of winning the rent. If entry into rent seeking is free, entry will continue to the point where the number of rent seekers, n, is such that the expected income of a rent seeker just equals that of a non–rent seeker.

$$E(Y) = \frac{1}{n}(Y - I + R) + \frac{n-1}{n}(Y - I) = Y, \tag{13.1}$$

---

1. That some expenditures to obtain rents may be transfers of one sort or another and not a pure social waste has been discussed by Brooks and Heijdra (1986). Congleton (1988) points out that the payment to the lobbyist is not simply a transfer, assuming that she could be employed doing something socially productive.
2. See Tullock (1980, 1985), Rogerson (1982), Hillman and Katz (1984), Corcoran and Karels (1985), Higgins, Shughart, and Tollison (1985), and Higgins and Tollison (1986).

from which it follows that

$$Y - I + R + (n - 1)(Y - I) = nY \qquad (13.2)$$

and thus that

$$R = nI. \qquad (13.3)$$

Entry continues to the point where the number of rent seekers is such that the total amount invested in rent seeking fully dissipates the rents to be received.

When one relaxes any of the three assumptions, (1) that rent seekers are risk-neutral, (2) that they are in symmetric positions, or (3) that there is free entry into rent seeking, then one can obtain results showing that the total funds invested are either more or less than the potential rent.

Consider first the effect of dropping the risk-neutrality assumption. Hillman and Katz (1984) illustrate the effects of risk aversion by rent seekers for the special case in which risk aversion is introduced by assuming that each individual has a logarithmic utility function. Table 13.1 is taken from their paper. The X/A's are the rents to be gained relative to a rent seeker's initial wealth. The n's are the numbers of rent seekers. Note that when the rents to be won are small relative to the rent seeker's initial wealth (e.g., less than 20 percent), over 90 percent of the value of the rents is dissipated by the competition to obtain them. This result holds when risk aversion is introduced by assuming other forms of utility functions (Hillman and Katz, 1984, pp. 105–7).

Much of the rent-seeking literature discusses the process as if rent seekers were individuals acting on their own behalf. In these cases, it is sometimes reasonable to assume that the value of the sort of rents sought is large relative to the initial assets of the rent seekers. But in most instances of rent seeking through the public sector, and probably in private sector rent seeking too, the size of the rents sought will be small relative to the assets of the rent seekers. If we assume that the stockholders of a corporation are the ultimate recipients of its profits, then the rents that the airline would earn by having a monopoly over an air route between two cities must be compared to the aggregate wealth of the stockholders of the airline. The rents that milk farmers earn from an increase in the price supports for milk must be divided by the assets of all the milk farmers. In public sector rent seeking, the ratio of potential rents to initial assets of the relevant rent-seeking groups should be small, and the relevant rows of Table 13.1 are one and maybe two. Competitive rent seeking can be expected to result in nearly a full dissipation of the rents even when the rent seekers are risk-averse.

The issue of the size of the rent seekers' assets becomes more complicated when we recognize the principal-agent problem in the joint stock company or the other forms of interest groups. The decision to invest airline revenues to

Table 13.1. *Competitive rent dissipation, logarithmic utility,* A = 100

| | | | | *n* | | | |
X/A	2	3	5	10	50	100	1,000
0.10	98	97	96	96	95	95	95
0.20	95	94	93	92	91	91	91
0.50	88	85	83	82	81	81	81
1.00	76	74	72	70	70	69	69
5.00	32	34	35	36	36	36	36
10.00	18	21	22	23	24	24	24

Source: Hillman and Katz (1984).

win a monopoly on an air route is made by the airline's managers. To whose wealth should the investment be compared?

When the manager-agents of shareholders are the relevant actors in the rent-seeking game, the assumption that these actors are risk-averse is no longer very plausible. The bulk of the money that the airline's management is investing belongs to the company's shareholders, and this fact will induce managers to take greater risks (Jensen and Meckling, 1976). When rent seekers are agents investing the money of their principals, risk-taking behavior is more plausible than risk aversion, and an overdissipation of rents can be expected. Similar considerations probably apply to the rent-seeking actions of the agents of other interest groups (labor unions, farm associations).

Frank Knight (1934) argued that the self-selection process for choosing entrepreneurs made entrepreneurs as a group risk takers. He thus predicted that aggregate profits would on average be negative owing to the overcompetition for profits by risk-taking entrepreneurs. Since profits and rents are one and the same to the individual entrepreneur, Knight's assumption would again lead one to expect that entrepreneurial rent seeking under competitive conditions more than fully dissipates all potential rents. Moreover, this conclusion should hold whether the rents sought come from private market investments (e.g., advertising, patenting), or from political markets (campaign expenditures, lobbying). The principal-agent problem should, if anything, exaggerate this tendency.

Relaxing any of the perfect competition assumptions of free entry and symmetric investment opportunities leads to less than full dissipation of the rents, as one might expect. The more the game is rigged in favor of a few players, the less they and others find it profitable to invest (Rogerson, 1982).

The amount of rent dissipation that occurs also depends upon the relationship between the amount a single rent seeker invests and the probability of winning the rent. The implicit assumption in much of the work seems to be that the probability of winning the rent is linear in the amount invested, as it is, for example, when the probability of winning equals the proportion of the total investment in rent seeking. With risk-neutral rent seekers, the amount invested in rent seeking expands to equal the total amount of the rents even when the number of rent seekers is fixed. Let S be the total amount invested in rent seeking and I the investment of a particular rent seeker. The probability of her winning R is then I/S, and the expected gain from investing another dollar is simply R/S. This ratio exceeds one as long as $R > S$, and so investment expands until $S = R$. As with the size of the firm under constant returns to scale, the amount the rent seeker invests is indeterminate when both utility and the probability of winning the rent are assumed to be linear, but the residual of rents over total investment in rent seeking is not. It is zero.

The situation changes if we assume that the probability of winning rises more or less proportionately to the amount invested. Consider, for example, a process for allocating a rent R, whereby each rent seeker filed an application at a fixed cost F, the rent was allocated by a random draw among the applicants, and no one was allowed to file more than one application. Under this procedure, no one would spend more than F to win the rent. With risk-neutral rent seekers and free entry, the number of applicants would increase, as shown in equations (13.1) to (13.3), until total rents were dissipated. But if the total number of applicants were constrained to some level $\bar{n}$, less than the n satisfying $R = nF$, then this procedure would not result in a full dissipation of the rents through internal competition among the rent seekers. More generally, the assumption of diminishing increases in the probability of winning R to increases in I results in a determinant, optimal investment in rent seeking by each rent seeker, just as the assumption of diminishing returns to scale results in a determinant optimal-sized firm. With n constrained, this diminishing-returns assumption prevents the rent seekers from competing away all rents. Free entry and symmetry again produce a full dissipation of rents.

Finally, consider a process for awarding R, which gives R to the rent seeker making the highest I. If the other investments are fixed, it always pays to invest slightly more than the highest investment that any other rent seeker has made up to the point where $I = R$. A competition to make the highest I could ensue until the aggregate funds invested in rent seeking were nearly nR. At this point all rent seekers would drop out and the competition would begin again. No Nash equilibrium in pure strategies exists for this game, but the discontinuously increasing returns-to-scale property of the game does create the danger that aggregate investments will greatly exceed the potential rent to be won (Tullock, 1980). Hillman and Samet (1987) show that a mixed-strategy equilibrium exists that, with risk-neutral players, is again character-ized by full dissipation of all rents.

The extent to which any rents are fully dissipated through rent-seeking expenditures obviously depends on so many factors that no general conclu-sions can be offered that cover all cases. But the assumption cannot be sustained that rent-seeking investments are likely to be small relative to the rents sought.

B.   Rent seeking through regulation

The traditional economic rationale for regulation sees the regulated industry as a "natural monopoly" with falling long-run average costs. The classic, bridge example is a polar case of the natural monopoly situation. A single bridge is needed, and once built, the marginal cost of allowing additional cars to cross it is zero (crowding aside). The optimal toll on the bridge is then zero. However, if a private firm operates the bridge, it will set the price at the revenue-maximizing level, and the result will be a socially inefficient under-utilization of the bridge. Any industry with continuously falling long-run average costs is a "natural monopoly" in the sense that only one firm is needed to supply all of the industry's output. Regulation is said to be needed to restrain that one firm from taking advantage of its monopoly position. In terms of Figure 13.1, regulation is thought to be necessary to help consumers capture some fraction of the consumers' surplus triangle L.[3]

In the regulatory process, producer and consumer interests are opposed. The higher the price that the regulators set, the bigger the monopoly rent rectangle going to the producers. Since regulation is a political bureaucratic process, it is reasonable to assume that the sellers of a regulated product place some pressure on the regulators to raise price, and increase the size of the rectangle. In a seminal contribution to the regulation debate, George Stigler (1971) shifted attention away from largely normative discussions of what price should be to minimize L, to a positive analysis of how the struggle to secure R determines price. Although predating the rent-seeking literature, Stigler's paper draws attention to the rent-creating powers of regulators and the rent-seeking efforts of those regulated.

In an important extension of Stigler's argument, Sam Peltzman (1976) integrated both consumers and producers into the rent-seeking struggle. He depicted regulation as being supplied by a vote-maximizing politician. Let V, the number of votes the politician receives, be a function of the utilities

3. In practice, regulation in the United States has tended to resemble average cost pricing more than marginal cost pricing so that some welfare triangle losses have occurred even when regulation has worked well (Kahn, 1970).

of both the regulated producers, U_R, and the consumers of the regulated product, U_C.

$$V = V(U_R, U_C), \quad \frac{\partial V}{\partial U_R} > 0, \quad \frac{\partial V}{\partial U_C} > 0. \tag{13.4}$$

For simplicity, assume consumer and regulator utilities are linear in R and L; that is,

$$U_R = R \ , \ U_C = K - R - L, \tag{13.5}$$

where K is an arbitrary constant. Then assuming that the proper second-order conditions hold to ensure an interior maximum, the vote-maximizing regulator sets price, P, to satisfy

$$\frac{dV}{dP} = \frac{\partial V}{\partial U_R} \frac{dR}{dP} - \frac{\partial V}{\partial U_C} \frac{dR}{dP} - \frac{\partial V}{\partial U_C} \frac{dL}{dP} = 0 \tag{13.6}$$

or

$$\frac{\partial V}{\partial U_R} \frac{dR}{dP} = \frac{\partial V}{\partial U_C} \left(\frac{dR}{dP} + \frac{dL}{dP} \right) \tag{13.7}$$

The vote-maximizing regulator sets a price such that the marginal gain in support from the producers for an increment in monopoly rents, R, is just offset by the loss in consumer votes from a combined rise in R and L.

Although most regulated industries are not monopolies, the number of sellers is generally small. It is certainly small relative to the number of consumers. The costs of organizing the producers and the concentration of the benefits, R, on each producer are likely to combine to make $\partial V/\partial U_R$ large relative to $\partial V/\partial U_C$, at least over an initial range of values for R (Olson, 1965; Stigler, 1971; Peltzman, 1976). Stigler (1971) stresses this point in arguing that the main beneficiaries of regulation are the regulated firms. Price will be raised until dR/dP falls sufficiently far, or $\partial V/\partial U_C$ becomes sufficiently large to bring (13.7) into equality. But note also that as long as $\partial V/\partial U_C > 0$ – that is, as long as there is some loss in votes from reducing consumer utility – (13.7) will not be satisfied at the rent-maximizing price, where $dR/dP = 0$. When $dR/dP = 0$, dL/dP is greater than zero, and that combined with $\partial V/\partial U_C > 0$ makes the right-hand side of (13.7) positive. The vote-maximizing politician may favor the regulated industry's producers, but stops short of setting price at the rent-maximizing level (Peltzman, 1976, pp. 222–41; Becker, 1976). Peltzman derives several interesting implications from his analysis. One is that "*either* naturally monopolistic or naturally competitive industries are more politically attractive to regulate than an oligopolistic hybrid" (1976, pp. 223–4, italics in original). Equation (13.7) implies that regulation brings price to a level somewhere between the pure monopoly and pure competition prices. Assuming oligopoly prices tend to lie intermediate between monopoly and competitive levels, then oligopolists and their consumers have less to gain from regulation than do the consumers of a natural monopoly product, or the producers of a competitive product. By this argument, Peltzman helps to explain the ubiquitous regulation of agriculture around the world and other interventions in seemingly competitive industries like trucking and taxicabs in the United States.

Stigler (1971) emphasized the strength of the regulated groups in using the regulatory process to enhance their incomes, and several studies are supportive of this view of regulation (e.g., Shepherd, 1978; Paul, 1982; Ulrich, Furtan, and Schmitz, 1987). Peltzman (1976) stressed the trade-off between consumer and regulator interests in the final vote-maximizing equilibrium. In trying to test the Peltzman generalization of the Stigler theory, scholars have generally tried to find variables that measure both producer-seller and consumer interests. Leffler (1978), Keeler (1984), Primeaux, et al. (1984), and Becker (1986) all present evidence consistent with the view that both consumer and producer interests receive some weight in the final regulatory outcomes. Ippolito and Masson (1978) show that regulation in the milk industry redistributes rents from one group of producers to another, and from one group of consumers to another. Finally, there is evidence that in some cases (e.g., the passage of legislation regulating the stock exchanges in the 1930s) consumers have received substantial redistributive gains (Schwert, 1977). The redistributive gains from regulation are a prize, which all can pursue and win.

Although the Stigler–Peltzman model focuses on the rents of monopoly and their distribution through regulation, the process by which the interest groups influence the regulators, and vice versa, is not developed. The issue of whether R is competed away through wasteful rent-seeking expenditures or remains a pure transfer is not addressed.

There are several reasons to expect that some if not all of R is competed away. As Hirshleifer (1976) pointed out, regulators – that is, those people who regulate within existing legislation as opposed to those who vote on the legislation – are typically bureaucrats not politicians. Although their decisions may be sensitive to public opinion on both sides, they are not actually trying to win votes. Both consumers and producer interests devote resources trying to convince the regulator-bureaucrats to set prices in a manner favorable to them. Since they are arguing for opposite changes in price, at least one side's expenditures must be wasted, in the sense that they are made in an effort to move the price away from a welfare-maximizing price, however that is defined.

Regulation can also lead to waste when it controls one level of competition but not some others. A good example was airline regulation in the United

States under the Civil Aeronautics Board (CAB). The CAB controlled price competition, but allowed airlines to compete for customers by offering non-price frills like free drinks, movies, and half-empty planes. The airlines competed away, through additional costs, the rents granted them by the prices the CAB set (Douglas and Miller, 1974).

Rent seeking can also occur at the time when the initial legislation establishing or altering a regulatory process is voted upon. Here a vote-maximizing model of the regulator-politician is appropriate. If all that the interest groups supplied was votes, there would be no social waste. But interest groups may try to influence electoral outcomes by lobbying, campaign contributions, and the other potentially wasteful outlays that we have discussed. To the extent that they do, rent seeking through regulation is part of these generally wasteful rent-seeking activities.

Richard Posner (1975), in an influential contribution to the rent-seeking literature, emphasized the wastes from rent seeking in regulated industries. Assuming that the entire rectangle R is dissipated, he used estimates of the rise in price brought about by regulation in several industries to calculate $R + L$ as a measure of the social costs of regulation. Posner's figures are reproduced in Table 13.2. The η_1 column presents demand elasticities calculated under the assumption that the industry sets price so as to maximize monopoly rents, $(P - MC)/P = 1/\eta$, using the independent estimates of the price rise under regulation. The estimates in the η_2 column are from econometric studies of demand elasticity for the industries. The C_1 and C_2 columns are measures of $R + L$ made using the η_1 and η_2 estimates, respectively. They are all fairly large, both in an absolute sense and relative to existing estimates of the social cost of monopoly in the private sector that rely only on measures of L.

C.   Rent seeking through tariffs and quotas

Few issues elicit greater agreement among economists than the proposition that society's welfare is maximized when there is free trade.[4] Yet tariffs, quotas, and other restrictions on international trade abound, and trade policy is a constant subject of political debate. As with regulation policies, one suspects that the allocative efficiency gains from free trade so obvious to the economist have been sacrificed to provide the equally obvious rents and redistributive gains that restrictions on trade engender.

To see what is involved, consider Figure 13.2. Let S_M be the supply of imports of product X, and S_D the supply of domestic production. S_T and D are the total supply and demand schedules in the domestic country. Under free

---

4. For a review of the caveats, see Findlay and Wellisz (1986, pp. 221–2).

Table 13.2. *Social costs of regulation*

	Regulatory price increase (%)	Demand elasticity		Costs (as % of industry sales)	
		η_1	η_2	C_1	C_2
Physicians' services	0.40	3.500	0.575	0.42	0.31
Eyeglasses	0.34	0.394	0.450	0.39	0.24
Milk	0.11	10.00	0.339	0.15	0.10
Motor carriers	0.62	2.630	1.140	0.57	0.30
Oil	0.65	2.500	0.900	0.60	0.32
Airlines	0.66	2.500	2.360	0.60	0.19

Source: Posner (1975, p. 84). See original for references to sources for the various estimates.

trade, X_F is purchased at a price P_F, with output divided between domestic production, D_F, and imports, M_F.

Now let a tariff be imposed on imports that shifts the import supply schedule including the tariff to S'_M. Total supply shifts to S'_T, and X_R divided into M_R and D_R is sold at a price P_R.

The tariff brings about the welfare loss represented by the consumers' surplus triangle L on the forgone consumption $X_F - X_R$. In addition, factor owners and producers in the domestic industry earn rents of $R(P_R P_F EG)$, assuming that they are specialized in the production of X, and the government receives tariff revenue T ($P_R CBA$). Both R and T represent income flows that might stimulate a demand for the tariff by those in the protected industry, or those in government.

The outcome of X_R sold at a price P_R can also be brought about by imposing a quota on imports restricting them to M_R. The domestic industry receives R in rents again, but the rectangle T now represents rents received by the importers "lucky" enough to get licenses for the M_R units of imports. Thus, political pressure from domestic sellers will be the same whether the trade restriction is a quota or a tariff (assuming the same level of imports results), but pressure for quotas will come from importers, while pressure for tariffs will come from those in government, or from the eventual beneficiaries of the increase in government revenue.

Not all industries receive protection from import competition, and those that do receive it in varying degrees. As with the Stigler–Peltzman theory of regulation, one expects industries to be favored over consumers, and industries with concentrated market structures and geographically concentrated production patterns to be more successful at gaining protection.

Both of these predictions have found some empirical support. Marvel and

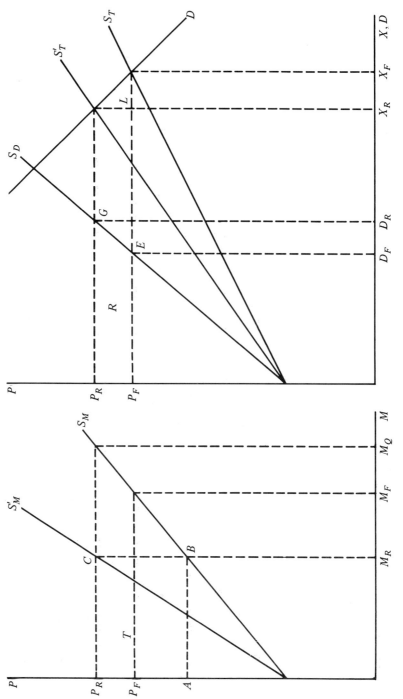

Figure 13.2. Imports and domestic production under tariffs and quotas.

Ray (1983) found tariffs to be higher in consumer goods industries. Pincus (1975) and Marvel and Ray (1983) found them to be higher in concentrated industries. Caves (1976) found a negative relationship between concentration and tariff levels in Canada, however.

Beyond these rather direct measures of interest group strength, the most important explanatory variables explaining protectionism have measured the degree of competitive pressure, and thus the short-run losses of income and rents of factor owners from international competition. Unemployment rates have been found to be positively and significantly related to tariffs (Baldwin, 1985, pp. 142–80), to escape clause petitions to the International Trade Commission (ITC) (Takacs, 1981), and to the number of dumping cases filed with the U.S. Bureau of Customs (Magee, 1982). Industries experiencing relatively high import penetration or unfavorable trade balances also make more escape clause petitions to the ITC (Takacs, 1981). Baldwin (1985, pp. 142–80) argues that the importance of unemployment rates and the percentage of low-paid workers in explaining tariffs and other measures of protectionism suggests more long-run and altruistic motivations on the part of either voters or their representatives than hypothesized in the interest group models.

The potential of gaining R or a larger R can lead to investments that may constitute a social waste: lobbying, providing information to the news media, contributing to political campaigns, and the like. T can also induce rent-seeking outlays. At P_R, M_Q units of the imported good could be profitably sold, but only M_R units can receive licenses. Anne Krueger (1974, pp. 52–54) enumerated the forms these wasteful outlays could take: (1) construction of excess plant capacity, when licenses are awarded in proportion to firms' plant capacities; (2) excessive entry and therefore less than optimal-sized firms, when licenses are allocated pro rata to applicants; (3) lobbying efforts and bribes in the form of hiring relatives of customs officials who are less productive than their earnings, to obtain import licenses; (4) the wasteful competition among those in the government to be in a position to receive the bribes.

Given these wasteful outlays to secure import licenses, Krueger favored tariffs over quotas as a means of restricting imports. But competition can arise between those both within and outside of government with regard to sharing in T, when T is the revenue raised by a tariff. The iron law of rent seeking is that wherever a rent is to be found, a rent seeker will be there trying to get it.

When one starts from a first-best equilibrium, rent-seeking activities that both create rents and dissipate them must leave society worse off, since both L and R and perhaps T are lost. But when one starts in a second-best situation, rent seeking can sometimes improve welfare, for example, when it succeeds in eliminating a trade barrier to bring about a first-best allocation of resources (Bhagwati and Srinivasan, 1980; Bhagwati, 1982). Although a comforting possibility, because rectangles and trapezoids are so much larger than triangles, rent seeking must typically reduce welfare whenever the rents are substantially dissipated.

Krueger presented data on the rents generated from several categories of licenses in India, the largest of which was imports, indicating a potential loss from rent seeking in 1964 of 7.3 percent of national income. Figures for 1968 for import licenses in Turkey imply a waste of resources equivalent to 15 percent of GNP (Krueger, 1974, pp. 55–7). As with Posner's calculations, these estimates are rough, but nonetheless impressive.

An important component of rent-seeking expenditures in competitive democracies should be contributions by the potential beneficiaries of restrictive legislation to the parties or candidates. These contributions should in turn influence the way the recipients vote. Three studies have tested for the effect of the level of campaign contributions on the direction of a congressman's vote on protective legislation. Baldwin (1985, pp. 59–69) examined the effect of union contributions to congressmen on their vote on the Trade Act of 1974. Coughlin (1985) examined the effect of contributions from labor on congressional voting on the Automotive Products Act of 1982, a piece of domestic content legislation. Tosini and Tower (1987) analyze the effect of contributions by interest groups from the textile industry on congressional voting on the Textile Bill of 1985. All three studies find a positive and significant effect of the size of political contributions from the interest group, and the probability that a congressman voted in favor of the protective legislation. Other significant variables in these studies measure the importance of the industries that would be protected in the congressman's district or state, the unemployment rate in the state, and the congressman's party affiliation. These studies of voting on trade legislation along with those reviewed earlier confirm the hypothesis that interest groups can buy votes through their campaign contributions. When these votes are on rent-creating or rent-preserving legislation, the possibility that they contribute to the wasteful bidding away of the rents that the legislation effects must be entertained.

D.   Rent seeking in governmental contracting

Regulation and trade restrictions are but two ways in which government alters the distribution of income. Direct transfers are a third, and they too can give rise to investments to change their size and the direction of their flow (Tullock, 1971d). More generally, Aranson and Ordeshook (1981, pp. 81–2) stress that even the production of a good with public good characteristics, like a highway, has distributional effects that may significantly influence the collective decision to provide the good:

> A larger view of production would embrace the idea that some contractor must build a road to the exclusion of other contractors. Some concrete

manufacturer receives a subcontract while other manufacturers do not. Some bureaucrats must receive the wages for planning and overseeing construction, while another bureaucrat (or his agency) or even private sector taxpayers do not. And, those who speculate correctly on land in one area gain a windfall over those who speculate incorrectly elsewhere. In sum, a federally funded interstate highway system in production can be much like a private good; its supply is limited and subject to exclusion.

The entire federal budget can be viewed as a gigantic rent up for grabs for those who can exert the most political muscle.

The distributional consequences of government contracting can be expected to influence the flow of lobbying and campaign expenditures as in the rent-seeking models. Campaign expenditures should come from those seeking government contracts, and contracts should flow to those making contributions. Zardkoohi (1985) has found that the amount of campaign contributions a firm makes is positively and significantly related to the percentages of federal and state government outputs purchased by the firm's industry, and whether or not industry-specific regulation was applicable to the firm's industry. Wallis (1986) found that large states used their numerical advantages in the House to garner greater shares of federal relief programs than the Senate was willing to award in the 1930s. The flow of funds from federal and state budgets is a prize to be sought, and those who can benefit from and determine its allocation are aware of this fact, and act accordingly.

E. Rent seeking and the political process

Although much of the rent-seeking literature regards the government as the main instrument for the creation and distribution of rents, little attention is devoted to the implications of this assumption with respect to the workings of government institutions. The paper by Wallis (1986) is an exception, as is the book by McCormick and Tollison (1981).

Building on a paper by Stigler (1976), McCormick and Tollison develop a set of models of the political process. A fundamental assumption they make is that all legislation consists of wealth transfers. Legislatures are organized to transfer wealth efficiently. Each individual or interest group is a potential supplier of wealth transfers, and at the same time a potential demander. The legislatures take from those who are least capable of resisting the demands for wealth transfers and give to those who are best organized for pressing their demands. Thus, like the Stigler–Peltzman theory of regulation, McCormick and Tollison's (1981, chs. 1–3) theory builds on Olson's (1965) theory of group formation.

To succeed in securing a wealth transfer, an interest group must win a majority of votes in both houses of a bicameral legislature. The more seats there are in each house, the more resources that must be devoted to winning legislator votes. Moreover, assuming that there are diminishing returns to securing votes in any house, holding the total number of seats constant, it will be easier to win legislator votes the more evenly divided the total number of seats in the two houses is. McCormick and Tollison (1981, pp. 45–55) find that these two variables, number of seats and the ratio of seats in the two houses, are significantly related to the degree of economic and occupational regulation across the states, and to the total number of bills enacted. They go on to analyze the determinants of legislator wages, gubernatorial salaries, and other issues (1981, chs. 4–7).

Complementing the McCormick–Tollison models of government is the theory of the independent judiciary put forward by William Landes and Richard Posner (1975). They too see legislators as selling legislation for "campaign contributions, votes, implicit promises of future favors, and sometimes outright bribes" (p. 877). In this setting, an independent judiciary can increase the value of the legislation sold today by making it somewhat immune from short-run political pressures that might try to thwart or overturn the intent of the legislation in the future. And this is apparently what the founding fathers had in mind when they established an independent judiciary in the Constitution. In the Landes–Posner theory, the First Amendment emerges "as a form of protective legislation extracted by an interest group consisting of publishers, journalists, pamphleteers, and others who derive pecuniary and non-pecuniary income from publication and advocacy of various sorts" (p. 893). By such fruit has the dismal science earned its reputation.

F.   Reforms

Rent seeking is a relatively new addition to the analytical tool kit of the student of markets and politics. Economists, in particular, are prone to seeing the world as a continuum of markets, to assuming that most markets work well if unfettered by external constraints, and to believing that increases in the competitiveness of a market generally improve its performance. But this view of the world is derived largely from the analysis of price competition in private goods markets. When competition uses up resources, as in all non-price modes of competition, more competition need not improve social welfare on net, even when the advertising or research and development does generate useful information and improved products, since the costs of this competition can exceed the benefits it creates. When no benefits are created, as in distributional struggles or pure rent seeking, the costs of competition are all waste, and the more competition there is, the greater the social waste there will be. This fundamental insight from the rent-seeking literature has yet to penetrate fully the Weltanschauungen of those who see competitive markets as the solutions to most social problems.

Rents are omnipresent. They exist wherever information and mobility asymmetries impede the flow of resources. They exist in private good markets, factor markets, asset markets, and political markets. Where rents exist, rent seeking can be expected to exist. The task of reform is to design institutions that allow and encourage those forms of competition that create rents by creating additional consumer and citizen surpluses, and discourage competition designed to gain and retain existing rents.

The task of eliminating wasteful rent seeking is not an easy one. Had price supports for milk and other agricultural products never been introduced, one might be able to convince farmers and the other beneficiaries of these programs to refrain from pursuing them on the grounds that they and everyone else in society benefits from free market competition. But the programs are now in place. Investments have been made to secure the price supports and investments in land, capital, and training have been made under the presumption that the price supports would be in effect. To eliminate them now would inflict severe adverse wealth effects on some groups. These groups resist these changes with alacrity.

To temper the resistance of these groups to the losses they would experience by eliminating those programs that facilitate rent seeking, even greater gains must be offered. Perhaps this observation explains why it is sometimes politically easier to eliminate or reduce a large group of restrictions on trade than just a few. The deregulation movement in the United States has had the success it has to date because it attacked regulations in many industries. To come fully to grips with the rent-seeking problem, one must think in terms of radical reforms; fundamental redefinitions of property rights (Buchanan, 1980b).

In some areas, modest changes in institutional structures could have beneficial effects, however. Having a committee award grants or licenses instead of a single administrator can discourage rent seeking by increasing the number of individuals who must be won over to achieve the award (Congleton, 1984). Similarly, commissions that are responsible for regulating several industries are less likely to be captured by a single industry, and thus are more likely to be responsive to the diffuse interests of consumers and consumer advocates (Miller, Shughart, and Tollison, 1984).

Finally, the best and simplest way to avoid the rent-seeking problem is to avoid establishing the institutions that create rents, that is, the regulations and regulatory agencies that lead to rent seeking. Anderson and Hill (1983) point out that auctioning off public lands or publicly owned mineral rights reduces rent seeking because it assigns the task of allocating the rents to those who have the residual claim to them. These individuals, unlike officials in a public regulatory agency, have an incentive to ensure that the allocation process does not dissipate the rents, since they are the claimants to them.

Laws that encourage rent seeking can be avoided by constitutionally requiring that certain types of legislation receive supramajorities. A constitutional amendment guaranteeing free trade could, for example, stipulate that legislation imposing tariffs, quotas, domestic content requirements, price ceilings, price floors, and the like requires a two-thirds or three-fourths majority to pass. We are back to the need for fairly fundamental constitutional reforms to attack rent seeking seriously.

Bibliographical notes

The seminal contributions of Tullock (1967c) and Krueger (1974) along with several others have been brought together in a rent-seeking anthology by Buchanan, Tollison, and Tullock (1980). A second anthology by the same individuals is planned.

Robert Tollison (1982) has written a useful survey of the literature.

For an excellent review of the public choice literature concerning the determinants of protectionism, see Frey (1984, chs. 2, 3) and in German Frey (1985, chs. 2, 3).

To the extent that bribes are pure transfers, they do not strictly belong to the wasteful rent-seeking category. But they do belong to the seamy tail of the distribution of activities rent seekers pursue. Susan Rose-Ackerman's (1978) seminal book, *Corruption,* analyzes these activities from a public choice perspective. Her book is a good complement to the rent-seeking literature.

CHAPTER 14

The supply of government output

There can be no doubt, that if power is granted to a body of men, called representatives, they, like any other men, will use their power, not for the advantage of the community, but for their own advantage, if they can.

James Mill

Each official is evidently more active within the body to which he belongs than each citizen within that to which he belongs. The government's actions are accordingly influenced by the private wills *of its members* much more than the sovereign's [citizenry's] by those of its members – if only because the official is almost always individually responsible for some specific function of government, while the citizen is not individually responsible for any specific function of sovereignty. (Italics in original)

Jean-Jacques Rousseau

The preceding chapters have focused upon the demand side of public choice. Individual preferences, be they of the citizen voter or the interest group member, determine outcomes in the public sector. Government, like the market in a pure exchange economy, is viewed simply as an institution for aggregating or balancing individual demands for public policies. Those in government, the candidates and representatives, have been depicted as single-mindedly seeking to be elected. To do so they must please voters and interest group members, so that those in government are merely pawns of those outside in a competitive political system. Only in the rent-seeking literature just reviewed does one begin to obtain a glimpse of another side of government. Politicians may not live by votes alone. They, too, may seek wealth and leisure. Their preferences may impinge on the outcomes of the public sector.

In this chapter we examine several models that give those in government a role in determining policies beyond that of simply carrying out the revealed demands of the citizens. These may be viewed as models of the supply of government policies. The assumption that government actors are selfish utility maximizers is retained, but they are allowed to have more in their objective functions than just the desire to be elected. Indeed, a main actor in the government, the bureaucrat, does not need to be elected at all, and so a modeling of this functionary's behavior must start from a different premise.

Max Weber (1947) assumed that the bureaucrat's natural objective was

247

power. "Power" is a concept frequently employed by political scientists and sociologists, and totally ignored by economists[1] and practitioners of public choice. Given Weber's stature as a social scientist, it seems prudent to pay some heed to his thinking on this matter. As we shall see in the following section, there is an interpretation of political power that not only is prominent in the political science and sociology literature, but also fits in well with the analysis of government and bureaucracy in public choice. We begin by developing this concept, and then turn to models that grant the government an increasing degree of power over the citizens.

A.   Uncertainty, information, and power

At the most intuitive level, the word "power" connotes the ability or capacity to do something (Wagner, 1969, pp. 3–4).[2] But "something" can stand for a variety of objects, each of which leads to a different kind of power. Physical power is the ability to apply force. Economic power is the capacity to purchase goods, and so on. Political power must be defined as the ability to achieve certain ends through a political process. To observe the exercise of political power, some actors must have conflicting goals. If all members of a committee, including A, favor x over y and x is chosen, we cannot say that A has exercised power. If only A favors x and x is chosen, A has political power.

Bertrand Russell (1938) defined three ways in which an individual can exert influence in a political context: (1) by exercising direct physical power, for example, by imprisonment or death, (2) by offering rewards and punishments, and (3) by exerting influence on opinion through the use of education and propaganda. The first two are closely related to a more general type of political power, which we might call procedural power. A might achieve his choice of x because the rules of the committee make him dictator, or grant him the right to set an agenda by which the committee is led to choose x. The procedural power granted the agenda setter will figure prominently in one of the models we examine next. But it is the third source of influence Russell listed that is most closely related to a more general notion of political power. Education, propaganda, and persuasion are all forms of information. Information has value, or grants power, only in the presence of uncertainty. Uncertainty creates the potential to exercise power; information provides the capacity to do so.

Political power means inducing someone to do something that they did not want to do, as when A gets a committee to choose x when all but A favor feasible alternative y (Simon, 1953; Dahl, 1957, p. 80). In the agenda-setter

1. Market power, the ability to raise price, is a limited use of the term by economists.
2. This section borrows heavily from Mueller (1980).

example discussed in Chapter 5, it was not simply the authority A has to set the agenda that brought about this outcome. It was the *knowledge A* had of every other committee member's preferences, coupled with their *ignorance* of the sequence of votes that would be taken. Given this uncertainty on the part of all committee members save A, A could induce the committee to choose z over y, z' over z, and so on until x was reached. But if all committee members save A favor y over x, they could impose y by not voting for z against y. Their lack of information compared to A gave A the power to use his position as agenda setter to bring about x's victory.

Returning to Russell's list of sources of power, we can see that it is the uncertainty that surrounds a dictator's use of physical power or a supervisor's issuance of rewards and punishments that allows these people to control their subordinates. If B knows with certainty that A will give him a reward if B does X, as the rules require it, then B in carrying out X exercises as much power over A as A does over B. In a bureaucracy in which no uncertainty existed, lines of authority might exist, but no real power would accompany authority. All employees would know all of the possible events that might occur and all could predict the eventual outcomes or decisions that would follow each. Employee grievance procedures would be completely codified and both the supervisor's and the employee's reaction to any situation would be perfectly predictable. In a world of complete certainty, all individuals are essentially acting out a part, "going by the rules," and those at the top of the bureaucracies are as devoid of discretionary power as those at the bottom. All power is purely procedural (see Simon, 1953, p. 72).

This type of situation comes close to the conditions existing in the French monopoly that Michel Crozier (1964) described in *The Bureaucratic Phenomenon*. As Crozier depicts it, the monopoly does operate in a world of certainty – with one exception – the machines sometimes break down. This places the women operating the machines completely under the power of the mechanics responsible for repairing them, since the women have a quota of output for each day and must work harder to make up for any downtime. More interesting, the supervisors who nominally have more authority also have less power than the mechanics. Since the mechanics know how to repair the machines, and the supervisors do not, the supervisors are unable to exert any real control over the mechanics (Crozier, 1964, pp. 98–111).

It is instructive to note the tactics used by the mechanics to preserve their power. The operators were severely scolded for "tinkering" with their machines in an effort to keep them going or to repair them. Only the mechanics knew how to repair the machines; each machine was different, and just how it needed to be fixed was known only to the mechanics. Repairing them was an art, not a science. When clashes arose between the mechanics and the supervisors, it was over whether the latter could, on occasion, work at repairing the machines. The supervisors were further hampered in this endeavor by the continual "mysterious" disappearance of machine blueprints from the factory. The mechanics always worked without the aid of blueprints.

One sees in the power exerted by the mechanics in Crozier's case study a modest form of the power of experts in a bureaucracy. Max Weber emphasized the power of expertise, and it will appear again in the models discussed next. More generally, we shall see that all incorporate in various ways assumptions regarding the power stemming from asymmetric possession of information in a world of uncertainty.

B.   The budget-maximizing bureaucrat

Bureaucratic man pursues power. Economic man pursues profit. In Frank Knight's (1921) theory of profit, profit exists because of uncertainty and is earned by those who possess the daring and *information* to allow them to make correct decisions under uncertainty. Thus, there is a close link between the economic theory of profit and the political theory of power. Both exist owing to uncertainty; both accrue to the possessors of information.

In the modern corporation, the information gatherers and processors of information are the managers. They are the possessors of power. A major difference between the business corporation and the public bureau is that the power of managers can be monetarized. The business of corporations is making profits, and managers as information gatherers are its main recipients.

Legally, however, corporations belong to the stockholders, and the custom persists that they are the rightful recipients of corporate profits. Thus, managers are unable to pay themselves all of the profits they create. They are forced to claim corporate profits in less conspicuous ways than simply salaries and cash bonuses. Numerous substitute goals have been put forward: on-the-job consumption, excess staff and emoluments (Williamson, 1964), security (Fisher and Hall, 1969; Amihud and Lev, 1981), and a host of nonpecuniary goals that one can lump together under the heading of X-inefficiency (Leibenstein, 1966; Comanor and Leibenstein, 1969).

Many of the nonpecuniary goals of managers are likely to be correlated with the size or growth in size of the corporation (Baumol, 1959; Marris, 1964, ch. 2). Large size can also be used as a justification for higher compensation packages, and thus can allow managers to justify greater direct cash payments to themselves. The bigger and more complex the firm is, the more difficult it is for stockholders to monitor the activities of managers, and the more power managers have. Thus, size and growth in size are plausible goals, along with profits, of corporate managers.

The pursuit of profits is not the perceived legitimate goal of public bureaus, and thus it is even more difficult for public bureaucrats to convert the power they have into income. The nonpecuniary goals of management become the logical objectives of the public bureaucrat. Among these, size and risk aversion have received the most attention. The first systematic effort to study bureaucracies within a public choice framework was made by William Niskanen,[3] and we turn now to his model of bureaucracy.

1. Environment and incentives

One of the key characteristics of a government bureau is the nonmarket nature of its output (Downs, 1967, pp. 24–5). Indeed, a bureau does not typically supply a number of units of output as such, but levels of *activities* from which output levels must be inferred (Niskanen, 1971, pp. 24–6). Thus, the Department of Defense maintains numbers of combat personnel and weapon systems, although it supplies various degrees (units) of defensive and offensive capabilities. Its budget is defined over the activities it maintains, even though the purchasers – the taxpayers and their representatives – are ultimately interested only in the "final outputs" of combat capabilities that these activities produce. The reason for this is obvious: It is easier to count soldiers and airplanes than it is units of protection. This "measurement problem," inherent in so many of the goods and services that public bureaus provide, creates a monitoring problem for the funding agency. Given the unmeasurable nature of a bureau's outputs, how can the purchaser monitor the efficiency of their production?

The monitoring problem is intensified by the bilateral monopoly nature of the bureau–sponsor relationship (Niskanen, 1971, p. 24). That the buyer of a bureau's output would be a monopsonist follows almost from the nature of the good sold. A public good is by definition consumed by all of the people, and the agent of all of the people is a monopsonist buyer on their behalf. Of course, we have seen that the government may not engage in the supply of only pure public goods, but, nevertheless, it remains the sole agent of whatever interest group it represents in dealing with public bureaucracies. Even if the government acts as the sole agent for the population, or an interest group, it does have to buy from a single source, although this is often the case. The usual reason for granting a bureau a monopoly on the provision of a given service is to avoid wasteful duplication. Although there is certainly some validity in this justification, the monopoly nature of most bureaus also frees them from competitive pressure to be efficient and denies the funding agency

---

3. Niskanen's book (1971) was preceded by two insightful looks at bureaucracy by Gordon Tullock (1965) and Anthony Downs (1967). Although written by two of the founding fathers of the public choice field, these earlier works do not attempt to develop a theory or model of bureaucracy from a public choice perspective. Instead, they use the economics methodology to examine various facets of bureaucratic organizations.

an alternative source of information by which to gauge the efficiency of the monopolist bureaus, thus compounding the monitoring problem inherent in the nature of the bureau's output.

Inefficient production of a bureau's services is further induced by the scheme of compensation of bureaucrats. While managers in a private corporation can usually claim a share of the savings (profits) generated by an increase in efficiency, public bureaucrats' salaries are either unrelated or indirectly, and perhaps inversely (Warren, Jr., 1975), related to improved efficiency. Thus, the public bureau is characterized by weak external control on efficiency and weak internal incentives.

If the bureaucrat has no financial incentive to pursue greater efficiency, what are his goals, and how are they related to efficiency? Niskanen (1971, p. 38) lists the following possible goals of a bureaucrat: "salary, perquisites of the office, public reputation, power, patronage, output of the bureau, ease of making changes, and ease in managing the bureau."[4] He then asserts that all but the last two are positively and monotonically related to the size of the budget.

2.   *The model*

The bureau receives a budget from its funding agency (say, Congress or the Parliament), which is a function of the *perceived* output of the bureau's service

$$B = B(Q), B' > 0, B'' < 0. \tag{14.1}$$

This function may be thought of as a public benefit or utility function. Public benefits are assumed to increase, but at a diminishing rate, with increasing output.

The bureau has a cost function for producing its output that, over the relevant range at least, increases at an increasing rate like a competitive firm's cost schedule.

$$C = C(Q), C' > 0, C'' > 0. \tag{14.2}$$

This cost schedule is known only to the bureau's members (or a subset thereof). This is how the monitoring problem arises. The funder knows its total benefit schedule (14.1), but sees only an activity budget from the bureau. Therefore it cannot determine whether this output is being supplied Pareto efficiently, that is, if, at the margin, public benefits equal public costs. The funder sees only the total output of the bureau and its total budget. This frees the bureau to maximize its budget subject to the constraint that its budget

4. Downs also devotes a good deal of space to the goals of bureaucrats (1967, pp. 81–111).

cover the costs of production. If we assume that the bureau does not turn money back to the funder, this constraint is satisfied as an equality and the bureau's objective function is

$$O_B = B(Q) + \lambda(B(Q) - C(Q)), \tag{14.3}$$

whose first-order conditions yield

$$B'(Q) = \frac{\lambda}{1 + \lambda} C'(Q) \tag{14.4}$$

$$B(Q) = C(Q). \tag{14.5}$$

Optimality from the point of view of the funder requires that the marginal benefit of an extra unit of output to the funder equals its marginal cost to the bureau

$$B'(Q) = C'(Q). \tag{14.6}$$

The Lagrangian multiplier represents the marginal utility of an expansion of the budget constraint to the bureau and is positive. Thus, (14.4) implies that $B' < C'$. The budget is expanded beyond the point where marginal public benefits equal marginal costs. If B and C are quadratic, B' and C' become straight lines and we have the situation depicted in Figure 14.1, taken from Niskanen (1971, p. 47). Instead of requesting a budget that would result in the output Q_0, and thereby maximize the net benefits of the funder, the bureau will request the larger budget consistent with the output Q^*. At Q^* triangle E equals triangle F. All of the consumer surplus gains from the production of the inframarginal units of output up to Q_0 are balanced out against the excess of marginal costs over marginal benefits on the units between Q_0 and Q^*. Note here that Niskanen's description of the public bureaucracy's behavior vis-à-vis the government is quite analogous to Breton's description of the behavior of the government vis-à-vis the citizens (discussed in Section E). The monopoly bureau uses its position to recapture the consumer surplus on its monopolized service just as the government exploits its monopoly on particular services by tying other outputs to them.

Niskanen also discusses the possibility that the funder's demand schedule would be so far to the right, or inelastic, that the marginal benefit of Q to the funder would fall to zero before F grew as large as E. The constraint that total budget equals total cost would not be operative then, and the bureau would simply request the output level at which the funder is satiated. This situation is represented by the B_s' schedule and Q_s quantity in Figure 14.1.

The possibility that a funder might become satiated from a given public good before a bureau had exhausted all of the consumer surplus it is capable of exploiting could lead a budget-maximizing bureaucrat to propose other

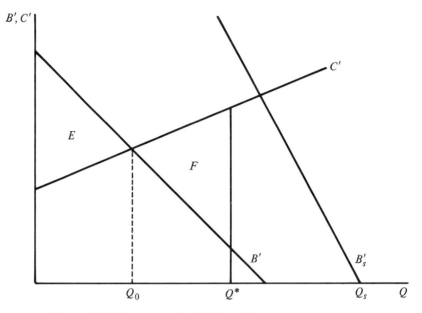

Figure 14.1. The oversupply of a bureau's output.

outputs besides the one for which it is solely responsible. This could take the form of radical innovations, or more plausibly, infringements of one bureau onto another bureau's domain, or onto the domain of the private market.

Niskanen develops his model of the budget-maximizing bureau to explore this and other cases. He also attempts to integrate the public bureau and the review process in a representative democracy into a median voter model, where the median voter in this case is an elected representative (1971, chs. 13–16). In some cases, the extensions tend to mitigate the tendency for bureaucratic budgets to be too large; in some cases they reinforce them. For example, the practice of choosing as the head of a bureau an individual who was (and/or is likely to become) an executive in companies that sell to this bureau strengthens the bureau's interests in larger budgets. The congressional practice of appointing representatives of high-demand users of a bureau's output (interest groups) to the subcommittees charged with reviewing a bureau's performance weakens the potential for curtailing the expansion of the bureau's budget through this outside monitoring process.

C.   Extensions of the model

The power of the bureaucracy to obtain budgets greater than those desired by the sponsor stems from three important characteristics of the bargaining situation assumed by Niskanen: (1) the bureau is a monopolist supplier, (2) it alone knows its true cost schedule, and (3) it is institutionally allowed to make take-it-or-leave-it budget proposals. Relaxing any of these assumptions weakens the bureau's position vis-à-vis the sponsoring agency.

1. *Alternative institutional assumptions*

The ability to make only take-it-or-leave-it budget proposals gives the bureau an extremely strong agenda-setting role, a fact that presumably occurs to the sponsor. The sponsor might reasonably request that the bureau state the costs of a range of outputs from which the sponsor then chooses. If the sponsor is still ignorant of the bureau's true costs and the bureau knows the sponsor's true demand, this new arrangement can leave the bureau in the same position as before, but it can alternatively force the bureau to announce its true marginal cost schedule.

Suppose that the bureau must announce a unit price P at which it will supply output Q, with the sponsor free to choose Q. The budget of the bureau is now

$$B = PQ, \tag{14.7}$$

with $Q = f(P)$ being the sponsor's demand schedule, which is known to the bureau. The bureau then chooses a P to maximize (14.7) subject to the constraint $B \geq C(Q)$. The first-order condition for this problem is simply

$$\frac{dB}{dP} = Q + P\frac{dQ}{dP} = 0, \tag{14.8}$$

from which one obtains

$$\eta = \frac{P}{Q}\frac{dQ}{dP} = 1. \tag{14.9}$$

If the constraint $B \geq C(Q)$ is not binding, the bureau chooses the unit price at the point on the bureau's demand schedule where its demand elasticity, η, equals unity. If the constraint is binding, the bureau selects the *lowest* price for which the budget covers its total costs. The possibilities, assuming a straight-line demand schedule and constant marginal costs, are depicted in Figure 14.2. With the low marginal cost schedule C_L', the bureau can announce the price P_1 at which revenue under the demand schedule is maximized. When marginal costs exceed P_1, however, the bureau is forced to reveal its true marginal costs to obtain the maximum budget possible, for example, $P_H = C_H'$. Thus, when the bureau must declare a unit price or price schedule, instead of a take-it-or-leave-it proposal, its ability to force a higher than optimal budget on the sponsor depends upon the elasticity of the sponsor's demand. If marginal costs intersect demand in the elastic portion of the

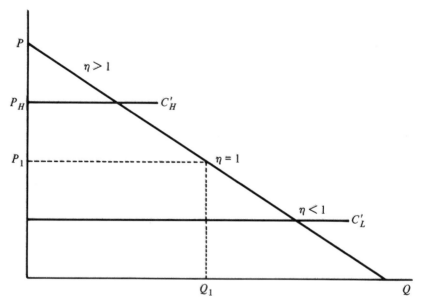

Figure 14.2. Options for a price-setting bureau.

demand schedule, the bureau honestly declares true costs. Only when the demand for its services is inelastic can the bureau expand its budget beyond the sponsor's preferred level by announcing a higher price for its output than its true costs (Breton and Wintrobe, 1975; Bendor, Taylor, and Van Gaalen, 1985).

Considerable power resides with the bureau owing to its ability to conceal its costs. In practice, this too is limited. Monitoring agencies, like the U.S. General Accounting Office, may detect budget excesses and report them to the sponsor. Whistle-blowers within the bureau inform sponsors from time to time of budget excesses. Thus, in declaring a $P > C'(Q)$, the bureau runs the risk of incurring a penalty in the form of a future reduction in budget, or direct sanctions on personnel (curtailed discretionary budget items, lost promotions, dismissal).

Let the expected penalty from announcing a $P > C'$ be $\pi(P)$, $\pi' > 0$. If π is defined in units comparable to B, then the bureau's objective can be written as the maximization of

$$O = B - \pi(P),\tag{14.10}$$

from which the condition

$$\eta = \frac{P}{Q}\frac{\mathrm{d}Q}{\mathrm{d}P} = 1 - \pi'\tag{14.11}$$

is obtained. If the constraint $B \geq C(Q)$ is not binding, the bureau announces a price lower than P_1, that is, a price in the inelastic portion of its demand schedule, to reduce the probability of incurring the penalty (Bendor et al., 1985). Wherever the sponsor can partially monitor and penalize the bureau, the bureau is forced to declare a price closer to its true marginal costs.

This conclusion is strengthened if we assume, as is often done, that bureaucrats are risk-averse. If bureaucrats are risk-averse, each additional dollar of budget provides lower marginal utility while each additional increase in price raises the expected penalty from being caught, causing increasing marginal disutility. The risk-averse bureaucrat will thus declare a still lower price than the risk-neutral bureaucrat (Bendor et al., 1985).

Allowing the sponsor to monitor the bureau and gather information shifts power from the bureau to the sponsor compared with the original situation in which the bureau knows the sponsor's demand but the sponsor is ignorant of the bureau's cost. The sponsor's position can be further strengthened if one assumes that the sponsor can conceal its demand from the bureau. Miller and Moe (1983) show how this assumption can also force the bureau to reveal its true costs.

Finally, the bureau's hand is weakened if it must compete for budget funding with other bureaus. If each bureau must announce prices at which it will supply output, then the sponsor can use the bids of other bureaus as information to gauge a bureau's true costs. In effect, the competing bureaus serve as monitors of a bureau activity, forcing it to declare lower prices.[5]

Thus, relaxing any of the assumptions of the original budget-maximizing-bureau model shifts the outcome away from the excessive budget result, and in several cases yields the optimally sized budget.

2. *Alternative behavioral assumptions*

Migue and Belanger (1974) have pointed out that the relentless use of budget funds to expand the bureau's output would conflict with one of the presumed objectives for having larger bureau budgets – to pursue other goals. Weatherby, Jr. (1971), has suggested, à la Oliver Williamson (1964), that the expansion of personnel would be one of the additional goals pursued by bureaucrats. Of the many goals put forward in the managerial literature, X-inefficiency and risk aversion seem the most plausible additions to the list of possible bureaucratic goals.

The addition of unnecessary personnel and more general examples of X-inefficiency raise the costs of a bureau's output. Thus, these goals lead to an

---

5. McGuire, Coiner, and Spancake (1979); Bendor et al. (1985). Niskanen (1971, chs. 18–20) emphasizes the potential for competition between bureaus as well as between bureaus and the private sector as a restraining force on a bureau's discretionary power.

expansion of the bureau's budget without an increase in output, if the demand for the budget is inelastic. If the sponsor's demand is elastic, X-inefficiency by raising unit costs (price) results in a decline in a bureau's output and budget size from the optimal level. Thus, inefficient bureaus may actually supply *too little* output.

The effects of risk aversion on a bureau's performance are more difficult to gauge. In Section 1, we noted that risk aversion may move a budget-maximizing bureau back toward the efficient bureau size. But risk aversion can induce bureaus to avoid projects that their sponsors would want them to undertake, if the sponsors could costlessly monitor all bureau activities. Gist and Hill (1981) reported that officials of the Department of Housing and Urban Development allocated funds to cities with less risky investment projects to avoid the criticism that the projects were not successful. Yet the purported goal of the program was to help "distressed" cities, that is, cities for which the risks in housing programs were high.

Cotton Lindsay (1976) gathered data indicating that risk-averse Veterans Administration hospital officials concentrate on providing outputs that are easily measured (hospital beds, patient days) at the cost of quality of service, an unmeasurable dimension of output. Here again we see the importance of information. The sponsor is not without some power to control the bureaucracy, since some dimensions of bureau performance can be measured. But if all dimensions cannot be monitored, then some power to skimp on these attributes rests with those in the bureau, who can use the savings to forward their own interests.

Breton and Wintrobe (1982, pp. 96–7) have argued that bureaucrats, like corporate managers, are not totally free to pursue their own goals; indeed, they may have less discretionary power than their private sector counterparts. They operate in an environment in which considerable competition for promotions exists. If anything, public bureaucrats are more mobile than corporate managers; this suggests that the market for public bureaucrats is more competitive than the market for company managers. Bureau sponsors, the elected representatives of parliament and the executive, also function in a competitive environment. They must stand for periodic reelection. Thus, they are under continuous pressure to control bureaucratic excesses to the best of their ability. How well they do this remains an empirical question.

3.   *Bargaining between sponsor and bureau*

Sponsors compete for votes on the basis of how well government programs have served the interests of voters. Bureaucrats compete for promotions, and bureaus compete for funds on the basis of how well they are judged to have supplied the outputs sponsors desire. The interests of the two main actors conflict, and the most general way to view the sponsor–bureau conflict over the size of the bureau's budget and other characteristics of its output mix is as a bargaining game between sponsor-demander and bureau-supplier (Breton and Wintrobe, 1975, 1982; Miller, 1977; Eavey and Miller, 1984). The bureau has monopoly power to some degree and information (expertise) on its side. But the sponsor controls the purse strings. It can offer rewards and punishments, gather information to an extent, and conceal its own hand. The most plausible outcome, as in most bargaining models, is a compromise. The bureau's budget falls short of the bureaucrat's target, but is greater than the sponsor would want. Slack and inefficiency are present to a degree. To what degree is an empirical question to which we now turn.

D.   Empirical tests

1.   Power of the agenda setter

The hypothesis that bureau budgets exceed the optimum levels of their parliamentary review committees is difficult to test directly, since output is hard to measure and the optimum levels for the review committee cannot be established. In Oregon, however, school budgets are determined by a process that allows one to observe the budget-maximizing bureaucrat in action. Each school district has a budget maximum determined by law. School boards can increase the budget size, however, by proposing larger budgets at an annual referendum. If the newly proposed budget gets more than 50 percent of the votes cast, it replaces the legally set limit. If the school board's budget fails, the budget reverts back to the level set by the law.

This situation allows one to test hypotheses regarding school board officials' motivation, if one assumes that the optimum level of expenditures would be that most preferred by the median voter, if voting were on all possible expenditure levels. Figure 14.3 depicts the utility function of the median voter defined over school expenditures G. Let G_r be the level of expenditures to which the school budget reverts if the referendum fails. While the median voter's most preferred expenditure is G_m, she would be willing to vote for G_b rather than see the budget revert to G_r. Thus, when the reversion level for the school budget is below the most favored budget of the median voter, the school board can force the median voter to vote for a larger budget than the one she prefers by forcing her to choose between this higher budget and the reversion level.

Romer and Rosenthal (1978, 1979b, 1982) have analyzed and tested a model of the Oregon school budget referenda process. They predict the budget expenditures that the median voter would demand using a standard median voter model and find that, where the reversion levels are below the levels

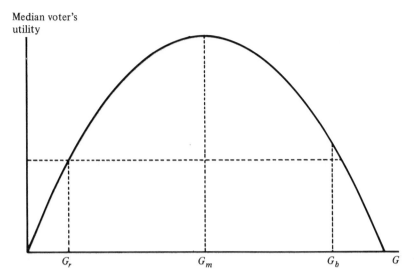

Figure 14.3. Options for the budget-maximizing agenda setter.

necessary to keep the school system viable, referenda pass providing school budgets anywhere from 16.5 to 43.6 percent higher than those most preferred by the median voter. Further corroboration for the budget-maximizing school bureau hypothesis is contained in the data for the 64 districts that either failed to hold a referendum or failed to pass one. When the reversion budget exceeds the level favored by the median voter, one expects that the school board does not call an election, and simply assesses the full 100 percent of its statutorily set base. The mean assessment for these 64 districts was over 99 percent of their bases.[6]

The Oregon school budgeting system provides school officials an unusually attractive opportunity to increase budget sizes by the power granted them to make take-it-or-leave-it referendum proposals. But, as noted earlier, most bureau budgets are the outcome of a bargaining process between the bureau

6. See also Filimon (1982).

   Additional evidence of the use of discretionary power by public officials is provided by Shapiro and Sonstelie (1982), who show that Proposition 13 in California took away discretionary funds from local officials and forced them to choose different budget expansion paths.

   Vernon Ruttan (1980) points to the agricultural research program of the U.S. Department of Agriculture (USDA) as an important counterexample to the budget-maximizing bureau story. The high rates of return on agricultural research estimated in numerous studies imply a significant underinvestment in agricultural research. This finding would be consistent with higher unit costs for the USDA, if the demand for this service were highly elastic.

and its sponsors. Using classroom experiments, Eavey and Miller (1984) have shown that merely granting the sponsor-demanders the right to confer and form coalitions increases their power vis-à-vis the agenda setter. The Eavey–Miller experiments produced outcomes falling in a bargaining range between the review committee's most preferred choice and that of the agenda setter. Fort (1988) found that for nonrepeated hospital bond issues, the outcomes did not differ from what one would expect from the median voter hypothesis.

Weingast and Moran (1983) provide evidence implying that congressional committees have considerable influence over the bureaus they monitor. They assume that House and Senate committees play the role of agenda setters for the full House and Senate. As in the Romer–Rosenthal model, a high-demand subcommittee can force the full assembly to vote for higher expenditures than the median voter would prefer by limiting the assembly's choices to high expenditure bills and others that the assembly finds even less attractive. They show that the ideological predilections of the membership of the House and Senate committees that oversee the Federal Trade Commission have a significant impact on the composition of the cases coming before the commission. The more liberal the chairman and House and subcommittee members are (as measured by their Americans for Democratic Action scores on their past voting records), the greater the percentage of cases favored by liberals (measured as truth-in-lending cases) that come before the commission. Faith, Leavens, and Tollison (1982) also found that FTC decisions tended to go in favor of firms located in the districts of members of the FTC review subcommittees.

2. Cost differences between publicly and privately provided services

In some cases, the nature of a bureau's services makes it difficult to expand its output beyond the level that the community demands. A school system cannot educate more children than are sent to school; the sanitation department cannot collect more garbage than the community puts out to be collected. In this situation, a bureau's members still have an incentive to increase a bureau's budget by providing the fixed output demanded by the community at a higher cost than necessary. The extra costs could reflect higher than competitive salaries, more personnel than are needed to provide the service, or general X-inefficiency. Numerous studies have compared the provision of similar services by public and private firms. Table 14.1 summarizes the findings for some 50 studies. In only 2, in which the quality of service was held constant, were public firms found to be more efficient than their private counterparts. In over 40 studies public firms were found to be significantly less efficient than

Table 14.1. *Cost and productivity indices: alternative organizational forms*

Activity: author	Unit/organizational forms	Findings
1. Airlines		
Davies (1971, 1977)	Australia/sole private domestic vs. its lone public counterpart	Efficiency indices of private 12–100% higher
2. Banks		
Davies (1982)	Australia/one public vs. one private bank	Sign and magnitude of all indices of productivity, response to risk, and profitability favor private banks
3. Bus service		
Oelert (1976)	Municipal vs. private bus service in selected West German cities	Cost public bus service 160% higher per km than private equivalents
4. Cleaning services		
Bundesrechnungshof (1972)	Public production vs. private contracting out in West German post office	Public service 40–60% more costly
Hamburger Senat (1971), Fishcer-Menshausen (1975)	Public production vs. private contracting out in West German public building	Public service 50% more costly than private alternative
5. Debt collection		
Bennett and Johnson (1980)	U.S. General Accounting Office Study/federal government supplied service vs. privately contracted-for equivalents	Government 200% more costly per dollar of debt pursued
6. Electric utilities		
Meyer[a] (1975)	Sample of 60–90 U.S. utilities/public vs. private firms	Very weak indication of higher costs of private production
Moore (1970)	Sample of U.S. utilities/27 municipal vs. 49 private firms	Overcapitalization greater in public firms; total operating costs of public production higher
Spann[b] (1977b)	Four major U.S. cities/public (San Antonio, Los Angeles) vs. private (San Diego, Dallas) firms	Private firm adjusted for scale as efficient and probably more so with respect to operating cost and investment (per 1,000 kWh)
Wallace and Junk (1970)	By regions in U.S./public vs. private firms	Operating costs 40–75% higher in public mode; investment (per kWh 40%) more in public mode

Table 14.1. *(cont.)*

Activity: author	Unit/organizational forms	Findings
7. Fire protection		
Ahlbrandt (1973)	Scottsdale, Arizona (private contract) vs. Seattle area (municipal) fire departments	Municipal fire departments 39–88% higher cost per capita
8. Forestry		
Bundesregierung Deutschland (1976)	Public vs. private forest harvesting in West Germany, 1965–75	Operating revenues 45 DM per hectare higher in private forests
Pfister (1976)	Private vs. public forests in state of Baden-Wurttemberg	Labor input twice as high per unit of output in public compared with private firms
9. Hospitals		
Clarkson (1972)	Sample of U.S. hospitals/private nonprofit vs. for profit	"Red tape" more prevalent in nonprofits; greater variation in input ratios in nonprofits; both suggest higher cost of nonprofit outputs
Lindsay[a] (1976)	U.S. Veterans Administration vs. proprietary hospitals	Cost per patient day less in V.A. hospital unadjusted for type of care and quality less "serious" cases and longer patient stays in V.A. preference for minority group professionals compared with proprietary hospitals
Rushing (1974)	Sample of 91 short-stay hospitals in U.S. mid-South region/private nonprofits vs. for-profit	Substitution among inputs and outputs more sluggish in nonprofit hospitals
Wilson and Jadlow (1978)	1,200 U.S. hospitals producing nuclear medicine/government vs. proprietary hospitals	Deviation of proprietary hospitals from perfect efficiency index less than public hospitals
10. Housing		
Muth (1973)	Construction costs in U.S. cities private vs. public agencies	Public agencies 20% more costly per constant quality housing unit
Rechnungshof Rheinland-Pfalz (1972)	Public vs. private cost of supplying large public building projects in the West German state of Rheinland-Pfalz	Public agencies 20% more costly than private contracting

(continued)

Table 14.1. *(cont.)*

Activity: author	Unit/organizational forms	Findings
Schneider and Schuppener (1971)	Public vs. private firm construction costs in West Germany	Public firms significantly more expensive suppliers
11. Insurance sales and servicing		
Finsinger[b] (1981)	5 public vs. 77 private liability and life firms in West Germany	Same rate of return and no obvious cost differences between organizational forms
Kennedy and Mehr (1977)	Public car insurance in Manitoba vs. private insurance in Alberta	Quality and services of private insurances higher than those of the public one
12. Ocean tanker repair and maintenance		
Bennett and Johnson (1980a)	U.S. General Accounting Office/Navy vs. commercial tankers and oilers	U.S. Navy from 230 to 5,100% higher
13. Railroads		
Caves and Christensen[b] (1980)	Canadian National (public) vs. Canadian Pacific (private) railroads	No productivity differences recently, but CN less efficient before 1965, the highly regulated period
14. Refuse collection		
Collins and Downes[b] (1977)	53 cities and municipalities in the St. Louis County area, Missouri/public vs. private contracting-out modes	No significant cost differences
Columbia University Graduate School of Business Studies: Savas (1974, 1977a, 1977b, 1980), Stevens (1978), Stevens and Savas (1978) and Edwards and Stevens (1976)	Many sorts of U.S. cities/ municipal vs. private monopoly franchise vs. private nonfranchise firms	Public supply 40–60% more expensive than private, but monopoly franchise only 5% higher than private nonfranchised collectors
Petrovic and Jaffee (1977)	83 cities in Midwestern U.S./ public vs. private contracting out modes	Cost of city collection is 15% higher than the price of private contract collectors
Hirsch[b] (1965)	24 cities and muncipalities in the St. Louis City-County area, Missouri/public vs. private firms	No significant cost differences
Kemper and Quigley (1976)	101 Connecticut cities/private monopoly contract vs. private nonfranchise vs. municipal firms	Municipal collection costs 14–43% higher than contract, but private nonfranchise 25–36% higher than municipal collection
Kitchen (1976)	48 Canadian cities/municipal vs. private firms	Municipal suppliers more costly than proprietary firms

Table 14.1. *(cont.)*

Activity: author	Unit/organizational forms	Findings
Savas[b] (1977c)	50 private vs. 30 municipal firms in Minneapolis	No significant cost differences
Pier, Vernon, and Wicks[a] (1974)	26 cities in Montana/municipal vs. private firms	Municipal suppliers more efficient
Pommerehne (1976)	102 Swiss municipalities/public vs. private firms	Public firms 15% higher unit costs
Spann (1977b)	Survey of various U.S. cities/municipal vs. private firms	Public firms 45% more costly
Bennett and Johnson (1979)	29 private firms vs. one public trash collection authority in Fairfax County, Virginia	Private firms more efficient
15. Savings and loans		
Nicols (1967)	California Savings and Loans/cooperative or mutuals vs. stock companies	Mutuals have 13–30% higher operating costs
16. Slaughterhouses		
Pausch (1976)	Private vs. public firms in 5 major West German cities	Public firms significantly more costly because of overcapacity and overstaffing
17. Water utilities		
Crain and Zardkoohi (1978)	112 U.S. firms/municipal vs. private suppliers; case study of two firms that each switched organizational form	Public firms 40% less productive with 65% higher capital–labor ratios than private equivalents; public firm that became private experienced an output per employee increase of 25%; private firm that became public experienced an output per employee decline of 40%
Mann and Mikesell (1976)	U.S. firms/municipal vs. private suppliers	Replicates Meyer's (1975) electricity model, but adjusts for input prices; found public modes more expensive by 20%
Morgan (1977)	143 firms in six U.S. states/municipal vs. private suppliers	Costs 15% higher for public firms
18. Weather forecasting		
Bennett and Johnson (1980a)	U.S. General Acounting Office study/U.S. Weather Bureau vs. private contracted-for service	Government service 50% more costly

[a]Public sector less costly or more efficient.   [b]No signficant difference in costs or efficiencies.
Source: Borcherding, Pommerehne, and Schneider (1982, pp. 130–3).

private firms supplying the same service. The evidence that public provision of a service reduces the efficiency of its provision seems overwhelming.[7]

E.   The government as a monopolist

In Albert Breton's (1974) theory of representative democracy, the government is the party in control of the legislature. This theory is thus more applicable to parliamentary systems such as those that exist in Europe and Canada, where the parliamentary majority is allowed to "form the government" and includes the executive branch. The governing party has an objective function, which includes the probability of being reelected, but also can include "variables such as personal pecuniary gains, personal power, [its] own image in history, the pursuit of lofty personal ideals, [its] personal view of the common good" (p. 124), and so on.[8] To achieve these goals, the governing party takes advantage of its position as a monopoly supplier of certain highly desired public goods, for example, defense, police and fire protection, highways. A monopolist of a private good can often increase his profits by tying other products that he does not monopolize to the monopolized product. As long as the consumer's surplus on the package of tied products exceeds that available on other packages, the consumer will buy the tied products to get the monopolized one. In the same way, the government can often achieve the varied objectives of its members by packaging rather narrowly defined issues that benefit only small groups of voters along with the broadly popular services it monopolizes.

In exploiting its monopoly position, the governing party is constrained by the threat of entry by the opposition party or parties (Breton, 1974, pp. 137–9). To ward off this threat, the governing party

> can engage in one or more of four basic activities: it can (1) enact and implement discriminatory policies as well as policies that have the characteristics of pure private goods, including changes in tax rates, basic exemptions, tax credits, loopholes, etc.; (2) discriminatorily adjust the penalties levied against and the probability of apprehending those committing legal offenses; (3) engage in implicit logrolling, combined with full-line supply by combining policies in such a way as to elicit or maintain political support; and (4) seek to alter the preferences of citizens so as to reduce the differences that exist between them and thus make them more homogeneous. (Breton, 1974, p. 143)

Breton's theory of monopoly government is broadly consistent with the Downsian model of representative democracy. Both Downs (1957) and

---

7. For additional discussion of the results reported in Table 14.1, see Borcherding, Pommerehne, and Schneider (1982). See also Borcherding (1977b) and Orzechowski (1977).
8. See also Donald Wittman (1973, 1977).

Tullock (1967a) predicted that majority rule would lead to logrolling and the serving of special interests. Tullock (1959) went on to conclude from his initial analysis of logrolling under majority rule that the size of the government would be too large. However, Tullock's conclusion was directly challenged by Downs (1961) himself, who argued that the tendency for government to oversupply special interest legislation would be more than offset by the tendency to undersupply general interest (public good) legislation owing to the free-rider problem and the complementary lack of incentives for voters to become informed about this type of legislation.[9]

The Downsian model of majority rule representative democracy was extended by Bernholz (1966) to derive specific predictions as to which special interests are likely to be served: for example, producers, low-profit industries, slow-growth and high-unemployment districts.[10] This list could easily be joined with Breton's to obtain a predictive theory of representative government.

There is little in the way of direct testing of the theory of government as monopolist at the national level. Several studies at the local level have been made, however. Robert Deacon (1979) has estimated a median voter model for total expenditures, police protection, and street maintenance for a sample of 64 small cities in the Los Angeles area. In some cases, services like police protection and street maintenance are bought from neighboring cities; in others they are bought from the cities' own monopoly bureaus. The costs of cities that buy services on contract were 86, 58, and 70 percent of the noncontracting cities' costs, respectively, for the three categories of expenditures. Mehay (1984) and Mehay and Gonzales (1985) also present evidence indicating that the costs of the suppliers of contract services are lower even for the services that they supply to their own municipalities. Thus, having to compete for contracts from other municipalities makes a bureau more efficient at supplying the demands of its own constituents.

The Tiebout model analyzed in Chapter 9 implies that an important constraint on the monopoly power of a local government is the existence of competing local governments to which citizens can move. Restrictions on entry into the local government "industry," that is, restrictions on the rights of local communities to incorporate, should then raise the costs of the existing, protected governments. Martin and Wagner (1978), Mehay (1981), and DiLorenzo (1981) all present evidence that restrictions on the creation of new government units raises the costs of existing ones.

These studies at the local level consistently support the view that governments do act as monopolists whenever they can, and that competition where it exists does tend to have the same salutary effect on efficiency that competition

9. For Tullock's reply, see (1961).
10. See also Bernholz (1974b).

among firms does. These studies also suggest that introducing competition among government bureaus, as Niskanen (1971, ch. 18) has recommended, would increase the efficiency of the government provision of goods and services.[11]

F.   The government as Leviathan

1.   *Theory*

Geoffrey Brennan and James Buchanan (1980) have pushed the monopoly-government model a step further. They assume with Breton that every government is and behaves like a monopolist. Political competition is thought to provide an ineffective constraint on governments owing to the rational ignorance of voters, the uncertainties inherent in majority rule cycling, and outright collusion among elected officials (Brennan and Buchanan, 1980, pp. 17–24). As in Niskanen's model, they assume that the government's primary objective is revenue maximization.

Although political competition cannot constrain the government's desire to expand, constitutional limitations on sources of tax revenue and on debt and money creation can. Brennan and Buchanan assume that the only truly effective constraints on government in the long run are contained in constitutional rules limiting government's power to tax, issue debt, and print money.

With the government viewed as a malevolent revenue maximizer rather than a benevolent public good provider, many of the traditional propositions of the public finance tax literature are stood on their heads (Brennan and Buchanan, 1980, p. 2). Traditional analysis assumes that the purpose of government is to raise a *given amount of revenue* subject to certain efficiency and equity constraints; Brennan and Buchanan assume that citizens seek to impose constraints on the government bureaucracy limiting its revenues to a given amount. To see the difference, consider the familiar problem of how to tax income without discriminating against leisure. Let *AB* in Figure 14.4 represent an individual's opportunity locus in the absence of any tax. An "ideal tax" would shift the individual's opportunity locus toward the origin without distorting his choice between income and leisure, say, to *CD,* by taxing an individual's *capacity* to earn income and not just the income actually earned. If the taxing authority is free to raise revenue only by means of a tax on earned income, however, it must raise the equivalent amount of revenue, *AC,* by imposing a much higher effective tax rate on earned income, as is

---

11. For some modeling implying that competition between bureaus would increase efficiency and some empirical evidence suggesting that the Antitrust Division of the Justice Department and the Federal Trade Commission do not compete, see Higgins, Shughart, and Tollison (1987).

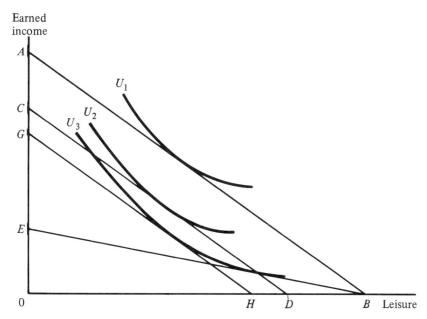

Figure 14.4. Alternative strategies for taxing income and leisure.

implicit in the opportunity line, *EB*. If the amount of tax revenue to be raised were a fixed amount, as the normative literature on optimal taxation assumes, the tax on the more comprehensive tax base would be preferred, since $U_2 >$ U_3. But, if the budget-maximizing bureaucrat were free to tax both earned income and leisure, there is no reason to assume he will stop with a tax revenue of *AC*. If the citizen would tolerate a reduction in utility by the taxing authority to U_3, then the budget-maximizing bureaucrat would push tax rates up sufficiently to raise *AG*. The difference between a comprehensive definition of income and a restricted definition is not the level of utility of the voter-taxpayer for a given tax revenue, but the amount of tax revenue taken at a given utility level under the grasping Leviathan view of government.

If the voter always finished up at the same utility level whatever the definition of the tax base, he would be indifferent to the resolution of this question. Brennan and Buchanan assume, however, that there are physical and institutional limits to how high nominal tax rates on a given revenue base can be raised. Given such limits, the bureaucracy's capacity to tax the citizenry is weaker under a narrow definition of the tax base than under a broad one. A citizen who expected bureaucrats to maximize their budgets would constrain their ability to do so by constitutionally restricting the kinds of income and wealth that could be taxed.

The Brennan–Buchanan model also turns the standard analysis of excess burden in taxation on its head. With the amount of revenue to be raised by taxation fixed, the optimal tax is the one that induces the minimum amount of distortion, which falls on the most inelastic sources of revenue. With the amount of revenue to be raised the maximand, the citizen seeks to limit the government to more elastic tax bases and shelter parts of his income and wealth from taxation entirely.

When Brennan and Buchanan apply their analysis to other aspects of taxation, they sometimes reach conclusions analogous to those existing in the normative tax literature, but the underlying logic is quite different. We have seen from the Downs–Breton model that the government will introduce special tax concessions favoring narrowly defined interest groups in pursuit of its own objectives. A citizen writing a tax constitution to constrain Leviathan would require that the government impose tax schedules that are uniform across persons to limit the government's capacity to engage in tax price discrimination as a means of expanding its revenue. Thus, "horizontal equity" would be favored at the constitutional stage because it limits the government's degrees of freedom, and not for any other ethical reasons. Similar logic leads in general to a preference for progressive over regressive taxes: Less revenue can typically be raised by tax schedules imposing high marginal rates than by schedules imposing low ones.

The Leviathan model also provides an additional justification for Wicksell's (1896) prescription that expenditure proposals be tied to the taxes that would finance them. Although to Wicksell this proposal seemed to be an obvious requirement to ensure informed choices as to benefits and costs by citizens, when governments seek to maximize revenue the proposal has the added advantage of ensuring budget balance and forcing the government to provide some public benefit to secure more revenue (Brennan and Buchanan, 1980, pp. 154–5). Bridges and roads must be built for government to collect the tolls.

Although traditional analyses of debt and money creation have assumed that government's motivation is benign, in the hands of a Leviathan seeking ever new sources of revenue, both of these policy instruments become extremely dangerous. Balanced budget constitutional amendments follow naturally, as do restrictions on the government's capacity to print money (chs. 5, 6, 10), with the ultimate restriction – "denying government the power to create money under any circumstances at all" (p. 130) – being possibly the best means to control the abuse of this power.

In the Brennan–Buchanan model of the state, the citizens have lost almost all control over government. They set government on its way, when they forge the constitutional constraints on government at its inception. The government's power to pursue its own objectives is greatly aided by the "rational ignorance" of voters of their true tax bills, the full impact of debt and money creation. The information-power nexus reappears in the Leviathan model as fiscal illusion and rational ignorance. From time to time, citizens may perceive that the government Leviathan has gone too far in pursuing its own ends and may rise from their lethargy to reforge certain bonds on government, as in the tax and debt revolts of the seventies. But between these surges of citizen control the government proceeds on its revenue-maximizing course within whatever constraints the Constitution effectively allows.

2.   *Empirical testing*

The central hypothesis of the Leviathan model is that only constitutional constraints on the sources of revenue or levels of expenditure can curb the appetite for growth by those in government. As yet, little in the way of direct testing of this hypothesis exists. Michael Nelson (1986, p. 293) has found that those states that tax personal income have significantly larger government sectors as implied by the Leviathan model, although causality may run the other way. Nelson also found that the relative size of the government sector varied inversely with the number of local government units. If one assumes that having more local government units signifies a stronger federalist structure and more intensive constraints on government through intergovernmental competition, then this result also supports the Leviathan model, as do the studies by Deacon (1979), Mehay (1984), and Mehay and Gonzales (1985). Marlow's (1988) finding that total government size varies inversely with the relative importance of a local government is also consistent with the Leviathan hypothesis. Several cross-national studies have also found that federalist structures inhibit government growth (Cameron, 1978; Saunders, 1986; Schneider, 1986).

Wallace Oates (1985) concluded that having a federalist constitutional structure had a negative, but statistically insignificant effect, on the growth rates of developed countries. Oates also found that the degree of centralization of tax revenue, a source of fiscal power emphasized by Brennan and Buchanan (1980, p. 185), was either not statistically significantly related to government growth or inversely related at both cross-national and cross-state levels of growth. The same result was observed by Nelson (1986) in his cross-sectional analysis of state data. As so often happens in the social sciences, a bold new theory loses much of its shine as it is dragged through the muddy waters of empirical analysis.

G.   Autocratic government

Gordon Tullock has remarked on several occasions that most governments around the world at any one point in time, or over the course of history, have not been democratic by any reasonable interpretation of this word. The most common form of government is some form of hierarchical, authoritarian structure with a single person at the top. Autocracy. The exclusive focus of public choice on democratic rules and institutions represents a provincial preoccupation with a nonmodal form of government. Tullock's (1987) book *Autocracy* begins to redress this imbalance.

Tullock does not develop a model of autocracy in the mold of Niskanen or Brennan and Buchanan, in which an objective of the autocrat is first hypothesized and then the logical implications of his maximizing this objective function are derived. Rather, the study proceeds more as an inductive historical account of autocracies from which insights and hypotheses are gleaned. However, the perspective is definitely that of public choice.

One of the explanations for the pursuit of growth by corporate managers and public bureaucrats is to achieve the nonpecuniary rewards associated with "empire building." But even Nissan, Shell, and the U.S. Department of Defense are dwarfed in relative magnitude by the empires that Alexander and Napoleon succeeded in building. Certainly maximizing the size of the state must have been a primary objective of these autocrats, and presumably many more.

But Tullock does not focus upon these exceptional cases. His concern is more with the garden variety of dictator or monarch, whose objectives are more reasonably described as (1) first getting into power, (2) hanging on to it, and (3) gaining some enjoyment while possessing it. Although creating an empire would fall under the third heading, most autocrats seem content to pursue security of tenure and rather high living standards while in office (and afterward if the nature of their exit from office does not preclude this possibility).

Thus, autocracies do share some characteristics with electoral systems. Getting into office and staying there is the primary task of many autocrats, as it is for elected officials. Empire building and other "misuses" of the revenues raised from citizens are characteristics of utility maximizers, be they autocrats, elected officials, or appointed bureaucrats. Only the scales on which these goals can be pursued may differ.

How badly do autocracies do at satisfying the preferences of the citizens? Tullock shrinks from trying to answer this question, but does note that many citizens seem to acquiesce in being governed by an autocrat even when they might prefer a democratic system. We encounter again the free-rider problem. No citizen is likely to have a significant impact on the structure of government, and few try to change it. Both democratic and autocratic systems survive perhaps more out of inertia fed by citizen lethargy than because of their inherent superiority (Tullock, 1987, ch. 9). The most frequent cause of a change from one form to another is defeat by a foreign power, which imposes the change in governmental structure.

Tullock's book raises as many questions as it answers. When, where, and how did democratic institutions first emerge? What fosters a nonexternally imposed shift from autocracy to democracy? What induces the reverse change? These are central questions of current, indeed, interminable relevance. Tullock's book constitutes a first step on the road to answering them.

H.   Conclusions

Most of the public choice literature is in the citizen-over-the-state tradition. Just as the individual consumer is sovereign in the marketplace, ultimate authority is assumed to rest with the citizens.

But the word "sovereign" did not originate as a synonym for citizen. Historically, the word has referred to a single person ruling the people as head of a monarchy. The state was something separate from, indeed above, the people it ruled.

This second view of the state has reappeared most vividly in Tullock's book on autocracy, and in Brennan and Buchanan's work on Leviathan models. But elements of this view are present also in the monopoly-state and bureaucracy models. Which model best explains the outcomes of the polity probably depends both on the outcomes that one wishes to explain and on the polity. The same model is unlikely to work equally well in describing the public policies of the Swiss canton of Appenzell and the German Democratic Republic.

How well each model works in explaining public policies in those countries, which are generally regarded as democracies, remains an empirical question. We have touched upon some of this evidence in this chapter. We consider more in later chapters, particularly in Chapter 17, which deals with the size of government.

Bibliographical notes

John Chubb (1985) develops the sponsor–bureau monitoring problem as an example of the principal-agent problem and presents evidence of its nature.

The agenda control model of bureaucracy has been extended to more than one government activity by Mackay and Weaver (1981).

For an analysis of the history of the state in the spirit of the government as monopolist, see Auster and Silver (1979).

PART IV

Applications

CHAPTER 15

Political competition and macroeconomic performance

All political history shows that the standing of the Government and its ability to hold the confidence of the electorate at a General Election depend on the success of its economic policy.

Harold Wilson (as quoted in Hibbs, 1982c)

In this part of the book we present four applications of the public choice approach to explaining real world phenomena. We shall see that the rational self-interest assumption with respect to individual behavior does fairly well at the macro level in explaining election outcomes, government stabilization policies, and macro growth rates; that it does less well but still offers some insight into differences in the size of governments and their growth rates; and performs rather dismally at the most micro level in explaining individual voting behavior. We begin with the hypothesis that has received the most impressive empirical support to date, and end with the one that has received the least support.

A. The political business cycle

The simplest way to operationalize the assumption that voters maximize their utilities is to assume that there is but one argument in their utility functions, say, income or wealth. Selfish voters will then support the party that they expect will maximize their income or wealth.

Although some redistribution may win more votes than it loses, redistribution is a game all parties can play, so it is difficult to achieve an unmatchable edge on the other parties by only promising to redistribute what is already there. A more difficult strategy to match is to create new income and wealth. In the long run, the growth of income and wealth in society is a function of the rate of technological change and population growth, variables that are difficult to change by government policy. But in the short run, incomes can be changed by changing the rates at which the existing stocks of capital and labor are employed. Thus, one strategy that a vote-maximizing party might follow is to adopt short-run macroeconomic policies to change the rate of unemployment or growth in national income. Both variables have figured prominently in the political business cycle literature and are in fact highly correlated. We concentrate for the moment on unemployment.

Although the levers of macro policy can be used to lower unemployment, reductions in unemployment come at the price of higher rates of inflation. The standard device for depicting the inflation–unemployment trade-off is the Phillips curve. Although the accuracy of this curve as a depiction of the long-run relationship between the rates of inflation and unemployment is much questioned today, that such a trade-off exists was widely believed by government leaders and their economic advisers during much of the period, which the empirical work reviewed here analyzes. Thus, it remains a useful analytic tool for studying the policies of the past, whatever its potential for depicting the trade-offs of the future.

Although the long-run effects of inflation on individual incomes are largely neutral, individual voters regard inflation as a serious economic problem. Kiewiet (1983, p. 84), for example, reports figures from biannual surveys of citizens in the United States between 1958 and 1980 in which individuals were asked to name the nation's most important economic problem. On average, 11.6 percent of the population named unemployment as the most important economic problem during this period, while almost twice that number (21.6 percent) named inflation.

An increase in the unemployment rate makes those individuals who become unemployed worse off. It also can increase the anxiety of other citizens that they will become unemployed. More generally, higher unemployment levels signify underutilized resources and slower growth in real incomes. These considerations suggest that both inflation and unemployment are arguments in a voter's utility function. Since both are bad, voter indifference curves are concave to the origin in Figure 15.1. Indifference curves closer to the origin represent higher utility levels.

If inflation and unemployment were the only variables in the voter's utility function, and the long-run Phillips curve (LL) were the effective opportunity set for two political parties, then competition for votes between the parties would lead to a single vote-maximizing point along LL. While each voter's indifference map might lead her to favor a different point along LL, with only U and P in the utility function, the inverse relationship between U and P inherent in the Phillips curve reduces the issue set to a single dimension, the choice, say, of U. Voters' preferences are single-peaked along LL, and the median voter theorem applies.[1] If I_1 and I_2 are indifference curves of the

---

1. If other issues enter the utility function, a multidimensional issue space arises, and an equilibrium from a generalized median voter theorem is unlikely. If parties are uncertain about voter responses, an equilibrium pair of strategies for the two parties may exist, however, in which both parties promise the same levels of inflation and unemployment (see Chapter 11).

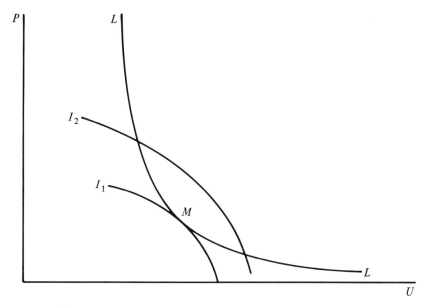

Figure 15.1. The trade-off between inflation (P) and unemployment (U).

median voter, then both parties will strive to adopt macro stabilization policies that bring the economy to point M on the Phillips curve.

Considerable evidence exists indicating that voters do judge governing parties and presidents on the basis of their ability to provide low levels of unemployment and inflation. Table 15.1 lists those studies that have tested whether U and P affect the percentage of the vote that a party or government receives. Included also are those studies that focus on national income rather than unemployment, since this variable has in some ways more justification as an argument in the voter's utility function, and is in any event highly correlated with U. Table 15.2 lists studies that have tested for a relationship between the government's or president's popularity, as measured by pollsters, and the macroeconomic variables. Although each variable is not significant in every study, and the coefficients bounce around a bit,[2] the number of times in which the coefficients on P, U, and Y are statistically significant and of the right sign compares favorably with other macroempirical relationships, which are generally assumed to hold. A pattern of results as consistent as these across so many countries is fairly impressive.

P – inflation   Y – income
U – unemployment

2. The instability of the relationships is stressed in Stigler's (1973) and Arcelus and Meltzer's (1975a) attacks on Kramer (1971) and Mueller (1970). See, also, Bloom and Price (1975), Goodman and Kramer (1975), and Arcelus and Meltzer (1975b).

Table 15.1. *The effect of macroeconomic conditions on votes for parties or presidents*

Country dependent variable	Author(s)	Time period	Lagged dependent variable	Inflation rate (P)
United States				
Republicans in House elections	Kramer (1971)	1896–1964		$-0.56^{**}\Delta P_t/P_{t-1}$
Republicans in House elections	Stigler (1973)	1896–1970		$-0.21^{**}(P_t - \bar{P})$
Ln (presidential candidate in office)	Niskanen (1979)	1896–1972		
Democratic presidential candidates	Fair (1982)	1961–80		$-0.68\|P_t - P_{t-2}\|/2P_{t-1}$
Presidential candidate in office	Kirchgässner (1981)	1896–1976	0.49^{**}	$-0.12^{**}P_t^2$
Denmark				
Deviation from long-term trand of bigger party in power	Madsen (1980)	1920–73		$-0.43^{*}P_t$
Norway				
Deviation of governing party from long-term average	Madsen (1980)	1920–73		$-0.36P_t$
Sweden				
Deviation of government party from long-term trend	Madsen (1980)	1920–73		$-0.22P_t$
France				
Left opposition parties	Rosa (1980)	1920–73	0.20^{*}	$\left(\dfrac{P_t + P_{t-1} + P_{t-2}}{3} \right)$

Note: *Significant at 0.05 level, **at 0.01 level, two-tailed tests. Variable definitions differ across studies (e.g., real national income versus nominal national income). The reader must consult the original studies. X_t is current value of X, X_{t-i} is X lagged i periods, $\Delta X_t = X_t - X_{t-1}$, $\bar{X}$ is a mean or trend value for X.

Sources: Schneider and Frey (1988, Table 1). Reprinted with permission of Duke University

Unemployment rate (U)	National income (Y)
$-0.14\Delta U_t$	$0.46^{**}\Delta Y_t/Y_{t-1}$
	$0.17^{*}(Y_t - \bar{Y})$
	$1.51^{*}\ln\left(\dfrac{Y_t + Y_{t-1} + Y_{t-2} + Y_{t-3}}{4}\right)$
	$0.98^{**}\Delta Y_t/Y_{t-1}$
$0.19\Delta U_t$	
$-0.10U_t$	
$-2.40^{*}(\Delta U_t - \Delta U_{t-1})$	$0.73^{**}Y_t$
$+0.02^{**}\left(\dfrac{U_t + U_{t-1} + U_{t-2}}{3}\right)$	$-0.08^{**}\left(\dfrac{Y_t + Y_{t-1} + Y_{t-2}}{3}\right)$

Press. Fair (1982) has been substituted for Fair (1978). Although it is unfair to Stigler's argument to include an equation from his paper, the one included must be close to what he would regard as the best formulation. Also relevant are the principal components analysis of presidential votes by Crain, Deaton, and Tollison (1978), and the analysis of forecasts from the Kramer model by Atesoglu and Congleton (1982).

281

Table 15.2. *The effect of macroeconomic conditions on party (presidential) popularity*

Country dependent variable[a]	Author(s)	Time period	Lagged dependent variable	Inflation rate (P)	Unemployment rate (U)	National income (Y)
United States						
Presidential, Q	Schneider (1978)	1961:1–1968:4		$-2.61*P_{t-2}$	$-5.43**U_{t-2}$	
Presidential, Q	Schneider (1978)	1969:1–1976:4		$-2.15*P_{t-2}$	$-3.89**U_{t-2}$	
ln[POP/(100-POP)] POP = presidential, Q	Hibbs (1982c)	1961:1–1980:1	0.84^b	$-0.017**\ln(P_t/P_{t-1})$	$-0.017**\ln(U_t/U_{t-1})$	$0.015**\ln(Y_t/Y_{t-1})$
ln[POP(100-POP)], Q POP = presidential popularity among	Hibbs (1987)	1961:1–1984:1				
Democrats			0.83^b	$-0.028**\ln(P_t/P_{t-1})$	$-0.030**\ln(U_t/U_{t-1})$	$0.011**\ln(Y_t/Y_{t-1})$
Republicans			0.77^b	$-0.039**\ln(P_t/P_{t-1})$	$-0.025**\ln(U_t/U_{t-1})$	$0.018**\ln(Y_t/Y_{t-1})$
Independents			0.84^b	$-0.031**\ln(P_t/P_{t-1})$	$-0.015**\ln(U_t/U_{t-1})$	$0.015**\ln(Y_t/Y_{t-1})$
France						
Presidential, M	Lewis–Beck (1980)	1960:1–1978:4		$-1.89**P_{t-2}$	$-0.56*U_{t-2}$	
Presidential, Q ln[POP/(100-POP)]	Hibbs (1981)	1969:4–1978:4	0.8^b	$.004**P_t$	$-0.01**U_t$	$0.017**Y_t$
Presidential, M ln[POP/(100-POP)]	Lafay (1984)	1974:10–1983:12		$-0.028**P_t$	$-0.103**U_{t-1}$	$0.029**Y_{t-1}$
Australia						
Governing parties, Q	Schneider–Pommerehne (1980)	1960:2–1977:2	$0.66**$	$-0.47*P_{t-1}$	$-1.13**U_{t-1}$	$0.05*Y_{t-1}$

Denmark						
Governing parties, Q	Paldam–Schneider (1980)	1957:2–1968:1	$0.67**$	$-0.41*(P_t - P_{t-4})$	$-0.73**(U_t - U_{t-4})$	$0.19*(Y_t - Y_{t-4})$
Germany						
Governing party, M	Kirchgässner (1976)	1951:1–1966:10	$0.67**$	$-0.20**P_t$	$-0.43**U_t$	
Governing parties, M	Kirchgässner (1977)	1970:3–1976:10	$0.61**$	$-0.09*P_t$	$-0.31**U_t$	
Governing parties, Q $\ln[\text{POP}(100\text{-POP})]$	Hibbs (1982c)	1957:4–1978:4	0.88^b	$-0.0044**\ln(P_t/P_{t-1})$	$-0.006**\ln(U_t/U_{t-1})$	$0.0051**\ln(Y_t/Y_{t-1})$
Great Britain						
Government lead, Q ($\text{POP}_{\text{GOV}}\text{-POP}_{\text{OPP}}$)	Pissarides (1980)	1955:3–1977:4	$0.52**$	$-0.57*(P_t - P_{t-1})$	$4.55*(1/U_{t-2})$	$0.26**Y_t$
Governing parties, Q $\ln[\text{POP}/(100\text{-POP})]$	Hibbs (1982c)	1959:4–1978:4	0.88^b	$0.0038***\ln(P_t/P_{t-1})$	$-0.21**\ln(U_t/U_{t-1})$	$0.0081\Delta\ln(Y_t/Y_{t-1})$
Government lead, Q ($\text{POP}_{\text{GOV}}\text{-POP}_{\text{OPP}}$)	Minford–Peel (1982)	1959:1–1975:3		$1.95P^c_{t+1}$		$0.53Y^c_{t+1}$
Japan						
Governing parties (30 observations)	Inoguchi (1980)	1960–76		$-0.68***P_t$		$0.59*Y_{t-2}$
New Zealand						
Government lead, Q ($\text{POP}_{\text{GOV}}\text{-POP}_{\text{OPP}}$)	Ursprung (1983)	1970:1–1981:4	0.28	$-0.35**(P_t - P_{t-1})$	$-2.12**U_t$	$0.07\, Y_t/Y_{t-1}$

(continued)

Table 15.2. (cont.)

Country dependent variable[a]	Author(s)	Time period	Lagged dependent variable	Inflation rate (P)	Unemployment rate (U)	National income (Y)
Sweden						
Social Democrats, M	Jonung and Wadensjoe (1979)	1967:3–1976:9	0.88**	$-0.10*P_{t-1}$	$-0.73**U_{t-1}$	
The Netherlands Popularity of 3 parties, M	Renaud and van Winden (1987a)	1970:1–1981:12				
Christian Democrats			0.83*	$-2.23*P_t$	$-1.09*U_t$	
Social Democrats			0.83*	$-1.67*P_t$	$-0.57*U_t$	
Liberal Conservatives			0.83*	$-0.78*P_t$	$-0.36*U_t$	

Note: See Table 15.1.
[a]Q = quarterly; M = monthly.
[b]Estimated by iterative search for minimum sum of squared errors.
[c]Projected value assuming rational expectations.
Source: Schneider and Frey (1988, Tables 2, 3) with additions and amendments. Reprinted with permission of Duke University Press.

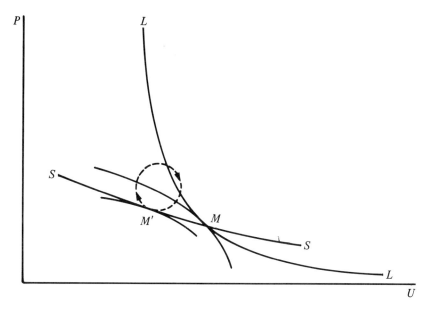

Figure 15.2. The political business cycle.

If quantities respond more rapidly to changes in macroeconomic conditions than prices (Okun, 1981), the government can manipulate the macroeconomic levers so as to reduce unemployment in the short run, with the full inflationary effect coming some time later. Governments face a short-run Phillips curve like SS in Figure 15.2. If voters ignore or heavily discount the future inflation that a movement along SS to the left of M must eventually bring, then the party in government can raise a substantial majority of voters' utilities in the short run by adopting policies that move the economy cut along SS to, say, M'. The party in control of the government is in a position to increase its chances for reelection by reducing unemployment just before an election. In countries in which the government has some discretion in choosing when to call an election, the party in power has an even further advantage over the opposition in ensuring that elections occur under favorable economic conditions (Frey and Schneider, 1978b; Lächler, 1982).

Of course, after the election inflation rises and the economy returns to LL. But this higher inflation may be inherited by the opposition party, and even if the incumbent party wins, it can wring the inflation out of the economy after the election by sufficiently deflationary policies. Thus, the prediction emerges that incumbent parties deliberately create a political business cycle with falling unemployment (rising national income) prior to an election, rising unemployment (falling inflation) afterward, as depicted, say, by the dashed line in

Figure 15.2 (Nordhaus, 1975; Lindbeck, 1976; MacRae, 1977; Fair, 1978; Tufte, 1978).

The political business cycle assumes that voters are myopic. They vote for the government at M' as if this combination of U and P were sustainable, even though the economy will soon change and bring them to lower levels of utility than at either M' or M. This assumption of voter myopia is difficult to reconcile with the assumed rational expectations of all economic agents in recent economic modeling. Despite the popular appeal of the rational expectations assumption and the evidence in its support (Barro, 1977), the facts seem incontrovertible that politicians do act in ways that imply that they believe voters are extremely myopic. Tufte (1978, pp. 39–44) documents the governmental strategy of moving transfer payments checks forward by one or even two months in election years so that they arrive just prior to the election. Can such efforts be explained without assuming an extremely high voter discount rate? For a full decade between 1957 and 1966 public works projects, jobs, and transfers were distributed according to the electoral cycle in such a way as to create a "biennial lurch," or expansion, before the election and contraction afterward (Averch, Koehler, and Denton, 1971).

It is much easier to time the mailing of checks than it is to coordinate macroeconomic policies to achieve an expanding economy just before an election. Thus, the evidence that governments behave as predicted by the political business cycle model is more mixed. Tufte (1978, ch. 1) examines the evidence for the world's 27 democracies and finds it consistent with the predictions of the political business cycle hypothesis. Paldam (1979, 1981b), on the other hand, looks at data for 17 OECD countries, and finds the patterns of inflation and income growth inconsistent with the hypothesis. McCallam (1978,), Beck (1982a), and Hibbs (1987, ch. 8) all reject the political business cycle hypothesis using rigorous econometric tests. Although there exists clear evidence that some governments in some countries at some points in time have behaved as the political business cycle model predicts, the evidence is not strong enough to warrant the conclusion that this type of behavior is a general characteristic of democratically elected governments.

B.   Ideology and electoral competition

The two-party competition model described above assumes that voters have no loyalty to any party and parties have no loyalties toward specific groups of voters. Political competition is, like market competition, impartial. Voters vote for the party coming closest to their position on inflation and unemployment; parties court all voters with equal alacrity.

A large body of evidence exists indicating that voters' choices of party are not as fluid as the above characterization suggests. Moreover, parties do not

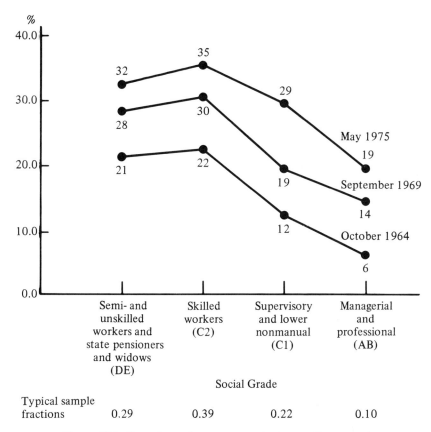

Figure 15.3. Percentage of survey respondents regarding unemployment as a "most serious problem." *Source:* Hibbs (1982b, p. 262).

promise exactly the same policies, but rather consistently pursue different objectives with regard to macroeconomic policies. This attraction of voters for particular parties and ideological inertia of party goals can be explained by an extension of the voter-self-interest-party-competition model.

Blue-collar and unskilled workers are more likely to become unemployed and stay unemployed than are white-collar and professional groups. Thus, it is rational for lower-skilled groups to be more concerned about unemployment. That they are is illustrated in Figure 15.3 taken from Hibbs (1982b) (see also Tufte, 1978, pp. 83–4; and for the United States, Hibbs, 1979, p. 715, and 1987, p. 139). The vertical axis gives the percentage of individuals of a given occupational group who regarded unemployment as "a particularly important issue" or the "most important problem" at the time. Not surprisingly, unem-

Table 15.3. *Changes in support for the U.S. president and U.K. governing party in response to macroeconomic performance*

Occupational group	Inflation rate	Unemployment rate	Real income growth rate
Gallop poll approval, U.S. presidents (1960–79)			
Blue-collar	−3.3	−2.2	+2.7
White-collar	−3.6	−1.6	+2.1
Nonlabor force	−3.2	−0.45	+1.2
Political support for U.K. governing party (1962–78)			
Semi- and unskilled workers, widows, and state pensioners	−1.9	−2.85	+1.0
Skilled workers	−1.8	−3.3	+1.3
Nonmanual employees	−1.7	−1.55	+0.55

Sources: Hibbs (1982a, Table 4; 1982b, Table 3). Figures are Hibbs's figures for a 2 percentage point increase divided by 2. All figures are values for complete adjustment except U.K. real income change figure, which is after 8 quarters.

ployment is regarded as a more important issue in 1975 when the unemployment rate stood at 4.2 percent, than in 1969 or 1964 when the rates were 2.5 and 1.8 percent, respectively. But at any given point in time, the lower-status occupational groups show a greater concern about unemployment than the managerial and professional group.

Given their greater relative concern about unemployment, it is perhaps not surprising to find that the lower-status groups' support for the president or government in office is more sensitive to unemployment levels. Table 15.3 reports estimates of the effects of changes in unemployment, inflation, and real income on support for the president in the United States and governing party in the United Kingdom. In both countries, the response to changes in unemployment differs to a greater extent across occupational groups than it does for inflation. Indeed, there is little difference in the response of the different groups to changes in inflation within either country, while the responses to changes in unemployment differ by a factor of more than four in the United States and two in the United Kingdom. Note also that the coefficients on inflation are much higher relative to those on unemployment in the United States than in the United Kingdom. According to Hibbs's estimate, Americans on average are more concerned about inflation relative to unemployment than the British population.

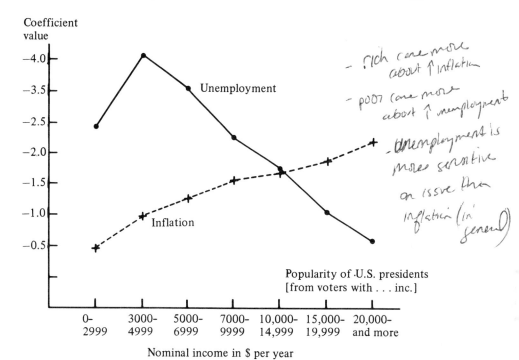

Figure 15.4. Coefficients for unemployment and inflation in U.S. presidential popularity equations (1969–76), seven income groups. *Source:* Schneider (1978); Schneider and Frey (1988).

Figure 15.4 plots the coefficients on unemployment and inflation by income group in a presidential popularity function estimated by Schneider (1978). Consistent with the relationship across occupational groups reported in Table 15.3, one finds that the support for the president is more sensitive to changes in unemployment the lower the group's income.[3] Conversely, support for the president is more sensitive to changes in inflation rates the higher a group's income is. Although there is more variability in the coefficients on inflation in Schneider's results than in Hibbs's, the line connecting the inflation coefficients in Figure 15.4 is flatter than the one connecting the unemployment coefficients. The differential response to unemployment changes is greater across income groups than is the differential response to inflation. Note that Schneider's results indicate a greater relative concern for unemploy-

3. The anomalous coefficient for the lowest income group may come about because this group contains a disproportionate fraction of retirees, who may be less concerned about unemployment.

Table 15.4. *Macroeconomic performance of U.S. economy under Republican and Democratic presidents (1952–85)*

Year	U	P	Year	U	P
1952	3.0	0.9	1972	5.6	4.4
1956	4.1	2.9	1976	7.7	4.8
1960	5.5	1.5	1980	7.1	12.4
1964	5.2	1.2	1984	7.5	4.0
1968	3.6	4.7	1987	6.1	4.4

Changes in U and P by party of president for presidential terms

	Republican					Democratic			
	ΔU		ΔP			ΔU		ΔP	
Term	ABS.	%	ABS.	%	Term	ABS.	%	ABS.	%
52–56	+1.1	+31	+2.0	+105	60–64	−.3	−6	−.3	−22
56–60	+1.4	+29	−1.4	−64	64–68	−1.6	−36	+3.5	+119
68–72	+2.0	+43	−1.3	−32	76–80	−.6	−8	+7.6	+88
72–76	+2.1	+32	+1.4	+34					
80–84	+.4	+5	−8.4	−102					
Average	1.4	+28	−1.5	−12		−.8	−17	3.6	+62

Changes in U and P by uninterrupted party control of presidency

	ΔU	ΔP
Republican administrations		
Eisenhower (1952–60)	$2.5	+.6
Nixon–Ford (1968–76)	+4.1	+.1
Reagan (1980–7)	−.9	−8.0
Cumulative	+5.7	−7.3
Democratic administrations		
Kennedy–Johnson (1960–68)	−1.9	+3.2
Carter (1976)	−0.6	+7.6
Cumulative	−2.5	+10.8

Source: Council of Economic Advisers, *Annual Report 1988,* Washington, D.C.: Government Printing Office, 1989.

ment among Americans than Hibbs's results. The absolute value of the coefficient on inflation is higher than that for unemployment for only two of the seven income groups.

Parties of the left draw their political support from lower occupational status and income groups. These groups are more concerned about unemployment, and their support is more sensitive to changes in unemployment. Parties of the right draw their support from groups more concerned about and responsive to inflation. A direct analysis of left-of-center party membership should find them more responsive to unemployment, right-of-center members to inflation, and it does. An increase in unemployment lowered the percentage of Democrats who approved of the president's performance by two to three times as much as the reduction for Republicans. On the other hand, an increase in the inflation rate reduces a president's approval among Republicans by somewhat more than it does among Democrats, although the differences are less dramatic (Hibbs, 1982a, Table 4; 1987, pp. 175–82).

C. Party ideology and macroeconomic policies

Those most concerned about unemployment are drawn to parties on the left, those concerned about inflation to parties on the right. Is this party allegiance rational? It would appear to be, if one judges the parties on the basis of what they say must be done and the promises they make. A content analysis of the annual *Economic Report of the President* and the *Council of Economic Advisers* along with party platforms reveals far more emphasis on unemployment by the Democrats, far more emphasis on inflation by Republicans (Tufte, 1978, pp. 71–83). Good evidence exists that the same differences are present in other countries (Kirschen et al., 1964; Kirschen, 1974).

Despite the vagaries of macroeconomic policy making in a country in which the executive and legislative branches are separated, U.S. presidents have succeeded to a considerable extent in matching the macro performance of the economy during their terms of office to the rhetoric of their parties. Table 15.4 reports unemployment (U) and inflation (P) rates in the fourth years of every presidential term since 1952. This period is particularly relevant to the issue, since a familiarity with Keynesian and monetarist macro policies existed throughout the period, and each party took turns in an almost perfect eight-year cycle in occupying the White House. The middle portion of the table indicates that each of the five Republican presidential terms resulted in a 1.4 percentage point increase in the unemployment rate, an increase of 28 percent of the figure in the year before the presidential term began. Inflation was reduced by an average of 1.5 percentage points, on the other hand.[4] The three Democratic presidential terms brought unemployment down by an average of 0.8 percentage points per term, while raising inflation by 3.6 percentage points.

Perhaps the most revealing figures are at the bottom of the table for the three sustained periods of Republican control of the White House and the two

---

4. The percentage change in inflation during Eisenhower's first term (1952–6) seems to contradict the hypothesis. But inflation in the year before Eisenhower took office was an unusually low 0.9 percent, a figure artificially depressed by Korean War wage and price controls.

periods of Democratic control. Since 1952 Republican presidential administrations have added 5.7 percentage points to the unemployment rate, while taking 7.3 percentage points off the rate of inflation. Democrats have added 10.8 percentage points to inflation while lowering unemployment by 2.5 percentage points.

Similar conclusions are obtained from Hibbs's time-series model for predicting unemployment and real output levels. Using quarterly data from 1953:1 through 1983:2, Hibbs estimates that Democratic administrations have a long-run impact on the economy that tends to reduce unemployment by 2 percentage points and increase real output by around 6 percent (Hibbs, 1987, pp. 224–32).

One can argue that Republicans concentrate on inflation when they take office because it is the most serious macro problem the country faces at the time, and for the same reason the Democrats concentrate on unemployment. But since Republicans take over from Democrats, and Democrats from Republicans, this observation hardly contradicts the hypothesis. Particularly revealing in this regard is the performance of the Reagan administration. One can argue that both unemployment (7.1 percent) and inflation (12.4 percent) were serious problems when Reagan took office. But it was inflation that received the highest priority. By the administration's second year the inflation rate had been cut by more than two-thirds, while unemployment had risen to its highest level since World War II, 9.5 percent. It was six years before the unemployment rate fell below the level when Reagan took office.

A similar dichotomy is apparent in other countries. Hibbs (1977) presents data on unemployment and inflation rates for 12 Western democracies (Belgium, Canada, Denmark, Finland, France, Italy, the Netherlands, Norway, Sweden, the United Kingdom, the United States, and West Germany) and compares them with the percentage of time from 1945 to 1969 in which Socialist-Labor parties were in office. The correlation between left-of-center control and unemployment is -0.68. The correlation between left-of-center control and inflation is $+0.74$ (see also Beck, 1982b).

These differences in performance in dealing with unemployment have not gone unnoticed by voters. In the United States, those who are more personally affected by unemployment, or who regard unemployment as a serious national issue, are more likely to vote Democratic, ceteris paribus (Kiewiet, 1981, 1983; Kuklinski and West, 1981). In Germany, high unemployment increases the percentage of the vote going to the left-of-center Social Democratic Party at the expense of the right-of-center Christian Democrats (Rattinger, 1981). In France, high unemployment increases the share of votes going to left-of-center parties, which are in opposition; high income lowers their share (Rosa, 1980).

Thus, competition for votes does not lead competing parties to converge on the same target with respect to unemployment and inflation rates. The prediction of a simple form of the median voter theorem applied to macroeconomic policy is not supported. What accounts for this observation?

One possible explanation is that the distribution of voter preferences is not unimodal. Douglas Hibbs has emphasized the importance of economic class in explaining voter support for political parties and the link between this support and macroeconomic policies. The existence of significant class distinctions might be interpreted as resulting in either a bi- or multimodal distribution of voter preferences with respect to unemployment and inflation. If voters abstain from supporting a party whose position is too far from their most favored position, competition for votes can pull party platforms away from one another, toward the other modes in the distribution (see Downs, 1957, pp. 118–22; Davis et al., 1970; and Chapter 12 of this volume). The threat of abstention is likely to be particularly effective in parliamentary systems with proportional representation, since the voter often has party options on both the left and the right of a given party, and new parties can more easily form than in the United States. Thus, one finds European parties to be more ideological than the two U.S. parties, and voters more closely tied to their parties (e.g., Hibbs, 1982c).

Another way to account for differences in macroeconomic performance by political parties is to assume that governments (presidents) manipulate the levers of macroeconomic policies to maximize their popularity only when their popularity is low or the election near, but when their popularity is high they adopt policies tied to their party ideology. Such a model was first developed by Frey and Lau (1968) in one of the pioneering contributions to the political business cycle literature. They posited that left-wing governments would spend more and right-wing governments less when their popularity was high. Both would try to lower unemployment and expand national income as the election approached and/or their popularity fell below a critical value (assumed to be 52 percent approval in empirical work). Thus, lower average unemployment rates and higher average inflation rates for left-of-center governments emerge from the Frey–Lau model as an indirect, Keynesian consequence of their ideological predilection to greater spending. Empirical support for variants on this model, modified to capture country-specific economic and institutional factors, has been found for the United States (Frey and Schneider, 1978a), the United Kingdom (Frey and Schneider, 1978b, 1981a), West Germany (Frey and Schneider, 1979), and Australia (Schneider and Pommerehne, 1980; Pommerehne and Schneider, 1983).[5]

5. The discretionary spending part of the model when government popularity is high was not supported for Australia. Schneider and Pommerehne argue that that is because the time between elections in Australia (typically, 2 to 2½ years) is too short to allow governing parties the luxury of pursuing ideological goals.

Chrystal and Alt (1981) have challenged the Frey and Schneider results for the United Kingdom. See also their reply (Frey and Schneider, 1981a).

Although Frey, Lau, Pommerehne, and Schneider emphasize the difference between vote-maximizing policies around election time and the pursuit of ideological goals at other times, the differences between these two strategies may be more in the nature of a difference between short- and long-run vote maximization. Hibbs (1981, 1982a,c, 1987) emphasizes that the support of blue-collar workers for left-of-center parties, and white-collar managerial personnel for conservative parties, is *rational* since these parties cater to these groups' respective interests. His estimates also imply that voters have long memories when evaluating party performance. What parties in office may do immediately following an election victory, or any time their popularity is high, is invest in long-run vote maximization by pursuing policies that will strengthen the loyalty of their traditional supporters. When the election is near, they pursue the votes of those citizens who are independents and/or have short memories of party performance records.

D.   Other policy variables and ideological goals

The hypothesis common to these studies is that macroeconomic variables affect the popularity of, and at election time votes for, the governing parties and party leaders. Governments select macroeconomic policies with these relationships in mind. The levels of unemployment and inflation are universally regarded as primary indexes of macroeconomic performance, and these variables constitute the common thread running through the political business cycle literature. But other policy variables can affect votes, and thus a complete model of government behavior should include these.

As we noted at the beginning of this chapter, the simplest way to operationalize the voter self-interest postulate is to assume that income is the only argument in the voter's utility function. "The quickest way to produce an acceleration of real disposable income is for the government to mail more people larger checks" (Tufte, 1978, p. 29). Transfer policies might be favored over more general macroeconomic policies because their timing can be better controlled and their impact pinpointed. Transfer payments are among the expenditures the Frey–Lau–Schneider–Pommerehne model assumes are varied according to the governing party's ideology. Tufte (1978, ch. 2) and Hibbs (1987, chs. 7, 9) give ample evidence of their use in the United States.

Many studies have also included national income along with or instead of unemployment in their models (see Table 15.1). Although it is often significant and sometimes outperforms unemployment, its performance is less consistent than the simple logic and Tufte's more micro evidence might lead one to expect. The difficulty with this more macroempirical work may come because increased transfer payments only increase the incomes of some voters. Although their incomes and possibly support for the government may change dramatically, there may be too many other random elements affecting national income and government popularity to ensure that the result holds up consistently over time across different studies.

Whereas short-run increases in transfers may increase government popularity, increases in taxes reduce it. Not surprisingly, transfer payment increases tend to be financed by tax increases, and the usual sequence is for the transfer increases to take effect just before the election, the tax increases afterward (Tufte, 1978, ch. 2). According to Mikesell (1978), the tax-policy cycle at the state level is most likely to lean toward tax increases in off-election years, least likely to do so in gubernatorial election years.

If expenditures increase just before elections and taxes do not, then the government's deficit must increase. Consistent with Mikesell's (1978) evidence of a state tax-policy cycle, Baber and Sen (1986) report results implying a debt-policy cycle. State debt issues expand prior to elections. Moreover, they expand more in states with intense two-party competition for the gubernatorial seat.

More generally, Buchanan and Wagner (1977) have argued that transfer and expenditure increases are so much more attractive to vote-seeking politicians than tax increases that budget deficits are a natural consequence of political competition. Indeed, deficits are such an obvious temptation to the politician seeking votes, that one expects that large deficits would be common in most countries if sanctions did not exist to prevent them. During the nineteenth century, running a deficit in the United States came to be regarded by the public as almost an immoral act. Politicians transgressed this norm with great peril since their political opponents were always ready to bring any government profligacy to the public's attention. This norm of fiscal responsibility was often buttressed at state and local levels by constitutional prohibitions against deficits. But the Keynesian revolution destroyed this norm by making deficits not only acceptable, but in times of unemployment desirable. With the balanced-budget norm removed, the natural proclivity of politicians to spend more than they raise in taxes took over, and the ballooning budget deficits of the seventies and eighties ensued.

Deficits can be financed by issuing government bonds or printing money. Examples abound of countries in which the government has chosen to finance expenditures by printing money, and in which the government's propensity to spend and print money has resulted in triple-digit inflation. The same conservative norms against budget deficits have led countries like the United States, United Kingdom, and West Germany to separate the Central Bank from the Treasury and give the former considerable institutional independence. But "political pressures also impinge on the decisions of monetary authorities" and being utility maximizers like everyone else they can be expected to go along with government deficit running by printing additional money to finance the deficits (Buchanan and Wagner, 1977, pp. 116–18). Buchanan and Wagner (1977, p. 115) report figures showing a strong positive correlation between changes in the money supply and the size of the government deficit between 1947 and 1974. Further corroboration for the hypothesis that the Federal Reserve accommodates politically motivated deficits by expanding the money supply is provided by Laney and Willett's (1983) modeling of Federal Reserve behavior from 1960 through 1976. Hibbs (1987, pp. 248–54) finds that the Fed's open market policies are in line with the administration's target macro policies. Frey and Schneider's (1981b) model of the West German Central Bank indicates that it accommodates government expansionary fiscal policies at election times by printing more money. Consistent, but weaker, evidence exists for Canada (Winer, 1984).

Thus, the political competition model can be extended to account for government deficits and monetary policy. Since the additional outlays that lead to the deficits are often transfers, redistribution policy is also a natural extension of the model, as is the question of the size of the government itself. But these two questions are important enough to warrant separate treatment (see Chapters 17 and 23).

E.   Unresolved issues

1.   *What variables affect voter decisions?*

Kramer's (1971) seminal effort to explain the percentage of the vote going to Republican candidates for the House of Representatives between 1896 and 1964 elicited a fierce bombardment from George Stigler (1973). Stigler reasoned (1) "that a rational voter should not give much weight to short-run fluctuations in economic conditions . . . [since they] may be due to developments . . . beyond the powers or responsibilities of the party" in office. (2) Thus, if macroeconomic performance is to figure at all in a rational voter's calculations, it should be as a forecast based on accumulated experience, with the most recent past receiving greater weight. (3) But, since "there is no difference between the Republicans and Democrats with respect to the ardent pursuit of high levels of employment and high and steady rates of growth of real income," the rational voter should ignore these general macroeconomic conditions when deciding which party to vote for, and should focus instead upon their differences with respect to redistribution policies.

Stigler's critique directly raises two issues concerning the explanation of voter behavior, and indirectly a third: (1) What variables affect voter decisions, macroeconomic variables like changes in national income or micro variables like changes in the voter's own income? (2) Is it the current level of the relevant variable, a weighted sum of past levels, or the anticipated future level that is relevant? (3) Do different variables affect voter decisions in House elections, than in Senate or presidential elections?

Stigler's answer to the first question is that macroeconomic variables are not important (1) because the two parties do not differ in their positions on macroeconomic policy, and (2) because Stigler's own examination of the distribution of votes in House elections between 1896 and 1970 reveals no stable relationship among the variables. Stigler's assertion that the two parties do not differ in their macroeconomic policies was challenged by Arthur Okun (1973) in his comment on Stigler's paper, and seems to be effectively refuted by the evidence reviewed in Section C and by Tufte (1978, pp. 71–83). The large number of studies that have found a relationship between macroeconomic variables and voter decisions cited in Tables 15.1 and 15.2 makes it difficult to dismiss these variables from consideration on the basis of one or two sets of contradictory results.

The answer to question 3 may help to remove some of the contradiction between Stigler's results and those in Tables 15.1 and 15.2. Suppose that a voter is concerned about both national income changes and changes in her own income as affected by government redistribution policies. She might reasonably believe that her representative in the House is more directly responsible for the flow of redistribution dollars to and from her, while the president is more directly responsible for macroeconomic policy. Stigler's critique of the importance of macroeconomic variables is thus perhaps more relevant to the explanation of voting in House races than in Senate and presidential contests (Crain, Deaton, and Tollison, 1978; Kuklinski and West, 1981). The bulk of the studies in Table 15.1 are for U.S. presidential elections, or governing party votes in non-U.S. parliamentary systems.

In addition to the instabilities Stigler and Arcelus and Meltzer (1975a) report, there exist several cross-sectional analyses of panel survey data that fail to discern much of a relationship between voting in House elections and macroeconomic variables (Fiorina, 1978; Weatherford, 1978; Kinder and Kiewiet, 1979). Although Kramer (1983) is probably correct in arguing that errors in observation are particularly likely to obscure the relationship between the economic performance variables and voting in micro cross-sectional analyses, these studies do nonetheless uncover the predicted relationships in Senate and presidential voting.[6]

Even in the studies explaining the vote or popularity of the president or governing party, however, the coefficients on the key variables are not always

---

6. Kuklinski and West (1981) present comparative results for House and Senate voting, Fiorina (1978, 1981) for House and presidential voting. The economic performance variables perform much better in presidential voting equations estimated for the same years. Kiewiet (1981, 1983) presents considerable evidence from survey results indicating that they help to explain presidential voting.

of the correct sign and vary considerably in magnitude. There are at least two plausible, econometric explanations for this behavior. As in almost all time-series work, the key "independent" variables in these equations are highly correlated. Indeed, a premise of much of the literature is that unemployment and inflation are functionally related via the Phillips curve. Given the high degree of multicollinearity among the right-hand-side variables in the equations, it is not unusual to find the magnitudes of their coefficients and levels of significance sensitive to both the specification of the equation (which variables are in it) and time period. The effects of multicollinearity are readily apparent in Stigler's (1973) paper.

The standard practice throughout this literature is to estimate linear or log-linear regressions. This specification presumes in the linear case that an increase in unemployment from 3 to 4 percent has the same impact on presidential or government popularity as an increase from 9 to 10 percent. The log-linear specification assumes that the elasticities are constant. But the importance of unemployment and inflation as economic problems varies with the levels of these variables (see Figure 15.3). Therefore we can expect the coefficients on these variables to vary over time. This variability is apparent in Hibbs's (1982c) estimates for the United States, United Kingdom, and West Germany. With the exception of the coefficient on inflation in the United Kingdom, the elasticities on unemployment, inflation, and both real and nominal income are much higher for the 1970s, when macroeconomic conditions were relatively bad in all three countries, than they were for the 1960s. If the coefficients on the independent variables vary with the levels of these variables, then one's estimates of these coefficients will be sensitive to the choice of time period.

2.   *How much weight do voters place on past performance?*

This issue is important, not merely because it affects the equations' goodness of fit to the data. The assumptions one makes about the weights that voters place on the past performances of the competing parties are directly related to one's assumptions about the inherent rationality or forgetfulness of the voter. On this issue the literature splits right down the middle.

Of course, the truly rational voter is most interested not in a party's past performance but in its likely future performance. Support for the inherent rationality of the voter can thus be claimed from those few studies of cross-sectional panel data that have found expectations about financial conditions perform better in explaining voter decisions than current or past levels (Kuklinski and West, 1981; Fiorina, 1981, ch. 8). But data on voter expectations are not available for aggregate time-series studies. Here current and past levels of performance must be used as a proxy for voter expectations.

As Stigler (1973) notes, it is reasonable to assume that a rational voter forms an expectation of a party's future performance from its past performance, giving greater weight to more recent periods. Stigler's notion of rationality corresponds to that formulated by Fiorina (1977a, 1981) in his theory of the retrospective voter. Hibbs (1981, 1982a,b,c, 1987) incorporates the same view of the rational voter into his models. In deciding which party to vote for, the individual evaluates the performances of the competing parties on the issues of highest salience to the individual. For low-income and status groups this issue tends to be unemployment, for higher-income and status groups inflation. The former groups are drawn rationally to the left-of-center parties, because these parties have better records at reducing unemployment, just as the higher-income and status groups are drawn to the right-of-center parties owing to their better performance at reducing inflation. Party leaders maintain a distance from one another on these economic issues so as to maintain the long-run support of their traditional constituencies.

Although both Stigler and Hibbs assume essentially the same model of rational voter behavior, Stigler sees competing parties as offering the same macroeconomic policies. He thus concludes that rational voters ignore macroeconomic conditions when voting. Hibbs assumes that the different attitudes of voters on these issues drive an ideological wedge between the competing parties, thereby dividing voter support for the parties along class lines.

Paldam's (1979, 1981b) critique of the political business cycle hypothesis is compatible with Hibbs's view of the political process. Paldam sees the increases in expenditures generally occurring in the second year after a government is elected as efforts by the government to make good on its campaign promises and reward its supporters. That parties feel compelled to keep their campaign promises in this way – despite the fact that by doing so they risk worsening the performance of the economy at the next election and lowering their chances of reelection – indicates that party leaders believe voters have a memory and expect campaign promises to be filled.[7]

Both Stigler and Hibbs assume that the rational voter "votes his pocketbook." For Stigler, this implies judging the parties on the basis of their differences on redistributional issues. Although Hibbs also believes that distributional issues are important in determining voter choices, he regards differences in party positions on unemployment as important (1) because different occupational groups face differing probabilities of being unemployed and thus rationally weight this issue differently, and (2) because levels of unemployment are important determinants of the distribution of income between economic classes (Hibbs, 1987, chs. 2, 7).

Two logical difficulties exist with respect to this inherently plausible model

---

7. Pomper (1971) presents evidence that U.S. administrations do deliver on a substantial fraction of their campaign pledges.

of a rational, long-run–oriented voter. If a voter is sufficiently rational to weigh the probability of becoming unemployed under each party's governance and to base these calculations on the comparative performances of both parties over several previous terms in office, then this voter is rational enough to calculate that her vote will not have an appreciable impact on the election's outcome. She should then rationally decide not to vote. The Achilles' heel to the assumption that voters are rational is the observation that they choose to vote. The second difficulty concerns the long-run nature of the formation of voter preferences. As noted above, numerous actions that governments take can be explained only by assuming that government leaders assume that voters place very heavy weight on events affecting their personal position, or the economy, months, weeks, even days before the election. Are politicians less rational than voters?

The best explanation for why most individuals vote seems to be because of some moral obligation or civic duty (see Chapter 18). Although it is possible that voters go to the polls out of a sense of civic duty and then vote their narrow self-interest once they are there, it is also possible that elements of civic duty affect how an individual votes. Some individuals may vote against a party whose policies have produced high inflation and unemployment not because they personally have been adversely affected by either event, but because they feel others are adversely affected and think a government that produces these economic ills is bad for the country. It is interesting that variables that measure both a voter's personal economic position and perceptions of the nation's problems have proven significant in explaining voter party preferences (Fiorina, 1978, 1981; Kiewiet, 1981, 1983; Kirchgässner, 1985).

Once one admits that a voter's presence at the polls is not explained as a rational act based on narrow self-interest, an element of unpredictability arises regarding whether the voter's choice of party is such an act. Although not necessarily being an irrational act, the voter's choice of party at an election may reflect less careful calculation of gains and losses under the competing parties than the above discussion of a rational voter presumes. Civic duty may be a strong enough moral obligation to induce a citizen to vote without bringing her to expend much effort gathering and weighing information about the parties. Ignorance of the issues is the rational individual's optimal position, whether she votes or not (Downs, 1957, chs. 11–13). The rational but civic-minded voter might then choose to vote for that party whose policies seem best for the nation or herself using information readily at hand to make her choice. The present state of the economy, the government's handling of the economy as evaluated in the news media, and recent changes in the voter's economic status are the likely variables that a rational but not fully informed voter considers.

Buchanan and Wagner (1977) emphasize that the rational individual lacks the incentive to make superrational calculations of the consequences of government policies. A check in the mail, an announced cut in taxes, a fall in the unemployment rate are easily noticed and much publicized manifestations of government policies. The future inflation or future tax liabilities that these policies foreshadow are indeed dimly perceived shadows that do not receive the same weight in the voter's party choice. This fact is perceived by politicians competing for votes, and leads to an imbalance between taxes and expenditures, government deficits, and inflation.

Although not necessarily concurring in the dire conclusions and predictions reached by Buchanan and Wagner, the political business cycle literature concurs in emphasizing the backwardly myopic, if not naive, behavior of voters.

The empirical results do not, unfortunately, resolve the controversy. Hibbs (1982c, 1987), in his U.K. study, estimated that the weight placed on past performance may be as high as 0.88. Fair (1978) suggests that only the current values of the variables are important in explaining the vote for president. Of the studies that evaluate popularity functions, however, only one estimates a weight on the past quarter's performance of less than 0.5; the bulk of the estimates fall between 0.66 and 0.88. Taking 0.67 as a modal estimate of the declining weight placed on past performance, we find that 80 percent of the impact of a performance variable on a voter's preferences is recorded in the first 8 quarters following a change in performance. Ninety-six percent of the impact is felt after 16 quarters. A candidate (party) running for reelection after four years in office would be evaluated almost exclusively on its performance over the previous four years, not on the basis of the successes or failures of the other party in previous terms in office. Voter preferences depend on more than the state of the economy at election time, but not on what has happened more than four years before the election.

F.   Cycles or trends?

In Section A we described a scenario in which party competition for votes led to a stable political business cycle as hypothesized by McRae (1977). Now consider Figure 15.5. Assume again that we start at point M and that the government seeks to win more votes by moving out along the short-run unemployment inflation trade-off curve S_1S_1. The election occurs at point 1. Now assume, however, that the economy reacts sufficiently slowly to macroeconomic changes so that it is not possible to go full circle within an election cycle. As the next election approaches, the government finds itself at, say, N, and the best that it can do is move out along S_2S_2 to point 2. The following election cycle takes it to O, with optimal short-run point now 3. Eventually, inflation rises so high that even a small increase in inflation at

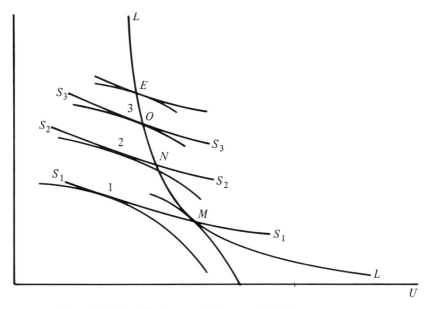

Figure 15.5. Equilibrium at a high rate of inflation.

election time in exchange for a large reduction in unemployment costs the government votes (*E*). *E* is then the equilibrium, and the political business cycle strategy can no longer be pursued (this scenario resembles that proposed by Nordhaus, 1975).

Now suppose that there is no long-run Phillips curve trade-off. The Phillips curve is a vertical straight line, as in Figure 15.6. Let *M* be an initial equilibrium point with the expectations of economic actors being such as to sustain *M*. Let it be possible to "fool" economic agents, however, and temporarily reduce unemployment by moving out along S_1S_1 to 1. A vote-maximizing government faced by myopic voters could then increase its chances of winning in the short run by going to point 1. Economic agents would then adjust their expectations of future inflation rates upward and one would return to *LL* at some higher point, *N*. If a new government could again surprise economic agents, one would move to point 2, and then, say, to *O*. As long as governments can find new ways to fool economic agents, an upward drifting business cycle might again ensue and continue until inflation got so high that no short-run gains from reducing unemployment could be obtained, or until economic agents could no longer be fooled. This last scenario resembles that described by Buchanan and Wagner (1977).

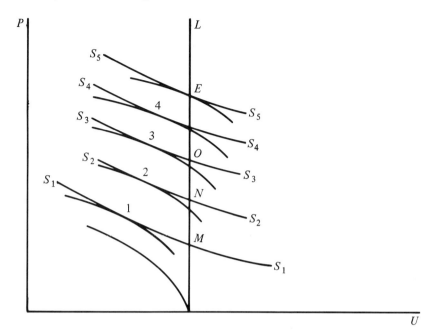

Figure 15.6. Equilibrium in the absence of a Phillips curve.

Buchanan and Wagner (1977) place more emphasis on government expenditure and tax policies as devices for winning votes, and Tufte (1978) presents considerable evidence on the selective use of these weapons. The Frey–Lau–Schneider model assumes that it is expenditures that vary according to the ideological predilections of the government; Paldam's (1979, 1981b) findings corroborate their econometric results. While generally rejecting the Frey–Lau–Schneider model, Alt and Chrystal (1983, pp. 231–4) nevertheless find that Labour governments in Great Britain do differ from Conservative governments in providing greater transfer payments. Thus, several studies link government competition for votes to expenditure policies.

If votes are positively related to expenditure increases and to tax cuts, competition for votes can produce budget deficits. Government popularity is enhanced if these deficits are at least partly covered by expansions in the money supply, and so they are. The results are higher inflation and government deficits, and these calculations follow whether one assumes a Keynesian–Phillips curve dynamics or a monetarist one.

Table 15.5 presents government deficits as a percentage of gross domestic product, inflation, and unemployment rates for industrialized countries from

Table 15.5. *Government deficits, inflation, and unemployment rates for 21 industrial countries, 1951–85*

Country	1951–5 D^a	P	U	1956–60 D	P	U	1961–5 D	P	U
Australia	1.5	9.1	—	0.6	2.9	a	−1.7	1.8	—
Austria	−0.2	9.3	7.2	−1.8	2.0	4.8	−1.4	4.0	2.8
Belgium	—	2.2	10.5	−4.1^b	1.8	7.6	−2.7	2.5	3.0
Canada	0.9	2.6	3.5	−0.9	1.9	5.6	−0.9	1.6	5.4
Denmark	−0.7	4.5	9.8	0.9	2.4	6.5	1.0	5.0	3.4
Finland	0.2	3.2	—	0.0	6.8	2.3^b	−1.4	8.4	1.4
France	−4.7	5.8	—	−3.1	4.6	—	−1.1	3.7	—
Germany	0.6	2.0	7.4	−0.6	1.8	2.9	−0.4^b	2.8	0.7
Iceland	0.8^b	7.4	—	0.1	6.0	—	0.8	10.9	—
Ireland	−6.3	4.9	8.2	−4.0	2.7	8.0	−6.0	4.2	5.8
Israel	—	21.0	—	−5.2	4.0	—	−6.9	7.1	3.4
Italy	−4.1	4.2	9.6	−2.1	1.9	8.9	−2.6	4.9	4.7
Japan	—	6.4	1.3	1.4	1.9	1.3	−0.8	6.2	1.3
Netherlands	1.8	3.6	2.3	0.3	2.7	1.5	−1.0	3.4	0.9
New Zealand	−2.4	7.1	—	−3.3	2.9	—	−3.6	2.7	—
Norway	−2.9^b	6.3	1.3	−1.4	2.8	1.8	−1.0	4.1	1.4
Spain	—	2.9	—	—	8.3	—	−1.0	5.4	1.7^b
Sweden	−1.3	2.6	2.4	−2.0	3.7	1.9	0.2	3.7	1.5^b
Switzerland	0.1	1.7	0.8	0.8	1.2	—	0.3	3.2	—
United Kingdom	−2.3	5.4	1.6	−0.3	2.7	1.8	−0.3	3.1	1.8
United States	0.0	2.2	3.7	−0.4	2.2	5.2	−0.8	1.3	5.5
Average (omitting Israel)	−1.1	4.7	5.0	−1.0	3.4	4.3	−1.2	4.5	3.0

Note: D = government deficit as percentage of Gross Domestic Product; P = percentage change Consumer Price Index; U = unemployment rate. — signifies data missing.
^{a}Deficit figures are for general government expenditures where available for most years, when not available for central government.
^{b}Data for all five years were not available. Average is for the years which are.

1951 to 1985.[8] Considerable variation in all variables exists across the countries. Nevertheless a general pattern is apparent. The first five-year period (1951–55) has more countries with government budgets in surplus than any other five-year period. The large deficits for France, Ireland, and Italy pull the average deficit up to slightly more than that for 1956–60. Starting with this five-year period, the average deficit rises steadily until by the early 1980s it is

8. The list of industrial countries follows the International Monetary Fund (IMF) classification with Luxembourg omitted because of missing data and Israel added because of its relatively industrialized economy, and because there is convincing evidence of the use of economic policies to win votes in this country (Ben-Porath, 1975).

1966–70			1971–5			1976–80			1981–5		
D	P	U	D	P	U	D	P	U	D	P	U
−1.5	3.2	1.5	−0.4	10.3	2.5	−3.1	10.6	5.8	−2.3	8.3	7.9
−2.0	3.2	2.7	−2.1	7.3	1.8	−5.0	5.3	2.0	−4.3[b]	4.9	3.7
−2.4	3.4	3.5	−3.5	8.5	4.1	−6.7	6.4	8.2	−12.1[b]	7.0	11.0
−0.5	3.9	4.6	−2.1[b]	7.4	6.1	−4.0	8.8	7.7	−5.4	7.2	8.5
1.3	5.0	3.4	1.4	9.3	2.6	−1.0	10.4	6.4	−6.6	7.9	9.8
−0.1	4.6	2.6	0.6	11.8	2.2	−1.6	10.8	5.7	−1.7[b]	9.6	5.9
−0.5	4.5	—	−1.2	8.9	—	−1.8	10.5	—	−3.2[b]	8.4	8.7
−0.5	2.7	1.2	−2.1	6.1	2.1	−3.5	4.0	4.2	−3.9[b]	3.9	7.1
—	12.3	3.8[b]	−4.2[b]	26.2	0.5	−2.7	42.2	0.4	−2.5[b]	49.7	—
−5.7	5.3	6.6	−8.5	13.4	8.5	−11.2	14.1	10.9	−13.2	12.4	14.8
−17.1	4.1	6.4	−18.9	24.8	3.0	−13.8	65.2	3.8	−17.8[b]	212.2	—
−3.4	3.0	5.6	−11.3[b]	11.5	5.9	−11.5	16.4	7.3	−13.2[b]	13.8	9.1
−1.2	5.5	1.2	—	11.7	1.4	—	6.6	2.1	—	2.7	2.5
−2.4	5.0	1.5	−1.1[b]	8.7	3.0	−3.6	6.1	5.3	−7.0	4.2	11.5
−2.5	3.4	—	−4.4	10.3	—	−5.9	14.8	—	−7.9[b]	12.1	—
−2.0	5.0	0.9	−2.9	8.4	1.0	−7.3	8.4	1.3	0.3	9.1	2.7
−1.8	5.1	1.0	−1.2	12.1	2.5	−2.9	18.1	7.9	−6.3[b]	12.4	17.8
−2.0	4.4	1.9	−3.8	8.0	2.3	−4.9	10.5	1.9	−9.4[b]	9.0	3.0
0.0	3.5	—	−0.6	7.7	—	−0.4	2.3	—	−0.3	4.3	—
−0.3	4.6	2.2	−4.9	13.2	3.2	−5.6	14.4	6.2	−3.5	7.2	10.3
−0.9	4.2	3.9	−1.8	6.6	6.1	−2.9	8.9	6.7	−4.7	5.5	9.6
−1.5	4.6	2.8	−2.8	10.8	3.3	−4.5	11.5	5.3	−5.6	10.0	8.5

Sources: Deficit and inflation data are from International Monetary Fund, *Financial Statistics*, October 1986, and Supplements on Economic Indicators, 1985, 1972 (Washington, D.C.). Unemployment data are from OECD, *Main Economic Indicators*, July 1983, July 1986 (Paris), and *Main Economic Indicators*, Historical Statistics, 1960–79, 1955–71 (Paris). United Nations, *Statistical Yearbook*, 1956, 1961, 1966, 1971, 1976, 1981 (New York).

running at a level of 5.6 percent of Gross Domestic Product. What is true of the average is also true of the individual countries. Over the first 15 years of this period more than half of the countries (54 percent) either ran surpluses on average or had deficits of less than 1 percent of GDP. In the last 15 years, only 12 percent of the countries accomplished this feat. Sixteen of 18 countries had greater deficits in the early 1980s than in the period 1951–55; 17 had larger deficits than in 1956–60.[9]

9. Webber and Wildavsky (1986, ch. 5 and p. 562 ff.) claim that states have confronted the problem of their revenues falling short of their expenditures throughout their history.

Average inflation rates also dropped between 1951–5 and 1955–60, but then rose steadily up through 1976–80. The inflation rate dropped for the first time in 25 years in the early 1980s, but was still in double figures on average across the industrial countries.

Even though budget deficits ran at over 5 percent of GDP and inflation rates averaged 10 percent, unemployment was higher during the first half of the 1980s than in any other five-year period following World War II.

The premise of Keynesian economics is that government policy can determine macroeconomic performance. If one accepts this premise, then the governments of the industrialized nations must be held responsible for the macroeconomic performance illustrated in Table 15.5.

The models of political competition reviewed in this chapter, although they differ in many respects, all assume that parties compete for votes, and that their success at winning votes depends on the unemployment, inflation, expenditure, and tax policies they bring about. The macroeconomic outcomes depicted in Table 15.5 must be assumed to be the direct or indirect consequence of the competition for votes between political parties. The only two countries in the early eighties with budget deficits of less than 1 percent of GDP are oil-rich Norway (which ran a slight surplus), and Switzerland. Switzerland is the only country in the table for which parties do not compete for the privilege of controlling the central government. It is also the only country in the table never to run a deficit greater than 1 percent of GDP for any five-year period between 1951 and 1985.

Bibliographical notes

This literature is huge and many works have been slighted. Several good surveys fortunately exist. In English, see Paldam (1981a), Alt and Chrystal (1983), and Schneider and Frey (1988). In German, see Frey (1977) and Schneider (1978, 1982).

The Frey–Lau–Schneider model is reviewed in general terms and put into a general political economy model by Frey (1978, 1979).

Frans van Winden (1983) has developed and simulated a complete model of private-public sector interaction allowing separate roles for labor, firms, the public bureaucracy, interest groups, and political parties.

CHAPTER 16

The logic of collective action and macroeconomic performance

The diversity in the faculties of men, from which the rights of property originate, is not less an insuperable obstacle to a uniformity of interests. The protection of these faculties is the first object of government. From the protection of different and unequal faculties of acquiring property, the possession of different degrees and kinds of property immediately results; and from the influence of these on the sentiments and views of the respective proprietors, ensues a division of the society into different interests and parties.

The latent causes of faction are thus sown in the nature of man; and we see them everywhere brought into different degrees of activity, according to the different circumstances of civil society. A zeal for different opinions concerning religion, concerning government, and many other points, as well of speculation as of practice; an attachment to different leaders ambitiously contending for pre-eminence and power; or to persons of other descriptions whose fortunes have been interesting to the human passions, have, in turn, divided mankind into parties, inflamed them with mutual animosity, and rendered them much more disposed to vex and oppress each other than to co-operate for their common good. So strong is this propensity of mankind to fall into mutual animosities, that where no substantial occasion presents itself, the most frivolous and fanciful distinctions have been sufficient to kindle their unfriendly passions and excite their most violent conflicts. But the most common and durable source of factions has been the various and unequal distribution of property. Those who hold and those who are without property have ever formed distinct interests in society. Those who are creditors, and those who are debtors, fall under a like discrimination. A landed interest, a manufacturing interest, a mercantile interest, a moneyed interest, with many lesser interests, grow up of necessity in civilized nations, and divide them into different classes, actuated by different sentiments and views. The regulation of these various and interfering interests forms the principal task of modern legislation, and involves the spirit of party and faction in the necessary and ordinary operations of the government.

James Madison

The literature reviewed in Chapter 15 links various measures of macroeconomic performance to competition between parties for votes. In this chapter we delve below the level of party competition to examine the factors affecting interest group formation and the effects of interest groups on macroeconomic performance. We focus on the hypotheses put forward in two books by

Mancur Olson (1965, 1982) and on the literature that has addressed these hypotheses.

A.   The logic of collective action

Interest groups come in a wide variety of institutional forms and sizes. Some seek to further the objectives of their members as factors of production or producers. Labor unions, farmer associations, professional associations (doctors, dentists, accountants), retail trade associations (groceries, hardware, liquor), and industrial trade associations (petroleum, cement, coal) are examples of these. Others seek to influence public policy or public opinion with respect to particular public good–externality issues. Peace groups, environmental groups, and the National Rifle Association are examples of these. Often a group is organized to pursue one objective, and then once organized turns to other forms of activity of benefit to its members. Labor unions came into being to improve the bargaining power of workers vis-à-vis management. But once the large initial costs of organization had been overcome, unions engaged in additional activities of interest to their members, such as lobbying for legislation, which improves the position of workers. Still other groups seek to advance *all* the interests of particular groups of people who belong to given ethnic, religious, or geographic groups. Most recently, groups have appeared to promote the interests of members of a given sex, or those with particular sexual affinities. In every case the driving force behind the formation of an interest group is the belief that its members have *common* interests and goals, be they higher wages for truck drivers or for women, or cleaner rivers for those whose consumption activities are enhanced by this public policy (pp. 5–8).[1]

The commonality of the goals of an interest group's members makes the achievement of these goals a public good for the group, and thus gives rise to the same incentives to free-ride as exist in all public good–prisoners' dilemma situations. The individual steelworker and steel manufacturer benefit from a tariff on steel, whether they have contributed to the efforts to bring about the tariff or not (pp. 9–16).

Two important conclusions can be drawn from this observation. (1) It is easier to form an interest group when the number of potential members is small than when the number is large (pp. 9–16, 22–65). An effective interest group can be organized more readily for two dozen steel producers than for two hundred thousand steel workers. (2) Thus, the appearance of organizations that effectively represent large numbers of individuals requires that "*separate and 'selective' incentive(s)*" be used to curb free-riding behavior (p.

---

1. Page references in this section are to Olson (1965) unless otherwise noted.

51, italics in original). The archetypal example of the use of selective incentives is the labor union. Unions have fought to have employers deduct dues from union members' wages, and for "closed shop" contracts forbidding employers from hiring nonunion labor (pp. 66–97). Where they have succeeded in forcing employers to abide by these rules, as in many states in the United States and in the United Kingdom, union membership has been relatively high and union workers have earned higher wages. In France, where these selective incentives encouraging union participation are absent, union membership is much lower and largely ineffective.[2] Perhaps the best evidence that such selective incentives are needed to avoid free-riding behavior is the importance union leaders place on getting legislation and/or contractual stipulations requiring closed shop contracts, the collection of union dues, and the like. Worker solidarity does not suffice.

Where the benefits from collective action are not the same across all group members, "*there is a systematic tendency for 'exploitation' of the great by the small*" (p. 29). To see this, consider the following example. The automobile industry has four firms producing the following numbers of cars each year:

$$X_G = 4,000,000 \text{ cars}$$
$$X_F = 2,000,000 \text{ cars}$$
$$X_C = 1,000,000 \text{ cars}$$
$$X_A = 500,000 \text{ cars}.$$

Compliance with fuel economy standards issued by the Environmental Protection Agency (EPA) would raise the costs of producing cars by an average of $1 per car. Each firm independently considers opening up a lobbying office in Washington to lobby the EPA to delay enforcement of the fuel economy standard by one year. The cost of running a lobbying office is $250,000 for the year. The probability that the industry will be successful in its lobbying effort increases with the number of lobbying offices opened, being .25 for one office, .4 for two, .5 for three, and .55 for four. Firm G realizes that if it does not profit from opening a lobbying office, no firm will. Its expected profit increase from opening a lobbying office is .25 times $4 million, which exceeds the $250,000 cost of the office. Firm F realizes that it will not profit from opening an office unless G does and thus calculates its profits from opening the second lobbying office for the industry. The incremental probability that the lobbying will succeed is .15, which when multiplied by F's $2 million cost saving gives an expected profit increase of $300,000 for F. This saving exceeds the $250,000 cost of the lobbying office so that F, too, opens an office. Given that G and F have opened offices, neither C nor A find it profitable to do so, however. Both choose to free-ride on G and F's lobbying

---

2. For a discussion of France in the context of Olson's work, see Asselain and Morrison (1983).

efforts, receiving, respectively, $400,000 and $200,000 increases in expected profits from G and F's lobbying. In this way the weak "exploit" the strong.

Note also that the amount of lobbying effort that arises from independent decisions is suboptimal from the point of view of the industry. A third and fourth lobbying office would bring the industry $750,000 and $375,000 in expected profits, respectively. But these additional offices will be opened only if G and F can bribe C and A to do so. Moreover, since C and A know that G and F will open lobbying offices regardless of whether C and A do so, C and A can hold out for subsidies from G and F, which maintain their favorable ratio of benefits to costs.[3]

Olson reviewed various evidence on this idea and related hypotheses in his first book. Relevant, too, is the recent experimental literature on the free rider problem. Numerous studies now exist testing the extent to which individuals free-ride in prisoners' dilemma situations. The main results of this research can be summarized as follows: (1) Some but not all individuals free-ride in a prisoners' dilemma situation. (2) Free riding occurs to the smallest extent on the first play of a series of prisoners' dilemma games, or in a one-play game, but increases in quantitative importance as prisoners' dilemma games are repeated with the same players, when the players do not possess information on the individual contributions of other players. (3) After repeated plays of the game, contributions may rise, if players have information on the individual contributions of other players. (4) Free riding increases as the number of players expands, at least if the return to a player declines as group size increases.[4] These results suggest the following scenario for an interest group that relies entirely on voluntary participation and contributions from its membership. The organization begins with fairly substantial attendance and contributions at the first few meetings. Then, attendance and contributions tail-off until the organization shrinks to a "hard core" of activists dedicated to the "cause," or it folds entirely. Both scenarios should be familiar to those who have joined voluntary organizations.

---

3. For example, if C agrees to pay only $\frac{1}{7}$ of the cost of its lobbying office with G and F paying $\frac{6}{7}$, since that is the ratio of their benefits; and A agrees to pay only $\frac{1}{15}$ of the cost of its lobbying office, with the other three sharing in proportion to their benefits, then C and A wind up enjoying 13.3 and 6.7 percent of the benefits from lobbying while paying but 6.9 and 1.7 percent of the costs, respectively.
4. The only studies to test for the influence of group size on free rider behavior are Isaac, Walker, and Thomas (1984) and Isaac and Walker (1988). These papers along with the work of Kim and Walker (1984), and Isaac, McCue, and Plott (1985) are among the most recent contributions to this literature and contain references to earlier works. Sell and Wilson (1988) report rising contributions when players have information on the individual contributions of other players.

B.   The rise and decline of nations

In *The Rise and Decline of Nations*, Olson built on his earlier analysis of interest group formation to explain differences in growth rates across nations and that malady peculiar to the latter part of the twentieth century, stagflation. Olson's concern was with those interest groups that seek redistributive objectives. Business, trade, and professional associations are primary examples of such groups, as are unions. In each case, much of the activity of these groups, insofar as it impinges on others in society, is devoted to creating or preserving monopoly positions, Medical associations seek to restrict entry into medical schools and the licensing of foreign-trained physicians. Unions seek to force employers to hire only union members and to determine wages and other employee benefits by bargaining with the union. Business associations and unions both seek to protect their members from foreign competition by obtaining tariffs and quotas on imports; and by obtaining regulations requiring that the government favor domestic producers in its purchases, government workers favor the nation's flagship airline in their travel, and the like. Thus, much of the activity of the economically oriented interest groups falls under the heading of rent seeking (p. 44).[5]

Many interest groups, which are not organized along business, trade, or occupational lines, nevertheless have goals that are, at least in part, distributional. The objectives of associations of the handicapped, the aged, and welfare recipients are largely distributional. Women's and ethnic groups have sought legislation imposing de facto if not de jure hiring quotas on employers.

The heavy emphasis that interest groups place on distributional goals has the consequence that their activities lead largely to jockeying for positions along the utility possibility frontier, not to shifts outward in the frontier. Moreover, each restriction on entry, each quota, each regulation creates an efficiency loss, which shifts inward the utility possibility frontier (pp. 41–7). As more and more energy is devoted to carving up the pie, the pie gets smaller. (A MisAllocation of pRoductive Resources)

Olson uses this redistribution–efficiency loss argument to explain differences in growth rates across nations. Not only does the activity of interest groups (Olson names them "distributional coalitions") shift the production possibility frontier inward, it retards the speed at which it moves outward as a result of the normal growth process. Interest groups tend to be democratic in varying degrees and thus are slow to reach decisions. They are therefore slow to respond to change, and impede the speed with which the organizations that they affect can react to or implement changes. The consequence is that "*dis-*

5. All remaining page references in this chapter are to Olson (1982) unless otherwise noted.

tributional coalitions slow down a society's capacity to adopt new technologies and to reallocate resources in response to changing conditions and thereby reduce the rate of economic growth."[6]

From this important proposition it follows that a country's growth rate varies inversely with the level of interest group activity ceteris paribus. It takes time to overcome free rider inertia and to discover the combinations of collective benefits and selective incentives that can induce active involvement in interest group activities. Long periods over which the social and political environment of a country remains stable are conducive to the appearance of new interest groups and the strengthening of existing ones. Periods of social and political stability should give rise to growing numbers of interest groups, growing distributional conflicts, and a slowing of economic growth. Conversely, a country whose interest groups were somehow destroyed or institutionally constrained from pursuing their institutional objective would grow faster than one heavily burdened by interest group activity, with again the important ceteris paribus proviso. Olson uses this argument to explain differences in growth rates over the first 25 years after the Second World War across developed democracies. Germany, Italy, and Japan suffered the greatest devastation to their economic and political institutions, and their growth performance was among the best of the developed countries up through 1970. The occupied, continental European countries also had their interest group structures disrupted to a degree by the war, and then the strength of their interest groups was further eroded by the formation of the Common Market. They, too, had impressive growth rates in the fifties and sixties. Ironically, or so it would seem, it was the countries whose economies and social-institutional structures were least damaged by the war (Australia, New Zealand, the United Kingdom, and the United States) that performed most poorly in terms of economic growth up through the early seventies.[7] The power in Olson's thesis comes in explaining why this fact should *not* be viewed with surprise. Indeed, it is precisely because the fabric of interest group structures existing prior to the war was left untorn that these Anglo-Saxon countries performed so poorly relative to both the countries suffering defeat in the war and those that suffered occupation (ch. 4).

Olson employs the logic of his thesis to shed light on several important issues: the exhilarating effect on economic performance of forming a larger economic federation or customs union (ch. 5); the debilitating effects of

---

6. Bowles and Eatwell (1983) question the leap from arguments related largely to static efficiency to conclusions regarding dynamic performance. Olson defends himself on pages 61–5, and also cites Hicks (1983) in support.

7. See, e.g., Pryor (1983), Tables 5.3 and 5.4, p. 99. Logically, Canada might also be expected to be in this group, since its borders were not crossed during the war. But its growth performance, although not above the average, was also not below.

discriminatory practices (ch. 6); and the micro foundations of stagflation (ch. 7). We shall return to the latter topic in Section D. Let us pause here to consider Olson's explanation for India's poor economic development performance alongside that of some of its Asian neighbors.

Olson attributes India's relatively poor economic performance to an important degree to the rigidities growing out of the caste system. Castes appear to have emerged from guilds and other occupational groupings and have functioned like other distributional coalitions trying to protect whatever monopoly or monopsony power its members have. Restricting marriages to members of one's own caste was a form of entry barrier to control the size of the caste and protect its monopoly position. The heavy concern with distributional issues as reflected in the caste system has had the same debilitating effect on India's growth that the distributional struggles among organized interests have had on India's former ruler, Great Britain (pp. 152–61).

C. Empirical evidence

Several attempts have been made to test Olson's theory empirically. The chief challenge comes in trying to measure the strength of interest group activity (Abramovitz, 1983; Pryor, 1983). In initially setting forth the theory, Olson argued that Italy, Germany, and Japan's strong postwar economic performance could be explained by the destruction of their interest group structures wrought by the war and immediate postwar occupation. These examples suggest the hypothesis that interest group strength can be measured by the length of time that has elapsed since a nation's inception, or since its rebirth following a war or revolution. Most tests of the thesis have thus used some time-dependent proxy for interest group strength. Kwang Choi (1983) constructed an index of "institutional sclerosis" for 18 OECD countries based on (1) the point in time when common-interest groups begin to accumulate, (2) what and when the major disruptions occurred, and how long they lasted, and (3) how strong each disruption was. An example of the results Choi obtained is presented as equation (16.1) (Choi, 1983, p. 73, equation 14).

$$Y = 7.75 - 0.074 \, IS \qquad R^2 = 0.59, \, n = 18. \qquad (16.1)$$
$$ (8.81) \quad (4.78)$$

The dependent variable is the growth in per capita income from 1950 to 1973 and IS is one of Choi's measures of institutional sclerosis, defined to fit a logistic curve so that it already incorporates a diminishing impact of time on interest group strength after some point. The negative and significant impact of institutional sclerosis proved resilient to (1) how this variable was measured, (2) the choice of dependent variable, and (3) the composition of the sample.

The best example of a nation suffering from acute institutional sclerosis is the United Kingdom. The best examples of nations rejuvenated by the destruction of their interest group structures are the three axis nations. Peter Murrell (1983) presented yet another test of the hypothesis by more closely examining the U.K. and West German economies.

Murrell reasoned that interest group strength in the United Kingdom would be weakest in the newest industries to have formed, since in these industries interest groups have had the shortest time to develop. Thus, the performances of U.K. industries should be the most comparable to that of West Germany in "young" industries, the furthest behind in "old" industries.

To test the hypothesis, Murrell compared the growth rates of young (j) and old (k) industries in the United Kingdom (UK) and West Germany (WG), standardizing for differences in the average (A) growth rate in each country. The hypothesis was that the growth rates of young industries in the United Kingdom would be relatively higher; that is, the inequality in (16.2) would hold, where G stands for an industry or commodity growth rate from 1969 through 1973.

$$\frac{G_j^{UK} - G_k^{UK}}{G_A^{UK}} > \frac{G_j^{WG} - G_k^{WG}}{G_A^{WG}} . \tag{16.2}$$

The proportions of cases in which (16.2) is satisfied are all significantly above the 0.5 predicted by the null hypothesis, and thus support the hypothesis that institutional sclerosis in the United Kingdom is most advanced in the older industries.

Olson reported results analogous to those obtained by Choi for the OECD for the 48 contiguous states in the United States. A representative example is presented as equation (16.3).[8]

$$Y = 10.01 - 2.69 \text{ STACIV1} \qquad R^2 = 0.52, \text{ n} = 48. \tag{16.3}$$
$$(7.02)$$

The dependent variable is the growth rate of per capita private nonfarm income during 1965–78. STACIV1 is the number of years since statehood divided by 178, with all Confederate states having been assumed to be reborn in 1865. As with Choi's results for the OECD, the significant negative effect of a state's age remains reasonably robust to changes in the definition of the dependent and independent variables (Olson, 1982, pp. 98–108).

One of the criticisms that has been leveled against the empirical testing of Olson's theory is the lack of consideration of other possible explanations of growth rate differences (Abramovitz, 1983; Pryor, 1983). Richard Vedder

---

8. Equation (24), Table 4.1, p. 104. Olson credits Kwang Choi with having done the regression work.

and Lowell Gallaway (1986) have recently tested the Olson theory using data for the 48 continental states, and allowing for 11 additional explanatory variables. Number of years since statehood has a highly significant negative coefficient in explaining personal income growth and is fairly robust to specification sensitivity tests.[9] Corroborative evidence using state data was also presented in an earlier study by Dye (1980). Gray and Lowery (1986), on the other hand, find a complete collapse of the Olson model using state data when it is tested over a later time period and other variables are added to the equation, as do Wallis and Oates (1988) when population growth by state is treated as an exogenous variable. Nardinelli, Wallace, and Warner (1987) find little support for Olson's hypothesis, once differences in income across states are included.

In stark contrast to these results using state data, those of Jan-Erik Lane and Svante Ersson (1986), from cross-national data, indicate that Choi's measure of institutional sclerosis maintains its significance as other variables are placed alongside of it and the dependent variable is measured over different time periods. Several additional studies have reported evidence for the Olson hypothesis based on cross-national comparisons (Paloheimo, 1984a,b; Datta and Nugent, 1985; Lange and Garrett, 1985; Lehner, 1985; Weede, 1986; McCallum and Blais, 1987).

An important assumption in most tests of the Olson hypothesis is that interest group strength increases with the number of years over which a country experiences political stability. Peter Murrell (1984) provided empirical support for this assumption by showing that the *number* of interest groups in a country increases with the number of years of political stability. Kennelly and Murrell (1987) also show that interest group numbers are larger in those industries in which the redistributive gains from interest group action are potentially larger.

Only one study claims to have directly contradicted the Olson hypothesis using cross-national data. Frederic Pryor (1983) did not test for the impact of some time-of-stability variable on growth, but rather tested for the impact of several additional variables that should be correlated with growth if Olson's theory is correct: population size, communist rule, ethnic heterogeneity, and religious heterogeneity. None of these had a significant impact on the growth rates of the sample countries.

To what extent this finding challenges Olson's theory is difficult to access. Although communist countries are not beset by interest group distributional struggles, the heavy bureaucratic hand that guides their economies quite likely

---

9. A dummy variable for South has the correct sign, but is not significant. The inclusion of unionization as a separate, independent variable clouds the significance of this finding, since both statehood and South should explain unionization by the Olson thesis.

more than offsets this advantage. Ethnic and religious heterogeneity can be measured only approximately. What Pryor's results underline is not so much the invalidity of Olson's theory, but the difficulty in testing it using rough proxies for the key explanatory variable, interest group strength,[10] the same conclusion Gray and Lowery (1986) reach from their negative findings using state data.[11]

Most of the empirically based objections to Olson's theory stem from observations of a given country, whose growth record and interest group structures do not accord with what Olson's theory seems to predict, or that argue for a more complicated formulation of the theory (Asselain and Morrison, 1983; Lehner, 1983; Rogowski, 1983; Schuck, 1984; Gustafsson, 1986; Rasch and Sorensen, 1986). Of particular interest in this regard is the case of Switzerland. Switzerland had the fourth highest index of institutional sclerosis in Choi's list of 18 OECD countries (1983, p. 70), and "has a very differentiated, pluralist structure of interest organization" (Lehner, 1983, p. 204). Yet, its degree of tariff protection was lowest among the 18 OECD countries (Olson, 1982, p. 134), and its growth rate above average over the fifties and sixties (Lehner, 1983, p. 70). The explanation for this apparent inconsistency with Olson's theory is found in the strong federalist nature of its political structure, and the importance of direct democracy at the cantonal level or in the form of the referendum. Since legislative decisions either must be subjected to a referendum vote or can be petitioned to a referendum vote, interest groups cannot strike a bargain with the parties in Parliament or with members of key legislative committees, and obtain redistributional favors, unless a majority of the citizens are willing to ratify the bargain. With the outcomes of referenda being hard to predict, forming a minimum winning coalition is a precarious strategy, and the legislature strives for consensual policies (Lehner, 1983). The result is that redistributional struggles do not figure prominently in Swiss political life, despite the strength of their interest group structure.

10. Pryor also cites the poor growth performance of Australia and New Zealand as contradicting Olson's theory, since they are both relatively young democracies (pp. 99–100). But surely these countries are exceptions that prove the rule. Presumably because of their British heritage, these countries have been able to play "catch-up" in developing interest group structures that rival that of their parent in their complexity and in their enervating effect on allocative efficiency. The two countries are at the top of Olson's list of countries ranked by height of tariff protection (p. 134). Unions in Australia are every bit as powerful and disruptive as those in the United Kingdom, while New Zealand stands in the second tier of labor unrest somewhat behind the United Kingdom and Australia (Paloheimo, 1984a, p. 20).

11. Gray and Lowery (1986) do *not* find a relationship between the age of a state and the number of interest groups in the state, which perhaps helps to explain the breakdown of the hypothesis when state data are used. In contrast, Peter Murrell (1984) has established that the number of organized interest groups in a country is positively related to the number of years that a country has had a modern political system receptive to pressure from interest groups.

The conclusion one draws is that Switzerland does not run counter to the main tenets of Olson's theory. The political institutions of Switzerland protect it from the undesirable consequences of the distributional struggles that would otherwise ensue given its fractionalized interest group structure. But the example of Switzerland does point to an important lacuna in Olson's argument. Olson focuses almost exclusively on interest groups and leaves out an analysis of how interest group pressure is channeled by the political and economic institutions of a country to produce the outcomes his theory predicts (Paloheimo, 1984a,b; Lehner, 1985).

D.   Interest groups and stagflation

One of the great imponderables for neoclassical economics has been how unemployment could grow so large and persist as long as it did in the Great Depression. Keynes's theory explained the existence of unemployment with the help of the assumption of "sticky wages." But lacking an explanation for why inflexible wages were in the interests of workers and employers, Keynes's argument fell short of a truly *general* theory, and met with increasing resistence over time.[12] The appearance of high levels of unemployment along with high inflation rates in the seventies left Keynesians and non-Keynesians dumbfounded and embarrassed. Olson sees the problem as a further consequence of the efforts of distributional coalitions to advance their interests at the expense of others.

Consider first the question of why involuntary unemployment exists. Figure 16.1 is taken from Olson (p. 199). Curves M and N represent the demand (marginal revenue product) and supply schedules for labor in the economy. OQ is the quantity of labor that would be bought at a competitive equilibrium. Suppose, however, that we observe that only OX amount of labor is employed. We can say that the quantity of labor XQ is involuntarily unemployed in the sense that there are contracts that could be struck between the employers and workers that could make both better off. Employers are willing to offer wages greater than or equal to the wages workers are willing to accept. What then prevents employers from making these offers and/or workers from accepting them once made?

The answer to the question becomes more apparent if we restate it slightly. Assume that we are on the labor demand schedule with a wage of w_H and a quantity demanded of OX. In whose interest could it be to block the agreements between employers and workers that would expand employment to OQ and reduce the wage to w_C? When thus stated, the answer is obvious. It is not in the interests of those workers who are employed at a wage above the level that would clear the market to see the labor market equilibrate. If these

12. See Olson's discussion, pp. 181–7.

Marginal revenue
product, wage

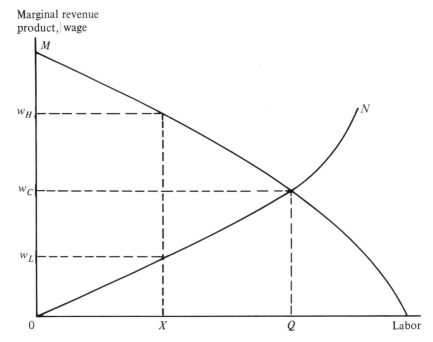

Figure 16.1. "Involuntary unemployment" from interest group activity.

workers are members of a union that can bar employers from hiring anyone at a wage less than w_H, they have an incentive to do so.

One could observe a wage below w_H, at the employment level OX, at say w_L, if it was not the workers who had organized a cartel, but the employers. It could be in the collective interests of the employers to form a monopsonistic cartel and force workers to accept a wage of w_L. In either case, the existence of OX as an equilibrium outcome depends on the ability of a coalition of workers or employers forming and successfully blocking the additional trades between employers and workers that would carry the economy to an equilibrium at OQ (pp. 196–202).

Because distributional coalitions employ democratic procedures to determine their basic policies and often employ consensual collective decision procedures, they are slow to react to changes in the economic environment. The greater the number of industries in which distributional coalitions and interest groups determine prices, either directly or with the help of government interventions and regulations, the less able the economy is to respond smoothly and quickly to demand and supply shocks. An economy with a well-developed interest group structure that has been experiencing some inflation and suddenly undergoes a deflationary shock can be expected to continue to exhibit inflationary price increases while unemployment rises–stagflation–or perhaps to collapse into a deep depression, as occurred during the Great Depression (pp. 203–16).

The empirical implications of the interest group–stagflation hypothesis are analogous to those regarding growth rate differences. Countries with highly developed and fractionalized interest group structures should have worse performances on stagflation than those without. Olson again cites the United States and the United Kingdom as poor performers with respect to stagflation, and finds West Germany on the plus side (pp. 216–19). But a full testing of this hypothesis would have to control for other variables, and is as yet lacking.

E.　Conclusions

The free rider problem pervades all of collective choice. It necessitates the passage of laws, the raising of taxes, and the hiring of police. It deters citizens from becoming informed about public issues, and even from voting. It undermines the normative properties of any voting procedure used by a large electorate.

Mancur Olson has used the free rider principle as the foundation for a theory of interest group formation. From this theory he has derived implications regarding various dimensions of macroeconomic performance. The assumptions and logic of the theory are simple and yet the implications are broad. This combination constitutes both the beauty and the weakness of the theory. With such broad implications built upon such a streamlined logical foundation, counterexamples and qualifications are all but inevitable. Nonetheless, one is drawn to the conclusion that Olson has produced an important component of the answers to the questions he addresses. That a microbased theory of public choice could make considerable headway in explaining macroeconomic phenomena, phenomena that existing macro theories do not explain, is no small feat.

CHAPTER 17

The size of government

Politicians are the same all over. They promise to build a bridge even where there is no river.

Nikita Khruschev

I sit on a man's back, choking him and making him carry me, and yet assure myself and others that I am very sorry for him and wish to lighten his load by all possible means – except by getting off his back.

Leo Tolstoi

Much attention in both lay and academic discourse has been given to the question of the proper size of government and the reasons for its growth. Public choice, the economic analysis of political institutions, would seem to be the natural tool for answering these questions, and in recent years it has frequently been employed in this task. A review of these efforts follows.

A.   The facts

That government has grown, and grown dramatically in recent years, cannot be questioned. Total government expenditure in the United States in 1987 as a percentage of GNP was 34.8 percent, up from 23 percent in 1949 and 10 percent in 1929 (see Table 17.1). Moreover, this growth is confined neither to this century nor to the United States. Federal government expenditures as a percentage of national income in the United States were only 1.4 percent of national income in 1799. They rose to double that figure by the end of the nineteenth century, but were still only 3 percent of GNP in 1929. Starting in the 1930s, however, federal expenditures took off, rising sevenfold as a percentage of GNP over the next 50 years (Table 17.1).

Table 17.2 presents comparable data for the United States and other OECD countries. Although spanning a much shorter time period, these data reveal across-the-board increases in the relative size of government in every OECD country. The smallest government sector, in Switzerland, accounts for 30 percent of GDP. In contrast, government expenditures in Sweden and the Netherlands absorbed more than 60 percent of GDP in 1985. Nor is the growth of government outside the United States limited to the post–World War II period. Neck and Schneider (1988) report an increase in the ratio of

320

Table 17.1. *Government expenditure in relation to national income and GNP in the United States, 1799–1987*

Year	Total federal expen- ditures[a] (1)	Total federal expen- ditures[b] (2)	Total federal expen- ditures[c] (3)	Total federal expen- ditures[c] (4)	Federal, state, and local expen- ditures[a] (5)	Federal, state, and local expen- ditures[c] (6)
1799	10	1.4				
1809	10	1.1				
1819	21	2.4				
1829	15	1.6				
1839	27	1.6				
1849	42	1.7				
1859	66	1.5				
1869	316	4.6	5.0			
1879	267	3.7	3.2			
1889	309	2.9	2.6			
1899	563		3.4			
1909	694		2.3			
1919	12,402		16.7			
1929	3,100		3.0	3.0	10,300	10.0
1939	8,800		11.7	9.7	17,600	19.4
1949	38,800		16.2	15.0	59,300	23.0
1959	92,100			18.9	131,000	26.8
1969	183,600			19.4	286,800	30.4
1979	503,500			20.8	750,800	31.1
1984	851,800			23.3	1,258,100	34.4
1987	1,074,200			23.7	1,574,400	34.8

[a]In millions of current U.S. dollars.
[b]As percentage of national income.
[c]As percentage of GNP.
Sources: Figures for columns 2 and 3 are from Kendrick (1955, pp. 10–12). Figures for columns 4, 5, and 6 are from United States, *Economic Report of the President*, 1985 and 1989, Table B-1, B-72, and B-79.

central state budget expenditures to GDP for Austria from 11.4 percent in 1870 to 18.4 percent in 1913. Table 17.3 presents data for three European countries and the United States that indicate a considerably smaller government sector before World War I than after it and a considerably smaller government sector after World War I than after World War II.

Dennis C. Mueller, "The Growth of Government," *IMF Staff Papers*, March 1987, p. 115–49. © International Monetary Fund.

Table 17.2. *General government expenditure and revenue in relation to Gross Domestic Product at current prices in OECD countries (percent)*

Country	1960		1985	
	Outlays	Receipts	Outlays	Receipts
Australia (1960–84)	21.4	25.4	36.6	33.3
Austria	35.7	34.4	50.7	47.7
Belgium	30.3	27.5	54.4	46.5
Canada	28.9	26.0	47.0	38.9
Denmark	24.8	27.3	59.5	57.0
Finland	26.6	29.7	41.5	40.5
France	34.6	34.9	52.4	48.5
Germany, Federal Republic of	32.4	35.0	47.2	45.4
Greece	17.4[a]	21.1	43.2[a]	34.6
Iceland	28.2	36.4	35.6	33.4
Ireland (1960–84)	28.0	24.8	54.6	44.3
Italy	30.1	28.8	58.4	44.1
Japan	18.3[b]	20.7	32.7	31.2
Luxembourg (1960–82)	30.5	32.5	56.4	53.0
Netherlands	33.7	33.9	60.2	54.4
Norway	29.9	33.1	48.1	56.1
Portugal (1960–81)	17.0	17.6	43.9	33.3
Spain (1964–84)	18.8[b]	18.1	39.3	33.2
Sweden	31.0	32.1	64.5	59.4
Switzerland	17.2[a]	23.3	30.9[a]	34.4
Turkey (1962–8)	18.0[b]	19.1[b]	21.9	21.8
United Kingdom (1960–84)	32.3	30.0	47.8	42.8
United States	27.0	26.3	36.7	31.1
Mean (unweighted)	26.6	27.7	47.3[c]	42.9[c]

[a]Current disbursements only.
[b]Taken from Saunders and Klau (1985, p. 29).
[c]Omitting Turkey.
Source: Organization for Economic Cooperation and Development, *OECD Economic Outlook: Historical Statistics, 1960–1985*, Paris, 1987, p. 64.

The figures in these tables suggest three questions. What caused the increase in the relative size of government over the past two centuries? What caused the growth of government to accelerate after World War II? What explains the large disparities in levels and rates of growth in government among countries?

B.   Explanations for the size and growth of government

The same explanations that have been given for why government exists should, logically, explain why it attains a given size in one country and not in

Table 17.3. *Tax levels in the major Western countries in relation to national income, 1900–1 to 1924–5 (percent)*

Country	1900-1	1913-14	1924-5
France	14.96	14.11	20.01
Germany, Federal Republic of	7.99	10.51	29.21
United Kingdom	9.99	11.29	24.77
United States	7.76	6.68	11.06

Source: Seligman (1925, ch. 1), as reported in Tanzi (1986b, p. 5).

another, or why it starts to grow at a more rapid rate at a particular time. Thus, in reviewing the hypothesized causes for the size and growth of government, one is essentially also reviewing the explanations for the existence of government. If each explanation is represented as a variable or a variable set, then differences in size and rates of growth in size must be explained by differences in these variables.

1. The government as provider of public goods and eliminator of externalities

The traditional explanation for why governments exist is that they exist to provide public goods and to eliminate or alleviate externalities. Let us assume that this is the only function governments perform. Each citizen can then be posited to have a demand for the public goods, which is a function of the individual's income, the relative price of public to private goods, and perhaps other taste variables. If it is assumed that voting takes place using majority rule, that citizens vote directly on the government expenditure issue, and that the only issue to be decided is the level of government expenditures, then one can apply the median voter theorem and write government expenditures as a function of the characteristics of the median voter.[1] Letting X be a composite of private goods and G the composite of public goods (with P_x and P_g being their respective prices), Y_m the income of the median voter, and Z a vector of taste parameters, then one can write a government expenditure equation in logarithms for the median voter:

$$\ln G = a + \alpha \ln P_g + \beta \ln Y_m + \gamma \ln Z + \mu . \qquad (17.1)$$

An explanation for the relative growth of government can be obtained from equation (17.1) if any of the following conditions are met:

1. See Barr and Davis (1966), Davis and Haines (1966), Borcherding and Deacon (1972), Bergstrom and Goodman (1973), and Deacon (1977a,b).

The demand for public goods is inelastic $(-1 < \alpha < 0)$, and P_g has risen relative to P_x.

The demand for public goods is elastic $(-1 > \alpha)$, and P_g has fallen relative to P_x.

Because Y_m has been increasing over time, if changes in Y_m are to explain growing G relative to X, β must be greater than unity.

Some taste variable could change in the appropriate way, given the sign of $\dot{\gamma}$.[2]

Let us start with the last possibility. The very definitions of public goods and externalities connote geographic proximity. The smoke from a factory harms more individuals in a densely populated community than in a population thinly dispersed around the factory. A park is easier to reach and probably of more utility in a densely populated community than in a rural area. Increasing urbanization has occurred throughout the last century in every developed country and has been taking place for well over a century in most. Urbanization or population density is an obvious choice for a Z variable with a predicted positive sign on its γ. It is surprising, therefore, to find so little empirical support for this hypothesis.[3] No other "taste" variable has garnered both compelling a priori and empirical support.

Nor can one account for much of the relative increase in government size from increasing personal income. Although some estimates of the income elasticity of demand for $G(\beta)$ are greater than one,[4] a greater number are less than one, and very few indeed are significantly greater than one.[5]

2. For discussion of these possibilities relative to the growth of government issue, see Borcherding (1977a, 1985), Buchanan (1977), and Bennett and Johnson (1980b, pp. 59–67).

3. See Borcherding (1977a, 1985), and Deacon (1977b), but for a critique of this literature, see Oates (1988a). Most work in estimating equation (17.1) has been at the local governmental unit level, and many problems in public goods and externalities may be resolved at higher levels of governmental aggregation. But Mueller and Murrell (1985) did not find a positive relationship between government expenditures and urbanization across countries.

4. Deacon (1977b) has noted that in most studies park and recreation expenditures appear to be income-elastic.

5. There is good reason to believe that existing estimates of the income elasticity of demand for G, based on state and local cross-sectional data, are biased downward. Most studies assume that the cost of providing government services is the same across communities. But a given level of safety may be provided more cheaply in a wealthy community than in a poor one. Thus the price of safety is lower in wealthy communities and, given that the price elasticity of this service is less than unity, wealthy communities will consume less, other things being equal. With the price of government services held constant across all communities, this wealth–price effect is shifted to the income elasticity, biasing it downward (Hamilton, 1983). Schwab and Zampelli (1987) observed a jump in β from near zero to unity when this income–price relationship was properly estimated. But in terms of accounting for the long-run growth of government, this adjustment merely shifts some of the explanation of government growth, using equation (17.1), from the price term to the income term. The Hamilton–Schwab–Zampelli

Existing studies all estimate β using data from state and local government jurisdictions.[6] Most redistribution takes place at the national level, however, and redistribution has been one of the most rapidly growing components of federal expenditures. Estimates of β based on state and local government data may not be reasonable approximations of the income elasticity of redistribution expenditures at the national level. But estimates of the income elasticity of charity contributions also tend to lie below unity, suggesting that this adjustment also would not account for the growth of government (Clotfelter, 1985, ch. 2).

The remaining candidate for explaining government growth is the price elasticity of demand. Most estimates of α suggest that it is significantly greater than -1 and thus imply a relative growth in government if there has been a relative increase in its price. Baumol (1967a) has argued that we might expect a relative increase in the price of government-provided "goods," given that many of them (education, police protection) are services. Because productivity increases come largely from technological change, and this in turn is typically embodied in capital equipment, there is less potential for productivity advances in service sectors such as the government.

Although the argument has intuitive plausibility, it is not clear how far it can be pushed. The military services are quite capital-intensive today and spend vast sums on productivity-enhancing research and development. Similarly, computers, xerography, and other innovations have brought productivity increases in many white-collar jobs. Thus it is not apparent a priori that productivity increases in government could not keep pace with those in the private sector, at least with those in the private service sector. But it appears that they have not. A fair consensus exists among studies of government productivity that suggests that government productivity lags private sector productivity and may in fact be zero or negative.[7] As Buchanan (1977, pp. 8–9) has noted, lagging productivity in the government sector may be more symptomatic of why government growth is a "problem" than the cause of it.

Whatever the cause of the relative rise in the price of government-provided goods, this rise does appear to account for some of the growth of government. Estimates of significant "Baumol effects" have been obtained for the United

critique implies that the growth of income should, other things being equal, bring down the cost of providing government services, thus partly offsetting the Baumol effect on price. The total effect of changes in income on expenditures measured by Schwab and Zampelli was roughly zero.

6. Mueller and Murrell (1986) estimated government size relative to GDP at the national level. Although always positive and often significant, the coefficients on income in their equations were too small to provide much of an explanation of the growth of government.

7. See in particular Fuchs (1968), Gollop and Jorgenson (1980), Ross and Burkhead (1974, ch. 6), and the discussion in Pommerehne and Schneider (1982, pp. 312–13).

States (Tussing and Henning, 1974; Berry and Lowery, 1984), Switzerland (Pommerehne and Schneider, 1982), Sweden (Henrekson, 1988), and Austria (Neck and Schneider, 1988). Lybeck (1986, ch. 5) finds support for the Baumol effect in his pooled, cross-sectional time-series analysis of 12 OECD countries, as well as in 9 of the 12 individual countries examined: Australia, Austria, Belgium, Canada, Federal Republic of Germany (weak), Italy, the Netherlands, Norway, and the United Kingdom. The effect was not found in France, Sweden, or the United States (my judgment, according to results for supply equations explaining government expenditures *excluding* transfers).

Given that significant Baumol effects exist, the next question is how much of the growth of government can they explain? Some parts of the government budget (for example, pure transfers and interest payments) are difficult to think of as "goods" whose price rises relative to private goods. The budget component for which Baumol's effect seems most appropriate is perhaps what the OECD characterizes as "final consumption" – that is, the goods and services actually absorbed by government. Final consumption expenditures for the OECD countries from 1960 through 1983 are presented in Table 17.4. If it is assumed that the price of government goods and services rose relative to the price of private goods by 2 percent a year, government services would be 61.6 percent more expensive relative to private goods in 1983 than they were in 1960. If the price elasticity of demand for government services was -0.5,[8] then the Baumol effect would imply a 12 percent relative increase in final consumption expenditures. This figure comes close to the 14 percent increase actually observed for the United States between 1960 and 1983, but it falls considerably short of the average increase of 50 percent observed across all of the countries listed in Table 17.4. Thus, at best, the Baumol effect seems capable of explaining about a quarter of the increase in final consumption expenditures for the average OECD country.

2.   *The government as redistributor of income and wealth*

The government giveth and it taketh away.

Several writers have criticized the view that government exists to provide public goods and alleviate externalities, arguing that this is essentially a normative description of government – a theory of what government ought to do – not a description of what it actually does. These writers argue that a positive theory of government must analyze the redistributive nature of government activity. Aranson and Ordeshook (1981) pressed the point most

8. This figure seems reasonable from the studies surveyed by Borcherding (1977a, p. 49; 1985, pp. 364–5), although he prefers Deacon's (1978) -0.4 estimate.

Table 17.4. *Total final consumption expenditure of government in relation to GDP, 1960–83 (percent)*

Country	1960	1971	1975	1983
Canada	13.6	19.2	20.0	21.0
France	13.0	13.4	14.4	16.3
Germany, Federal Republic of	13.4	16.9	20.5	20.0
Italy	12.8	15.5	15.4	19.5
Japan	8.0	8.0	10.1	10.2
United Kingdom	16.4	17.8	21.8	22.0
United States	16.9	18.5	19.1	19.3
Average of the above	13.4	15.6	17.3	18.3
Australia	9.4	12.5	15.4	17.6
Austria	13.0	14.8	17.2	18.7
Belgium	12.4	14.1	16.4	17.7
Denmark	13.3	21.3	24.6	27.2
Finland	11.9	15.2	17.1	19.4
Greece	11.7	12.5	15.2	18.8
Iceland	8.5	10.0	11.1	12.3
Ireland	12.5	15.2	18.6	20.2
Luxembourg	9.8	11.7	14.9	17.3
Netherlands	12.8	16.0	17.4	17.7
New Zealand	10.7	12.9	14.8	17.0
Norway	12.9	17.9	19.3	19.5
Portugal	10.5	13.5	15.0	14.6
Spain	7.4	8.6	9.2	12.3
Sweden	15.8	22.5	23.8	28.5
Switzerland	8.8	10.9	12.6	13.5
Turkey	10.5	13.4	12.6	10.8
Average of the above	11.3	14.3	16.2	17.8
Overall average	11.9	14.7	16.7	17.9

Source: OECD, as reported in Tanzi (1986b, p. 17).

forcefully, emphasizing that all government expenditures have a redistributive component. Roads must be built in this location or that. The contracts to construct the roads must be given to one set of firms, to the loss of all others. As Aranson and Ordeshook view it, to understand what government is and why it grows, one must analyze its redistributive activities.

Meltzer and Richard (1978, 1981, 1983) have presented perhaps the simplest and yet most elegant public choice analysis of the growth of government. Their model presumes that all government activity consists in redistribution. This redistribution occurs by means of per capita lump-sum grants of r, financed from a proportional tax of t levied on all earned income. If $\bar{y}$ is mean per capita income, a balanced government budget implies

$$r = t\bar{y}. \tag{17.2}$$

An individual's utility depends on his consumption, c, and leisure, l. Letting n be the fraction of total time worked, we have the identities

$$l = 1 - n \tag{17.3}$$

$$c = (1 - t)y + r. \tag{17.4}$$

Meltzer and Richard assumed that income depends on an ability or productivity factor x, which is randomly distributed across the population. Given the hours one works, n, one's income is higher the higher one's x factor:

$$y = nx. \tag{17.5}$$

Given t and r, an individual's only choice is how much to work, n. Maximizing $U(c,l)$ with respect to n, given equations (17.3)–(17.5), one gets, as a first-order condition,

$$U_c(1 - t)x = U_l \tag{17.6}$$

or

$$\frac{U_l}{U_c} = (1 - t)x. \tag{17.7}$$

The marginal rate of substitution between leisure and consumption is equated to the net-of-tax marginal product of an individual's time. From equation (17.7) one can obtain the number of hours an individual works. For the specific case of a Stone–Geary utility function, $U = \ln(c + \gamma) + a \ln(l + \lambda)$, one obtains for optimal n

$$n = \frac{(1 - t)(1 + \lambda)x - a(r + \gamma)}{(1 - t)(1 + a)x}. \tag{17.8}$$

The denominator of equation (17.8) must be positive, but with small enough x the numerator can be negative. Obviously n cannot be negative; thus there is a critical level of ability, x_0, at which optimal $n = 0$, at or below which an individual chooses not to work. Letting $n = 0$, we can see from equation (17.8) that

$$x_0 = \frac{a(r + \gamma)}{(1 - t)(1 + \lambda)}. \tag{17.9}$$

Although r and t are exogenous from the point of view of the individual, they are endogenous to the political system. Substituting equation (17.8) back into the individual's utility function demonstrates that the individual's utility ultimately depends on r and t. When choosing r and t, the rational voter considers this and takes into account the relationship between r and t given by equation (17.2). Now $\partial \bar{y}/\partial t < 0$. Mean income falls as the tax rate rises because of the negative incentive effects of higher taxes on effort.[9] Thus r is a function of t, rising at a diminishing rate until $-d\bar{y}/dt = \bar{y}/t$ and then falling (see Figure 17.1). Voters who work have positively sloped indifference curves such as U^1 and $U^2(U^2 > U^1)$, since higher taxes lower utility and increased subsidies raise it. Voters who do not work do not have their utilities affected by changes in t. Their indifference curves are horizontal straight lines such as U^3 and U^4, with $U^4 > U^3$. Each rational voter recognizes that $r = \bar{y}t$ constitutes the opportunity set in choosing t (or r). Each voter chooses the $t - r$ combination along the $r = \bar{y}t$ curve that maximizes her utility. Voters who do not work all choose the t_o that maximizes the lump-sum transfer. The voter with $x > x_o$ favors a lower t than t_o. If all voters have the same utility function and differ only in their ability factors, x, voters with a higher x have steeper utility functions and favor a lower t. The voters are in essence confronted with a one-dimensional choice, with t uniquely defining r. A variant on the median voter theorem, first proved by Roberts (1977), can be used to establish the existence of an equilibrium under majority rule. If U^1 and U^2 are indifference curves for the median voter, then $t_m - r_m$ is the optimal tax-subsidy combination.

Meltzer and Richard suggested that one explanation for the secular growth in government in this country and around the world over the past two centuries has been the expansion of suffrage. Those added to the voting rolls are more often than not those with incomes (ability levels) below the median. Thus the median voter changes to someone with a flatter indifference map in Figure 17.1, with tangency further to the right. A decline in the income of the median voter relative to the mean has the same effect. Thus Meltzer and Richard gave increased inequality of income as well as increased suffrage as the primary causes for the growth of government and presented some empirical support for their hypothesis.

Peltzman (1980) has also presented an explanation for the growth of government that depends on the shape of the distribution of income. Peltzman did not, however, make use of the median voter theorem in developing the argument. Rather, he envisaged a form of representative government in which candidates compete for votes by promising to redistribute income toward those voters or groups of voters that agree to join the candidate's coalition of supporters. Peltzman reasoned that the more equal the distribution of income

---

9. Note that as t rises more individuals choose not to work:

$$\partial x_o/\partial t = a(r + \gamma)/(1 + \lambda)(1 - t)^2 > 0.$$

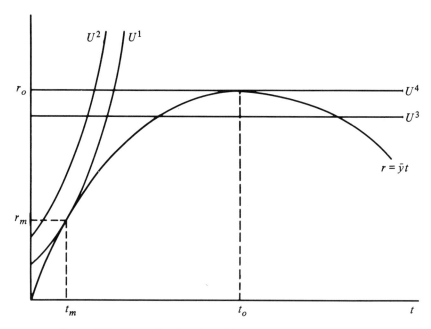

Figure 17.1. The optimal choice of t.

among the potential supporters of a candidate, the more bargaining strength they would have. Thus the candidate must promise a greater amount of redistribution the more equal is the initial distribution of income among voters. Peltzman pointed to the spread of education as an important factor increasing the equality of pretransfer incomes and thus leading to a growth in the size of government. Peltzman's hypothesis depends on increasing equality of income to drive the growth of government, whereas Meltzer and Richard's rests on increasing inequality. But Peltzman, too, found empirical support for his hypothesis in the data he examined.

Both the Meltzer–Richard and Peltzman papers discussed the role of government as if government was exclusively engaged in redistribution. Aranson and Ordeshook (1981), Brunner (1978) and Lindbeck (1985) also placed primary emphasis on government's redistributive activities. But if redistribution is the primary activity of government, then some additional logical arguments are missing to explain the growth in government to the sizes now observed in different countries. Alternatively, government activity is not exclusively redistributive.

Government has grown to far greater size than is necessary just to achieve redistribution. If one group or a coalition of groups can make use of the democratic machinery of government to achieve a greater share of the pie, then one would think that the group or coalition ought to be able to do so in such a way as not to use up such a large fraction of the pie in bringing about the redistribution. The number of programs and people making up government seems much larger than necessary just to achieve redistribution (see, for example, Table 17.4).

An additional conceptual difficulty surrounds Meltzer and Richard's reliance on the extension of suffrage as an explanation of the growth of government. The addition of individuals with productivity and income below the median changes the identity of the median voter, making the former median voter no longer decisive and worse off than before the extension of suffrage. Thus an extension of suffrage that would result in a new median voter of lower income would never be approved under majority rule.[10] If the size of government is endogenous to a political process that uses majority rule and the median voter theorem is applicable, then the extension of suffrage cannot be endogenous to the same political system.

This difficulty can be circumvented by assuming that changes in suffrage are governed by some other form of voting rule, such as a constitutional amendment. But this way out of the logical problem raises other difficulties. Constitutional changes require even more support than a simple majority. How can these changes come about given their redistributional implications in a world of rational, self-interested voters? Moreover, other constitutional changes with important redistributional implications have occurred, such as the amendment to the U.S. Constitution allowing Congress to levy an income tax. Several writers have emphasized the importance of the falling transactions costs of taxation that have accompanied the increasing use of income taxes in industrial countries, and the increased proportion of income that is easily reached through income taxation (e.g., Becker, 1985; North, 1985). Kau and Rubin (1981) provide empirical support for this hypothesis. But if this eventual growth of government was unwanted, or wanted by but a bare majority, how could the supramajority needed to amend the constitution be garnered?

Meltzer and Richard and Peltzman[11] assumed that all redistribution is from

10. Of course an expansion of suffrage that added voters with above-median income to the list of voters would also change the identity of the median voter. Such an expansion should also be opposed by the median voter and all voters with lower incomes – if the higher-income individuals who would be added to the voter rolls were already paying taxes – since the new voters would favor lower taxes and transfers, making the previous majority worse off. But the addition of higher-income citizens to the tax base – say, after the annexation of a wealthy community – might be favored by a previous winning majority, even though such addition would change the identity of the median voter, since the expansion of the tax base might more than make up for the loss in capacity to choose the tax-subsidy rates (see Chapter 9).

11. Peltzman (1980) backed away from this assumption at the end of his paper (pp. 285–7).

rich to poor. But this characterization of the redistribution that government induces does not fit the facts. Some redistribution is in the direction of the rich,[12] and much redistribution is difficult to categorize in terms of rich or poor. Indeed, if all government activity can be characterized as some form of redistribution, the most salient feature of this process of redistribution is probably its lack of a single-directional flow.[13]

The multidimensional character of government redistribution makes it difficult to rationalize *all* government activity as *purely* redistributionally motivated. If all government programs simply take from one group and give to another, and if all citizens participate at both ends of the redistributional process, who gains from the process? Why do not the citizens simply abolish the government and save the tremendous deadweight losses from zero-sum redistribution? Either there must be some clear gainers from the redistributional process, who are in a position to sustain and enlarge their gains, or all government activity is not purely redistributional in character. If the former possibility explains the growth of government, who are those gaining from government and how do they achieve their goals within the rules of a democratic process? If some not insignificant proportion of government activity is not purely redistributional, but, say, is directed at providing public goods, then one again has a logical problem in explaining government growth as a result of redistributional struggles. Once it is admitted that a large component of government expenditure is to provide public goods, then all redistributional objectives can be achieved simply by changing the tax shares of individuals or groups of individuals.[14] One typically does not have to spend money on, or give money to, a group to give that group greater command over private goods.

An assumption of both the Meltzer–Richard and Peltzman models is that the beneficiaries of government growth support government growth. In the Meltzer–Richard model, all voters with incomes below the median favor increased government transfers. Yet, survey evidence indicates that obvious beneficiaries of government growth, such as public employees and welfare

---

12. Fratianni and Spinelli (1982) have noted the increasing importance of special programs to help business in their discussion of the growth of government in Italy.
13. Aranson and Ordeshook (1981) emphasized the multidimensional character of the redistributional process, as did Brunner (1978) to some extent.
14. See Mueller and Murrell (1985). Of course those groups that pay no taxes to finance the public goods portion of the budget can be subsidized further only by an expenditure or transfer program, but not enough groups such as this exist to account for current government activity in most countries. One might object that tax cuts cannot always be designed to benefit specific groups, but the number of tax loopholes and the complexity of tax-loophole legislation belies this point.
  Hettich and Winer (1988) analyze the effect of political pressure to achieve redistribution on tax structure.

recipients, do not have significantly different preferences for tax limitation proposals from other voters (Courant, Gramlich, and Rubinfeld, 1981; Gramlich and Rubinfeld, 1982b).

Despite these criticisms, it is difficult to suppress the impression that an important component of the explanation for the growth of government lies in government's redistributional activities, so substantial has been the growth in the transfer component of government budgets, as Table 17.5 shows (see also the discussion in Tanzi (1986a)). But these arguments make clear that the hypotheses put forward so far, which attempt to explain the growth of government in simple redistributional terms, are inadequate. Some additional elements are needed to complete the story. Two villains often mentioned as instrumental in the growth of government are interest groups and bureaucrats.

3. Interest groups and the growth of government

The pioneering public choice analysis of the question of government size might be regarded as Tullock's (1959) classic discussion of majority rule. Tullock presented an example in which a community of 100 farmers votes on proposals to repair access roads, each of which benefits only a few farmers. Using a majority rule, a coalition of 51 farmers is predicted, with a political outcome in which the only roads repaired are those that service the 51 farmers in the winning coalition. Because these 51 farmers pay only 51 percent of the costs of repairing their roads, they vote to have them maintained at a higher level of repair than they would if they had to cover the full costs. Thus, majority rule might be said to lead to a level of government expenditures that is excessive, relative to the Pareto-optimal level that would occur under the unanimity rule, in one of two senses. First, more is spent repairing those roads than would be spent under the unanimity rule. Second, if the unanimity rule were in use, there would be no incentive to have the government (that is, the community to which the 100 farmers belong) repair the roads at all. Each small group of farmers could agree among themselves to repair their own roads. The repair of access roads would not be a public issue at all in the community of 100.[15]

Whereas Tullock's example of road repair nicely illustrates how government may become too large under majority rule, it also illustrates some of the troublesome questions raised earlier. If a coalition of 51 farmers can impose taxes on their neighbors without the neighbors receiving any benefits, why do not the 51 simply take the money as a cash transfer and repair the roads themselves at the optimal level, rather than make suboptimally large road repairs through the government?

15. For a modeling of the pork-barrel process that demonstrates inefficiently large budgets, see Weingast et al. (1981).

The logrolling under majority rule that Tullock describes resembles the kind of pork-barrel logrolling under majority rule that one often associates with pressures from interest groups. Virtually every study that discusses the growth of government mentions interest groups as a possible cause and then goes on to discuss some other cause for the growth of government, leaving the role of interest groups in limbo. The questions of whether, how, and why interest groups contribute to the growth of government remain largely unanswered.

If one begins to ask these questions, the first issue one confronts is whether interest groups pursue redistributive favors from government or the provision of public goods and alleviation of externalities. A moment's reflection brings to mind the names of interest groups with each objective. A farmers' cooperative seeking price supports would seem to belong to the category of a redistribution-oriented interest group; a naturalists' club wanting to save the whales is in the category of a club seeking a public good. Thus, in terms of the overt objectives of interest groups, it would seem possible, if such groups do play an important role in explaining government growth, that interest groups expand either the redistributive or the public good–expenditure components, or both.

Becker (1983, 1985) has developed a model of the influence of interest groups (or, as he calls them, pressure groups) that is relevant to the issue at hand. At first glance it appears that Becker is analyzing the purely redistributive gains of interest groups. He states that "the basic assumption of the analysis is that taxes, subsidies, regulations, and other political instruments are used to raise the welfare of more influential pressure groups" (pp. 373–4). He assumes a single good, income, to be distributed among the interest groups, with some groups getting a subsidy S and others paying a tax R. The summation of the subsidies received over all interest groups is less than the taxes paid, however, because of the transaction costs of collecting and distributing subsidies and the deadweight losses from adverse incentive effects when incomes are taxed and subsidies granted.

Each group applies pressure to increase (reduce) its subsidies (taxes). With diminishing returns to applying pressure assumed, an equilibrium is obtained in which the pressure to increase subsidies just equals the opposing pressure to reduce taxes. For each group the marginal cost of applying additional pressure just equals the marginal gain from reduced taxes or increased subsidies. Several not totally obvious propositions follow from this analysis. One is that "competition among pressure groups favors efficient methods of taxation" (Becker, 1983, p. 386). Those groups that can be cheaply subsidized or are expensive to tax do better. In particular, "politically successful groups tend to be small relative to the size of the groups taxed to pay their subsidies" (Becker, 1983, p. 385).

Although Becker's analysis is entirely couched in terms of taxes, subsidies, and regulations – as if all government activity were of a redistributive nature – one of the implications of the analysis is that the government does provide public goods and alleviate externalities whenever the collective gains from these activities exceed the transaction costs of bringing them about. "Political policies that raise efficiency are more likely to be adopted than policies that lower efficiency" (Becker, 1983, p. 384). This proposition has broad implications for the types of activities that are subsidized and taxed and for the types of interest groups helped and harmed. If education has positive spillover effects, teachers' unions will have more success winning public support for their "industry" than, say, a plumbers' union. Moreover, the support is more likely to take the form of more funds for more teachers than of higher wages for existing teachers. Factor owners in the liquor and cigarette industries are more likely to suffer from excise taxes than are factor owners in the plumbing goods industry because of the perceived negative externalities from drinking alcohol and smoking tobacco.

Becker's paper gives insight into how interest group activity and government activity might be linked. It also demonstrates that the expenditures and taxes that interest groups bring about have more than merely redistributive characteristics. Groups whose interests have public good or externality attributes are more likely to be successful than those seeking pure redistribution. Groups whose productive activities have negative externalities are more likely to be taxed.

North and Wallis (1982) have linked the growth of government to interest group activity. They drew a parallel between the growth of government and the growth of white-collar and managerial employment in the private sector. Both were seen as a response to the greater transaction costs from organizing a market economy with increasing specialization (see also North, 1985): "Growing specialization also created a host of new interest groups" (North and Wallis, 1982, p. 340). The demands that these groups press on government are not simply for a redistributive handout but are to alleviate the transaction costs these groups bear within an increasingly specialized society. Thus, as with Becker's analysis, the influence of interest groups on government activity is seen as having both an efficiency-enhancing dimension as well as a redistributive dimension. North and Wallis presented the data in Table 17.5, taken from Peltzman (1980), to illustrate that nondefense, nontransfer expenditures of government have grown faster than total government has grown since World War II, and almost as fast as transfers.

The transaction costs explanation for the growth of government is the most general. Our analysis in Chapter 2 revealed that the existence of externalities and public goods was not sufficient to warrant the creation of the state. Rather, the state emerged as the lowest transaction costs institution for provid-

Table 17.5. *Government expenditures in relation to GDP in the United States and fifteen developed countries (DCs), 1953–74 (percent)*

Expenditure category	1953–4	1958–9	1963–4	1968–9	1973–4
Total government					
United States	27.0	27.5	28.0	31.1	32.2
Average of 15 DCs	28.9	29.9	31.7	35.8	39.4
SD of 15 DCs	4.1	4.3	4.8	5.9	7.2
CV of 15 DCs	14.1	14.2	15.0	16.6	18.3
Defense					
United States	12.25	9.9	8.45	8.95	5.7
Average of 15 DCs	4.05	3.3	3.24	2.83	2.51
SD of 15 DCs	2.46	1.55	1.32	1.13	1.03
CV of 15 DCs	60.7	46.5	40.7	39.9	41.1
Transfers[a]					
United States	5.5	6.7	7.5	8.7	11.0
Average of 14 DCs	11.9	12.9	13.8	16.2	18.8
SD of 14 DCs	4.3	4.2	4.3	4.9	5.9
CV of 14 DCs	36.4	32.5	31.0	30.3	31.6
Nontransfer, nondefense					
United States	9.2	10.9	12.05	13.4	15.5
Average of 15 DCs	12.64	13.54	14.7	16.61	18.37
SD of 15 DCs	2.89	2.32	2.11	3.27	3.47
CV of 15 DCs	22.9	18.5	14.4	19.7	18.9

Note: Sample countries are Australia, Austria, Belgium, Canada, Denmark, Finland, France, the Federal Republic of Germany, Italy, Japan, the Netherlands, Norway, Sweden, Switzerland, and the United Kingdom. SD of 15 countries is the standard deviation for the 15- (14-) country sample; CV is the coefficient of variation.

[a]Transfer payments were not broken down separately for Switzerland.

Sources: Peltzman (1980), as reported in North and Wallis (1982). All sample data are from national accounts of OECD countries; U.S. data are from United States, *Economic Report of the President*.

ing public goods and eliminating externalities. Logically, falling transaction costs are thus the best explanation for the growth in the state. But the very generality of the transaction costs notion makes it difficult to pinpoint more accurately the particular transaction costs that have fallen and the budget items that will grow. For example, all industrialized countries can make use of income taxation, yet this efficient source of revenue collection leads to vastly different government sizes in Japan and Switzerland compared with Sweden and Holland. Do the transaction costs of organizing interest groups differ greatly across countries?

Mueller and Murrell (1985, 1986) presented empirical evidence that interest groups affect the size of government. They described a political process in which parties supply interest groups with favors in exchange for the interest groups' support. When these favors take the form of goods targeted to specific interest groups, but with some spillovers for other groups, government grows larger. The number of organized interest groups in a country was shown to have a positive and significant effect on the relative size of the government sector in a cross-sectional sample of OECD countries for the year 1970.

Lybeck (1986, pp. 88–96) found that the relative size of government in Sweden varied over time with the relative fraction of employees who were members of interest groups. McCormick and Tollison (1981, pp. 45–9) found that the extent of economic regulation within a state varied directly with the number of trade associations registered in the state.

The analyses of Becker and Mueller and Murrell are essentially static, describing an equilibrium in which interest group pressures are in balance, an equilibrium in which government is bigger than it would be in the absence of the influence of interest groups. They do not describe a process in which interest group influence leads to growing government size. Olson (1982) has discussed the conditions favoring the growth of interest groups, however, and Murrell (1984) has presented evidence consistent with Olson's hypotheses concerning the causes of interest group formation. The stable economic and political environment in Western developed countries since World War II will have facilitated the growth in interest groups, according to Olson's thesis, and this growth in turn may help to explain the relatively poor macroeconomic performance of some countries in the 1970s and 1980s. If the number of effective interest groups in developed countries has grown since World War II, then their growth could help to explain the relative growth of government. Government growth and macroeconomic inefficiency would, in turn, be tied together. Unfortunately, however, the possible interrelationships of interest groups, government growth, and macroeconomic performance remain largely unexplored.[16]

4. Bureaucracy and the growth of government

Government programs do not come into existence merely because some interest group wants them and the legislature authorizes them. They must be

16. Mueller and Murrell (1985, 1986) made allowance for interest groups and government size both being endogenous variables.

Wallis and Oates (in press) provide an indirect test of the hypothesis linking the size of government to the growth of interest groups. Following Olson (1982), they assume stronger interest groups in old states. Following Mueller and Murrell, they assume bigger government sectors in states with stronger interest groups. Yet they find the government sectors to be larger in *younger* states, thus contradicting one of the links in the causal chain. Gray and Lowery's (1986) results suggest that it is the relationship between age of state and number of interest groups that breaks down.

"manufactured." More often than not, the supplier of a program is part of the government itself, a government bureau. Government may grow not only because increasing expenditures are demanded by citizens, interest groups, or legislators, but also because they are demanded by the bureaucracy supplying government programs. The government bureaucracies are an independent force, which possibly may lead to increasing government size.

In Chapter 14 we examined several hypotheses as to why bureaucrats might seek a larger budget and considered some evidence in a specific situation when the bureaucrats have the power to set the agenda where they do. Thus, the bureaucracy appears to be a plausible candidate as an independent source for the growth of government.

Nevertheless, some logical difficulties exist when applying the bureaucracy models to explain the size of government and its growth. The Niskanen (1971) model predicts a government budget as much as twice as large as that demanded by the bureau's sponsor. It is easy to see why a bureau would wish to charge a higher price for a given output. The extra revenue could be used to offer higher salaries, more leisure (because of a large staff), more perquisites (paid travel to conventions), and a whole host of amenities that might make a bureaucrat's life on and off the job more pleasant. But the power of the bureaucracy to obtain these benefits should not be exaggerated. Salary increases are very visible exercises of bureaucratic power; travel and other perquisites can often be easily monitored. A wise legislature should be capable of exercising some control over such budget items.

One way sometimes used to justify a larger salary is to expand the bureau's output, and then to demand higher salaries that allow for the expanded demands placed on the bureaucracy. Niskanen (1971, p. 38) postulated that a bureaucrat's "salary, perquisites of the office, public reputation, power [and] patronage" are all positively related to the size of the bureau. Niskanen uses this postulate to analyze the consequences of assuming that bureaucrats maximize the size of their budgets. Not surprisingly, the model implies larger budgets than are desired by the legislative demanders. Niskanen's analysis has become the theoretical underpinning for an important part of the literature on the growth of government.

The model of the budget-maximizing bureaucrat has a certain resonance with models of the corporation that assume that managers maximize the corporation's size, its growth in size, or other size-related variables such as white-collar staff (Baumol, 1959; Marris, 1964; Williamson, 1964). The behavioral underpinning and empirical support for these models can to some extent be cited in support of the postulate of the budget-maximizing bureaucrat. But one must not be too quick to generalize.

The manager of a company with $10 billion in sales may be able to justify to the board of directors and stockholders a larger salary than he could if the company had sales of $1 billion and company size and managerial compensation were positively correlated. But the head of a bureau with a budget of $10 billion does not necessarily get paid more than the head of a bureau with a budget of $1 billion. Salaries across government bureaucracies tend to be much more uniform than are salaries across companies. Moreover, the top officers in bureaus are typically political appointees, who stay at the bureau for four years at most. Thus expanding the size of the bureau, even if size and salary were positively related, would not be likely to benefit directly the bureaucrat who brought about the increase. If the growth of bureaus benefits the top members of the bureaucracy, it must in general be from the nonpecuniary dimensions of a bureaucrat's rewards that accompany the growth in a bureau's size.

Even at middle levels, salaries do not differ much across bureaus. Undersecretaries earn the same regardless of which department they are in. But the chances for promotion in a rapidly growing bureau are certainly greater than in a shrinking one. Thus, middle-level bureaucrats do have a financial incentive to encourage the rapid expansion of their bureaus because it increases the likelihood of their promotion to a higher rank. Career bureaucrats are also likely to be with the bureau long enough to benefit directly from the expansion, unlike their short-term superiors.

Although this analysis provides a rationale for the promotion of growth in size by middle-level career bureaucrats, it greatly complicates the story of why these individuals are allowed to fulfill their goals to the loss of society. If the bureaucrats at the top of the bureau do not benefit from the growth in bureau size, why do they not curtail its growth? Are middle-level bureaucrats able to deceive both the legislative overseers of the bureau and their superiors within the bureau about the true magnitudes of the quantities of bureau output supplied and their unit costs?[17]

Bureaucrats and interest groups stand equally high on all lists of the causes of the growth of government, and much case study evidence is consistent with this hypothesis. For example, Gary Miller's (1981, ch. 3) study of city incorporations in Los Angeles County reveals both city and county bureaucrats to be driven by the goal of expanding the size and scope of their jurisdictions, and resisting attempts to contract them. But more systematic support for the bureaucracy-size relationship is sparse and contradictory. Henrekson (1988) finds that public employment is positively related to local levels of government consumption expenditures in Sweden, but not to transfers. This result seems plausible, since bureaucrats are presumably more interested in increasing the money spent within government than the money passing through it.

17. For further critical discussion of the hypothesis linking the size of government to the bureaucracy, see Musgrave (1981, pp. 91–5).

But then how can one rationalize the entirely opposite results for Holland (Renaud and van Winden, 1987b)? Borcherding, Bush, and Spann (1977) present evidence supporting the bureaucrat–interest group hypothesis for the United States; Lowery and Berry (1983) present evidence contradicting it. Neck and Schneider (1988) are not able to sustain the hypothesis on Austrian data.

Perhaps the best direct evidence in favor of the hypothesis that bureaucratic power increases the size of government is that indicating that government bureaucracies do have higher unit costs than private firms when they supply measurable outputs, such as tons of garbage collected. Borcherding (1977a, p. 62) describes this as "the Bureaucratic Rule of Two" – "removal of an activity from the private sector will double its unit costs of production."[18] If unit costs rise by this much when direct comparisons with private sector alternatives are possible, how much more are they inflated when the bureaucracy knows it cannot be subjected to a comparison with private market alternatives?

The bureaucracy models of Niskanen (1971), Romer and Rosenthal (1978, 1979b, 1982), and others are static. They explain why government might be larger than the legislature would prefer if it knew the unit costs of the outputs it thought it was buying, and why the level of outputs might be larger than the median voter's most preferred quantity. They do not directly explain why government grows.

Indirectly, however, they perhaps do offer an explanation. The bureaucracy's ability to expand the budget beyond the amount the legislature or citizens demand depends in part on its ability to misrepresent the true prices and quantities of publicly provided goods. The ability to misrepresent is likely to depend in turn on the size and complexity of the budget itself. The bigger the bureaucracy, the more difficult it is for outsiders to monitor its activity, and the more insiders there are who are working to increase the size of the bureaucracy. Thus the growth of the bureaucracy is likely to depend on its absolute size.

To see this relationship, let us define G_t as the amount of publicly provided goods that the citizens or legislature truly demand. Let B_t be the total size of the budget. B_t is greater than G_t to the extent to which the bureaucracy is capable of forcing a greater expenditure of resources toward the bureaucracy than is demanded; that is,

$$B_t = \alpha_t G_t, \; \alpha_t > 1 \; . \tag{17.10}$$

Now let

$$\alpha_t = e^{aB_t} \tag{17.11}$$

18. For summaries of the evidence, see Orzechowski (1977) and Borcherding, Pommerehne, and Schneider (1982).

and let the amount of publicly provided goods demanded grow at a constant rate n equal to, say, the growth in national income:

$$G_t = ce^{nt}. \tag{17.12}$$

Then

$$B_t = ce^{aB_t}e^{nt}. \tag{17.13}$$

The growth in the budget, g, is then

$$g = \ln B_t - \ln B_{t-1} = a(B_t - B_{t-1}) + n. \tag{17.14}$$

The growth rate of the budget both exceeds the growth in national income, n, and increases with the absolute difference between this period's and last period's budget. Other functional forms for α_t will yield other relationships between g and B_t; as long as α_t increases with budget size, however, the growth in the size of the budget can be expected to increase with its absolute size.

Equation (17.13) is broadly consistent with the pattern of growth of government expenditure observed in the United States over the past two centuries: slow but steady initial growth, gradually shifting into more rapid rates of growth. But this same pattern could be expected from any process that resulted in an S-shaped growth path for government. S-shaped growth paths for organizations are sufficiently common that one should not claim too much for a hypothesis that bureaucratic power increases the size of government merely because the hypothesis is consistent with at least the initial segment of the S, and so, too, are the data. Government growth cannot outpace national income indefinitely, and so there must be the subsequent slowdown in growth, which the logistic S-curve predicts. Indeed, the conservative governments that in recent years have taken office in the United States, the United Kingdom, the Federal Republic of Germany, and several other developed countries may have already initiated the slowdown.

This consideration raises a more general point. Given the steady growth in government both since World War II and over the past two centuries, any variable exhibiting a steady growth over the same period, or for that matter any variable with a stable trend factor, is likely to be highly correlated with government growth. Tullock (1983) has made a similar point in his critique of Meltzer and Richard's (1983) empirical support for their hypothesis. A key variable in their model is the ratio of median to mean income. This ratio has been virtually constant since World War II, yet it "explains" a significant fraction of the growth of government.

Testing hypotheses by using time-series data that have strong trend components incurs familiar problems. That they are present in the literature on the growth of government is unfortunate, if unsurprising. The absence of a consistent pattern of results when one looks across the individual country time-series analyses is thus also predictable. These time-series inconsistencies reinforce the importance of those studies that try to explain levels of government expenditure by using cross-sectional data, even though these studies typically do rely on static rather than dynamic models of government size.

5.   *Fiscal illusion*

The hypothesis that bureaucratic power increases the size of government presumes that the bureaucracy can deceive the legislature about the true costs of supplying different levels of output. The fiscal illusion hypothesis presumes that the legislature can deceive the citizens about the true size of government. Tanzi (1980) has traced the argument back to Mill and also cites Pareto as a source for the hypothesis. But it is to Puviani (1897, 1903) that credit must go for emphasizing the importance of fiscal illusion to a positive theory of government (see also the discussion in Buchanan, 1967, pp. 126–43).

The fiscal illusion explanation for government size assumes that citizens measure the size of government by the size of their tax bill. To bring about an increase in government size, for which the citizens are not willing to pay voluntarily, the legislative-executive entities must increase the citizens' tax burden in such a way that the citizens are unaware that they are paying more in taxes, or be willing to pay the price of citizen displeasure at the next election. If tax burdens can be disguised in this way, citizens have the illusion that government is smaller than it actually is, and government can grow beyond the levels citizens prefer.

Although this proposition seems reasonable enough, to develop it into a model to be used for explaining the size and growth of government one must make some specific assumptions about the kinds of tax burdens that can be disguised. Mill (1970, pp. 220–1) felt that direct taxes were more visible and, by implication, that excessive government growth would have to rely on indirect taxes. But the citizens of Boston had no illusions about the burden of the British tax on tea two centuries ago, and one can argue that employer withholding of income taxes, like bank collection of property taxes with mortgage payments, makes these forms of direct taxation less visible than some types of indirect taxation, such as liquor and cigarette taxes. The issue of what sources of revenue are less visible to citizens, as well as the magnitude of any fiscal illusion caused, must be regarded as largely empirical.

The empirical literature on fiscal illusion is too large to be reviewed here. Fortunately, Oates (1988b) has recently completed a comprehensive review of it. He breaks the fiscal illusion argument into five subhypotheses: (1) a tax burden is more difficult to judge the more complex the tax structure; (2)

renters are less able to judge their share of property taxes in the community than are homeowners; (3) built-in tax increases because of the progressivity of the tax structure are less clearly perceived than are legislated changes, making elastic tax structures more conducive to government growth than are inelastic structures; (4) the implicit future tax burdens inherent in the issuance of debt are more difficult to evaluate than are equivalent current taxes; (5) citizens do not treat lump-sum cash subsidies to their government as being as much theirs as they would a cash subsidy to themselves (the "flypaper" effect). Each of these hypotheses implies a relationship between the size or growth of government and the relevant fiscal illusion variable. Oates carefully examined the evidence in support of each and concluded "that although all five cases entail plausible illusion hypotheses, none of them have very compelling empirical support" (Oates, 1988b). Fiscal illusion, like the other hypotheses reviewed in this paper, does not by itself provide a persuasive explanation for the growth of government.

The lack of strong empirical support for the fiscal illusion hypothesis, despite its intuitive appeal, may be due to the rather vague way in which fiscal illusion has been defined and modeled in the literature. For example, it is not clear from the literature whether fiscal illusion is a kind of short-run myopia on the part of voters that allows for temporary increases in expenditures, or a permanent astigmatism indefinitely obscuring the true size of government. The latter is obviously a much stronger hypothesis. The tax revolts in Europe and the United States in the 1970s, and the deficit revolt of the 1980s, symbolized so dramatically by the Gramm–Rudman–Hollings legislation in the United States, suggest that fiscal illusion may not permanently impair voters' vision. Eventually, they may see the light and rise up to chain Leviathan.

From a public choice perspective, the most serious deficiency in the literature on fiscal illusion is the gap between the potential existence of fiscal illusion on the part of voters and its consequences for the size of government. Who is it within the government that takes advantage of the fiscal illusion, bureaucrats or elected politicians? Is it perhaps groups outside of government who gain – interest groups, for example? If it is insiders, why do they not simply increase their salaries rather than expand personnel and programs? Although fiscal illusion explains why government *could* grow larger than citizens prefer, it does not provide an explanation for why it *would*. Such an explanation can be found only in the other theories of government growth examined here. To account for government growth completely, fiscal illusion must be combined with some other hypothesis that can supply the driving force behind the growth of government. Some suggestions are presented in the concluding section. (For further discussion of the fiscal illusion hypothesis, see Musgrave, 1981, pp. 98–104; and Oates, 1988b.)

C.   Conclusions

The five possible explanations of government size reviewed in this chapter stem from two quite different conceptualizations of the state. The first three hypotheses (the government as a provider of public goods and eliminator of externalities, the government as a redistributor of income and wealth, and interest groups as inducers of government growth) are essentially drawn from a classical theory of the democratic state (Pateman, 1970). Ultimate authority lies with the citizens. The state exists to carry out "the will of the people." State policies are reflections of the preferences of individual voters. In the public choice literature, the state often appears as simply a voting rule that transforms individual preferences into political outcomes. Most of the classic works on public choice – beginning with Arrow (1951), Downs (1957), Black (1958), and Buchanan and Tullock (1962) right up to Groves and Ledyard (1977a) – are based on this citizen-over-state view of the polity.

The fourth and fifth hypotheses reviewed here (bureaucratic power as inducer of government growth, fiscal illusion as enhancer of government growth) place the state above the citizens. It is the preferences of the state, or of the individuals in the government, that are decisive. Citizens and political institutions constitute at most (loose) constraints against which political leaders and bureaucrats pursue their own personal interests. This state-rules-citizen view of politics underlies Puviani's (1903) work and characterizes that of Niskanen (1971) and Brennan and Buchanan (1980).

If either of these two conceptions of the state is fully accurate,[19] then the other must be rejected – and so, too, the set of hypotheses associated with it in this chapter. But both views might be correct to some degree. Government officials and bureaucrats may have some discretionary power to advance their own interests at the citizens' expense, but citizens' preferences, as registered through existing political institutions, may also constitute a consequential constraint. If so, then all five hypotheses may help to explain the size and growth of government.

Only a couple of studies have attempted to test for the relative strengths of demand and supply factors. Henrekson (1988) found evidence of both the Baumol effect and the voting power of government bureaucrats in his time-series analysis of Sweden. Although the fiscal illusion variables did not prove to be very robust, the supply side variables did have somewhat more explanatory power than the demand variables.

Johann Lybeck (1986) has also estimated an integrated demand and supply of government model for 12 OECD countries. Demand factors appeared to

---

19. Tanzi (1980) has discussed both of these conceptions of the state – as well as a third, the paternalistic state – in the context of the fiscal illusion issue.

dominate in Sweden and the United Kingdom; supply factors in Canada, France, and the United States; and both were of about equal importance in the remaining countries (Australia, Austria, Belgium, the Federal Republic of Germany, Italy, the Netherlands, and Norway). Impressive support for the Baumol effect was again found. Interest group strength, as measured by the number of interest groups in a time-series analysis of Sweden (Lybeck, 1986, pp. 58–82), and by the degree of unionization in a pooled cross-sectional time-series analysis of all 12 countries (pp. 96–106), was highly significant. The number of public employees, another interest group measure, proved significant in several countries. In the pooled regressions, population size (negatively related) and unemployment (positively related) were the remaining significant variables. The former appears in the demand side of the model and implies that government size does decline relatively as population grows, as one would expect if government output resembles a pure public good. The unemployment rate appears in the supply side of the model, as hypothesized in political-business-cycle models. Other hypotheses (Wagner's law, redistribution, fiscal illusion) received very mixed support.

Pommerehne and Schneider (1982) tested a model that incorporated both of the views of the state discussed here. These authors first estimated the demand for government for 48 Swiss municipalities that operate under direct (as opposed to representative) democracy. They then used the estimated coefficients from this equation to simulate what the levels of government expenditure would be in the 62 Swiss municipalities that have representative democracy. They found that *all* of the individual spending categories are underestimated from the parameter estimates based on the direct democracies. The representative democracies spent 28 percent more than one would predict on the basis of the expenditure equation estimated over the direct democracies. The use of a representative form of government changes the nature of the political outcomes substantially, making government considerably larger than it would be if citizens directly determined outcomes. Moreover, in those Swiss municipalities in which representative democracy exists, the size of government is smaller if the citizens have the right to call a referendum and thereby reverse a government decision. These results of Pommerehne and Schneider suggest rather strongly that the existence of a layer of representative government between the citizens and political outcomes expands the size of the public sector considerably. They would appear to support the state-over-citizen view of government, and Pommerehne and Schneider (1982, pp. 319–22) interpret their results as indicating the importance of "the supply side of local services." This inference may be warranted, but it is also possible that the existence of representative democracy facilitates the attainment of private gains by interest groups. Both Peltzman (1980) and Mueller and Murrell (1985, 1986) have seen the growth of government as a by-product of the competition for votes between candidates and parties. Thus government growth (or size) in these models is dependent on the representative nature of the democratic process, although the models assume that citizens' preferences, as channeled by interest group representation, are the driving force behind government programs.

Regardless of which of these interpretations is correct, Pommerehne and Schneider's results forcefully demonstrate what may be regarded as the single most important message that public choice has to teach – namely, the rules of the game *do* affect the outcomes of the game. Institutions matter. In Switzerland, the more direct the citizen influence on political outcomes, the smaller is the scale of government. Among the developed countries, citizens of Switzerland are able to exercise control over government more effectively than anywhere else. Only Switzerland makes much use of direct democracy and the referendum, and it has the strongest federalist system in the world. It also has the smallest public sector among the developed countries (see Table 17.2). The results of Pommerehne and Schneider suggest that these facts are related.[20]

Cross-sectional studies such as that of Pommerehne and Schneider (1982) help to answer the third of the three questions posed at the beginning of this chapter: What explains cross-country differences in the relative size of government? They are less useful, however, in explaining the growth of government. Several authors have thus resorted to time-series analysis of individual countries. Although the results for a single country often appear plausible and statistically defensible, when one compares the different time-series studies one finds little overlap in the key explanatory variables. Thus, little consensus exists in what the key determinants of the growth of government are. Some variables, like the relative rise in the price of publicly provided goods, appear to be significant determinants of government growth. But even a generous allowance for their impact leaves much of the growth in government, or relative disparities in government sizes across countries, unexplained (Borcherding, 1977a, 1985). What appears to be needed are new theories to explain the growth of government, or more imaginative testing of existing theories (Lowery and Berry, 1983).

Three promising candidates are suggested by the literature. The hypothesis that bureaucratic power leads to larger budget sizes is yet to be tested. Most studies test for the *voting* power of bureaucrats. But true bureaucratic power arises in the control that bureaucrats have over information, rests in their

---

20. Santerre (1986) provides additional evidence indicating that direct democracies better satisfy the preferences of citizens.

   Several studies have found that more federalized or decentralized government structures constrain the size or growth in size of government (Cameron, 1978; Saunders, 1986; Schneider, 1986). But see Oates (1985).

ability to "manipulate" the budgetary agenda. Only the Romer and Rosenthal (1982) study of Oregon school budgets bears directly on this issue. In general, bureaucratic power is probably related to bureaucratic size. Growth in size is then a function of absolute size, which leads to the prediction that government grows exponentially. The bureaucratic power hypothesis might also explain the rachet effect in government growth, to which attention was first drawn by Peacock and Wiseman (1961). The expansion of government bureaucracy in response to an external shock such as a war increases the bureaucracy's discretionary power, allowing it to achieve a permanent increase in size. The Peacock–Wiseman study might be regarded as evidence in support of the bureaucratic power hypothesis, but more direct testing is needed.

If all the growth of government cannot be explained by shifts in the demand for government output or the costs in supplying it, then this growth must result from shifts in the *costs of registering* demands and in the opposition to such growth. The transaction costs explanation of the growth of government has the potential for explaining many of the unanswered questions about the growth of government (North, 1985). What is now needed is an empirical realization of this potential.

The transaction costs of using government depend in part on "the rules of the game" in which government operates. These rules differ across countries, and their efficacy changes over time as the economic and political environment of a country change. The citizen's role in a representative democracy is more passive than in a direct democracy, and Pommerehne and Schneider's (1982) work suggests that even this difference leads to a significant fillip to government size. Today's citizen, confronted by expanded and more complex government structures at the local, state, and federal levels, must feel that he is more of a passive spectator of the democratic process, as he watches a campaign commercial on television, than did the citizen of 150 years ago. How much of the growth of government in the intervening years can be explained by a slackening of the reins of government in citizens' hands, and how much is a reflection of the preferences of citizens transmitted through the political process, remains, along with so many other important issues in this unsatisfying literature, an open question.

CHAPTER 18

The paradox of voting

When we move . . . away from the private concerns of the family and the business office into those regions of national and international affairs that lack a direct and unmistakable link with those private concerns, individual volition, command of facts and method of inference soon cease to fulfill the requirements of the classical doctrine. What strikes me most of all and seems to me to be the core of the trouble is the fact that the sense of reality is so completely lost. Normally, the great political questions take their place in the psychic economy of the typical citizen with those leisure-hour interests that have not attained the rank of hobbies, and with the subjects of irresponsible conversation. These things seem so far off; they are not at all like a business proposition; dangers may not materialize at all and if they should they may not prove so very serious; one feels oneself to be moving in a fictitious world.

This reduced sense of reality accounts not only for a reduced sense of responsibility but also for the absence of effective volition. One has one's phrases, of course, and one's wishes and daydreams and grumbles; especially, one has one's likes and dislikes. But ordinarily they do not amount to what we call a will – the psychic counterpart of purposeful responsible action. In fact, for the private citizen musing over national affairs there is no scope for such a will and no task at which it could develop. He is a member of an unworkable committee, the committee of the whole nation, and this is why he expends less disciplined effort on mastering a political problem than he expends on a game of bridge. . . .

Thus the typical citizen drops down to a lower level of mental performance as soon as he enters the political field. He argues and analyzes in a way which he would readily recognize as infantile within the sphere of his real interests. He becomes a primitive again. His thinking becomes associative and affective. And this entails two further consequences and ominous significance.

First, even if there were no political groups trying to influence him, the typical citizen would in political matters tend to yield to extra-rational or irrational prejudice and impulse. . . . Moreover, simply because he is not "all there," he will relax his usual moral standards as well and occasionally give in to dark urges which the conditions of private life help him to repress. But as to the wisdom or rationality of his inferences and conclusions, it may be just as bad if he gives in to a burst of generous indignation. This will make it still more difficult for him to see things in their correct proportions or

Dennis C. Mueller, "The Voting Paradox," *in* Charles K. Rowley, ed. *Democracy and Public Choice,* New York: Basil Blackwell, © Basil Blackwell, Ltd.

even to see more than one aspect of one thing at a time. Hence, if for once he does emerge from his usual vagueness and does display the definite will postulated by the classical doctrine of democracy, he is as likely as not to become still more unintelligent and irresponsible than he usually is. At certain junctures, this may prove fatal to his nation.

Joseph Schumpeter

The Americans . . . are fond of explaining all the actions of their lives by the principle of self-interest rightly understood; they show with complacency how an enlightened regard for themselves constantly prompts them to assist one another and inclines them willingly to sacrifice a portion of their time and property to the welfare of the state. In this respect . . . they frequently fail to do themselves justice; for in the United States as well as elsewhere people are sometimes seen to give way to those disinterested and spontaneous impulses that are natural to man; but the Americans seldom admit that they yield to emotions of this kind; they are more anxious to do honor to their philosophy than to themselves.

Alexis de Tocqueville

The distinguishing characteristic of public choice is the assumption that individuals in the political arena as in the marketplace behave rationally and in their own self-interest. We have examined models of candidate competition and bureaucratic behavior based on this assumption, but as yet have said little about the key actor in the political drama, the individual voter. This chapter fills that void.

A.   The rational voter hypothesis

1.   Expected utility maximization

The rational voter hypothesis was first developed by Anthony Downs (1957, chs. 11–14) and later was elaborated by Gordon Tullock (1967a, pp. 110–14) and William Riker and Peter Ordeshook (1968, 1973). In deciding between two parties or candidates, the voter envisages the different "streams of utility" to be derived from the policies promised by each candidate. The voter calculates the expected utility from each candidate's victory, and naturally votes for the candidate whose policies promise the highest utility. Thus, voting is a purely instrumental act in the theory of rational voting. One votes to bring about the victory of one's preferred candidate. The benefit from voting is the difference in expected utilities from the policies of the two candidates. Call this difference B.

Of course, it is unlikely that one's vote decides the outcome of the election. One's vote has an impact on the outcome only when (1) the votes of all other voters are evenly split between the two candidates, or (2) one's preferred candidate would lose by one vote if one did not vote. Call the probabilities of these two events occurring P_1 and P_2, respectively. If one's preferred candidate has a 50/50 chance of eventually winning should the first election end in a draw, then the probability that a single individual's vote will be instrumental in bringing about the victory of the voter's preferred candidate is $P = P_1 + \frac{1}{2} P_2$. The expected benefits from voting are PB.

P is a subjective probability and depends on how close the voter expects the election to be. Let p be the voter's expectation of the percentage of the vote that his or her preferred candidate will get, that is, the probability that any one voter will vote for the candidate. Then

$$P = \frac{3e^{-2(N-1)(p-\frac{1}{2})^2}}{2\sqrt{2\pi(N-1)}} . \tag{18.1}$$

P declines as N increases, and as p diverts from $\frac{1}{2}$.[1] Even when $p = \frac{1}{2}$, however, the probability that a single vote will decide the election is but .00006, when there are 100,000,000 voters. If there were some cost, C, to voting, then the expected benefits from one's preferred candidate's victory would have to be large indeed to make the voter's calculus produce an expected utility gain from voting $(PB - C > 0)$.

Several people have noted that the probability of being run over by a car going to or returning from the polls is similar to the probability of casting the decisive vote.[2] If being run over is worse than having one's preferred candidate lose, then this potential cost of voting alone would exceed the potential gain, and no rational self-interested individual would ever vote. But millions do, and thus the paradox.

If voting cannot be explained as a rational, self-interested act, then it must either be irrational or not self-interested. We shall argue below that it is the former, but first we examine three attempts to reconcile it with the rationality postulate, and then arguments that voting is an ethical, altruistic, selfless act.

---

1. Owen and Grofman (1984) derive the following formula for the probability that a voter's vote breaks a tie when N is odd

$$P_{OG} = \frac{2e^{-2(N-1)(p-1/2)^2}}{\sqrt{2\pi(N-1)}} .$$

Now P_1 is simply the probability that N will be odd (.5) times P_{OG}, and P_2 is the same. Thus, $P \approx \frac{1}{2}P_{OG} + \frac{1}{4}P_{OG}$, which is the formula in the text. See also Beck (1975), Margolis (1977), Mayer and Good (1975).

2. B. F. Skinner (1948, p. 265) appears to be the first to have used the probability of an auto accident as a foil to puncture the rational voter hypothesis, writing some nine years before Downs, cited in Goodin and Roberts (1975). Meehl (1977) also uses it.

2.   A taste for voting

One way to reconcile voter rationality with the act of voting is to posit the existence of benefits stemming from the act itself, but not dependent on the consequence of the act, that is, not depending on whether the vote is decisive. Individuals may have a patriotic or civic itch, and voting helps scratch that itch, yielding benefits (utility) D.[3] Thus, a person votes if $PB + D - C > 0$. With PB tiny, the act of voting is explained by the private gains (psychic income) from the act of voting itself, D, exceeding the personal costs of going to the polls, C. Voting is not undertaken as an instrumental act to determine the winning candidate, but as a private, or symbolic act from which satisfaction is derived independent of the outcome of the election.

This modification of the rational voter hypothesis does reconcile the act of voting with individual rationality, but does so by robbing the rational, self-interest hypothesis of its predictive power. Any hypothesis can be reconciled with any conflicting piece of evidence with the addition of the appropriate auxiliary hypothesis. If I find that the quantity of Mercedes autos demanded increases following an increase in their price, I need not reject the law of demand, I need only set it aside, in this case by assuming a taste for "snob appeal." But in so doing I weaken the law of demand, as a hypothesis let alone as a law, unless I have a tight logical argument for predicting this taste for snob appeal.

So it is with rescuing the rational, self-interested voter hypothesis by assuming a taste for civic duty. If this taste explains the act of voting, what else might it explain? If the voter is carried to the polls by a sense of civic duty, what motivation guides her actions once there? Does she vote for the candidate, whose policies advance the voter's narrow interests, or does her sense of civic duty lead her to vote for the candidate, whose victory is most beneficial to the general, public interest? If voters can be moved by civic duty, why not politicians and bureaucrats? Without a theory explaining the origin, strength, and extent of an individual's sense of civic duty, merely postulating a sense of civic duty "saves" rational egoism by destroying its predictive content.

3.   Voting as a game of cat and mouse

If each rational voter were to decide not to vote because her vote has too small of a chance of affecting the outcome, and all voters were rational, no one would vote. But then any one voter could determine the outcome of the

3. See Riker and Ordeshook (1968). Tullock (1967a, p. 110) described these personal, psychic gains from voting as a negative cost, C.

election by voting. Whether it is in fact rational for an individual to abstain depends upon whether other voters are abstaining. The greater the number of other voters I expect will rationally abstain, the more rational it is for me to vote. The result is an n-person, noncooperative game, in which each person's strategy, to vote or to abstain, is dependent on her expectations with regard to the other voters' decisions. Under some assumptions, the solutions to this game involve positive numbers of individuals voting (Ledyard, 1981, 1984; Palfrey and Rosenthal, 1983). But when individuals are uncertain about the costs of voting of other citizens and the size of the electorate is large, a rational individual votes only if the psychic benefits from voting exceed the costs (Palfrey and Rosenthal, 1985). This effort to rescue the rational voter hypothesis by resorting to game theory does not succeed. Let us examine another.

4.   *The rational voter as minimax-regret strategist*

In a much discussed article, John Ferejohn and Morris Fiorina (1974, p. 525) set out "to show one means of rescuing rational choice theorists from this embarrassing predicament" of the voting paradox. They recognize that the Achilles' heel of rationality is the tiny but positive probability that a vote will change the outcome of an election. They then posit that voters may be using a decision strategy that does not weigh each possible event by its probability, but rather gives all events equal weight, like the minimax-regret strategy. Under this decision rule, one calculates not the actual payoff for each strategy choice and state-of-the-world combination, but the regret, that is, the loss one would experience in choosing the given strategy should this state of the world occur, as opposed to the best alternative strategy under this state of the world. One then chooses the action that minimizes the regret. Voting for one's second choice is not surprisingly a dominated strategy. So the decision reduces to whether to vote for one's first choice or to abstain. There are essentially two relevant states of the world to consider: S_I, the outcome of the election, is independent of whether one votes; S_D, by voting the individual, produces the victory of one's preferred candidate by either breaking a tie or forcing a runoff, which the candidate wins. If one votes and the outcome is independent of one's vote, one regrets voting because one has incurred C to no avail (see Matrix 18.1, cell a). If the outcome is independent of one's vote and one abstains, one has no regrets (b); the same is true if one votes and casts the decisive vote (c). If the net gains from having one's candidate's victory (B) are at least double the costs of voting, C, then one's maximum regret occurs when one abstains and one's vote would have been decisive (d). The minimax-regret strategy is to vote.

The minimax-regret strategy is extremely conservative and leads to rather

Matrix 18.1. *Minimax-regret options*

		States	
		S_I	S_D
Strategies	Vote	(a) C	(c) 0
	Abstain	(b) 0	(d) B − C

bizarre behavior when applied to other decisions or even when extended within the voting context, as several critics have stressed.[4] Suppose, for example, that a voter is indifferent between the Republican and Democratic candidates. His minimax-regret strategy is then to abstain. Suppose now that the Nazi Party enters a candidate. Now the minimax-regret criterion forces the voter to the polls to avoid the possible, although highly unlikely, event that the Nazi candidate will win, *and will do so by a single vote.*

Few situations in everyday life in which individuals routinely employ minimax-regret strategies come to mind. Indeed, it is easier to think of examples where people exhibit the reverse tendency. Losing one's home and possessions must be a disaster at least comparable to having one's second choice for president win, and probably occurs with no less probability than that one's vote decides an election. Yet most people do not protect themselves against losses from floods even when insurance is sold at rates below actuarial value (Kunreuther et al., 1978). Is it reasonable to assume that the same person is a risk taker with respect to home and personal possessions but becomes minimax-regret conservative when deciding whether or not to vote?

Ferejohn and Fiorina seem to think so. They cite Levine and Plott (1977) in support of the "possibility that individuals act as if they vary their decision rules in response to the decision context" (1975, p. 921). People also vote. The issue is not whether these things happen, but whether they can be explained and predicted using the rational egoism postulate. If individuals commonly switch from extremely risk-averse strategies to risk-taking strategies, how are we to predict their behavior? What theory tells us which situations elicit which strategy? To rationalize a given action ex post as possibly consistent with the use of a particular decision strategy in this situation does not suffice to justify the rational egoism postulate as the foundation of a *general* behavioral theory, unless one has a theory to predict which decision strategies are chosen in which situations.

4. Beck (1975), Goodin and Roberts (1975), Mayer and Good (1975), and Meehl (1977).

B.   The rational voter hypothesis: the evidence

Ferejohn and Fiorina's major defense of their thesis rests upon empirical evidence. The key determinant of voter turnout under the minimax-regret hypothesis is $B - C$. The costs of voting are difficult to define and measure, but data on the perceived differential between candidates are gathered in surveys like those conducted by the University of Michigan Survey Research Center. These may be used as a measure of B. B also figures prominently in the Downsian expected utility model, as does P. Ferejohn and Fiorina's test of the minimax-regret hypothesis is to see whether differences in B and P are significantly related to voter abstentions. Under minimax-regret, only B should be related to voter turnout; the probability of the voter being decisive does not matter. Under Downsian expected utility maximization, both B and P should be related. The choice between the hypotheses rests on whether, P, the probability that a voter's vote will be decisive is systematically related to abstentions.

Examining pre- and postelection survey results for 1952, 1956, 1960, and 1964, they find the minimax-regret hypothesis supported five times, the Downsian hypothesis only once (1975). In their sample, about 90 percent of the respondents claimed to have voted. This is a much higher percentage than is typical of the United States and suggests a nonrandom sample or misrepresentation of voter behavior. More important, the variation in abstention rates is likely to be too small to allow one to run tests against other variables. A look at some additional evidence is warranted.

One of the first papers to present empirical evidence in support of the full rational voter hypothesis is by Riker and Ordeshook (1968), from which we have taken the $R = PB + D - C$ formulation of this hypothesis. Riker and Ordeshook examine 4,294 responses to the 1952, 1956, and 1960 prepresidential SRC questionnaires. They cross-tabulate responses to see whether P, B, and D have a significant impact on the probability of an individual's voting. They find that when one holds the levels of the other two variables fixed, P, B, and D all tend to have a significant impact on the probability of voting in the way that the rational voter hypothesis predicts. Thus, the Riker–Ordeshook results support both the instrumental-vote portion of the rational voter hypothesis (PB matters), as well as the tastes (D) matter portion.

Although P, B, and D all seem related to voter behavior in the manner that the rational voter hypothesis predicts, the quantitative importance of D in the Riker–Ordeshook data set is much greater than that of either P or B. The difference in probability of voting between those with high P (i.e., those who thought the election would be close) and those with low P, ignoring both B and D, is 78 percent versus 72 percent. Eighty-two percent of those with high values for B voted, as opposed to 66 percent of those with low Bs. However,

87 percent of those with high Ds voted against only 51 percent of those with low Ds. D was operationalized by Riker and Ordeshook through questions related to citizen duty. Thus, a high sense of citizen duty has a much larger quantitative impact on voter turnout, over a low sense of citizen duty, than do high values of either P or B over low values of these variables. Both parts of the rational voter hypothesis are supported in the Riker–Ordeshook study, but the tastes component has the greatest quantitative impact.

Among the most ambitious tests of the rational voter hypothesis in terms of both sample size and number of variables included is that of Orley Ashenfelter and Stanley Kelley, Jr. (1975). They examine the responses of 1893 individuals surveyed by the Survey Research Center (SRC) in connection with the 1960 and 1972 presidential elections. They relate individual answers to the question, "Did you vote?" to a large set of variables grouped under the headings

1. Personal characteristics
2. Cost variables
3. Strategic value of voting
4. Interest in campaign
5. Obligation toward voting.

These variables can be related to the rational voter hypothesis

$$R = PB + D - C,$$

with C obviously related to group 2 variables; P and B both related to 3; B and possibly D related to 4; and D and 5 related. The personal characteristics of each individual (education, income, age, etc.) could be related to any one of the components of R, and do not clearly discriminate among the hypotheses.

Ashenfelter and Kelley's results give mixed support for the rational voter hypothesis. Several measures of the cost of voting are statistically significant and of the right sign. Most important among these were the existence of a poll tax and literacy tests, legal in 1960 but abolished by 1972. A six-dollar poll tax in 1960 reduced the probability of an individual voting by 42 percent (Ashenfelter and Kelley, Jr., 1975, p. 708). This result gives one a rough idea of what the distribution of $PB + D$ is for a large fraction of voters. Several of the other variables introduced as proxies for the costs of voting do not perform well, although multicollinearity among the cost variables is a problem.

Turning to proxies for P and B, Ashenfelter and Kelley (1975, p. 717) did not find that a voter's perception of whether the race is close or not had a statistically significant relationship to the probability of voting. On the other hand, this proxy for P was of the correct sign (t value of 1.4 in the pooled regression), and the difference in the percentage of voters who thought the 1972 Nixon landslide would be close and the percentage that thought the

Nixon–Kennedy 1960 election would be close was so great (10 percent versus 60 percent), that the difference in the levels for this variable between 1960 and 1972 is enough to explain 40 percent of the change in turnout between 1960 and 1972 (pp. 720–1). Both of these findings are of considerable importance in explaining an otherwise perplexing inconsistency in the literature on voter participation, and we shall return to them.

Of the variables that might measure an individual's perception of the differences between the candidates, B, the answer to the question, "How do you think you will vote?" proved to have the most explanatory power. If, at the time of the survey, an individual was undecided as to how she would vote, there was a 40 percent lower probability that this individual would vote at all (p. 717). If an individual's indecision arises because of a small perceived difference between the two candidates, a small B, then this result offers considerable support for the rational voter hypothesis. But if indecision concerning how one will vote stems from indecision over whether one will vote – that is, one is not interested in the election – then the impact of the finding is less clear. Some people may simply prefer to remain aloof from the political process.

Individuals who felt a "strong obligation" to vote did so with a 30 percent higher probability, those with a "very strong obligation" voted 38 percent more often (pp. 719–20). These variables, measuring a sense of obligation to vote, had substantial explanatory power. Their impressive performance underlines the importance of the D term in the rational voter's calculus.

Ashenfelter and Kelley (1975, p. 724) conclude, "The theory of voting that is best supported by our results is that which posits a sense of duty or obligation as the primary motivation for voting. The variables with the greatest quantitative impact on voting are education, indecision, the dummy variables representing the sense of an obligation to vote, and certain cost variables." This study offers rather strong support for the Tullock–Riker–Ordeshook interpretation of rational voting, which sees the D and C terms in the $BP + D - C$ equation as dominating the voting decision. As noted earlier, indecision might arise from a small B term, but indecision might also detract from the D term, if the sense of obligation to vote is weakened by not knowing who to vote for. Education should ceteris paribus reduce the importance of the BP term, since higher education levels should make one less susceptible to the misconception that one's vote makes a difference (that P is large). Education's positive impact on voting must then come through the D and C terms. We shall consider education's role in explaining voting again.

A very similar pattern of results appears in Morris Silver's (1973) analysis of 959 SRC questionnaires from the 1960 election survey. Several cost variables are significant, as are interest in the campaign, sense of citizen duty, and education. Whether the individual thinks the election will be close or not did not have a significant impact on the probability of voting. Thus, the only support for the *BP* portion of the rational voter hypothesis in Silver's results comes through the "interest in the campaign" responses, if one assumes that these measure *B*, although Silver regards them as an index of *D*.

The same general picture of the voter's decision reappears in the analysis of survey results for some 2,500 voters in the 1968 presidential election using Opinion Research Corporation and SRC data by Brody and Page (1973). In explaining abstentions they focus upon the importance of indifference – the perceived difference between candidates, and alienation – the difference between a voter's position and her preferred candidate's position. Abstentions do increase with both indifference and alienation, but not by enough to confirm a purely instrumentalist interpretation of the act of voting. Forty-three percent of the 201 individuals who saw no difference between the candidates ($B = 0$) voted nonetheless. Forty-four percent of the 174, who were both alienated and indifferent, chose to vote (Brody and Page, 1973, p. 6). For these voters and probably for many of the others, the *D* and *C* terms of *R* must explain the decision to vote.

A fifth test of the rational voter hypothesis using SRC data, although explicitly built on Downs's formulation, is more difficult to interpret. Frohlich et al. (1978) construct proxies for *B*, *P*, and *D* from the SRC questions by combining various questions using different weights. They then make various assumptions about the distribution of the unknown *C* variable, and use combinations of *B*, *P*, *D*, and C^5 to predict both turnout and choice of candidate for the 1964 presidential election. The assumption that *C* is lognormally distributed works best, and with this assumption they can predict turnout with an R^2 of .847.[6] But Frohlich et al. do not report their results in such a way to allow one to gauge the relative importance of *BP*, *D*, and *C* in explaining turnout, although the assumption concerning the distribution of *C* is important. However, the individual's opinion as to the efficacy of her vote (the proxy for *P*) does appear important, suggesting that *P* plays a bigger role in explaining turnout in the study by Frohlich et al. than it did in those of Ferejohn and Fiorina, and Ashenfelter and Kelley.

The five preceding studies relate the characteristics and opinions of an individual voter to that person's decision to vote. A second set of studies tests the rational voter hypothesis by relating aggregate figures on voter turnout, at, say, the state level, to characteristics of the population of voters in that state. These studies have basically tested to see whether *P*, the probability that a voter's vote changes the outcome, has a significant impact on voter turnouts.

---

5. They formulate the $R = BP + D - C$ equation slightly differently, but their formulation and the one used here are equivalent.
6. As with the Ferejohn and Fiorina SRC sample, a whopping 90.9 percent of the subjects reported having voted, raising issues of representativeness or misrepresentation.

They have done so, by regressing turnout figures on p, the expected vote of the leading candidate, and N the size of the jurisdiction. Reference to the formula for P

$$P = \frac{3e^{-2(N-1)(p-\frac{1}{2})^2}}{2\sqrt{2\pi(N-1)}}$$

indicates that both p and N are inversely related to P in a nonlinear way. Table 18.1 summarizes the results of 11 studies, abstracting from the functional form used to introduce p and N. Each study differs from the others with respect to choice of functional form and choice of other variables included. But we focus here on just p and N. A negative coefficient for each variable is interpreted as being consistent with what the rational voter hypothesis predicts. Only signs and significance levels are given in the table. Cebula and Murphy (1980) attempt an ex ante measure of p by limiting their sample to states with a Democratic majority in the lower house and estimating p as the fraction of the house that is Democratic. Foster's (1984) last set of results employs a similar ex ante measure of p, but for both Republican and Democratic majorities. All other studies assume rational expectations on the part of voters and measure p by the actual split in the vote between the candidates on election day.

Considering first the studies in the upper half of the table, we observe that both p and N generally are of the correct sign and more often than not have statistically significant coefficients. From these studies one is inclined to conclude that voter turnouts are positively related to the probability of a single vote's being decisive.

The bottom half of the table summarizes the results of Carroll Foster's (1984) reestimation of the models from four studies as well as the estimates for his own model using data for the 1968, 1972, 1976, and 1980 presidential elections. Instability in the coefficient estimates for cross sections precluded pooling the data to reestimate the Barzel–Silberberg and Kau–Rubin models, so the results for the individual cross sections are presented. In general, voter turnouts are not related to p or N in Foster's retesting of the rational voter hypothesis. Outside of the Nixon landslide in 1972, p does quite badly. N performs only moderately more consistently.

Foster (1984, p. 688) concludes "that the perceived probability of a tied election at the state level is not a powerful or reliable factor in explaining across-state variation in voter participation rates in presidential elections." This conclusion seems justified. But p and N have the predicted sign more often than not, and when their coefficients are significant they are, with but one exception, of the correct sign. Here the Ashenfelter–Kelley results with regard to voter perceptions of the closeness of an election should be recalled. They found that there was a statistically weak and quantitatively small posi-

Table 18.1. *Impact of the probability of a vote's being decisive on voter turnouts*

Study	Sample (time period)	p	N
Barzel and Silberg (1973)	122 gubernatorial elections, 1962, 1964, 1966, 1968	−(.01)	−INS
Silberman and Durden (1975)	400 congressional districts, 1962	−(.01)	−(.01)
Tollison, Crain, and Paulter (1975)	29 gubernatorial elections, 1970	−(.10)	+INS
Kau and Rubin (1976)	50 states, 1972 presidential	+INS	−(.01)
Settle and Abrams (1976)	26 national presidential elections, 1868–1972, omitting 1944	−(.01)	
Crain and Deaton (1977)	50 states, 1972 presidential	−(.01)	−INS
Cebula and Murphy (1980)	35 states, 1976 presidential	−(0.1)[a]	
Chapman and Palda (1983)	Electoral districts in 5 Canadian provinces, 1972–8	−(.05)[b]	
Patterson and Caldeira (1983)	46 states, 1978, 1980 gubernatorial elections	−(.05)	
Darvish and Rosenberg (1988)	108 municipalities in Israel, 1978, 1983	−(.01)	
Foster (1984) Barzel–Silberg	50 states,		
	1968 presidential	+(.05)	+INS
	1972 presidential	−(.01)	−INS
	1976 presidential	−INS	−INS
	1980 presidential	+INS	−INS
Foster (1984) Kau–Rubin	50 states,		
	1968 presidential	+(.05)	−INS
	1972 presidential	−(.01)	−INS
	1976 presidential	+INS	+INS
	1980 presidential	−INS	−INS

(*continued*)

Table 18.1. (*cont.*)

Study	Sample (time period)	p	N
Foster (1984)			
Silberman–Durden	200 states pooled, 1968, 1972, 1976, 1980 presidential	−INS	−(.10)
Foster (1984)			
Crain–Deaton	200 states pooled, 1968, 1972, 1976, 1980 presidential	−INS	−(.01)
Foster (1984)			
Wolfgram–Foster	200 states pooled, 1968, 1972, 1976, 1980 presidential	−(.10)[a]	−INS

Note: p = expected (actual) percentage of vote for leading candidate; N = size of jurisdiction.
[a]Proxy for ex ante measure of closeness used, proportion of Democrats in the lower house for all states with more than 50 percent Democratic representation.
[b]Significant in 6 of 10 provincial elections, of wrong sign and insignificant in 3 of 10.

tive effect on the chances of an individual voting if the individual thought that the election was close. Changes in voter perception of the closeness of an election should vary considerably from one election to another. A preelection Gallup poll projection of a candidate's getting 60 percent of the vote makes the candidate's victory a virtual certainty. Few would bet against a candidate with preelection poll percentages in the 54 to 56 range. The difference in prior probabilities between an election that is "too close to call," like the 1960 Kennedy–Nixon contest and the 1972 Nixon landslide over McGovern, is the difference between a coin flip and a sure bet. With these shifts in odds, even if only some voters are weakly influenced by changes in their perception of the closeness of the contest, large changes in turnout may ensue. This consideration may explain why the closeness of the race in each state seems to have had a significant impact on voter turnouts in Nixon's 1972 landslide win (Crain and Deaton, 1977; Foster–Barzel–Silberberg, and Foster–Kau–Rubin, 1984), and why efficacy affected voter turnouts in Johnson's 1964 landslide (Frohlich et al., 1978).

In some ways the weak performance of differences in P in explaining voter turnouts supports the overall view of the voter as a rational egoist more than it contradicts this image. Even when the probability of each voter's voting for one of the candidates is .5, the probability of a single vote being decisive in a polity of 100,000,000 is only .00006. As Riker and Ordeshook (1968) note regarding their finding that voter turnout is responsive to changes in P, this

finding implies an unusually elastic response by voters to changes in probabilities. If drivers responded to changes in the probability of accidents to the
same degree, heavy rain would find the roads abandoned. Riker and Ordeshook (1968, pp. 38–9) suggest that the highly elastic response of voters to
changes in P may be due to the persuasive impact of television and radio
announcements claiming that "your vote counts." Consistent with this explanation for the importance of *perceived* closeness of the election are the results
of Tollison et al. (1975). They found an enhanced impact for the closeness
variable in states with relatively large newspaper circulation. "Information
concerning the expected outcome [tends] to make more people vote in close
races" (p. 45). But if voters are so easily misled concerning the importance of
their vote, one's confidence in the intelligence of the rational voter is weakened. Although naïveté and rationality are not strictly opposites, the existence
of the former does undermine the importance of the rationality assumption
somewhat.

The results reviewed here suggest that the relationship between changes in
P and voter abstentions is weaker than Riker and Ordeshook conclude. If so,
then voters are less naive about their ability to change the outcome of the
election, and thus behave in what seems like a more sophisticatedly rational
way. But in so doing they confirm the more cynical interpretation of voter
rationality, that is, the noninstrumentalist view that voting is determined
solely by its entertainment-psychic income value (D), and private costs (C).
This interpretation raises the issue, in deriving a theory of voting, of the
determinants of D and C.

Whence springs a sense of civic duty, and how does one predict its variability across individuals and over time? We now examine two answers to this
question.

C.   The ethical voter hypothesis

Unless one escapes the voting paradox in the tautological way of postulating a
taste for (psychic income from) voting (the D term), one must reject the postulate either that voters are rational or that they act in their (narrowly defined)
self-interest. One group of scholars has chosen the second alternative.[7] They
view the voter as having two sets of preferences, an ethical set and a selfish
set. The latter includes only one's own utility, the former includes the utilities
of others, or one's perception thereof. In some situations – for example, the
consumer in the marketplace – one uses one's selfish preferences to decide.

7. See Goodin and Roberts (1975), Margolis (1982b), and Etzioni (1986). Harsanyi's (1955)
   approach is the same, although he does not discuss the act of voting. See also Arrow's (1963,
   pp. 81–91) discussion.

One maximizes one's utility as conventionally defined. In others, one employs one's ethical preferences. Voting is assumed to be one of those situations in which one's ethical preferences govern. Voting is presumed to improve the welfare of others by, say, improving the quality of the outcomes of the political process (better outcomes arise when all vote), or by helping to maintain democratic institutions. The D term in $R = PB + D - C$ is essentially the effect of one's vote on the welfare of all others.[8]

This Jekyll and Hyde view of man's nature has a long and distinguished ancestry. The importance of "a sense of civic duty" in explaining voting resonates with this "ethical voter" hypothesis. But the ethical voter hypothesis suffers from the same deficiency as the "taste for participation" as an explanation for voting. Instead of providing us with a hypothesis with which we can develop a theory of voting and perhaps of other cooperative-social behavior, it provides an ex post rationalization for the act. It provides the end for a story about voting, not the beginning for a behavioral theory of voting.

The kind of ethical-selfish dichotomy presumed in the ethical theory of voting might be operationalized as a predictive theory by assuming that each individual i maximizes an objective function of the following form:[9]

$$O_i = U_i + \theta \sum_{j \neq i} U_j. \tag{18.2}$$

A purely selfish voter would set $\theta = 0$; a fully altruistic voter would set $\theta = 1$, as in Harsanyi (1955). In either case, the individual is behaving rationally in the sense of maximizing an objective function. In either case, the analyst benefits from the most important advantage of the rationality assumption, clear predictions about human behavior, in this case in the form of first-order conditions to the maximization of (18.2) with θ equal to either zero or one. But the first-order conditions for (18.2) differ, in general, if one sets $\theta = 0$, or $\theta = 1$. How does one know which assumption to make? From the SRC surveys it would appear that some individuals think of voting as a selfish act ($\theta = 0$), others as an ethical one ($\theta = 1$). How does one differentiate between selfish and ethical voters? Moreover, in situations where the ethical decision variable is continuous (e.g., how much to contribute voluntarily to the provision of a public good), rather than 0, 1, as with voting, it appears that some θ less than 1 but greater than 0 is required to make an individual's observed behavior consistent with the maximization of (18.2). How can one predict when an individual will behave selfishly and when ethically, or the degree to which one's ethical preferences govern one's actions, when ethical behavior is not a simple either-or decision? To make these predictions, one needs to do

8. This is the way Frohlich et al. describe the term in their Downsian test also.
9. This approach is elaborated upon in Mueller (1986a).

more than merely posit the existence of ethical preferences; one needs a theory of how ethical preferences are formed, what determines their strength, what triggers their use. One needs a theory of learning, which probably must be found in the areas of psychology of sociology.

D.   Ethical preferences as selfish behavior

Behavioral psychology seems to offer the best description of the learning process.[10] Actions followed by rewards increase in frequency. Actions followed by punishment decline in frequency. Man learns to avoid doing that which brings about pain, and to do that which produces pleasure. When one observes how man learns, it is difficult to reject the postulate that man is innately a selfish animal. The same principles appear to describe the learning processes of all animals. Man differs from other animals not in how he learns but in what he learns. Man is capable of learning far more complex behavioral patterns than are other creatures.

Ethical behavior is learned. Much of this learning takes place when we are children. When we commit acts that harm others we are punished by our parents, teachers, and other adult supervisors. Actions that benefit others are rewarded. Ethical behavior patterns learned as children can be maintained at high frequency levels through adulthood by only occasional positive and negative reinforcement.[11] What we normally describe as ethical behavior is inherently no more or less selfish than what we call selfish behavior. It is a conditioned response to certain stimuli governed by past reinforcement experience.

There are several advantages to using behavioral psychology to explain ethical behavior. First, it allows us to work with a single conceptualization of man, a conceptualization consistent with the selfish-egoism postulate underlying both economics and public choice. Second, it allows us to develop a purely positive theory of behavior, free from the normative prescripts that often accompany the Jekyll and Hyde view of man. Third, it gives us some insight into what variables might explain why some individuals behave in what is commonly described as an ethical manner, and some do not. Home environment during childhood, educational experience, religion, community stability, and any other factors that might affect an individual's ethical learning experience become possible candidates as explanatory variables in a positive theory of ethical behavior. Thus, ethical behavior like voting can be explained if one retains the self-interest assumption of public choice and drops, or at least relaxes, the rationality assumption.

10. For reviews of the basic principles of behavioral psychology, see Notterman (1970), and Schwartz and Lacey (1982, chs. 1–6).
11. Ibid.

Equation (18.2) can be used to describe behavior in situations involving ethical choices, if one assumes that individuals act *as if* they were maximizing (18.2), with some θ not necessarily equal to zero or one. The argument is similar to Alchian's (1950) argument that competition eliminates less profitable firms, leaving only the most profitable, whose actions resemble those they would have chosen had they consciously been maximizing profit even when they were not. It is in society's collective interest in certain contexts to establish institutions that condition people to behave as if they were maximizing (18.2) with $\theta = 1$. Although this degree of cooperative behavior is seldom achieved, the conditioning process is usually successful in eliciting some degree of cooperation. Observed behavior thus resembles what one would expect if individuals consciously maximized (18.2) with some $\theta > 0$, even though (because) individual behavior is governed by social conditioning.[12] Under this interpretation θ is a behavioral parameter to be explained by the individual's or group's conditioning history, not a choice variable set equal to zero or one depending on whether the individual has chosen today to be Hyde or Jekyll.

E.   The selfish voter

Normally, when we model individual behavior, an individual's past history plays no part in the analysis. Sunk costs are sunk, bygones are bygones, and all that matters are the future consequences of an individual's action. With respect to voting, this conceptualization of the voting act boils the number of relevant variables down to three: the benefits from the preferred candidate's victory, B; the probability that one's vote will bring about this victory, P; and the costs of getting to the polls, C.

Modeling individual behavior as conditioned by past learning shifts one's attention from the future payoffs from different actions to the past history of the individual. The list of potential explanatory variables is expanded considerably.

We have already made the point that years of education might, if voters were purely rational and egoistic, be expected to be negatively related to the probability of voting. The uneducated might be duped by television advertisements to believe their vote would count, but the more educated should remain rationally cynical regarding the efficacy of their vote.

One learns more than probability theory in school, however. One also

---

12. Darwinian selection will play a role in determining which social institutions survive or even which social groups. If the collective gains from cooperation are large, those groups that are more successful at eliciting cooperative behavior (inducing individuals to behave as if $\theta = 1$) will have higher survival chances. Evolutionary forces may also select gene structures more conducive to the teaching and learning of cooperative behavior, when cooperation raises individual survival chances.

learns to cooperate. Number of years of successfully completed schooling measures the amount and strength of conditioning in the numerous cooperative games played in a school environment. By the time one graduates one has been rewarded again and again for going by the rules, and doing what is expected, and one has usually been punished on those occasions when one has broken the rules. One expects those with more education to behave more cooperatively, to break fewer rules, be they driving laws or social mores, and to do more of what is expected of them as a citizen. Years of education have proven to be positively and significantly related to voter turnout in virtually every study of voter participation.[13]

Income is another variable which invariably picks up the wrong sign in explaining voter turnout from what a straightforward application of the rational egoism postulate would imply. The higher one's income, the higher the opportunity cost of time, and ceteris paribus the lower the probability that one goes to the polls.[14] Yet income is consistently, positively correlated with the probability of voting.[15]

Income, like a graduation certificate, is a mark of success at playing by certain rules of the societal game. (Of course, some individuals accumulate income by successfully breaking the rules, but I doubt that many of these persons are part of the SRC survey panels.) Individuals with high income are more likely to go by the rules, and to live within the social mores. Moreover, their high incomes are evidence that they have been rewarded for doing so, since money is society's chief token reinforcer. High-income individuals, like the highly educated, can be expected to break fewer rules and to behave in other socially cooperative ways, like voting.

There are other explanations for why income and education might be positively related to political participation, of course. For example, education may reduce the cost of gathering information about candidates and thus be positively related to voting as predicted by the rational voter model.[16] Without

13. Campbell et al. (1964, pp. 251–4), Milbrath (1965), Kelley, Ayres, and Bowen (1967), Verba and Nie (1972, pp. 95–101), Silver (1973), Brody and Page (1973), Ashenfelter and Kelley (1975), and Chapman and Palda (1983).

 Education appears to have a strong positive effect on voting in the Patterson and Caldeira (1983) study, also, when correlated separately with voting. Its failure to have a significant impact when income is included is probably due to multicollinearity, a problem observed in several studies.

14. See discussion of Russell, Fraser, and Frey (1972), and Tollison and Willett (1973).

15. Dahl (1961) and Lane (1966) as cited by Frey (1971), Milbrath (1965), Kelley et al. (1967), Dennis (1970), Verba and Nie (1972, pp. 95–101), Silver (1973), Silberman and Durden (1975), Ashenfelter and Kelley (1975), Crain and Deaton (1977), and Foster (1984).

 An important exception is Chapman and Palda (1983), the only study to my knowledge to get a significant negative coefficient, as predicted by the rational voter hypothesis.

16. See in particular Frey (1971), and ensuing interchange among Russell (1972), Fraser (1972), Frey (1972), Tollison and Willett (1973), and Chapman and Palda (1983).

denying the possible relevance of these explanations, I nevertheless favor starting from a behavioralist view toward voting and other forms of cooperative behavior, both because this approach offers a more natural explanation for why these and other background characteristics of the voter matter, and because this approach offers greater potential for developing additional hypotheses about individual behavior in situations like voting when narrowly self-interested behavior is inconsistent with the behavior that social conditioning dictates.

If education is positively related to voting because it reduces the costs of political participation, for example, one would expect a secular rise in participation rates since education levels have been rising. Yet since the early 1960s voter participation in the United States has declined steadily and dramatically. Abramson and Aldrich (1982) attribute at least two-thirds of this decline to two factors: (1) weakening voter identification with the political parties, and (2) declining beliefs in the responsiveness of government. Both of these factors may in turn be explained as the result of negative rewards from voting in presidential elections since 1960. In a normal presidential election, over half of the voters are rewarded for going to the polls in that this action is followed by their preferred candidate's victory. In this way, majority rule tends to sustain political participation. Since 1960, however, three presidents have been elected whose performance in office must have been a great disappointment to their supporters: Johnson because of Vietnam, Nixon because of Watergate, Carter because of an overall poor performance. Thus, voting for the winning candidate was punished, and this punishment may explain the drop in the frequency with which individuals go to the polls.

F.   Normative implications

All of the public choice literature as it pertains to the outcomes of committee voting or elections assumes that voters vote, whether sincerely or strategically, to attain that outcome promising them the highest benefits. All of public choice is based on the assumption that it is the attainment of B in the equation $R = PB + D - C$, which determines the way in which an individual votes.

The logical foundation for this assumption is significantly undermined in elections or committees in which the number of voters is large. P is then infinitesimal, the PB term vanishes, and considerations other than the instrumental value of the vote determine whether or not an individual votes, or at least they ought to if the individual is both rational and sufficiently intelligent to make a reasonable guess as to the magnitude of P.

The empirical literature reviewed here is reassuring with respect to both the intelligence and rationality of voters in that it indicates that P has a rather weak (statistically) and inconsistent relationship to the decision to vote. The primary explanation for why individuals vote comes from the D and C terms in R, as Downs (1957) and Tullock (1967a) first asserted. What then are the implications of this conclusion for the rest of the public choice literature that assumes voters are voting to maximize B? If PB does not explain why individuals vote, can B explain how they vote? If it does not, what does?

Brennan and Buchanan (1984) have posed these questions recently. They emphasize that the knowledge that one's vote has a negligible effect on the outcome of the election frees one to vote in ways inconsistent with one's own interest. One can vote in a totally whimsical fashion secure in the knowledge that the satisfaction of this whim through voting will not affect one's welfare in any other way.

Given the apparent importance of the D term in explaining why individuals vote, we need to draw out the implications of this "taste" variable for the question of how they vote. Do individuals who are motivated to vote because of D nevertheless vote to bring about some purely, selfishly determined B once they get to the polls, or do they perhaps give some weight to the impact of the outcomes on the welfare of others?

A few studies exist that examine the rationality of an individual's vote in improving the voter's narrowly defined self-interest. One of the easiest of these to interpret is Jeffrey W. Smith's (1975) analysis of voting in Oregon intermediate election districts. Voting takes place on whether the tax burdens of the districts should be equalized or not, with equalization raising the tax rates of some districts and lowering those of others. A simple application of the self-interest hypothesis implies a vote for equalization if it lowers one's taxes, against it if it raises them. The percentage favoring equalization was positively related to whether one gained from equalization, and was larger for large gains (Smith, 1975, p. 64).

Percentage of large[17] gainers favoring equalization	60.7
Percentage of small gainers favoring equalization	52.9
Percentage of small losers favoring equalization	46.1
Percentage of large losers favoring equalization	32.7

Bloom's (1979) analysis of voting on tax classification in Massachusetts provides similar support for a private interest explanation for voting. Caution should be exercised in generalizing from these results, however. In each case the voter is essentially confronted with the question of whether he prefers a higher or lower tax rate ceteris paribus. Such issues must raise the importance of private interest to its highest level. Yet in Smith's study over 40 percent of

17. Large gainers (losers) had their tax rates lowered (raised) by equalization by more than $1 per $1,000 of assessed value.

the population voted to raise their tax rates. Some factors beyond private interest must have influenced the voting of this substantial fraction of citizens.

A tougher test of the private interest explanation for voting comes on issues where the "public interest," that is, the welfare of others, is clearly affected by an issue as well as one's own welfare. Transfer payments present a good example. The narrow private interest assumption is that all recipients of transfers vote for them, all payers against them. This assumption underlies Meltzer and Richard's (1981) model of the growth of government using the median voter theorem, and Peltzman's (1980) explanation based on candidate competition. Gramlich and Rubinfeld (1982b) found from an examination of the responses of 2,001 households to a telephone survey in Michigan that transfer recipients (the aged, unemployed, and those on welfare) had only a moderately higher tendency to vote against a tax limitation proposal than nonrecipients. A more significant difference occurred for public employees; yet even here, 42 percent of those voting voted to *restrict* expenditures. In general, self-interest voting models have not done well in explaining voting on Proposition 13 issues (Lowery and Sigelman, 1981). Rather, votes for these proposals seem better treated as "symbolic acts" against "bad government" by citizens seeking improved government efficiency, the kinds of actions one might expect from a civic-minded voter.

The propensity to vote against the president or governing party when unemployment and inflation are high, and for them when macro conditions are good, also seems to be partly motivated out of concern for the interests of others. Even voters whose own personal economic position has not been or is not anticipated to be adversely affected by high unemployment vote in greater percentages against incumbents when unemployment is high (Fiorina, 1978, 1981; Kiewiet, 1981, 1983; Kirchgässner, 1985).

Sears et al. (1980) examined Center for Political Studies survey data for the 1976 presidential election. Their concern was "to assess the relative roles of self-interest and symbolic attitudes in producing policy attitudes and issue voting on four controversial policy areas (unemployment, national health insurance, busing of school children for racial integration, and crime)." They concluded that "in general, symbolic attitudes (liberalism-conservatism, party identification, and racial prejudice)[18] had strong effects, while self-interest

---

18. The importance of racial prejudice as a determinant of voter behavior (Sears, Hensler, and Speer, 1979) reinforces the case for using behavioral psychology to explain individual actions in social interaction situations, like prisoners' dilemmas, as opposed to a pure, rational-egoist-game-theoretic explanation, or a dual preference explanation.

The typical rational-egoist explanation for cooperative behavior, as in a prisoners' dilemma, is to posit an indefinite sequence, prisoners' dilemma supergame with each player playing the tit-for-tat strategy (Taylor, 1976; Axelrod, 1984). Such an explanation is consistent with $O_i = U_i + \theta \sum_{j \neq i} U_j$ over the supergame with $\theta = 1$.

had almost none" (p. 679). They also reviewed several studies reaching similar conclusions with respect to the relative importance of self-interest. Although survey results are susceptible to different interpretations, this literature strongly suggests that considerations beyond one's narrowly defined self-interest influence a citizen's vote, once they have gotten to the polling booth.

If individuals vote because they believe it is their civic duty to do so, because they believe the community functions better under strong democratic institutions, and their voting strengthens the community's democratic institutions, then voting can be regarded as a conditioned response of individuals to being in situations in which behavior benefiting others has been previously rewarded. When voting, individuals would then act as if they were maximizing (18.2) with $\theta > 0$. If the trip to the polls is best explained as an implicit maximization of (18.2) with $\theta > 0$, then it is tempting to assume that individuals behave analogously once inside the voting booth. Furthermore, it is tempting to characterize the objective function $O_i = U_i + \theta \sum_{j \neq i} U_j$ as i's (implicit) conceptualization of the public interest. That is, to interpret the literature reviewed above as suggesting that voters, who vote because of a sense of civic duty, vote according to a (conditioned) conceptualization of the public interest. If this interpretation were to be sustained, it would leave us with the following paradox. Suppose we take as given the assumption that candidates act as if maximizing their self-interest and not the public interest when campaigning and in office and do so by choosing policies to maximize their expected votes. If, however, voters vote for that candidate who comes closest to their conception of the public interest, then candidates will adopt policies consistent with a particular conception of the public interest, albeit not necessarily their own, personal conception. The public interest conception of politics is pulled from the ashes by the selfish, but ethically conditioned, voter's behavior (Tullock, 1984).

It is fitting that we close this chapter with a paradox.

Racial prejudice can be characterized as *as-if* maximization of O_i with $\theta < 0$ for some racial group. That racial prejudice is a conditioned behavioral response to certain stimuli is an easily defended proposition. But what kind of supergame and supergame strategies lead one to behave as if one maximizes O_i with negative θ?

Just as one could explain cooperative behavior as the maximization of a second set of ethical preferences, one could explain racial prejudice by assuming yet a third set of preferences. Now we have Mr. Hyde, Dr. Jekyll, and Simon Legree. To explain sexism, we assume a fourth set of preferences, and so on. However useful this approach is to characterizing different behavior in different situations, it does not take one anywhere in developing a theory to explain and predict behavior.

PART V

Normative public choice

CHAPTER 19

Real-valued social welfare functions

> The interest of the community then is – what? The sum of the interests of the
> several members who compose it.
>
> Jeremy Bentham

Whereas one can speak of *the* positive theory of public choice, based upon
economic man assumptions, one must think of normative *theories* of public
choice, for there are many views of what the goals of the state *should be,* and
how to achieve them. This potential multiplicity has been the focus of much
criticism by the positivists, who have argued for a "value-free" discipline. For
the bulk of economics, it might be legitimate to focus on explanation and
prediction, and leave to politics the explication of the goals of society. For the
study of politics itself, in toto, to take this position is less legitimate; thus the
interest in how the basic values of society are or can be expressed through the
political process. The challenge that normative theory faces is to develop
theorems about the expression and realization of values, based on generally
accepted postulates, in the same way that positive theory has developed
explanatory and predictive theorems from the postulates of rational egoistic
behavior. Part V reviews some efforts to take up this challenge.

A.   The Bergson–Samuelson social welfare function

The traditional means for representing the values of the community in economics is to use a social welfare function. The seminal paper on social
welfare functions is by Abram Bergson (1938), with the most significant
further explication by Paul Samuelson (1947, ch. 8). The social welfare
function can be written as follows:

$$W = W(z_1, z_2, \cdots, z_n),$$

where W is a real valued function of all variables, the z_i's, that might affect
social welfare. The z_i's and W are chosen to represent the ethical values of the
society, or of the individuals in it (Samuelson, 1947, p. 221). The objective is
to define a W and set of z_i's, and the constraints thereon, to yield meaningful
first- and second-order conditions for a maximum W. Although in principle
any variables might be included in the social welfare function that are related

to a society's well-being (e.g., crime statistics, weather data, years of schooling), economists have focused on economic variables. Thus, the social welfare function literature has adopted the same assumptions about consumers, production functions, and so on, that underlie the bulk of economics and public choice and has made these the focal point of its analysis.

The only value postulate upon which general agreement has been possible has been the Pareto postulate. This postulate suffices to bring about a set of *necessary* conditions for the maximization of W, which limit social choices to points along the generalized Pareto frontier. The proof is analogous to the demonstration that movement from off the contract curve to points on it can be Pareto improvements, and the necessary conditions are also analogous. With respect to production, these conditions are

$$\frac{\partial X_i / \partial V_{1i}}{\partial X_k / \partial V_{1k}} = \cdots = \frac{\partial X_i / \partial V_{mi}}{\partial X_k / \partial V_{mk}} = \frac{T_{xk}}{T_{xi}}, \tag{19.1}$$

where $\partial X_i / \partial V_{mi}$ is the marginal product of factor V_m in the production of output X_i, and T is the transformation function defined over all products and inputs (Samuelson, 1947, pp. 230–3).

> In words this takes the form: *productive factors are correctly allocated if the marginal productivity of a given factor in one line is to the marginal productivity of the same factor in a second line as the marginal productivity of any other factor in the first line is to its marginal productivity in the second line. The value of the common factor of proportionality can be shown to be equal to the marginal cost of the first good in terms of the (displaced amount of the) second good.* (Samuelson, 1947, p. 233; italics in original)

These conditions ensure that the economy is operating on the production possibility frontier. If these conditions were not met, it would be possible to transfer factors of production from one process to another and obtain more of one product without giving up any amounts of another. Such possibilities are ruled out by the Pareto principle.

The necessary conditions for consumption require that the marginal rate of substitution between any two private goods, i and j, be the same for all individuals consuming both goods

$$\frac{\partial U^1 / \partial X_i}{\partial U^1 / \partial X_j} = \frac{\partial U^2 / \partial X_i}{\partial U^2 / \partial X_j} = \cdots = \frac{\partial U^s / \partial X_i}{\partial U^s / \partial X_j}, \tag{19.2}$$

where $(\partial U^k / \partial X_i)/(\partial U^k / \partial X_j)$ is voter k's marginal rate of substitution between i and j (Samuelson, 1947, pp. 236–8). If (19.2) were not fulfilled, gains from trade would exist, again violating the Pareto postulate. Thus, choice is limited to points along the production possibility frontier – distributions of final products that bring about equality between the marginal rate of transformation of one product into another, and individual marginal rates of substitution (Samuelson, 1947, pp. 238–40).

Through the appropriate set of lump-sum taxes and transfers it is possible to sustain any point along the Pareto-possibility frontier as a competitive equilibrium. Thus, the normative issue to be resolved with the help of the social welfare function is which point along the generalized Pareto-possibility frontier should be chosen; what set of lump-sum taxes and subsidies is optimal. Both Bergson and Samuelson speak of solving this question with the help of a variant of the social welfare function in which the utility indexes of each individual are direct arguments in the welfare function

$$W = W(U^1, U^2, \ldots, U^s). \tag{19.3}$$

The issue then arises as to what form W takes, and what the characteristics of the individual utility functions are. In particular, one wants to know whether ordinal utility functions are sufficient, or whether cardinal utility indexes are required, and if the latter, whether interpersonal comparability is required as well. Since the evolution of utility theory over the last century has led to an almost unanimous rejection of cardinal, interpersonally comparable utility functions throughout much of economics, the hope is, of course, that they will not be needed here also. But, alas, that hope is in vain.

To see why this is so consider the following simple example: Six apples are to be divided between two individuals. On the basis of knowledge of the positions of the two individuals, their tastes for apples, and the ethical values and norms of the community, we believe that social welfare will be maximized with an even division of the apples. The question then is whether an ordinal representation of individuals 1 and 2's preferences can be constructed that always yields this result. Consider first the additive welfare function

$$W = U^1 + U^2. \tag{19.4}$$

We wish to select U^1 and U^2 such that

$$U^1(3) + U^2(3) > U^1(4) + U^2(2). \tag{19.5}$$

Equation (19.5) implies

$$U^2(3) - U^2(2) > U^1(4) - U^1(3). \tag{19.6}$$

If U^1 is an ordinal utility function, it can be transformed into an equivalent ordinal function by multiplying it by k. This transformation multiplies the right-hand side of (19.6) by k, however, and given any choice of U^2 that is bounded, a k can always be found that will reverse the inequality in (19.6), assuming $U^1(4) - U^1(3) > 0$.

The same holds if W is multiplicative. We then seek a U^1 and U^2 such that

$$U^1(3) \cdot U^2(3) > U^1(4) \cdot U^2(2), \tag{19.7}$$

which is equivalent to

$$\frac{U^2(3)}{U^2(2)} > \frac{U^1(4)}{U^1(3)} \; . \tag{19.8}$$

But, the ordinality of U^2 is not affected by adding a constant to it, so that (19.8) should also hold for

$$\frac{U^2(3) + k}{U^2(2) + k} > \frac{U^1(4)}{U^1(3)} \; . \tag{19.9}$$

But, the left-hand side of (19.9) tends toward one as k becomes large, and the inequality will thus reverse for some sufficiently large k, if individual 1 experiences some positive utility from consuming the fourth apple.

Other algebraic forms of W are possible, but it should be obvious that the pliability of an ordinal utility function is such that these, too, will be incapable of yielding a maximum at (3, 3) under every possible transformation that preserves the ordinality of the U's. The same arguments could be repeated with respect to a comparison of the distribution (4, 2) with (5, 1), and the distribution (5, 1) and (6, 0). The only way we will get a determinant outcome from a social welfare function whose arguments are ordinal utility indicators is to define it lexicographically, that is, to state that society prefers any increase in 1's utility, however small, to any increase in 2's utility, however large, and have this hold independently of the initial utility levels (distribution of income and goods). Which is to say, a social welfare function defined over ordinal utility indexes must be dictatorial if it is to select a single outcome consistently. This result was first established by Kemp and Ng (1976) and Parks (1976) with proofs that follow the Arrow impossibility proofs discussed in Chapter 20 (see also Hammond, 1976; Roberts, 1980c).

The very generality of the ordinal utility function, which makes it attractive for the analysis of *individual* decisions, makes it unsuitable for the analysis of *social* decisions, where trade-offs *across individuals* are envisaged. To make these trade-offs, *either* the relative positions of individuals must be compared directly in terms of the bundles of commodities or command over these commodities they enjoy using the ethical norms of the community, or, if utility indexes are employed, these must be defined in such a way as to make cardinal, interpersonal comparisons possible.

All of this would appear to have been known for some time. Although Bergson's initial exposition of the social welfare function seems to have led to some confusion over the need for cardinal utilities and interpersonal comparisons,[1] this need was emphasized by Lerner (1944, ch. 3) and clearly

---

1. At several places Bergson emphasizes that only ordinal utility indexes are required when deriving the optimality conditions for the social welfare function, and he states directly, "In my opinion the utility calculus introduced by the Cambridge economists [i.e., cardinality] is not a useful tool for welfare economics" (1938, p. 20). From these statements undoubtedly

addressed by Samuelson (1947, p. 244) in his initial exploration of the social welfare function:

> An infinity of such positions [points along the generalized contract locus] exists ranging from a situation in which all of the advantage is enjoyed by one individual, through some sort of compromise position, to one in which another individual has all the advantage. Without a well-defined *W* function, i.e., without assumptions concerning interpersonal comparisons of utility, it is impossible to decide which of these points is best. In terms of a given set of ethical notions which define a *Welfare function* the best point on the generalized contract locus can be determined, and only then. (Italics in original)

And we have Samuelson's (1967) subsequent proof that cardinality alone will not suffice; that is, cardinality *and* interpersonal comparability are required. The issue of whether the arguments of the social welfare function can be ordinal utility indexes would seem to be finally closed with the appearance of the papers by Kemp and Ng and Parks, were it not that these articles have sparked a controversy over precisely the cardinality–ordinality issue involving, perhaps surprisingly, Paul Samuelson (and indirectly Bergson also). Given the personages involved and the issues at debate, it is perhaps useful to pause and examine their arguments.

The main purpose of Samuelson's (1977) attack on the Kemp–Ng and Parks theorems is, as the title of his note states, to reaffirm the existence of "reasonable" Bergson–Samuelson social welfare functions. And the note is clearly provoked by the claims by Kemp and Ng and Parks of having established nonexistence or impossibility theorems. In criticizing their theorems, Samuelson focuses on the particular form of axiom Kemp and Ng use to capture ordinality in a Bergson–Samuelson social welfare function, an axiom

arises the view that Bergson claimed that welfare judgments could be based on ordinal utility indicators. Thus, for example, we have Arrow (1963, p. 110) stating, "It is the great merit of Bergson's 1938 paper to have carried the same principle [Leibnitz's principle of the identity of indiscernibles] into the analysis of social welfare. The social welfare function was to depend only on indifference maps; in other words, welfare judgments were to be based only on interpersonally observable behavior." But the clauses preceding and following "in other words" are not equivalent. And, in fact, Bergson goes on following his attack on the Cambridge economists' use of cardinal utility to argue not for the use of ordinal utility indexes or "interpersonally observable *behavior*," but for interpersonal comparisons of "relative economic positions" and "different commodities." Thus, in rejecting cardinal utility, Bergson opts not for a *W* defined over ordinal *U*s but for *W* defined over the actual physical units, that is, $W(z_1, z_2, \cdots, z_n)$. This leaves the status of *W* defined over individual, ordinal utility indexes indeterminate, at best.

In his discussion of Arrow's theorem in 1954, Bergson states quite clearly, to my mind, that interpersonal cardinal utility comparisons are required (see, in particular, his discussion of the distribution of wine and bread on pp. 244–5, and n. 8), but Arrow (1963, pp. 111–12) would not agree.

that implies that the social welfare function must be lexicographic. Samuelson is obviously correct in deriding an axiom that makes one individual an "ethical dictator," but his criticism of the theorems of Kemp, Ng, and Parks is misplaced. As Parks's proof most clearly shows, all Bergson–Samuelson social welfare functions based on ordinal preferences make one individual an ethical dictator.

A careful reading of the Kemp and Ng and Parks papers indicates that they do not claim the nonexistence of *all* reasonable Bergson–Samuelson social welfare functions, but only of those whose arguments are ordinal, individual utility indicators. Interestingly enough, Kemp and Ng (1976, p. 65) cite Samuelson himself as one of those holding "the apparently widely held belief that Bergson–Samuelson social welfare functions can be derived from individual ordinal utilities." They cite page 228 of the *Foundations,* the same page, incidentally, that Arrow (1963, pp. 10, 110, n. 49) cities, to indicate that the social welfare function *is* based on ordinal utilities. On this page appears the following:

> Of course, if utilities are to be added, one would have to catch hold of them first, but there is no need to add utilities. The cardinal utilities enter into the W function as independent variables if assumption (5) [individuals' preferences are to "count"] is made. But the W function is itself only ordinally determinable so that there are an infinity of equally good indicators of it which can be used. Thus, if one of these is written as
>
> $$W = F(U^1, U^2, \ldots),$$
>
> and if we were to change from one set of cardinal indexes of individual utility to another set $(V^1, V^2, \ldots)$, we should simply change the form of the function F so as to leave all social decisions invariant.

This passage clearly states that W is ordinal, and seems to imply that the individual utility arguments need not be interpersonally comparable. But the passage appears in the section in which the necessary conditions defining points *along the generalized Pareto-possibility frontier* are derived, and is obviously superseded, or amplified by the passage appearing later in the book on p. 244 and quoted above, where Samuelson makes clear that one *must* "catch hold" of the individual utilities and compare them if a single point out of the Pareto set is to be chosen. However, subsequent statements by Samuelson and his vigorous attack on the Kemp–Ng–Parks theorems would seem to imply that he believes that Bergson–Samuelson social welfare functions are well defined even when they have the ordinal utility functions of individuals as arguments.[2] The theorems of Kemp and Ng (1976), Parks (1976), Hammond (1976), Roberts (1980c), and still others deny this interpretation.

2. See Samuelson (1967, 1977, 1981). Samuelson also attributes this position to Bergson (Samuelson, 1967, pp. 44–5, 48–9), but see my discussion in n. 1.

Rather, one must conclude (1) that ordinal utility functions are sufficient as arguments of W when deriving the necessary conditions for a Pareto optimum, but (2) that cardinal, interpersonally comparable arguments are required to select a single, best point from among the infinity of Pareto optima.

B.   The form of the welfare function

Given that the Bergson–Samuelson SWF must be defined over cardinal, interpersonally comparable individual utility indexes or their equivalent, if a single socially preferred allocation is to be determined, the next questions to be answered are how these cardinal utilities are to be measured, and what form W is to take.

Let us set the question of measurability aside for a moment and consider the functional form of W. Two alternatives stand out, the additive and the multiplicative forms:

$$W = U^1 + U^2 + \cdots + U^s \tag{19.10}$$

$$W = U^1 \cdot U^2 \cdot \cdots \cdot U^s. \tag{19.11}$$

Both have a venerable position in welfare theory. The additive W can be traced back to the great utilitarian Jeremy Bentham, the multiplicative to the great game theorist John Nash (1950). If the social choice is defined as the outcome that maximizes W, then both satisfy the Pareto postulate. They also satisfy anonymity, in the sense that interchanging the utility indexes for individuals i and j does not alter the level of W. The choice between defining W by (19.10) or by (19.11) hinges on whether it should be the difference between i's utility levels in states G and M that are compared to the difference between j's utility levels in these two states, or whether it is the ratios that are compared. Although the distinction may seem trivial, its implications are not.

Let the entries in Matrix 19.1 represent cardinal, interpersonally comparable utility levels, that is, the utility levels achieved after allowing for diminishing marginal utility of income or consumption. Individual i's income in state G might then be 3, 4, or 10 times her income in M, but her achieved utility level in G is only double her utility in M. If a social choice had to be made between G and M, which state should be chosen? An additive W selects M, a multiplicative G.

Regardless of which choice the reader makes, it should be obvious that it is possible that other readers will make the opposite choice. To see this point more clearly, assume that i and j are really the same person at two different times in her life, and G and M are two alternative career paths. Path G is a job in government with somewhat lower income and utility at the start than later. Path M is a career in medicine with lower utility at the start than the govern-

Matrix 19.1.

	i	j
G	2	3
M	1	5

ment job, but much higher utility later. Given full knowledge of the utility payoffs to each career choice, it is conceivable that some rational, self-interested individuals favor the career in government, others medicine. If this is true, then some will probably prefer a multiplicative welfare function, others an additive.

As this example suggests, the choice of the multiplicative welfare function is likely to hinge on one's values with regard to how egalitarian the distribution of *utilities* ought to be. Recall that the entries in Matrix 19.1 are in utilities, not income. If the marginal utility of income declines, the difference in the utility levels i and j experience is smaller than the difference in their incomes. A choice of G over M as a state of the world (career) indicates a strong preference for egalitarian outcomes.

With a multiplicative social welfare function, a doubling of i's utility is offset by a halving of j's. An increase in i's utility from 100 to 200 is fully offset by a decline in j's from 100 to 50. Requiring that such trade-offs be made in the social welfare function has been criticized by Yew-Kwang Ng (1981b) on the grounds that it can lead some individuals to make very large sacrifices to avoid very small *absolute* declines in utility for others. Suppose, for example, that a society of five faces the choice among the three states of the world A, B, and C as in Matrix 19.2. In state A, all five experience a relatively modest level of welfare. In B, one is utterly miserable (almost to the point of suicide), two is ecstatic, and the other three individuals are as in state A. In C, one is again miserable, but all four of the other individuals are 10 times better off than in A. An additive welfare function ranks B above C, and places both above A. The multiplicative regards A, B, and C as socially indifferent.

Those who object to the choice of B over A argue that the use of the additive welfare function in this situation allows individual 1 to be used as a means to 2's gain in violation of Kant's fundamental dictum.[3] Indeed, with an additive W, a maximum could arise at which some individuals have zero or negative

---

3. See, in particular, Rawls (1971). Sen's (1979a) critique of welfarism is also relevant here. Rawls does not argue for a multiplicative welfare function, but rather a lexicographic one (setting aside his objections to utilitarianism). Rawls's theory is discussed in Chapter 21.

Matrix 19.2.

	Individuals				
	1	2	3	4	5
A	1		1	1	1	1
B	0.0001	10,000	1	1	1
C	0.0001	10	10	10	10

utilities. Killing a wealthy invalid and redistributing her property to the healthy poor could easily raise an additive W. If j is a sadist, then j's torture of i so that i has negative utility (wishes he were dead) could raise W. With a multiplicative W, no state with any $U^i \leq 0$ could ever be chosen as long as some states are feasible for which all $U^i > 0$.

As a counterargument to these examples, note that although increases in W can easily be envisaged as involving murder and torture, that maximum W would occur at these points is less plausible. If i is not a masochist, then a less costly (in terms of the interpersonally comparable U's) way of increasing U^j is probably available, than by letting j torture i.

The same logic and arithmetic that makes A and B equal with multiplicative W, makes C no better than A, although here the exchange of making four people considerably better off for making one modestly worse off in absolute terms may strike some as reasonable. Note again that one could well imagine individuals making such a trade-off for themselves. If at the age of 21 the reader were given a choice between living the next 50 years at, say, the poverty line, versus living 10 of those years at the margin of existence, and 40 in the affluence of the upper middle class, it is more than conceivable that the reader would make the Faustian choice for the second alternative. If these options are represented reasonably by the utility numbers in rows A and C in Matrix 19.2, then the reader has made the choice using a criterion that is closer to the additive than to the multiplicative welfare function. If the reader would make choices such as these by implicitly adding the different utility levels, why ought not society to use the same criterion?

One possible reply to this question is to argue that, although it is perfectly acceptable for an individual to make choices by adding her utility levels at different points in time, since she is making choices for herself and may compare her utilities at different points in time anyway she wants, when the welfares of different persons are to be compared, the trade-offs inherent in the additive W are unacceptable for the means-ends reason given above. A different criterion, one more protective of individual rights as in the multiplicative

W, is required when one makes interpersonal welfare choices, from that which may be reasonable or acceptable for making intrapersonal choices.

This reply raises indirectly the issue of the context in which the social welfare function is used. Many observers seem to think of the SWF as an analytic tool to be used by a policy maker, who plugs in the U^i's and then maximizes; that is, some unknown third party is making social choices *for* society. In this setting, the issues of how the U^i's are measured and what trade-offs in utility are allowed across individuals are salient. Constraints on the choices that protect individuals from having their welfares lowered for the benefit of others in the community, as introduced through a multiplicative W, have much appeal.

An alternative way to view W, however, is to see it as a guide to writing the constitution, the set of rules by which the society makes collective decisions. If one views these rules as being chosen by self-interested individuals who are uncertain of the future positions they will hold when the rules are in effect, then in choosing an SWF (i.e., a set of rules to implement an SWF), one is not making an interpersonal choice but rather an *intra*personal one. One is choosing a set of rules to maximize one's own welfare, given that one is uncertain about what position and utility function one will possess. In this context, an additive W would seem appropriate as a social welfare function, if individual choices tend to be made by comparing differences in utility levels at different points in time.

The context in which the SWF is to be used is also relevant to the issue of whether and how cardinal utilities are to be measured. The abhorrence of economists for the concept of cardinal utility would seem to stem from a fear that some bureaucrat would go about metering and somehow combining individual utilities to reach decisions on social policies. Evidence from the psychological literature and sensitivity studies that indexes of cardinal utility can be constructed might from this perspective be viewed more with alarm than enthusiasm.

But if one views the SWF as a construct to guide an individual's choice in selecting a constitution, a choice made from behind a veil of ignorance concerning one's future position and utility function, then the issue is whether people can conceptualize being a slave and a slave owner, and compare their utilities in both roles. If they can, then choosing a set of rules to implement a W of whatever functional form is at least a hypothetical possibility. This is the setting in which Rawls (1971) and Buchanan and Tullock (1962) envisage a set of constitutional rules being chosen, and Harsanyi (1955) a social welfare function. It is the context in which the concept of an SWF seems most useful to the study of collective decision making. Therefore, we defer further discussion of the functional form of the SWF until we take up constitutional decision making in Chapters 21 and 22.

Bibliographical notes

Following the pioneering papers by Parks (1976) and Kemp and Ng (1976), several papers have appeared reestablishing the impossibility of a Bergson–Samuelson SWF with ordinal utility arguments, or the necessity of using cardinal, interpersonally comparable utility indexes (D'Aspremont and Gevers, 1977; Pollak, 1979; Roberts, 1980a,b,c), and for a survey see Sen (1977b).

I have been of the opinion, ever since I read Bergson (1938) and Samuelson (1947, ch. 8) on social welfare functions, that cardinal, interpersonal utility comparisons were necessary to select a single allocation as best among those in the Pareto set. Moreover, I believe this opinion was commonly shared among welfare–public choice theorists. The papers of Kemp and Ng (1976) and Parks (1976) appeared to me to be important not so much because they brought startling new results to light, but because they proved formally what had been known or suspected for some time. I thus confess to some befuddlement at the nature and tone of the Samuelson (1977, 1981) and Kemp and Ng (1977, 1987) debate.

Section B draws heavily on Ng (1981b). See also Bergson (1938), Samuelson (1947), Little (1957), Sen (1979a), and Ng (1981a).

The literature on experimentally measuring utilities is reviewed in Vickrey (1960) and Ng (1975).

CHAPTER 20

Axiomatic social welfare functions

The only orthodox object of the institution of government is to secure the greatest degree of happiness possible to the general mass of those associated under it.

Thomas Jefferson

A really scientific method for arriving at the result which is, on the whole, most satisfactory to a body of electors, seems to be still a *desideratum*.

Charles Dodgson
(Lewis Carroll)

The Bergson–Samuelson social welfare function has been constructed analogously to the individual's utility function. Just as the individual chooses bundles of commodities to maximize his utility, society must choose an allocation of commodities across individuals to maximize its welfare. That consumers make choices to maximize their utility follows almost tautologically from the definition of rationality. In extending the idea of maximizing an objective function to the level of society, however, more is involved than just rationality. Embedded in the characteristics of the welfare function and the nature of the data fed into it are the value judgments that give the social welfare function its normative content, as the discussions of Bergson (1938) and Samuelson (1947, ch. 8) make clear.

An alternative way of analyzing individual behavior from assuming that individuals maximize their utility is to assume various postulates about individual rationality that suffice to define a preference ordering, and allow one to predict which bundle an individual will choose from any environment. Again by analogy, one can make various postulates about social decision making and analyze society's decisions in terms of social preference orderings. What choice should a society make from any environment? Again, however, in shifting from the individual to the societal level, the postulates change from simply defining rationality to expressing the ethical norms of the community. This is important to keep in mind, because some of the axioms *sound as if* they simply require collective rationality, and some writers have so interpreted them. This is not the course followed here. In discussing each axiom, we emphasize its normative content.

The first and most important attempt to define a social welfare function in

384

terms of a few, basic ethical axioms was made by Kenneth Arrow in 1951 (rev. ed. 1963). Although some of Arrow's discussion of the individual axioms seems to mix ethical and rational considerations, the overriding objective of the inquiry is normative, and our emphasis on the normative characteristics of the axioms does not seem out of place. Arrow, himself, has accepted the interpretations of these axioms as indicating the basic value judgments to be incorporated in the community's social contract or constitution,[1] and this is perhaps the best way to look at them. The question then is this. What ethical norms are we to impose on the social choice process, and what collective choice processes satisfy these axioms? The answer is disappointing. Given but a few, fairly weak, and ethically uninspiring axioms, no process (voting, the market, or otherwise) exists that satisfies them.

We begin by briefly stating the axioms and sketching the impossibility proof, after which we turn to a more detailed examination of the axioms.

A.   Logic of the proof

I follow William Vickrey's (1960) restatement of the postulates and proof, since they are simpler and shorter.

1.   *Unanimity* (the Pareto postulate): If an individual preference is unopposed by any contrary preference of any other individual, this preference is preserved in the social ordering.
2.   *Nondictatorship:* No individual enjoys a position such that whenever he expresses a preference between any two alternatives and all other individuals express the opposite preference, his preference is always preserved in the social ordering.
3.   *Transitivity:* The social welfare function gives a consistent ordering of all feasible alternatives. That is, $(aPbPc) \rightarrow (aPc)$, and $(aIbIc) \rightarrow (aIc)$.
4.   *Range:* (unrestricted domain): There is some "universal" alternative u such that for every pair of other alternatives x and y and for every individual, each of the six possible strict orderings of u, x, and y is contained in some admissible ranking of all alternatives for the individual.[2]

---

1. This interpretation was first put forward by Kemp and Asimakopulos (1952) and was subsequently endorsed by Arrow (1963, pp. 104–5).
2. Arrow's statement of the axiom is as follows:

> Among all the alternatives there is a set S of three alternatives such that if any set of individual orderings $T_1,...,T_n$ of the alternatives in S, there is an admissible set of individual orderings $R_1,...,R_n$ of all alternatives such that, for each individual i, xR_iy if and only if xT_iy for x and y in S. (Arrow, 1963, p. 24)

5. *Independence of irrelevant alternatives:* The social choice between any two alternatives must depend only on the orderings of individuals over these two alternatives, and not on their orderings over other alternatives.[3]

Condition 4 perhaps requires an additional word of explanation. The notion of a universal alternative is not crucial here. What is implied by the range axiom is that the social choice process allows any possible ordering of the three alternatives x, y, and u. The process is not established in such a way as to rule out possible orderings.

The theorem states that no social welfare function satisfies these five postulates. To understand the significance of the theorem, it is useful to run through the proof, again following Vickrey. We first define a decisive set D.

Definition of decisive set: *A set of individuals* D *is decisive, for alternatives* x *and* y *in a given social welfare function, if the function yields a social preference for* x *over* y, *whenever all individuals in* D *prefer* x *to* y, *and all others prefer* y *to* x.

PROOF:

Step	*Justification*
1. Let D be a set of individuals decisive for x and y	Assumption
2. Assume for all members of D $xPyPu$, and for all others (those in C) $yPuPx$	Range
3. For society xPy	Definition of D
4. For society yPu	Unanimity
5. For society xPu	Transitivity
6. But for only members of D is xPu	Assumption
7. Society must prefer x to u regardless of changes in rankings of y or any other alternatives	Independence
8. D is decisive for x and u	Definition
9. D is decisive for all pairs of alternatives	Repetition of steps 2–8
10. D must contain two or more persons	Nondictatorship

3. Vickrey states this postulate somewhat differently, but his proof relies on it in this form. This statement of the axiom also differs from Arrow's original statement of it, and others existing in the literature. Arrow's statement is as follows:

Let $R_1,...,R_n$ and $R'_1,..., R'_n$ be two sets of individual orderings and let $C(S)$ and $C'(S)$ be the corresponding social choice functions. If, for all individuals i and all x and y in a given environment S, xR_iy if and only if xR'_iy, then $C(S)$ and $C'(S)$ are the same. (Arrow, 1963, p. 27)

For a statement of the axiom in the present way, and impossibility proofs based on it, see Sen (1970a,b).

11. Divide D into two nonempty subsets A and B Assumption

12. Assume for A $xPyPu$

      for B $yPuPx$ Range

      for C $uPxPy$

13. Since for members of A and B, yPu, for   Definition of D

     society yPu

14. If for society yPx, B is decisive for y Definition of D

     and x

15. If for society xPy, then for society xPu Transitivity

16. But then A is decisive for x and u Definition of D

In either case, one of the proper subsets of D is decisive for a pair of issues, and therefore by step 9 for all issues. Steps 10–16 can be repeated for this new decisive set, and then continued until the decisive set contains but one member, thus contradicting the nondictatorship postulate.[4]   □

The intuition underlying the proof runs as follows: The unrestricted domain assumption allows any possible constellation of ordinal preferences. When a unanimously preferred alternative does not emerge, some method for choosing among the Pareto preferred alternatives must be found. The independence assumption restricts attention to the ordinal preferences of individuals for any two issues, when deciding those issues. But, as we have seen in our discussions of majority rule, it is all too easy to construct rules that yield choices between two alternatives but produce a cycle when three successive pairwise choices are made. The transitivity postulate forces a choice among the three, however. The social choice process is not to be left indecisive (Arrow, 1963, p. 120). But with the information at hand – that is, individual ordinal rankings of issue pairs – there is no method for making such a choice that is not imposed or dictatorial.

B.   Relaxing the postulates

To avoid the impossibility result, the postulates must be relaxed. Before doing so, however, let us consider the significance of the theorem as it stands, for its significance stems precisely from the weakness of the postulates as now stated. Although, as we shall see, these axioms are somewhat stronger than they might first appear, they are far weaker than one would wish to impose at the constitutional stage to satisfy reasonable notions of distributional equity.

4. This literature is replete with this form of "Chinese boxes" proof to uncover the dictator. For an important variant thereon with infinite numbers of voters, see Kirman and Sondermann (1972).

For example, there is nothing in the axioms to preclude one group of individuals, as long as it has more than one member, from tyrannizing over the others, if it stays on the Pareto frontier.[5] Even allowing this and still other violations of our ideas of equity, we cannot find a process to choose from among the Pareto optimal set that satisfies these axioms.

Space precludes a complete review of all modifications of the postulates that have been made to produce either possibility theorems or new impossibility results. Instead, we focus on modifications of particular relevance to public choice.

Relaxing unanimity and nondictatorship hardly seem worth discussing if the ideals of individualism and citizen sovereignty are to be maintained.[6] These two axioms clearly illustrate that what we are engaged in here is a normative exercise. There is nothing particularly irrational about selecting one individual and allowing him to make all decisions for the community; indeed, arguments for an omniscient dictator have been around at least since Plato's eloquent defense of this alternative in *The Republic*.[7] But such arguments are inconsistent with our most basic democratic ideals. Special mention should also be made of Hobbes's defense of monarchy (1651). To Hobbes, there was one issue on which all preferences were identical: Life in anarchy was terrible and inferior to life under a unanimously accepted dictator. If one made the other postulates part of the Hobbesian contract, one might construct a new defense of autocracy. And, of course, in practice the dictatorial solution to the uncertainties and deadlocks of social choice is very popular. Empirically, it might be interesting to investigate the frequency with which dictatorial governments replace democratic ones following apparent deadlocks of the latter stemming from voting paradoxes. The other three axioms require more detailed discussion.

1.   *Transitivity*

Arrow's reasons for requiring that the social choice process produce a consistent social ordering appear to be two: (1) "That some social choice be made from any environment" (1963, p. 118), and (2) that this choice be independent of the path to it (p. 120). These are in fact different requirements, and neither of them requires the full force of transitivity.

The requirement that the social choice process should be able to make some

---

5. See Sen's amusing example (1977a, p. 57).
6. But see Little (1952).
7. Daniel Bell (1973) presents the modern version of this position. After citing Arrow's proof at a number of places to indicate the difficulty that purely democratic processes have reaching decisions, he opts for choice by technocratic experts, who form the ruling elite in the postindustrial society.

choice from any environment seems the easiest to defend, deadlocks of democracy being an open invitation to dictatorship. But to achieve this goal one does not have to assume the existence of a social preference ordering defined on the basis of all individual preference orderings. To make choices one needs only a *choice function* that allows one to select a best alternative from any set of feasible alternatives (Sen, 1970a, pp. 47–55; Plott, 1971, 1976). Transitivity is not required. Either quasi transitivity or acyclicity will suffice (Sen, 1970a, pp. 47–55). Both of these conditions are milder than transitivity. Quasi transitivity requires transitivity of the preference relation, but not of indifference; acyclicity allows x_1 to be only "at least as good as" x_n even though $x_1 P x_2 P x_3, \ldots, x_{n-1} P x_n$. Possibility theorems have been proven by replacing transitivity by either of these and retaining the other Arrow axioms. Gibbard (1969) has shown, however, that requiring a quasi-transitive ordering of the social choice function produces an oligarchy, which can impose its unanimous preference on the rest of the community; and Brown (1975) has shown that acyclicity gives veto power to *every* member of a subset of the committee that Brown calls a "collegium."[8] Thus, as one relaxes the consistency requirement from transitivity to quasi transitivity, and then to acyclicity, dictatorial power becomes spread and transformed, but does not disappear entirely. Requiring the social decision process to be decisive in some sense vests one individual or a subset of individuals with the power to decide, or at least block, any outcome.[9]

Although relaxing the transitivity axiom has some advantage in spreading dictatorial power across a wider group, it incurs the additional cost of introducing a degree of arbitrariness into the process (Sen, 1970a, pp. 47–55). Under quasi transitivity, for example, *aIb* and *bIc* can exist along with *aPc*. Then, in a choice between *a* and *b,* society can pick either, but if *c* is added to the set, society must pick only *a*. If *a, b,* and *c* are points on the Pareto frontier, there will be distributional consequences to the choice of any one. Those favored under *b* may question the ethical underpinnings of a process that makes their fate dependent in such a seemingly capricious way on the set of alternatives under consideration.

The gain from relaxing the transitivity axiom is further reduced when one considers the restrictions that must be placed on the patterns of individual preference orderings to ensure that either quasi transitivity or acyclicity holds. For majority rule, at least, the conditions that are necessary and sufficient for acyclicity are the same as those required for quasi transitivity, and these in turn will also ensure transitivity when the number of individuals is odd.[10]

8. See also Blau and Deb (1977).
9. For further discussion of this point, see Brown (1973), Plott (1976, pp. 543–6), and Sen (1977a, pp. 58–63).
10. See Sen and Pattanaik (1969), Inada (1970), and Sen (1977a).

Thus, if the property of having a choice made from every environment is to be maintained, there appears to be little lost by sticking to the full transitivity requirement.

The intuition behind requiring the final outcome to be independent of the path to it is somewhat different. Here, to begin with, a *path to* the final outcome is obviously assumed. That is, a choice is not made from the full set of all possible candidates, but instead winners are selected from subsets of the full issue set. These in turn are pitted against one another in some manner, and a given path is followed until a final choice set is found. The requirement that the social choice process should be path independent amounts to the requirement that the final choice set should be independent of how the initial subsets are formed out of the full issue set (Plott, 1973).

Path independence is related to and in fact implies another condition that has received much attention in the literature, Sen's (1969) property α. Property α states that if x is a member of the choice set defined over the full set of alternatives S, then x is a member of the choice set of any proper subset of S of which it is a member. Property α is one of a group of *contraction-consistent* properties that have been investigated.[11] As the set of alternatives is contracted, x must continue to be chosen as long as it is one of the alternatives. The intuitive notion here is perhaps obvious: If x is the best chess player in the world, then he is also the best chess player in London. Path independence in this context requires that x's emergence as champion be independent of how the original runoff matches were ordered. This latter requirement is obviously stronger than the former, which explains why path independence implies the α-property, but not the reverse.

Complementary to α and the other contraction-consistent properties are a set of *expansion*-consistent properties such as the β property (Sen, 1969, 1970a, 1977a). The β property states that if x and y are both members of the choice set for some subset S_1 of the full set S, then x can be a member of the choice set of S if and only if y is. Returning to our chess champion examples, if x and y tie for the chess championship of England, then the β property requires that they be among those who tie for the chess championship of the world. As Sen pointed out, it is quite plausible in examples such as these for two individuals to tie in a local contest, but one goes on to beat all others and emerge the world champion. Thus, although β may be a reasonable constraint to place on some choice processes, as when contestants are measured in a single dimension like weight, it does not seem as reasonable when the candidates are measured (or compete) in several dimensions. Since issues arising in a social choice context are likely to take the latter form, it is quite possible that a social decision process would violate property β and still not seem inherently irrational or unfair.

11. See Sen (1977a, pp. 63–71).

Thus, of the two types of properties, the intuitive support for contraction-consistent or path-independent properties seems much stronger than for expansion-consistent properties of the β type. What we seek is the social choice, or set of choices, that defeats all others. Having found such a choice, it would be comforting to know that its selection was independent of the chance way in which earlier contests were established (path independence), and that it could compete again against any subset of losers and still emerge a winner (α-property). But, unfortunately, it is path independence and the α-properties, even in their weakest forms, that lead to dictatorial or oligarchical social preference orderings; the only possibility theorems that have been proven impose only expansion-consistent properties of the β type.[12]

Let us consider somewhat further what is at stake if we abandon all vestiges of the transitivity axiom. Requiring that the social choice process satisfy this axiom is motivated in part by the desire to avoid the embarrassment of inconsistency and arbitrariness. But this view in turn seems to stem from the belief that, just as it is *irrational* for an individual to exhibit inconsistent preference orderings, it is *wrong* for society to do so. James Buchanan (1954a) made an early attack on Arrow's generalization of the concept of individual rationality to collective choice processes focusing precisely on this axiom, and Charles Plott (1972) has extended and generalized this line of criticism. If the transitivity axiom is to earn a place in our constitutional set of constraints on the social choice process, then it must do so by demonstrating that the arbitrary outcomes arising from cyclic preference orderings violate some basic ethical norm. This need not be true. Small committees often resort to random processes such as the flip of a coin, or the drawing of straws to resolve issues of direct conflict. Although obviously arbitrary, the general popularity of random decision procedures to resolve conflictual issues suggests that "fairness" may be an ethical norm that is more basic than the norm captured by the transitivity axiom for decisions of this sort. One might then think of replacing Arrow's notion of collective rationality with the requirement that the social decision process be fair. Transitivity could then be relaxed by simply declaring society indifferent to all choices along the Pareto frontier. Any choice among them will be somewhat arbitrary, but if just might meet with general acceptance. The winners of chess, tennis, and similar elimination tournaments may on occasion be dependent on the particular set of drawings (paths) occurring. This does not seem to detract from the widespread acceptability of this form of tournament for determining the "best" player, however, since the method of determining a sequence of play is regarded as fair, and the nature of the process precludes the determination of which of the contests were in fact path dependent. Thus, it is possible that a social decision process which was intransitive or path dependent, but had

12. Plott (1976, pp. 569–75); Sen (1977a, pp. 71–5).

additional desirable properties, such as fairness perhaps, could be widely acceptable. If there is more general agreement concerning these rules than for transitivity or the other consistency properties, the Arrow problem is solved (Kemp, 1954).

2.   *Unrestricted domain*

The justification for requiring this axiom is something akin to freedom of choice or expression. Each individual should be free to have any preference ordering he might select and the collective choice process should be capable of reflecting these preferences in accordance with the other axioms. Although freedom of choice strikes a responsive chord, we have seen how quickly conflict can arise when individuals have different preference orderings even over how a given piece of public land is to be used. A set of cyclic preferences is quite possible, and if we also require transitivity, we are well on the way to an impossibility result. It should be obvious that some preference orderings are diametrically opposed to one another. This must almost of necessity follow from Axiom 1, which limits consideration to points along the Pareto frontier, that is, to pure distributional issues. Establishing a committee procedure to resolve these issues, without placing any constraints on the preferences that the individuals can express, seems doomed to failure from the start.

There are two ways around this problem. One is to replace unrestricted domain with other axioms limiting the types of preference orderings that the collective choice process is capable of reflecting. In the context of public choice, this implies placing constitutional constraints on the types of issues that can come up before the collective. The protection of certain property rights is one example of this type of constraint. Everyone can be a member of the community, but not every preference can be satisfied or necessarily even recorded as part of the collective choice process. The alternative solution is to restrict entry into the community to those having preference orderings that do make collective choices possible.

We have discussed a number of collective choice results that rely on a restricted domain assumption. Single-peakedness ensures that majority rule produces an outcome, namely the median, and single-peakedness along with the other four axioms produces a nondictatorial social welfare function. But this way out of the dilemma requires strict restrictions on both the selection of issues to be decided and the voters to decide them (Slutsky, 1977b). Issues must all be of the one-dimensional variety: the number of guns, the number of schoolbooks. The voters cannot simultaneously consider both the number and kind of books. And their preferences must be single-peaked in this one dimension. If fate provides voters of this type, these kinds of issues can be resolved by majority rule without violating the other axioms, although we are still left with a plethora of multidimensional issues to resolve in some other way. If some individuals have multiple peaks, they must somehow be isolated and excluded from the community, or an impossibility result can again emerge.

The single-peakedness condition implicitly introduces a degree of homogeneity of tastes assumption, for there must be a consensus over how things are arranged for single-peakedness to occur.[13] More generally, the experimental work on majority rule cycles reviewed in Chapter 5 indicates that the probability of a cycle occurring decreases as voter preferences become more "homogeneous," and increases with increasing voter "antagonism" (Plott, 1976, p. 532). These results suggest searching for ways of restricting membership in the polity to those with sufficiently homogeneous or complementary preferences to avoid the impossibility result. The theories of clubs and voting-with-the-feet describe processes by which groups of homogeneous tastes might form. In the absence of externalities across clubs (local communities), and perfect mobility, free entry, and so on, such a process might avoid the Arrow problem. But, as we have seen, when spillovers exist, some decisions may have to be made by the aggregate population, and the impossibility problem will apply here, even when "solved" in the smaller ones. In such likely circumstances, homogeneity of preferences can be brought about only if individuals adopt, or already have, a common set of values (Bergson, 1954). Appeals to reason, à la Kant, or uncertainty, à la Rawls and Harsanyi to be discussed in Chapters 21 and 22, are along these lines.

3.　　*Independence of irrelevant alternatives*

Of all the axioms, the independence of irrelevant alternatives has been the subject of the most discussion and criticism.[14] In justifying this axiom Arrow (1963, p. 110) made the following argument:

> The Condition of Independence of Irrelevant Alternative extends the requirements of observability one step farther. Given the set of alternatives available for society to choose among, it could be expected that ideally, one could observe all preferences among the available alternatives, but there would be no way to observe preferences among alternatives not feasible for society . . . clearly, social decision processes which are independent of irrelevant alternatives have a strong practical advantage. After all, every known electoral system satisfies this condition.

Here Arrow defends the axiom in terms of limiting attention to feasible alternatives only, and this objective of the axiom has led Plott (1971, 1976) to restate and rename the axiom specifically in terms of infeasible alternatives.

13. Arrow (1963, p. 80), and Sen (1970a, pp. 166–71).
14. As noted in n. 3, Arrow's statement of the axiom differs from the one presented here.

But in his original discussion of the axiom, Arrow presents an example using the rank-order or Borda method discussed above, in which candidates are ranked according to their position in each voter's preferences. In the example Arrow (1963, p. 27) gives, x wins from a slate of x, y, z, and w, but draws with z when y is dropped from the list. Thus, under the Borda method the outcome depends on the nature of the full list of candidates. One of Arrow's objectives for invoking the axiom would appear to be to eliminate procedures like the rank-order so that "Knowing the social choices made in pairwise comparisons in turn determines the entire social ordering and therefore the social choice function $C(S)$ for all possible environments" (p. 28). Now this is precisely what the independence axiom stated above (condition 5) achieves, and it does eliminate procedures like the Borda method from consideration. Thus, our use of this form of the independence axiom would appear to be fully consistent with Arrow's objectives in introducing this axiom.[15] The question then is, what is the normative value to limiting the informational content of collective choice processes in this way?

The outcomes under the Borda procedure and similar schemes depend on the specific (and full) set of issues to be decided. Thus, abandonment of the independence axiom raises the importance of the process that selects the issues to be decided in a way that its acceptance does not. When the choice between x and y can be made by considering voter preferences on only x and y, the rest of the agenda need not be known. This property of the independence axiom has an appealing economy to it, but it is this property that opens the door to endless cycling over these *other* items in the agenda.

By restricting the choice between two alternatives to information on individual rankings of these two alternatives, the independence axiom excludes all information with which one might cardinalize and interpersonally compare utilities (Sen, 1970a, pp. 89–91). It was the desire to establish a welfare function that was not based upon interpersonal utility comparisons that first motivated Arrow (1963, pp. 8–11, 109–11). There would appear to be two distinct justifications for wishing to exclude cardinal utility information from a collective choice process. The first is that the measurement of cardinal utilities is difficult and arbitrary, and any process that was based on combining interpersonally comparable, cardinal utilities would be vulnerable to abuse by those making the cardinal utility measurements. This would appear to be Arrow's chief fear (pp. 8–11). It rests on Arrow's view of the collective

15. As Plott (1971, 1976) and Ray (1973) have shown, however, Arrow's original statement of the axiom as given in n. 3 does not exclude the Borda procedure limited to outcomes in the feasible set. It does eliminate the Borda procedure when the ranks are assigned over the set of all possible alternatives, feasible and infeasible, and thus does limit some of this procedure's scope for strategic behavior (Plot, 1976). For additional comment on this axiom, see Bergson (1954); Blau (1972); Hansson (1973); Kemp and Ng (1987).

choice process as one in which information is gathered by public officials, who make the actual choices for the collective (pp. 106–8). Allowing these officials to engage in cardinal, interpersonal utility comparisons would vest them with a great deal of discretionary power and might be something to be avoided.

The danger of an abuse of discretionary power does not arise, however, if the cardinal utility information is provided by the voters themselves, as when they take part in the process using the Borda method, vote trading, or point voting. Now a different problem arises, however. These procedures are all vulnerable to strategic misrepresentation of preferences. The independence axiom eliminates not only these strategy-prone procedures, but all voting procedures that are vulnerable to strategizing. This property is sufficiently important to warrant separate treatment.

4.   Strategy-proof social welfare functions

The above discussion indicates that an important objective of Arrow's in imposing the independence of irrelevant alternatives axiom was to eliminate the possibility that individuals could be made better off under a collective decision procedure if they did not state their true preferences as inputs into the collective decision process. William Vickrey (1960, pp. 517–19) speculated that immunity to strategic manipulation and satisfying the independence axiom were logically equivalent, and subsequently this insight was rigorously established by A. Gibbard (1973) and M. A. Satterthwaite (1975).

The relationship between independence of irrelevant alternatives (*IIA*) and strategy proofness (*SP*) is brought out most clearly by Blin and Satterthwaite (1978).

Strategy proofness (SP): Let M_i be the message i supplies the voting procedure when she states her true preferences. Let M_i' be any misstatement of i's preferences. Let x be the social outcome from the voting procedure when i states M_i and all other voters j state their true preferences M_j. Let y be the social outcome when i states M_i' and all other voters state their true preferences M_j. Then a voting procedure is strategy-proof if and only if for all possible M_i' there exists no y such that yP_ix.

Another way to think of strategy proofness is that every profile of true preferences must be a Nash equilibrium under the voting procedure (Blin and Satterthwaite, 1978, p. 257, n. 10).

Blin and Satterthwaite first prove an Arrow-type impossibility theory for the three axioms, nondictatorship (*ND*), Pareto optimality (*PO*), *IIA*, and two not yet defined axioms, rationality (*R*) and positive association (*PA*). *R* states simply that the voting procedure must define a social preference ordering, and

Table 20.1. *Six of 36 possible orderings of two voters' preferences over three issues*

1	2	1	2	1	2	1	2	1	2	1	2
x	*x*	*x*	*x*	*x*	*y*	*x*	*y*	*x*	*z*	*x*	*z*
y	*y*	*y*	*z*	*y*	*x*	*y*	*z*	*y*	*x*	*y*	*y*
z	*z*	*z*	*y*	*z*	*z*	*z*	*x*	*z*	*y*	*z*	*x*

subsumes transitivity. *PA* requires that if *x* is chosen under one profile of individual preferences, then it must also be chosen under a second profile of preferences, which differs from the first only in that *x* has gone up in one or more individuals' preference orderings.[16]

They then show that the three axioms *R*, *IIA*, and *PA* are equivalent to *R* and *SP*. Thus, *SP* and *IIA* are not equivalent, but when one demands that the voting process be rational, that is, that it define a consistent social preference ordering, they come close to being so.

Since *R*, *IIA*, and *RP* are equivalent to *R* and *SP*, and it is impossible to have a voting procedure that satisfies *R*, *IIA*, *RP*, *ND*, and *PO*, it is impossible to have a voting procedure that satisfies *R*, *SP*, *ND*, and *PO*. To see the logic of this result, consider a simple example, where we have but two voters (1 and 2) and three alternatives (x, y, z).[17] Each voter can order the three alternatives in six possible ways. Thus, there are 36 possible combinations of the two voters' preference orderings, of which six are presented in Table 20.1. Voter 1's preferences are the same in all six cases, xP_1yP_1z, and 2's preferences run through the full set of six possible orderings. In the first two combinations or orderings, both voters rank *x* highest. Thus, by the Pareto principle, *x* must be the social choice if both voters state either of these sets of preferences. By further application of the Pareto principle, we establish the following restrictions on the social choice for the six combinations of preferences.

$$x \quad x \quad x \text{ or } y \quad x \text{ or } y \quad x \text{ or } z \quad x \text{ or } y \text{ or } z.$$

Voter 1's preferences are the same in all six cases. If 1 honestly states this preference ordering, then any differences in the outcomes that come about must be due to differences in 2's stated preferences. Now consider the third case, where 2's preferences are yP_2xP_2z. This preference ordering in conjunc-

16. Note that this axiom is not the same as the positive responsiveness axiom used in May's (1952 (ch. 6)) theorem on majority rule. Rather, it resembles nonnegative responsiveness as defined by Sen (1970a, pp. 68–9, 74–7).

17. With this example we follow the exposition of Feldman (1979), pp. 465–72. Kalai and Muller (1977) show that a strategy proof SWF exists for a group of $n > 2$, if and only if it exists for a group of two. Thus, a full proof for a committee of two would suffice for the general case.

tion with 1's must yield either x or y as the social choice to be consistent with the Pareto principle. Suppose from this third case the social outcome were x. Voter 2 prefers y to x, under the preferences given in this third case. If they are his true preferences, and the voting rule were such that y would be the outcome if 2 stated any of the preferences 4, 5, or 6, then the procedure would not be strategy-proof. 2 would then state that preference ordering that produced y, given 1's honestly stated ordering. Thus, given that x is the social outcome in case 3, y cannot be the outcome in cases 4, 5, and 6, and we now have the following constraints on the social outcome imposed by strategy proofness.

$$x \quad x \quad x \quad x \quad x \text{ or } z \quad x \text{ or } z.$$

Under the preferences of case 4 (yP_2zP_2x), 2 prefers z to x. Were these 2's true preferences, and z were the social choice for either case 5 or 6, 2 would again have an incentive to misstate his preferences so they appear as in either 5 or 6 when they are really as in 4. Thus, strategy proofness requires x to be the social choice for the pairs of preference orderings in cases 5 and 6. But that implies that x is the social choice when 1's preferences are xP_1yP_1z regardless of what 2's preferences are, which is to say that 1 is a dictator.

Had we assumed that y was the outcome from case *3*, we could have shown that nonmanipulation required 2 to be a dictator. The remaining 30 cases can be handled in a similar manner.

The close relationship between strategy proofness and independence of irrelevant alternatives is apparent from this example. In the third combination of individual preferences depicted in Table 20.1, two individuals disagree only with respect to whether x is better than y, or the reverse. The independence axiom confines the social choice to using only information from the two individuals' rankings of this pair when choosing the socially preferred outcome. If the social choice process picks x in this situation, it effectively makes 1's preferences dominant over 2's, and 1 becomes the dictator. If y is the social choice, 2 is effectively a dictator.

If the voting procedure's selection of an alternative is sensitive to the voter's full statement of preferences over the 3 or more issues in the issue set, the scope for strategic manipulation of the procedure exists *unless* one voter is treated as a dictator. The dictator has an incentive to be honest, and the preferences of the other voters do not matter. When the voting procedure processes information on only individual, ordinal preferences on issue pairs, as required by the independence axiom, and the procedure is positively responsive, voters will honestly state their true preferences. But information on ordinal preferences on issue pairs does not in general suffice to determine a consistent social preference ordering over the full set of issues. One must make one voter a dictator to ensure transitive social preferences.

The public choice literature builds on the behavioral postulate that individuals rationally and slavishly pursue their self-interest. Whenever the outcome of a voting procedure can be manipulated by cheating, this postulate requires that we assume that voters will cheat. Thus, the concern in the public choice literature with finding cheat-proof voting procedures, and the importance of the theorems establishing the impossibility of defining such procedures.

But the negative side to these theorems should not be overdrawn. We have seen in Chapter 18 that the rational, self-interest assumption regarding voter behavior does not give us a very satisfactory predictive theory. Individuals appear to be conditioned to behave in ways that do not fit a narrow definition of self-interested behavior. To what extent individuals who vote out of a sense of "civic duty" would vote strategically is not clear, even if they could figure out what a strategic vote would be.

The more sophisticated voting procedures discussed above require manipulative strategies that may go beyond the capacities of most voters of normal rationality. The obvious strategy of overloading one's vote points on one's most preferred candidates is curbed in Hylland and Zeckhauser's version of point voting by the use of a square-root aggregation procedure. The demand revelation process is strategy-proof, although perhaps not Pareto optimal.[18] Voting by veto is strategy-proof, but does not define a social preference ordering.[19] The significance of the impossibility results regarding strategy proofness must be examined in each case. Vernon Smith's (1977) experimental results indicating that students using the auction method of voting did not behave strategically must again be cited as evidence showing that what one can prove to be a certain hypothetical possibility does not always happen.

5.   Implications for public choice

The Arrow theorem rests on five axioms that appear to be fairly moderate and reasonable restrictions to place on the collective choice process. The theorem states that no process can exist that satisfies all five axioms simultaneously. In designing a collective choice process, writing our political constitution, we must violate one or more of the axioms – although in so doing we may be able to satisfy the others – and still more to be added to the list.

From a public choice perspective, two promising avenues might be fol-

---

18. The demand revelation process also violates the unrestricted domain assumption by placing certain constraints on individual preferences; e.g., they prefer paying less taxes than more. See Sugden (1981), pp. 164–5.

19. Voting by veto attaches probabilities to the outcomes in the feasible set rather than defining a social ordering over them (Mueller, 1984). In general, probabilistic voting rules that are positively responsive, as is voting by veto, fare much better with regard to strategy proofness than do deterministic rules. See Gibbard (1977) and Barbera (1977). Note also the similarity between this finding and the results for the political competition models (Chapters 10 and 11).

lowed out of the Arrow paradox. One is to drop the transitivity axiom and abandon the search for a *best* alternative, *the* social preference. In its place could then be substituted the requirement that the social choice process be fair or democratic or accord with some other generally held value. For example, one of the probabilistic voting procedures with desirable normative properties like voting by veto could be substituted for the deterministic ones (see n. 19). Alternatively, if a social ordering must be made, then either the independence axiom or unrestricted domain must be relaxed.

If we continue to interpret these axioms as restrictions on the collective choice process written into the constitution, then these conclusions have the following implications. Axiom 1 limits consideration to points along the Pareto frontier. But a choice from among these involves distributional issues directly, and cycles will occur under any voting process requiring less than full unanimity. Thus, if the majority rule or any other less-than-unanimity rule is chosen, some fair or otherwise generally accepted way for breaking cycles must be included in the constitution.

Relaxing the unrestricted domain assumption to allow only single-peaked preferences does not seem to be a very promising way out of the paradox, since so few issues can realistically be thought of as unidimensional. More realistically, one can think of designing the constitution in such a way as to allow for the revelation of preferences for public goods via voluntary association in private and local clubs. This solution solves the problem by imposing a form of unanimity condition, but leaves aside all distributional considerations, and the problems of resolving differences of opinion on globally public goods.

Where strategic behavior is not a problem, one of the procedures that gathers information on the voters' preferences over the full set of alternatives, like the Borda procedure or point voting, can be used. As we noted in Chapter 8, however, the normative properties of these procedures depend heavily upon what issues are allowed into the decision set. Thus, relaxing either the unrestricted domain assumption or independence of irrelevant alternatives raises questions as to what issues are to be decided, who is to decide, and of those who decide, which preferences shall be weighed and with what weights. Such choices directly or indirectly involve interpersonal utility comparisons, and must rest on some additional value postulates, which, if explicitly introduced, would imply specific interpersonal utility comparisons. The latter cannot be avoided, if a preferred social choice is to be proclaimed.[20]

And so, we close our discussion of the Arrow axiomatic social welfare function at the same point we were at with the Bergson–Samuelson real-valued social welfare function.

20. Kemp and Asimakopulos (1952); Hildreth (1953); Bergson (1954); Sen (1970a, pp. 123–5, 1974, 1977b).

C.   The impossibility of a Paretian liberal

1.   The theorem

Arrow's theorem states that it is impossible to satisfy four reasonable constraints on the social choice process without making one person a dictator over all social choices. Amartya Sen (1970a,b) sought to allow each person to be dictator over a single "social" choice, for example, the color of paint in one's own bathroom, and arrived at yet another impossibility theorem.

More specifically, Sen (1976 p. 217) set out to find a social decision function that would satisfy the following property:

> Acceptance of personal liberty: there are certain personal matters in which each person should be free to decide what should happen, and in choices over these things whatever he or she thinks is better must be taken to be better for the society as a whole, no matter what others think.

He formalizes this condition by allowing each individual to be decisive for the social choice over one pair of alternatives, and shows that this condition, unrestricted domain, and the Pareto principle are sufficient to produce a cyclic social decision function (1970a,b). The theorem is remarkable, as in the Arrow case, in that it achieves so much from so few constraints. Neither transitivity (only acyclicity) nor the independence of irrelevant alternatives are involved (but see below).

Sen illustrates his theorem with the following example: A copy of *Lady Chatterley's Lover* is available to be read and the following three social states are possible:

a.   *A* reads *Lady Chatterley's Lover,* and *B* does not.
b.   *B* reads *Lady Chatterley's Lover,* and *A* does not.
c.   Neither reads it.

A, the prude, prefers that no one reads it, but would rather read it himself than have *B* read it. Lascivious *B* prefers most that prudish *A* read the book, but would rather read it himself than see it left unread, that is,

for *A cPaPb,* and
for *B aPbPc.*

Invoking the liberal rule to allow *B* to choose whether he reads the book or not results in

bPc.

Doing the same for *A* results in

cPa.

But, both *A* and *B* prefer *a* to *b;* thus, by the Pareto principle

aPb

and we have a cycle.

2. *Rights over Pareto*

There are several ways out of or around the paradox, of which we discuss but two.

Sen's own preferred solution is to require that the Pareto principle defer to liberal rights in certain situations.

> Let me be the "prude" (Mr. A) . . . , while you are "lascivious" (Mr. B). I would rather not read the stuff myself (i.e. I prefer *c* to *a*), and I would rather you would not (i.e. I prefer *c* to *b*), but I decide to "respect" your tastes on what I agree is your benighted business (while wondering whether "respect" is quite the word), conceding that my preference for *c* over *b* be ignored. My dislike of your gloating over "muck" was so strong that I would have preferred to read the work myself to stop you from falling into this (i.e., I preferred *a* to *b*), but being a consistent kind of a man, I notice that, if I insist that my preference for *c* over *a* should count as well as my preference for *a* over *b*, then there is not much point in my "renouncing" my preference for *c* over *b*. So I may decide not to want my preference for *a* over *b* to count, even though the choice over the pair (*a, b*) is not exclusively your business.
>
> On a similar ground, you might not want your preference for *a* over *b* to count, since you do wish your preference for *b* over *c* to count and decide not to want that your preference for *a* over *c* should count (since it is my business). But the Pareto preference for *a* over *b* is built on counting my preference and yours over *a* and *b*. (Sen, 1976, 1982, pp. 313–4; case designation altered to conform to our example)

Thus, Sen solves the paradox by assuming that the individuals, although meddlesome in nature, have liberal values that they impose upon themselves so that parts of their preferences "do not count" or receive "different weight." Liberal *B* might state that the only choice relevant for him is *b* or *c,* and state

liberal *B* bPc

while liberal *A* states

liberal *A* cPa

The social ordering is now transitive with the liberally constrained outcome being the plausible one that *B* reads *LCL* and *A* does not.

Sen chooses to treat the meddlesome preferences of *A* and *B* as in some sense their "true" preferences for the purposes of defining Pareto optimality, with liberalism a constraint or weight placed on true preferences. Alternatively, one could regard meddlesomeness and liberalism as both attributes of a single set of preferences with one dominating the other.

Liberal A might simply state that if B prefers reading LCL to not reading, A as a liberal is willing to respect that choice so his ordering of the three social states becomes

liberal A $aP'bP'c$

and likewise for liberal B

liberal B $bP'cP'a$.

Their preferences are diametrically opposed. All social outcomes are Pareto optimal. Since B can impose b unilaterally, while A cannot impose a, b is the likely social outcome as before. If A and B are liberals, the expected liberal solution emerges without violating the Pareto principle.

The same outcome emerges if we assume liberalism is a part of preferences or a constraint upon them. Which way one views the problem is an issue of methodological preference. I enjoy a cigarette after dinner, and always smoke one when I dine alone. But tonight I am dining with you, and you are offended by the smoking of others. I choose not to smoke. Is this choice best described as the unconstrained maximum of my utility function, which includes as arguments both my pleasure from smoking and my displeasure from watching your reaction to my smoking, or as the maximum to my utility function that includes only my pleasure from smoking, but with the solution being derived under the constraint that I not cause you discomfort?[21]

Our first solution to the liberal paradox solves the paradox by assuming that the individuals themselves are willing to behave in such a way as to avoid what would otherwise be a paradox. Were individuals resolutely selfish and meddlesome, a conflict between liberal principles and Pareto optimality would remain. But if both of the individuals' behavior (preferences) is (are) controlled by liberal principles, no inconsistency with a (un)constrained Pareto principle arises. The next solution to the paradox relies entirely on the selfish, meddlesome interests of the individuals.

3.   *Pareto trades*

In the original example, a certain degree of extra conflict is introduced by assuming that there is but one copy of the book to read. This assumption ensures that each individual who is making a choice is choosing between two

---

21. The paradox can be avoided, if only one individual is a liberal, but the social outcome can depend on which individual is the liberal (Suzumura, 1978). However, modifications of the liberalism and Pareto criteria can produce an existence theorem as long as *any* one individual is a liberal (Austen-Smith, 1982).

Matrix 20.1.

		B, the lascivious	
		Does not read LCL	Reads LCL
A, the prude	Reads LCL	a	d
	Does not read LCL	c	b

social states, since if he is free to choose between reading the book or not the other individual cannot be reading it. But this makes somewhat artificial the presentation of this choice to both individuals, since both cannot decide to read the book at the same time. The decision of who reads the book is obviously a collective decision from the start, and cannot be a purely personal matter for both individuals at the same time (see Buchanan, 1976b).

This difficulty can be gotten around by assuming that the book is available to both, and redefining the liberalism axiom to require that each individual is decisive over an element pair (whether he reads *Lady Chatterley* or not) in all possible social states, that is, independent of the other's choice.[22] The decision options can now be illustrated by Matrix 20.1 in which the possibility

> d. Both A and B read *Lady Chatterley's Lover*

has been added. Whereas Sen's condition grants A the choice of either row *given that B is constrained to the first column*, the modified liberalism condition gives A the choice of row regardless of what column B chooses, and assigns the analogous right to B with respect to the choice of column.

Since this new liberalism condition is stronger than Sen's, it obviously does not overturn his theorem. Applying the condition to A, we have

$$(c, b)P(a, d)$$

and from B's preference ordering

$$(d, b)P(a, c).$$

The intersection of these two choice sets is b, which is Pareto inferior to a. Notice that Pareto-optimal a is the only social state ruled out entirely by the application of this modified liberalism principle.

Although this new liberalism principle does not solve the liberal's paradox, it does suggest a way out of it. Matrix 20.1 is the prisoners' dilemma matrix,

22. Bernholz (1974c); Seidl (1975); Buchanan (1976b); Breyer (1977); Craven (1982).

and the Parcto-inferior outcome at *b* comes about from each individual's *independent* decision to exercise his own liberal rights without regard for the externalities that this decision inflicts on the other.[23] The way out of the dilemma, as in the case of other externalities, is to invoke another liberal axiom – all individuals are free to engage in mutually beneficial trades – and allow *A* and *B* to form a contract in which *B* agrees not to read the book in exchange for *A*'s reading it (Coase, 1960). The power to form such contracts requires that the liberalism axiom be redefined to allow an individual either to exercise his assigned right or trade it away, that is, agree not to exercise it.[24]

Sen (1986, pp. 225–8) raises two objections to allowing individuals to trade away their liberal rights to achieve Pareto optimality. First, if *A* and *B* have liberal values, they might refuse to form such a contract despite its seeming attractiveness. Sen's preferred solution to the paradox may dominate the trading alternative. In either case, the paradox is resolved, however, and, as noted above, whether one regards this solution as a violation of the Pareto principle or a consistent application of it depends on whether one regards an individual's liberal values as a part of his preferences or a constraint upon them.

Second, the needed contract is difficult if not impossible to enforce. Prudish *A* may feign reading the book but avert his eyes at the juiciest passages. Lascivious *B* may surreptitiously devour a purloined copy of the book. Moreover, the enforcement of such a contract by even an impartial third party would in itself violate liberal values in a most fundamental way. Consider just how carefully and continuously *B* would have to be monitored to ensure that he never read the book.

This second objection to the trading solution to the paradox is certainly valid, but in accepting it the paradox in not achieving Pareto optimality vanishes. We have seen in our discussion of externalities and public goods in Chapter 2 that Pareto-optimal allocations of resources are always in principle attainable through unanimous agreements among all concerned parties. "All" that stands in the way of reaching these agreements are transactions costs. The failure to achieve potentially Pareto-optimal allocations due to transactions costs does not constitute a paradox. It is a fact of our collective lives. Indeed, one might better describe the resulting allocations as Pareto optimal *given the existence of transactions costs* (Dahlman, 1979).

The costs of making and enforcing a contract to produce the Pareto-preferred outcome *a* could prevent its realization *even in the absence of liberal rights*. If every decision as to who would read what had to be made as a

---

23. Fine (1975); Buchanan (1976b).
24. Gibbard (1974); Kelly (1976); Buchanan (1976b); Nath (1976); Breyer (1977); Barry (1986).

collective agreement between A and B and neither had the *right* to do anything on his own, the prisoners' dilemma nature of their preference structure would still provide incentives for both to cheat on the agreement to obtain a. The problem of enforcing such a contract exists with or without the assignment of liberal rights.

4.   Implications for public choice

The literature on the liberal paradox treats both liberal rights and the meddlesome preferences of individuals as exogenous. The desirability of enforcing liberal rights of one form or another is taken for granted. The possibility of individuals with meddlesome preferences is assumed, and a paradox ensues. As such, the theorems derived seem more relevant for the science of ethics than for collective choice. If society wishes to avoid the paradox, individuals must (ought to) make their meddlesome tastes subservient to liberal values. A liberal society should count this set of preferences but not that set.

The theorems can take on relevance for collective choice when we think of liberalism not as a value to which I, the ethical observer, think society should conform, but as a value that members of society share and agree to uphold. Liberalism is then endogenous to the preferences or ethical beliefs of the individuals who make up society. If all individuals were like A and B, and all books like *Lady Chatterley's Lover*, it would be difficult to see how a liberal right to read what one wishes would ever emerge. In such a society, who reads what would be of concern to everyone and would presumably be treated as other public good–externality decisions.

If, however, most people are not like A and B and most books are not like *LCL*, then having to reach a collective decision on who reads what for every book and person in society would involve tremendous decision-making costs. Rational, self-interested individuals might agree to treat the choice of book that an individual reads as a purely personal matter. Society economizes on transactions costs and thus is better off in the long run if each individual is free to make this choice himself.

In the presence of such a long-run liberalism condition, books like *Lady Chatterley's Lover* and individuals like A and B may from time to time come along and lead to a short-run conflict between this liberalism condition and the Pareto principle. The individuals in society may agree, however, that their long-run interests are best served by also establishing the liberal right to waive or trade one's right to read what one chooses, when such trades are mutually beneficial. When such trades are possible and can be enforced, Pareto optimality is achieved in the short run. When the costs of making and enforcing such trades prevent them, the liberal right to read what one chooses may be seen as helping to block a situation that would be Pareto preferred were it to come about. In this sense, liberalism may be seen as overriding the Pareto principle.[25]

But if we assume that individuals act in their enlightened self-interest, and that liberal rights are collectively agreed upon by the individuals who will exercise them, then there cannot be a conflict between liberal rights and a long-run definition of the Pareto principle. If liberal rights can produce Pareto inefficiencies in the short run and yet be Pareto efficient in the long run, the issue arises as to how or by what criteria these rights are chosen. To establish a long-run rule allowing each individual to read what he chooses as being socially preferred, the set of all likely books to appear and all individual preference functions must somehow be envisaged and weighed. Interpersonal utility comparisons will be involved. The solution to Sen's paradox as with Arrow's paradox rests ultimately on the use of cardinal, interpersonally comparable utility information (Ng, 1971).

D.   Axiomatic social welfare functions and collective choice

The Arrow and Sen theorems and the many impossibility theorems and paradoxes that have followed in their wake raise fundamental questions about the possibility of establishing collective choice procedures satisfying minimally appealing normative properties, and about the possibility of granting individuals liberal rights without foreclosing unanimously preferred options. But the negative side of the theorems should not be overemphasized. We have suggested that both sorts of paradoxes might be avoided with the use of cardinal, interpersonally comparable utility information.

Arrow explicitly eschewed the use of such information, and the independence of irrelevant alternatives axiom was imposed to rule out voting procedures that might make use of such information, in part out of a fear that such procedures might be vulnerable to strategic manipulation. The Pareto principle and the liberalism axiom, at least as Sen uses them, also "slip in" a form of the independence axiom, since both are defined in terms of issue pairs (Sen, 1970a, p. 84; Blau, 1975). As argued above, the possibility that a voting procedure can be strategically manipulated does not constitute an inevitability that it will be. Several voting procedures have been put forward that violate either the independence axiom or one of the other Arrow axioms, but nevertheless have attractive properties. In some cases, as for example point voting, interpersonal utility comparisons will have to be made at the constitu-

25. In addition to Sen (1970a, pp. 83–5; 1976, pp. 235–7; 1979a, 1986), Rowley and Peacock (1975) and Wriglesworth (1985, ch. 5) have been willing to give liberalism priority over the Pareto principle, at least in some instances.

tional stage when the number of votes each individual gets and constraints on the issue set are decided. But these are interpersonal utility comparisons the citizens themselves must make, when envisaging the possible issues and their own preferences that may arise in the future. It is possible that the citizens may be trusted to make these comparisons in an ethically acceptable way. Similarly, decisions as to which choices are to be left to the individual and which are to be reserved for collective action must be made by the citizens themselves when they establish the constitutional structure in which social interaction takes place. The utilities that they are comparing under different definitions of individual rights are their own.

If interpersonal utility comparisons must be made at the constitutional stage of decision making, the question arises as to whether these comparisons can be made in an ethically acceptable way. It is the question that concerns us in Chapters 21 and 22.

Bibliographical notes

The difference between Arrow's social welfare function and the Bergson–Samuelson social welfare function has been the subject of much discussion (Arrow, 1963, pp. 23–4; Samuelson, 1967; Sen, 1970a, pp. 33–6).

Numerous books and articles survey and extend the impossibility result first established by Arrow. See, in particular, Riker (1961, 1982b), Rothenberg (1961), Arrow (1963, ch. 8), Sen (1970a, 1977a,b), Pattanaik (1971), Taylor (1971), Fishburn (1973), Plott (1976), Kelly (1978), MacKay (1980), and Suzumura (1983).

Sen's original six-page note posing the liberal paradox has spawned an immense literature. Sen (1976) surveys the results up through 1976. Wriglesworth (1985) provides a most recent and complete review of the terrain.

For a more optimistic statement concerning the potential for embedding liberal values in a set of democratic institutions, see Riley (1985).

CHAPTER 21

A just social contract

> A republican constitution is a constitution which is founded upon three principles. First, the principle of the *freedom* of all members of a society as men. Second, the principle of the *dependence* of all upon a single common legislation as subjects, and third, the principle of the *equality* of all as *citizens*. This is the only constitution which is derived from the idea of an ongoing contract upon which all rightful legislation of a nation must be based. (*Italics in original*)
>
> Immanuel Kant

One of the most influential studies of the first stages of the social choice process in recent years has been John Rawls's *A Theory of Justice* (1971). This book is at once a contribution to moral and to political philosophy. Rawls relies on work and results appearing in various branches of the social sciences, however, and applies his theory to several of the major issues of the day. For this reason, Rawls's work has been widely read and discussed and has had a substantial impact on the economics literature in general, and on collective choice in particular.

Rawls's theory differs from those that we have discussed up until now in its focus on the *process* or *context* in which decisions are made as much as, if not more than, on the outcomes of this process. The goal is to establish a set of just institutions in which collective decision making can take place. No presumption is made that these institutions or the decisions emerging from them will in any sense maximize the social good (Rawls, 1971, pp. 30–1, 586–7). Here we see a clear break with the social welfare function approach. More generally, Rawls challenges the utilitarian philosophy that underlies the social welfare function methodology and that has reigned in discussions of these topics over the past two centuries.[1]

---

1. Bruce Ackerman (1980) is critical of both utilitarianism and contractarianism as approaches to deriving principles of justice. Instead, he emphasizes dialogue as the *process* by which these principles are established.

   His criticism of contract theory seems overdrawn, however. Unless dialogue eventually leads to a consensus on the principles that underlie the liberal state, the liberal state can never come into being. If agreement on principles is ultimately achieved, that agreement becomes a form of social contract that binds the citizens of the liberal state together. Dialogue is an important part of the process by which agreement is obtained, but not a substitute for the agreement.

Rawls sets out to develop a set of principles to apply to the development of "the basic structure of society. They are to govern the assignment of rights and duties and regulate the distribution of social and economic advantages" (p. 61). These principles form the foundation of the social contract, and Rawls's theory is clearly one of the major, modern reconstructions of the contractarian argument. The theory is developed in two parts: First, the arguments in favor of the contractarian approach are established. Here the focus is upon the characteristics of the original position from which the contract is drawn. The moral underpinning of the social contract rests on the nature of the decision process taking place within the *original position*, which in turn depends upon the setting in which the original position is cast. The second part of the theoretical argument develops the actual principles embedded in the social contract. Rawls emphasizes the independence of these two arguments. One can accept either part without necessarily committing oneself to the other (pp. 15 ff.). This point is important to keep in mind since the different parts have been attacked in different ways and one might feel more comfortable about one set of arguments than another. This two-part breakdown forms a natural format by which to review Rawls's theory. Following this review, we examine some of the criticisms of the theory that have been made.

(REVIEW) → *TO BE FOLLOWED BY CRITISMS. PART D*

A.   The social contract

Perhaps the easiest way to envisage how the social contract comes about in Rawls's theory is to think of a group of individuals sitting down to draw up a set of rules for a game of chance, say, a game of cards, in which they will subsequently participate.[2] Prior to the start of the game, each individual is ignorant of the cards to be dealt to him and uncertain of his skills relative to those of other players. Thus, each is likely to favor rules that are neutral or fair with respect to the chances of each player, and all might be expected to agree to a single set of fair rules for the game. Here again the incentive "to get on with the game" can be expected to encourage this unanimous agreement.

In Rawls's theory, life is a game of chance in which Nature deals out attributes and social positions in a random or accidental way (Rawls 1971, pp. 15, 72, 102 ff.). Now this natural distribution of attributes and chance determination of social position is neither just nor unjust (p. 102). But it is unjust for society simply to accept these random outcomes, or to adopt institutions that perpetuate and exaggerate them (pp. 102–3). Thus, a set of just institu-

---

2. The analogy between a social contract or constitution and drawing up rules for a parlor game is often used by James Buchanan. See, e.g., Buchanan (1966), Buchanan and Tullock (1962, pp. 79–80).

tions is one that mitigates the effects of chance on the positions of individuals in the social structure.

To establish such a set of institutions, individuals must divorce themselves from knowledge of their own personal attributes and social positions by stepping through a *veil of ignorance* that screens out any facts that might allow an individual to predict his position and benefits under a given set of principles (pp. 136 ff.). Having passed through the veil of ignorance, all individuals are in an *original position* of total equality in that each possesses the same information about the likely effects of different institutions on his own future position. The original position establishes a status quo of universal equality from which the social contract is written (pp. 3–10).

Individuals in the original position about to choose a set of principles to form a social contract resemble individuals about to draw up rules for a game of chance, with one important difference. Individuals choosing rules for a game of chance are ignorant of their future positions by necessity, and thus can be expected to adopt fair rules out of self-interest. Individuals in the original position are ignorant of their present and likely future positions, because they consciously suppress this information by voluntarily passing through the veil of ignorance. Although they may choose institutions out of self-interest once they are in the original position, the act of entering the original position is a moral one, whose ethical content rests on the argument that information about the distribution of certain "factors [is] arbitrary from a moral point of view" (p. 72). Justice is introduced into the social contract via the impartiality incorporated into the collective decision process through the nature of the information made available to individuals in the original position. Thus emerges the fundamental notion of *justice as fairness.*

What, then, is the nature of the information screened out by the veil of ignorance? Rawls's views here are rather strict. Not only is knowledge of their natural talents, tastes, social position, income, and wealth denied them, but also information about the generation to which they belong, the state of economic and political development of their society, and other fairly general information, which Rawls argues might nevertheless bias an individual's choice in the direction of one set of principles over another. For example, knowledge of the generation in which an individual lives might lead him to favor a particular type of public investment policy, or social discount rate, thereby benefiting his generation at the expense of others. Given the very general nature of the information that individuals have in the original position, it is plausible to assume that the principles on which they agree are impartial with respect to the advantages they provide, not only for specific individuals, or individuals in well-defined positions, but even for individuals in different generations and living under different economic and political systems. Since all individuals have access to the same information once they have passed

[Handwritten at top: ✳ REMOVES CONFLICT OF INTEREST IN BARGAINING.]

through the veil of ignorance, all will reach the same conclusions as to the set of just principles that ought to be embedded in the social contract. Equality in the original position leads to unanimity over the social contract.

[Handwritten right margin: (?) DOES IT REALLY. ARE people HOMOG EVEN IF THIER ENVIRONMENT IS. ∫ THEY HAD Exp. WHICH SHAPED WHO THEY ARE THEN THE VIEL OF IGN. WOULD NOT SUFFICE.]

B. The two principles of justice

Given the information available in the original position, Rawls argues that the following two principles will be chosen as the pillars of the just social contract.

> *First:* each person is to have an equal right to the most extensive basic liberty compatible with a similar liberty for others.

[Handwritten left margin: DIFF. PRINCIPAL MAXIMIN.]

> *Second:* social and economic inequalities are to be arranged so that they are both (a) reasonably expected to be to everyone's advantage, and (b) attached to positions and offices open to all. (p. 60)

> [These] two principles (and this holds for all formulations) are a special case of a more general conception of justice that can be expressed as follows. All social values–liberty and opportunity, income and wealth, and the bases of self-respect–are to be distributed equally unless an unequal distribution of any, or all, of these values is to everyone's advantage. (p. 62)

It is perhaps intuitively obvious that something like the "more general conception of justice" appearing on page 62 would emerge from a collective decision process in which the individuals were ignorant of their future positions and thus were induced to act impartially. Indeed, in some ways the setting of the original position resembles the familiar cake-cutting problem in which one individual divides the cake and the other chooses the first piece. By analogy with this example, one would expect the principles emerging from the original position to have an egalitarian tone, as is present in the more general conception. Rawls adds flesh to his theory, however, by deriving the two, more specific principles quoted above as part of the *special* conception of justice that is thought to hold once a society has reached a point of moderate scarcity, and by further arguing that these two principles will be chosen in lexicographical order. The first principle always has precedence over the second (pp. 61 ff., 151 ff., 247–8).

Rawls defends the lexicographical ordering of these two principles as follows:

> Now the basis for the priority of liberty is roughly as follows: as the conditions of civilization improve, the marginal significance for our good of further economic and social advantages diminishes relative to the interests of liberty, which become stronger as the conditions for the exercise of the equal freedoms are more fully realized. Beyond some point it becomes and then

remains irrational from the standpoint of the original position to acknowledge a lesser liberty for the sake of greater material means and amenities of office. Let us note why this should be so. First of all, as the general level of well-being rises (as indicated by the index of primary goods the less favored can expect) only the less urgent wants remain to be satisfied by farther advances, at least insofar as men's wants are not largely created by institutions and social forms. At the same time the obstacles to the exercise of the equal liberties decline and a growing insistence upon the right to pursue our spiritual and cultural interests asserts itself. (pp. 542–3)

Thus, Rawls sees society as better able to "afford" the extension of equal liberties to all citizens as it develops; that is, he sees liberty as essentially a luxury good in each individual's preference function. With increasing levels of income, the priority of liberty over other psychological and material needs rises, until at some level of development it takes complete precedence over all other needs.

The second principle of justice, which Rawls names the difference principle, also contains a lexicographic ordering. The welfare of the worst-off individual is to be maximized before all others, and the only way inequalities can be justified is if they improve the welfare of this worst-off individual or group. By simple extension, given that the worst-off is in his best position, the welfare of the second worst-off will be maximized, and so on. The difference principle produces a lexicographical ordering of the welfare levels of individuals from lowest to highest. It is important to note that Rawls defines welfare levels not in terms of utility indexes or some similarly subjective concept, but in terms of primary goods. These are defined as the basic "rights and liberties, powers and opportunities, income and wealth," which a society has to distribute (p. 62; see also pp. 90–5). Here we have another example of the break that Rawls is trying to establish between his theory and classical utilitarianism. The principles embedded in the social contract must be general. They must apply to all and be understandable by all (p. 132). This requirement places a bound on the complexity that can be allowed to characterize the basic principles of the social contract. The lexicographical nature of the difference principle and its definition in terms of objectively discernible primary goods make it easy to apply.

The difference principle is closely related to the maximin strategy of decision theory. This strategy dictates that an individual should always choose that option with the highest minimum payoff regardless of what the other payoffs are or the probabilities of obtaining them. The force of the strategy can easily be seen in an example Rawls himself uses when discussing the principle (pp. 157–8). Let W and B be two possible states of the world, say, the drawing of a white or black ball from a sack. Let S_1 and S_2 be the strategy options with prizes as given in Table 21.1. The maximin strategy requires that

Table 21.1.

	W	B
S_1	0	n
S_2	$1/n$	1

one always pick strategy S_2, regardless of the value of n and regardless of the probability, p, of a white ball being drawn, as long as $n < \infty$, and $p > 0$. One will never pay an amount, however small, to win a prize, however large, no matter what the probability of winning is, as long as it is not a sure thing.

Given the conservatism inherent in the maximin decision rule, Rawls goes to great pains to rationalize incorporating this rule into his basic principle of distributive justice. His reasons are three:

> First, since the rule takes no account of the likelihoods of the possible circumstances, there must be some reason for sharply discounting estimates of these probabilities. (p. 154)

> Now, as I have suggested, the original position has been defined so that it is a situation in which the maximin applies [and] the veil of ignorance excludes all but the vaguest knowledge of likelihoods. The parties have no basis for determining the probable nature of their society, or their place in it. Thus they have strong reasons for being wary of probability calculations if any other course is open to them. They must also take account of the fact that their choice of principles should seem reasonable to others, in particular their descendants, whose rights will be deeply affected by it. (p. 155)

> The second feature that suggests the maximin rule is the following: the person choosing has a conception of the good such that he cares very little, if anything, for what he might gain above the minimum stipend that he can, in fact, be sure of by following the maximin rule. It is not worthwhile for him to take a chance for the sake of a further advantage, especially when it may turn out that he loses much that is important to him. This last provision brings in the third feature, namely, that the rejected alternatives have outcomes that one can hardly accept. The situation involves grave risks. (p. 154)

Thus Rawls's arguments for the difference principle rest heavily upon his assumptions about the information available in the original position, and the economic conditions facing society. Society is in a state of "moderate scarcity," the poor can be made better off without great sacrifice to the rich (pp. 127–8). The assumption of moderate scarcity also plays an important role in justifying the lexicographic priority of the liberty principle over the difference principle, as already noted (pp. 247–8). Obviously, situations could be envisaged in which an individual would be willing to give up a certain degree of liberty for an increase in material goods, or risk being slightly poorer for a chance to be substantially richer. Rawls assumes, however, that the marginal utility of material gains declines rapidly enough as prosperity increases, and that society is already wealthy enough, so that these trade-offs and gambles at unknown odds are no longer appealing.

C.   Extensions of the theory to other political stages

Rawls extends his theory to consider the characteristics of subsequent stages in the political process: the constitutional stage, the parliamentary stage, and administrative and judicial stages. In each subsequent stage, the veil of ignorance is lifted to some extent and individuals are given more information with which to make collective decisions. For example, in the constitutional stage, individuals are allowed to know the type of economic system with which they are dealing, the state of economic development, and so on. At each subsequent stage, however, knowledge of specific individual positions and preferences is denied to individuals making collective decisions. Impartiality is thus preserved, and the two principles of justice continue on into subsequent stages of the political process in precisely the same form in which they appear in the social contract. Thus, the social contract forms the ethical foundation for all subsequent political stages. As with the social contract stage itself, Rawls does not envisage actual political processes at work, but rather a form of *Gedanken experiment* in which individuals reflect upon the principles that *ought* to underlie the social contract, constitution, or subsequent stages. In the original position, as defined for the constitutional stage, a hypothetical, just constitution is drafted in the same way that a hypothetical, just social contract is drafted by individuals at this earlier stage. This just constitution, once drafted or conceptualized, can then be compared with actual constitutions to determine in what respect they are in accord with the ethical principles contained in this hypothetical constitution. Of course, once one has specified the principles underlying a just constitution, and assuming that all can agree on them, one would be free to redraft actual constitutions to conform to these principles. But the leap from hypothetical constitutions formulated introspectively to actual constitutions written by individuals with real conflicts of interest may be a great one.

D.   Critique of the Rawlsian social contract

A Theory of Justice has precipitated so much discussion and critical evaluation that we cannot hope to survey all of this material here. Instead, we focus on those issues that are most relevant to the public choice literature. Again the material can be most easily organized around Rawls's arguments in favor of the contractarian approach and the two principles underlying the contract formed.

1.   The social contract

Until the appearance of Rawls's book, social contract theory had fallen into disrepute. The historical version of the theory had been fully discredited for over a century, and as a purely theoretical account for the existence of the state it was thought by many to be redundant.[3] This latter criticism is certainly valid from a public choice perspective. The theory of public goods, the prisoners' dilemma, externalities, the existence of insurable risks, and a variety of similar concepts suffice to explain why individuals might out of self-interest reach unanimous collective agreements. Now a contract is nothing more than a unanimous collective agreement to the provisions specified in the contract. Thus, any decision that can be explained via the creation of a contract can probably be explained just as well as a unanimous collective decision (vote). Not all public good and prisoners' dilemma situations require the existence of a state, of course. But one does not have to think very long to come up with *some* public goods with sufficiently strong joint supply and nonexclusion properties to require the participation of *all* members of a given geographic area. If such collective goods exist, then we have an explanation for a unanimous agreement to provide them.[4]

We have seen, however, how the provision of public goods is plagued by the free rider problem; the cooperative solution to the prisoners' dilemma game is dominated. The notion of a social contract, with the connotation of mutual obligations and rewards and penalties for abiding by the contract, may serve a useful purpose in winning adherence to the provisions of the collective agreement.

Rawls is concerned throughout much of the latter part of his book with the problem of obtaining a stable, well-ordered, just society (pp. 453–504). To do so, individuals must adhere to the principles of justice incorporated in the social contract not only in the original position, but also, by and large, in daily life when they are cognizant of their actual positions. One of the important advantages claimed for the principles derived from the original position is that they stand a greater chance of compliance in the real world than any of their competitors (pp. 175–80). For this to be true, however, it is necessary that the principles be formulated so that all individuals can determine fairly readily

---

3. For a review of this literature, see Gough (1957).

4. For a reluctant demonstration that this is so for at least one category of public goods, see Robert Nozick (1974).

what conduct compliance requires, and, of course, all must be compelled by the nature of the arguments for compliance based upon a consensus reached in the original position.

To see that the first condition may be a problem in the Rawlsian system, consider the following example presented by H. L. A. Hart (1973). The application of Rawls's (1971, pp. 201–5) first principle requires that one liberty be constrained only for the advancement of another. This requires that individuals in the original position trade off the benefits from advancing one liberty against the costs of constraining another. Private property, including the right to own land, is one of the possible freedoms that Rawls allows in his system. But the right to own land might be defined to include the right to exclude trespassers, and this in turn would conflict with the right of free movement. Thus, rights to exclude trespassers and rights to free movement are among those that would have to be sorted out at the original position. Now suppose that a farmer and a hiker get into conflict over the hiker's right to cross the farmer's field. The priority of liberty principle will do nothing to promote compliance with the social contract if the farmer and hiker, or any two people selected at random, are not likely to agree on whose right is to be preserved upon adopting the reflective frame of mind called for in the original position. But, as defined, the original position does not seem to contain enough information to allow one to sort out the priority of different liberties, and thus compliance with these important stipulations of the social contract cannot be presumed.[5]

It might be possible to resolve this kind of conflict from the original position if more information were available to individuals in this position. If they knew the amount of land available, population densities, the impact of trespassing on agricultural productivity, the alternatives to trespassing and their costs, and the like, they might be able to specify whether the right to own property took precedence or not, or even work out mixed cases in which trespassing was prohibited on land smaller than some size, but public pathways were required on larger plots. However, allowing this kind of information would in effect allow individuals to make probability calculations, and this is precluded from the original position by the characteristics of the veil of ignorance. Thus, at the level of generality at which they are derived, the principles inherent in Rawls's social contract may be an imperfect guide for compliance.

The problem of compliance can be likened to the existence of a core in a game in which individuals behind tne veil of ignorance choose principles to

5. Ackerman raises similar criticisms of the problem of conceptualizing what principles the impartial or ethical observer arrives at, even assuming that one is able to assume an impartial frame of mind (1980, pp. 327–42).

govern the distribution of resources once the veil is lifted. If a core exists, no individual or coalition of individuals will choose to return behind the veil of ignorance and draft new principles. Howe and Roemer (1981) show that the difference principle, defined as maximizing the *incomes* of the lowest income group, yields a core to the game if all individuals are extremely risk-averse in the sense that they will join a new coalition only when they can *guarantee* themselves a higher income. Less extreme risk aversion leads to less extreme (egalitarian) principles of justice.

Rawls (1971, p. 172) explicitly rejects a defense of the difference principle based on individual attitudes toward risk and similar utilitarian concepts. Rather, he argues for greater compliance with his social contract than with a set of principles based on utilitarianism on the grounds that one could not expect compliance from the poor under any set of principles requiring them to make sacrifices for the rich, as might occur under a set of utilitarian principles (pp. 175–80). But, under the difference principle, the rich are to be asked to make sacrifices (possibly quite large) for the benefit (possibly quite small) of the poor. This could lead to a problem of noncompliance by the rich.[6] Rawls (1974, p. 144) has responded to this form of criticism by noting that the "better situated . . . are, after all, more fortunate and enjoy the benefits of that fact; and insofar as they value their situation relatively in comparison with others, they give up much less." However plausible this argument is in its own right, it does not seem adequate as a part of a defense of the difference principle within the context of Rawls's theoretical framework. The latter would seem to dictate that the appeal for compliance rests on the inherent justness (fairness) of the principle's application and the proposition that the rich would agree to this principle from behind the veil of ignorance. But here we have a difficulty. The gains to the rich are excluded from consideration under alternative distributions because probability information is barred from the original position.

The exclusion of probability information cannot entirely be defended on the grounds that it would lead to principles favoring one *individual against another*. Knowing the numbers of rich and poor in the country and yet not knowing one's own income could still lead one to select a set of rules that were impartial with respect to one's own future position. But these rules would undoubtedly not include the difference principle.[7] As Rawls's three arguments in defense of the difference principle indicate, in the presence of general knowledge about probabilities something more akin to a utilitarian principle of distribution giving some weight to the interests of rich as well as

---

6. Nagel (1973, p. 13); Scanlon (1973, pp. 198 ff.); Klevorick (1974); Mueller et al. (1974a); Nozick (1974, pp. 189–97).
7. Nagel (1973); Mueller et al. (1974a); Harsanyi (1975a).

poor would be selected. Rawls's chief reason for ruling out information about probabilities from the original position would thus appear to be to remove rational calculations of an average utility sort. But, as Thomas Nagel has pointed out (1973, pp. 11–12), the elimination of competing principles is supposed to be a *consequence* of the working out of the justice-as-fairness concept, not a presupposition of the analysis.[8] Note also that Rawls does allow individuals in the original position certain pieces of information that are particularly favorable to the selection of his twin principles—for example, a period of moderate scarcity reigns, and individuals care little for what they receive above the base minimum. A utilitarian might ask that this information be excluded from the original position along with the general probability information that serves to handicap the selection of utilitarian rules. In any event, the construction of the arguments in favor of the difference principle is such that an individual more favorably situated than the worst-off individual in the society might question whether his interests have been fairly treated in the original position. If he does, we have a compliance problem. Rawls's (1971, pp. 175–80) social contract and his arguments in support seem to be constructed entirely for the purpose of achieving the compliance of only one group, the worst-off individuals.

Problems of compliance could also arise among the various candidates for the worst-off position (Klevorick, 1974). As Arrow (1973) and Harsanyi (1975a) have noted, these are likely to include the mentally and physically ill and handicapped as well as the very poor. But with the set of primary goods defined over several dimensions, individuals in the original position will be forced into interpersonal utility comparisons of the type Rawls seeks to avoid (Arrow, 1973; Borglin, 1982). Should individuals disagree in their rankings, then the problem of noncompliance could again arise, since those who fail to qualify as the worst off under Rawls's difference principle receive no weight whatsoever in the social outcome. If someone truly believed that the affliction he bore was the worst that anyone could possibly bear, it is difficult to see how one could make a convincing argument to him that his position was ignored in the meting out of social justice, on the grounds that from an original position, in which he did not know he had this affliction, he would weigh it below some other. He in fact has it, and the knowledge this imparts to him convinces him that he is the worst off.

Inevitably, in trying to justify an actual implementation of the difference principle and win compliance, one is led to appeal for compliance by one individual by pointing to another who is unquestionably worst off. This resembles Hal Varian's (1974, 1976) suggestion that the difference principle should be defined in terms of envy; the worst-off individual is the one that no one envies. Here, of course, we can still have conflicts. The blind may envy

8. See, also, Hare (1973, pp. 90–1); Lyons (1974, pp. 161 ff.).

those who are paralyzed but can see, and the latter may envy those who can walk but are blind. Even if the envy relationship is, from behind the veil of ignorance, transitive, the risk here is that the individual selected as the worst off will be someone who is very bad off indeed–someone perhaps like the pathetic creature in Trumbo's *When Johnny Comes Marching Home*. Literal application of the procedure to someone in this position could lead to the expenditure of immense resources to achieve a very modest improvement in individual welfare. Arrow is undoubtedly right in arguing that this is the type of special case to which Rawls's (1973) principles are not meant to apply. But the number of special cases is likely to be large, and it is particularly awkward to set aside these often pitiable and ethically difficult cases from the application of the principles of justice, because it is precisely these kinds of cases that one would like an ethical theory to handle.

These problems are all variants on the general problem of compliance raised in the example of the rich and poor. Much of Rawls's discussion of the difference principle seems to be couched in a comparison of *the* rich and *the* poor, as if there were but two groups to compare and one criterion by which to compare them. But in reality there are many possible groupings of individuals and many possible dimensions over which their welfares can be defined. Thus, a line must be drawn on the basis of some sort of interpersonal utility comparisons, around those who are to be categorized as *the* worst off. Unless a fair consensus exists on where this line is to be drawn, compliance with the principles of justice may not be forthcoming (Klevorick, 1974), for the difference principle treats all of those outside of the line, the rich and the not so rich, as being equally rich. This may lead to compliance problems among the very rich, who have to make great sacrifices for the worst off, and among the fairly poor, who receive no special treatment at all. In this way, a utilitarian principle, which weighed each individual's welfare to some degree, might achieve greater compliance than the difference principle, which ignores the welfare of all but a single group (Harsanyi, 1975a).

2.   The two principles of justice

Even if we accept the above criticisms of the social contract aspect of Rawls's theory, it is still possible to consider the two principles of justice based on the justice-as-fairness argument as candidates for a set of political institutions. The question then is, can the arguments behind these two principles be sustained?

The ethical support for these two principles is derived from the impartiality characterizing the original position and the unanimity that stems from it. Is, then, the original position truly impartial with respect to all competing principles of justice? In setting up the problem as one in which "free and equal persons" voluntarily assent to principles to govern their lives, liberty seems to receive a prominent position from the start.[9] It is perhaps no surprise, there-fore, that liberty is "chosen" as the top-priority principle from the original position.

A similar argument has been made by Robert Nozick (1974, pp. 198–9) against the difference principle: "A procedure that founds principles of dis-tributive justice on what rational persons who know nothing about themselves or their histories would agree to *guarantees that end-state principles of justice will be taken as fundamental*" (italics in original). Given that people know nothing about the economic structure of society, about how primary goods and the other outcomes of economic and social interaction are produced, they have no choice but to ignore these intermediate steps, and any principles of justice that might govern them, and focus on final outcomes, the end distribu-tion of primary goods. Nozick argues that this conceptualization of the setting for choosing principles of justice excludes consideration of principles that would govern the *process* of economic and social interaction. In particular, it excludes consideration of an *entitlement* principle of distributive justice, in which individuals are entitled to their holdings as long as they came to them via voluntary transfers, exchanges, and cooperative productive activity, that is, by legitimate means (pp. 150–231). To choose such a principle, one would have to know something about how the society functions, information un-available in the original position.

The flavor of Nagel's and Nozick's criticisms can possibly be captured by returning to our example of the rule-making card game. In this particular example, it is highly unlikely that the players choose rules to bring about particular end-state distributions. If they did, they would probably agree to have all players wind up with an equal number of chips, or points. But this would destroy much of the purpose of the game, which is presumably to match each player or couple's skill against that of the other players, given the chance distribution of the cards. The fun of the game is in the playing, and *all* of the rules would govern the *process* by which winners are selected and not the *final positions* of the winners.

My point here is not to argue that life is like a game of cards and thereby defend Nozick's entitlement theory. But it is valid to argue that individuals may want to consider the *context* and *process* by which outcomes are deter-mined, perhaps along with these outcomes, in choosing principles of jus-tice.[10] It is ironic that Rawls's theory, which derives its conception of justice from the process by which principles are chosen, rules out all consideration of

9. Nagel (1973, pp. 5–11). The quoted words are from Rawls (1971, p. 13).
10. "The suppression of knowledge required to achieve unanimity is not equally fair to all the parties. . . . [It is] less useful in implementing views that hold a good life to be readily achievable only in certain well-defined types of social structure, or only in a society that works concertedly for the realization of certain higher human capacities and the suppression of baser ones, or only certain types of economic relations among men" (Nagel, 1973, p. 9).

principles that deal with the subsequent process of social interaction (except for those contained in the equal liberty principle) (Nozick, 1974, p. 207). Indeed, the theory based on the notion of justice as fairness seems to exclude the selection of a principle of justice that would give to each individual anything that he had acquired by fair means, a principle that does resemble Nozick's entitlement principle.

Even if we accept Rawls's constraints on the information available in the original position and view the problem as one of selecting an end-state distribution principle, it is not clear that the difference principle is the one that would necessarily be chosen. As Harsanyi (1975a) has argued, in the absence of objective probability information, we implicitly and almost instinctively apply subjective probability estimates, or act as if we do, when making decisions. Suppose that the prize for correctly identifying the color of the ball drawn from a bag in our previous example is $5, and nothing is paid, or charged, if the color is incorrectly guessed. Since the game is free, even a maximin risk averter will play. If he chooses white, he is implicitly assuming that the probability of a white ball being chosen is equal to or greater than .5. If he chooses black, the reverse. If he is indifferent between the choice of color and perhaps uses a fair coin to decide, he is implicitly applying the principle of insufficient reason. Harsanyi argues that it is difficult to believe that individuals in the original position will not form probability estimates of this sort, perhaps to eliminate the awkward special cases of physical and mental illness discussed above, and if they do they are unlikely to choose the maximin rule.

Using arguments such as these, several writers have questioned the plausibility of claiming that all would choose the maximin rule from behind the veil of ignorance.[11] This skepticism is reinforced by experimental work of Frohlich, Oppenheimer, and Eavey (1987). They presented students with four possible redistribution rules (Rawls's rule of maximizing the floor, maximizing the average, maximizing the average subject to a floor constraint, and maximizing the average subject to a range constraint). The students were made familiar with the distributional impacts of the four rules and were given time to discuss the merits and demerits of each rule. In 44 experiments in which students were uncertain of their future positions in the income distribution, the five students in each experiment reached unanimous agreement on which redistributive rule to use to determine their final incomes in every case. Not once did they choose Rawls's rule of maximizing the floor. The most popular rule, chosen 35 out of 44 times, was to maximize the average subject to a floor constraint.

Hoffman and Spitzer (1985) also found that students in an experimental

---

11. Sen (1970a, pp. 135–41); Arrow (1973); Hare (1973); Nagel (1973); Mueller et al. (1974a); Harsanyi (1975a).

setting employ a principle of distributive justice that is neither straight Rawlsian egalitarianism nor simple utilitarianism. Rather, in the context of their experiment students employed what appeared to be a "just desserts" principle, a principle consistent with Nozick's entitlements principle.

It is possible, under the assumptions Rawls makes about the original position, that utilitarianism would give outcomes rather similar to those of Rawls's system.[12] The assumption that "the person choosing has a conception of the good such that he cares very little, if anything, for what he might gain above the maximum stipend that he can, in fact, be sure of by following the maximin rule" is equivalent to rapidly diminishing marginal utility of income (primary goods). Incorporated into von Neumann–Morgenstern utility indexes, it would imply extreme risk aversion and would undoubtedly lead to fairly egalitarian redistribution rules, although probably not the difference principle as long as individuals do care something for what lies above the minimum. More generally, under the rather favorable economic conditions that exist when the special conception of justice, including the difference principle and the lexicographic ordering of the two principles, is chosen, it is likely that utilitarianism would also favor liberty and redistribution greatly. Arrow (1973) points out that an additive social welfare function will order liberty lexicographically over all other wants, if all individuals do, as they might given enough wealth. Rawls's arguments that utilitarianism would produce significantly different outcomes, for example, slavery, often seem to rest on the assumption that utilitarianism is operating in the harsher economic environment under which only Rawls's *general* conception of justice applies. But this general conception of justice also allows trade-offs between liberty and economic gain and thus resembles utilitarianism to this extent (Lyons, 1974).

As a final example of the close relationship between Rawls's theory and utilitarianism, consider a purely utilitarian theory of redistribution, Hochman and Rodgers's (1969) theory of Pareto-optimal redistribution. In their theory, rich Jeff gives to poor Mutt because Mutt's utility is an argument in Jeff's utility function. Assuming that Mutt's utility is positively related to his income, we can write Jeff's utility as a function of both Jeff's and Mutt's incomes:

$$U_J = U(Y_J, Y_M).$$

Given such a utility function, we can expect rich Jeff to make voluntary transfers to poor Mutt, if the latter figures heavily enough in Jeff's utility function. In a world of more than one Mutt, Jeff will receive the highest marginal utility from giving a dollar to the poorest Mutt. Thus, although the

---

12. Arrow (1973); Lyons (1974); Harsanyi (1975a).

Pareto-optimal approach to redistribution does not fully justify the maximin principle, it does justify a redistribution policy that focuses sole attention on the worst-off individual or group (von Furstenberg and Mueller, 1971). An altruistic utilitarian and a Rawlsian will both consider the welfare of only the worst-off individual(s) in society.[13]

E.   Conclusions

The reader is by now weary of these criticisms of Rawls's theory. Renewed admiration and perhaps even enthusiasm for the social contract approach can be obtained, however, by reading Rawls's book. It is a most inspiring and rewarding adventure. Nevertheless, the criticisms raised in the literature are so numerous and often sufficiently weighty to suggest that our quest for a theory of the unanimous agreement to the rules and principles underlying the collective choice process may not be at an end. Let us proceed, therefore, to some of its competitors.

13. For still another defense of the difference principle that differs from Rawls's, see Buchanan (1976a).

CHAPTER 22

Utilitarian contracts

The individuals themselves, each in his own personal and sovereign right, entered into a compact with each other to produce a government; and this is the only mode in which governments have a right to arise and the only principle on which they have a right to exist.

Thomas Paine

The ideally perfect constitution of a public office is that in which the interest of the functionary is entirely coincident with his duty. No mere system will make it so, but still less can it be made so without a system, aptly devised for the purpose.

John Stuart Mill

Several works that have appeared within economics and public choice bear a resemblance to Rawls's theory in their use of the idea of impartiality and the unanimity rule. John Harsanyi (1953, 1955, 1977) and William Vickrey have used impartiality to derive a social welfare function; James Buchanan and Gordon Tullock (1962) and Harvey Leibenstein (1965) have applied the impartiality notion to the analysis of collective decision making. These works form a bridge between John Rawls's contribution to moral philosophy and the welfare economics and public choice literature. We begin with the work of Harsanyi.

A.   The just social welfare function

Harsanyi's social welfare function is based on highly individualistic postulates. An organic view of the state never appears, even by implication. Harsanyi distinguishes between an individual's *personal* preferences and his *ethical* preferences. The first are what he uses to make his day-to-day decisions. The second are used on those more seldom occasions when he makes moral or ethical choices. In making the latter decisions, the individual must weigh the consequences of a given decision on other individuals, and thus must engage in interpersonal utility comparisons. In making his everyday decisions, of course, he simply considers his own preference function.

Harsanyi derives a social welfare function on the basis of the following three assumptions:

424

1. Individual personal preferences satisfy the von Neumann–Morgenstern–Marschak axioms of choice.
2. Individual moral preferences satisfy the same axioms.
3. If two prospects P and Q are indifferent from the standpoint of every individual, they are also indifferent from a social standpoint.

He then uses these three postulates to prove the following theorem concerning the form of the social welfare function, W:

Theorem: W *is a weighted sum of the individual utilities of the form*

$$W = \sum_i a_i U_i,$$ (22.1)

where a_i *stands for the value that* W *takes when* $U_i = 1$ *and* $U_j = 0$; *for all* $j \neq i$ *(Harsanyi, 1955, p. 52).*

This is clearly a rather powerful result given the three postulates. The additive social welfare function has, of course, had a long and venerable history in economics. But since the work of Bergson (1938) and Samuelson (1947), the idea that *the* social welfare function would *necessarily* take this form has not been popular. Harsanyi's theorem reintroduces the Benthamite conception of social welfare on seemingly weak postulates. As always, when powerful results follow from weak premises one must reexamine these premises to see whether they perhaps contain a wolf in disguise.

The first assumption simply guarantees a form of individual rationality in the face of risk and seems rather innocuous as such. It allows each individual's utility to be expressed as a von Neumann–Morgenstern utility index.

The second assumption extends the concept of rationality from an individual's own personal preferences to his moral preferences. The same rationality axioms apply when an individual makes ethical, interpersonal utility comparisons such as those that apply when he makes selfish intrapersonal ones. This assumption can be criticized in the same way that Buchanan (1954) criticized the Arrow postulates, as an illegitimate extension of the notion of individual rationality, and this criticism has been made by Pattanaik (1968, pp. 1164–5), who focused on the transitivity axiom, as did Buchanan. But this objection seems to carry less weight against Harsanyi's generalization of the concept of individual rationality than against Arrow's. Harsanyi is assuming *individual* evaluations in both cases; no aggregate will or organic being is even implicitly involved. The W in Harsanyi's theory is a subjective W in the mind of an individual. If individuals differ in their subjective evaluations, there will be different W's for different individuals. A collective W need not exist.

The von Neumann–Morgenstern–Marschak axioms as applied to social choices raise another issue not raised by the Arrow analysis. The social choice becomes directly dependent on individual attitudes toward risk. Arrow himself raised this criticism prior to Harsanyi's work, but in clear anticipation that the then newly invented von Neumann–Morgenstern cardinal utility indexes would be used by someone to create a social welfare function (Arrow, 1951, 2d ed. 1963, pp. 9–11):

> This [the von Neumann–Morgenstern theorem] is a very useful matter from the point of view of developing the descriptive economic theory of behavior in the presence of random events, but it has nothing to do with welfare considerations, particularly if we are interested primarily in making a social choice among alternative policies in which no random elements enter. To say otherwise would be to assert that the distribution of the social income is to be governed by the tastes of individuals for gambling. (Arrow, 1963, p. 10)

More generally, as Sen (1970, p. 97) notes, the use of the von Neumann–Morgenstern–Marschak axioms introduces a degree of arbitrariness, which is inherent in all cardinalization of utilities.

Whether social choices *should* depend on individual attitudes toward risk is a knotty question. It raises, also, the more general question of whether certain individual preferences (for pornography, for education) are to be given more or less weight in the social welfare function. The only way that this issue can be dodged is if *all* preferences, including those toward risk, are allowed to affect the social choice. The knowledge that an individual would pay X for a p probability of winning Y tells us something about his preferences for X and Y, just as the knowledge he prefers Y to X does. The former knowledge actually contains more information than the latter, and this information does not seem a priori inherently inferior to knowledge of simple preference orderings. At least the inferiority of the former sort of information would seem to require further justification.[1] Under the assumption that individuals make decisions involving risk by maximizing the expected value of their subjective utilities, Ng (1984a) has established an equivalence between von Neumann–Morgenstern utility indices and subjective utility indices. This important theorem further strengthens the case for treating von Neumann–Morgenstern utilities on a par with other measures of cardinal utility when making social choices. Since Harsanyi assumes that individual ethical preferences satisfy the Marschak axioms (i.e., the preferences used to calculate W), Ng's theorem is applicable to the Harsanyi welfare function, and the U_i's can be treated as either subjective or von Neumann–Morgenstern utilities.

The third postulate introduces the individualistic values that underlie Harsanyi's social welfare function. It is this postulate that forces an additive

---

1. For additional criticism and discussion of the role of risk preferences in the Harsanyi social welfare function, see Diamond (1967), Pattanaik (1968), and Sen (1970a, pp. 143–5).

characterization onto the social welfare function. What is remarkable about Harsanyi's theorem is that he has been able to derive the intuitively plausible, additive social welfare function by introducing such a modest amount of individualism as contained in the third postulate.

Knowing that the social welfare function is additive is only the first, even though large, step in determining the social outcome, however. The weights to be placed on each individual's utility index must be decided, and the utility indexes themselves must be evaluated. It is here that Harsanyi derives the ethical foundation for his social welfare function. He suggests that each individual evaluate the social welfare function at each possible state of the world by placing himself in the position of every other individual and mentally adopting the preferences of the other individuals. To make the selection of a state of the world impartial, each individual is to assume that he has an equal probability of being any other in the society (Harsanyi, 1955, p. 54).

The selection of a state of the world is to be a lottery with each individual's utility index (evaluated using his own preferences) having an equal probability. "This implies, however, without any additional ethical postulates that an individual's impersonal preferences, if they are rational, must satisfy Marschak's axioms and consequently must define a cardinal social welfare function equal to the arithmetic mean of the utilities of all individuals in the society" (Harsanyi, 1955, p. 55). Thus, the *Gedanken experiment* of assuming that one has an equal probability of possessing both the tastes and position of every other person solves both of our problems: The utility functions are evaluated using each individual's own subjective preferences, and the weights assigned to each, the a_i, are all equal. The social welfare function can be written simply as the sum of all individual utilities:

$$W = \sum_i U_i, \tag{22.2}$$

Of course, the practical problems of getting people to engage in this form of mental experiment, of evaluating states of the world using other individuals' subjective preferences, remain, and Harsanyi (1955, pp. 55–9; 1977, pp. 57–60) is aware of them. Nevertheless, he holds the view that with enough knowledge of other individuals, people could mentally adopt the preferences of other individuals, and the U_i terms in each individual's evaluation of social welfare would converge. Thus, the mental experiment of adopting other individuals' preferences combined with the equiprobability assumption would produce the same kind of homogeneity of ethical preferences and unanimity as to the best state of the world to choose as Rawls achieves via the veil of ignorance (1955, p. 59). All individuals would arrive at the same, impartial social welfare function.

The latter conclusion has been challenged by Pattanaik (1968) and Sen

Table 22.1. *Outcomes in dollars*

State of the world	T	W
Person		
R	60	100
P	40	10

(1970a, pp. 141–6). Even under the assumption that all individuals are able to adopt the subjective preferences of other voters (agree on the values for all U_i), Pattanaik and Sen question whether all individuals will accept a fair gamble at being in everyone else's position.

To see the problem, consider the following example. Let there be two individuals in the community, rich (R) and poor (P), and two possible states of the world, with a progressive tax (T), and without one (W). Table 22.1 gives the possible outcomes in *dollar* incomes.

By way of illustration, Table 22.2 presents the von Neumann–Morgenstern utility indexes for R and P at each level of income scaled in such a way, let us say, to make them interpersonally comparable. R is assumed to have constant marginal utility of income, P diminishing marginal utility. If each individual now assumes that he has an equal probability of being R or P in either state of the world, then the von Neumann–Morgenstern–Marschak postulates of rationality dictate the following evaluation of the two possible states:

$$W_T = 0.5(0.6) + 0.5(0.4) = 0.5$$
$$W_W = 0.5(1) + 0.5(0.2) = 0.6.$$

The state of the world without the progressive tax provides the highest expected utility and would, according to Harsanyi, be selected by all impartial individuals. But, reply Pattanaik and Sen, P might easily object. He is clearly much worse off under W than T, and experiences a doubling of utility in shifting to T; (while) R loses less than $\frac{1}{2}$. The utility indexes in Table 22.2 reveal P to be risk-averse. Given a choice, he might refuse to engage in a fair gamble at having R or P's utility levels under T and W, just as a risk averter refuses actuarially fair gambles whose prizes are in monetary units. Although the Harsanyi welfare function incorporates each individual's risk aversion into the evaluations of the U_i, it does not allow for differences in risk aversion among the impartial observers who determine the social welfare function values. If they differ in their preferences toward risk, so, too, will their evaluations of social welfare under the possible alternative states of the world,

Table 22.2. *Outcomes in utility units*

State of the world	T	W
Person		
R	0.6	1
P	0.4	0.2

and unanimous agreement on the social welfare function will not be possible (Pattanaik, 1968).

The Pattanaik–Sen critique basically challenges Harsanyi's assumption that the Marschak axioms can reasonably be assumed to hold for the ethical choices that an individual makes when uncertain of his future position. In defense of postulating that these axioms hold at this stage of the analysis, one can reiterate that the utilities that make up the arguments of W already reflect individual attitudes toward risk. To argue that special allowance for risk aversion must be made in determining W from the individual U_i's one is insisting that social outcomes be discounted twice for risk, a position that requires its own defense (Harsanyi, 1975b; Ng, 1984a).

Part of the objective for placing individuals behind a veil of ignorance in Rawls's work is to achieve a consensus on the social choices. If a consensus on W cannot be reached, because of different attitudes toward risk behind the veil of ignorance, then the veil has been defined too thinly. An alternative response to the Pattanaik–Sen critique is to extend the logic of the Rawls–Harsanyi mental experiment and assume that each individual uses not his own risk preferences, but that he has an equal probability of having the risk preferences of every other individual. Suppose that in our example one individual was risk-neutral (N), the other risk-averse (A). Their evaluations of the alternative states of the world might then look something like the figures presented in Table 22.3.

The elements of row N represent the simple expected values of states T and W occurring, assuming an individual has the same probability of being R or P and is risk-neutral. Row A presents the lower evaluations that a risk averter might place on these possible outcomes. The social welfare levels under these two states of the world, assuming each individual had an equal probability of being rich or poor *and of being risk-averse or risk-neutral*, would then be

$$W_T = 0.5(0.5) + 0.5(0.44) = 0.47$$
$$W_W = 0.5(0.6) + 0.5(0.42) = 0.51.$$

Table 22.3. *Outcomes in utility units (second round of averaging)*

State of the world	T	W
Person		
N	0.5	0.6
A	0.44	0.42

The state of the world without the tax is again preferred, although by a narrower margin.

The same objection to this outcome can be raised, however, as was raised to the first. A risk averter will recognize that the tax alternative favoring the rich has a greater likelihood of occurring under risk-neutral preferences than under risk-averse preferences. He might then object to being forced to accept a gamble that gave him an equal chance of having risk-neutral or risk-averse preferences, in the same way that he would reject a fair gamble of experiencing the utility levels of the rich and poor. However, this objection can be met in the same way as the previous objection. Reevaluate the two states of the world assuming each individual has an equal probability of being risk-neutral or risk-averse using the utility levels from the previous round of averaging as this round's arguments for the utility functions. If the utility functions are smooth and convex, convergence on a single set of values for W_T and W_W can be expected.[2]

Here the reader may begin to feel his credulity stretching. Not only is our ethical observer supposed to take on the subjective preferences of all other citizens, these preferences must be defined over both physical units (like apples and money) and the interpersonally comparable cardinal utility units of each individual, and he must be prepared to engage in a potentially infinite series of mental experiments in arriving at *the* social welfare evaluation to which all impartial individuals agree. The price of unanimity is high.

Although this type of criticism cannot be readily dismissed, it must be kept in mind that what we seek here is not a formula for evaluating social outcomes

2. Vickrey was the first to suggest repeated averaging of welfare functions to bring about consensus (1960, pp. 531–2). Mueller (1973) and Mueller et al. (1974a) have proposed using this technique explicitly with respect to answering Pattanaik and Sen's objections to the Harsanyi welfare function. Vickrey (1960) sets up the problem of maximizing social welfare in terms of choosing a set of rules for a community that one is about to enter not knowing one's position in it. The setting is obviously similar to that envisaged by Harsanyi, and not surprisingly we find Vickrey arguing for a weighted summation of von Neumann–Morgenstern (or "Bernoullian") utility functions. He resorts to repeated averaging in the event that there will be disagreement over the values of these weighted sums.

that each individual can apply and come up with a unique number. What we seek is a way of conceptualizing the problem of social choice to which we all might agree, *and* which might help us arrive at agreement over actual social choices were we to apply the principles emerging from this form of mental experiment. In this context it pays to consider the Harsanyi approach alongside Rawls's theory.

Both Harsanyi and Rawls obtain an ethical foundation for their analysis by relying on the intuitive notion that certain social choices *ought* to be made impartially.[3] Impartiality is introduced by assuming that these social choices are made by someone uncertain of his future position. And, as in Rawls, some form of interpersonal comparison is required by the individual who assumes this impartial frame of mind. These are the elements that the two theories have in common. Harsanyi, however, would have the impartial observer try to envisage the subjective utility levels of each citizen under different social states and use these in making his (ethical) social choice. If we accept the above criticisms against an equal weighting of each individual's utility, then the Harsanyi approach would fall back to relying on some (unequal) weighted sum of the individual utilities, for the repeated averaging of the different utility indexes does nothing more than reweight the social welfare function in favor of the worse-off individuals. This can be seen most dramatically by assuming that one individual is maximin risk-averse. Repeated averaging will then result in the selection of that state of the world that maximizes the welfare of the worst-off individual (Mueller, Tollison, and Willett, 1974a). A social welfare function that gives enough weight to the most risk-averse individual preference function in the limit reflects this same extreme degree of risk aversion.

In evaluating the "realism" of the Harsanyi approach, therefore, the issues are these: (1) Can one envisage individuals obtaining sufficient information about the positions and psychology of other individuals to allow them to engage in the interpersonal comparisons inherent in the approach? (2) Can individuals assume an impartial attitude toward all individuals in the community, and from this impartial stance agree on a set of weights (a common attitude toward risk) to be attached to the positions of each individual when making the social choice?

Viewed in this light, one gains, perhaps, a better appreciation for Rawls's (1971, pp. 132, 320–5; 1974, p. 144) criticism of utilitarianism's greater complexity. Suppose, for example, that society did make social choices by applying Harsanyi's social welfare function. Now suppose that someone feels that his position is in reality worse off than it ought to be in a just society. To

3. For a highly critical discussion of the role intuitionism plays in Rawls's argument see Hare (1973).

answer this objection, one must say that one's position was evaluated using his own preferences in the original position, and that one's gains were weighed against those of all others using a consensual set of weights, or mean degree of risk aversion. But since any amount of redistribution is consistent with some degree of risk aversion, how can the unhappy citizen verify that his subjective preferences have been truly envisaged, that his position has received its proper weight? Here the comparative simplicity of Rawls's lexicographic orderings defined on primary goods – for all their faults – comes shining through.

The objections that have been raised to the work of Rawls, Harsanyi, and similar efforts along these lines suggest that the main value of these works, at least from the point of view of public choice, is not the principles that these theorists derive from their analyses,[4] or the real number one might assign to a social welfare function. Their main contributions lie instead in the insight they provide into how collective decisions, at least of some types, *ought* to be made, and the implications that these considerations have for actual democratic choice processes. Let us turn, therefore, to an approach to collective choice that is more positivistic in its orientation and yet that relies on the idea of impartiality.

B.   The just political constitution

James Buchanan and Gordon Tullock (1962) develop a theory of constitutional government in which the constitution is written in a setting resembling that depicted by Harsanyi and Rawls. Individuals are uncertain about their future positions and thus are led out of self-interest to select rules that weigh the positions of all other individuals (Buchanan and Tullock, 1962, pp. 77–80).[5] If we think of individuals at the constitutional stage as being utilitarians who implement the impartiality assumption by assuming that they have an equal probability of being any other individual, then the rules incorporated into the constitution can be thought of as maximizing a Harsanyi-type of social welfare function (Mueller, 1973). These constitutional rules, like Arrow's axioms, form the basis for the social welfare function.

The Buchanan–Tullock theory is at once positive and normative. Its authors state: "The uncertainty that is required in order for the individual to be led by his own interest to support constitutional provisions that are generally advantageous to all individuals and to all groups seems likely to be present at any constitutional stage of discussion" (Buchanan and Tullock, 1962, p. 78). And the tone of their entire manuscript is strongly positivist in contrast to,

---

4. Buchanan makes this point in his review of Rawls's book (1971).
5. Leibenstein (1965) achieves the same effect by envisaging collective decisions being made by a group of aging individuals for their descendants.

say, the works of Rawls and Harsanyi. But they also recognize the normative antecedents to their approach in the work of Kant and the contractarians (see, especially, Appendix 1). Indeed, they state that the normative content of their theory lies precisely in the unanimity achieved at the constitutional stage (p. 14).

One of the important contributions of Buchanan and Tullock's book is that it demonstrates the conceptual usefulness of the distinction between the constitutional and parliamentary stages of democratic decision making. If unanimous agreement can be achieved behind the veil of uncertainty that shrouds the constitutional stage, then a set of rules can be written at this stage that will allow individuals to pursue their own self-interest at the parliamentary stage in full possession of knowledge of their own tastes and positions. This obviously requires that any redistribution which is to take place be undertaken at the constitutional stage where uncertainty over future positions holds (Buchanan and Tullock, 1962, ch. 13). Here the similarity to Rawls is striking. Unlike Rawls, however, Buchanan and Tullock are able to allow individuals not just *more* information about themselves at the parliamentary stage, but full information. With redistribution and similar property rights issues out of the way, the only decisions left to decide at the parliamentary stage are allocational efficiency improvements of a prisoners' dilemma type. Unanimity out of pure self-interest is at least theoretically possible, and Wicksell's voluntary exchange theory of government can reign at this level of decision making.

Buchanan and Tullock do not argue for unanimity at the parliamentary stage, however, but instead develop their costs of decision-making framework for determining the optimal majority, as discussed in Chapter 4. They also develop other propositions about representative government (1962, chs. 15 and 16), and still others can be developed using the Buchanan and Tullock mode of analysis.

Despite its obvious importance to their theory, Buchanan and Tullock do not discuss the process by which the constitution gets written, or the procedure for selecting delegates to the constitutional convention to ensure that they all act in the disinterested manner required to achieve unanimity on the democratic rules and individual rights under which the society will operate. Although the long-run nature of these decisions would certainly move the individual's own calculus in the direction of an impartial observer, whether any group of delegates could abstract sufficiently from their own positions and ideologies to produce the kind of collective contract Buchanan and Tullock envisage must remain an open question.

C. Alternative axiomatic characterizations of SWFs

From a public choice perspective, it is more useful to think of real-valued SWFs not as formulas into which utility numbers are plugged, and out of which policy decisions are cranked, but rather as normative constructs for guiding the choice of voting rules and other decisions at the constitutional stage. Once this perspective is adopted, our interest turns to the normative axioms associated with each SWF, just as our interest with the Arrowian SWF was in the normative axioms underlying it. We have examined one set of axioms in Section A, those underlying the Harsanyi–Benthamite W. We now briefly consider several others.

The pioneering axiomatic treatment of SWFs was presented by Marcus Fleming (1952). Fleming proved that any SWF satisfying the Pareto principle and the elimination of indifferent individuals axiom (EII) must be of the following form:

$$W = f_1(U_1) + f_2(U_2) + \cdots + f_s(U_s). \tag{22.3}$$

Elimination of indifferent individuals: *Given at least three individuals, suppose that both* i *and* j *are indifferent between* x *and* x', *and between* y *and* y', *but* i *prefers* x *to* y *and* j *prefers* y *to* x. *Suppose that all other individuals are indifferent between* x *and* y, *and* x' *and* y' *(but not necessarily between* x *and* x', *and* y *and* y'). *Then social preferences must always go in the same way between* x *and* y *as they do between* x' *and* y'. *(Name and statement follow Ng's [1981b] simpler presentation.)*

EII has two important properties. First, as its name implies, it does eliminate all individuals who are indifferent between x and y in a choice between x and y. Second, it requires that whatever convention is used to decide whether i's preferences regarding x and y override j's, it must also decide the pair (x', y') given i and j's indifference between x and x', and y and y'.

The value of W in (22.3) is obviously independent of the ordering of individuals in the $1, s$ sequence, and so the theorem implies anonymity. But, it does not tell us much about the functional form of W. In particular, if

$$f_i(U_i) = a_i U_i, \tag{22.4}$$

then (22.3) becomes the additive W, with $a_i = 1$ for all i, a possible special case. If

$$f_i(U_i) = \log(U_i),$$

we have the multiplicative W.

Harsanyi (1955) provided conditions to support (22.4) as the representation of f. As the discussion of Chapter 19 makes clear, the arguments of W must be cardinal and in some way interpersonally comparable, if W is to have reasonable properties as an index of social welfare. Harsanyi chose to work with von Neumann–Morgenstern cardinal utility indexes.

Ng (1975) chose to work with "finite sensibility" units. The concept of a finite sensibility unit is built on "the recognition of the fact that human beings are not infinitely discriminative" (p. 545). Thus, for a small enough change in x to x' an individual is indifferent between x and x' even though $x \neq x'$. Individuals are capable of perceiving changes in x only for discrete intervals in x. These discrete steps in an individual's perceptions of changes in x become the building blocks for a cardinal utility index measured in finite sensibility units. To the finite sensibility postulate Ng adds the weak majority preference criterion, which states that if a majority prefers x to y, and all members of the minority are indifferent between x and y, then society prefers x to y. The latter incorporates the ethical values built into the social welfare function. It is obviously a combination of both the Pareto principle and the majority rule principle that is at once significantly weaker than both. In contrast to the Pareto criterion, it requires a majority to be better off, rather than just one, to justify a move. And, in contrast to majority rule, it allows the majority to be decisive only against an indifferent minority. In spite of this apparent weakness, the postulate nevertheless proves strong enough to support a Benthamite social welfare function whose arguments are unweighted individual utilities measured in finite sensibility units, that is, (22.2). For those who dismiss Harsanyi's theorem supporting (22.2), because of the introduction of risk preferences through the use of von Neumann–Morgenstern cardinal utility indexes, Ng's theorem offers a powerful alternative justification for the Benthamite SWF, which does not introduce risk in any way.

From the perspective of public choice, the theorems of Harsanyi and Ng are the most important justifications for the additive SWF since their basic axioms are easily interpretable as conditions one might wish to incorporate into a set of constitutional rules, and in Harsanyi's case, the whole context in which the SWF is derived resembles the constitutional setting of Rawls, Buchanan, and Tullock. In Chapter 19 we discussed the multiplicative SWF as an important alternative to the Benthamite SWF. What properties does it possess?

Although the multiplicative W is most closely associated with the name of John Nash, Nash (1950) actually proposed a solution to a two-person bargaining game. When generalized to s persons (see Luce and Raiffa, 1957, pp. 349–50) Nash's solution is of the form

$$W = (U_1 - U_1^*) (U_2 - U_2^*) \cdots (U_s - U_s^*). \tag{22.5}$$

The utilities that go into the welfare function are defined relative to a status quo point at which $U_i = U_i^*$, for all i. This formulation is natural for the bargaining problem that Nash first addressed. Should a bargain not be reached, the status quo is the outcome of the game. Selection of an outcome that maximizes (22.5) is sensitive to the characteristics of the status quo point.

On the other hand, the axioms needed to derive a social welfare function are few and rather innocuous. Cardinality, the Pareto postulate, the α-property of contraction defined in Chapter 20, and symmetry imply the Nash SWF.

Symmetry: *If an abstract version of a bargaining game places the players in completely symmetric roles, the arbitrated value shall yield them equal utility payoffs, where utility is measured in the units which make the game symmetric (Luce and Raiffa, 1957, p. 127).*

Nash's solution to the bargaining problem was put forward more as a description of the outcomes of the game than as a prescription as to what the outcome ought to be. On the other hand, Nash does argue that the outcome is fair, and it is because of the inherent fairness of the outcome, which should be apparent to both sides, that one expects the solution satisfying (22.5) to emerge (Luce and Raiffa, 1957, pp. 128–32). Indeed, Nash's SWF has the same tendency to produce egalitarian sharing of the gains from cooperation, that is, the gains over the status quo, that we noted in Chapter 19 with respect to the more general multiplicative SWF.

But the delimitation of the gains to be shared is sensitive to the choice of the status quo point. The important position played by the status quo in the Nash SWF has led to its criticism as a normative construct by Amartya Sen (1970a, pp. 118–21). If bargaining on social choices takes place, given market-determined income and wealth and presently defined property rights, then the scope for alleviating current inequities through collective action will be greatly restricted.

On the other hand, conceptualizing the problem of selecting a set of rules to govern the political game as a "bargaining problem" does seem to be a reasonable way to view the writing of the constitution or social contract. Were one to think of the social contract as being the set of rules selected from a hypothetical state of anarchy, then the status quo point would be the "natural distribution" of property that would exist in a state of anarchy (Bush, 1972; Buchanan, 1975a). The gains from cooperation would then be enormous and the rather egalitarian sharing of these gains as implied by the Nash SWF might indeed be deemed fair, as Nash thought it would be.

Viewing the status quo as the starting position in a state of anarchy resembles the setup in the Kaneko and Nakamura (1979) theorem. They derive conditions for an SWF of the Nash form as in (22.5), but $(U_1^*, U_2^*, \cdots, U_s^*)$ is defined not as the status quo, but as the worst possible state for each individual that we can imagine. It is doubtful if modern man were thrust into true anarchy that his utility would be much higher than that envisaged by Kaneko and Nakamura. As with all the SWFs that we have been considering, the Kaneko–Nakamura SWF satisfies anonymity and the Pareto postulate. They also assume a form of independence of irrelevant alternatives, but add to it the "fundamental assumption that we evaluate the social welfare by considering relative increases of individuals' welfare from the origin" (p. 426). This fundamental assumption combined with their use of von Neumann–Morgenstern utility indexes forces one to compare ratios of utilities across individuals rather than absolute differences and goes most of the way toward requiring an SWF in multiplicative form.

The most general characterization of a multiplicative SWF is by DeMeyer and Plott (1971). They measure intensity differences as ratios of utilities (relative utilities) and go on to derive an SWF of the form

$$W = U_1^K U_2^K \cdots U_s^K, \tag{22.6}$$

where K is a real number.

The theorems of Kaneko and Nakamura and of DeMeyer and Plott strongly suggest that the choice of some form of multiplicative SWF hinges in large part on whether it is ratios of individual utilities we wish to compare under different states of the world. The other properties of the multiplicative SWF (Pareto, anonymity, α-contraction, unanimous individual indifference implies social indifference) are properties one can also find with additive SWFs. If one prefers to compare absolute differences in utilities across individuals, then one is driven toward the additive SWF as the theorems of D'Aspremont and Gevers (1977) and Maskin (1978) demonstrate.

The theorems of Parks (1976) and Kemp and Ng (1976) indicate that cardinal, interpersonally comparable utility information of some sort is required to specify a meaningful SWF. The functional form of the SWF will in turn largely depend on whether it is utility information in ratio form that we choose to use, or information in absolute differences. The one leads naturally toward the multiplicative SWF, the other toward the additive.

D.   From social welfare function to constitution

Suppose that the individuals at our constitutional convention could unanimously agree on the form of the SWF, what then? How could they go from an additive or a multiplicative SWF to a set of rules for the political game, which would implement it?

In Chapter 8, we showed that the point-voting scheme of Hylland and Zeckhauser (1979) implicitly maximized an SWF of the form

$$W = \lambda_1 U_1 + \lambda_2 U_2 + \cdots + \lambda_s U_s, \tag{22.7}$$

where the $\lambda_i s$ depended on the number of points given to each voter, and thus his marginal utility of a vote point. If, then, we sought to implement an additive SWF in a direct democracy, and if we thought it was reasonable to assume from behind the veil of ignorance that each voter had the same potential utility gain from collective action, then we could implement an additive SWF with all λ_i equal by adopting the Hylland–Zeckhauser point-voting scheme and giving each voter an equal number of vote points. Alternatively, if objective criteria could be agreed upon for why some individuals have a greater stake in the collective choice outcomes – for example, individuals in the central city have a greater stake in the provision of public goods in the city than citizens in the outer suburbs – then these criteria could be used to implement an additive SWF with equal weights on voter utilities through an appropriate unequal allocation of vote points.

The demand revelation process allows individuals to cast dollar votes for quantities of public goods. If individuals at the constitutional stage were willing to assume that the marginal utility of a dollar was the same across all individuals, then the demand revelation process would maximize an additive SWF with equal weights on all individuals (Tullock, 1977b).[6] If they assumed that all individuals had the same utility function, and the marginal utility of income declined with increasing income, then the demand revelation process would implicitly maximize an additive SWF with the weights on individuals positively related to their income levels.

The multiplicative SWF is more protective of individual welfares and leads to more egalitarian outcomes. If all individual utility functions were of the form $U_i = a_i Y_i^\alpha$, then a multiplicative SWF would distribute Y equally across all individuals regardless of the a_is, while an additive SWF would distribute Y in proportion to the a_is. The veto that each voter gets in voting by veto helps protect a voter from proposals that would lower his welfare for the benefit of the other members of the group, and voting by veto produces an equal division of a given sum of money in a simple divide-the-benefits game. While voting by veto does not generate a multiplicative welfare function in the same way that point voting generates an additive SWF, were the constitutional convention to prefer a multiplicative to an additive SWF, voting by veto would be a preferable choice to point voting or a demand-revealing process, ceteris paribus.

If one wished to use one of these procedures in a representative government to implement an SWF, one would need to write into the constitution some form of election procedure that leads to each group of citizens' preferences being represented in parliament, like the proportional representation (PR) or random selection procedures described in Chapter 12 (Mueller et al., 1972, 1976). Were a form of PR used in which different representatives had differ-

---

6. For an alternative justification for the equation of dollar income changes across individuals for welfare purposes, see Ng (1984c).

ent numbers of supporters, vote points in the case of point voting or vetoes in the case of voting by veto could be distributed to representatives in proportion to the number of votes that elected them.[7]

In Chapter 11 we saw that candidate competition for votes can lead candi-- dates to select platforms that effectively maximize an SWF, when candidates assume that it is the probability that a voter votes for him that is affected by the candidate's choice of platform. An alternative form of representative government that would yield an implicit SWF maximization would then be to establish in the constitution two-party democracy of the European variety, in which the executive and legislative branches are combined and the winning party has the power to implement its platform directly. As the models of Ledyard (1984) and Coughlin–Nitzan (1981a) show, whether the SWF im- plicitly maximized by party competition is multiplicative or additive depends on whether individual voter probabilities of voting for a given candidate are a function of the ratios of voter utilities under the two candidates' platforms, or the differences in utilities. Thus, in opting for this form of representative government a constitutional convention would effectively dodge the issue of which SWF it sought to maximize. This decision would emerge out of the competitive political process, and the way in which individual voters compare the two candidates' choices of platforms.

E.   Conclusions

Although public choice is not yet in a position to offer us a blueprint for a constitution that would maximize a given social welfare function or achieve a given conception of the good or just society, the above discussion illustrates that there do exist direct links between various normative principles as em- bodied in, say, a given SWF, and the voting rules one employs. In Chapter 19, it was made clear that no meaningful SWF can be derived from individual utility functions unless they are cardinally defined and in some sense interper- sonally comparable. The suggestion that any individual or political body would be empowered to make cardinal interpersonal utility comparisons on a day-to-day basis and then use these judgments to make allocative and re- distributive decisions for society is to most of us frightening. Not sur- prisingly, little consensus exists over what the institutions would be that would implement such a process.

However, the thought that individuals from behind a veil of ignorance might make interpersonal utility comparisons by mentally assuming the utility

---

7. The demand revelation procedure is more difficult to apply in a representative body because of its reliance on real money and a willingness to pay, but not necessarily actual payments. But see Clarke (1980).

functions of others, and might then use these interpersonal comparisons to derive a set of political rules that would govern society, seems far more palatable. But, if this escape from the nihilism of SWF impossibility theorems is to succeed, it must be possible to reach consensus at the constitutional stage. With respect to this possibility, it is hard to be optimistic. The main premise of Rawls's book is that consensus is possible from behind a veil of ignorance. Yet, no book in the general areas of philosophy, political science, and public choice has stirred more debate in the last generation than Rawls's book, with the two principles that Rawls thought all would agree on generating the most controversy. If Rawls's book is the first step toward reaching a consensus on basic principles, then we have a long way to go.

If Rawls has failed to derive principles of justice to which all can agree, his book and the work of Buchanan and Tullock do succeed in indicating the need for consensus on the basic principles and rules within which a society operates. Can a well-ordered society exist in which a consensus does not exist on the place of liberty and the principles governing distribution in the society? Can a political constitution sustain support if citizens do not accept its rules and distributional implications as fair and just?

Although no agreement exists on the principles that should enter a constitution, on the form the social welfare function should take, throughout the debate the ideas of justice as fairness, impartiality, and equiprobability have managed to survive largely unscathed. This is no mean achievement, for it suggests a shared view toward individualism, a shared view toward the setting in which social choice takes place, and further basic agreement on the underlying properties of the social decision problem. If agreement does exist at this intuitive level, then it should be possible to extend our shared intuitions and design a process for drafting a constitution that would achieve consensus. And, should the process ever get that far, public choice stands ready to offer specific suggestions as to the kinds of voting rules one might choose and their normative properties.

Bibliographical notes

The seminal contributions of John Harsanyi appeared in 1953 and 1955. The argument has been reviewed and alternative proofs to the theorem presented in Harsanyi (1977, ch. 4). This book also provides a more complete statement of the basic axioms.

The number of papers that have implicitly adopted the constitutional stage decision as a point of reference is large. See, in particular, Rae (1969); Mueller (1971, 1973); Mueller et al. (1974a,b, 1976); Abrams and Settle (1976).

Sugden and Weale (1979) link their SWF theorem directly to the constitutional-contractual setting. The theorem resembles Fleming's (1952).

Ng's (1975) original theorem, and subsequent elaborations thereon (1981b, 1982, 1983, 1984b, 1985a), constitute a most forceful defense of the additive SWF.

For axiomatic derivations of the Nash SWF, besides Nash's own (1950), and critiques, see Luce and Raiffa (1957, pp. 124–32, 349–50), and Sen (1970a, pp. 118–21, 126–8).

PART VI

Normative and positive theories of public choice compared

CHAPTER 23

Redistribution

When there is no middle class, and the poor greatly exceed in number, troubles arise, and the state soon comes to an end.

Aristotle

A decent provision for the poor is the true test of civilization.

Samuel Johnson

For Bruce Ackerman (1980) the fundamental question of the liberal state is that of distribution. How can one individual defend a claim to X when challenged by another?

Although the distributional question is not the only question a polity must resolve, it is an important one. And no other issue seems capable of stirring the passions quite like this one. We have examined several hypotheses of how the political process does (should) redistribute income or wealth. Before ending our journey, let us examine how these hypotheses of redistribution stack up against the data.

A.   Normative theories of redistribution

Both Rawls's theory of redistribution following the difference principle and the utilitarian alternative proposed by Harsanyi, Buchanan, and Tullock envisage redistribution under the unanimity rule. Individuals from behind a veil of ignorance that screens knowledge of their future positions unanimously agree on a redistribution formula. In Rawls's theory, this formula would maximize the claims on primary goods, say, income, of the worst-off individual in society. In the absence of negative incentive effects, this would lead to an egalitarian distribution of income.

So, too, would the utilitarian alternative. To see this, assume two income classes with $Y_2 > Y_1$. Let r be the number of rich in class 2, p the number of poor in class 1. An individual uncertain of her future position chooses a tax of T on the rich and a benefit subsidy B to the poor so as to maximize the following objective function:

$$0 = \pi_2 U_2(Y_2 - T) + \pi_1 U_1(Y_1 + B), \tag{23.1}$$

445

where π_2 and π_1 are the probabilities that she will be in classes 2 and 1, respectively ($\pi_2 = r/(r + p)$, $\pi_1 = p/(r + p)$). Assuming zero transaction costs in transferring income,

$$rT = pB. \tag{23.2}$$

Substituting for π_1, π_2, and T into (23.1) and maximizing with respect to B, we obtain

$$\frac{dO}{dB} = \frac{r}{r + p} \frac{dU_2}{dY} \left(-\frac{p}{r} \right) + \frac{p}{r + p} \frac{dU_1}{dY} = 0, \tag{23.3}$$

from which it follows that

$$\frac{dU_2}{dY} = \frac{dU_1}{dY}. \tag{23.4}$$

The impartial utilitarian chooses a distribution of income so as to equate the marginal utility of income across individuals. If the impartial utilitarian further assumes that all individuals have the same utility functions, she chooses taxes and subsidies to equate incomes across all individuals.[1]

As the last normative theory, consider the type of Pareto-optimal redistribution first analyzed by Hochman and Rodgers (1969). Under this approach, the rich are seen as transferring income to the poor, not because they are uncertain about whether they might become poor, or because of an imposed uncertainty, but out of empathy or similar altruistic motivation. This behavior can be analyzed using a similar framework to that just employed. Each member of the highest income group is envisaged as gaining some satisfaction from the utility gains of members of the lower classes. The highest income group acts as a sort of club that unanimously agrees to transfer income from itself to members of the lower group(s). Assuming three groups, with $Y_3 > Y_2 > Y_1$, then each member of group 3, when voting, can be seen as maximizing an objective function consisting of a weighted sum of the utilities of its own members, and those of members of lower-income groups:

$$0 = n_3 U_3(Y_3 - T) + \alpha_2 n_2 U_2(Y_2 + B_2) + \alpha_1 n_1 U_1(Y_1 + B_1), \tag{23.5}$$

where n_3, n_2, and n_1 are the numbers of individuals in groups 3, 2, and 1, respectively, T is the tax imposed on the richest group, and B_1 and B_2 are the per capita subsidies to the other two groups. Each member of the richest group places full weight on the utility of each member of its own group, and partial

---

1. Abba Lerner (1944, pp. 23–40) was the first to demonstrate that an equal distribution of income maximizes the expected utility of an individual uncertain of future position. See also Sen (1973) and Olson (1987).

weights ($\alpha_1 \leq 1$, $\alpha_2 \leq 1$) [2] on the utilities of members of other groups. Substituting from the budget constraint

$$n_3 T = n_2 B_2 + n_1 B_1 \tag{23.6}$$

and maximizing with respect to B_1 and B_2 yields

$$\frac{dO}{dB_1} = n_3 U_3' \left(\frac{n_1}{n_3} \right) + \alpha_1 n_1 U_1' = 0 \tag{23.7}$$

$$n_3 U_3' \left(\frac{n_2}{n_3} \right) + \alpha_2 n_2 U_2' = 0, \tag{23.8}$$

from which it follows that

$$U_3' = \alpha_2 U_2' = \alpha_1 U_1'. \tag{23.9}$$

If a member of the richest class places the same weight on the utilities of members of classes 1 and 2 ($\alpha_1 = \alpha_2$) and assumes that each derives the same utility from income, then (23.8) implies subsidies to members of classes 1 and 2 so as to equate their marginal utilities of income. Since $Y_1 < Y_2$, if the marginal utility of income falls with increasing income, then the incomes of the lowest class must be raised to equality with those of class 2 before any transfers are made to class 2 (von Furstenberg and Mueller, 1971).

A saintly altruist who assumed that her utility function was the same as that of others, and who placed equal weight on her own utility as on that of others ($\alpha_1 = \alpha_2 = 1$) would vote to equate everyone's income. Everyday altruists who place more weight on their own utility than on the utilities of others ($0 < \alpha < 1$) will not favor transfers so large as to bring their own incomes into equality with those to whom they make transfers.

Equation (23.9) could be used to predict the voting behavior of a member of the highest-income group on redistribution or the charitable contributions of such a person. Since charity is a purely voluntary act, whereas government redistribution programs are not, one wonders why, if all the members of group 3 do favor redistribution, reliance is not made on private charities (clubs) for redistribution.

As always, the argument for government intervention relies on the free-rider problem. If a member of group 3 wishes to see the welfare of all individuals in group 1 raised, and not just a few that she knows personally, she cannot achieve her goal alone. If all members of group 3 feel likewise, they can achieve their goal by joint-collective action. But if a voluntary

---

2. Malicious behavior can be modeled by $\alpha < 0$. The highest group can be thought of as forming a perfect cartel among themselves, and an imperfect cartel with members of lower-income classes when $\alpha_i < 1$. For a modeling of cartel behavior using this approach, see Mueller (1986b).

association is employed, free-riding may ensue, and less than the Pareto-optimal amount of redistribution may occur. The Pareto-optimal approach to redistribution sees redistribution through the government occurring as if only the rich voted, and when they did they used the unanimity rule.

B.   Positive theories of redistribution

But government redistribution is actually decided using majority rule, and the potential beneficiaries get to vote. Both facts can alter the outcomes even if some voters have ethical or altruistic motives as described in the preceding section.

The first problem one has in developing a positive description of redistributive outcomes is predicting which outcome will occur. Redistribution is a zero-sum game, and absent a core any outcome could occur. If one thinks of redistribution in spatial terms, then each individual or group's income becomes a separate vector, and one has as many dimensions in the outcome space as one has voters or groups of voters. Any majority coalition is almost certain to be vulnerable to the formation of a different majority coalition (see Chapter 5).

Two tricks have been employed to circumvent this difficulty. The first is to treat redistribution as a single-dimensional issue and employ the median voter theorem. Meltzer and Richard (1981) have assumed that redistribution takes the form of a lump-sum subsidy to all individuals and a proportional tax on all income (see discussion in Chapter 17). Given the population size, the choice of the tax rate determines the lump-sum subsidy. For low-income voters, the subsidy outweighs the tax and they favor higher taxes and transfers. High-income voters favor low taxes and transfers. The tax–transfer combination favored by the median voter is chosen under majority rule. The Meltzer–Richard model predicts rich-to-poor redistribution, with all voters with incomes below the median favoring more redistribution, and all voters above the median favoring less.

Tax and subsidy programs are generally more flexible than the Meltzer–Richard model assumes. Given a choice between taking only from the rich and taking from both the rich and the poor, the selfish median voter should take from both. The hypothesis that redistribution in a democracy is from the tails of the income distribution to the center has come to be known as Director's law, after Aaron Director, who first suggested it, and has been further developed by George Stigler (1970) and Gordon Tullock (1971b).

The second method of circumventing the problem of a lack of an equilibrium under majority rule voting on redistributional issues is the surest way of all. Assume that an equilibrium exists. Both Peltzman (1980) and Becker (1983) have simply assumed that equilibria exist in their models of interest group competition for redistributive gains. Theoretical justification for this assumption can be obtained from the probabilistic voting models reviewed in Chapter 11. Coughlin (1986) has proven the existence of an equilibrium under probabilistic voting when only redistributional issues are to be decided. Coughlin, Mueller, and Murrell (1988) have used the probabilistic voting model to analyze interest group influence in a two-party competition setting.

The interest group influence models of redistribution do not give very precise predictions as to the form and direction that redistribution will take. Relying on Olson's (1965) theory of groups, one can expect redistribution from broadly defined interests to narrowly defined ones, from unconcentrated industries to concentrated industries, from the disorganized to the organized. But which groups are sufficiently organized to win redistributive gains may vary from country to country and may even vary over time in one country. Weingast et al.'s (1981) model leads to the prediction that redistribution takes the form of overly large government budgets.

C.   The evidence

1.   Social insurance

If individuals agree to redistribution programs because they are uncertain of their future positions, they are effectively buying insurance. The normative theories of Rawls, Harsanyi, and Buchanan and Tullock assume that individuals self-impose uncertainty over future positions as an ethical act by stepping behind a veil of ignorance, which screens all specific information about individual positions. Uncertainty is also a characteristic of our everyday lives, however. We all run the risk of growing old. Unemployment is an event that occurs at some time during the working lives of many of us. Serious illnesses or accidents can befall all of us. Thus, rational individuals who consider only their own interests will purchase insurance and may vote for social insurance programs. Social insurance may come about as a result of either ethically motivated or selfishly motivated actions of individuals, or some combination of the two.

It is interesting in this regard to recall that the major social insurance programs in the United States were created during the Great Depression, a time when both the actualities and the probabilities of being unemployed or in poverty soared. Although the economic uncertainties of the Great Depression would lead many to favor government-provided insurance programs, they might also have impressed upon individuals the nature and magnitude of the general uncertainties we all face.

The same thing may have happened during World War II. Dryzek and Goodin (1986) remark upon the common risks all Britons experienced during

Table 23.1. *Comparative growth of insurance and antipoverty programs, 1965–83, in the United States (billions of dollars)*

Programs[a]	Expenditures		
	1965	1975	1983
Insurance			
Old age and survivors	17.501	60.396	152.999
Disability	1.687	8.789	18.177
Unemployment	3.003	13.836	25.350
Medicare	0.000	14.781	56.930
Totals	22.191	97.802	253.456
Antipoverty			
Aid to families with dependent children	1.660	9.211	13.839
Medicaid	1.367	13.502	36.327
Food stamps	0.036	4.694	11.727
Low-rent housing	0.235	1.456	6.659
Education[b]	0.055	1.414	3.766
Totals	3.353	30.277	72.318
Gross National Product[c]	705.1	1598.4	3405.7
Federal transfer payments[c]	41.3	189.6	435.1

Note: This includes Pell grants, supplementary grants, and college work-study.
[a]Source: Social Security Bulletin, Volume 49.
[b]Source: Statistical Abstract of the United States, 1987.
[c]Source: Annual Report, Council of Economic Advisers, 1987.

the bombings of Britain in World War II. They argue that these common risks made the British more aware of their ties with their fellow countrymen. The mental experiment of putting oneself in the position of one's neighbor became easier. "Partiality and impartiality [were] fused" and the British voted for expansions in social insurance programs covering not only damages from the war, but also all of the common risks that a society faces. Dryzek and Goodin (1986) present evidence linking the expansion of social insurance programs in Britain to World War II events. They also present cross-national evidence that the social insurance programs in other countries expanded in proportion to the war-related uncertainties a country endured.

Whatever the underlying motivations, social insurance programs constitute the largest fraction of redistribution in the modern welfare state. Between 1965 and 1983 in the United States, for example, they made up between 78 and 83 percent of all redistributive outlays (Table 23.1).

2.   Social welfare

The different motivations behind redistribution are difficult to disentangle. Does a wealthy individual favor a transfer to the poor because she (a) assumes as an ethical act that she has an equal probability of being rich or poor, (b) actually believes that she faces a positive probability of being poor, or (c) places a positive weight on the welfare of the poor out of ethical-altruistic motivation? Short of psychoanalysis, there may be no way to disentangle fully these three motivations.

One area that seems particularly well-suited to explanation by the Pareto-optimal approach to redistribution is in-kind transfers like housing, food, and medical care. Since recipients value in-kind transfers at less than their nominal value, a redistribution program that was based only on the giver's utility from seeing recipients have higher utility levels would consist of cash transfers (Aaron and von Furstenberg, 1971; Giertz, 1982). That some individuals are willing to contribute to the poor in the form of specific consumption items implies that it is the poor's level of housing, food consumption, and medical care that is of interest to the taxpayers. But more direct evidence supporting the Pareto-optimal approach over competing hypotheses is lacking.[3]

3.   Private welfare

The approaches that explain redistribution as the outcome of voting by selfish individuals on a single-dimensional issue differ in the directional flows, which they predict redistribution takes. Measuring the distributional impact of government policies is not easy, however. The distributional impact of taxes is easier to gauge than the impact of expenditures, but even here substantial

---

3. Larry Orr's (1976, 1978) valiant effort to convert the Pareto-optimal approach to a testable hypothesis is unfortunately marred by an unrealistic assumption in his model. Instead of assuming that the rich get utility from seeing both their fellow rich and the poor better off, he assumes that it is only increases in the incomes of the poor that give the rich utility. In terms of our model, his objective function for the rich takes the form

$$0 = U_2(Y_2 - T) + \alpha n_1 U_1(Y_1 + B),$$

assuming only two income classes (compare with our equation [23.5]). His optimal choice of B by the rich is then defined by the equation

$$\frac{n_1}{n_2} U_2' = \alpha n_1 U_1'.$$

Orr thus predicts lower levels of B with higher ratios of n_1/n_2, and higher levels of B with higher n_1, holding n_1/n_2 constant. But this model implies that if population were to grow and n_1/n_2 remain constant, the rich would eventually impoverish themselves in their efforts to see the poor better off. This implausible implication follows from the assumption that a member of disagreement often exists regarding the incidence of some taxes.[4] For expenditures, things are much worse. Are the benefits that the rich receive from police protection and national defense proportional to their tax payments? Should expenditures on police and defense be thought of as providing any final-consumption social benefits at all, or are they intermediate goods to be netted out when determining the final distribution of benefits and costs from government action (Meerman, 1980)?

Unfortunately, one's measure of the distributional impact of government policies is sensitive to what assumptions one makes. No consensus exists concerning the net distributional effects of the government. Werner Pommerehne (1975) concluded from his survey of studies up through the mid-1970s and from his own work on the canton of Basel Land, that redistribution is from the two tails of the income distribution to the middle. But Aaron and McGuire (1970) and Maital (1973, 1975), working with a model that makes specific assumptions about the utility functions of individuals, derive estimates implying that redistribution is *from the middle to the two ends*. Such a pattern violates Director's law, to say the least, and is consistent with *no* theory of redistribution that exists in the public choice literature. These estimates are sensitive to both the assumptions one makes regarding the spillovers from government output, and the shapes of individual utility functions (Gillespie and Labelle, 1978; Aaron and McGuire, 1970).

The most commonly reported pattern of redistribution shows a slight rich-to-poor effect of government taxes and expenditures. Table 23.2 presents estimates for the United States for 1984. Comparing the first and last lines of the table, we see that government policies reduce the share of income received by the highest-income quintile by roughly 15 percent, and raise the share of the lowest quintile by roughly 50 percent. Nevertheless, families in the highest-income quintile receive five times the average income of those in the lowest quintile, even after adjustments for the impact of government.

A similar conclusion is reached when one makes allowances for the benefits from other types of government expenditures. Table 23.3 reveals that government fiscal policies nearly double the average family income of the lowest-income bracket, whereas they reduce the incomes of the highest-bracket groups by around 10 percent. Similar results have been reported in several other studies (Gillespie, 1965, 1976; Dodge, 1975; Reynolds and Smolensky, 1977).

---

the rich class gets utility from seeing every member of the poor class better off, but no utility from seeing any member of the rich class better off, other than herself. Treating the rich as a club that is concerned with its joint welfare as well as that of the poor eliminates this problem, but unfortunately also eliminates the key variables in Orr's equations (n_2/n_1, and n_1).

4. See, for example, the survey by Peter Mieszkowski (1969).

Table 23.2. *Corrected family income distribution, 1984 (percent)*

	Share of income received by each quintile of families				
	1st (poorest)	2nd	3rd	4th	5th (richest)
Current population survey defini- tion (pretax, cash only)	4.7	11.0	17.0	24.4	42.9
Current population survey defini- tion less taxes	5.8	12.3	17.8	24.1	40.0
Current population survey defini- tion less taxes plus Medicare, Medicaid, and food stamps	7.2	12.2	17.7	24.3	38.7
Current population survey defini- tion less taxes plus Medicare, Medicaid, food stamps, and em- ployer fringe benefits	6.7	12.3	17.6	24.3	39.1
Line above adjusted for differences in family sizes across quintiles	7.3	13.4	18.1	24.4	36.8

Note: When 1984 census income statistics are corrected for taxes, in-kind government and private benefits, and family size, the family income distribution becomes moderately more equal.
Source: Levy (1987, p. 195).

4.   Special interests

The interest group theories predict targeted expenditures, regulations, and tax loopholes to benefit a particular well-organized, influential group. A good example of special interest redistributional gains are the benefits that farm groups have been able to secure from the government. Table 23.4 reports the distribution of farm incomes and program benefits during the mid-1960s in the United States. Although the largest 20 percent of the farms received 50 percent of farm income prior to the distribution of government benefits, they also tended to receive more than 50 percent of government program benefits. Table 23.5 presents the benefits by economic class, class I being the highest income class, class VI the lowest. Sixty-three percent of direct government benefits go to the farms in the highest two income groups, while only 9 percent go to the farms in the lowest two groups. Government programs double the incomes of the richest farms, while they raise the incomes of the poorest farms by "only" 50 percent. It is difficult to reconcile this pattern of government subsidies with any normative theory of redistribution. Rather, it seems obvious that the programs are designed to benefit the biggest and richest farms, and they do.

Other examples come readily to mind: licensing requirements for doctors,

Table 23.3. *Distribution of net benefits and burdens (net as percentage of total family income)*

	Income brackets[a]									
	Under $4,000	$4,000– $5,700	$5,700– $7,900	$7,900– $10,400	$10,400– $12,500	$12,500– $17,500	$17,500– $22,600	$22,600– $35,500	$35,500– $92,000	$92,000 and over
Federal										
1. Specific allocation	76.7	17.7	4.1	−1.9	−4.2	−5.6	−5.6	−5.1	−5.1	−5.1
2. General, variant A	4.3	2.7	1.0	0.7	0.6	−0.4	−0.1	−0.6	−1.0	−3.6
3. Total	81.0	20.5	5.1	−1.3	−3.6	−6.0	−5.6	−5.7	−6.1	−8.7
State and local										
4. Specific allocation	15.7	8.2	5.9	2.7	0.2	−1.4	−3.2	−3.7	−3.4	−4.4
5. General, variant A	−1.1	−0.8	−0.6	−0.5	−0.3	−0.1	0.2	0.4	1.1	1.2
6. Total	14.6	7.4	5.4	2.2	−0.1	−1.5	−3.0	−3.2	−2.3	−3.2
All levels										
7. Specific allocation	92.4	25.9	10.0	0.8	−4.0	−7.0	−8.8	−8.7	−8.5	−9.5
8. General, variant A	3.2	1.9	0.4	0.2	0.3	−0.5	0.1	−0.2	0.1	−2.4
9. Total	95.6	27.9	10.5	0.9	−3.7	−7.4	−8.6	−8.9	−8.4	−11.9

[a]Data are for 1968.
Source: Musgrave and Musgrave (1980), p. 276.

Table 23.4. *Distribution of farm income and commodity program benefits by farm size, mid-1960s (percentage of total income or benefits)*

Source and year	Farm size (percent)						Gini concentration ratio[a]
	Lower 20	Lower 40	Lower 60	Top 40	Top 20	Top 5	
Farm and farm manager total money income, 1963	3.2	11.7	26.4	73.6	50.5	20.8	0.468
Program benefits							
Sugarcane, 1965	1.0	2.9	6.3	93.7	83.1	63.2	0.799
Cotton, 1964	1.8	6.6	15.1	84.9	69.2	41.2	0.653
Rice, 1963	1.0	5.5	15.1	84.9	65.3	34.6	0.632
Wheat, 1964							
Price supports	3.4	8.3	20.7	79.3	62.3	30.5	0.566
Direct payments	6.9	14.2	26.4	73.6	57.3	27.9	0.480
Total	3.3	8.1	20.4	79.6	62.4	30.5	0.569
Feed grains, 1964							
Price supports	0.5	3.2	15.3	84.7	57.3	24.4	0.588
Direct payments	4.4	16.1	31.8	68.2	46.8	20.7	0.405
Total	1.0	4.9	17.3	82.7	56.1	23.9	0.565
Peanuts, 1964	3.8	10.9	23.7	76.3	57.2	28.5	0.522
Tobacco, 1965	3.9	13.2	26.5	73.5	52.8	24.9	0.476
Sugar beets, 1965	5.0	14.3	27.0	73.0	50.5	24.4	0.456
Agricultural conservation program, 1964							
All eligibles	7.9	15.8	34.7	65.3	39.2	n.a.	0.343
Recipients	10.5	22.8	40.3	59.7	36.6	13.8	0.271

n.a. = not available.

[a]The more closely the Gini concentration ratio approaches 1, the more unequal is the distribution; 0 represents a completely equal distribution.

Source: Schultze (1972, p. 98). © The Brookings Institution.

opticians, plumbers, and carpenters; depletion allowances for petroleum and other minerals. Indeed, all of the rent-seeking literature might be included as part of the process of government redistribution to special interests. That some government policies – taxes or expenditures – are intended to confer redistributional gains on particular interest groups cannot be questioned. What the literature does not illuminate is the amount of government activity explained in this way and its net impact on the distribution of income.

D.   Conclusions

The normative theories of redistribution envisage impartial or altruistic individuals unanimously agreeing to programs that redistribute income from

Table 23.5. *Distribution of farm program benefits and income by economic class, 1969*

| Item | Economic class | | | | | | | |
	I	II	III	IV	V	VI	I & II	V & VI
Aggregate benefits	(*billions of dollars*)							
Price supports	1.90	0.76	0.55	0.22	0.08	0.09	2.66	0.17
Direct payments	1.08	0.90	0.88	0.43	0.20	0.30	1.98	0.50
Total	2.98	1.66	1.43	0.65	0.28	0.39	4.64	0.67
Distribution of benefits	(*percentage of total*)							
Price supports	52.9	21.0	15.4	6.1	2.2	2.4	73.9	4.6
Direct payments	28.5	23.7	23.2	11.3	5.3	7.9	53.6	13.2
Total	40.3	22.5	19.4	8.8	3.8	5.3	62.8	9.1
Income and benefits per farm	(*thousands of dollars*)							
Farmer's net income	33.0	13.7	9.6	8.1	7.0	8.1	20.9	7.9
Net income from farming	27.5	10.5	6.5	3.6	2.1	1.1	16.8	1.3
Price supports	9.0	2.1	1.1	0.6	0.3	0.1	4.7	0.1
Direct payments	5.1	2.5	1.7	1.1	0.7	0.2	3.6	0.3
Total	14.1	4.6	2.8	1.7	1.0	0.3	8.3	0.4
Net income from farming under free market conditions	13.4	5.9	3.7	1.9	1.1	0.8	8.5	0.9

Source: Schultze (1972, p. 110). © The Brookings Institution.

themselves. These theories seem romantic and naive alongside the pragmatic public choice theories, which predict that the organizationally and numerically strong grab from unorganized minorities. But we have seen in Chapter 18 that the *narrow* self-interest model of voting does not explain well the voting behavior of many individuals. Nor does it explain all redistribution activity.

Social insurance programs, like old age and survivors' insurance and unemployment compensation, appear to have widespread popular support that goes beyond the rational decisions of a selfish individual calculating her retirement needs or the probability of losing her job (Rodgers, 1974, pp. 195–9). Even tenured economics professors may vote in favor of unemployment compensation programs out of a belief that their fellow citizens should be protected from the economic uncertainties of the labor market, rather than from the expectation that their own expected compensation benefits exceed their expected tax payments.

The rational, self-interest models of redistribution predict a sharp division between groups over governmental policies. If redistribution is from rich to poor, then all those with incomes above the median should vote against the redistribution policies, all of those with incomes below the median should vote in favor. But survey results again do not indicate such a clear dichotomy. Income is not closely related to voting behavior on Proposition 13 measures to stop government growth.[5]

On the other hand, many expenditures, subsidies, regulations, and tax measures can best be explained as the rewards to better organization and lobbying efforts by some groups. Although the self-interest model does not explain all redistribution activity of government, it certainly explains some. The best model of redistribution is one that combines elements of both the normative and positive public choice theories of redistribution (Rodgers, 1974).

Plotnick and Winters (1985) have developed such a model to explain aid to families with dependent children (AFDC) payments across states. AFDC is a means-test program of the type one might expect to see if the taxpayers wished to improve the positions of the worst-off in society. Plotnick and Winters thus include variables to capture the willingness of nonbeneficiaries from AFDC to pay taxes for such a program across states. They also hypothesize that the selfish interests of the poor get greater weight in states in which interparty competition is more intense. Variables related to both hypotheses turn out to be significant, implying that both the willingness of taxpayers to pay and the ability of the poor to take explain differences in AFDC levels across states.[6]

That no one redistributive model is clearly predominant suggests that efforts to explain redistribution in the future must either try to explain but a single aspect of redistribution, or must, as Plotnick and Winters argue, combine more than one theory of redistribution. This conclusion may also explain why the net distributional effects of government appear to be so small. The patterns that we have observed in this chapter might be explained as a modest amount of rich-to-poor redistribution for altruistic or impartial insurance motives and an indeterminant amount of selfishly motivated redistribution with no clear directional impact. Given the intensity of emotions raised by redistributional issues, more modeling and testing of public choice models of redistribution are certainly needed.

5. Gramlich and Rubinfeld (1982b). Mickey Levy (1975) reports results somewhat more favorable to the self-interest hypothesis, but he, too, found that households with incomes below $5,000 voted counter to their predicted self-interest, and households with incomes above $25,000 exhibited no systematic pattern on Proposition 13.

6. The variables that Plotnick and Winters use to test the Pareto-optimal approach part of the model, e.g., income per capita, do not really allow one to discriminate this approach from, say, the redistribution insurance approach. The willingness to buy insurance could also increase with income.

Bibliographical notes

This chapter benefited from my reading of the surveys of Rodgers (1974) and Oppenheimer (1979).

Frank Levy (1987) has written an interesting account of the changes in income distributional patterns that have occurred in the United States since World War II without focusing on the public choice process, however.

Douglas Rae (1981) and his associates have pulled together an interesting assortment of the different definitions of equality which underlie discussions of redistribution.

Robert E. Goodin (1988) analyzes and defends redistribution policies from a normative perspective.

CHAPTER 24

Allocation, redistribution, and public choice

Some men look at constitutions with sanctimonious reverence, and deem them like the ark of the covenant, too sacred to be touched. They ascribe to the men of the preceding age a wisdom more than human, and suppose what they did to be beyond amendment. I knew that age well; I belonged to it, and labored with it. It deserved well of its country. It was very like the present, but without the experience of the present; and forty years of experience in government is worth a century of book-reading; and this they would say themselves, were they to rise from the dead. I am certainly not an advocate for frequent and untried changes in laws and constitutions. I think moderate imperfections had better be borne with; because, when once known, we accommodate ourselves to them, and find practical means of correcting their ill effects. But I know also, that laws and institutions must go hand in hand with the progress of the human mind. As that becomes more developed, more enlightened, as new discoveries are made, new truths disclosed, and manners and opinions change with the change of circumstances, institutions must advance also, and keep pace with the times. We might as well require a man to wear still the coat which fitted him when a boy, as civilized society to remain ever under the regimen of their barbarous ancestors.

Thomas Jefferson

Rules for collective decision are needed, quite simply, because people live together. Their mere grouping into circumscribed geographic areas creates the potential and necessity for collective action. Some collective decisions can benefit all individuals involved; other decisions benefit only some. Even when everyone benefits, some do so more than others, raising an issue of how the "gains from trade" are shared. Thus, collective choices can be grouped into two categories: those benefiting all members of the community, and those benefiting some and hurting others. These two categories correspond to the familiar distinction between moves from off the Pareto frontier to points on it and moves along the frontier – that is, to allocation and redistribution.

The potential to make collective decisions benefiting all members of a community has undoubtedly existed for as long as it has been legitimate to call a group of humans living in proximity to one another a community. So, too, has the potential for redistribution. Did the state come into existence to enable its members to better achieve the allocative efficiency gains that social organization and technology made possible? Did the state come into existence

459

so that *some* members of the community could exploit their neighbors? Does the modern state grow by providing an ever-increasing amount of collective benefits to the community, or does its growth reflect an escalating series of programs for transferring wealth from one segment of the community to another? Do the rent-seeking and wealth-transferring efforts of different groups of society stifle the potential for making moves that benefit all of society? These questions have puzzled anthropologists, economists, and political scientists. They lie at the heart of the public choice literature.

It was one of Knut Wicksell's (1896) great insights to recognize the importance of the distinction between allocation and redistribution decisions, *and* to recognize the need to make these decisions by separate voting procedures. More fundamentally, his contribution to the literature can be seen as the recognition that the characteristics of the outcomes of government action, the allocation or redistribution decisions, cannot be discussed without taking into account the inputs from the citizens via the voting process bringing these outcomes about. This latter contribution was virtually ignored by the profession for half a century until the public choice literature began to appear. It may be regarded as one of the cornerstone postulates of this literature.

Although Wicksell made use of the distinction between allocation and redistribution decisions, his analysis focused on the former. The redistribution decisions were assumed to have been justly decided at some prior point in time. This left only the allocative efficiency improvements to resolve, decisions of potential benefit to all. Here Wicksell's work takes on a distinctly contractarian and individualistic tone. Each citizen took part in the collective decision process to advance his own ends, and via the quid pro quo of collective decision-making outcomes were reached to the mutual benefit of all. Voting achieved in the market for public goods the same outcome as exchange achieved in the markets for private goods. This contractarian, quid pro quo approach to government has underlain much of public choice and the public expenditure theory of public finance, most visibly in the work of Buchanan and Musgrave.

Often this literature takes on a very optimistic tone concerning the potential of collective decision making. In *The Calculus of Consent* Buchanan and Tullock describe government institutions that bear more than a passing resemblance to those of the United States and that seem capable of satisfying a society's collective wants. Redistribution decisions are separated from allocative efficiency decisions, however, and unanimously resolved at the constitutional stage. Thus, the day-to-day work of parliament is limited to deciding those issues in which unanimity is potentially possible. In the last 20 years several new and "superior" voting procedures have been put forward. All have attractive properties that seem to circumvent most if not all of the paradoxes of collective choice. All are capable of achieving this magic only when limited to deciding allocative efficiency improvements.

The literature that focuses upon redistribution, or ignores the distinction between redistribution and allocation, thereby implicitly combining the two, has a discernibly more pessimistic tone. Equilibria do not exist. Their absence enables agenda setters to dictate outcomes. Outcomes of all voting procedures can be manipulated by strategic misrepresentation of preferences unless someone is allowed to be dictator. Outcomes may be Pareto inefficient. The mood of this new "dismal" science is accurately captured by William Riker (1982b). Given the achievements of the social choice literature, the most society can hope for is to develop and maintain political institutions capable of deposing bad leadership – some of the time.

It is difficult to reject Riker's pessimistic interpretation of the implications of the social–public choice literature. Moreover, his examples and countless others that one could present illustrate too vividly that the instabilities, inefficiencies, manipulated agendas, and other diseases of democratic decision making, which public choice predicts, do occur. But I am reluctant to write off the achievements of the first 40 years of public choice as a catalogue of the deficiencies of democratic decision making. There are strands in this literature that suggest a more optimistic picture, a picture perhaps more of what might be than of what is. We close by sketching this picture.

To begin with, one must distinguish between decisions to improve allocative efficiency and to redistribute income and wealth. Certainly one of the major achievements of the public choice literature has been to underline the importance of this distinction first recognized by Wicksell. Not to make use of it when designing political institutions is to handicap the exercise from the start. Second, one must distinguish clearly between designing institutions for direct democracy and designing institutions for electoral politics.

Nowhere is the importance of the distinction between allocative efficiency and redistribution made more vivid than in the literature on clubs and voting-with-the-feet. Allocative efficiency can be improved when individuals with homogeneous tastes for bundles of public goods form clubs and local polities. When local polities attempt to provide redistribution programs and other programs unwanted by some taxpayers, individuals vote with their feet and move to communities where such programs do not exist. In a mobile society significant amounts of redistribution at the local level cannot occur if those who must pay for the redistribution are unwilling to do so. Just as redistribution proposals would be screened out under a unanimity rule leaving only proposals to improve allocative efficiency, the unanimity achieved silently through voting-with-the-feet eliminates redistribution programs from local budgets. If significant redistribution is to occur, it must take place at higher levels of government.

Much of the pessimism regarding the potential of democratic institutions stems from Arrow's theorem and the flood of theorems in its aftermath. The objective of Arrow's search was to find a social welfare function that based its rankings of alternatives on the aggregation of individual ordinal rankings. That none was found indicates that interpersonal utility comparisons must be made either directly via the decision rule, or indirectly through restrictions placed on the preference domain, the types of issues that can be decided, or in some equivalent manner.

The same conclusion emerges from the literature on real-valued welfare functions. Ordinal utility functions plus the Pareto postulate do not allow one to choose from among the set of points along the Pareto frontier. To make such a choice, additional postulates must be introduced incorporating stronger value judgments than contained in the Pareto postulate. Most writers have shied away from making these additional value judgments, have stopped short of defining a social welfare function that will select from among the Pareto-preferred set. Those who have introduced additional value postulates, for example, Harsanyi (1955) and Ng (1975), have invariably come up with additive social welfare functions whose arguments are the cardinal, interpersonally comparable utilities of the citizens.

Several of the new voting procedures aggregate cardinal utility information supplied by the voters (the demand revelation process, Smith's auction process, Hylland and Zeckhauser's point voting). If restricted to use on decisions that could improve allocative efficiency, they contain the potential for achieving Pareto-optimal allocations of resources. Experimental work and some limited applications indicate that they can work as theory predicts. Although each is potentially vulnerable to strategic and coalitional manipulation, such strategic behavior is both complicated and risky. The extent to which these procedures would be manipulated needs to be demonstrated experimentally rather than assumed on the basis of hypothetical examples and impossibility proofs. Voting by veto is strategy-proof and relies only on ordinal utility information. It thus provides another option for achieving a Pareto-optimal allocation of resources in deciding public good–externality issues, an option that would allow one to avoid the implicit weighting of cardinal utilities in proportion to initial incomes inherent in the demand revelation and auction procedures.

These new voting procedures all assume that voting is by those whose welfare is affected by the outcomes of the voting process, as in a direct democracy. Were these procedures to be employed by a committee of representatives, then these representatives should be chosen in such a way that each group of citizens is represented in proportion to their number in the polity. A form of proportional representation is required. To ensure that the representatives did vote in accordance with the preferences of those they represent, their (re)election should depend upon their record of voting only on the public good–externality issues to be decided. The function of choosing a government (executive) should be separated from that of deciding allocative efficiency issues. Under such a reform the ideal proportional representation system would differ from those now extant. So be it. The proportional representation systems functioning today reflect the best ideas of political theorists one century ago. We know more today than we did then. We know that deciding levels of national defense, police protection, and other public goods are positive-sum games in which all can possibly gain. Forming a cabinet by majority rule is a zero-sum game in which nearly half of the parties represented must lose. The same institution and voting rule are not optimal for both tasks.

If one assumes that political institutions can be designed to reveal preferences on allocative efficiency changes adequately, the question remains, how to resolve redistributional questions. In answering this question it is again critical to recognize that the procedures required are different from those employed for allocative efficiency gains. Beyond this important insight, the public choice literature points in two distinct directions. First, the uncertainty inherent in the long-run nature of constitutional decisions can induce individuals, out of self-interest, to incorporate certain redistributional measures and the protection of civil liberties into the constitution. The potential for this kind of redistribution could be enhanced by organizing a constitutional convention in such a way as to maximize uncertainty over future positions or impartiality (e.g., have the constitution not go into effect until several years after ratification). Parliaments could be freed to concentrate on allocative efficiency improvements by confining redistributional measures to constitutional guarantees.

The literature on majority rule suggests a second way of handling redistributional property rights issues. When these issues are of a binary nature, and equal intensities can be assumed by individuals on both sides, then majority rule can be an attractive rule for settling distributional questions. The requirement that issues be binary immediately suggests a court of law, and the Supreme Court in the United States has used majority rule to resolve distributional questions (e.g., abortion and desegregation of schools). Other institutional arrangements can be envisaged, once one recognizes the need to resolve redistributional questions using a procedure different from that used for allocative efficiency improvements.

An alternative to institutionally separating allocative efficiency and redistribution issues and allowing the citizens to decide them directly is to limit the citizen's role to that of selecting an agent or set of agents, and to have the agent(s) decide the issues. The models of Chapters 10 and 11 are relevant here, and this literature contains a more optimistic view of the results of voting than does the literature on committee voting in the Arrow tradition. When voting is limited to a pair of candidates or parties that compete for the privilege of running (forming) the government, an equilibrium pair of platforms exists (Chapter 11). The properties of this equilibrium (Pareto optimality, the maximization of a particular social welfare function) are not obviously inferior to those achieved by (claimed for) the market, or to those one might reasonably demand of a collective choice process. These results place the outcomes from collective decision procedures in a radically different light.

There is much evidence consistent with this model of electoral competition. Although the cycling literature implies that a candidate forced to run on her record is always doomed to defeat, incumbents generally face much better odds. The evidence reviewed in Chapters 11, 13, and 15 indicates that intense efforts are made by candidates to win votes and interest groups to influence candidates. Political competition is real and results in predictable and stable outcomes with reasonable normative properties.

Competition between candidates increasingly takes the form of spending money to "buy" votes. This money comes from interest groups, which seek to "buy" legislation. The weights given to individual utilities in the social welfare function that political competition maximizes depend on the resources and organizational skills of the interest groups to which individuals belong. Although the process of competition for votes may achieve a welfare maximum of sorts, it is not one in which all will be happy with the weights their interests receive in the resulting equilibrium.

Moreover, the money candidates spend does not really buy votes. It buys television commercials, posters, placards and buttons, pollsters, canvassers, and consultants. It buys all of the instruments that modern marketing can devise to influence how an individual votes on election day. But in the end it is the decision the voter makes that determines the outcome of the election. The quality of these outcomes rests on the quality of this choice.

An important implication of the rational choice approach to politics is that it is irrational for an individual to vote if the act of voting is predicated on the assumption that the individual's vote will affect the outcome of the election. Given this observation, voting must be explained as satisfying some motivation of individuals other than one directly tied to the outcomes of the election. We have argued that voting is one of those acts that individuals are conditioned to perform for the good of the community. Although social conditioning may carry voters to the polls, it is not evident that this conditioning induces them to gather sufficient information to make a discriminating choice once they get there. Nor is the "information" supplied to them by the candidates likely to aid in this task. Candidate competition may lead to an equilibrium set of platforms defined over an "issue" space, but the nature of the issues over which this competition takes place is undefined. So too, therefore, is the significance of the welfare maximum achieved through this competition.

The candidate competition models help to dispel concern over the existence of an equilibrium in policy space. They raise questions, however, about the nature of the policy space over which competition takes place, and about the weights given to individual preferences in the welfare function that this competition implicitly maximizes. More generally, they suggest that the emphasis in public choice research needs to shift from the outputs of the political process to its inputs, to shift from an emphasis upon the quality of the aggregation process to the quality of the choices aggregated. Much of the public choice literature has analyzed outcomes of procedures in which each individual's vote(s) receives equal weight and all voters are well-informed about the issues. But in representative democracies, rules of representation and the nature of competition give radically different weights to voter interests, and these are often poorly defined and expressed.

Thus, a number of important issues in public choice require further research. But the field remains young. In its first 40 years, a rich harvest of results has been brought forth. Most do seem to be rather disheartening descriptions of how political institutions function and malfunction. But I have tried to suggest that there is also a brighter side to the public choice literature. Some parts offer insights into when and why political institutions work well. Other parts make proposals to improve the performance of political institutions. To some, this latter literature will appear utopian. And so it is. But the constitutional governments of Switzerland and the United States today would have seem utopian to a vassal living in Europe during the Middle Ages, and even today must seem utopian to some citizens of communist and developing country dictatorships.

Indeed, what is most utopian of all is the idea that knowledge is cumulative, and that from a knowledge of past mistakes we can design institutions that will avoid similar mistakes in the future. Public choice does provide us with this knowledge. Because of this, I remain optimistic that the field will continue to attract fine scholars, that the future harvests of their work will be of high quality, and even about the possibility that this research may someday help to improve the democratic institutions by which we govern ourselves.

References

Aaron, H. and von Furstenberg, G. M. "The Efficiency of Transfers in Kind," *Western Economic Journal,* June 1971, *9,* pp. 184–91.

Aaron, H. and McGuire, M. C. "Public Goods and Income Distribution," *Econometrica,* November 1970, *38,* pp. 907–20.

Abramovitz, M. "Notes on International Differences in Productivity Growth Rates," in Mueller (1983, pp. 79–89).

Abrams, B. A. and Settle, R. F. "A Modest Proposal for Election Reform," *Public Choice,* Winter 1976, *28,* pp. 37–53.

Abrams, R. "The Voter's Paradox and the Homogeneity of Individual Preference Orders," *Public Choice,* Summer 1976, *26,* pp. 19–27.

Abramson, P. R. and Aldrich, J. H. "The Decline of Electoral Participation in America," *American Political Science Review,* September 1982, *76,* pp. 502–21.

Ackerman, B. A., *Social Justice in the Liberal State,* New Haven: Yale University Press, 1980.

Ahlbrandt, R. S., Jr. "Efficiency in the Provision of Fire Services," *Public Choice,* Fall 1973, *16,* pp. 1–15.

Aivazian, V. A. and Callen, J. L. "The Coase Theorem and the Empty Core," *Journal of Law and Economics,* April 1981, *24,* pp. 175–81.

Alchian, A. A. "Uncertainty, Evolution and Economic Theory," *Journal of Political Economy,* June 1950, *58,* pp. 211–21.

Alt, J. E. and Chrystal, K. A. *Political Economics,* Brighton: Wheatsheaf Books, 1983.

Amihud, Y. and Lev, B. "Risk Reduction as a Managerial Motive for Conglomerate Mergers," *Bell Journal of Economics,* Autumn 1981, *12,* pp. 605–17.

Anderson, T. L. and Hill, P. J. "Privatizing the Commons: An Improvement?" *Southern Economic Journal,* October 1983, *50,* pp. 438–50.

Aranson, P. H. and Ordeshook, P. C. "Spatial Strategies for Sequential Elections," *Decision-Making,* Columbus: Merrill, 1972.

"Regulation, Redistribution, and Public Choice," *Public Choice,* 1981, *37*(1), pp. 69–100.

Arcelus, F. and Meltzer, A. H. "The Effect of Aggregate Economic Variables on Congressional Elections," *American Political Science Review,* December 1975a, *69,* pp. 1232–65.

"Aggregate Economic Variables and Votes for Congress–Reply," *American Political Science Review,* December 1975b, *69,* pp. 1266–9.

Arrow, K. J. *Social Choice and Individual Values,* New York: John Wiley and Sons, 1951, rev. ed. 1963.

"Some Ordinalist-Utilitarian Notes on Rawls' *Theory of Justice,*" *Journal of Philosophy,* May 1973, *70,* pp. 245–63.

Arrow, K. J. and Scitovsky, T., eds. *Readings in Welfare Economics,* Homewood, Ill.: Richard D. Irwin, 1969.

Ashenfelter, O. and Kelley, S., Jr. "Determinants of Participation in Presidential Elections," *Journal of Law and Economics,* December 1975, *18,* pp. 695–733.

466

Asselain, J.-C. and Morrison, C. "The Political Economy of Comparative Growth Rates: The Case of France," in Mueller (1983, pp. 157–75).

Atesoglu, H. S. and Congleton, R. "Economic Conditions and National Elections, Post-Sample Forecasts of the Kramer Equations," *American Political Science Review*, December 1982, *76*, pp. 873–75.

Austen-Smith, D. "Voluntary Pressure Groups," *Economica*, May 1981a, *48*, pp. 143–53.

"Party Policy and Campaign Costs in a Multi-Constituency Model of Electoral Competition," *Public Choice*, 1981b, *37*(3), pp. 389–402.

"Restricted Pareto Rights," *Journal of Economic Theory*, February 1982, *26*, pp. 89–99.

"Interest Groups, Campaign Contributions, and Probabilistic Voting," *Public Choice*, 1987, *54*(2), pp. 123–39.

Auster, R. D. and Silver, M. *The State as a Firm*, Boston: Kluwer, 1979.

Averch, H. A., Koehler, J. E. and Denton, F. H. *The Matrix of Policy in the Philippines*, Princeton: Princeton University Press, 1971.

Axelrod, R. *Conflict of Interest*, Chicago: Markham, 1970.

The Evolution of Cooperation, New York: Basic Books, 1984.

Baber, W. R. and Sen, P. K. "The Political Process and the Use of Debt Financing by State Governments," *Public Choice*, 1986, *48*(3), pp. 201–15.

Baldwin, R. E. *The Political Economy of U.S. Import Policy*, Cambridge, Mass.: MIT Press, 1985.

Balinski, M. L. and Young, H. P. "Stability, Coalitions and Schisms in Proportional Representation Systems," *American Political Science Review*, September 1978, *72*, pp. 848–58.

Fair Representation, New Haven: Yale University Press, 1982.

Barbera, S. "The Manipulation of Social Choice Mechanisms That Do Not Leave 'Too Much' to Chance," *Econometrica*, October 1977, *45*, pp. 1573–88.

Barr, J. L. and Davis, O. A. "An Elementary Political and Economic Theory of the Expenditures of Local Governments," *Southern Economic Journal*, October 1966, *33*, pp. 149–65.

Barro, R. J. "Unanticipated Money Growth and Unemployment in the United States," *American Economic Review*, March 1977, *67*, pp. 101–15.

Barry, B. *Political Argument*, London: Routledge and Kegan Paul, 1965.

Lady Chatterley's Lover and Doctor Fischer's Bomb Party: Liberalism, Pareto Optimality, and the Problem of Objectionable Preferences," in Elster and Hylland (1986), pp. 11–43.

Barzel, Y. "Private Schools and Public School Finance," *Journal of Political Economy*, January 1973, *81*, pp. 174–86.

Barzel, Y. and Deacon, R. T. "Voting Behavior, Efficiency, and Equity," *Public Choice*, Spring 1975, *21*, pp. 1–14.

Barzel, Y. and Silberberg, E. "Is the Act of Voting Rational?" *Public Choice*, Fall 1973, *16*, pp. 51–8.

Baumol, W. J. *Business Behavior, Value and Growth*, New York: Macmillan, 1959.

"Macroeconomics of Unbalanced Growth: The Anatomy of Urban Crisis," *American Economic Review*, June 1967a, *57*, pp. 415–26.

Welfare Economics and the Theory of the State, 2d ed., Cambridge: Harvard University Press, 1967b.

"On Taxation and the Control of Externalities," *American Economic Review*, June 1972, *62*, pp. 307–22.

Beck, N. "The Paradox of Minimax Regret," *American Political Science Review*, September 1975, *69*, p. 918.

"Does There Exist a Business Cycle: A Box-Tiao Analysis," *Public Choice*, 1982a, *38*(2), pp. 205–9.

468   References

"Parties, Administrations, and American Macroeconomic Outcomes," *American Political Science Review*, March 1982b, *76*, pp. 83–93.

Becker, G. S. "Comment" (on Peltzman, 1976), *Journal of Law and Economics*, August 1976, *19*, pp. 245–8.

"A Theory of Competition among Pressure Groups for Political Influence," *Quarterly Journal of Economics*, August 1983, *98*, pp. 371–400.

"Public Policies, Pressure Groups, and Dead Weight Costs," *Journal of Public Economics*, December 1985, *28*, pp. 329–47.

Becker, G. "The Public Interest Hypothesis Revisited: A New Test of Peltzman's Theory of Regulation," *Public Choice*, 1986, *49*(3), pp. 223–34.

Bell, D. *Coming of Post-Industrial Society*, New York: Basic Books, 1973.

Bell, R., Edwards, D. V. and Wagner, R. H., eds. *Political Power*, New York: Free Press, 1969.

Bendor, J., Taylor, S. and Van Gaalen, R. "Bureaucratic Expertise versus Legislative Authority: A Model of Deception and Monitoring in Budgeting," *American Political Science Review*, December 1985, *79*, pp. 1041–60.

Bennett, E. and Conn, D. "The Group Incentive Properties of Mechanisms for the Provision of Public Goods," *Public Choice*, Spring 1977, *29*, pp. 95–102.

Bennett, J. T. and Johnson, M. H. "Public versus Private Provision of Collective Goods and Services: Garbage Collection Revisited," *Public Choice*, 1979, *34*(1), pp. 55–64.

"Tax Reduction without Sacrifice: Private-Sector Production of Public Services," *Public Finance Quarterly*, October 1980a, *8*, pp. 363–96.

The Political Economy of Federal Government Growth, 1959–1978, College Station: Texas A&M University Press, 1980b.

Ben-Porath, Y. "The Years of Plenty and the Years of Famine – A Political Business Cycle?" *Kyklos*, 1975, *28*, pp. 400–3.

Bental, B. and Ben-Zion, U. "Political Contributions and Policy: Some Extensions," *Public Choice*, Winter 1975, *19*, pp. 1–12.

Bentley, A. F. *The Process of Government*, Chicago: University of Chicago Press, 1907.

Ben-Zion, U. and Eytan, Z. "On Money, Votes, and Policy in a Democratic Society," *Public Choice*, Spring 1974, *17*, pp. 1–10.

Bergson, A. "A Reformulation of Certain Aspects of Welfare Economics," *Quarterly Journal of Economics*, February 1938, *52*, pp. 314–44.

"On the Concept of Social Welfare," *Quarterly Journal of Economics*, May 1954, *68*, pp. 233–53.

Bergstrom, T. C. "When Does Majority Rule Supply Public Goods Efficiently?" *Scandinavian Journal of Economics*, October 1979, *81*, pp. 217–26.

Bergstrom, T. C. and Goodman, R. P. "Private Demands for Public Goods," *American Economic Review*, June 1973, *63*, pp. 280–96.

Bernholz, P. "Economic Policies in a Democracy," *Kyklos*, 1966, *19*(1), pp. 48–80.

"Logrolling, Arrow Paradox and Cyclical Majorities," *Public Choice*, Summer 1973, *15*, pp. 87–95.

"Logrolling, Arrow Paradox and Decision Rules – A Generalization," *Kyklos*, 1974a, *27*, pp. 49–61.

Grundlagen der Politischen Okonomie, Band II, Tübingen: Mohr (Siebeck), 1974b.

"Is a Paretian Liberal Really Impossible?" *Public Choice*, Winter 1974c, *20*, pp. 99–107.

"Logrolling and the Paradox of Voting: Are They Logically Equivalent?" *American Political Science Review*, September 1975, *69*, pp. 961–2.

"Prisoner's Dilemma, Logrolling and Cyclical Group Preferences," *Public Choice*, Spring 1977, *29*, pp. 73–84.

"On the Stability of Logrolling Outcomes in Stochastic Games," *Public Choice*, 1978, *33*(3), pp. 65–82.

Berry, W. O. and Lowery, D. "The Growing Cost of Government: A Test of Two Explanations," *Social Science Quarterly*, September 1984, *65*, pp. 735–49.

Bhagwati, J. N. "Directly Unproductive, Profit-seeking (DUP) Activities," *Journal of Political Economy*, October 1982, *90*, pp. 988–1002.

Bhagwati, J. N. and Srinivasan, T. N. "Revenue Seeking: A Generalization of the Theory of Tariffs," *Journal of Political Economy*, December 1980, *88*, pp. 1069–87.

Black, D. "On the Rationale of Group Decision Making," *Journal of Political Economy*, February 1948a, *56*, pp. 23–34, reprinted in Arrow and Scitovsky (1969, pp. 133–46).
"The Decisions of a Committee Using a Special Majority," *Econometrica*, July 1948b, *16*, pp. 245–61.
The Theory of Committees and Elections, Cambridge: Cambridge University Press, 1958.

Blau, J. H. "A Direct Proof of Arrow's Theorem," *Econometrica*, January 1972, *40*, pp. 61–7.
"Liberal Values and Independence," *Review of Economic Studies*, July 1975, *42*, pp. 395–402.

Blau, J. H. and Deb, R. "Social Decision Functions and the Veto," *Econometrica*, May 1977, *45*, pp. 871–9.

Blin, J.-M. and Satterthwaite, M. A. "Individual Decisions and Group Decisions," *Journal of Public Economics*, October 1978, *10*, pp. 247–67.

Bloom, H. S. "Public Choice and Private Interest: Explaining the Vote for Property Tax Classification in Massachusetts," *National Tax Journal*, December 1979, *32*, pp. 527–34.

Bloom, H. S. and Price, H. D. "Voter Response to Short-Run Economic Conditions: The Asymmetric Effect of Prosperity and Recession," *American Political Science Review*, December 1975, *69*, pp. 1266–76.

Bohm, P. "Estimating Demand for Public Goods: An Experiment," *European Economic Review*, March 1972, *3*, pp. 111–30.

Borcherding, T. E., ed. *Budgets and Bureaucrats: The Sources of Government Growth*, Durham, N.C.: Duke University Press, 1977a.
"One Hundred Years of Public Spending, 1870–1970," 1977b in Borcherding (1977a, pp. 19–44).
"The Causes of Government Expenditure Growth: A Survey of the U.S. Evidence," *Journal of Public Economics*, December 1985, *28*, pp. 359–82.

Borcherding, T. E., Bush, W. C. and Spann, R. M. "The Effects of Public Spending on the Divisibility of Public Outputs in Consumption, Bureaucratic Power, and the Size of the Tax-Sharing Group," in Borcherding (1977a, pp. 211–28).

Borcherding, T. E. and Deacon, R. T. "The Demand for the Services of Non-Federal Governments," *American Economic Review*, December 1972, *62*, pp. 891–901.

Borcherding, T. E., Pommerehne, W. W. and Schneider, F. "Comparing the Efficiency of Private and Public Production: The Evidence from Five Countries," *Zeitschrift für Nationalökonomie*, 1982, *89*, pp. 127–56.

Bordley, R. F. "A Pragmatic Method for Evaluating Election Schemes through Simulation," *American Political Science Review*, March 1983, *77*, pp. 123–41.

Borglin, A. "States and Persons – On the Interpretation of Some Fundamental Concepts in the Theory of Justice as Fairness," *Journal of Public Economics*, June 1982, *18*, pp. 85–104.

Borooah, V. and van der Ploeg, F. *Political Aspects of the Economy*, Cambridge: Cambridge University Press, 1983.

Bowen, H. R. "The Interpretation of Voting in the Allocation of Economic Resources," *Quarterly Journal of Economics*, February 1943, *58*, pp. 27–48, reprinted in Arrow and Scitovsky (1969, pp. 115–32).

Bowles, S. and Eatwell, J. "Between Two Worlds: Interest Groups, Class Structure, and Capitalist Growth," in Mueller (1983, pp. 217–30).

Braithwaite, R. B. *Theory of Games as a Tool for the Moral Philosopher*, Cambridge: The University Press, 1955.

Brams, S. J. *Game Theory and Politics*, New York: Free Press, 1975.

Brams, S. J. and Fishburn, P. C. "Approval Voting," *American Political Science Review*, September 1978, *72*, pp. 831–47.

Approval Voting. Boston: Birkhäuser, 1983.

Brennan, G. and Buchanan, J. M. *The Power to Tax: Analytical Foundations of a Fiscal Constitution*, Cambridge: Cambridge University Press, 1980.

"The Logic of the Levers," George Mason University, July 1983, mimeo.

"Voter Choice: Evaluating Political Alternatives," *American Behavioral Scientist*, November/December 1984, *28*, pp. 185–201.

Brennan, G. and Lomasky, L. E. "Large Numbers, Small Costs: The Uneasy Foundations of Democratic Rule," VPI & SU, November, 1982, mimeo.

Brennan, G. and Walsh, C. "A Monopoly Model of Public Goods Provision: The Uniform Pricing Case," *American Economic Review*, March 1981, *71*, pp. 196–206.

Breton, A. *The Economic Theory of Representative Government*, Chicago: Aldine, 1974.

Breton, A. and Galeotti, G. "Is Proportional Representation Always the Best Electoral Rule?" *Public Finance*, 1985, *40*(1), pp. 1–16.

Breton, A. and Scott, A. *The Economic Constitution of Federal States*, Toronto: University of Toronto Press, 1978.

Breton, A. and Wintrobe, R. "The Equilibrium Size of a Budget Maximizing Bureau," *Journal of Political Economy*, February 1975, *83*, pp. 195–207.

The Logic of Bureaucratic Control, Cambridge: Cambridge University Press, 1982.

Breyer, F. "Sen's Paradox with Decisiveness over Issues in Case of Liberal Preferences," *Zeitschrift für Nationalökonomie*, 1977, *37*(1–2), pp. 45–60.

Brittan, S. "The Economic Contradictions of Democracy," *British Journal of Political Science*, April 1975, *5*, pp. 129–59.

Brody, R. A. and Page, B. I. "Indifference, Alienation and Rational Decisions," *Public Choice*, Summer 1973, *15*, 1–17.

Brooks, M. A. and Heijdra, B. J. "In Search of Rent-Seeking," University of Tasmania, 1986, mimeo.

Brown, D. J. "Acyclic Choice," Cowles Foundation, New Haven, 1973.

"Aggregation of Preferences," *Quarterly Journal of Economics*, August 1975, *89*, pp. 456–69.

Brubaker, E. R. "On the Margolis 'Thought Experiment,' and the Applicability of Demand-Revealing Mechanisms to Large-Group Decisions," *Public Choice*, 1983, *41*(2), pp. 315–19.

"Efficient Allocation and Unanimous Consent with Incomplete Demand Disclosures," *Public Choice*, 1986, *48*(3), pp. 217–27.

Brueckner, J. K. "A Test for Allocative Efficiency in the Local Public Sector," *Journal of Public Economics*, December 1982, *19*, pp. 311–31.

Brunner, K. "Reflections on the Political Economy of Government: The Persistent Growth of Government," *Schweizerische Zeitschrift für Volkswirtschaft und Statistik*, September 1978, *114*, pp. 649–80.

Buchanan, J. M. "The Pure Theory of Government Finance: A Suggested Approach," *Journal of Political Economy*, December 1949, *57*, pp. 496–506.

"Federalism and Fiscal Equity," *American Economic Review*, September 1950, *40*, pp. 583–600.

"Federal Grants and Resource Allocation," *Journal of Political Economy,* June 1952, *60,* pp. 201–17.

"Social Choice, Democracy, and Free Markets," *Journal of Political Economy,* April 1954a, *62,* pp. 114–23.

"Individual Choice in Voting and the Market," *Journal of Political Economy,* August 1954b, *62,* pp. 334–43.

"An Economic Theory of Clubs," *Economica,* February 1965a, *32,* pp. 1–14.

"Ethical Rules, Expected Values, and Large Numbers," *Ethics,* October 1965b, *76,* pp. 1–13.

"An Individualistic Theory of Political Process," in D. Easton, ed., *Varieties of Political Theory,* Englewood Cliffs, N.J.: Prentice-Hall, 1966, pp. 25–37.

"Notes for an Economic Theory of Socialism," *Public Choice,* Spring 1970, *8,* pp. 29–43.

"Principles of Urban-Fiscal Strategy," *Public Choice,* Fall 1971, *11,* pp. 1–16.

The Limits of Liberty: Between Anarchy and Leviathan, Chicago: University of Chicago Press, 1975a.

"Public Finance and Public Choice," *National Tax Journal,* December 1975b, *28,* pp. 383–94.

"A Hobbesian Interpretation of the Rawlsian Difference Principle," *Kyklos,* 1976a, *29,* pp. 5–25.

"An Ambiguity in Sen's Alleged Proof of the Impossibility of a Pareto Libertarian," Blacksburg, 1976b, mimeo.

"Why Does Government Grow?" in Thomas E. Borcherding, ed., *Budgets and Bureaucrats: The Sources of Government Growth,* Durham, N.C.: Duke University Press, 1977, pp. 3–18.

"Rent Seeking and Profit Seeking," in Buchanan, Tollison, and Tullock (1980a, pp. 3–15).

"Reform in the Rent-Seeking Society," in Buchanan, Tollison, and Tullock (1980b, pp. 359–67).

Liberty, Market and State, New York: New York University Press, 1986.

Buchanan, J. M. and Goetz, C. J. "Efficiency Limits of Fiscal Mobility: An Assessment of the Tiebout Model," *Journal of Public Economics,* April 1972, *1,* pp. 25–43.

Buchanan, J. M., Rowley, C. K. and Tollison, R. D., eds. *Deficits,* Oxford: Basil Blackwell, 1987.

Buchanan, J. M. and Stubblebine, W. C. "Externality," *Economica,* November 1962, *29,* pp. 371–84, reprinted in Arrow and Scitovsky (1969, pp. 199–212).

Buchanan, J. M. and Tollison, R. D., eds. *Theory of Public Choice,* Ann Arbor: University of Michigan Press, 1972.

Buchanan, J. M., Tollison, R. D. and Tullock, G., eds. *Toward a Theory of the Rent-Seeking Society,* College Station: Texas A&M Press, 1980.

Buchanan, J. M. and Tullock, G. *The Calculus of Consent,* Ann Arbor: University of Michigan Press, 1962.

Buchanan, J. M. and Wagner, R. E. "An Efficiency Basis for Federal Fiscal Equalization," in Margolis, J., ed., *The Analysis of Public Output,* New York: National Bureau of Economic Research, 1970.

Democracy in Deficit, New York: Academic Press, 1977.

Bundesrechnungshof. Bemerkungen des Bundesrechnungshofs zur Bundeshaushaltsrechnung (einschliebblich Bundesvermogensrechnung) für das Haushaltsjahr 1972, Bundestagsdrucksache 7/2709, pp. 110–111.

Bundesregierung Deutschland. Agrarbericht 1976. Bundestagsdrucksache 7/4680, pp. 63–65; Bundestagsdrucksache 7/4681, p. 146.

Burns, M. E. and Walsh, C. "Market Provision of Price-excludable Public Goods: A General Analysis," *Journal of Political Economy,* February 1981, *89,* pp. 166–91.

472   **References**

Bush, W. C. "Individual Welfare in Anarchy," in G. Tullock ed., *Explorations in the Theory of Anarchy*, Blacksburg: Center for the Study of Public Choice, 1972, pp. 5–18.

Bush, W. C. and Mayer, L. S. "Some Implications of Anarchy for the Distribution of Property," *Journal of Economic Theory*, August 1974, *8*, pp. 401–12.

Calvert, R. *Models of Imperfect Information in Politics*, Chur: Harwood Academic, 1986.

Cameron, D. R. "The Expansion of the Public Economy: A Comparative Analysis," *American Political Science Review*, December 1978, *72*, pp. 1243–61.

Campbell, A., Converse, P. E., Miller, W. E. and Stokes, D. E. *The American Voter*, New York: Wiley, 1964.

Campbell, D. E. "On the Derivation of Majority Rule," *Theory and Decision*, June 1982, *14*, pp. 133–40.

Caves, D. W. and Christensen, L. R. "The Relative Efficiency of Public and Private Firms in a Competitive Environment: The Case of Canadian Railroads," *Journal of Political Economy*, October 1980, *88*, pp. 958–76.

Caves, R. E. "Economic Models of Political Choice: Canada's Tariff Structure," *Canadian Journal of Economics*, May 1976, *9*, pp. 278–300.

Cebula, R. J. *The Determinants of Human Migration*, Lexington, Mass.: Lexington Books, 1979.

Cebula, R. J. and Kafoglis, M. Z. "A Note on the Tiebout–Tullock Hypothesis: The Period 1975–1980," *Public Choice*, 1986, *48*(1), pp. 65–9.

Cebula, R. J. and Murphy, D. R. "The Electoral College and Voter Participation Rates: An Exploratory Note," *Public Choice*, 1980, *35*(2), pp. 185–90.

Chamberlin, J. R. and Courant, P. N. "Representative Deliberations and Representative Decisions: Proportional Representation and the Borda Rule," *American Political Science Review*, September 1983, *77*, pp. 718–33.

Chapman, R. G. and Palda, K. S. "Electoral Turnout in Rational Voting and Consumption Perspectives," *Journal of Consumer Research*, March 1983, *9*, pp. 337–46.

"Assessing the Influence of Campaign Expenditures on Voting Behavior within a Comprehensive Electoral Market Model," *Marketing Science*, 1984, *3*, pp. 207–26.

Chappell, H. W. Jr. "Campaign Contributions and Voting on the Cargo Preference Bill: A Comparison of Simultaneous Models," *Public Choice*, 1981, *36*(2), pp. 301–12.

"Campaign Contributions and Congressional Voting. A Simultaneous Probit–Tobit Model," *Review of Economics and Statistics*, February 1982, *64*, pp. 77–83.

Choi, K. "A Statistical Test of Olson's Model," in Mueller (1983, pp. 57–78).

Chrystal, K. A. and Alt, J. E. "Some Problems in Formulating and Testing a Politico-Economic Model of the U.K.," *Economic Journal*, September 1981, *91*, pp. 730–6.

Chubb, J. E. "The Political Economy of Federalism," *American Political Science Review*, December 1985, *79*, pp. 994–1015.

Clarke, E. H. "Multipart Pricing of Public Goods," *Public Choice*, Fall 1971, *11*, pp. 17–33.

"Multipart Pricing of Public Goods: An Example," in S. Mushkin, ed., *Public Prices for Public Products*, Washington: Urban Institute, 1972, pp. 125–30.

"Some Aspects of the Demand-Revealing Process," *Public Choice*, Spring 1977, *29*, pp. 37–49.

Demand Revelation and the Provision of Public Goods, Cambridge: Ballinger, 1980.

Clarkson, K. W. "Some Implications of Property Rights in Hospital Management," *Journal of Law and Economics*, October 1972, *15*, pp. 363–84.

Clotfelter, C. T. *Public Spending for Higher Education*, College Park: University of Maryland Press, 1976.

Federal Tax Policy and Charitable Giving, Chicago: University of Chicago Press, 1985.

Coase, R. H. "The Nature of the Firm," *Economica*, 1937, *4*, pp. 386–405.

"The Problem of Social Cost," *Journal of Law and Economics*, October 1960, *3*, pp. 1–44.

Cohen, L. "Cyclic Sets in Multidimensional Voting Models," *Journal of Economic Theory*, February 1979, *20*, pp. 1–12.

Coleman, J. S. "Foundations for a Theory of Collective Decisions," *American Journal of Sociology*, May 1966a, *71*, pp. 615–27.

"The Possibility of a Social Welfare Function," *American Economic Review*, December 1966b, *56*, pp. 1105–22.

"Political Money," *American Political Science Review*, December 1970, *64*, pp. 1074–87.

"Internal Processes Governing Party Positions in Elections," *Public Choice*, Fall 1971, *11*, pp. 35–60.

"The Positions of Political Parties in Elections," in Niemi, R. G. and Weisberg, H. F., eds., *Probability Models of Collective Decision-Making*, Columbus: Merrill, 1972.

"Recontracting, Trustworthiness, and the Stability of Vote Exchanges," *Public Choice*, 1983, *40*(1), pp. 89–94.

Collins, J. N. and Downes, B. T. "The Effect of Size on the Provision of Public Services: The Case of Solid Waste Collection in Smaller Cities," *Urban Affairs Quarterly*, March 1977, *12*, pp. 333–47.

Comanor, W. S. "The Median Voter Rule and the Theory of Political Choice," *Journal of Public Economics*, January–February 1976, *5*, pp. 169–77.

Comanor, W. S. and Leibenstein, H. "Allocative Efficiency, X-Efficiency and the Measurement of Welfare Losses," *Economica*, August 1969, *36*, pp. 304–9.

Congleton, R. D. "Committees and Rent-Seeking Effort," *Journal of Public Economics*, November 1984, *25*, pp. 197–209.

"Evaluating Rent-Seeking Losses: Do the Welfare Gains of Lobbyists Count?" *Public Choice*, 1988, *56*(2), pp. 181–4.

Conn, D. "The Scope of Satisfactory Mechanisms for the Provision of Public Goods," *Journal of Public Economics*, March 1983, *20*, pp. 249–63.

Corcoran, W. J. and Karels, G. V. "Rent-Seeking Behavior in the Long Run," *Public Choice*, 1985, *46*(3), pp. 227–46.

Cornes, R. and Sandler, T. *The Theory of Externalities, Public Goods and Club Goods*, Cambridge: Cambridge University Press, 1986.

Coughlin, C. C. "Domestic Content Legislation: House Voting and the Economics of Regulation," *Economic Inquiry*, July 1985, *23*, pp. 437–48.

Coughlin, P. "Pareto Optimality of Policy Proposals with Probabilistic Voting," *Public Choice*, 1982, *39*(3), pp. 427–33.

"Expectations about Voter Choices," *Public Choice*, 1984, *44*(1), pp. 49–59.

"Elections and Income Redistribution," *Public Choice*, 1986, *50*(1-3), pp. 27–99.

Coughlin, P., Mueller, D. C. and Murrell, P. "Electoral Politics, Interest Groups, and the Size of Government," University of Maryland, 1988, mimeo.

Coughlin, P. and Nitzan, S. "Electoral Outcomes with Probabilistic Voting and Nash Social Welfare Maxima," *Journal of Public Economics*, 1981a, *15*, pp. 113–22.

"Directional and Local Electoral Equilibria with Probabilistic Voting," *Journal of Economic Theory*, April 1981b, *24*, pp. 226–39.

Courant, P. N., Gramlich, E. M. and Rubinfeld, D. L. "Why Voters Support Tax Limitations Amendments: The Michigan Case," *National Tax Journal*, 1980, *33*, pp. 1–20.

Coursey, D. L., Hoffman, E. and Spitzer, M. L. "Fear and Loathing in the Coase Theorem: Experimental Tests Involving Physical Discomfort," *Journal of Legal Studies*, January 1987, *16*, pp. 217–48.

474   **References**

Crain, W. M. and Deaton, T. H. "A Note on Political Participation as Consumption Behavior," *Public Choice*, Winter 1977, *32*, pp. 131–35.

Crain, W. M., Deaton, T. H. and Tollison, R. D. "Macroeconomic Determinants of the Vote in Presidential Elections," *Public Finance Quarterly*, October 1978, *6*, pp. 427–38.

Crain, W. M. and Tollison, R. "Campaign Expenditures and Political Competition," *Journal of Law and Economics*, April 1976, *19*, pp. 177–88.

Crain, W. M. and Zardkoohi, A. "A Test of the Property-Rights Theory of the Firm: Water Utilities in the United States," *Journal of Law and Economics*, October 1978, *21*, pp. 395–408.

Craven, J. "Liberalism and Individual Preferences," *Theory and Decision*, December 1982, *14*, pp. 351–60.

Crozier, M. *The Bureaucratic Phenomenon*, Chicago: University of Chicago Press, 1964.

Dahl, R. A. "The Concept of Power," *Behavioral Science*, 1957, *2*, pp. 201–15, reprinted in Bell, Edwards and Wagner (1969), pp. 79–93.

　Who Governs? Democracy and Power in an American City, New Haven: Yale University Press, 1961.

Dahlman, C. J. "The Problem of Externality," *Journal of Law and Economics*, April 1979, *22*, pp. 141–62.

Daniels, N. *Reading Rawls*, New York: Basic Books, 1974.

Darvish, T. and Rosenberg, J. "The Economic Model of Voter Participation: A Further Test," *Public Choice*, 1988, *56*(2), pp. 185–92.

D'Aspremont, C. and Gevers, L. "Equity and the Informational Basis of Collective Choice," *Review of Economic Studies*, June 1977, *44*, pp. 199–209.

Datta, S. K. and Nugent, J. B. "Adversary Activities and Per Capita Income Growth," University of Southern California, 1985, mimeo.

Davies, D. G. "The Efficiency of Public versus Private Firms: The Case of Australia's Two Airlines," *Journal of Law and Economics*, April 1971, *14*, pp. 149–65.

　"Property Rights and Economic Efficiency: The Australian Airlines Revisited," *Journal of Law and Economics*, April 1977, *20*, pp. 223–26.

　"Property Rights and Economic Behavior in Private and Government Enterprises: The Case of Australia's Banking System," *Research in Law and Economics*, 1981, *3*, pp. 111–42.

Davis, J. R. "On the Incidence of Income Redistribution," *Public Choice*, Spring 1970, *8*, pp. 63–74.

Davis, O. A., DeGroot, M. H. and Hinich, M. J. "Social Preference Orderings and Majority Rule," *Econometrica*, January 1972, *40*, pp. 147–57.

Davis, O. A. and Haines, G. H., Jr. "A Political Approach to a Theory of Public Expenditures: The Case of Municipalities," *National Tax Journal*, September 1966, *19*, pp. 259–75.

Davis, O. A., Hinich, M. J. and Ordeshook, P. C. "An Expository Development of a Mathematical Model of the Electoral Process," *American Political Science Review*, June 1970, *64*, pp. 426–48.

Deacon, R. T. "Private Choice and Collective Outcomes: Evidence from Public Sector Demand Analysis," *National Tax Journal*, December 1977a, *30*, pp. 371–86.

　"Review of the Literature on the Demand for Public Services," in *National Conference on Nonmetropolitan Community Services Research*, papers prepared for U.S. Senate, Committee on Agriculture, Nutrition and Forestry, 95th Cong., 1st sess., July 12, 1977b, Washington: Government Printing Office, pp. 207–30.

　"A Demand Model for the Local Public Sector," *Review of Economics and Statistics*, May 1978, *60*, pp. 184–92.

　"The Expenditure Effect of Alternative Public Supply Institutions," *Public Choice*, 1979, *34*(3–4), pp. 381–98.

de Borda, J. C. "Memorie sur les Elections au Scrutin," *Historie de l'Academie Royale des Sciences,* 1781.

de Condorcet, M. *Essai sur l'Application de L'Analyse à la Probabilité des Décisions Rendues à la Pluraliste des Voix,* Paris, 1785.

de Jouvenal, B. "The Chairman's Problem," *American Political Science Review,* June 1961, *55,* pp. 368–72.

DeMeyer, F. and Plott, C. "The Probability of a Cyclical Majority," *Econometrica,* March 1970, *38,* pp. 345–54.

"A Welfare Function Using Relative Intensity of Preference," *Quarterly Journal of Economics,* February 1971, *85,* pp. 179–86.

DeNardo, J. *Power in Numbers: The Political Strategy of Protest and Rebellion,* Princeton: Princeton University Press, 1985.

Dennis, J. "Support for the Institution of Elections by the Mass Public," *American Political Science Review,* September 1970, *64,* pp. 269–80.

Denzau, A. and Grier, K. "Determinants of Local School Spending: Some Consistent Estimates," *Public Choice,* 1984, *44*(2), pp. 375–83.

Denzau, A. and Kats, A. "Expected Plurality Voting Equilibrium and Social Choice Functions," *Review of Economic Studies,* June 1977, *44,* pp. 227–33.

De Swaan, A. "A Classification of Parties and Party Systems according to Coalitional Options," *European Journal of Political Research,* 1975, *3,* pp. 361–75.

De Swaan, A. and Mokken, R. J. "Testing Coalition Theories: The Combined Evidence," in Leif Lewin and Evert Vedung, eds., *Politics as Rational Action,* Dordrecht: Reidel, 1980, pp. 199–215.

Diamond, P. "Cardinal Welfare, Individualistic Ethics, and Interpersonal Comparisons of Utility: A Comment," *Journal of Political Economy,* October 1967, *75,* pp. 765–6.

DiLorenzo, T. J. "The Expenditure Effects of Restricting Competition in Local Public Service Industries: The Case of Special Districts," *Public Choice,* 1981, *37*(3), pp. 569–78.

Dodge, D. R. "Impact of Tax, Transfer and Expenditure Policies of Government on the Distribution of Personal Income in Canada," *Review of Income and Wealth,* March 1975, *21,* pp. 1–52.

Dodgson, C. L. "A Method of Taking Votes on More than Two Issues," 1876, reprinted in Black (1958, pp. 224–34).

Douglas, G. W. and Miller, J. C. III. *Domestic Airline Regulation: Theory and Policy,* Washington, D.C.: Brookings Institution, 1974.

Downs, A. *An Economic Theory of Democracy,* New York: Harper and Row, 1957.

"In Defense of Majority Voting," *Journal of Political Economy,* April 1961, *69,* pp. 192–9.

Inside Bureaucracy, Boston: Little, Brown, 1967.

Drèze, J. H. and de la Vallée Poussin, D. "A Tâtonnement Process for Public Goods," *Review of Economic Studies,* April 1971, *38,* pp. 133–50.

Dryzek, J. and Goodin, R. E. "Risk-Sharing and Social Justice: The Motivational Foundations of the Post-War Welfare State," *British Journal of Political Science,* January 1986, *16,* pp. 1–34.

Dye, T. R. "Taxing, Spending and Economic Growth in American States," *Journal of Politics,* November 1980, *42,* pp. 1085–1107.

Eavey, C. L. and Miller, G. J. "Bureaucratic Agenda Control: Imposition or Bargaining?" *American Political Science Review,* September 1984, *78,* pp. 719–33.

Eberts, R. W. and Gronberg, T. J. "Jurisdictional Homogeneity and the Tiebout Hypothesis," *Journal of Urban Economics,* September 1981, *10,* pp. 227–39.

Edel, M. and Sclar, E. "Taxes, Spending, and Property Values: Supply Adjustment in a Tiebout-Oates Model," *Journal of Political Economy,* September/October 1974, *82,* pp. 941–54.

Edwards, F. R. and Stevens, B. J. "Relative Efficiency of Alternative Institutional Arrangements for Collecting Refuse: Collective Action vs. the Free Market," New York: Columbia University Press, 1976, mimeo.

Elections Research Center, *America Votes, 1984,* Washington, D.C., 1985.

Ellickson, B. "A Generalization of the Pure Theory of Public Goods," *American Economic Review,* June 1973, *63,* pp. 417–32.

Elster, J. and Hylland, A., eds. *Foundations of Social Choice Theory,* Cambridge: Cambridge University Press, 1986.

Enelow, J. M. and Hinich, M. J. *The Spatial Theory of Voting,* Cambridge: Cambridge University Press, 1984.

Enelow, J. M. and Koehler, D. H. "Vote Trading in a Legislative Context: An Analysis of Cooperative and Noncooperative Strategic Voting," *Public Choice,* 1979, *34*(2), pp. 157–75.

Epple, D., Zelenitz, A. and Visscher, M. "A Search for Testable Implications of the Tiebout Hypothesis," *Journal of Political Economy,* June 1978, *86,* pp. 405–25.

Escarraz, D. R. "Wicksell and Lindahl: Theories of Public Expenditure and Tax Justice Reconsidered," *National Tax Journal,* June 1967, *20,* pp. 137–48.

Etzioni, Amitai. "The Case for a Multiple Utility Conception," *Economics and Philosophy,* October 1986, *2,* pp. 159–83.

Fair, R. C. "The Effect of Economic Events on Votes for President," *Review of Economics and Statistics,* May 1978, *60,* pp. 159–73.

   "The Effect of Economic Events on Votes for President: 1980 Results," *Review of Economics and Statistics,* May 1982, *64,* pp. 322–5.

Faith, R. L., Leavens, D. L., and Tollison, R. D. "Antitrust Pork Barrel," *Journal of Law and Economics,* October 1982, *25,* pp. 329–42.

Farquharson, R. *Theory of Voting,* New Haven: Yale University Press, 1969.

Feld, S. L., Grofman, B., Hartly, R., Kilgour, M., Miller, N. and Noviello, N. "The Uncovered Set in Spatial Voting," *Theory and Decision,* 1987, *23,* pp. 129–55.

Feldman, A. "Manipulating Voting Procedures," *Economic Inquiry,* July 1979, *17,* pp. 452–74.

Fenno, R. F., Jr. *Home Style: House Members in Their Districts,* Boston: Little, Brown, 1978.

Ferejohn, J. *Pork Barrel Politics: Rivers and Harbors Legislation, 1947–1968,* Stanford: Stanford University Press, 1974.

Ferejohn, J. A. and Fiorina, M. P. "The Paradox of Not Voting: A Decision Theoretic Analysis," *American Political Science Review,* June 1974, *68,* pp. 525–36.

   "Closeness Counts Only in Horseshoes and Dancing," *American Political Science Review,* September 1975, *69,* pp. 920–25.

Ferejohn, J., Forsythe, R. and Noll, R. "Practical Aspects of the Construction of Decentralized Decision-Making Systems for Public Goods," in Cliff S. Russell, ed., *Collective Decision Making,* Baltimore: Johns Hopkins University Press, 1979.

Filimon, R. "Asymmetric Information and Agenda Control," *Journal of Public Economics,* February 1982, *17,* pp. 51–70.

Findlay, R. and Wellisz, S. "Tariffs, Quotas and Domestic Content Protection: Some Political Economy Considerations," *Public Choice,* 1986, *50*(1–3), pp. 221–42.

Fine, B. J. "Individual Liberalism in a Paretian Society," *Journal of Political Economy,* December 1975, *83,* pp. 1277–82.

Finney, L. D. "A Rational Choice Theory of Revolution and Political Violence," Ph.D. dissertation, University of Maryland, 1987.

Finsinger, J. "Competition, Ownership and Control in Markets with Imperfect Information: The Case of the German Liability and Life Insurance Markets," Berlin: International Institute of Management, 1981, mimeo.

Fiorina, M. P. "An Outline for a Model of Party Choice," *American Journal of Political Science*, August 1977a, *21*, pp. 601–25.

Congress: Keystone of the Washington Establishment, New Haven: Yale University Press, 1977b.

"Economic Retrospective Voting in American National Elections: A Micro-Analysis," *American Journal of Political Science*, May 1978, *22*, pp. 426–43.

Retrospective Voting in American National Elections, New Haven: Yale University Press, 1981.

Fiorina, M. P. and Plott, C. R. "Committee Decisions under Majority Rule: An Experimental Study," *American Political Science Review*, June 1978, *72*, pp. 575–98.

Fisch, O. "Optimal City Size, the Economic Theory of Clubs and Exclusionary Zoning," *Public Choice*, Winter 1975, *24*, pp. 59–70.

Fischer-Menshausen, H. "Entlastung des Staates durch Privatisierung von Aufgaben," *Wirtschaftsdienst*, 1975, *55*, pp. 545–52.

Fishburn, P. C. *The Theory of Social Choice*, Princeton: Princeton University Press, 1973.

Fishburn, P. C. and Brams, S. J. "Approval Voting, Condorcet's Principle, and Runoff Elections," *Public Choice*, 1981a, *36*(1), pp. 89–114.

"Efficacy, Power, and Equity under Approval Voting," *Public Choice*, 1981b, *37*(3), pp. 425–34.

Fishburn, P. C. and Gehrlein, W. V. "Social Homogeneity and Condorcet's Paradox," *Public Choice*, 1980, *35*(4), pp. 403–19.

Fisher, I. W. and Hall, G. R. "Risk and Corporate Rates of Return," *Quarterly Journal of Economics*, February 1969, *83*, pp. 79–92.

Flatters, F., Henderson, B. and Mieszkowski, P. "Public Goods, Efficiency, and Regional Fiscal Equalization," *Journal of Public Economics*, May 1974, *3*, pp. 99–112.

Fleming, M. "A Cardinal Concept of Welfare," *Quarterly Journal of Economics*, August 1952, *66*, pp. 366–84.

Fort, R. D. "The Median Voter, Setters, and Non-Repeated Construction Bond Issues," *Public Choice*, 1988, *56*(3), pp. 213–31.

Foster, C. B. "The Performance of Rational Voter Models in Recent Presidential Elections," *American Political Science Review*, September 1984, *78*, pp. 678–90.

Fraser, J. "Political Participation and Income Level: An Exchange," *Public Choice*, Fall 1972, *13*, pp. 115–18.

Fratianni, M. and Spinelli, F. "The Growth of Government in Italy: Evidence from 1861 to 1979," *Public Choice*, 1982, *39*(2), pp. 221–43.

Frey, B. S. "Why Do High Income People Participate More in Politics?" *Public Choice*, Fall 1971, *11*, pp. 101–5.

"Political Participation and Income Level: An Exchange, Reply," *Public Choice*, Fall 1972, *13*, pp. 119–22.

Modern Politische Okonomie, Munich: Piper-Verlag, 1977.

"Politico-Economic Models and Cycles," *Journal of Public Economics*, April 1978, *9*, pp. 203–20.

"An Econometric Model with an Endogenous Government Sector," *Public Choice*, 1979, *34*(1), pp. 29–43.

International Political Economics, Oxford: Basil Blackwell, 1984.

Internationale Politische Okonomie, Munich: Verlag Vahlen, 1985.

Frey, B. S. and Lau, L. J. "Towards a Mathematical Model of Government Behavior," *Zeitschrift für Nationalökonomie*, 1968, *28*, pp. 355–80.

Frey, B. S. and Schneider, F. "An Empirical Study of Politico-Economic Interaction in the U.S.," *Review of Economics and Statistics*, May 1978a, *60*, pp. 174–83.

"A Politico-Economic Model of the United Kingdom," *Economic Journal*, June 1978b, *88*, pp. 243–53.

"An Econometric Model with an Endogenous Government Sector," *Public Choice*, 1979, *34*(1), pp. 29–43.

"A Politico-Economic Model of the U.K.: New Estimates and Predictions," *Economic Journal*, September 1981a, *91*, pp. 737–40.

"Central Bank Behavior: A Positive Empirical Analysis," *Journal of Monetary Economics*, May 1981b, *7*, pp. 291–315.

Frohlich, N. and Oppenheimer, J. A. "I Get By with a Little Help from My Friends," *World Politics*, October 1970, *23*, pp. 104–20.

Frohlich, N., Oppenheimer, J. A. and Eavey, C. L. "Laboratory Results on Rawls's Distributive Justice," *British Journal of Political Science*, January 1987, *17*, pp. 1–21.

Frohlich, N., Oppenheimer, J. A., Smith, J., and Young, O. R. "A Test of Downsian Voter Rationality: 1964 Presidential Voting," *American Political Science Review*, March 1978, *72*, pp. 178–97.

Fuchs, V. R. *The Service Economy*, New York: Columbia University Press, 1968.

Furstenberg, G. M. von and Mueller, D. C. "The Pareto Optimal Approach to Income Redistribution: A Fiscal Application," *American Economic Review*, September 1971, *61*, pp. 628–37.

Garman, M. B. and Kamien, M. I. "The Paradox of Voting: Probability Calculations," *Behavioral Science*, July 1968, *13*, pp. 306–17.

Gehrlein, W. V. and Fishburn, P. C. "Condorcet's Paradox and Anonymous Preference Profiles," *Public Choice*, Summer 1976a, *26*, pp. 1–18.

"The Probability of the Paradox of Voting: A Computable Solution," *Journal of Economic Theory*, August 1976b, *13*, pp. 14–25.

Gibbard, A. "Intransitive Social Indifference and the Arrow Dilemma," 1969, mimeo.

"Manipulation of Voting Schemes: A General Result," *Econometrica*, July 1973, *41*, pp. 587–602.

"A Pareto-Consistent Libertarian Claim," *Journal of Economic Theory*, April 1974, *7*, pp. 388–410.

"Manipulation of Schemes That Combine Voting with Chance," *Econometrica*, April 1977, *45*, pp. 665–8.

Giertz, J. F. "A Limited Defense of Pareto Optimal Redistribution," *Public Choice*, 1982, *39*(2), pp. 277–82.

Gillespie, W. I. "Effect of Public Expenditures on the Distribution of Income," in Richard A. Musgrave, ed., *Essays in Fiscal Federalism*, Washington, D.C.: Brookings Institution, 1965, pp. 122–86.

"On the Redistribution of Income in Canada," *Canadian Tax Journal*, July/August 1976, *24*, pp. 419–50.

Gillespie, W. I. and Labelle, J. B. "A Pro-Poor or Pro-Rich Redistribution of Income," *National Tax Journal*, June 1978, *31*, pp. 185–9.

Gist, J. R. and Hill, R. C. "The Economics of Choice in the Allocation of Federal Grants: An Empirical Test," *Public Choice*, 1981, *36*(1), pp. 63–73.

Glantz, S. A., Abramowitz, A. I. and Burkart, M. P. "Election Outcomes: Whose Money Matters?" *Journal of Politics*, November 1976, *38*, pp. 1033–8.

Glashan, R. *American Governors and Gubernatorial Elections, 1775–1978*, Westport: Meckler Books, 1979.

Gollop, F. M. and Jorgenson, D. W. "U.S. Productivity Growth in Industries, 1947–73," in John W. Kendrick and Beatrice N. Vaccara, eds., *New Developments in Productivity Measurement and Analysis*, Chicago: University of Chicago Press, 1980, pp. 17–124.

Goodin, R. E. *Reasons for Welfare,* Princeton: Princeton University Press, 1988.

Goodin, R. E. and Roberts, K. W. S. "The Ethical Voter," *American Political Science Review,* September 1975, *69,* pp. 926–8.

Goodman, S. and Kramer, G. H. "Comment on Arcelus and Meltzer," *American Political Science Review,* December 1975, *69,* pp. 1277–85.

Gough, J. W. *The Social Contract,* 2d ed. Oxford: Clarendon Press, 1957.

Gramlich, E. M. "The Effects of Grants on State-Local Expenditures: A Review of the Econometric Literature," National Tax Association, *Proceedings of the Sixty-Second Annual Conference on Taxation, 1969* (1970), pp. 569–93.

Gramlich, E. M. and Rubinfeld, D. L. "Micro Estimates of Public Spending Demand Functions and Tests of the Tiebout and Median-Voter Hypothesis," *Journal of Political Economy,* June 1982a, *90,* pp. 536–60.

"Voting on Spending," *Journal of Policy Analysis and Management,* Summer 1982b, *1,* 516–33.

Gray, V. and Lowery, D. "Interest Group Politics and Economic Growth in the American States: Testing the Olson Construct," University of North Carolina, Chapel Hill, 1986, mimeo.

Green, J. and Laffont, J.-J. "Characterization of Satisfactory Mechanisms for the Revelation of Preferences for Public Goods," *Econometrica,* March 1977a, *45,* pp. 427–38.

"Imperfect Personal Information and the Demand Revealing Process: A Sampling Approach," *Public Choice,* Spring 1977b, *29,* pp. 79–94.

Incentives in Public Decision-Making, Amsterdam: North-Holland, 1979.

Greenberg, J., Mackay, R. and Tideman, N. "Some Limitations of the Groves-Ledyard Optimal Mechanism," *Public Choice,* Spring 1977, *29,* pp. 129–37.

Groves, T. "Incentives in Teams," *Econometrica,* July 1973, *41,* pp. 617–31.

"Efficient Collective Choice When Compensation Is Possible," *Review of Economic Studies,* April 1979, *46,* pp. 227–41.

Groves, T. and Ledyard, J. "Optimal Allocation of Public Goods: A Solution to the 'Free Rider' Problem," *Econometrica,* May 1977a, *45,* pp. 783–809.

"Some Limitations of Demand Revealing Processes," *Public Choice,* Spring 1977b, *29,* pp. 107–24.

"Reply," *Public Choice,* Spring 1977c, *29,* pp. 139–43.

Groves, T. and Loeb, M. "Incentives and Public Inputs," *Journal of Public Economics,* August 1975, *4,* pp. 211–26.

Guha, A. S. "Neutrality, Monotonicity and the Right of Veto," *Econometrica,* September 1972, *40,* pp. 821–6.

Gunning, J. P. "An Economic Approach to Riot Analysis," *Public Choice,* Fall 1972, *13,* pp. 31–46.

Gustafsson, A. "Rise and Decline of Nations: Sweden," *Scandinavian Political Studies,* March 1986, *9,* pp. 35–50.

Haas, J. *The Evolution of the Prehistoric State,* New York: Columbia University Press, 1982.

Haefele, E. T. "A Utility Theory of Representative Government," *American Economic Review,* June 1971, *61,* pp. 350–67.

Hamburger Senat, *Abschlubbericht des Beauftragten zur Gebaudereinigung,* Hamburg, 1974.

Hamilton, B. W. "The Effects of Property Taxes and Local Public Spending on Property Values: A Theoretical Comment," *Journal of Political Economy,* June 1976, *84,* pp. 647–50.

"The Flypaper Effect and Other Anomalies," *Journal of Public Economics,* December 1983, *22,* pp. 347–61.

Hamilton, B. W., Mills, E. S. and Puryear, D. "The Tiebout Hypothesis and Residential Income Segregation," in Edwin S. Mills and Wallace E. Oates, eds., *Fiscal Zoning and Land Use Controls,* Lexington, Mass.: Lexington Books, 1975, pp. 101–18.

480   **References**

Hamlin, A. P. *Ethics, Economics and the State,* New York: St. Martin's Press, 1986.

Hammond, P. J. "Why Ethical Measures of Inequality Need Interpersonal Comparisons," *Theory and Decision,* October 1976, *7,* pp. 263–74.

Hansson, B. "The Independence Condition in the Theory of Choice," *Theory and Decision,* September 1973, *4,* pp. 25–49.

Hansson, I. and Stuart, C. "Voting Competitions with Interested Politicians: Platforms Do Not Converge to the Preferences of the Median Voter," *Public Choice,* 1984, *44*(3), pp. 431–41.

Hardin, R. "Collective Action as an Agreeable n-Prisoners' Dilemma," *Behavioral Science,* September 1971, *16,* pp. 472–81.

Collective Action, Baltimore: Johns Hopkins University Press, 1982.

Hare, R. M. "Rawls' Theory of Justice," *Philosophical Quarterly,* April 1973, *23,* pp. 144–55, reprinted in Daniels (1974, pp. 81–107).

Harrison, G. W. and Hirshleifer, J. "Experiments Testing Weakest-Link/Best-Shot Models for Provision of Public Goods," UCLA Working Paper 372A, February 1986.

Harrison, G. W. and McKee, M. "Experimental Evaluation of the Coase Theorem," *Journal of Law and Economics,* October 1985, *28,* pp. 653–70.

Harsanyi, J. C. "Cardinal Utility in Welfare Economics and in the Theory of Risk-Taking," *Journal of Political Economy,* October 1953, *61,* pp. 434–5.

"Cardinal Welfare, Individualistic Ethics, and Interpersonal Comparisons of Utility," *Journal of Political Economy,* August 1955, *63,* pp. 309–21, reprinted in Arrow and Scitovsky (1969, pp. 46–60).

"Can the Maximin Principle Serve as a Basis for Morality? A Critique of John Rawls' Theory," *American Political Science Review,* June 1975a, *69,* pp. 594–606.

"Nonlinear Social Welfare Functions," *Theory and Decision,* August 1975b, *6,* pp. 311–32.

Rational Behavior and Bargaining Equilibrium in Games and Social Situations, Cambridge: Cambridge University Press, 1977.

Harstad, R. M. and Marrese, M. "Behavioral Explanations of Efficient Public Good Allocations," *Journal of Public Economics,* December 1982, *19,* pp. 367–83.

Hart, H. L. A. "Rawls on Liberty and Its Priority," *University of Chicago Law Review,* Spring 1973, *40,* pp. 534–55, reprinted in Daniels (1974, pp. 230–52).

Head, J. G. "Public Goods and Public Policy," *Public Finance,* 1962, *17,* pp. 197–221.

"Lindahl's Theory of the Budget," *Finanzarchiv,* October 1964, *23,* pp. 421–54.

Henderson, J. V. "Theories of Group, Jurisdiction, and City Size," in Peter Mieszkowski and Mahlon Straszheim, eds., *Current Issues in Urban Economics,* Baltimore: Johns Hopkins University Press, 1979, pp. 235–69.

Henrekson, M. "Swedish Government Growth: A Disequilibrium Analysis," in J. A. Lybeck and M. Henrekson, eds., *Explaining the Growth of Government,* Amsterdam: North-Holland, 1988, pp. 93–132.

Hettich, W. and Winer, S. L. "Economic and Political Foundations of Tax Structure," *American Economic Review,* September 1988, *78,* pp. 701–12.

Hibbs, D. A., Jr. "Political Parties and Macroeconomic Policy," *American Political Science Review,* December 1977, *71,* pp. 1467–87.

"The Mass Public and Macroeconomic Performance: The Dynamics of Public Opinion toward Unemployment and Inflation," *American Journal of Political Science,* November 1979, *23,* pp. 705–31.

"Economics and Politics in France: Economic Performance and Mass Political Support for Presidents Pompidou and Giscard d'Estaing," *European Journal of Political Research,* 1981, *9,* pp. 133–45.

"The Dynamics of Political Support for American Presidents among Occupational and Partisan Groups," *American Journal of Political Science,* May 1982a, *26,* pp. 312–32.

"Economic Outcomes and Political Support for British Governments among Occupational Classes: A Dynamic Analysis," *American Political Science Review,* June 1982b, *76,* pp. 259–79.

"On the Demand for Economic Outcomes: Macroeconomic Performance and Mass Political Support in the United States, Great Britain, and Germany," *Journal of Politics,* May 1982c, *44,* pp. 426–62.

The Political Economy of Industrial Democracies, Cambridge, Mass.: Harvard University Press, 1987.

Hibbs, D. A., Jr. and Fassbender, H., eds. *Contemporary Political Economy,* Amsterdam: North-Holland, 1981.

Hicks, J. "Structural Unemployment and Economic Growth: A 'Labor Theory of Value,'" in Mueller (1983, pp. 53–6).

Higgins, R. S., Shughart II, W. F. and Tollison, R. D. "Free Entry and Efficient Rent Seeking," *Public Choice,* 1985, *46*(3), pp. 247–58.

"Dual Enforcement of the Antitrust Laws," in R. J. Mackay, J. C. Miller III and B. Yandle, eds., *Public Choice and Regulation,* Stanford: Hoover Institution, 1987, pp. 154–80.

Higgins, R. S. and Tollison, R. D. "Life among the Triangles and Trapezoids: Notes on the Theory of Rent Seeking," George Mason University, 1986, mimeo.

Hildreth, C. "Alternative Conditions for Social Orderings," *Econometrica,* January 1953, 21, pp. 81–94.

Hillman, A. I. and Samet, D. "Dissipation of Contestable Rents by a Small Number of Contenders," *Public Choice,* 1987, *54*(1), pp. 63–82.

Hillman, A. L. and Katz, E. "Risk-Averse Rent Seekers and the Social Cost of Monopoly Power," *Economic Journal,* March 1984, *94,* pp. 104–10.

Hinich, M. J. "Equilibrium in Spatial Voting: The Median Voter Result Is an Artifact," *Journal of Economic Theory,* December 1977, *16,* pp. 208–19.

Hinich, M. J., Ledyard, J. O. and Ordeshook, P. C. "Nonvoting and the Existence of Equilibrium under Majority Rule," *Journal of Economic Theory,* April 1972, *4,* pp. 144–53.

"A Theory of Electoral Equilibrium: A Spatial Analysis Based on the Theory of Games," *Journal of Politics,* February 1973, *35,* pp. 154–93.

Hinich, M. J. and Ordeshook, P. C. "Plurality Maximization vs. Vote Maximization: A Spatial Analysis with Variable Participation," *American Political Science Review,* September 1970, *64,* pp. 772–91.

Hirsch, W. Z. "Cost Functions of Urban Government Services: Refuse Collection," *Review of Economics and Statistics,* February 1965, *47,* pp. 87–92.

Hirschman, A. O. *Exit, Voice, and Loyalty,* Cambridge, Mass.: Harvard University Press, 1970.

Hirshleifer, J. "Comment" (on Peltzman, 1976), *Journal of Law and Economics,* August 1976, *19,* pp. 241–4.

"From Weakest-Link to Best-Shot: The Voluntary Provision of Public Goods," *Public Choice,* 1983, *41*(3), pp. 371–86.

"The Voluntary Provision of Public Goods – Descending-Weight Social Composition Functions," UCLA Working Paper 326, May 1984.

Hobbes, T. *Leviathan,* London, 1651. Reprinted in *The English Philosophers,* New York: Modern Library, 1939, pp. 129–234.

Hochman, H. M. and Rodgers, J. D. "Pareto Optimal Redistribution," *American Economic Review,* September 1969, *59,* pp. 542–57.

"Pareto Optimal Redistribution: Reply," *American Economic Review,* December 1970, *60,* pp. 997–1002.

Hoffman, E. and Spitzer, M. L. "The Coase Theorem: Some Experimental Tests," *Journal of Law and Economics,* April 1982, *25,* pp. 73–98.

482 **References**

"Entitlements, Rights, and Fairness: An Experimental Examination of Subjects' Concepts of Distributive Justice," *Journal of Legal Studies*, June 1985, *14*, pp. 259–97.

"Experimental Tests of the Coase Theorem with Large Bargaining Groups," *Journal of Legal Studies*, January 1986, *15*, pp. 149–71.

Holcombe, R. G. "An Empirical Test of the Median Voter Model," *Economic Inquiry*, April 1980, *18*, pp. 260–74.

Hotelling, H. "Stability in Competition," *Economic Journal*, March 1929, *39*, pp. 41–57.

Howe, R. E. and Roemer, J. E. "Rawlsian Justice as the Core of a Game," *American Economic Review*, December 1981, *71*, pp. 880–95.

Hoyer, R. W. and Mayer, L. "Comparing Strategies in a Spatial Model of Electoral Competition," *American Journal of Political Science*, August 1974, *18*, pp. 501–23.

Hume, D. *Treatise of Human Nature* (1739), Oxford: Oxford University Press, 1941.

An Inquiry Concerning the Principles of Morals (1751), Indianapolis, Bobbs-Merrill, 1957.

Hurwicz, L. "On Allocations Attainable through Nash Equilibria," *Journal of Economic Theory*, August 1979, *21*, pp. 140–65.

Hylland, A. and Zeckhauser, R. "A Mechanism for Selecting Public Goods When Preferences Must Be Elicited," KSG Discussion Paper 70D, Harvard University, August 1979.

Inada, K.-I. "The Simple Majority Decision Rule," *Econometrica*, July 1969, *37*, pp. 490–506.

"Majority Rule and Rationality," *Journal of Economic Theory*, March 1970, *2*, pp. 27–40.

Inman, R. P. "Testing Political Economy's 'As If' Proposition: Is the Median Income Voter Really Decisive?" *Public Choice*, 1978, *33*(4), pp. 45–65.

"The Fiscal Performance of Local Governments: An Interpretive Review," in Peter Mieszkowski and Mahlon Straszheim, eds., *Current Issues in Urban Economics*, Baltimore: Johns Hopkins University Press, 1979, pp. 270–321.

"Markets, Governments, and the 'New' Political Economy," in A. J. Auerbach and M. Feldstein, eds., *Handbook of Public Economics*, Amsterdam: North Holland, 1987, pp. 647–777.

Inoguchi, T. "Economic Conditions and Mass Support in Japan," in P. Whiteley, ed., *Models of Political Economy*, London: Sage, 1980, pp. 121–54.

Intriligator, M. D. "A Probabilistic Model of Social Choice," *Review of Economic Studies*, October 1973, *40*, pp. 553–60.

Ippolito, R. A. and Masson, R. T. "The Social Cost of Government Regulation of Milk," *Journal of Law and Economics*, April 1978, *21*, pp. 33–65.

Isaac, R. M., McCue, K. F. and Plott, C. R. "Public Goods Provision in an Experimental Environment," *Journal of Public Economics*, February 1985, *26*, pp. 51–74.

Isaac, R. M. and Walker, J. M. "Group Size Effects in Public Goods Provision: The Voluntary Contributions Mechanisms," *Quarterly Journal of Economics*, February 1988, *103*, pp. 179–99.

Isaac, R. M., Walker, J. M. and Thomas, S. H. "Divergent Evidence on Free Riding: An Experimental Examination of Possible Explanations," *Public Choice*, 1984, *43*(2), pp. 113–49.

Jacobson, G. C. "The Effect of Campaign Spending in Congressional Elections," *American Political Science Review*, June 1978, *72*, pp. 469–91.

"Money and Votes Reconsidered: Congressional Elections, 1972–1982," *Public Choice*, 1985, *47*(1), pp. 7–62.

Jensen, M. and Meckling, W. H. "The Theory of the Firm: Managerial Behavior, Agency Costs and Ownership Structure," *Journal of Financial Economics*, October 1976, *3*, pp. 305–60.

Johansen, L. "Some Notes on the Lindahl Theory of Determination of Public Expenditures," *International Economic Review*, September 1963, *4*, pp. 346–58.

Johnston, R. J. "Campaign Spending and Votes: A Reconsideration," *Public Choice,* 1978, *33*(3), pp. 83–92.

Jonung, L. and Wadensjo, E. "The Effect of Unemployment, Inflation and Real Income Growth on Government Popularity in Sweden," *Scandinavian Journal of Economics,* 1979, *81*(2), pp. 343–53.

Joslyn, R. A. "The Impact of Decision Rules in Multi-candidate Campaigns: The Case of the 1972 Democratic Presidential Nomination," *Public Choice,* Spring 1976, *25,* pp. 1–17.

Kadane, J. B. "On Division of the Question," *Public Choice,* Fall 1972, *13,* pp. 47–54.

Kahn, A. E. *The Economics of Regulation,* vol. 1, New York: Wiley, 1970.

Kalai, E. and Muller, E. "Characterizations of Domains Admitting Nondictatorial Social Welfare Functions and Nonmanipulable Voting Procedures," *Journal of Economic Theory,* December 1977, *16,* pp. 457–69.

Kalt, J. H. and Zupan, M. A. "Capture and Ideology in the Economic Theory of Politics," *American Economic Review,* June 1984, *74,* pp. 279–300.

Kaneko, M. and Nakamura, K. "The Nash Social Welfare Function," *Econometrica,* March 1979, *47,* pp. 423–35.

Kats, A. and Nitzan, S. "Global and Local Equilibrium in Majority Voting," *Public Choice,* Summer 1976, *26,* pp. 105–6.

Kau, J. B., Keenan, D. and Rubin, P. H. "A General Equilibrium Model of Congressional Voting," *Quarterly Journal of Economics,* May 1982, *97,* pp. 271–93.

Kau, J. B. and Rubin, P. H. "The Electoral College and the Rational Vote," *Public Choice,* Fall 1976, *27,* pp. 101–07.

"Self-Interest, Ideology, and Logrolling in Congressional Voting," *Journal of Law and Economics,* October 1979, *22,* pp. 365–84.

"The Size of Government," *Public Choice,* 1981, *37*(2), pp. 261–74.

Congressmen, Constituents, and Contributors, Boston: Martinus Nijhoff, 1982.

Keeler, T. E. "Theories of Regulation and the Deregulation Movement," *Public Choice,* 1984, *44*(1), pp. 103–45.

Kellett, J. and Mott, K. "Presidential Primaries: Measuring Popular Choice," *Polity,* Summer 1977, *9,* pp. 528–37.

Kelley, S., Jr., Ayres, R. E. and Bowen, W. G. "Registration and Voting: Putting First Things First," *American Political Science Review,* June 1967, *61,* pp. 359–79.

Kelly, J. S. "Rights Exercising and a Pareto-Consistent Libertarian Claim," *Journal of Economic Theory,* August 1976, *13,* pp. 138–53.

Arrow Impossibility Theorems, New York: Academic Press, 1978.

Kemp, M. C. "Arrow's General Possibility Theorem," *Review of Economic Studies,* 1954, *21*(3), pp. 240–3.

Kemp, M. C. and Asimakopulos, A. "A Note on 'Social Welfare Functions' and Cardinal Utility," *Canadian Journal of Economic Political Science,* May 1952, *18,* pp. 195–200.

Kemp, M. C. and Ng, Y.-K. "On the Existence of Social Welfare Functions: Social Orderings and Social Decision Functions," *Economica,* February 1976, *43,* pp. 59–66.

"More on Social Welfare Functions: The Incompatibility of Individualism and Ordinalism," *Economica,* February 1977, *44,* pp. 89–90.

"Arrow's Independence Condition and the Bergson-Samuelson Tradition," in G. Feiwel, ed., *Arrow and the Foundations of the Theory of Economic Policy,* London: Macmillan, 1987, pp. 223–41.

Kemper, P. and Quigley, J. M. *The Economics of Refuse Collection,* Cambridge, Mass.: Ballinger, 1976.

Kendall, W. *John Locke and the Doctrine of Majority Rule*. Urbana: University of Illinois Press, 1941.

Kendrick, M. S. *A Century and a Half of Federal Expenditures*, New York: National Bureau of Economic Research, 1955.

Kennedy, K. F. and Mehr, R. I. "A Case Study in Private versus Public Enterprise: The Manitoba Experience with Automobile Insurance," *Journal of Risk and Insurance*, 1977, *4*, pp. 595–621.

Kennelly, B. and Murrell, P. "The Sources of Collective Action: An Empirical Investigation of the Relationship between Industry Characteristics and Interest Group Formation," University of Maryland, 1987, mimeo.

Kiewiet, D. R. "Policy-Oriented Voting in Response to Economic Issues," *American Political Science Review*, June 1981, *75*, pp. 448–59.

Macroeconomics and Micropolitics, Chicago: University of Chicago Press, 1983.

Kim, O. and Walker, M. "The Free Rider Problem: Experimental Evidence," *Public Choice*, 1984, *43*(1), pp. 3–24.

Kinder, D. R. and Kiewiet, D. R. "Economic Discontent and Political Behavior: The Role of Personal Grievances and Collective Economic Judgments in Congressional Voting," *American Journal of Political Science*, August 1979, 23, pp. 495–517.

Kirchgässner, G. *Rationales Wählerverhalten und optimales Regierungsverhalten*, Ph.D. dissertation, University of Constance, 1976.

"Wirtachtslage und Wählerverhalten," *Politische Vierteljahresschrift*, 1977, *18*, pp. 510–36.

"The Effect of Economic Events on Votes for President – Some Alternative Estimates," Swiss Federal Institute of Technology, Zurich, 1981, mimeo.

"Causality Testing of the Popularity Function: An Empirical Investigation for the Federal Republic of Germany, 1971–1982," *Public Choice*, 1985, *45*(2), pp. 155–73.

Kirman, A. P. and Sondermann, D. "Arrow's Theorem, Many Agents, and Invisible Dictators," *Journal of Economic Theory*, October 1972, *5*, pp. 267–77.

Kirschen, E. S., ed. *Economic Policies Compared: West and East*, vol. 1, *General Theory*, Amsterdam: North-Holland, 1974.

et al. *Economic Policy in Our Time*, Amsterdam: North-Holland, 1964.

Kitchen, H. M. "A Statistical Estimation of an Operating Cost Function for Municipal Refuse Collection," *Public Finance Quarterly*, January 1976, *4*, pp. 56–76.

Klevorick, A. K. "Discussion," *American Economic Review*, May 1974, *64*, pp. 158–61.

Knight, F. H. *Risk, Uncertainty and Profit*, New York: Harper and Row, 1965; 1st ed. 1921.

"Profit" in *Encyclopedia of Social Sciences*, 1934, reprinted in Fellner, William and Haley, Bernard F., *Readings in the Theory of Income Distribution*, Philadelphia: Blakiston, 1950, pp. 533–46.

Koehler, D. H. "Vote Trading and the Voting Paradox: A Proof of Logical Equivalence," *American Political Science Review*, September 1975, *69*, pp. 954–60.

Koford, K. J. "Centralized Vote-Trading," *Public Choice*, 1982, *39*(2), pp. 245–68.

Kormendi, R. C. "A New Remedy for the Free Rider Problem? – Flies in the Ointment," *Research in Law and Economics*, 1979, *1*, pp. 115–30.

"Further Thoughts on the Free Rider Problem and Demand Revealing Processes," *Research in Law and Economics*, 1980, *2*, pp. 219–25.

Kragt, A. J. van de, Orbell, J. M. and Dawes, R. M. "The Minimal Contributing Set as a Solution to Public Goods Problems," *American Political Science Review*, March 1983, *77*, pp. 112–22.

Kramer, G. H. "Short Run Fluctuations in U.S. Voting Behavior, 1896–1964," *American Political Science Review*, March 1971, *65*, pp. 131–43.

"Sophisticated Voting over Multidimensional Choice Spaces," *Journal of Mathematical Sociology*, July 1972, *2*, pp. 165–80.

"On a Class of Equilibrium Conditions for Majority Rule," *Econometrica*, March 1973, *41*, pp. 285–97.

"A Dynamic Model of Political Equilibrium," *Journal of Economic Theory*, December 1977, *16*, pp. 310–34.

"The Ecological Fallacy Revisited: Aggregate- versus Individual-level Findings on Economics and Elections, and Sociotropic Voting," *American Political Science Review*, March 1983, *77*, pp. 92–111.

Kramer, G. H. and Klevorick, A. J. "Existence of a Local Cooperative Equilibrium in a Class of Voting Games," *Review of Economic Studies*, October 1974, *41*, pp. 539–47.

Krueger, A. O. "The Political Economy of the Rent-Seeking Society," *American Economic Review*, June 1974, *64*, pp. 291–303, reprinted in Buchanan, Tollison, and Tullock (1980, pp. 51–70).

Kuga, K. and Nagatani, H. "Voter Antagonism and the Paradox of Voting," *Econometrica*, November 1974, *42*, pp. 1045–67.

Kuklinski, J. H. and West, D. M. "Economic Expectations and Voting Behavior in United States House and Senate Elections," *American Political Science Review*, June 1981, *75*, pp. 436–47.

Kunreuther, H., et al. *Disaster Insurance Protection*, New York: Wiley, 1978.

Lächler, U. "On Political Business Cycles with Endogenous Election Dates," *Journal of Public Economics*, February 1982, *17*, pp. 111–17.

Lafay, J.-D. "Important Political Change and the Stability of the Popularity Function: Before and after the French General Election of 1981," University of Poitiers, 1984, mimeo.

Laffont, J.-J. and Maskin, E. "A Differential Approach to Dominant Strategy Mechanisms," *Econometrica*, September 1980, *48*, pp. 1507–30.

Landes, W. M. and Posner, R. A. "The Independent Judiciary in an Interest-Group Perspective," *Journal of Law and Economics*, December 1975, *18*, pp. 875–901.

Lane, J.-E. and Ersson, S. "Political Institutions, Public Policy and Economic Growth," *Scandinavian Political Studies*, March 1986, *9*, pp. 19–34.

Lane, R. E. "Political Involvement through Voting," in B. Seasholes, ed., *Voting, Interest Groups, and Parties*, Glenview, Ill.: Scott, Foresman, 1966.

Laney, L. O. and Willett, T. D. "Presidential Politics, Budget Deficits, and Monetary Policy in the United States: 1960–76," *Public Choice*, 1983, *40*(1), pp. 53–69.

Lange, P. and Garrett, G. "The Politics of Growth: Strategic Interaction and Economic Performance in the Advanced Industrial Democracies, 1974–80," *Journal of Politics*, August 1985, *47*, pp. 792–827.

Ledyard, J. O. "The Paradox of Voting and Candidate Competition: A General Equilibrium Analysis," in G. Hornwich and J. Quirk, eds., *Essays in Contemporary Fields of Economics*, West Lafayette: Purdue University Press, 1981.

"The Pure Theory of Large Two-Candidate Elections," *Public Choice*, 1984, *44*(1), pp. 7–41.

Leffler, K. B. "Physician Licensure: Competition and Monopoly in American Medicine," *Journal of Law and Economics*, April 1978, *21*, pp. 165–86.

Lehner, F. "Pressure Politics and Economic Growth: Olson's Theory and the Swiss Experience," in Mueller (1983, pp. 203–14).

"The Political Economy of Distributive Conflict in the Welfare State," Ruhr University, Bochum, 1985, mimeo.

Leibenstein, H. "Long-Run Welfare Criteria," in J. Margolis, ed. *The Public Economy of Urban Communities*, Baltimore: Johns Hopkins University Press, 1965, pp. 539–57.

486   **References**

"Allocative Efficiency vs. X-Efficiency," *American Economic Review,* June 1966, *56,* pp. 392–415.

"Organizational or Frictional Equilibria, X-Efficiency, and the Rate of Innovation," *Quarterly Journal of Economics,* November 1969, *83,* pp. 600–23.

Lerner, A. P. *Economics of Control.* New York: Macmillan, 1944.

Levine, M. E. and Plott, C. R. "Agenda Influence and Its Implications," *Virginia Law Review,* May 1977, *63,* pp. 561–604.

Levy, F. *Dollars and Dreams: The Changing American Income Distribution,* New York: Basic Books, 1987.

Levy, M. "Voting on California's Tax and Expenditure Limitation Initiative," *National Tax Journal,* December 1975, *28,* pp. 426–36.

Lewis-Beck, M. S. "Economic Conditions and Executive Popularity: The French Experience," *American Journal of Political Science,* May 1980, *24,* pp. 306–23.

Libecap, G. D. and Wiggins, S. N. "The Influence of Private Contractual Failure on Regulation: The Case of Oil Field Unitization," *Journal of Political Economy,* August 1985, *93,* pp. 690–714.

Lindahl, E. "Just Taxation – A Positive Solution," first published in German, Lund, 1919. English translation in Musgrave and Peacock (1958, pp. 168–76).

Lindbeck, A. "Stabilization Policy in Open Economies with Endogenous Politicians," *American Economic Review,* May 1976, *66,* pp. 1–19.

"Redistribution Policy and the Expansion of the Public Sector," *Journal of Public Economics,* December 1985, *28,* pp. 309–28.

Lindeen, J. W. "An Oligopoly Model of Political Market Structures," *Public Choice,* Fall 1970, *9,* pp. 31–7.

Lindsay, C. M. "A Theory of Government Enterprise," *Journal of Political Economy,* October 1976, *87,* pp. 1061–77.

Little, I. M. D. "Social Choice and Individual Values," *Journal of Political Economy,* October 1952, *60,* pp. 422–32.

A Critique of Welfare Economics, 2d ed., Oxford: Clarendon Press, 1957.

Locke, J. "An Essay Concerning the True Original Extent and End of Civil Government," reprinted in *The English Philosophers,* New York: Random House, 1939.

Loeb, M. "Alternative Versions of the Demand-Revealing Process," *Public Choice,* Spring 1977, *29,* pp. 15–26.

Lowery, D. and Berry, W. D. "The Growth of Government in the United States: An Empirical Assessment of Competing Explanations," *American Journal of Political Science,* November 1983, *27,* pp. 665–94.

Lowery, D. and Sigelman, L. "Understanding the Tax Revolt: Eight Explanations," *American Political Science Review,* December 1981, *75,* pp. 963–74.

Lowi, T. J. *The End of Liberalism,* New York: W. W. Norton, 1969.

Luce, R. D. and Raiffa, H. *Games and Decisions,* New York: Wiley, 1957.

Lybeck, J. A. *The Growth of Government in Developed Economies,* Gower: Hants, 1986.

Lyons, D. "Nature and Soundness of the Contract and Coherence Arguments," in Daniels (1974, pp. 141–67) based on material from "Rawls versus Utilitarianism," *Journal of Philosophy,* October 1972, *69,* pp. 535–45, and "The Nature of the Contract Argument," *Cornell Law Review,* *59*(6) 1974.

McCallam, B. T. "The Political Cycle: An Empirical Test," *Southern Economic Journal,* January 1978, *44,* pp. 504–15.

McCallum, J. and Blais, A. "Government, Special Interest Groups, and Economic Growth," *Public Choice,* 1987, *54*(1), pp. 3–18.

McConnell, G. *Private Power and American Democracy,* New York: Alfred A. Knopf, 1966.

McCormick, R. E. and Tollison, R. D. *Politicians, Legislation, and the Economy,* Boston: Martinus Nijhoff, 1981.

McGuire, M. "Private Good Clubs and Public Good Clubs: Economic Models of Group Formation," *Swedish Journal of Economics,* March 1972, *74,* pp. 84–99.

"Group Segregation and Optimal Jurisdictions," *Journal of Political Economy,* January/February 1974, *82,* pp. 112–32.

McGuire, M. and Aaron, H. "Efficiency and Equity in the Optimal Supply of a Public Good," *Review of Economics and Statistics,* February 1969, *51,* pp. 31–8.

McGuire, T., Coiner, M. and Spancake, L. "Budget-Maximizing Agencies and Efficiency in Government," *Public Choice,* 1979, *34*(3–4), pp. 333–57.

MacKay, A. F. *Arrow's Theorem: The Paradox of Social Choice,* New Haven: Yale University Press, 1980.

Mackay, R. J. and Weaver, C. L. "Agenda Control by Budget Maximizers in a Multi-Bureau Setting," *Public Choice,* 1981, *37*(3), pp. 447–72.

McKelvey, R. D. "Intransitivities in Multidimensional Voting Models and Some Implications for Agenda Control," *Journal of Economic Theory,* June 1976, *12,* pp. 472–82.

"Covering, Dominance, and Institution-Free Properties of Social Choice," *American Journal of Political Science,* May 1986, *30,* pp. 283–314.

McKelvey, R. D. and Ordeshook, P. C. "Symmetric Spatial Games without Majority Rule Equilibria," *American Political Science Review,* December 1976, *70,* pp. 1172–84.

"Vote Trading: An Experimental Study," *Public Choice,* 1980, *35*(2), pp. 151–84.

McKelvey, R. D., Ordeshook, P. C. and Winer, M. "The Competitive Solutions for N-Person Games without Transferable Utility, with an Application to Committee Games," *American Political Science Review,* June 1978, *72,* pp. 599–615.

McMillan, M. L. "Toward the More Optimal Provision of Local Public Goods: Internalization of Benefits or Intergovernmental Grants?" *Public Finance Quarterly,* July 1975, *3,* pp. 229–60.

MacRae, D. C. "A Political Model of the Business Cycle," *Journal of Political Economy,* April 1977, *85,* pp. 239–63.

Madsen, H. J. "Electoral Outcomes and Macro-Economic Policies: The Scandinavian Cases," in Paul Whiteley, ed., *Models of Political Economy,* London: Sage, 1980, pp. 15–46.

Magee, Stephen P. "Protectionism in the United States," University of Texas, Austin, 1982, mimeo.

Maital, S. "Public Goods and Income Distribution: Some Further Results," *Econometrica,* May 1973, *41,* pp. 561–4.

"Apportionment of Public Goods Benefits to Individuals," *Public Finance,* 1975, *30*(3), pp. 397–415.

Malinvaud, E. "Procedures pour la Determination d'un Programme de Consommation Collective," *European Economic Review,* Winter 1970–71, *2,* pp. 187–217.

Mann, H. M. and McCormick, K. "Firm Attributes and the Propensity to Influence the Political System," in John J. Siegfried, ed., *The Economics of Firm Size, Market Structure and Social Performance,* Washington, D.C.: Federal Trade Commission, 1980, pp. 300–13.

Mann, P. C. and Mikesell, J. L. "Ownership and Water Systems Operations," *Water Resources Bulletin,* 1976, *12,* pp. 995–1004.

Margolis, H. "Probability of a Tied Election," *Public Choice,* Fall 1977, *31,* pp. 135–8.

"A Thought Experiment on Demand-Revealing Mechanisms," *Public Choice,* 1982a, *38*(1), pp. 87–91.

Selfishness, Altruism, and Rationality. Cambridge, Mass.: Cambridge University Press, 1982b.

"A Note on Demand-Revealing," *Public Choice,* 1983, *40*(2), pp. 217–25.

488 References

Marlow, M. L. "Fiscal Decentralization and Government Size," *Public Choice*, 1988, *56*(3), pp. 259–69.

Marris, R. *The Economic Theory of Managerial Capitalism*, New York: Free Press, 1964.

Martin, D. and Wagner, R. "The Institutional Framework for Municipal Incorporation: An Economic Analysis of Local Agency Formation Commissions in California," *Journal of Law and Economics*, October 1978, *21*, pp. 409–25.

Marvel, H. P. and Ray, E. J. "The Kennedy Round: Evidence on the Regulation of International Trade in the United States," *American Economic Review*, March 1983, *73*, pp. 190–7.

Maskin, E. "A Theorem on Utilitarianism," *Review of Economic Studies*, February 1978, *45*, pp. 43–6.

May, K. O. "A Set of Independent, Necessary and Sufficient Conditions for Simple Majority Decision," *Econometrica*, October 1952, *20*, pp. 680–4.

Mayer, L. S. and Good, I. J. "Is Minimax Regret Applicable to Voting Decisions?" *American Political Science Review*, September 1975, *69*, pp. 916–17.

Mayhew, D. R. *Congress: The Electoral Connection*, New Haven: Yale University Press, 1974.

Meade, J. E. "External Economies and Diseconomies in a Competitive Situation," *Economic Journal*, March 1952, *62*, pp. 54–67, reprinted in Arrow and Scitovsky (1969, pp. 185–98).

Meehl, P. E. "The Selfish Citizen Paradox and the Throw Away Vote Argument," *American Political Science Review*, March 1977, *71*, pp. 11–30.

Meerman, J. "Are Public Goods Public Goods?" *Public Choice*, 1980, *35*(1), pp. 45–57.

Mehay, S. L. "The Expenditure Effects of Municipal Annexation," *Public Choice*, 1981, *36*(1), pp. 53–62.

"The Effect of Governmental Structure on Special District Expenditures," *Public Choice*, 1984, *44*(2), pp. 339–48.

Mehay, S. L. and Gonzalez, R. A. "Economic Incentives under Contract Supply of Local Governmental Services," *Public Choice*, 1985, *46*(1), pp. 79–86.

Meltzer, A. H. and Richard, S. F. "Why Government Grows (and Grows) in a Democracy," *Public Interest*, Summer 1978, *52*, pp. 111–18.

"A Rational Theory of the Size of Government," *Journal of Political Economy*, October 1981, *89*, pp. 914–27.

"Tests of a Rational Theory of the Size of Government," *Public Choice*, 1983, *41*(3), pp. 403–18.

Merrill, S. III. "Strategic Decisions under One-Stage Multi-Candidate Voting Systems," *Public Choice*, 1981, *36*(1), pp. 115–34.

"A Comparison of Efficiency of Multicandidate Electoral Systems," *American Journal of Political Science*, February 1984, *28*, pp. 23–48.

"A Statistical Model for Condorcet Efficiency Based on Simulation under Spatial Model Assumptions," *Public Choice*, 1985, *47*(2), pp. 389–403.

Meyer, R. A. "Publicly Owned versus Privately Owned Utilities: A Policy Choice," *Review of Economics and Statistics*, November 1975, *57*, pp. 391–9.

Midlarsky, M. I. "Political Stability of Two-Party and Multiparty Systems: Probabilistic Bases for the Comparison of Party Systems," *American Political Science Review*, December 1984, *78*, pp. 929–51.

Mieszkowski, P. "Tax Incidence Theory," *Journal of Economic Literature*, December 1969, *7*, pp. 1103–24.

Migue, J.-L. and Belanger, G. "Towards a General Theory of Managerial Discretion," *Public Choice*, Spring 1974, *17*, pp. 27–43.

Mikesell, J. L. "Election Periods and State Tax Policy Cycles," *Public Choice*, 1978, *33*(3), pp. 99–106.

Milbrath, L. W. *Political Participation*, Chicago: Rand McNally, 1965.

Mill, J. S. *Considerations on Representative Government,* New York: Bobbs-Merrill, 1958 (first publication, 1861).

Principles of Political Economy, Harmondsworth, England: Penguin Books, 1970 (first publication, 1848).

Miller, G. J. "Bureaucratic Compliance as a Game on the Unit Square," *Public Choice,* Spring 1977, *19,* pp. 37–51.

Cities by Contract, Cambridge, Mass.: MIT Press, 1981.

Miller, G. J. and Moe, T. M. "Bureaucrats, Legislators, and the Size of Government," *American Political Science Review,* June 1983, *77,* pp. 297–322.

Miller, J. C. III, Shughart, W. F. and Tollison, R. D. "A Note on Centralized Regulatory Review," *Public Choice,* 1984, *43*(1), pp. 83–8.

Miller, N. R. "Logrolling, Vote Trading, and the Paradox of Voting: A Game Theoretical Overview," *Public Choice,* Summer 1977, *30,* pp. 51–75.

Miller, N. R. "A New Solution Set for Tournaments and Majority Voting: Further Graph-Theoretical Approaches to the Theory of Voting," *American Journal of Political Science,* February 1980, *24,* pp. 68–96.

"The Covering Relation in Tournaments: Two Corrections," *American Journal of Political Science,* May 1983, *27,* pp. 382–5.

Milleron, J. C. "Theory of Value with Public Goods: A Survey Article," *Journal of Economic Theory,* December 1972, *5,* pp. 419–77.

Minford, P. and Peel, D. "The Political Theory of the Business Cycle," *European Economic Review,* February 1982, *17,* pp. 253–70.

Mishan, E. J. "The Postwar Literature on Externalities: An Interpretative Essay," *Journal of Economic Literature,* March 1971, *9,* pp. 1–28.

Mitchell, W. C. "Schumpeter and Public Choice, Part I: Precursor to Public Choice?" *Public Choice,* 1984a, *42*(1), pp. 73–88.

"Schumpeter and Public Choice, Part II: Democracy and the Demise of Capitalism: The Missing Chapter in Schumpeter," *Public Choice,* 1984b, *42*(2), pp. 161–74.

Moore, T. G. "The Effectiveness of Regulation of Electric Utility Prices," *Southern Economic Journal,* April 1970, *36,* pp. 365–75.

Morgan, W. D. "Investor Owned vs. Publicly Owned Water Agencies: An Evaluation of the Property Rights Theory of the Firm," *Water Resources Bulletin,* August 1977, *13,* pp. 775–82.

Moulin, H. "Dominance Solvable Voting Schemes," *Econometrica,* November 1979, *47,* pp. 1337–51.

"The Proportional Veto Principle," *Review of Economic Studies,* July 1981a, *48,* pp. 407–16.

"Prudence versus Sophistication in Voting Strategy," *Journal of Economic Theory,* June 1981b, *24,* pp. 398–412.

"Voting with Proportional Veto Power," *Econometrica,* January 1982, *50,* pp. 145–62.

Mueller, D. C. "The Possibility of a Social Welfare Function: Comment," *American Economic Review,* December 1967, *57,* pp. 1304–11.

"Fiscal Federalism in a Constitutional Democracy," *Public Policy,* Fall 1971, *19,* pp. 567–93.

"Constitutional Democracy and Social Welfare," *Quarterly Journal of Economics,* February 1973, *87,* pp. 60–80.

"Allocation, Redistribution and Collective Choice," *Public Finance,* 1977, *32*(2), pp. 225–44.

"Voting by Veto," *Journal of Public Economics,* 1978, *10*(1), pp. 57–75.

"Power and Profit in Hierarchical Organizations," *Swedish Journal of Political Science,* 1980, *5,* pp. 293–302.

"Redistribution, Growth and Political Stability," *American Economic Review,* May 1982, *72,* pp. 155–9.

ed., *The Political Economy of Growth,* New Haven: Yale University Press, 1983.

490   **References**

"Voting by Veto and Majority Rule," in Horst Hanusch, ed., *Public Finance and the Quest for Efficiency*, Detroit, Mich.: Wayne State University Press, 1984, pp. 69–86.

"Rational Egoism versus Adaptive Egoism as Fundamental Postulate for a Descriptive Theory of Human Behavior," *Public Choice*, 1986a, *51*(1), pp. 3–23.

Profits in the Long Run, New York: Cambridge University Press, 1986b.

Mueller, D. C. and Murrell, P. "Interest Groups and the Political Economy of Government Size," in Francesco Forte and Alan Peacock, eds., *Public Expenditure and Government Growth*, Oxford: Basil Blackwell, 1985, pp. 13–36.

"Interest Groups and the Size of Government," *Public Choice*, 1986, *48*(2), pp. 125–45.

"The Voting Paradox," in C. K. Rowley, ed., *Democracy and Public Choice*, Oxford: Basil Blackwell, 1987, pp. 77–99.

Mueller, D. C., Philpotts, G. C. and Vanek, J. "The Social Gains from Exchanging Votes: A Simulation Approach," *Public Choice*, Fall 1972, *13*, pp. 55–79.

Mueller, D. C., Tollison, R. D. and Willett, T. D. "Representative Democracy via Random Selection," *Public Choice*, Spring 1972, *12*, pp. 57–68.

"The Utilitarian Contract: A Generalization of Rawls' Theory of Justice," *Theory and Decision*, February/April 1974a, *4*, pp. 345–67.

"On Equalizing the Distribution of Political Income," *Journal of Political Economy*, March/April 1974b, *82*, pp. 414–22.

"Solving the Intensity Problem in a Representative Democracy," in R. D. Leiter and G. Sirkin, eds., *Economics of Public Choice*, New York: Cyro Press, 1975, pp. 54–94, reprinted in R. Amacher, R. Tollison and T. Willett, *Political Economy and Public Policy*, Ithaca, N.Y.: Cornell University Press, 1976, pp. 444–73.

Mueller, J. E. "Presidential Popularity from Truman to Johnson," *American Political Science Review*, March 1970, *64*, pp. 18–34.

Munley, V. G. "An Alternative Test of the Tiebout Hypothesis," *Public Choice*, 1982, *38*(2), pp. 211–7.

Murrell, P. "The Comparative Structure of the Growth of the West German and British Manufacturing Industries," in Mueller (1983), pp. 109–31.

"An Examination of the Factors Affecting the Formation of Interest Groups in OECD Countries," *Public Choice*, 1984, *43*(2), pp. 151–71.

Musgrave, R. A. "The Voluntary Exchange Theory of Public Economy," *Quarterly Journal of Economics*, February 1939, *53*, pp. 213–38.

The Theory of Public Finance, New York: McGraw-Hill, 1959.

"Approaches to a Fiscal Theory of Political Federalism," National Bureau of Economic Research, *Public Finances: Needs, Resources and Utilization*, Princeton: Princeton University Press, 1961, pp. 97–122.

"Leviathan Cometh – Or Does He?" in Helen F. Ladd and T. Nicolaus Tideman, eds., *Tax and Expenditure Limitations*, Washington, D.C.: Urban Institute, 1981, pp. 77–120.

Musgrave, R. and Musgrave, P. B. *Public Finance in Theory and Practice*, 3d ed., New York: McGraw-Hill, 1980.

Musgrave, R. A. and Peacock, A. T., eds. *Classics in the Theory of Public Finance*, New York: St. Martin's Press, 1967.

Muth, R. F. *Public Housing: An Economic Evaluation*, Washington, D.C.: American Enterprise Institute, 1973.

Nagel, T. "Rawls on Justice," *Philosophical Review*, April 1973, *82*, pp. 220–34, reprinted in Daniels (1974, pp. 1–15).

Nardinelli, C., Wallace, M. S. and Warner, J. T. "Explaining Differences in State Growth," *Public Choice*, 1987, *52*(3), pp. 201–13.

Nash, J. F. "The Bargaining Problem," *Econometrica*, April 1950, *18*, pp. 155–62.

Nath, S. K. "Liberalism, Pareto Principle and the Core of a Society," University of Warwick, 1976.

Neck, R. and Schneider, F. "The Growth of the Public Sector in Austria: An Explanatory Analysis," in J. A. Lybeck and M. Henrekson, eds., *Exploring the Growth of Government,* Amsterdam: North-Holland, 1988, pp. 231–62.

Nelson, M. A. "An Empirical Analysis of State and Local Tax Structure in the Context of the Leviathan Model of Government," *Public Choice,* 1986, *49*(3), pp. 283–94.

Newman, P. *The Theory of Exchange,* Englewood Cliffs, N.J.: Prentice-Hall, 1965.

Ng, Y.-K. "The Possibility of a Paretian Liberal: Impossibility Theorems and Cardinal Utility," *Journal of Political Economy,* November/December 1971, *79,* pp. 1397–1402.

"The Economic Theory of Clubs: Optimal Tax/Subsidy," *Economica,* August 1974, *41,* pp. 308–21.

"Bentham or Bergson? Finite Sensibility, Utility Functions and Social Welfare Functions," *Review of Economic Studies,* October 1975, *42,* pp. 545–69.

Welfare Economics, New York: John Wiley, 1980.

"Welfarism: A Defense against Sen's Attack," *Economic Journal,* June 1981a, *91,* pp. 527–30.

"Bentham or Nash? On the Acceptable Form of Social Welfare Functions," *Economic Record,* September 1981b, *57,* pp. 238–50.

"Beyond Pareto Optimality: The Necessity of Interpersonal Cardinal Utilities in Distributional Judgements and Social Choice," *Zeitschrift für Nationalökonomie,* 1982, *42*(3), pp. 207–33.

"Some Broader Issues of Social Choice," in P. K. Pattanaik and M. Salles, eds., *Social Choice and Welfare,* Amsterdam: North-Holland, 1983, pp. 151–73.

"Expected Subjective Utility: Is the Neumann-Morgenstern Utility the Same as the Neoclassical's?" *Social Choice and Welfare,* 1984a, *1,* pp. 177–86.

"Interpersonal Level Comparability Implies Comparability of Utility Differences," *Theory and Decision,* 1984b, *17,* pp. 141–7.

"Quasi-Pareto Social Improvements," *American Economic Review,* December 1984c, *74,* pp. 1033–50.

"Some Fundamental Issues in Social Welfare," in G. Feiwel, ed., *Issues in Contemporary Microeconomics and Welfare,* London: Macmillan, 1985a, pp. 435–69.

"Equity and Efficiency vs. Freedom and Fairness: An Inherent Conflict," *Kyklos,* 1985b, *38*(4), pp. 495–516.

Nicols, A. "Stock versus Mutual Savings and Loan Associations: Some Evidence of Differences in Behavior," *American Economic Review,* May 1967, *57,* pp. 337–46.

Niemi, R. G. "Majority Decision-Making with Partial Unidimensionality," *American Political Science Review,* June 1969, *63,* pp. 488–97.

"Why So Much Stability?: Another Opinion," *Public Choice,* 1983, *41*(2), pp. 261–70.

"The Problem of Strategic Behavior under Approval Voting," *American Political Science Review,* December 1984, *78,* pp. 952–8.

Niemi, R. G. and Weisberg, H. F. "A Mathematical Solution for the Probability of the Paradox of Voting," *Behavioral Science,* July 1968, *13,* pp. 317–23.

Niskanen, W. A. Jr. *Bureaucracy and Representative Government,* Chicago: Aldine-Atherton, 1971.

"Bureaucrats and Politicians," *Journal of Law and Economics,* December 1975, *18,* pp. 617–43.

"Economic and Fiscal Effects on the Popular Vote for the President," in Douglas W. Rae and Thomas J. Eismeir, eds., *Public Policy and Public Choice,* London: Sage, 1979, pp. 93–120.

Nitzan, S. "Social Preference Ordering in a Probabilistic Voting Model," *Public Choice,* Winter 1975, *24,* pp. 93–100.

"The Vulnerability of Point-Voting Schemes to Preference Variation and Strategic Manipulation," *Public Choice,* 1985, *47*(2), pp. 349–70.

Nitzan, S., Paroush, J. and Lampert, S. I. "Preference Expression and Misrepresentation in Point Voting Schemes," *Public Choice,* 1980, *35*(4), pp. 421–36.

Nordhaus, W. D. "The Political Business Cycle," *Review of Economic Studies,* April 1975, *42,* pp. 1969–90.

North, D. C. "The Growth of Government in the United States: An Economic Historian's Perspective," *Journal of Public Economics,* December 1985, *28,* pp. 383–99.

North, D. C. and Wallis, J. J. "American Government Expenditures: A Historical Perspective," *American Economic Review, Papers and Proceedings of the Ninety-Fourth Annual Meeting of the American Economic Association,* May 1982, *72,* pp. 336–40.

Notterman, J. M. *Behavior: A Systematic Approach,* New York: Random House, 1970.

Nozick, R. *Anarchy, State, and Utopia,* New York: Basic Books, 1974.

Oakland, W. H. "Public Goods, Perfect Competition, and Underproduction," *Journal of Political Economy,* September/October 1974, *82,* pp. 927–39.

Oates, W. E. "The Effects of Property Taxes and Local Public Spending on Property Values: An Empirical Study of Tax Capitalization and the Tiebout Hypothesis," *Journal of Political Economy,* November/December 1969, *77,* pp. 957–71.

Fiscal Federalism, London: Harcourt Brace, 1972.

"Searching for Leviathan: An Empirical Study," *American Economic Review,* September 1985, *75,* pp. 748–57.

"On the Measurement of Congestion in the Provision of Local Public Goods," *Journal of Urban Economics,* 1988a, *24,* pp. 85–94.

"On the Nature and Measurement of Fiscal Illusion: A Survey," in G. Brennan et al., eds., *Taxation and Fiscal Federalism: Essays in Honour of Russell Mathews,* Canberra: Australian National University Press, 1988b, pp. 65–82.

Oelert, W. "Reprivatisierung des offentlichen Personalverkehrs," *Der Personenverkehr,* 1976, *4,* pp. 108–14.

Okun, A. M. "Comment" (on Stigler, 1973), *American Economic Review,* May 1973, *63,* pp. 172–7.

Prices and Quantities, Washington, D.C.: Brookings Institution, 1981.

Olson, M., Jr. *The Logic of Collective Action,* Cambridge: Harvard University Press, 1965.

The Rise and Decline of Nations: Economic Growth, Stagflation, and Social Rigidities, New Haven: Yale University Press, 1982.

"Why Some Welfare-State Redistribution to the Poor Is a Great Idea," in C. K. Rowley, ed. *Democracy and Public Choice,* Oxford: Basil Blackwell, 1987, pp. 191–222.

Oppenheimer, J. A. "Relating Coalitions of Minorities to the Voters' Paradox, or Putting the Fly in the Democratic Pie," paper presented at the Southwest Political Science Association meeting, 1972.

"Some Political Implications of 'Vote Trading and the Voting Paradox: A Proof of Logical Equivalence': A Comment," *American Political Science Review,* September 1975, *69,* pp. 963–6.

"The Democratic Politics of Distributive Justice: Theory and Practice," College Park, Md., 1979, mimeo.

Orbell, J. M. and Uno, T. "A Theory of Neighborhood Problem Solving: Political Action vs. Residential Mobility," *American Political Science Review,* June 1972, *66,* pp. 471–89.

Ordeshook, P. C. *Game Theory and Political Theory,* Cambridge: Cambridge University Press, 1986.

Orr, L. L. "Income Transfers as a Public Good: An Application to AFDC," *American Economic Review,* June 1976, *66,* pp. 359–71.

"Income Transfers as a Public Good: Reply," *American Economic Review*, December 1978, *68*, pp. 990–4.

Orzechowski, W. "Economic Models of Bureaucracy: Survey, Extensions, and Evidence," in Borcherding (1977a, pp. 229–59).

Ostrom, V. *The Political Theory of a Compound Republic*, Blacksburg: Public Choice Society, 1971.

Owen, G. and Grofman, B. "To Vote or Not to Vote: The Paradox of Nonvoting," *Public Choice*, 1984, *42*(3), pp. 311–25.

Palda, K. F. and Palda, K. S. "Ceilings on Campaign Spending: Hypothesis and Partial Test with Canadian Data," *Public Choice*, 1985, *45*(3), pp. 313–31.

Palda, K. S. "Does Advertising Influence Votes? An Analysis of the 1966 and 1970 Quebec Elections," *Canadian Journal of Political Science*, December 1973, *6*, pp. 638–55.

"The Effect of Expenditure on Political Success," *Journal of Law and Economics*, December 1975, *18*, pp. 745–71.

Paldam, M. "Is There an Electional Cycle? A Comparative Study of National Accounts," *Scandinavian Journal of Economics*, 1979, *81*(2), pp. 323–42.

"A Preliminary Survey of the Theories and Findings on Vote and Popularity Functions," *European Journal of Political Research*, June 1981a, *9*, pp. 181–99.

"An Essay on the Rationality of Economic Policy: The Test-Case of the Electional Cycle," *Public Choice*, 1981b, *37*(2), pp. 287–305.

Paldam, M. and Schneider, F. "The Macro-Economic Aspects of Government and Opposition Popularity in Denmark, 1957-78," *Nationaløkonomisk Tidsskrift*, 1980, *118*(2), pp. 149–70.

Palfrey, T. R. and Rosenthal, H. "A Strategic Calculus of Voting," *Public Choice*, 1983, *41*(1), pp. 7–53.

"Voter Participation and Strategic Uncertainty," *American Political Science Review*, March 1985, *79*, pp. 62–78.

Paloheimo, H. "Pluralism, Corporatism and the Distributive Conflict in Developed Capitalist Countries," *Scandinavian Political Studies*, 1984a, *7*, pp. 17–38.

"Distributive Struggle and Economic Development in the 1970s in Developed Capitalist Countries," *European Journal of Political Research*, 1984b, *12*(2), pp. 171–90.

Park, R. E. "The Possibility of a Social Welfare Function: Comment," *American Economic Review*, December 1967, *57*, pp. 1300–4.

Parks, R. P. "An Impossibility Theorem for Fixed Preferences: A Dictatorial Bergson-Samuelson Welfare Function," *Review of Economic Studies*, October 1976, *43*, pp. 447–50.

Pateman, C. *Participation and Democratic Theory*, Cambridge: Cambridge University Press, 1970.

Pattanaik, P. K. "Risk, Impersonality, and the Social Welfare Function," *Journal of Political Economy*, November 1968, *76*, pp. 1152–69.

Voting and Collective Choice, Cambridge: Cambridge University Press, 1971.

"Stability of Sincere Voting Under Some Classes of Non-Binary Group Decision Procedures," *Journal of Economic Theory*, June 1974, *8*, pp. 206–24.

Patterson, S. C. and Caldeira, G. A. "Getting Out the Vote: Participation in Gubernatorial Elections," *American Political Science Review*, September 1983, *77*, pp. 675–89.

Paul, C. W. II. "Competition in the Medical Profession: An Application of the Economic Theory of Regulation," *Southern Economic Journal*, January 1982, *48*, pp. 559–69.

Pauly, M. V. "Clubs, Commonality, and the Core: An Integration of Game Theory and the Theory of Public Goods," *Economica*, August 1967, *35*, pp. 314–24.

"Cores and Clubs," *Public Choice*, Fall 1970, *9*, pp. 53–65.

Pausch, R. *Möglichkeiten einer Privatisierung offentlicher Unternehmen*, Gottingen, 1976.

494   References

Peacock, A. T. and Wiseman, J. *The Growth of Public Expenditure in the United Kingdom*, Princeton, N.J.: Princeton University Press, 1961.

Peltzman, S. "Towards a More General Theory of Regulation?" *Journal of Law and Economics*, August 1976, *19*, pp. 211–40.

"The Growth of Government," *Journal of Law and Economics*, October 1980, *23*, pp. 209–88.

"Constituent Interest and Congressional Voting," *Journal of Law and Economics*, April 1984, *27*, pp. 181–210.

Pestieau, P. "The Optimality Limits of the Tiebout Model," in W. E. Oates, ed., *The Political Economy of Fiscal Federalism*, Lexington, Mass.: Lexington Books, 1977, pp. 173–86.

Peterson, G. M. *The Demand for Public Schooling*, Washington, D.C.: Urban Institute, 1973.

"Voter Demand for School Expenditures," in J. E. Jackson, ed., *Public Needs and Private Behavior in Metropolitan Areas*, Cambridge, Mass.: Harvard University Press, 1975, pp. 99–115.

Petrovic, W. M. and Jaffee, B. L. "Aspects of the Generation and Collection of Household Refuse in Urban Areas," Indiana University, Bloomington, 1977, mimeo.

Pfister, W. "Steigende Millionenverluste der Bayerischen Staatsforstverwaltung: Ein Dauerzustand?" *Mitteilungsblatt des Bayerischen Waldbesitzerverbandes*, 1976, *26*, pp. 1–9.

Philpotts, G. "Vote Trading, Welfare, and Uncertainty," *Canadian Journal of Economics*, August 1972, *3*, pp. 358–72.

"A Note on the Representation of Preferences in the Lindahl-Johansen Diagram," *American Economic Review*, June 1980, *70*, pp. 488–92.

Pier, W. J., Vernon, R. B. and Wicks, J. H. "An Empirical Comparison of Government and Private Production Efficiency," *National Tax Journal*, December 1974, *27*, pp. 653–6.

Pigou, A. C. *The Economics of Welfare*, London: Macmillan, 1920 (revised 1924, 1929, 1932).

Pincus, J. "Pressure Groups and the Pattern of Tariffs," *Journal of Political Economy*, August 1975, *83*, pp. 757–78.

Pissarides, C. A. "British Government Popularity and Economic Performance," *Economic Journal*, September 1980, *90*, pp. 569–81.

Pitkin, H. F. *The Concept of Representation*, Berkeley: University of California Press, 1967.

Pittman, R. "The Effects of Industry Concentration and Regulation on Contributions in Three U.S. Senate Campaigns," *Public Choice*, Fall 1976, *27*, pp. 71–80.

"Market Structure and Campaign Contributions," *Public Choice*, Fall 1977, *31*, pp. 37–52.

Plotnick, R. D. and Winters, R. F. "A Politico-Economy Theory of Income Redistribution," *American Political Science Review*, June 1985, *79*, pp. 458–73.

Plott, C. R. "A Notion of Equilibrium and Its Possibility under Majority Rule," *American Economic Review*, September 1967, *57*, pp. 787–806.

"Recent Results in the Theory of Voting," in M.D. Intriligator, ed., *Frontiers of Quantitative Economics*, Amsterdam: North-Holland, 1971, pp. 109–27.

"Ethics, Social Choice Theory and the Theory of Economic Policy," *Journal of Mathematical Sociology*, 1972, *2*, pp. 181–208.

"Path Independence, Rationality and Social Choice," *Econometrica*, November 1973, *41*, pp. 1075–91.

"Axiomatic Social Choice Theory: An Overview and Interpretation," *American Journal of Political Science*, August 1976, *20*, pp. 511–96.

Pollack, R. A. "Bergson-Samuelson Social Welfare Functions and the Theory of Social Choice," *Quarterly Journal of Economics*, February 1979, *93*, pp. 73–90.

Pommerehne, W. W. "Budgetäre Umverteilung in der Demokratie: Ein empirischer Test Alternative Hypothesen," Discussion Paper 64, Konstanz, 1975.

"Private versus Offentliche Mullabfuhr; Ein Theoretischer und Empirischer Vergleich," *Finanzarchiv,* 1976, *35,* pp. 272–94.

"Institutional Approaches to Public Expenditures: Empirical Evidence From Swiss Municipalities," *Journal of Public Economics,* April 1978, *9,* pp. 163–201.

Pommerehne, W. W. and Frey, B. S. "Two Approaches to Estimating Public Expenditures," *Public Finance Quarterly,* October 1976, *4,* pp. 395–407.

Pommerehne, W. W. and Schneider, F. "Unbalanced Growth between Public and Private Sectors: An Empirical Examination," in Robert H. Haveman, ed., *Public Finance and Public Employment,* Detroit, Mich.: Wayne State University Press, 1982, pp. 309–26.

"Does Government in a Representative Democracy Follow a Majority of Voters' Preferences?– An Empirical Examination," in Horst Hanusch, ed., *Anatomy of Government Deficiencies,* Berlin: Springer, 1983, pp. 61–84.

Pomper, G. M. *Elections in America,* New York: Dodd, Mead, 1971.

Poole, K. T. and Romer, T. "Patterns of Political Action Committee Contributions to the 1980 Campaigns for the United States House of Representatives," *Public Choice,* 1985, *47*(1), pp. 63–111.

Posner, R. A. "The Social Costs of Monopoly and Regulation," *Journal of Political Economy,* August 1975, *83,* pp. 807–27, reprinted in Buchanan, Tollison, and Tullock (1980, pp. 71–94).

Powell, G. B., Jr. "Party Systems and Political System Performance: Voting Participation, Government Stability and Mass Violence in Contemporary Democracies," *American Political Science Review,* December 1981, *75,* pp. 861–79.

Primeaux, W. J., Filer, J. E., Herren, R. S. and Hollas, D. R. "Determinants of Regulatory Policies toward Competition in the Electric Utility Industry," *Public Choice,* 1984, *43*(2), pp. 173–86.

Pryor, F. L. "A Quasi-test of Olson's Hypotheses," in Mueller (1983, pp. 90–105).

Puviani, A. *Teoria della illusione nelle netrate publiche,* Perugia, 1897.

Teoria della illusione Finanziaria, Palermo, 1903.

Rae, D. W. "Decision-Rules and Individual Values in Constitutional Choice," *American Political Science Review,* March 1969, *63,* pp. 40–56.

The Political Consequences of Electoral Laws, rev. ed., New Haven: Yale University Press, 1971.

"The Limits of Consensual Decision," *American Political Science Review,* December 1975, *69,* pp. 1270–94.

Equalities, Cambridge, Mass.: Harvard University Press, 1981.

Rapoport, A. and Chammah, A. *Prisoner's Dilemma,* Ann Arbor: University of Michigan Press, 1965.

Rasch, B. E. and Sorensen, R. J. "Organizational Behavior and Economic Growth: A Norwegian Perspective," *Scandinavian Political Studies,* March 1986, *9,* pp. 51–63.

Rattinger, H. "Unemployment and the 1976 Election in Germany: Some Findings at the Aggregate and the Individual Level of Analysis," in Hibbs and Fassbender (1981, pp. 121–35).

Rawls, J. A. *A Theory of Justice,* Cambridge, Mass.: Belknap Press, 1971.

"Some Reasons for the Maximin Criterion," *American Economic Review,* May 1974, *64,* pp. 141–6.

Ray, P. "Independence of Irrelevant Alternatives," *Econometrica,* September 1973, *41,* pp. 987–91.

Reid, T. R. "Congress: Best Little Soap Opera on Cable," *Washington Post,* April 29, 1984, p. B1.

Reimer, M. "The Case for Bare Majority Rule," *Ethics,* October 1951, *62,* pp. 16–32.

Renaud, P. and van Winden, F. "Political Accountability for Price Stability and Unemployment in a Multi-Party System with Coalition Governments," *Public Choice*, 1987a, *53*(2), pp. 181–6.

"Tax Rate and Government Expenditure," *Kyklos*, 1987b, *40*, pp. 349–67.

Reynolds, M. and Smolensky, E. *Public Expenditures, Taxes and the Distribution of Income*, New York: Academic Press, 1977.

Rheinland-Pfalz, R. *Jahresbericht über die Prüfung der Haushalts- und Wirtschaftsführung sowie der Landeshaushaltsrechnung 1971*, Drucksache 7/1750, 1972, pp. 81–4.

Riker, W. H. "Voting and the Summation of Preferences: An Interpretative Bibliographical Review of Selected Developments During the Last Decade," *American Political Science Review*, December 1961, *55*, pp. 900–11.

The Theory of Political Coalitions, New Haven and London: Yale University Press, 1962.

"Is 'A New and Superior Process' Really Superior?" *Journal of Political Economy*, August 1979, *87*, pp. 875–90.

"The Two-Party System and Duverger's Law: An Essay on the History of Political Science," *American Political Science Review*, December 1982a, *76*, pp. 753–66.

Liberalism Against Populism, San Francisco: W. H. Freeman, 1982b.

Riker, W. H. and Brams, S. J. "The Paradox of Vote Trading," *American Political Science Review*, December 1973, *67*, pp. 1235–47.

Riker, W. H. and Ordeshook, P. C. "A Theory of the Calculus of Voting," *American Political Science Review*, March 1968, *62*, pp. 25–42.

Introduction to Positive Political Theory, Englewood Cliffs, N.J.: Prentice-Hall, 1973.

Riley, J. "On the Possibility of Liberal Democracy," *American Political Science Review*, December 1985, *79*, pp. 1135–51.

Rob, R. "Asymptotic Efficiency of the Demand Revealing Mechanism," *Journal of Economic Theory*, December 1982, *28*, pp. 207–20.

Roberts, K. W. S. "Voting over Income Tax Schedules," *Journal of Public Economics*, December 1977, *8*, pp. 329–40.

"Possibility Theorems with Interpersonally Comparable Welfare Levels," *Review of Economic Studies*, January 1980a, *47*, pp. 409–20.

"Interpersonal Comparability and Social Choice Theory," *Review of Economic Studies*, January 1980b, *47*, pp. 421–39.

"Social Choice Theory: The Single-Profile and Multi-Profile Approaches," *Review of Economic Studies*, January 1980c, *47*, pp. 441–50.

Rodgers, J. D. "Explaining Income Redistribution," in Harold M. Hochman and George E. Peterson, eds., *Redistribution through Public Choice*, New York: Columbia University Press, 1974, pp. 165–205.

Rogerson, W. P. "The Social Costs of Monopoly and Regulation: A Game-Theoretic Analysis," *Bell Journal of Economics*, Autumn 1982, *13*, pp. 391–401.

Rogowski, R. "Structure, Growth and Power: Three Rationalist Accounts," *International Organization*, Autumn 1983, *37*, pp. 713–38.

Romer, T. and Rosenthal, H. "Political Resource Allocation, Controlled Agendas, and the Status Quo," *Public Choice*, Winter 1978, *33*(4), pp. 27–43.

"The Elusive Median Voter," *Journal of Public Economics*, October 1979a, *12*, pp. 143–70.

"Bureaucrats versus Voters: On the Political Economy of Resource Allocation by Direct Democracy," *Quarterly Journal of Economics*, November 1979b, *93*, pp. 563–87.

"Median Voters or Budget Maximizers: Evidence from School Expenditure Referenda," *Economic Inquiry*, October 1982, *20*, pp. 556–78.

Rosa, J. J. "Economic Conditions and Elections in France," in Paul Whiteley, ed., *Models of Political Economy*, London: Sage, 1980, pp. 101–20.

Rose-Ackerman, S. *Corruption,* New York: Academic Press, 1978.

Ross, J. P. and Burkhead, J. *Productivity in the Local Government Sector,* Lexington, Mass.: Lexington Books, 1974.

Rothenberg, J. *The Measurement of Social Welfare,* Englewood Cliffs, N.J.: Prentice-Hall, 1961.

Rousseau, J-J. *The Social Contract,* New York: Hafner, 1966 (original publication, 1762).

Rowley, C. K. and Peacock, A. T. *Welfare Economics,* London: Martin Robertson, 1975.

Runciman, W. G. and Sen, A. K. "Games, Justice and the General Will," *Mind,* October 1965, pp. 554–62.

Rushing, W. "Differences in Profit and Nonprofit Organizations: A Study of Effectiveness and Efficiency in General Short-Stay Hospitals," *Administrative Science Quarterly,* December 1974, *19,* pp. 474–84.

Russell, B. *Power,* New York: Norton, 1938.

Russell, K. P. "Political Participation and Income Level: An Exchange," *Public Choice,* Fall 1972, *13,* pp. 113–14.

Ruttan, V. W. "Bureaucratic Productivity: The Case of Agricultural Research," *Public Choice,* 1980, *35*(5), pp. 529–47.

Samuelson, L. "Electoral Equilibria with Restricted Strategies," *Public Choice,* 1984, *43*(3), pp. 307–27.

Samuelson, P. A. *Foundations of Economic Analysis,* Cambridge: Harvard University Press, 1947.

"The Pure Theory of Public Expenditure," *Review of Economics and Statistics,* November 1954, *36,* pp. 386–9, reprinted in Arrow and Scitovsky (1969, pp. 179–82).

"Arrow's Mathematical Politics," in S. Hook, ed., *Human Values and Economic Policy,* New York: New York University Press, 1967.

"Pure Theory of Public Expenditure and Taxation," in J. Margolis and H. Guitton, eds., *Public Economics,* New York: St. Martin's Press, 1969, pp. 98–123.

"Reaffirming the Existence of 'Reasonable' Bergson-Samuelson Social Welfare Function," *Economica,* February 1977, *44,* pp. 81–8.

"Bergsonian Welfare Economics," in S. Rosefielde, ed., *Economic Welfare and the Economics of Soviet Socialism,* Cambridge: Cambridge University Press, 1981, pp. 223–66.

Sandler, T. and Tschirhart, J. T. "The Economic Theory of Clubs: An Evaluation Survey," *Journal of Economic Literature,* December 1980, *18,* pp. 1481–1521.

"Mixed Clubs: Further Observations," *Journal of Public Economics,* April 1984, *23,* pp. 381–9.

Santerre, R. E. "Representative versus Direct Democracy: A Tiebout Test of Relative Performance," *Public Choice,* 1986, *48*(1), pp. 55–63.

Satterthwaite, M. A. "Strategy-Proofness and Arrow's Conditions: Existence and Correspondence Theorems for Voting Procedures and Social Welfare Functions," *Journal of Economic Theory,* April 1975, *10,* pp. 187–217.

Saunders, P. "Explaining International Differences in Public Expenditure: An Empirical Study," paper presented at Conference of Economists, Clayton, Victoria, 1986.

Saunders, P. and Klau, F. *The Role of the Public Sector: Causes and Consequences of the Growth of Government,* Economic Studies, No. 4, Paris: Organisation for Economic Co-operation and Development, 1985.

Savas, E. S. "Municipal Monopolies versus Competition in Delivering Urban Services," in W. D. Hawley and D. Rogers, eds., *Improving the Quality of Urban Management,* Beverly Hills, Calif., 1974, pp. 473–500.

Evaluating the Organization and Efficiency of Solid Waste Collection, Lexington, Mass.: Lexington Books, 1977a.

498   References

The Organization and Efficiency of Solid Waste Collection, Lexington, Mass.: Lexington Books, 1977b.

"Comparative Costs of Public and Private Enterprise in a Municipal Service," in W. J. Baumol, ed., *Public and Private Enterprise in a Mixed Economy*, New York and London, 1980, pp. 234–94.

Scanlon, I. M. "Rawls' Theory of Justice," in Daniels (1974, pp. 141–67) as adapted from "Rawls' Theory of Justice," *University of Pennsylvania Law Review*, May 1973, *121*, pp. 1020–69.

Schattschneider, E. E. *Politics, Pressures and the Tariff*, Englewood Cliffs, N.J.: Prentice-Hall, 1935.

Schelling, T. C. *Arms and Influence*, New Haven: Yale University Press, 1966.

Schneider, F. *Politisch-Okonomische Modelle: Theoretische und Empirische Ansätze*, Konigstein, Athenaeum, 1978.

"Politisch-ökonomische Modelle: Ubersicht und Nevere Entwicklungen," *Jahrbuch für Neue Politische Okonomie*, 1982, *1*, pp. 57–88.

Schneider, F. and Frey, B. S. "Politico-Economic Models of Macroeconomic Policy," in Thomas D. Willett, ed. *Political Business Cycle*, Durham, N.C.: Duke University Press, 1988.

Schneider, F. and Pommerehne, W. W. "Politico-Economic Interactions in Australia: Some Empirical Evidence," *Economic Record*, June 1980, *56*, pp. 113–31.

Schneider, H. K. and Schuppener, C. *Soziale Absicherung der Wohnungsmarktwirtschaft durch Individualsubventionen*, Gottingen, 1971.

Schneider, M. "Fragmentation and the Growth of Local Government," *Public Choice*, 1986, *48*(3), pp. 255–63.

Schofield, N. "Instability of Simple Dynamic Games," *Review of Economic Studies*, October 1978, *45*, pp. 575–94.

"The Relationship between Voting and Political Stability in an Electoral System," in Manfred J. Holler, ed., *Power, Voting and Voting Power*, Wurzburg: Physica Verlag, 1981.

"Coalitions in West European Democracies: 1945–1986," St. Louis: Washington University, 1987, mimeo.

Schotter, A. *The Economic Theory of Social Institutions*, Cambridge: Cambridge University Press, 1981.

Schuck, P. H. "The Politics of Economic Growth," *Yale Law and Policy Review*, Spring 1984, *2*, pp. 359–81.

Schultze, C. "The Distribution of Farm Subsidies," in K. E. Boulding and M. Pfaff, eds., *Redistribution to the Rich and the Poor*, Belmont, Calif.: Wadsworth, 1972, pp. 94–116.

Schumpeter, J. A. *Capitalism, Socialism and Democracy*, 3d ed., New York: Harper and Row, 1950.

Schwab, R. M. and Zampelli, E. M. "Disentangling the Demand Function from the Production Function for Local Public Services: The Case of Public Safety," *Journal of Public Economics*, July 1987, *33*, pp. 245–60.

Schwartz, B. and Lacey, H. *Behaviorism, Science, and Human Nature*, 1982, New York: Norton.

Schwartz, T. "Vote Trading and Pareto Efficiency," *Public Choice*, Winter 1975, *24*, pp. 101–9.

"The Universal-Instability Theorem," *Public Choice*, 1981, *37*(3), pp. 487–501.

The Logic of Collective Choice, New York: Columbia University Press, 1986.

Schwert, G. W. "Public Regulation of National Securities Exchanges: A Test of the Capture Hypothesis," *Bell Journal of Economics*, Spring 1977, *8*, pp. 128–50.

Scitovsky, T. "Two Concepts of External Economies," *Journal of Political Economy*, April 1954, *17*, pp. 143–51, reprinted in Arrow and Scitovsky (1969, pp. 242–52).

Scott, A. D. "A Note on Grants in Federal Countries," *Economica*, November 1950, *17*, pp. 416–22.

"Evaluation of Federal Grants," *Economica*, November 1952a, *19*, pp. 377–94.

"Federal Grants and Resource Allocation," *Journal of Political Economy*, December 1952b, *60*, pp. 534–6.

Sears, D. O., Hensler, C. P. and Speer, L. K. "Whites' Opposition to 'Busing': Self-Interest or Symbolic Politics?" *American Political Science Review*, June 1979, *73*, pp. 369–84.

Sears, D. O., Law, R. R., Tyler, T. R. and Allen, H. M., Jr. "Self-Interest vs. Symbolic Politics in Policy Attitudes and Presidential Voting," *American Political Science Review*, September 1980, *74*, pp. 670–84.

Segal, U. and Spivak, A. "On the Single Membership Constituency and the Law of Large Numbers: A Note," *Public Choice*, 1986, *49*(2), pp. 183–90.

Seidl, C. "On Liberal Values," *Zeitschrift für Nationalökonomie*, 1975, *35*, pp. 257–92.

Seligman, E. R. A. *Studies in Public Finance*, New York: Macmillan, 1925.

Sell, J. and Wilson, R. K. "Effects of Monitoring and Information on Public Goods Provisioning: Experimental Evidence," Rice University, 1988, mimeo.

Selten, R. "Anwendungen der Spielthoerie auf die Politische Wissenschaft," in H. Maier, ed., *Politik und Wissenschaft*, Munich: Beck, 1971.

Sen, A. K. "A Possibility Theorem on Majority Decisions," *Econometrica*, April 1966, *34*, pp. 491–9.

"Quasi-transitivity, Rational Choice and Collective Decisions," *Review of Economic Studies*, July 1969, *36*, pp. 381–94.

Collective Choice and Social Welfare, San Francisco: Holden-Day, 1970a.

"The Impossibility of a Paretian Liberal," *Journal of Political Economy*, January/February 1970b, *78*, pp. 152–7.

"On Ignorance and Equal Distribution," *American Economic Review*, December 1973, *63*, pp. 1022–4, reprinted in Sen (1982, pp. 222–5).

"Informational Basis of Alternative Welfare Approaches, Aggregation and Income Distribution," *Journal of Public Economics*, November 1974, *3*, pp. 387–403.

"Liberty, Unanimity and Rights," *Economica*, August 1976, *43*, pp. 217–45.

"Social Choice Theory: A Re-examination," *Econometrica*, January 1977a, *45*, pp. 53–89.

"On Weight and Measures: Informational Constraints in Social Welfare Analysis," *Econometrica*, October 1977b, *45*, pp. 1539–72.

"Personal Utilities and Public Judgments: Or What's Wrong with Welfare Economics," *Economic Journal*, September 1979a, *89*, pp. 537–58.

Choice, Welfare and Measurement, Cambridge, Mass.: MIT Press, 1982.

"Foundations of Social Choice Theory: An Epilogue," in Elster and Hylland (1986, pp. 213–48).

Sen, A. K. and Pattanaik, P. K. "Necessary and Sufficient Conditions for Rational Choice under Majority Decision," *Journal of Economic Theory*, August 1969, *1*, pp. 178–202.

Sen, M. "Strategy-Proofness of a Class of Borda Rules," *Public Choice*, 1984, *43*(3), pp. 251–85.

Settle, R. F. and Abrams, B. A. "The Determinants of Voter Participation: A More General Model," *Public Choice*, Fall 1976, *27*, pp. 81–9.

Shapiro, P. and Sonstelie, J. "Representative Voter or Bureaucratic Manipulation: An Examination of Public Finances in California before and after Proposition 13," *Public Choice*, 1982, *39*(1), pp. 113–42.

Shepherd, L. "Licensing Restrictions and the Cost of Dental Care," *Journal of Law and Economics*, April 1978, *21*, pp. 187–201.

500 References

Shepsle, K. A. "Institutional Arrangements and Equilibrium in Multidimensional Voting Models," *American Journal of Political Science*, February 1979, *23*, pp. 27–59.

Shepsle, K. A. and Weingast, B. R. "Structure-Induced Equilibrium and Legislative Choice," *Public Choice*, 1981, *37*(3), pp. 503–19.

Silberman, J. I. and Durden, G. C. "The Rational Behavior Theory of Voter Participation," *Public Choice*, Fall 1975, *23*, pp. 101–8.

"Determining Legislative Preferences on the Minimum Approach," *Journal of Political Economy*, April 1976, *84*, pp. 317–29.

Silver, M. "A Demand Analysis of Voting Costs and Voting Participation," *Social Science Research*, August 1973, *2*, pp. 111–24.

"Political Revolution and Repression: An Economic Approach," *Public Choice*, Spring 1974, *17*, pp. 63–71.

Simon, H. A. "Notes on the Observation and Measurement of Power," *Journal of Politics*, 1953, *15*, pp. 500–16, reprinted in Bell, Edwards and Wagner (1969, pp. 69–78).

Skinner, B. F. *Walden II*. New York: Macmillan, 1948.

Sloss, J. "Stable Outcomes in Majority Rule Voting Games," *Public Choice*, Summer 1973, *15*, pp. 19–48.

Slutsky, S. "A Characterization of Societies with Consistent Majority Decision," *Review of Economic Studies*, June 1977a, *44*, pp. 211–25.

"A Voting Model for the Allocation of Public Goods: Existence of an Equilibrium," *Journal of Economic Theory*, April 1977b, *14*, pp. 299–325.

"Equilibrium under α-Majority Voting," *Econometrica*, September 1979, *47*, pp.1113–25.

Smith, J. H. "Aggregation of Preferences and Variable Electorate," *Econometrica*, November 1973, *41*, pp. 1027–41.

Smith, J. W. "A Clear Test of Rational Voting," *Public Choice*, Fall 1975, *23*, pp. 55–67.

Smith, V. "The Principal of Unanimity and Voluntary Consent in Social Choice," *Journal of Political Economy*, December 1977, *85*, pp. 1125–39.

"An Experimental Comparison of Three Public Good Decision Mechanisms," *Scandinavian Journal of Economics*, 1979a, *81*(2), pp. 198–215.

"Incentive Compatible Experimental Processes for the Provision of Public Goods," in V. L. Smith, ed., *Research in Experimental Economics*, Greenwich, Conn.: JAI Press, 1979b, pp. 59–168.

"Experiments with a Decentralized Mechanism for Public Good Decisions," *American Economic Review*, September 1980, *70*, pp. 584–99.

Smithies, A. "Optimum Location in Spatial Competition," *Journal of Political Economy*, June 1941, *49*, pp. 423–39.

Spann, R. M. "Collective Consumption of Private Goods," *Public Choice*, Winter 1974, *20*, pp. 63–81.

"Rates of Productivity Change and the Growth of State and Local Government Expenditures," 1977a, in Borcherding (1977a, pp. 100–29).

"Public versus Private Provision of Governmental Services," 1977b, in Borcherding (1977a, pp. 71–89).

Stevens, B. J. "Scale, Market Structure, and the Cost of Refuse Collection," *Review of Economics and Statistics*, August 1978, *66*, pp. 438–48.

Stevens, B. J. and Savas, E. S. "The Cost of Residential Refuse Collection and the Effect of Service Arrangements," *Municipal Year Book*, 1978, *44*, pp. 200–5.

Stigler, G. J. "Director's Law of Public Income Redistribution," *Journal of Law and Economics*, April 1970, *13*, pp. 1–10.

"The Theory of Economic Regulation," *Bell Journal of Economics and Management Science*, Spring 1971, *2*, pp. 137–46.

"General Economic Conditions and Natural Elections," *American Economic Review*, May 1973, *63*, pp. 160–7.

"The Sizes of Legislatures," *Journal of Legal Studies*, January 1976, *5*, pp. 17–34.

Stokes, D. E. "Spatial Models of Party Competition," *American Political Science Review*, June 1963, *57*, pp. 368–77.

Sugden, R. *The Political Economy of Public Choice*, New York: Halsted Press, 1981.

"Free Association and the Theory of Proportional Representation," *American Political Science Review*, March 1984, *78*, pp. 31–43.

Sugden, R. and Weale, A. "A Contractual Reformulation of Certain Aspects of Welfare Economics," *Economica*, May 1979, *46*, pp. 111–23.

Suzumura, K. "On the Consistency of Liberal Claims," *Review of Economic Studies*, June 1978, *45*, pp. 329–42.

Rational Choice, Collective Decisions, and Social Welfare, Cambridge: Cambridge University Press, 1983.

Takacs, Wendy E. "Pressures for Protectionism: An Empirical Analysis," *Economic Inquiry*, October 1981, *19*, pp. 687–93.

Tanzi, V. "Toward a Positive Theory of Public Sector Behavior: An Interpretation of Some Italian Contributions," Washington, D.C.: International Monetary Fund, 1980, mimeo.

"Public Expenditure and Public Debt: An International and Historical Perspective," in John Bristow and Declan McDonagh, eds., *Public Expenditure: The Key Issues*, Dublin: Institute of Public Administration, 1986a, pp. 6–41.

"The Growth of Public Expenditure in Industrial Countries: An International and Historical Perspective," Washington, D.C.: International Monetary Fund, 1986b, mimeo.

Taylor, M. J. "Proof of a Theorem on Majority Rule," *Behavioral Science*, May 1969, *14*, pp. 228–31.

"Review Article: Mathematical Political Theory," *British Journal of Political Science*, July 1971, *1*, pp. 339–82.

Anarchy and Cooperation, New York: Wiley, 1976.

Taylor, M. J. and Herman, V. M. "Party Systems and Government Stability," *American Political Science Review*, March 1971, *65*, pp. 28–37.

Taylor, M. J. and Laver, M. "Government Coalitions in Western Europe," *European Journal of Political Research*, September 1973, *1*, pp. 205–48.

Taylor, M. and Ward, H. "Chickens, Whales, and Lumpy Goods: Alternative Models of Public-Good Provision," *Political Studies*, September 1982, *30*, pp. 350–70.

Thompson, E. A. "A Pareto Optimal Group Decision Process," in G. Tullock, ed. *Papers on Non-Market Decision Making*, Charlottesville: University of Virginia, 1966, pp. 133–40.

Tideman, T. N. "Ethical Foundations of the Demand-Revealing Process," *Public Choice*, Spring 1977, *29*, pp. 71–7.

"An Experiment in the Demand-Revealing Process," *Public Choice*, 1983, *41*(3), pp. 387–401.

Tideman, T. N. and Tullock, G. "A New and Superior Process for Making Social Choices," *Journal of Political Economy*, December 1976, *84*, pp. 1145–59.

"Some Limitations of Demand Revealing Processes: Comment," *Public Choice*, Spring 1977, *29*, pp. 125–8.

"Coalitions under Demand Revealing," *Public Choice*, 1981, *36*(2), pp. 323–8.

Tiebout, C. M. "A Pure Theory of Local Expenditures," *Journal of Political Economy*, October 1956, *64*, pp. 416–24.

Tollison, R. D. "Rent Seeking: A Survey," *Kyklos*, 1982, *35*(4), pp. 575–602.

Tollison, R. D., Crain, M. and Paulter, P. "Information and Voting: An Empirical Note," *Public Choice*, Winter 1975, *24*, pp. 43–9.

502   References

Tollison, R. D. and Willett, T. D. "Some Simple Economics of Voting and Not Voting," *Public Choice,* Fall 1973, *16,* pp. 59–71.

Tosini, S. C. and Tower, E. "The Textile Bill of 1985: The Determinants of Congressional Voting Patterns," *Public Choice,* 1987, *54*(1), pp. 19–25.

Tufte, E. R. *Political Control of the Economy,* Princeton: Princeton University Press, 1978.

Tulkens, H. "Dynamic Processes for Allocating Public Goods: An Institution-Oriented Survey," *Journal of Public Economics,* April 1978, *9,* pp. 163–201.

Tullock, G. "Some Problems of Majority Voting," *Journal of Political Economy,* December 1959, *67,* pp. 571–9, reprinted in Arrow and Scitovsky (1969, pp. 169–78).

"Reply to a Traditionalist," *Journal of Political Economy,* December 1961, *69,* pp. 200–3.

The Politics of Bureaucracy, Washington, D.C.: Public Affairs Press, 1965.

Toward a Mathematics of Politics, Ann Arbor: University of Michigan Press, 1967a.

"The General Irrelevance of the General Impossibility Theorem," *Quarterly Journal of Economics,* May 1967b, *81,* pp. 256–70.

"The Welfare Costs of Tariffs, Monopolies and Theft," *Western Economic Journal,* June 1967c, *5,* pp. 224–32, reprinted in Buchanan, Tollison and Tullock (1980, pp. 39–50).

"Federalism: Problems of Scale," *Public Choice,* Spring 1969, *6,* pp. 19–30.

"The Paradox of Revolution," *Public Choice,* Fall 1971a, *11,* pp. 89–100.

"The Charity of the Uncharitable," *Western Economic Journal,* December 1971b, *9,* pp. 379–92.

Logic of the Law, New York: Basic Books, 1971c.

"The Cost of Transfers," *Kyklos,* December 1971d, *4,* pp. 629–43, reprinted in Buchanan, Tollison, and Tullock (1980, pp. 269–82).

The Social Dilemma: Economics of War and Revolution, Blacksburg: Center for Study of Public Choice, 1974.

"Comment" (on Rae, 1975), *American Political Science Review,* December 1975, *69,* pp. 1295–7.

"Practical Problems and Practical Solutions," *Public Choice,* Spring 1977a, *29,* pp. 27–35.

"The Demand-Revealing Process as a Welfare Indicator," *Public Choice,* Spring 1977b, *29,* pp. 51–63.

"Demand-Revealing Process, Coalitions and Public Goods," *Public Choice,* Spring 1977c, *29,* pp. 103–5.

"Revealing the Demand for Transfers," in R. Auster and B. Sears, eds., *American Re-Evolution,* Tucson: University of Arizona, 1977d, pp. 107–23.

"Efficient Rent Seeking," in Buchanan, Tollison, and Tullock (1980, pp. 97–112).

"Why So Much Stability?" *Public Choice,* 1981, *37*(2), pp. 189–202.

"More Thoughts about Demand Revealing," *Public Choice,* 1982, *38*(2), pp. 167–70.

"Further Tests of a Rational Theory of the Size of Government," *Public Choice,* 1983, *41*(3), pp. 419–21.

"A (Partial) Rehabilitation of the Public Interest Theory," *Public Choice,* 1984, *42*(1), pp. 89–99.

"Back to the Bog," *Public Choice,* 1985, *46*(3), pp. 259–63.

Autocracy, Dordrecht: Kluwer Academic Publishers, 1987.

Tullock, G. and Campbell, C. D. "Computer Simulation of a Small Voting System," *Economics Journal,* March 1970, *80,* pp. 97–104.

Tussing, A. D. and Henning, J. A. "Long-Run Growth of Non-Defense and Government Expenditures," *Public Finance Quarterly,* 1974, *2,* pp. 202–22.

Ulrich, A., Furtan, W. H. and Schmitz, A. "The Cost of a Licensing System Regulation: An Example from Canadian Prairie Agriculture," *Journal of Political Economy,* February 1987, *95,* pp. 160–78.

United States, *Economic Report of the President, Transmitted to the Congress February 1985,* Washington, D.C.: Government Printing Office, 1985.

Economic Report of the President, Transmitted to the Congress February 1989, Washington, D.C.: Government Printing Office, 1989.

Ursprung, H. W. "Macroeconomic Performance and Government Popularity in New Zealand," Victoria University, Wellington, 1983, mimeo.

van Winden, F. *On the Interaction between State and Private Sector,* Amsterdam: North-Holland, 1983.

Varian, H. R. "Equity, Envy, and Efficiency," *Journal of Economic Theory,* September 1974, *9,* pp. 63–91.

"Two Problems in the Theory of Fairness," *Journal of Public Economics,* April–May 1976, *5,* pp. 249–60.

Vedder, R. and Gallaway, L. "Rent-seeking, Distributional Coalitions, Taxes, Relative Prices and Economic Growth," *Public Choice,* 1986, *51*(1), pp. 93–100.

Verba, S. and Nie, N. H. *Participation in America.* New York: Harper and Row, 1972.

Vickrey, W. "Utility, Strategy, and Social Decision Rules," *Quarterly Journal of Economics,* November 1960, *74,* pp. 507–35.

"Counterspeculation, Auctions, and Competitive Sealed Tenders," *Journal of Finance,* May 1961, *16,* pp. 8–37.

Wagner, R. H. "The Concept of Power and the Study of Politics," in Bell, Edwards, and Wagner (1969), pp. 3–12.

Wallace, R. L. and Junk, P. E. "Economic Inefficiency of Small Municipal Electric Generating Systems," *Land Economics,* February 1970, *46,* pp. 98–104.

Wallis, J. J. "Laws and Legislatures," College Park: University of Maryland, 1986, mimeo.

Wallis, J. J. and Oates, W. E. "Does Economic Sclerosis Set in with Age? An Empirical Study of the Olson Hypothesis," *Kyklos,* 1988, *41,* pp. 397–417.

Walsh, C. "Excludable Public Goods: On Their Nature and Significance," in R. Pethig, ed., *Public Goods and Exclusion,* Frankfurt: Peter Lang Verlag, 1986.

Ward, H. "The Risks of a Reputation for Toughness: Strategy in Public Goods Provision Problems Modelled by Chicken Supergames," *British Journal of Political Science,* January 1987, *17,* pp. 23–52.

Warren, R. S., Jr. "Bureaucratic Performance and Budgetary Reward," *Public Choice,* Winter 1975, *24,* pp. 51–7.

Warwick, P. "The Durability of Coalition Governments in Parliamentary Democracies," *Comparative Political Studies,* January 1979, *11,* pp. 465–98.

Weatherby, J. L., Jr. "A Note on Administrative Behavior and Public Policy," *Public Choice,* Fall 1971, *11,* pp. 107–10.

Weatherford, M. S. "Economic Conditions and Electoral Outcomes: Class Differences in the Political Response to Recession," *American Journal of Political Science,* November 1978, *22,* pp. 917–38.

Webber, C. and Wildavsky, A. *A History of Taxation and Expenditure in the Western World,* New York: Simon and Schuster, 1986.

Weber, M. *The Theory of Social and Economic Organization,* Talcott Parsons, ed., New York: Free Press, 1947.

Weede, Erich. "Catch-up, Distributional Coalitions and Government as Determinants of Economic Growth or Decline in Industrialized Democracies," *British Journal of Sociology,* June 1986, *37,* pp. 194–220.

Weingast, B. R. and Moran, M. J. "Bureaucratic Discretion or Congressional Control? Regulatory Policymaking by the Federal Trade Commission," *Journal of Political Economy,* October 1983, *91,* pp. 765–800.

504   **References**

Weingast, B. R., Shepsle, K. A. and Johnsen, C. "The Political Economy of Benefits and Costs: A Neoclassical Approach to Distribution Politics," *Journal of Political Economy*, August 1981, *89*, pp. 642–64.

Welch, W. P. "The Economics of Campaign Funds," *Public Choice*, Winter 1974, *20*, pp. 83–97.

"The Effectiveness of Expenditures in State Legislative Races," *American Politics Quarterly*, July 1976, *4*, pp. 333–56.

"The Allocation of Political Monies: Economic Interest Groups," *Public Choice*, 1980, *35*(1), pp. 97–120.

"Money and Votes: A Simultaneous Equation Model," *Public Choice*, 1981, *36*(2), pp. 209–34.

Wicksell, K. "A New Principle of Just Taxation," *Finanztheoretische Untersuchungen*, Jena, 1896, reprinted in Musgrave and Peacock (1967, pp. 72–118).

Williamson, O. E. *The Economics of Discretionary Behavior*, Englewood Cliffs, N.J.: Prentice-Hall, 1964.

Williamson, O. E. and Sargent, T. J. "Social Choice: A Probabilistic Approach," *Economic Journal*, December 1967, *77*, pp. 797–813.

Wilson, G. W. and Jadlow, J. M. "Competition, Profit Incentives, and Technical Efficiency in the Nuclear Medicine Industry," Bloomington: Indiana University, 1978, mimeo.

Wilson, R. "An Axiomatic Model of Logrolling," *American Economic Review*, June 1969, *59*, pp. 331–41.

"A Game-Theoretic Analysis of Social Choice," in B. Liebermann, ed., *Social Choice*, New York: Gordon and Breach, 1971a.

"Stable Coalition Proposals in Majority-Rule Voting," *Journal of Economic Theory*, September 1971b, *3*, pp. 254–71.

Winer, S. L. "Money and Politics in a Small Open Economy," Ottawa: Carleton University, 1984, mimeo.

Wittman, D. A. "Parties as Utility Maximizers," *American Political Science Review*, June 1973, *67*, pp. 490–8.

"Candidates with Policy Preferences: A Dynamic Model," *Journal of Economic Theory*, February 1977, *14*, pp. 180–9.

"Multi-Candidate Equilibria," *Public Choice*, 1984, *43*(3), pp. 287–91.

"Economic and Political Markets: Why Democracies are Efficient and Government Bureaucracies Are Not Too Large," University of California at Santa Cruz, 1986, mimeo.

Wriglesworth, J. L. *Libertarian Conflicts in Social Choice*, Cambridge: Cambridge University Press, 1985.

Young, H. P. "An Axiomatization of Borda's Rule," *Journal of Economic Theory*, September 1974, *9*, pp. 43–52.

Zardkoohi, A. "On the Political Participation of the Firm in the Election Process," *Southern Economic Journal*, January 1985, *51*, pp. 804–17.

Author index

505

Subject index